How to Do Everything with Adobe® Acrobat® 5.0

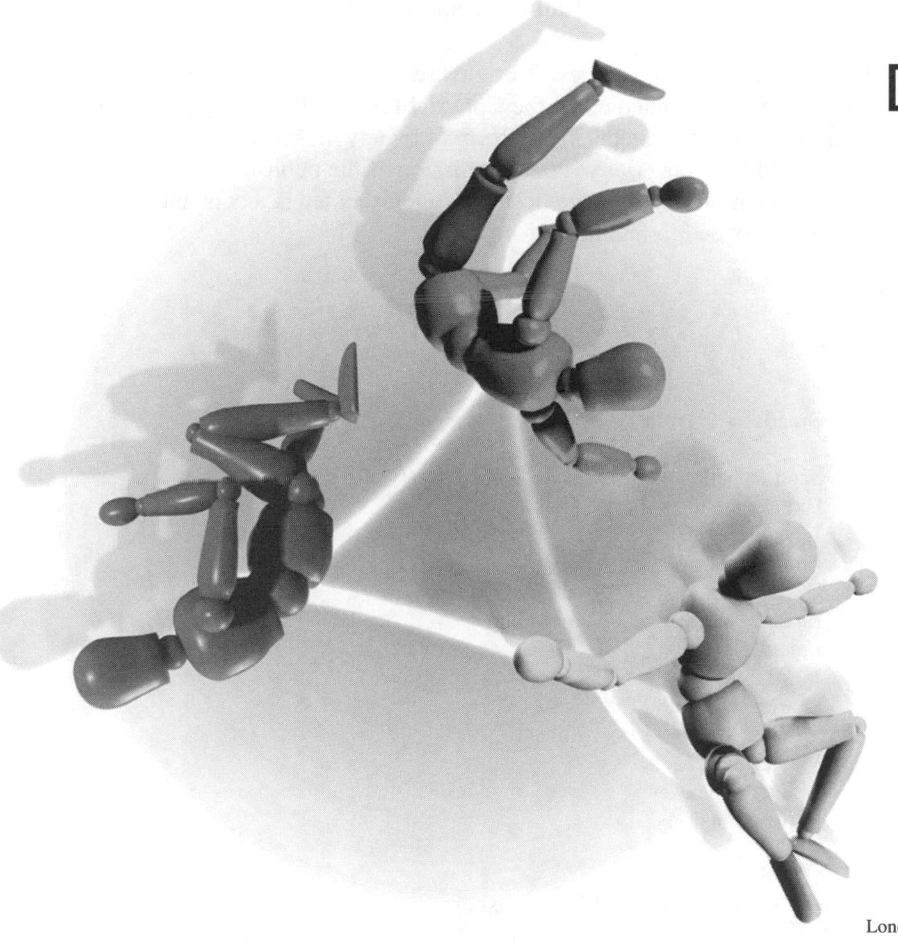

Doug Sahlin

McGraw-Hill/Osborne

New York Chicago San Francisco Lisbon
London Madrid Mexico City Milan New Delhi
San Juan Seoul Singapore Sydney Toronto

McGraw-Hill/Osborne
2600 Tenth Street
Berkeley, California 94710
U.S.A.

To arrange bulk purchase discounts for sales promotions, premiums, or fund-raisers, please contact **McGraw-Hill/**Osborne at the above address. For information on translations or book distributors outside the U.S.A., please see the International Contact Information page immediately following the index of this book.

How to Do Everything with Adobe® Acrobat® 5.0

4567890 FGR FGR 0198765432

ISBN 0-07-219511-8

Publisher: Brandon A. Nordin
Vice President & Associate Publisher Scott Rogers
Acquisitions Editor: Gretchen Ganser
Project Editor: Julie M. Smith
Acquisitions Coordinator: Emma Acker
Technical Editor: Dave Wraight
Copy Editors: Linda Marousek
Proofreader: Linda Medoff
Indexer: Jack Lewis
Computer Designers: Lauren McCarthy, Tara A. Davis
Illustrators: Michael Mueller, Lyssa Wald
Series Design: Mickey Galicia
Cover Series Design: Dodie Shoemaker
Cover Illustration: Eliot Bergnan

This book was composed with Corel VENTURA™ Publisher.

Dedication

This book is dedicated to the innocent people who perished during the September 11, 2001 attack on America. Peace-loving citizens of the free world mourn your passing and extend our heartfelt condolences to your families and loved ones.

About the Author

Doug Sahlin is an author, graphic designer and website designer living in Central Florida. He is the author of Carrara 1 Bible (Hungry Minds, Inc.), Carrara 1 for Dummies (Hungry Minds, Inc.), Flash 5 Virtual Classroom (Osborne/McGraw-Hill), Fireworks 4 for Dummies (Hungry Minds, Inc.) and Flash ActionScript for Dummies (Hungry Minds, Inc.). Doug has developed and authored an online Flash 4 course and has written numerous magazine articles and website tutorials about image editing and web design software.

Contents

Acknowledgments

Writing may be a solitary process, but the creation of a book is not possible without a team effort. Thanks and a tip of the mouse to the fine folks at Adobe for creating a wonderful application and for answering technical questions. I'd also like to extend my appreciation to Corel Corporation and ScanSoft Inc. for providing information on how their software is used to create PDF files.

Thanks to acquisitions editor Gretchen Ganser for making this book possible. Kudos to the lovely and talented Margot Maley-Hutchinson for being a literary agent extraordinaire and for ironing out the contractual issues. A bushel full of virtual flowers for Emma Acker for being the liaison between the author and Osborne's production staff. Copious amounts of gratitude to project editor Julie Smith and copy editor Linda Marousek for manicuring the text for final copy. A heaping cup of JavaScript and a pat on the back for the book's technical editor, the Acrobat wonder from down under, Dave Wraight.

I'd like to extend my appreciation to fellow Acrobat devotee and author Bonnie Blake for providing words of encouragement. I'd like to thank my friends and mentors for their support. And finally I'd like to thank my family for their love and support, especially you Karen and Ted.

Acknowledgments

Introduction

In today's electronic age, there are many ways of sharing information. There's the telephone, the Fax and e-mail. E-mail is becoming a favorite way to share information because of its immediacy. You type a message, attach a file, click a button and a few minutes later, your intended recipient has the information. Of course the information you attach to the e-mail message can take on many forms. It can be a photograph, a document, or a spreadsheet. All your recipient needs to open the attachment is software associated with the attachment. Of course if your recipients don't have the proper software, you will not be able to share the information with them. That is unless you convert the document to PDF format with Adobe Acrobat.

About Adobe Acrobat

Adobe Acrobat is software you use to convert documents to PDF format. The software consists of Acrobat, the core application, Acrobat Distiller, which is used to convert PS and EPS files to PDF format as well as function as a system printer, and Acrobat Catalog, which is used to create a searchable index of PDF files. The beauty of the Acrobat application is the end product, the PDF file. PDF is an acronym for Portable Document Format. A published PDF file retains the look and feel of the original document and can be viewed by anyone who has a copy of the free Acrobat Reader installed on their computer. If recipients of PDF documents have the full version of Acrobat, they can edit the document, add comments to the document and much more. To sum up, you can use Acrobat to electronically publish just about anything from a quick inter-office memo to a product manual complete with multi-media elements like movies and sound clips.

How to Get the Most from This Book

In this book you will find coverage of all the major aspects of Acrobat. If you are a beginner with Acrobat, start at the beginning to familiarize yourself with the software's working environment and read the chapters that apply to the type of documents you will be creating with Acrobat. If you want a full course, appetizer to demitasse serving of Acrobat, read the book from start to finish.

If you are an experienced Acrobat user, you may be tempted to skip the introductory chapters. However, in these chapters you will find material that is specific to new features in Acrobat 5.0. To quickly find information about a specific Acrobat feature or menu command, refer to the Table of Contents or the Index.

Acrobat 5.0 features extensive support of JavaScript. You will find coverage of JavaScript in certain sections of this book. However, this is a book on Acrobat not JavaScript. If every JavaScript object or method that can be effectively used with Acrobat were covered in this book, it would be too large and heavy to comfortably read —unless of course you are very fit and like to lift heavy things. If you need additional information about JavaScript, consider purchasing an Osborne JavaScript title at your local bookstore, or online at www.osborne.com. Alternatively you can refer to the Acrobat JavaScript Guide, a 295 page PDF document you can open within Acrobat by choosing Help | Acrobat JavaScript Guide.

How This Book is Organized

The information in this book is organized in four sections:

- **Welcome to Adobe Acrobat 5.0** In this section you'll find basic information about Adobe Acrobat, the Acrobat working space and how to use Acrobat and Acrobat Reader to view PDF documents.
- **Create PDF Documents** In this section, you'll find information on how to create PDF documents from within authoring applications, how to capture PDF documents from paper and Web sites, as well as how to create eBooks and PDF forms. This section also features a chapter on how to create navigation for your PDF documents.
- **Edit PDF Documents** In this section you'll find all the information you need to edit your PDF documents and annotate PDF documents created within a multi-author team. You'll also find out how to use Acrobat Security to limit access to your documents.

- **Distribute PDF Documents** In this section you'll find information on optimizing your documents for an intended destination, creating a searchable PDF index, and creating PDF documents for distribution on the Internet.

Conventions Used in this Book

Acrobat 5.0 is available for the Windows and Macintosh platforms. This book was written using the Windows version of Acrobat 5.0. However the book supports both the Windows and Macintosh versions of Acrobat. Whenever a dialog box or command is specific to the Macintosh platform, it is noted. When commands or keyboard sequences differ between the Windows and Macintosh versions of Acrobat they are noted; for example: right-click (Windows) or Control-Click (Macintosh).

Italic type is used to designate a new phrase or term.

SMALL CAPITAL LETTERS are used to designate keyboard entries such as CTRL, SHIFT, or ESC.

`COURIER` type is used to designate JavaScript code.

Paths to menu commands are separated with a pipe (|) symbol. For example Edit | Search | Query is the path to the command used to search a PDF index. The command is located on the Search menu, which is a submenu of the Edit menu.

Part 1

Welcome to Adobe Acrobat 5.0

Chapter 1

Get to Know Adobe Acrobat 5.0

How to...

- Utilize the Power of Acrobat
- Create PDF Documents
- Create PDF Documents for the Web
- Capture websites as PDF Documents
- Optimize PDF Documents

Most computer users are familiar with Acrobat in some form or another. Many think that Acrobat is the application that pops up when they double-click a file with the *PDF* (Portable Document Format) extension. That little gem is Acrobat Reader. But there's much more to Acrobat than the Reader. Major corporations, software manufacturers, and businesses use the full version of Acrobat to create and publish documents for electronic distribution. The fact that you are reading this book means that you either own the full version of Acrobat 5.0, or will soon purchase the program to create interactive electronic documents that retain the appearance of the original.

If you have used Acrobat before, you know that it is chock-full of features—so many features that it takes a while to learn them all. If you're brand new to Acrobat, the prospect of publishing sophisticated electronic documents might seem a bit daunting. As you read this book, you'll learn to harness the power of Acrobat to create documents you never thought possible. Whether you need to create a simple electronic memo, an employee manual, or an indexed electronic catalog, Acrobat is the tool for you. In the chapters that follow, you'll learn to harness the potential of Acrobat and use the program options to publish your documents in electronic format. In this chapter, you'll learn about the different components that come with Acrobat and the many uses for the software. If you are an experienced Acrobat user, you may be tempted to skip this chapter. However, even if you're an Acrobat publishing veteran, it is suggested that you browse through this chapter. You may discover an application for the program you never knew existed. As you read these pages, develop ideas how to best utilize Acrobat for your publishing needs.

About Adobe Acrobat

Adobe Acrobat isn't quite as old as dirt, but it has been around for some time. Adobe created the product for individuals and corporations that needed to publish documents for distribution in electronic format (also known as ePaper). The

1

premise of the product was to create a format for electronic documents that could be viewed by anyone, on any computer, with the only required software being the free Acrobat Reader. Adobe accomplished this goal and then some. Initially, the product found great favor with software manufacturers who used Acrobat to create online manuals for their products. The manuals could easily be bundled on program installation disks with a free copy of Acrobat Reader. Many software manufacturers opted to publish program manuals only in PDF format. Software companies, selling programs with manuals published in this manner, saved on packaging and shipping costs, enabling them to price their software more competitively. Help manuals published in PDF format are easy to navigate and read. Figure 1-1 shows the Adobe Acrobat Help manual as viewed in Acrobat Reader.

As Acrobat grew in popularity, Adobe added more features to the product. Newer versions of the software featured enhanced usability, the addition of document security, and the ability to create a searchable index of multiple PDF documents. Users of the software found new applications for PDF documents;

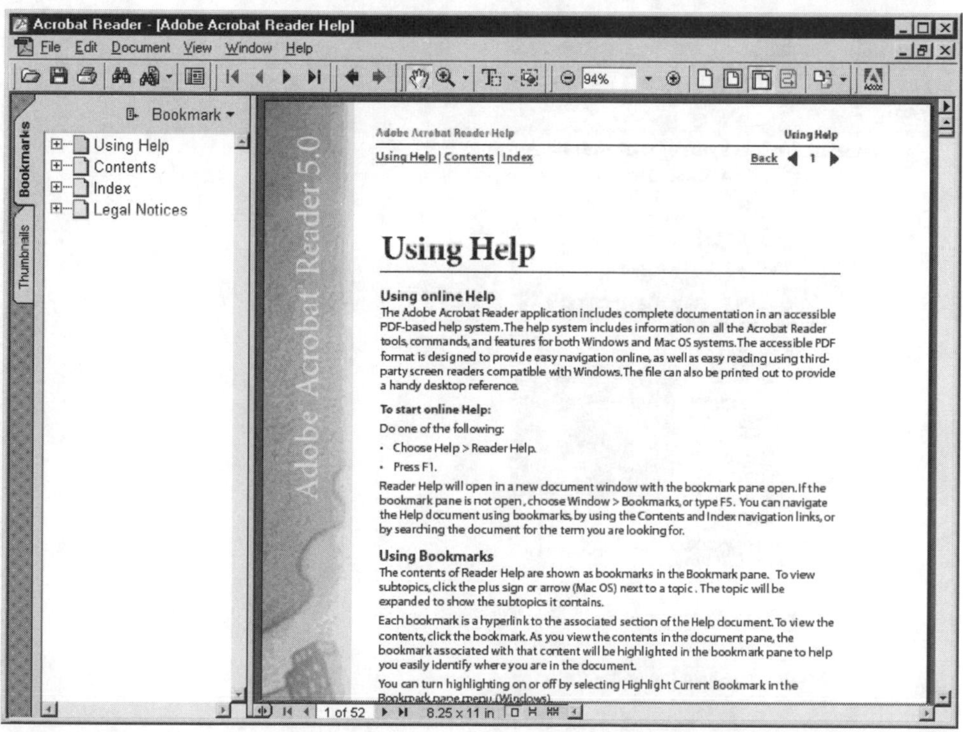

FIGURE 1-1 Many software manufacturers publish their help manuals in PDF format.

they soon appeared as corporate memos, portable product catalogs, and multimedia presentations for salespeople. The PDF acronym aptly describes the published file, as it is truly a portable document, viewable by anyone with Acrobat Reader installed on their computer.

You use Acrobat software to create and publish documents for electronic distribution in PDF format. You create PDF files by either importing into Acrobat documents authored in other applications or by converting documents created in authoring applications to (such as Microsoft Word, Microsoft PowerPoint, or Adobe PhotoShop) PDF documents. There are also several third party plug-ins available for creating PDF files.

When you create a PDF document, it retains the look and feel of the original. All of the fonts and images you used in the original document are carried over to the PDF document. Figure 1-2 shows a document in Microsoft Word; Figure 1-3 shows the same document after being converted to a PDF file. Other than the different interfaces, the documents look identical.

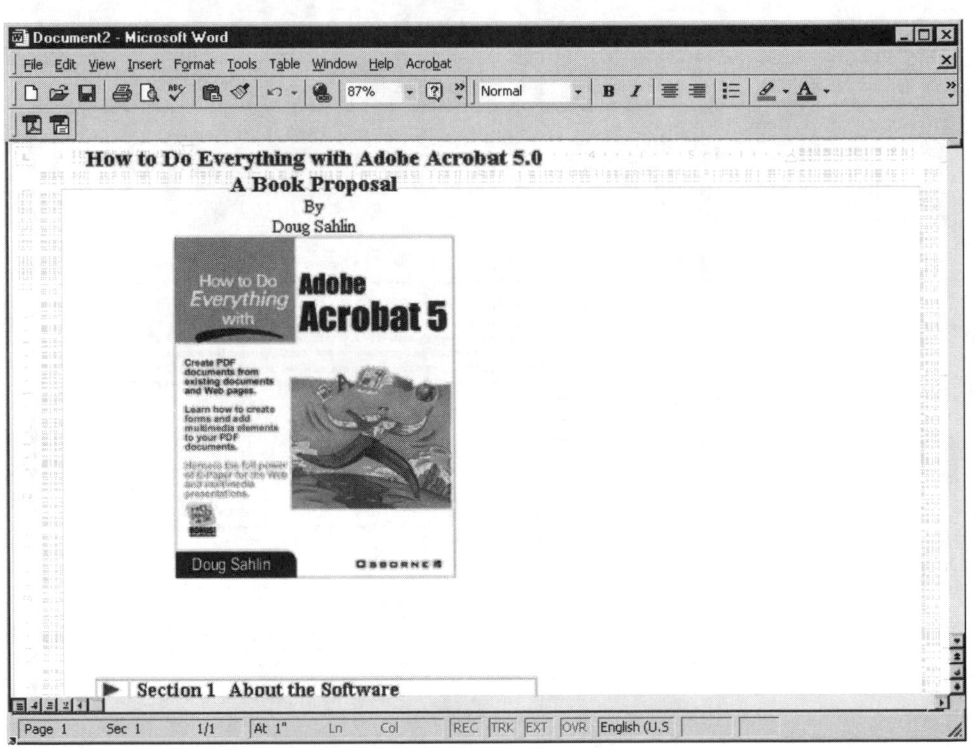

FIGURE 1-2 You can create PDF documents in an authoring program such as Microsoft Word.

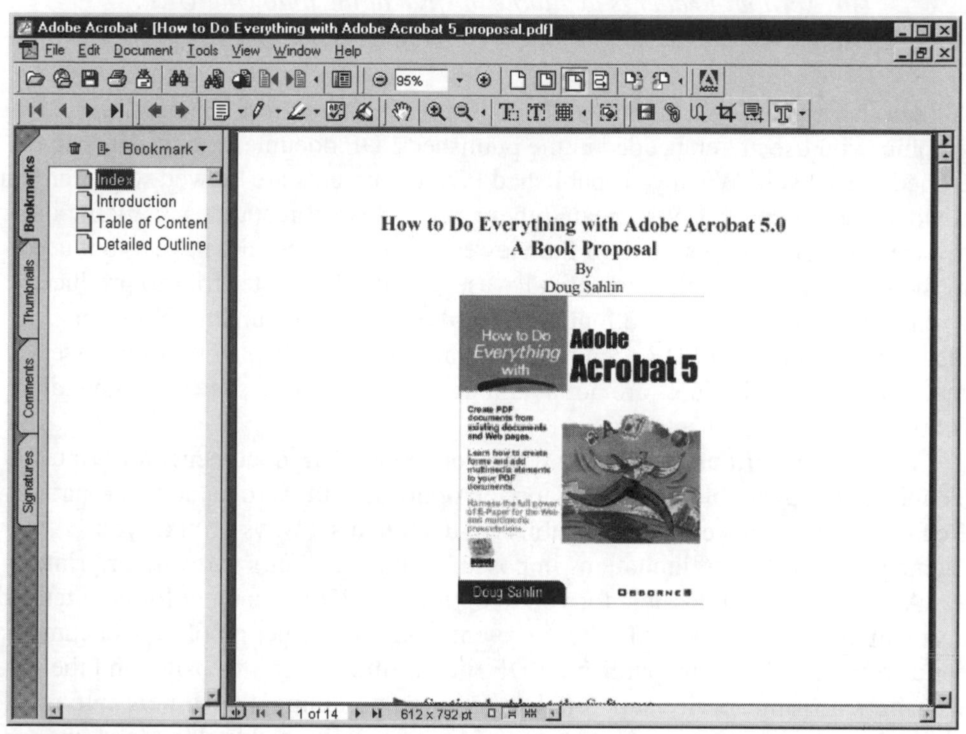

FIGURE 1-3 When you convert the document to PDF format, it maintains the look and feel of the original.

When you use different applications to publish documents for electronic distribution, the documents can only be read if the recipients have a copy of the authoring software installed on their computer. If you work for a large corporation and need to electronically distribute documents to a large number of coworkers, your employer ends up spending a fortune in software licensing fees. However, if you publish the document in PDF format, any coworker can read it as long as a copy of Acrobat Reader is installed on their computer. Adobe does not charge licensing fees when you distribute copies of Acrobat Reader. As you can see, sending documents in PDF format is a cost-effective way to distribute documents within large organizations.

If your published PDF documents are included on a website, most popular Web browsers are equipped with the proper plug-in to display PDF files within the browser. In the event that your viewer doesn't have Acrobat Reader installed, you can add a direct link from your website to the Adobe website where your viewer can download the Reader for free.

NOTE *The Acrobat Reader is available for free at the following URL: http://www.adobe.com/products/acrobat/readstep.html*

Another benefit you have as a PDF author is cross-platform compatibility. Any graphics you use are embedded in the published PDF document, and fonts can be embedded as well. When your published PDF documents are viewed with Acrobat Reader, they display as you created them, regardless of resources available on the viewer's operating system. If the viewer's machine does not have a font used in the PDF, Acrobat will automatically use a Multiple Master font to produce a reasonable facsimile of the fonts used in the original document. You can also embed fonts in a PDF document and the fonts will display on the viewer's machine, even if the fonts are not available on the viewer's system. Embedding fonts is covered in Chapter 14.

You also benefit using Acrobat when you create PDF documents for print. Thanks to the available formatting and job options, both Acrobat and Acrobat Reader software make sure your published documents always print as you intended, regardless of limitations imposed by the recipient's software or printer.

Acrobat makes it possible for you to optimize a PDF document for an intended destination whether it be a CD-ROM presentation, a customer proof, or a document for a website. When you publish a PDF file optimized for a website, and the website's hosting service supports *byteserving* (streaming a document into the viewer's web browser), you can be assured the file will quickly download into the viewer's web browser.

About the PDF Format

If you have used computers for any length of time, you are probably familiar with the PDF format. As mentioned previously, PDF is the acronym for Portable Document Format. PDF files are indeed portable. You can view them on any computer with the free Acrobat Reader. For example, if someone sends you a PDF file created on a Macintosh computer using Adobe PageMaker, you can view it on a PC (Personal Computer) that has Acrobat Reader. The file you view with Acrobat Reader on a PC looks identical to the Macintosh-created PDF file. All of the elements used to create the file on the Macintosh were saved when the author converted the file to PDF format. This is the reason it appears identical when viewed with Acrobat Reader on a PC. PDF files can also be viewed in supported web browsers where Acrobat Reader functions as a plug-in or helper application. Whenever a PDF file posted at a website is selected, Acrobat or Acrobat Reader launches in the viewer's web browser.

Many people confuse Acrobat with Acrobat Reader, the little program you download from the Adobe website. If you are new to Acrobat, you will quickly learn that Acrobat is a full-fledged application for publishing electronic documents in PDF format. If you have used previous versions of Acrobat, you are already familiar with the program's basic premise. In the sections to follow, you'll learn about the new features and uses for Acrobat 5.0.

About Adobe Acrobat 5.0

Acrobat 5.0 is an application you use to create electronic documents in PDF format. The software ships with the following components:

Adobe Acrobat

This is the core application. You use Acrobat to publish and edit PDF documents. In future chapters, you'll learn how to use the program features to create and publish PDF files for a variety of mediums. You'll also use Acrobat to capture web pages and save them as PDF files, as well as scan printed documents into Acrobat and save them as PDF files.

Acrobat Reader

This application is used to read published PDF documents. You don't need to install the reader; PDF documents can be read within the Acrobat application. Adobe includes the Acrobat Reader with the application CD-ROM so you can bundle it with applications you create for distribution on CD-ROM or zip disk. You can distribute Acrobat Reader without paying a licensing fee as long as you comply with the Adobe distribution policy that requires you to distribute the EULA (End User License Agreement) and information that is included with the installation utility.

Acrobat Distiller

Acrobat Distiller is used to create a PDF document from PostScript files in *EPS* (*Encapsulated PostScript*) or *PS* (*PostScript*) format. The Distiller *Job Options* help you optimize the document for its intended destination. Acrobat Distiller is a separate application that can also be accessed from the core application.

NOTE *You will find the installer utility for Acrobat Reader with the application CD-ROM. To include the Acrobat Reader installer with an application or presentation you have developed, copy the entire Acrobat Reader Install folder from the Acrobat CD-ROM to your application or presentation folder prior to copying the folder to the destination media. When you copy the Install folder to your application folder, you include all the necessary documentation Adobe requires to distribute this software without paying licensing fees.*

What's New in Adobe Acrobat 5.0

Acrobat 5.0 has many new features that enhance usability when creating files within a network environment. You can easily share your PDF documents within a team. Individual team members can modify PDF documents by creating annotations, adding audio and written comments, and much more. For example, you can easily create interactive forms to gather information from within a corporate environment. These forms can be printed out and filled in, or they can be filled in and submitted on a corporate intranet. Recipients of your form can use either Acrobat Reader or Acrobat to fill out a form. In the sections to follow, you'll learn the exciting new features at your disposal in Acrobat 5.0.

New Features

Previous versions of Acrobat were fragmented into Adobe Catalog, Adobe Acrobat, and Adobe Distiller. Acrobat 5.0 consists of two separate entities named Acrobat and Acrobat Distiller. Adobe Catalog is now a plug-in within the core application. You use the Catalog to create a searchable index of PDF files. Even though Acrobat Distiller is a separate program, used to create PDF files from EPS and PS files, you can now launch it from within Acrobat.

Veteran users of Acrobat will notice the *PDFWriter* is missing. In previous versions of Acrobat, the PDFWriter was added as a system printer. You could use the PDFWriter to print a file in PDF format from within another application. When you install Acrobat 5.0, Acrobat Distiller is added as a system printer. You can choose Distiller from an authoring application Print command to create a PDF file, or you can use the new Open As Adobe PDF command to convert text files and image files to PDF documents.

If you work on a PDF project with multiple authors, you and your team members can review and add comments to a PDF file from within a web browser via the Internet or a corporate intranet. When you open a PDF file within your web browser, every Acrobat commenting tool is at your disposal. You can freely annotate the PDF file and then save it, or share your comments with other authors through protocols such as *WebDAV* (Web-based distributed Authoring and Versioning). If your team is working on a corporate intranet, you can set up a shared data repository by setting up a shared network folder, using *ODBC* (*Open Database Connectivity*) for connecting to such databases as *MDB* (*Microsoft Data Base*) or *SQL Server* databases, or *Microsoft Office Server extensions.*

If you create PDF files that are shared in a workplace, you will be pleased to know that the software can publish a document that is accessible by workers with visual disabilities. Acrobat supports high-contrast monitor settings used by the visually impaired and a wide variety of screen readers.

With Acrobat 5.0, you can apply enhanced security features to the documents you create. Acrobat 5.0 features 128-bit encryption, which makes it possible for you to distribute confidential documents with complete peace of mind. If you author a confidential PDF document, you can limit access to the document by assigning a *password* to the file. You can also apply digital signatures to PDF documents. A *digital signature*, as shown next, is like an electronic fingerprint; it identifies which member of the team worked with the document and when.

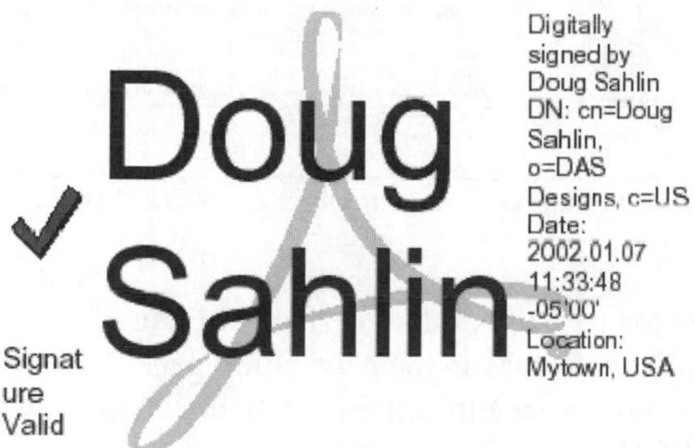

New User Interface

Acrobat 5.0 features an enhanced interface that you can easily customize to suit your working preferences. What was a tool palette on the left side of the workspace in Acrobat 4.0 is now a series of tool groups on the top of the large work area, as shown in Figure 1-4. The toolbars can be moved, grouped, and customized to suit your working preference. You'll learn about the Acrobat and Acrobat Reader interfaces in Chapter 2.

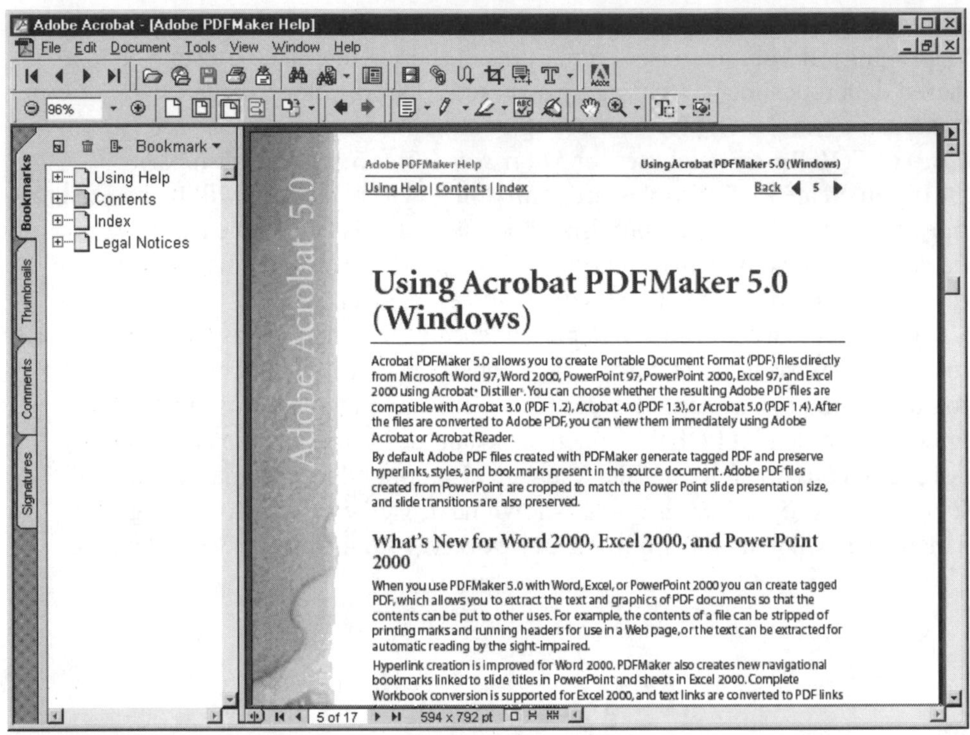

FIGURE 1-4 You can easily customize the Acrobat workspace to suit your preference.

The window on the left side of the interface in Figure 1-4 is the *Navigation pane*. You click the various tabs in the Navigation pane to open palettes that you use to advance to various elements within a PDF document. You'll learn how to navigate within a PDF document in Chapter 3.

New Acrobat Palettes

In Acrobat, you use palettes to perform various task,s such as navigating within the PDF document or displaying a list of elements used in the PDF file. In Acrobat 5.0, you have the following new palettes at your disposal:

- **Comments** The Comments palette is located in the Navigation pane on the left side of the interface. In previous versions of Acrobat, Comments were referred to as Annotations. You use the Comments palette to display a list of all comments within a PDF document and to navigate to their respective locations within the document.

- **Info** The Info palette is opened from the Window menu. This palette is a window that displays the x and y coordinates of the mouse. This palette is useful for aligning objects such as form fields. You'll learn how to create forms in Chapter 9.
- **Fields** The Fields palette is accessed from the Window menu. The Fields palette is used to display all form fields contained in a PDF document.
- **Tags** The Tags palette is opened from the Window menu. The Tags palette is used to display and edit tagged words, text blocks, objects, and pages in a PDF file.

Enhanced Export and Import Features

Acrobat 5.0 makes it possible to repurpose PDF content for other formats. You can use the Extract Images As command to extract images from PDF files in JPEG, PNG, or TIFF image formats. You can use the Save As menu command to export PDF content in EPS or PS format. You can also save the current PDF document as a JPEG, PNG, or TIFF file, as well as an *RTF* (*Rich Text Format*) file.

New Menu Commands

In Acrobat 5.0, you have new menu commands available to streamline workflow and increase productivity. In upcoming chapters, you will find in-depth information about the following new commands:

- **Batch Processing** The Batch Processing command is used to automate a task or sequence of tasks within Acrobat. You can choose from preset sequences, or you can create a custom sequence. After you choose a sequence, you can apply it to a single PDF file or a selection of PDF files. Batch Processing is covered in Chapter 11.
- **Catalog** The Catalog command is used to create a searchable index of selected PDF files. In previous versions of Acrobat, Catalog was a separate program; now you can use it from within the main application. Chapter 15 is devoted to Acrobat Catalog.
- **Distiller** The Distiller command is used to launch Acrobat Distiller. Acrobat Distiller is a separate program; however, with this menu command; you have the luxury of opening Distiller from within Acrobat. This option is useful if you are working on a PDF file and decide you want to append the document with an EPS or PS file that has not been distilled to PDF format. You will find information about Acrobat Distiller in Chapter 4.

- **Spelling** The Spelling command is used to check the spelling of form fields and comments within a PDF document. You'll learn how to create PDF documents with forms in Chapter 9.
- **Open As Adobe PDF** The Open As Adobe PDF command is used to convert a BMP, GIF, HTML, JPEG, PCX, PNG, TIFF, or text file (with a .txt or .text extension) into a PDF document. You can also use this command to append an open PDF document with a file in one of the formats just listed. In Chapter 4, you'll learn to use this command to create PDF documents.

Create a PDF Document

The flexible tools in Acrobat give you several different options for producing a PDF document. You can create PDF documents from within an authoring application, capture them from documents you scan, or capture them from websites.

After you create or open a PDF document created by another author, you can add interactive elements such as text hyperlinks; image hyperlinks; and multimedia elements, such as QuickTime movies and sound files. You can append a PDF file by inserting other documents. You can also do other housekeeping chores, such as extract graphic elements from a PDF file, crop the file to delete unwanted elements, or remove unnecessary pages from the document. Acrobat has a set of *Touch Up* tools that let you make minor modifications to graphic and text elements in the document. If you need to extensively modify text in a PDF document, it is better to save it as an RTF file and edit the RTF file in a word processing program. After you edit the file in your word processor, you can then use the Print command to access Acrobat Distiller and convert the edited RTF file to PDF format.

Create PDF Documents from Authoring Applications

The easiest way to create a PDF document is to create a file in an authoring application and then convert it to a PDF file. You can create PDF files from any of these popular Microsoft programs (Microsoft Office 97 or newer):

- **Microsoft Word** Microsoft Word is a word processing application. Within limits, you can add graphic elements to the content.
- **Microsoft Excel** Microsoft Excel is a spreadsheet program. Excel also has limited support for graphic elements.

- **Microsoft PowerPoint** Microsoft PowerPoint is software used to create presentations. A PowerPoint presentation is similar to a slide show. You can add graphic elements to your presentation and then convert it to a PDF file.

When you install Acrobat, it detects the Microsoft products previously listed and installs the PDFMaker shortcut shown on the following toolbar. The icon on the left converts the current document to a PDF file; the icon on the right converts it to a PDF file and launches your default e-mail program, enabling you to send the PDF file as an e-mail attachment. Acrobat also adds an Acrobat menu to the Microsoft Office application. This menu gives you two additional commands, one to view the result in Acrobat and another to change conversion settings. You'll learn how to convert Microsoft Office documents to PDF documents in Chapter 5.

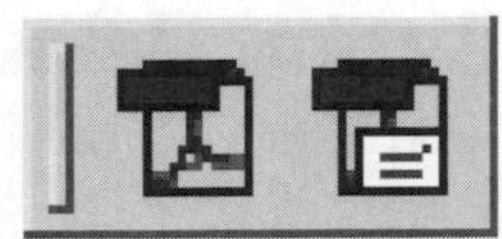

TIP

Older versions of Microsoft Office products use the PDFWriter icon to create a PDF file from within the application, similar to the method used in newer Office software by the more sophisticated PDFMaker. If Acrobat didn't install PDFMaker with your Microsoft Office software, you can do a custom install of Acrobat and choose only the PDFWriter.

If you own certain Adobe products such as PageMaker and Photoshop, you can use a plug-in to export a document in PDF format. Other illustration programs—such as CorelDraw, Quark, and Freehand—also have the capability to export files in PDF format.

You can publish PDF files from any other application you use to generate images, illustrations, or text files. When you install Acrobat, Acrobat Distiller is added as a system printer. To publish a PDF file directly from an authoring application, choose the Print command, and then choose Acrobat Distiller from the list of available printers. You can then open the PDF file in Acrobat to add enhancements such as links and form fields.

Create PDF Documents from EPS Files

If you create illustrations and documents in illustration or page layout programs, and publish files in EPS or PS format, you can convert these files to PDF format with Acrobat Distiller. After you open Distiller and select an EPS or PS file, select one of the preset Job Options in Distiller, or create your own Job Options. You use Job Options to optimize a PDF file for an intended destination, such as print, screen, or the Web. You can use Distiller to create complete PDF documents or to convert an illustration to PDF format. After you save the file in PDF format, you can then e-mail it to a client for approval.

TIP

You can quickly create a PDF document by dragging-and-dropping a supported file icon from your desktop onto the Acrobat shortcut icon. After you release the mouse button, the file will open in Acrobat. If the file is not supported, Acrobat displays the warning dialog box shown here. If you have the Distiller shortcut on your desktop, you can create a PDF document by dragging-and-dropping an EPS or PS file onto the icon.

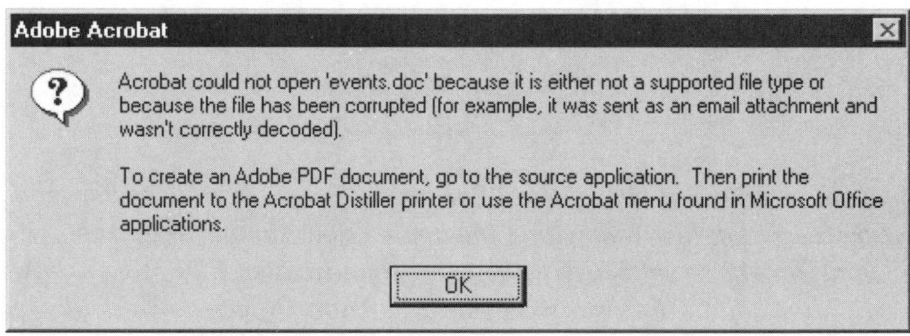
Adobe Acrobat
Acrobat could not open 'events.doc' because it is either not a supported file type or because the file has been corrupted (for example, it was sent as an email attachment and wasn't correctly decoded).
To create an Adobe PDF document, go to the source application. Then print the document to the Acrobat Distiller printer or use the Acrobat menu found in Microsoft Office applications.
OK

Create PDF Documents for the Internet

If you design websites, you can use PDF documents in a variety of effective ways. For example, you can create a product catalog, interactive PDF tutorials, or publish a manual—all in PDF format. The website visitor can choose to view the document in the web browser or download the complete file for future viewing. Most popular web browsers support Acrobat Reader as a plug-in or helper application. Figure 1-5 shows a published document as displayed in Internet Explorer. Note that the figure shows a document displayed in the full version of Acrobat, not the Acrobat Reader.

Send PDF Documents via E-Mail

You send a PDF document via e-mail when you need to share information with a coworker or client that may or may not have the program you used to create the original document. If you create the document in a Microsoft Office application

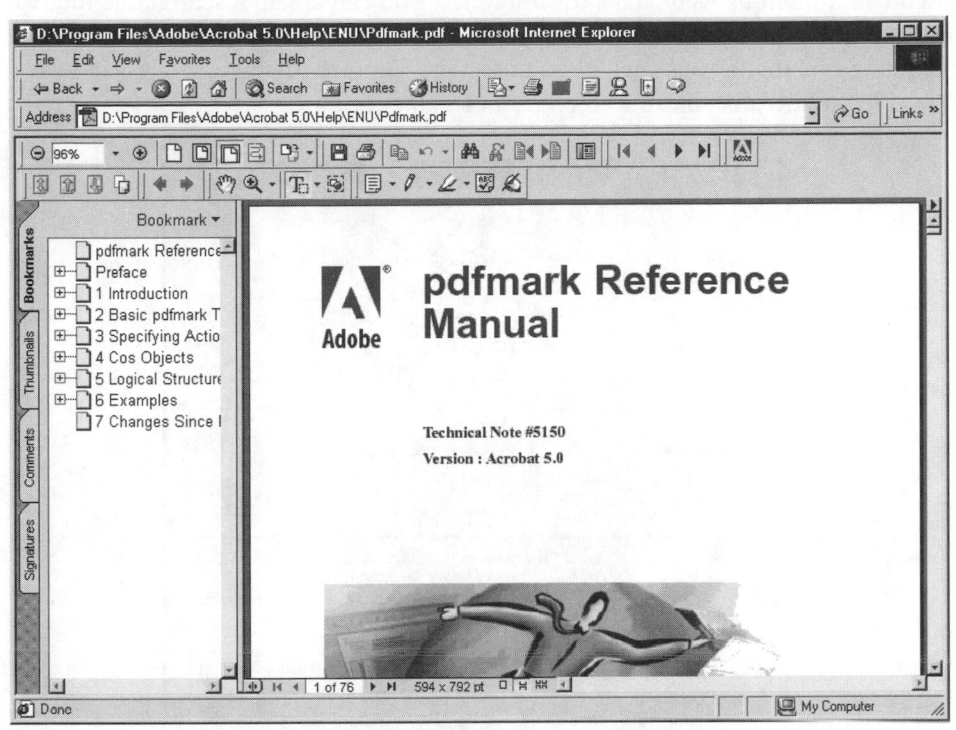

FIGURE 1-5 Acrobat is available as a plug-in or a helper application for most popular web browsers.

supported by PDFMaker, you can e-mail it directly from the authoring application; otherwise, you can open the file in Acrobat and e-mail it from there. Sending PDF documents via e-mail will be discussed in detail in Chapters 5 and 16.

Capture Websites as PDF Documents

If you do a lot of research on the Internet, you can capture web pages for future reference. When you capture a web page, Acrobat downloads the text and the graphic elements from the web page, complete with hyperlinks. If you want to add additional pages from the same site to the PDF file, simply click the hyperlink in the captured page and Acrobat will append the document by downloading the linked page. You can use the Acrobat *Web Capture* feature to download complex tutorials from the Internet and save them as PDF files for easy reference. If you download numerous web pages for reference, you can create a searchable index of your reference files with the *Catalog* command. The following illustration shows the dialog box that appears when you use Web Capture to download a web page. You'll learn how to capture web pages in Chapter 6.

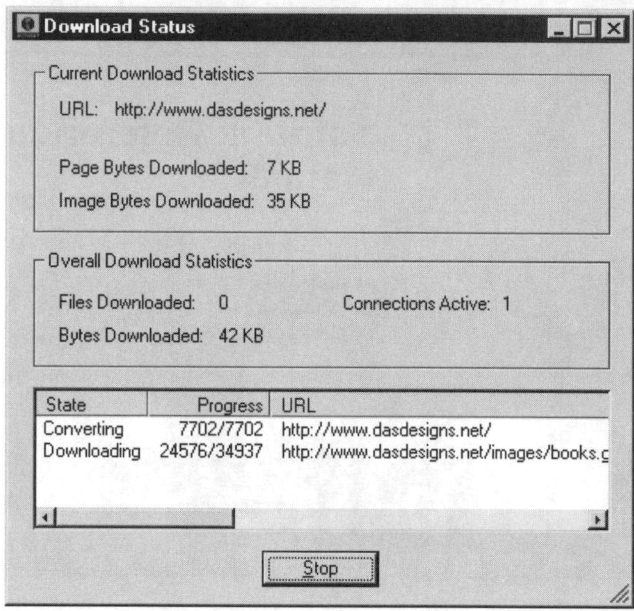

Convert Scanned Documents to PDF Format

If you have hard copies of documents, such as contracts or product brochures, that you need to share with coworkers or clients, Acrobat is very user-friendly. You could send the documents by fax, but in most cases what your recipient receives isn't anything near a reasonable facsimile of the original. To overcome the difference in resolution and quality of fax machines, create a PDF file for the document you want to share. If you have a scanner hooked up to your system, Acrobat copies the TWAIN information of the scanner. Then it's simply a matter of choosing Scan from the Import menu. After you scan the document into Acrobat, save it as a PDF file and then e-mail it. When your document is received and viewed in Acrobat Reader, it looks identical to what you scanned into Acrobat. As an example, you can also use the Scan command to archive dog-eared magazine articles for future reference in PDF format. You learn how to convert scanned documents to PDF files in Chapter 6.

TIP

To convert a scanned document into a PDF file with searchable text, you can use Acrobat Capture, a separate program available from Adobe, or upload the PDF document to the Adobe Create PDF Online service. As of this writing, you can use this online service to capture a limited number of documents for free. After you've used up your allotment of free captures, you can opt to subscribe to the service for unlimited access. For more information on the Create PDF Online service, go to http://createpdf.adobe.com.

Create PDF Documents for Print

In previous versions of Acrobat, you had few options to print a hard copy of a PDF file. After you optimize a file for print, Acrobat 5.0 gives you more options for sending the file to the output device. The Print dialog box in Acrobat 5.0 has an *Advanced* button. When you click the Advanced button, a separate dialog box opens allowing you to specify print options previously unavailable to Acrobat, such as trim marks, transparency levels, and the capability of omitting images to print a proof of the PDF file.

Create Interactive PDF Documents

When some Acrobat users create PDF documents for the first time, they tend to think that the document will be read in linear fashion. However, the Acrobat *Link* tool lets you create documents that can be navigated like web pages. You can use the Link tool to change static text or images into hyperlinks. When you create a link in a PDF document, it serves many purposes. You can use the link to open up another PDF document, to navigate to a specific page in the current PDF document, or to link to a URL on the Web, and much more. A link in a PDF document functions identically to a link in an HTML page. When you drag your mouse over the link, the cursor changes to a pointing hand, as shown in Figure 1-6. Interactive navigation for PDF documents is covered in Chapter 7.

Create PDF Documents for Multimedia Presentations

The age of electronic education is very much upon us. Fluctuating demands in the workplace make lifelong learning a necessity. People in all stages of life need to increase their knowledge base. Most lifelong learners don't have time for formal classroom education and use online education to learn at their own pace. Online learners can log on and take a lesson according to their schedule. Other lifelong learners purchase interactive CD-ROMs and play the discs in their spare time to educate themselves.

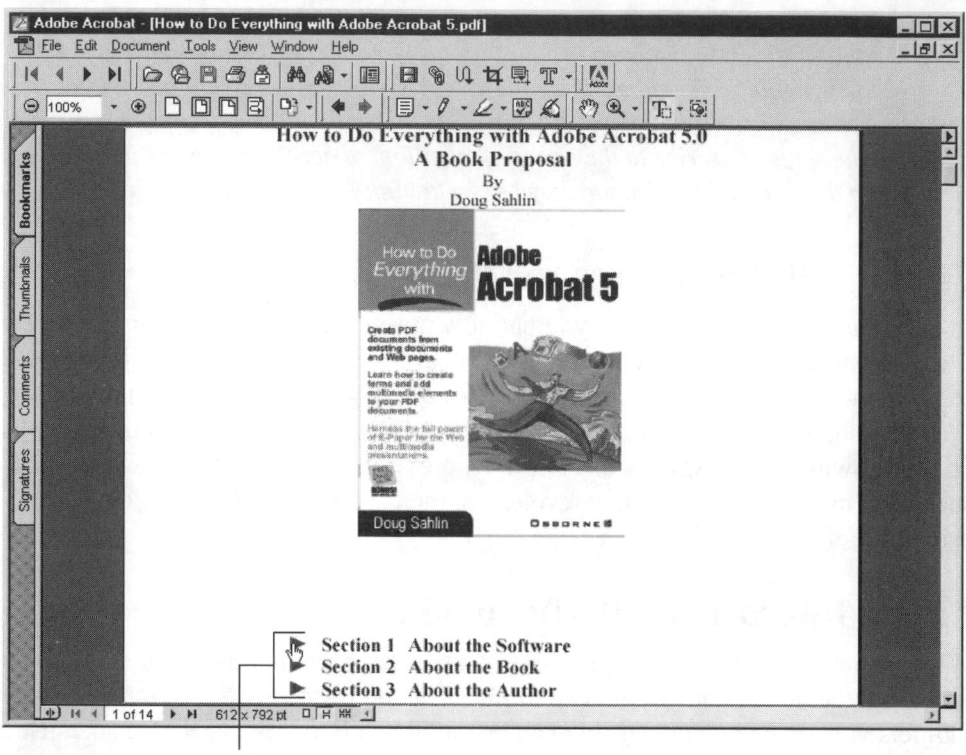

FIGURE 1-6 A link in a PDF document functions like a hyperlink in an HTML document.

Whether you need to create online or CD-ROM presentations, you can accomplish the task with Acrobat. When you create a PDF document for an online or CD-ROM presentation, Acrobat gives you the necessary tools to elevate your presentation to the next level. *Multimedia* is the current buzzword for online education, educational CD-ROMs, and business presentations. With Acrobat, you can create PDF documents with multimedia elements such as movie clips, music, and the spoken word. You can use the *Sound* tool in Acrobat to add a prerecorded sound clip to a document, or create a recording on the spot. After you add interaction, you can create links within the document to play multimedia clips, or you can have them play when the document is opened. In Chapter 10, you'll learn to create PDF files with multimedia elements. Figure 1-7 shows a QuickTime movie playing within a PDF document.

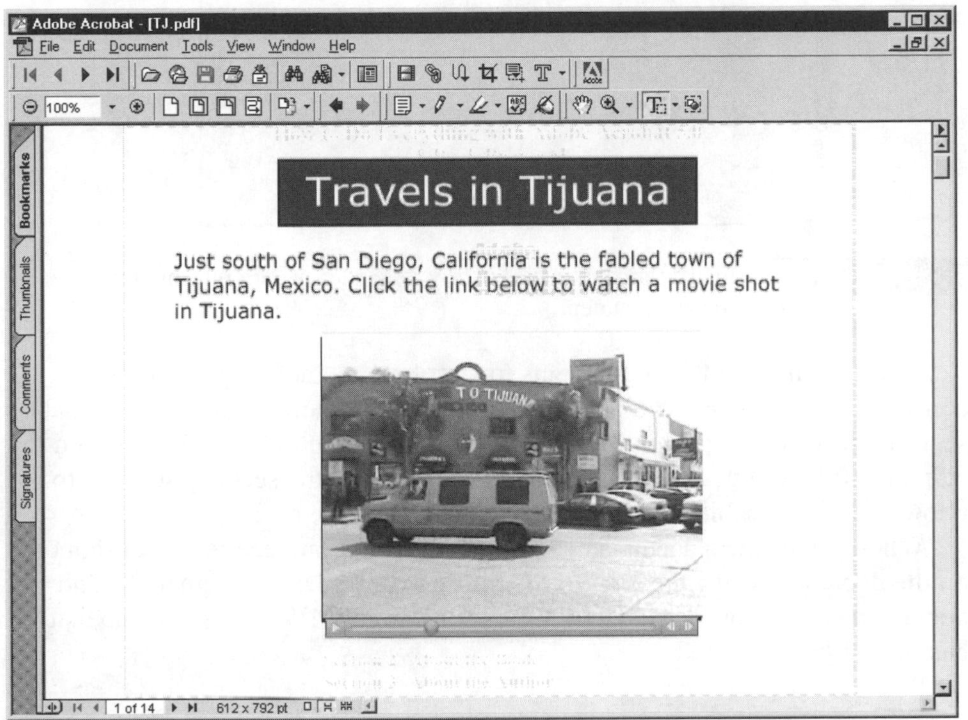

FIGURE 1-7 You can add elements, such as movies, to turn a PDF document into a multimedia experience.

Create PDF Documents for Internal Distribution

Many modern companies realize the futility of using paper to distribute information. Paper is bulky, it takes up room, and it is an expensive way to distribute written information with a short life span. If the company is a multi-location operation, there is also the cost of transporting published documents between locations. A much better solution for disseminating information is the PDF document. It can be efficiently distributed over the corporate intranet, sent via e-mail, or distributed on disk. An employee manual in print form might take up hundreds of pages plus a hefty portion of the employee's workspace. The same document can be created in PDF format and distributed to employees on a floppy disk, zip disk, or CD-ROM. A PDF employee manual uses fewer resources, is easier to distribute, and is easier to use. An employee looking for specific information can use the powerful Acrobat *Find* command (as shown in Figure 1-8) to navigate to specific information.

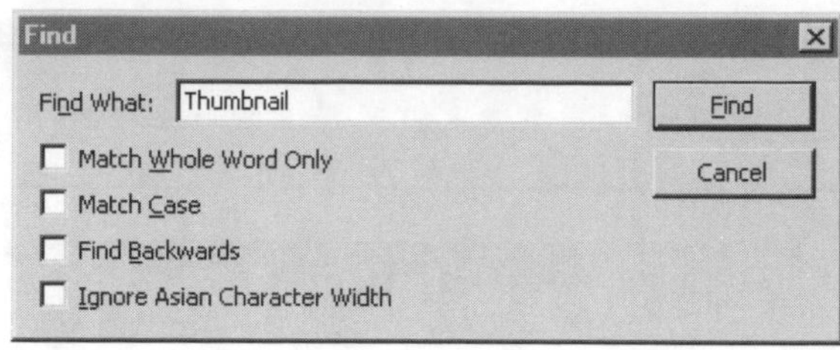

FIGURE 1-8 The Find command makes it easy to locate specific information in a multi-page document.

You can also use PDF documents to distribute memos. If you author a confidential memo, you can password protect the document and add Acrobat security measures to prevent editing by unauthorized personnel. If you need to edit a confidential document, you can always change the security settings to allow and then disable editing after you have made the changes.

When you create a document for internal distribution, recipients can sign off on the document using the *Digital Signature* feature. Digital Signatures and document security are discussed in Chapter 13. Figure 1-9 shows a memo that has been digitally signed.

Create a PDF Form

Acrobat 5.0 has advanced tools that you can use to create forms to accumulate data. You can create forms complete with text boxes for collecting data, radio buttons and check boxes for selecting form options, and buttons for navigating the form or submitting the form data to a web server. You can even create a drop-down list of form choices. You can use CGI (Common Gateway Interface) scripting options to route data from a form submitted over the Web to a server, or opt to have the completed document printed out as hard copy and submitted internally. You'll learn to create PDF forms in Chapter 9. Figure 1-10 shows a completed PDF form.

Create an eBook

The PDF format is well suited for creating and distributing books and manuals over the Internet. Books distributed over the Internet are also known as *eBooks*. You can create the content for an eBook in any page layout application and then use Acrobat Distiller to convert the file into PDF format. If you choose, you can distribute the content directly from a secure server. End users can also purchase eBook readers to view published eBooks, read them with Acrobat Reader, or

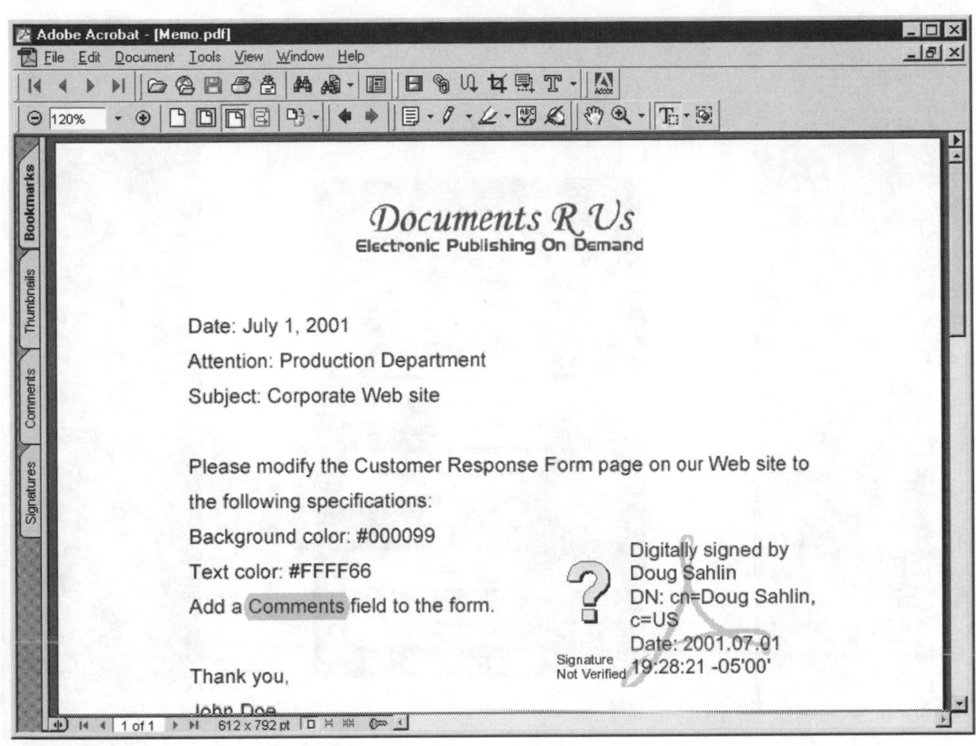

FIGURE 1-9 You can use PDF documents for internal memos and have them digitally signed.

download the free Adobe Acrobat eBook Reader. Unfortunately, once the document is paid for and downloaded, it can then be distributed freely to anyone with Acrobat Reader. A merchant or eBook publisher can control unauthorized distribution of downloaded ebooks by locking the document to hardware serial numbers. Adobe offers a service called *Content Server* that encrypts eBooks. End users who download secure eBooks use an Acrobat feature called *Web Buy* to download encrypted documents. eBooks and Web Buy are discussed in Chapter 8.

Create an Acrobat Catalog

If you create PDF documents in a corporate environment, you might end up publishing a large collection of related PDF documents. For example, if you create documents for your Human Resources department, you will end up with a collection of varied memos concerning employee procedures, benefits packages, and the like.

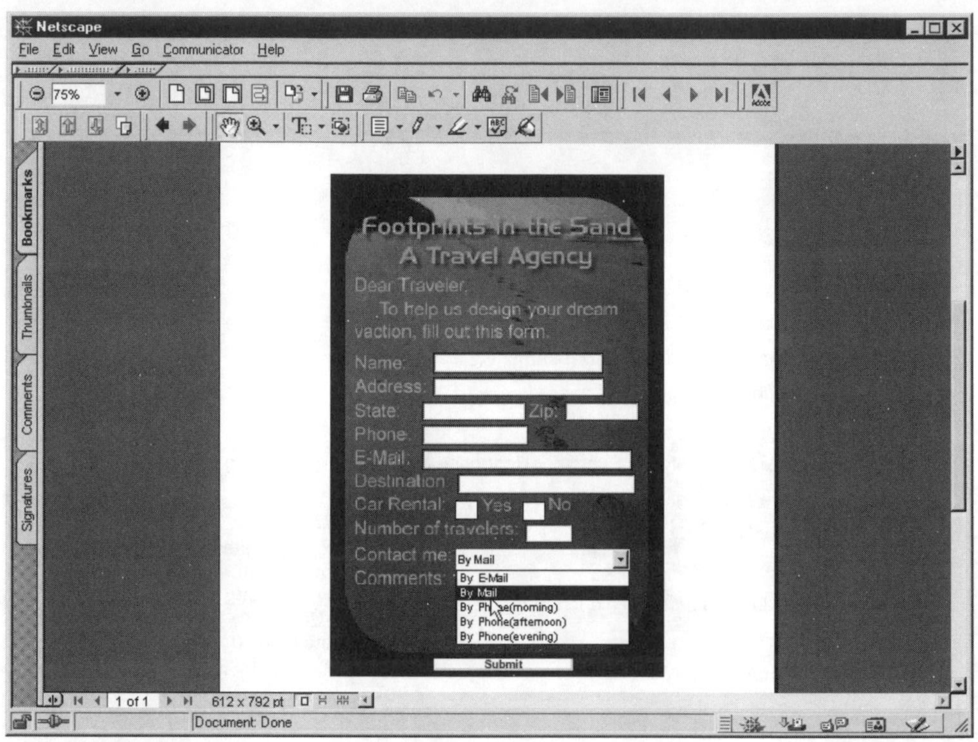

FIGURE 1-10 A PDF form is an ideal vehicle for collecting data.

When employees need to find specific information, they will end up using the Find command on numerous documents to find the data. The solution for this problem is to use *Acrobat Catalog* to create a searchable index of PDF files. After you create an index, use the Search command to find data related to a query. The following image is the Search dialog box. You'll learn to create a searchable index in Chapter 15.

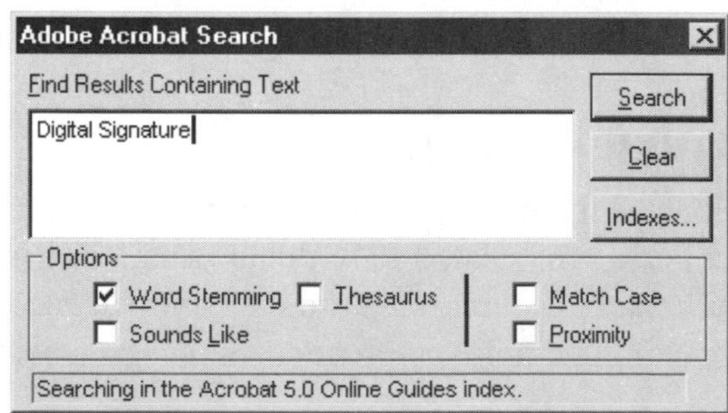

Optimize Documents for Distribution

If you have created images and documents for different destinations, you know that a file needs to be formatted correctly for the intended destination. The file you create for print has different requirements than the file you create for a website, both of which are different than the file you create for a multimedia CD-ROM presentation. When you create files for print, you need to optimize them for the output device, matching the file as closely as possible to the printer resolution. On the other hand, when you create a PDF file for a multimedia CD-ROM application, you only need to worry about screen resolution. When you create a document for the Web, you need to create a happy medium between image quality and bandwidth. Bandwidth is the amount of information that can be downloaded per second at a given connection speed, for example, 56 Kbps.

Acrobat Distiller comes with preset Job Options to optimize a document for an intended destination. Acrobat has several presets in the Job Options menu. If none of the presets suit the document you are publishing, you can modify a preset to create and save the parameters as a custom Job Options file. Chapter 14 is devoted to optimizing PDF documents.

Use Acrobat as a Publishing Solution

If you have read this chapter from the start, you are beginning to realize the power and diversity of Acrobat. You can use Acrobat as a publishing solution within a large corporation, use it to distribute documents over the Internet, and use it to share documents with clients who do not own the software you used to create the original document. Acrobat can be used to create a simple electronic interoffice memo, a form for collecting data, or a complex presentation with interactive navigation and multimedia elements. Acrobat makes it possible for you to create a single document in an authoring program such as Microsoft Excel, and publish the file as different PDF documents optimized for different destinations.

Chapter 2

Create PDF Documents

How to...

- Navigate the Acrobat Reader interface
- Navigate the Acrobat interface
- Customize the Acrobat interface
- Select Acrobat tools
- Set Acrobat preferences

When you launch Acrobat 5.0 for the first time, you are presented with a completely new interface. All of the tools you have grown accustomed to are no longer in their familiar places. It's like walking into your house after someone has completely rearranged it; you cannot find a thing. The change in the Acrobat interface marks a step forward. Although things may seem different, the interface does resemble the interface you used in Acrobat 4.0. After reading this chapter, you will be familiar with the layout. However, if you are a newcomer to Acrobat, things will be unfamiliar to you at first, but this will all change after you read this chapter.

In this chapter, you will discover what you can accomplish with the wide variety of tools on the Acrobat toolbar. As an author of PDF documents, you'll spend a good deal of time working in Acrobat. However, many (actually, most unless you collaborate with other employees) of the people who'll read your PDF files will do so with Acrobat Reader. You may not feel it is necessary to know everything about the Acrobat Reader interface, but the recipients of your PDF documents will. Many tools in Acrobat Reader are duplicated in Acrobat. In the first part of this chapter, the tools unique to Acrobat Reader are covered. In the second part, tools that are unique to Acrobat will be discussed.

Learn to Navigate the Acrobat Reader Interface

You use Acrobat Reader to read PDF files, print hard copies of PDF files, and save copies of PDF files. The Acrobat Reader shares a common look with Acrobat, but only has enough tools to read a document, navigate within a document, and select text and graphic elements within a document. In the upcoming sections, you'll learn about specific tools and how to select them. When information is common to both Acrobat Reader and Acrobat, for example—floating a toolbar—the information will be presented in the section about the Acrobat interface.

When you want to read a file in Acrobat Reader, you can open it by double-clicking the file with the PDF extension. If you have both Acrobat and Acrobat Reader installed on your machine, double-clicking a PDF file launches Acrobat. When you use this method to open a file in Acrobat, it appears in the workspace shown in Figure 2-1.

Notice that there are two windows within the workspace. The window on the left is known as the Navigation pane; the window on the right is the Document pane. The *Navigation pane*, as the name implies, is used to navigate to certain elements in the document.

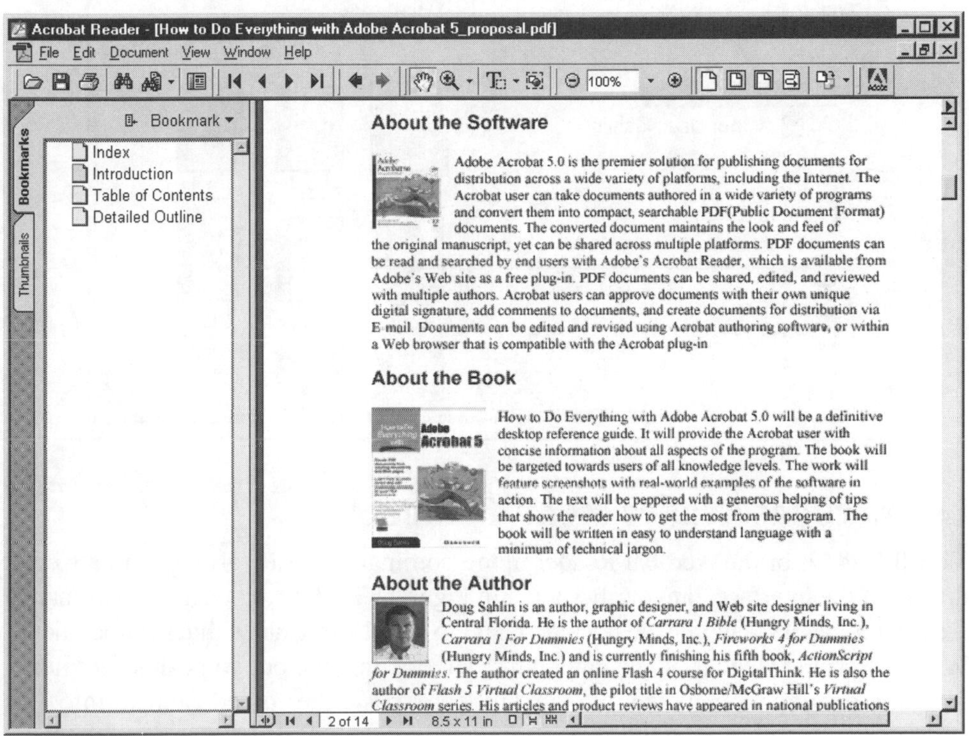

FIGURE 2-1 Use the Acrobat Reader to read PDF documents.

Use the Navigation Pane

In Acrobat Reader, the Navigation pane has two tabs, one for Bookmarks and one for Thumbnails. You open a pane by clicking its tab. Once the pane is open, you can use its elements to navigate within the document. Bookmarks are text links to specified parts of the document. Thumbnails are miniature versions of each page in the document. The following image shows the Bookmark and Thumbnail palettes side by side.

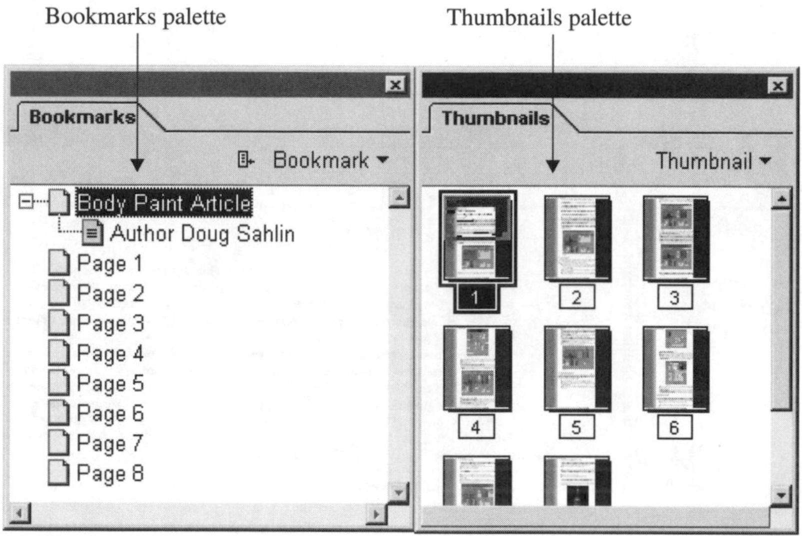

Use Acrobat Reader Menu Commands

You'll find all of the Acrobat Reader menu commands neatly arranged in a row at the top of the interface, previously shown in Figure 2-1. The various menu commands are used to navigate within the document and to select elements within the document. Within Acrobat Reader, you cannot edit PDF documents, but you can select items from the document, copy them to the clipboard, paste the copied element into another application, and edit them there. You have six Acrobat Menu groups to use when working with a PDF document in Acrobat Reader.

- **File** This menu group is used to open documents, save copies of documents, print documents, and gain information about the document itself and any security assigned to the document. You—or anyone reading your PDF documents in Acrobat Reader—cannot change security measures. Security measures can only be changed in Acrobat as discussed in Chapter 13.

- **Edit** The commands in this menu group are used to perform perfunctory edits on the page, such as copying text from the document to the clipboard, finding words in the document, and searching an index of PDF files. Several commands in this group function identically in the full version of Acrobat.
- **Document** The commands in this menu group are used to navigate within the document. Document Navigation is covered in detail in Chapter 3.
- **View** The commands in this menu group are used to change the way a document is displayed within the Document pane. You can zoom in or zoom out on a document, change the way the document fits within the pane, or change the number of pages that are displayed within the Document pane, as well as rotate a document page. These commands are covered in depth in Chapter 3.
- **Window** The commands in this menu group are used to display various elements in the Acrobat Reader workspace. There are commands in this group that can be used to display multiple documents, which is covered in Chapter 3.
- **Help** The commands in this menu group are used to get online help and basic information about Acrobat and Acrobat Reader.

TIP *To quickly gain more workspace, you can temporarily hide the Menu Bar by pressing F9. To reveal the hidden Menu Bar, press F9 again.*

Use the Acrobat Reader Toolbars

You use Acrobat Reader toolbars to perform many tasks while viewing a PDF document. When you initially launch Acrobat Reader, toolbars are arranged in a single row below the Menu Bar. The toolbars are arranged in groups (as shown in Figure 2-1), similar to the way the Menu Bar is laid out. You click a button to access a tool. Whenever you see a small black triangle pointing down to the right of a tool group, you can click the triangle to view more tools within the group or view more tool options. Hold your mouse over the triangle and a tooltip appears, telling you more tools are available. If the triangle shows more tools, a two-headed arrow appears that will expand the tool group when clicked. Acrobat Reader and Acrobat designate an expanded tool group with a triangle pointing to the left. Click the triangle to collapse the tool group. You can also float toolbars to suit your working preference. You'll learn how to float toolbars in the latter part of this chapter.

The toolbar groups as they appear on the command bar from left to right are as follows: File, Navigation View, View History, Basic Tools, Viewing, and Adobe

Online. You can show or hide an individual toolbar by choosing Window | Toolbars and then clicking the toolbar name to select or deselect it. Visible toolbars have a checkmark next to them, as shown in the following image.

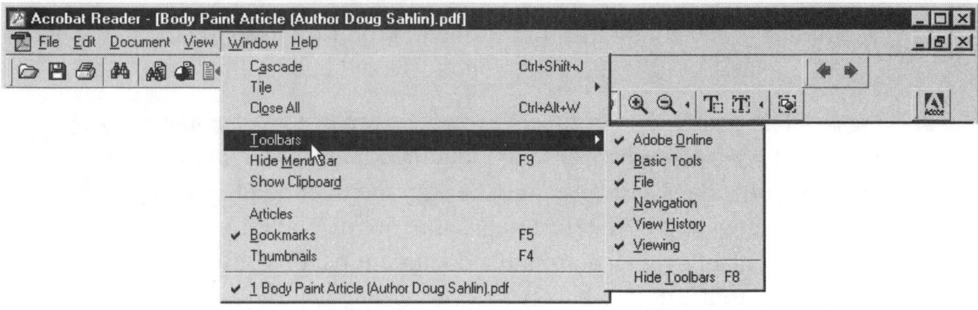

Use Acrobat Reader Tool Groups

The Acrobat Reader tool groups are shown in expanded form in Figure 2-2. In Chapter 3, you'll find an in-depth discussion on using the Navigation and View toolbars.

About the File Tool Group

The File tool group, in the following image, expands to nine buttons you use for file maintenance, printing, and search tasks. The parameters and options for these tools and their corresponding menu commands will be discussed in detail in Chapter 3.

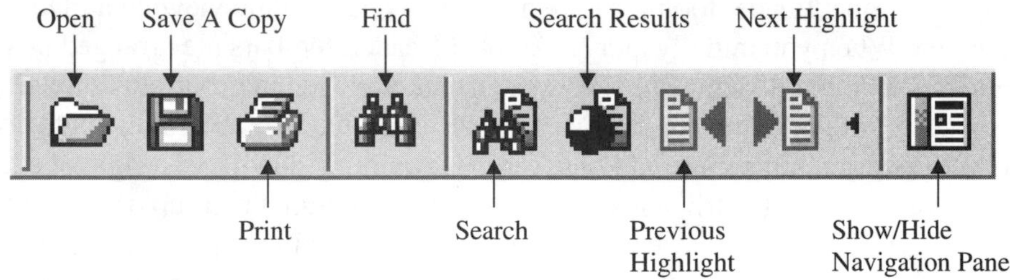

- **Open** This tool is used to open a PDF file from your hard drive. After you click the button, a dialog box opens that you use to navigate to the file you want to open. The Menu Bar equivalent for this tool is File | Open.

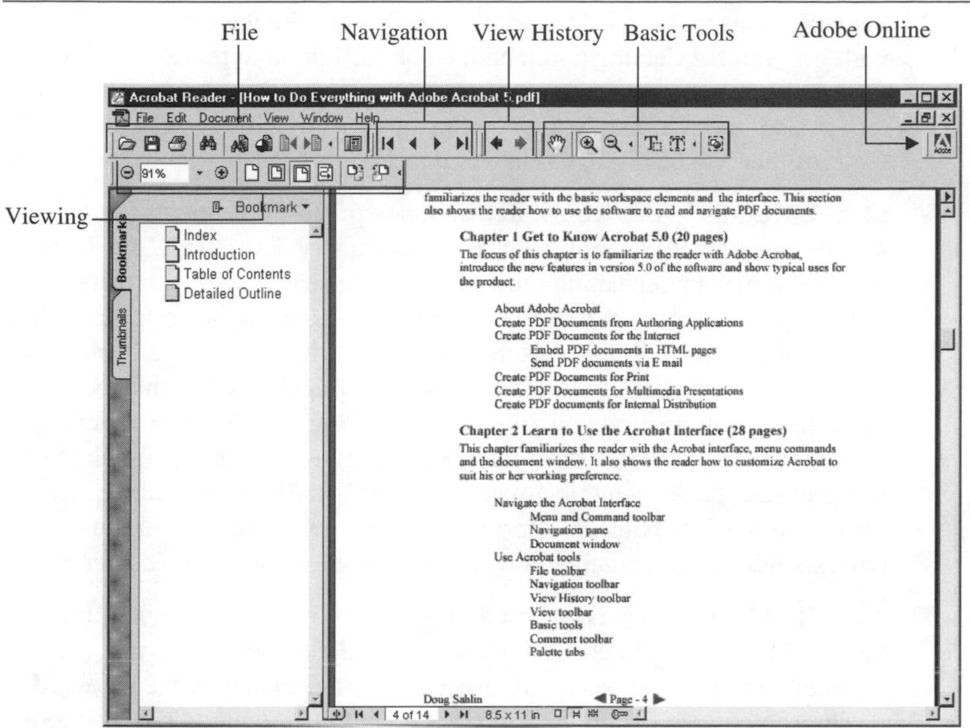

FIGURE 2-2 The Acrobat Reader tools are divided into six individual tool groups.

- **Save A Copy** This tool is used to save a copy of the PDF document you are viewing. Click the button to open a dialog box that prompts you for a filename and folder. This command comes in handy when you are viewing a PDF document that you have downloaded from the Internet into your Web browser and want to save for future reference. The Menu Bar equivalent for this tool is File | Save A Copy.
- **Print** This tool is used to print a hard copy of the document you are viewing with your system printer. Click the button to open a dialog box with several printing options. The Menu Bar equivalent for this tool is File | Print. If document security prohibits printing a hard copy of the document, this tool's icon is dimmed out.
- **Find** This tool is used to find a specific word or string of text within a document. Click the button to open a dialog box with search parameters. The Menu Bar equivalent for this tool is Edit | Find.

- **Search** This tool is used to search an index of PDF documents created with the Acrobat Catalog command. Click the button to reveal a dialog box that you use to enter search parameters. The Menu Bar equivalent for this tool is Edit | Search. The Search command has a number of very powerful features that will be discussed in detail in Chapter 3.
- **Search Results** After you search an index of PDF documents, you usually end up with several matches to your query. By default, the Search tool is dimmed out, meaning there are no more search results to display. After you use the Search tool, the Search Results dialog box appears with a list of the documents that match your query. After selecting a document, the file opens with the key words of your query highlighted. If the document contains the information you are looking for, you can close the Search Results dialog box. Click the Search Results button to reopen the dialog box and select a different document from the list. The Menu Bar equivalent for this tool is Edit | Search | Results. The features of this tool and its corresponding menu command will be discussed in detail in Chapter 3.
- **Next Highlight** This tool is used to navigate to the next match of the keyword or phrase you entered in the Search dialog box. If the tool is dimmed out, then your search returned only one instance of the keyword or phrase you specified in your query. On the File group toolbar, this tool is located before the Previous Highlight tool. After your initial search of an index, you use the Next Highlight tool before the Previous Highlight tool. The Menu Bar equivalent for this tool is Edit | Search | Next.
- **Previous Highlight** This button is used to return to the previous occurrence of the key word or phrase you entered in the Search dialog box. This tool is dimmed out when there is no previous occurrence of the key word or phrase in your query. The Menu Bar equivalent for this tool is Edit | Search | Previous.
- **Show/Hide Navigation Pane** This tool is used to display or hide the Navigation pane, which is the window on the left side of the interface.

TIP *You can also show or hide the Navigation pane by clicking the button with a double-headed arrow below the lower-left corner of the Document pane.*

About the Basic Tool Group

The tools in this group (as shown in the following image) are used to manually navigate to different parts of a document, activate links in the document, and change the magnification of the document. The enhanced features of these tools will be discussed in Chapter 3. This group also has tools used for selecting text and graphic elements in a document. Selecting text and graphics for use in other applications will be discussed in detail in an upcoming section of this chapter.

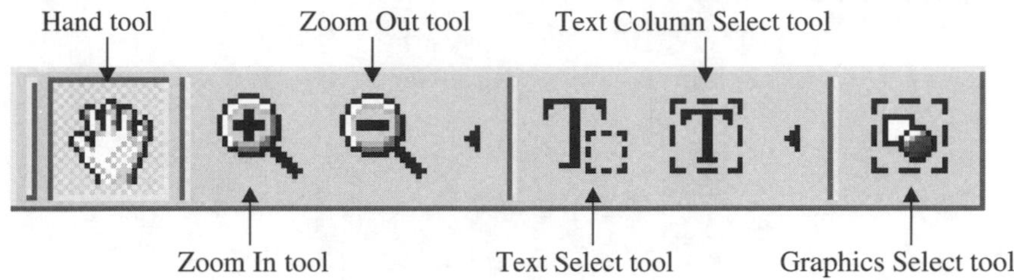

- **Hand** This aptly named tool is used to manually navigate through a page of a PDF document. Click the tool to select it. When you click to select this tool, your cursor becomes a closed hand. To navigate from the top to the bottom of a page, and vice versa, move the tool over the document, select the Hand tool, and then click and drag. When you select the hand tool and click within the Document pane, your cursor becomes a closed fist. Release the left mouse button to stop scrolling the page. The Hand Tool is also used to find and activate links within the document. When you pass your cursor over a document link or a bookmark in the Bookmark pane, the cursor becomes a pointing finger. Click the link or bookmark to navigate to the specified destination within the document.
- **Zoom In** This tool is used to magnify all or part of a document.
- **Zoom Out** This tool is used to zoom out to the next lowest level of magnification.
- **Text Select** This tool is used to select a block of text within a PDF document. You can copy the selected text to the clipboard and save it for use in another application.
- **Text Column Select** This tool is used to define and select a column of text within a document. After selecting a column of text, you can copy it to the clipboard and save it for use in another application.
- **Graphics Select** This tool is used to select graphics within a PDF document. You can then copy the selected graphics to the clipboard and save them for use in another application.

About the Navigation Tool Group

The tools from the appropriately named Navigation group (as shown in the following image) are used to go from page to page within a document and back again. There are also tools within this group that you use to navigate to the start or end of the document.

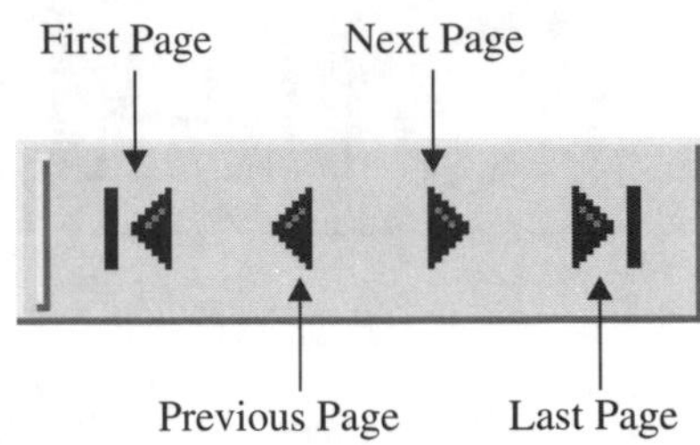

- **First Page** This button is used to navigate to the start of a PDF document. If you are at the start of the document, the tool is dimmed out.
- **Previous Page** This button is used to go to the previous page in a document. This button is dimmed out when you are viewing the first page of a document.
- **Next Page** This button is used to advance to the next page in a document. If you are viewing the last page of a document, the button is dimmed out.
- **Last Page** This button is used to navigate to the final page of a document. If you are already viewing the last page of a document, the button is dimmed out.

About the View History Tool Group

You use the tools in the View History group the same way you use the Forward and Back buttons in your favorite Web browser. However, the View History tools are a bit more sophisticated. The navigation buttons in your Web browser remember the last page you visited. The Acrobat and Acrobat Reader View History tools (as shown in the following illustration) return you to the last view you looked at (hence the tool's name), with the identical magnification you viewed the page at originally.

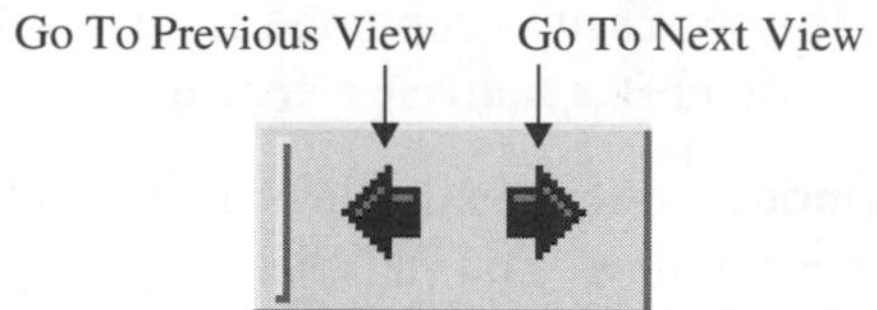

- **Go To Previous View** This button is used to return to the previous view of the last page you visited. It is the button that looks like a Back button in a Web browser. If you are at the start of a document, or have navigated to your first view of the document, the tool is dimmed out.
- **Go To Next View** This button is used to advance to the next available view you selected in a document. It is the button that looks similar to the Forward button in a web browser. If you are at the end of a document, the tool is dimmed out.

NOTE *You can also use the View History tools to navigate between documents; you can navigate from the last view in one document to the first view in the next document. If you have closed a document during an Acrobat or Acrobat Reader session and have navigated to the first view of the current document, you can use the Go To Previous View button to open the previous view of the closed document that you had open prior to the current document.*

About the Viewing Tool Group

You use the tools in this group to modify the view of the page you are reading. The use of these tools will be discussed in greater detail in Chapter 3. With the Viewing tool group, you have eight tools and the magnification window, as shown in the following image, that are used to modify your view of a document page.

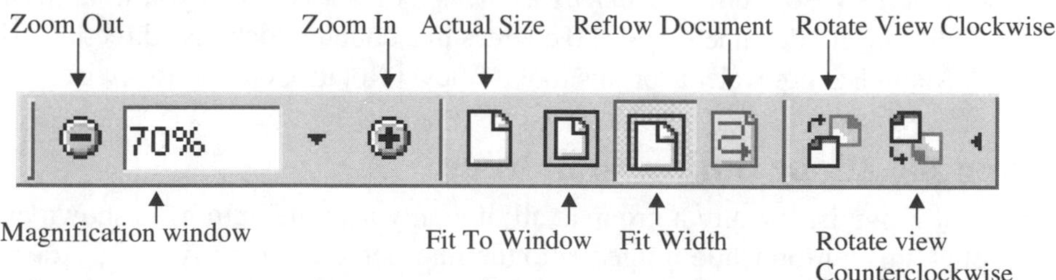

- **Zoom Out** This tool is used to zoom to the next lowest level of magnification. The Menu Bar equivalent for this tool is View | Zoom Out.
- **Magnification window** Acrobat displays the current percentage level of magnification in this window. You can click the triangle to the right of the window and select a magnification percentage from the drop-down menu, or you can enter the desired level of magnification directly into the window and then press enter or return to apply. You can also specify a magnification level by choosing View | Zoom To and then entering a value between 8.33% and 1600% in the Zoom To dialog box (the available range of magnification in Acrobat).
- **Zoom In** This tool is used to zoom to the next highest level of magnification. The Menu Bar equivalent for this tool is View | Zoom In.
- **Actual Size** This tool is used to return the document page to its originally published size. The Menu Bar equivalent for this tool is View | Actual Size.
- **Fit To Window** This button is used to zoom in or out to a level of magnification that displays a single page in the Document pane at its current width. The Menu Bar equivalent for this tool is View | Fit To Window.
- **Fit Width** This tool is used to conform the document width to the Document pane current width. The Menu Bar equivalent for this tool is View | Fit Width.
- **Reflow Document** This tool is used to reflow the contents of a page to fit the Document pane current width. The Menu Bar equivalent for this tool is View | Reflow.
- **Rotate View Clockwise** This tool is used to rotate the page you are viewing 90 degrees in a clockwise direction. The Menu Bar equivalent for this tool is View | Rotate Clockwise.
- **Rotate View Counterclockwise** This tool is used when you want to rotate the current document page 90 degrees in a counterclockwise direction. The Menu Bar equivalent for this tool is View | Rotate Counterclockwise.

About the Adobe Online Tool Group

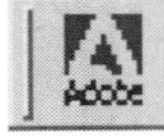

This tool group isn't really a group at all; it's only a single button, as shown at left. You click this button while logged onto the Internet to go directly to the Adobe Web site. This tool can come in handy if you need quick access to customer support, or information about any of Adobe's other programs.

To gain more working area, press F8 to momentarily hide all toolbars. Press F8 again to reveal the hidden toolbars.

Use Text and Graphics from PDFs in Other Applications

When you need to modify a document that you plan to distribute electronically, nothing beats the full version of Acrobat. However, if you work in an organization and need to share text and images that will be edited, then supplying an entire organization with a licensed version of Acrobat becomes cost prohibitive. There are times when you need to share editable text and graphic elements with clients who don't own the full version of Acrobat. If this describes your situation, you can teach recipients of your PDF documents how to use Acrobat Reader tools to select text and graphic elements from your document and use them in other applications.

Capturing text and graphic elements from a PDF document that you want to save for future editing can also come in handy if you are traveling and do not have a full version of Acrobat available. Select and copy text or graphic elements from PDF documents using another computer with Acrobat Reader installed, and then paste the copied elements into an application. Save the copied elements in a file format recognizable by software on your home or office computer, and then save the file to disk or e-mail it to yourself. You can also extract elements from a PDF document if you travel with a laptop equipped with Acrobat Reader. What you can do with Acrobat Reader is remarkable, especially when you consider it is distributed free of charge.

NOTE

You may not be able to capture text or graphic elements if Acrobat Security has been applied to the document.

Capture Text from a PDF Document

You can easily select any text elements in a PDF document with the Acrobat Reader *Text Select* tool. With the Text Select tool, you can select a single letter, a word, a sentence, an entire paragraph, or more. If there are graphic elements dispersed in the text you are selecting, Acrobat Reader will ignore them and select only text. To capture text from a PDF document,

1. Launch Acrobat Reader and open a PDF file.

2. Select the Text Select tool, shown at left from the Basic Tools group on the toolbar.

3. After you select the tool, drag it into the Document pane. Note that your cursor is now in the shape of an I-beam.
4. To select the text, click the point where you want to begin selecting text, drag your cursor to the right, and release it when you have selected the desired text. To select text from more than one line, click to define the beginning point, drag to the right, and then drag down to select contiguous sentences. Acrobat Reader highlights the selected text, as shown in Figure 2-3.

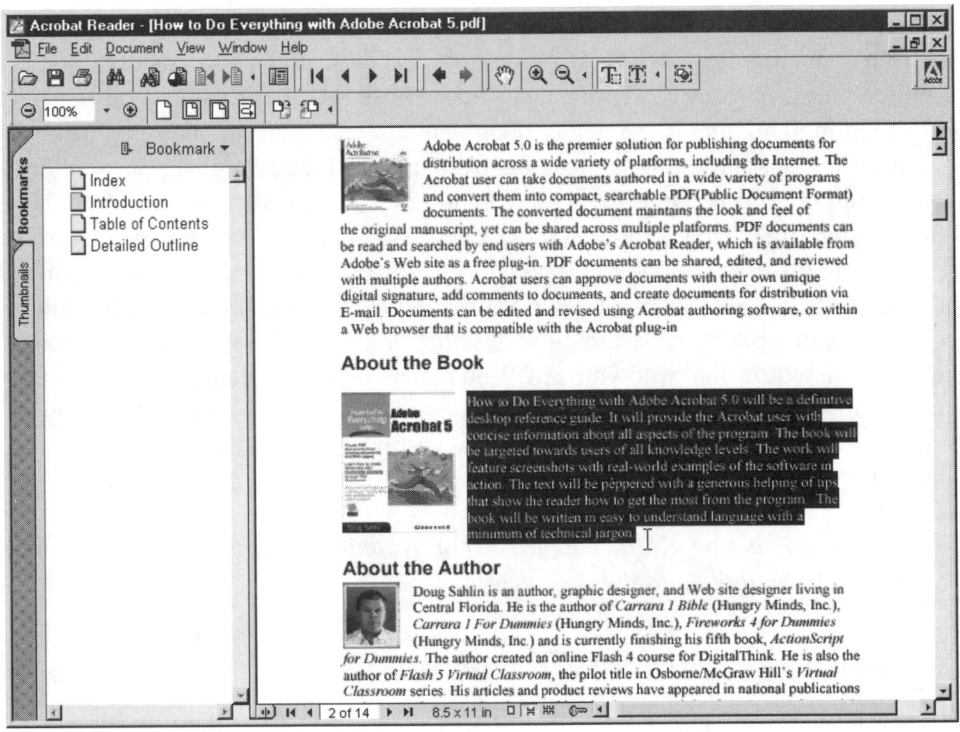

FIGURE 2-3 You can select text from a PDF document using the Acrobat Reader Text Select tool.

5. Choose Edit | Copy, and Acrobat copies the selected text to your system clipboard.
6. Open your favorite word processing program and choose the Paste command. You can now edit the pasted text and save it for future reference.

Capture a Block of Text from a PDF Document

Acrobat Reader has another text selection tool called the *Column Select* tool. With this tool you can define a block of text you want to capture. The tool works like the lasso tool you find in some graphics applications. You drag the tool down and to the right or left to select an area of text. To select a block of text with the Column Select tool, follow these steps:

1. Launch Acrobat Reader and open the file from which you want to select text.

2. Select the Column Select tool, as shownon the left, from the Basic Tools group on the toolbar. Note that the Column Select tool is on a flyout with the Text Select tool. If the Column Select tool is not visible, click the triangle to the right of the Text Select tool to expand the tool group and then select the tool.
3. Click to the above left (or right if you prefer) of the text you want to select, and then drag down and to the right (or left). As you drag the tool, a rectangular bounding box composed of dotted lines appears, defining the area you are selecting.
4. When the bounding box covers the text you want selected, release the mouse button and Acrobat highlights the selected text.
5. Choose Edit | Copy to copy the text to your system clipboard.
6. Open the application you plan to use the text in and choose the Paste command to work with the pasted text.

TIP *To view the contents of the clipboard, choose Window | Show Clipboard, and Acrobat displays the contents of the clipboard in a new window.*

Capture Graphic Elements from PDF Documents

When you receive a PDF document with embedded graphics, the PDF retains the look and feel of the graphics as they were originally created. If the PDF document has a relatively low level of compression applied, the graphic element will be crisp and clear. You can use the Acrobat Reader *Graphics Select* tool to select a graphic element, such as a photograph or logo, from a PDF document as follows:

1. Launch Acrobat Reader and open the PDF file that contains the graphic element(s) you want to select.

2. Select the Graphics Select tool, shown at left.
3. Within the PDF document, navigate to the page that contains the graphic you want to select. Note that your cursor becomes a crosshair once you move it to the Document pane.
4. Click to the above left (or above right) of the graphic you want to select, and then drag down and to the right (or left). As you drag, a dotted rectangular bounding box appears, giving you a preview of the area you selected.
5. When the bounding box surrounds the graphic, as shown in Figure 2-4, release the mouse button.
6. Choose Edit | Copy and Acrobat Reader copies the graphic to the system clipboard. You can now paste the graphic into any application that supports pasting from the system clipboard.

TIP *You can select a portion of a graphic (known in photo editing circles as cropping) by releasing the mouse button when the rectangle surrounds the desired portion of the graphic.*

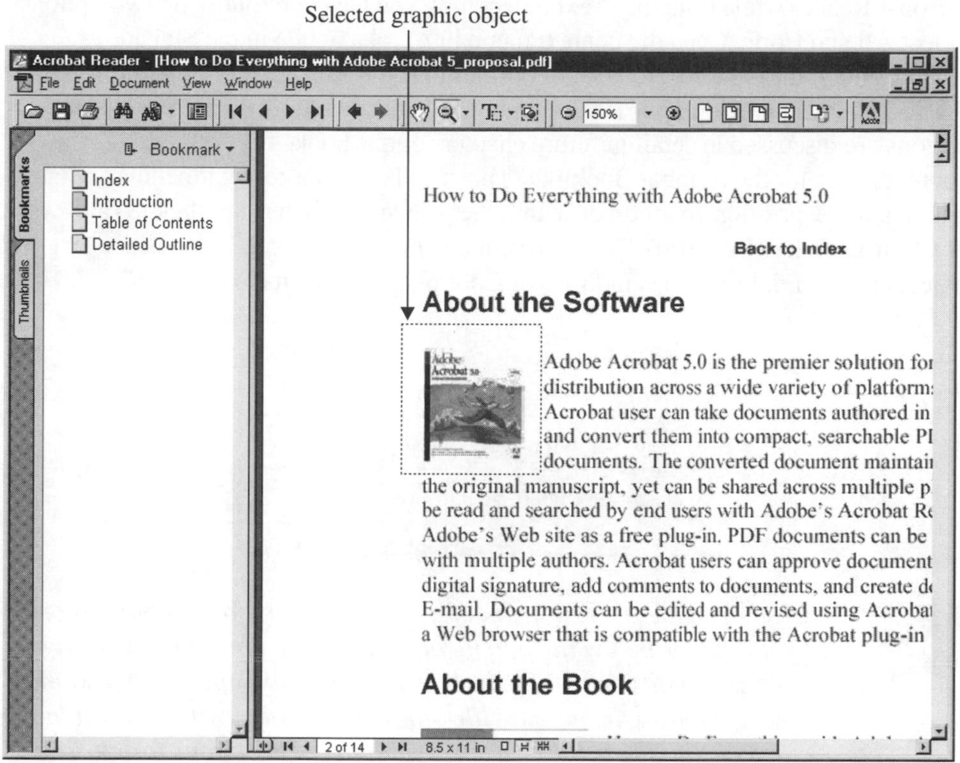

Selected graphic object
Acrobat Reader - [How to Do Everything with Adobe Acrobat 5_proposal.pdf]
File Edit Document View Window Help
150%
Bookmark
Bookmarks
Thumbnails
Index
Introduction
Table of Contents
Detailed Outline
How to Do Everything with Adobe Acrobat 5.0
Back to Index
About the Software
Adobe Acrobat 5.0 is the premier solution fo
distribution across a wide variety of platform
Acrobat user can take documents authored in
and convert them into compact, searchable P
documents. The converted document maintai
the original manuscript, yet can be shared across multiple p
be read and searched by end users with Adobe's Acrobat R
Adobe's Web site as a free plug-in. PDF documents can be
with multiple authors. Acrobat users can approve document
digital signature, add comments to documents, and create d
E-mail. Documents can be edited and revised using Acroba
a Web browser that is compatible with the Acrobat plug-in
About the Book
2 of 14
8.5 x 11 in

FIGURE 2-1 You use the Graphics Select tool to select graphic elements from a PDF document.

Save Time with Context Menus

Acrobat Reader and Acrobat have context menus that can streamline your production and speed up your workflow. Context menu options will vary depending upon the tool you use and the pane you work in. For example, if you access a context menu in

Acrobat Reader while using the Text Select tool, you have the following two options: Select All and Copy. Open the context menu in Acrobat while in the Signatures palette, and you have a different set of options that pertain to digital signatures within the document and their properties. Individual palette context menu commands and options are discussed in detail in future chapters of this book. The following is the context menu for the Acrobat Bookmarks palette. To open a context menu associated with a palette, position your cursor within the palette and then right-click (Windows) or Control-click (Macintosh). To open a context menu specific to an object, select the object and then right-click (Windows) or Control-click (Macintosh).

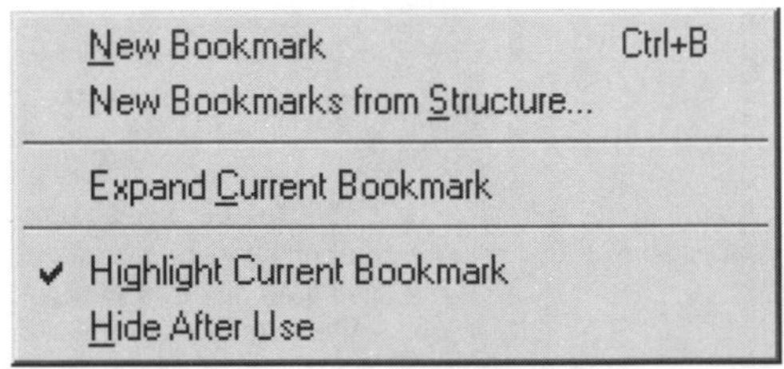

NOTE

When you open the context menu of a floating palette or toolbar, you must place your cursor below the palette or toolbar title bar before you right-click (Windows) or Control-click (Macintosh). If you open a context menu with your cursor on the palette title bar using Acrobat with the Windows operating system, the context menu displays system options for closing, moving, or resizing the palette. On a Macintosh system, no context menu is displayed when you Control-click with your cursor over the title bar.

Navigate the Acrobat Interface

Acrobat and Acrobat Reader interfaces look similar with one major exception—Acrobat's additional tools and palettes. When you open a document in Acrobat, you have two additional palettes in the Navigation pane and an extra row of tools on the toolbar, as shown in Figure 2-5. You use the additional palettes in the Navigation pane to advance to comments and digital signatures included in the document. You use the additional tools to add your own comments and digital signatures to a document and to add interactive elements such as links, multimedia elements, and much more. You will find additional information on how to use each tool in the remaining chapters of this book. In the sections that follow, the Acrobat tool groups will be discussed along with a brief explanation of each tool and its uses.

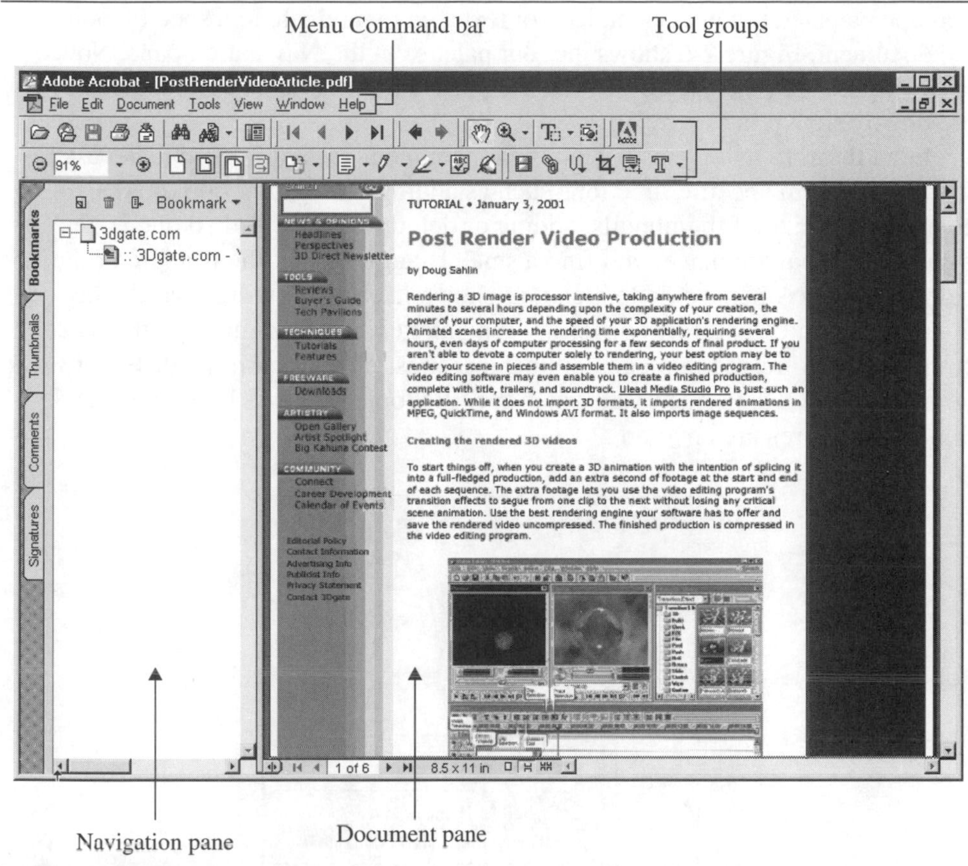

FIGURE 2-5 The Acrobat interface consists of two panes, a Menu Command bar, and several tool groups.

Use the Navigation Pane

The Acrobat Navigation pane has four tabs that are used to open palettes in order to navigate to specific items in a document. Open a palette by clicking its tab. You use the *Bookmarks* palette to display a list of the bookmarks in the document. Within the *Thumbnails* palette, you find thumbnail images of each page in the document. When you open the *Comments* palette, you'll see a list of all comments added to the document and the names of people who authored them. You open the *Digital Signatures* panel to review the list of digital signatures in the document. Whenever you open a palette, you click an icon or text area to navigate to a specific point in the document. Figure 2-6 shows the four palettes in the Navigation pane. Notice in this figure the palettes are floating as opposed to their default docked position previously shown in Figure 2-5.

In addition to using these palettes for document navigation, you also use them to perform specific functions such as adding or deleting bookmarks, changing the size of thumbnails, adding or deleting pages, and so on. To the right of each palette name, you find a small triangle. Click the triangle or the palette name to open a palette menu, as shown in the following image. The operations you can perform differ in each palette. You find many of the palette commands duplicated in menu command groups. You'll learn the different ways you can achieve the same result when specific topics such as bookmarks and digital signatures are covered.

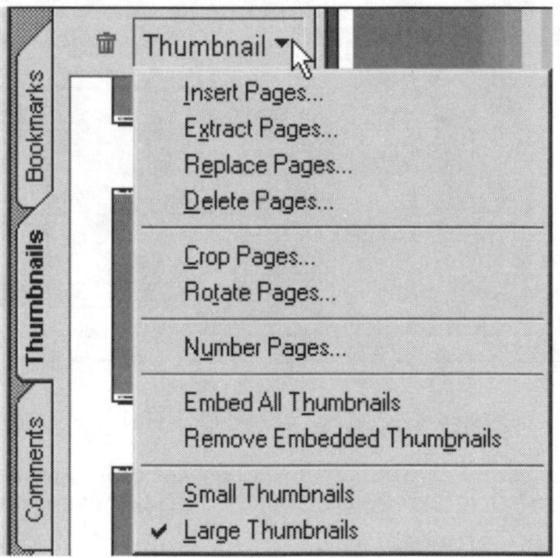

About the Document Pane

You use the Document pane (the large window to the right of the Navigation pane, previously shown in Figure 2-5) to edit a PDF document, as well as read it. At the bottom left of the Document pane is a toolbar that contains various information about the displayed PDF file, as well as tools you can use to navigate to a specific page and change the number of pages Acrobat displays in the Document pane. In Chapter 3, you'll learn how to use these tools.

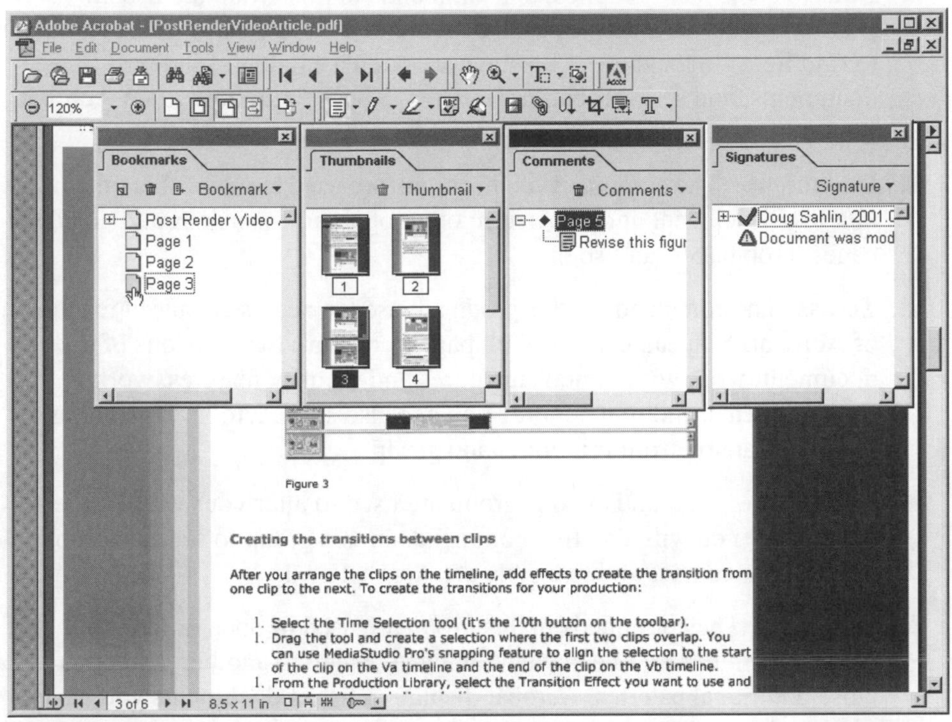

FIGURE 2-6 You use the Navigation pane to advance to specific elements in a PDF document.

Use the Acrobat Menu Commands

You find the Acrobat menu commands at the top of the interface, grouped by command type. Acrobat has seven command groups named File, Edit, Document, Tools, View, Window, and Help. Many of the commands function identically to those you use in Acrobat Reader. However, you have many additional commands that you use to unlock the powerful features of Acrobat, such as capturing Web pages. In upcoming chapters, individual menu commands will be presented in detail when they pertain to the topic of discussion. From left to right on the Menu Bar, you find the following command groups:

- **File** The commands in this list are used to open, close, and save documents. You also have additional commands to import comments, form data and scan documents, open Web pages, and view document information, as well as batch process.

- **Edit** As the name implies, the commands in this group are used to perform edits to the current PDF document. You also have Edit commands to find items in the current document, search a catalog of indexed PDF documents, and set Acrobat Preferences. You'll learn how to set Acrobat Preferences in an upcoming section of this chapter.
- **Document** The commands in this group are used to move about the pages in a PDF document and to perform other operations, such as add and delete pages, crop pages, and so on.
- **Tools** The commands in this group are used to access enhanced features of Acrobat. You can capture Web pages, compare two versions of a document, work with digital signatures and security features, work with form elements, and much more. You can also start Acrobat Distiller and Acrobat Catalog from this command group.
- **View** The commands in this group are used to alter your view of the document. You will also find commands in this group to set up a proof of a PDF document and to enable the Acrobat grid.
- **Window** The commands in this group are used to open or hide tool groups, switch from one Navigation pane palette to another, and open or close additional palettes. Acrobat displays a list of documents you have open at the bottom of this group.
- **Help** In this command group you find access to program help, links to Adobe online, the Adobe JavaScript guide, and other useful information.

Use Acrobat Tool Groups

The tools you use to unleash the full power of Acrobat are conveniently grouped and laid out on a toolbar. In each group, you find tools that perform operations related to an Acrobat feature such as Comments and Digital Signatures. In other groups, you find related tools to edit, view, navigate documents, and so on. Many of the tool groups are collapsed to save working space. A *collapsed group* is signified by a downward pointing triangle. Click the triangle to view other tools in the group, as shown in the following image. You can click the double-headed arrow to expand the group on the toolbar. *Expanded tool groups* are designated by a left-pointing triangle. Click the left-pointing triangle to collapse an expanded group.

You can do most of your work in Acrobat using the tool groups. If you prefer working with menus, most of the tools have equivalent menu commands. Most Acrobat users find it convenient to work with a combination of menu commands, tools, context menus, and shortcuts. For a complete list of Acrobat shortcuts, refer to Appendix A. Figure 2-7 shows the Acrobat tool groups. Note that all groups have been expanded and repositioned in this figure.

The following sections list certain tool groups as they appear on the toolbar. In each tool group section, individual tools are listed with a brief description of the task they accomplish. In future chapters, you'll find detailed information about using a specific tool in conjunction with a related task.

Many of the tool groups in Acrobat perform the same function as their counterpart in Acrobat Reader. In the upcoming sections, the only tool groups that will be discussed are those that differ.

About the File Tool Group

The File tool group, shown in the following image, expands to eleven tools that you use for file maintenance, printing, and search tasks. Many of the tools perform identical functions to their Acrobat Reader counterparts, with the exception of

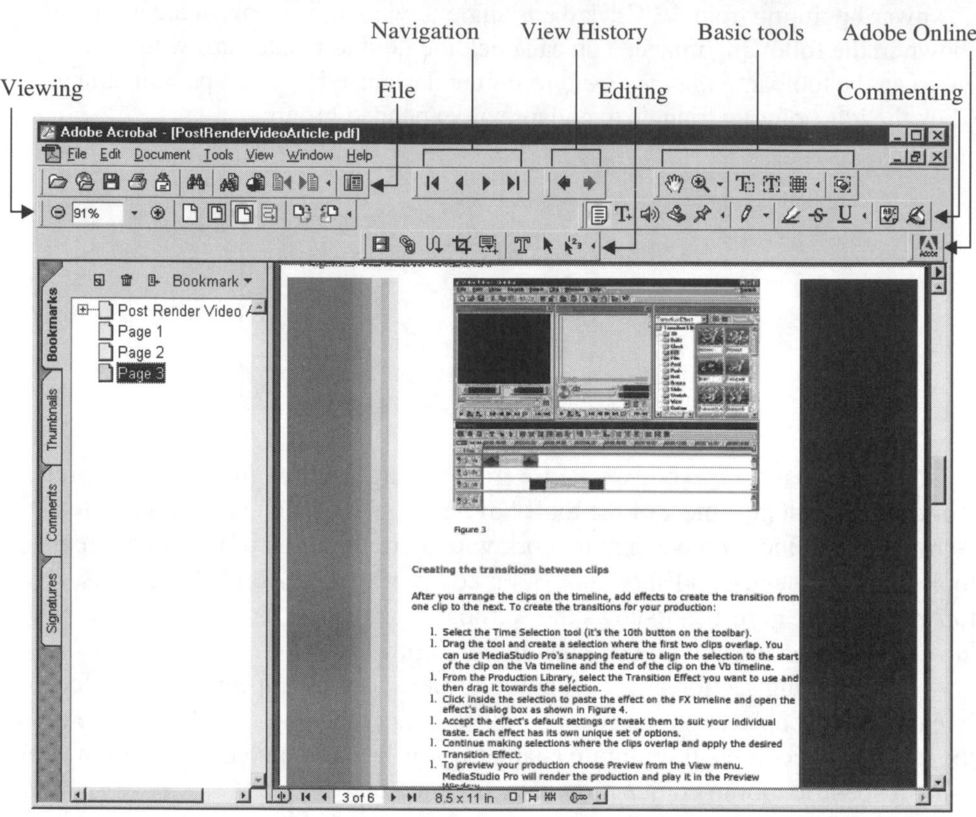

FIGURE 2-7 You use Acrobat tools to edit, navigate, and view PDF documents.

specialized tools that you use to open Web pages and e-mail a PDF document. The following list includes the tools that are unique to Acrobat.

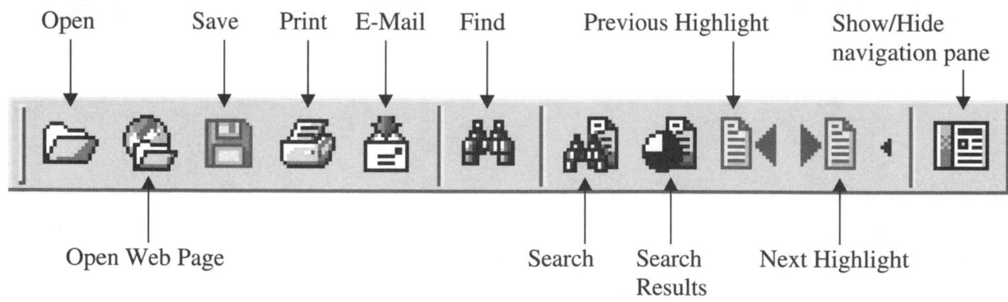

- **Open Web page** Click this button to download a web page into the Document pane. You must be connected to an Internet Service Provider for this tool to work. Converting web pages to PDF documents is covered in detail in Chapter 6.
- **Save** This tool is used to save the current PDF document. This tool functions similarly to its Acrobat Reader counterpart, Save A Copy. However, in Acrobat Reader, the Save A Copy command only allows you to save unedited copies of files; in Acrobat, you can save edited files. The Menu Bar equivalent for this tool is File | Save.
- **E-Mail** Click this button to send a PDF document as an e-mail attachment. You must be logged onto your Internet server for this tool to work properly. Information on sending PDF documents as e-mail attachments is presented in detail in Chapters 5 and 16.

About the Commenting Tool Group

You use the tools in this group to add comments (or, as they were referred to in early versions of Acrobat, annotations) to a PDF document. Your comments can be in the form of notes, free-form text, file attachments, and sound files. Within the tool group, you'll also find tools to add shapes to PDF documents, mark up text, and spell check form fields and comments, as well as add digital signatures. The tasks you perform with the commenting tools in this group are discussed in detail in Chapter 12; digital signatures and spell checking are discussed in Chapter 13. This group is divided into four sections. The first three are collapsed to save space; the fourth is expanded, as shown in Figure 2-8.

The first section of the Comments tool group is used to annotate a document. With the tools in this section (as shown in Figure 2-8), you can create written, visual, and audible comments to a PDF document.

- **Note** Click this button when you want to add a note or comment to a PDF file. After you create the note, an icon that looks like a sticky note appears in the document. Readers click the icon to read the note.
- **Text** Use this tool to add free-form text notes with or without a border to a document.
- **Sound Attachment** This tool is used to insert audio files in a document or to record an audio note. After you use this tool, a speaker icon appears in the document. When a viewer double-clicks the icon, the recorded note or sound plays.

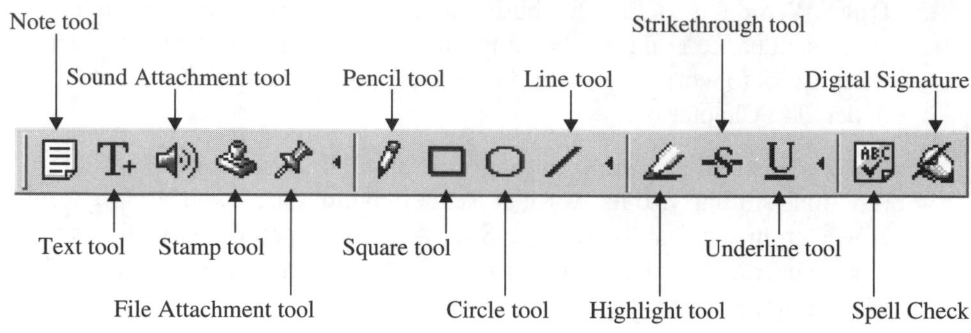

FIGURE 2-8 You use the tools in this group to annotate and add digital signatures to a PDF document.

- **Stamp** This tool is used to add your stamp of approval (or other annotations) to a document. Acrobat gives you four stamp categories with a variety of presets to use, such as Confidential, Draft, and Final. You can specify the color and size of the stamp, as well as create custom stamps. The Stamp tool is the electronic equivalent of a rubber stamp, without the messy inkpads.
- **File Attachment** This tool is used to attach a file to a PDF document. After you use this tool, an icon appears in the document. When the icon is double-clicked, the file opens up in the appropriate program (for example, Microsoft Word for a file with the .doc extension).

The next set of tools in the Commenting tool group is used to add graphic elements to a PDF file, such as straight lines, rectangles and ovals. You add graphic elements to draw attention to specific objects within a document, such as a paragraph that needs to be revised or deleted before the document is acceptable for publication. As explained in Chapter 12, each graphic element you add to a document can have a pop-up note attached.

- **Pencil** This tool is used to add a free-form line to a PDF file. You can modify the color and thickness of lines you draw. Your drawing skill with a mouse determines how straight or crooked the line is.
- **Square** This tool is used to add a square or rectangle to a PDF file. You can specify the thickness and color of the border and whether or not the shape is filled with color.

- **Circle** This tool is used to create circles and ovals. You can specify the thickness and color of the borders and whether or not the shape is filled with color.
- **Line** This tool is used to add straight lines to a PDF document. You specify the width and color of the line. You can even create a line with head and tail shapes, such as arrowheads or diamonds.

The next group of tools in the Commenting group is used to mark up text, as shown in Figure 2-8 as well. You can highlight text, create strikeouts, or underline text.

- **Highlight** This tool is used to highlight text. This tool is the electronic counterpart of a felt-tipped highlighter. You can change the color of a highlight from the Acrobat default yellow to any color available in your system color picker. You can also use the Highlight tool to create a note that pops up when a viewer clicks the highlighted text.
- **Strikeout** This tool is used to strikeout selected text. You can change the color of the strikeout and you can create a pop-up note with the Strikeout tool as well.
- **Underline** This tool is used to highlight text by underlining it. You can specify the color of the underline and use this tool to create a clickable pop-up as well.

The last two tools in this group (shown in Figure 2-8) are used to spell check forms and comments, as well as add digital signatures to a document.

- **Spell Check** This tool is used to check any comments and form fields in the document for spelling errors. After you click the button, a dialog box appears. When Acrobat finds a spelling error, the dialog box displays a list of corrections you can apply or ignore. You also have the option of adding the suspect word to the Acrobat dictionary.
- **Digital Signature** This tool is used to digitally sign a PDF document. When you add a digital signature to a document, a dialog box appears, prompting you to log in. Once you are logged in, you specify where in the document to add the signature.

About the Editing Tool Group

With the tools in this group, you can add quite a bit of interactivity to your PDF documents. You can create article threads, links, and form fields; crop document pages; and touch up text and graphic elements, as well as add movies to a document. The expanded tool group is shown here.

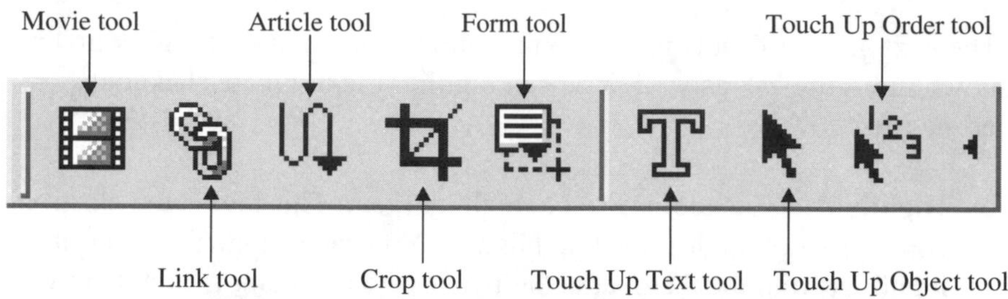

- **Movie** This tool is used to add movies to your PDF files. You specify the location where the movie will play in the document and the trigger used to begin the movie. You can choose to display the first frame of the movie, which, when clicked, will start play, or choose to leave the movie invisible until a button is clicked to begin play.
- **Link** This tool is used to add interactivity to your documents. You can create visible or invisible links. You can use document links for navigation or to trigger an event, such as opening a file or opening a Web page. Acrobat calls these events *Actions*, and you have a wide variety of Actions from which you can choose. Detailed uses for this tool are discussed in Chapter 7.
- **Article** This tool is used to select a portion of a PDF document and give it a name, known in Acrobat as an *Article*. An Article can be a single block of text, or several blocks of related text dispersed throughout the document. When readers view your document, they can follow the thread of the article.
- **Crop** This tool is used to reduce the size of the page or remove elements, such as unwanted graphics and extraneous text from a PDF document page. If you have used cropping tools in image editing programs, you'll find this tool performs in a similar manner.

- **Form** This tool is used to create form fields. After you define the area for the form field, you need to define the type. The types you can choose from are Button, Check Box, Combo Box, List Box, Radio Button, Signature, and Text. Forms will be discussed in detail in Chapter 9.
- **TouchUp Text** This tool is used to edit text in PDF documents. After you select a line of text with the tool, you can modify the text or delete it.
- **TouchUp Object** This tool is used to select graphic objects in PDF documents. You can then move or delete the objects.
- **TouchUp Order** This tool is used to change the order (or flow) of elements in a tagged PDF.

Customize the Workspace

As you become more comfortable with Acrobat, you'll find there are certain tools that you use more often than others. Adobe has engineered flexibility into the program, making it possible for you to customize the workspace to suit your working preference. You can customize the workspace by floating toolbars and palettes, as well as expanding toolbars that you frequently use.

Float Toolbars

When you edit PDF documents and perform the same task numerous times, reaching up to select a tool from the command bar can be distracting. If this is the case, or if you prefer working with a certain toolbar in a different position, you can float any toolbar to a different position. To float a toolbar, click the vertical line at the left edge of the toolbar and drag it. Release the mouse button when the toolbar is where you want it. To move a floating toolbar, click its title bar, drag it to a new position, and release the mouse button. Figure 2-9 shows several floating toolbars in the Document pane.

NOTE *To dock a floating toolbar to the command bar, click the horizontal line below the title bar. You cannot dock a toolbar if you drag it by its title bar. When you close a floating toolbar, it does not redock itself. When you open the toolbar again, it floats in the last position you left it.*

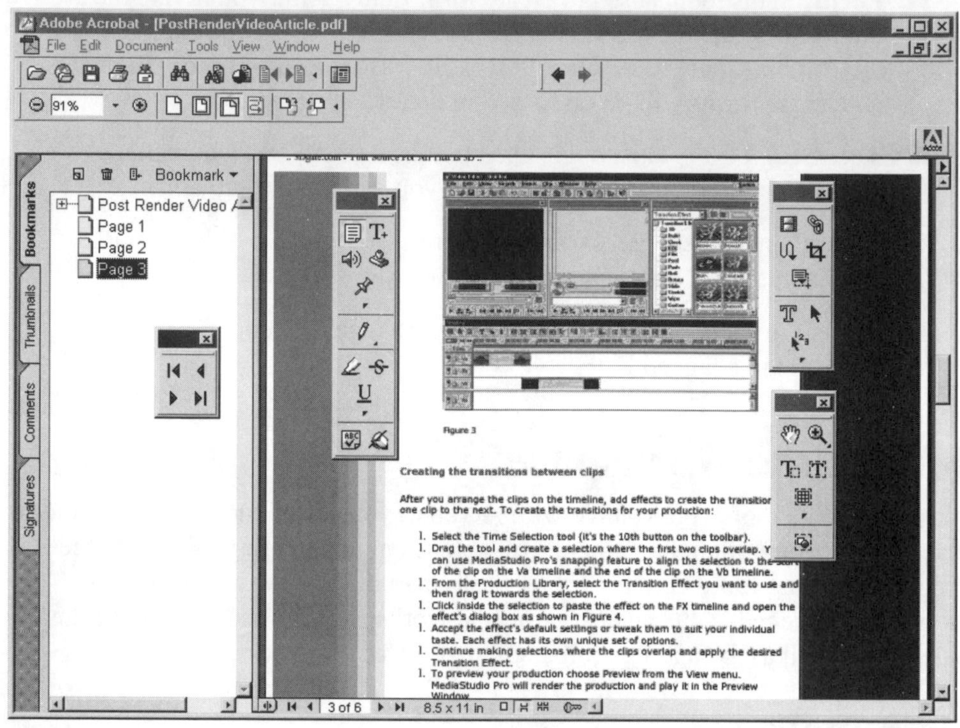

FIGURE 2-9 You can float a toolbar by clicking and dragging it to another position.

Create a Floating Toolbar Group

After you have floated a few toolbars, you can combine them into a group. To dock one toolbar to another, click the horizontal line below the tool group title bar and drag it into the other floating tool group. Release the mouse button and the two groups become one. Repeat the procedure to dock additional toolbars to the group. A custom tool group is shown next.

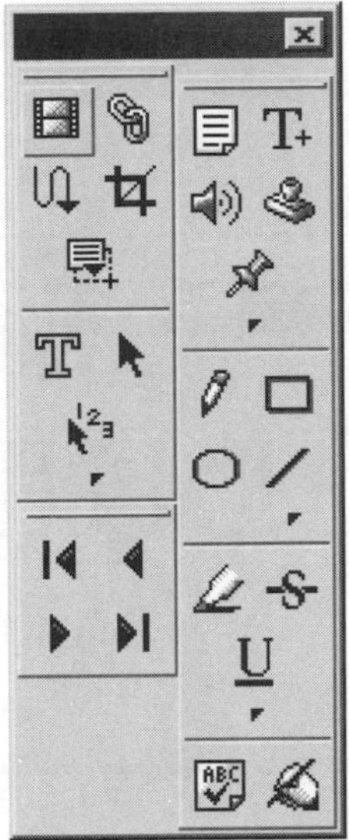

NOTE *You cannot dock a custom tool group to the Command bar. You can drag the custom tool group by its title bar and move it anywhere in the workspace; however, the moment you click and drag the horizontal line at the top of an individual tool group, you move it out of the custom tool group.*

Float Palettes

You can float any palette in the Navigation pane by clicking its name and dragging it out of the Navigation pane. Release the mouse button when the palette is in the desired position. After you float a palette, you can change its height by clicking and dragging the horizontal bar at the base of the palette. You change the width of a floating palette by clicking and dragging the vertical bar on the left or right side of the palette. Figure 2-10 shows two floating palettes in the Document pane. The palette on the right has been resized.

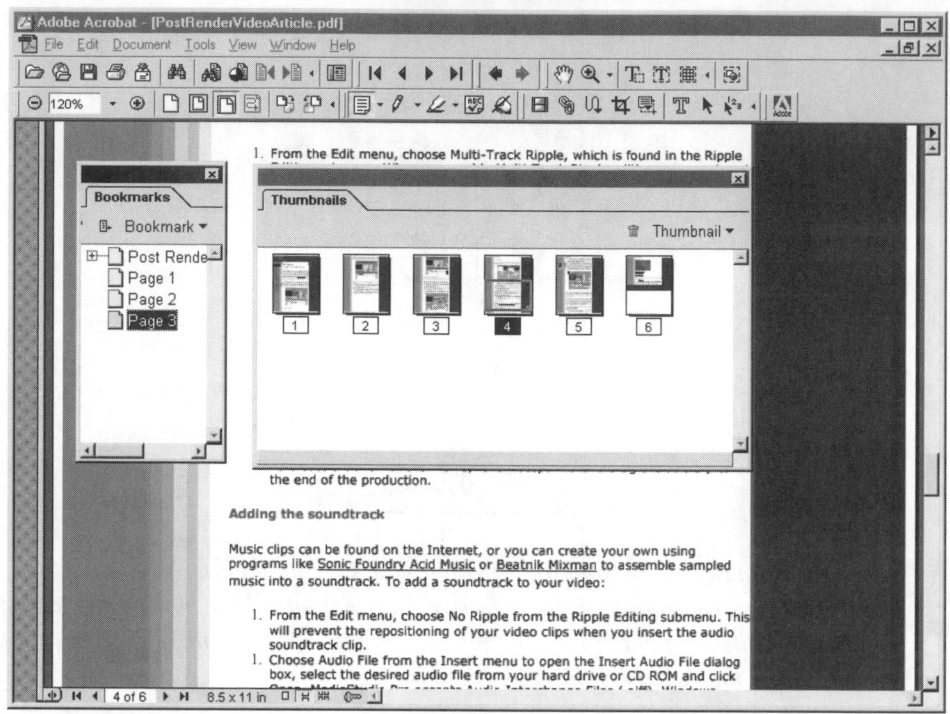

FIGURE 2-10 You can float and resize palettes to suit your working preference.

To redock a palette in the Navigation pane, click the palette name and then drag-and-drop it into the palette. Note that when you redock a palette, it appears at the bottom of the pane, regardless of its original position.

Group Palettes

When you have more than one palette floating in the Document pane, you can group them to conserve monitor space. To create a palette group, click the name of a floating palette and drag it into another palette. You can group as many palettes as needed. To access an individual palette in a group, click its tab. Note that you can combine Navigation pane palettes with palettes opened from menu commands such as the Info and Articles palettes. In Figure 2-11, you see a custom palette group consisting of Navigation pane palettes and palettes accessed from the Window menu.

2

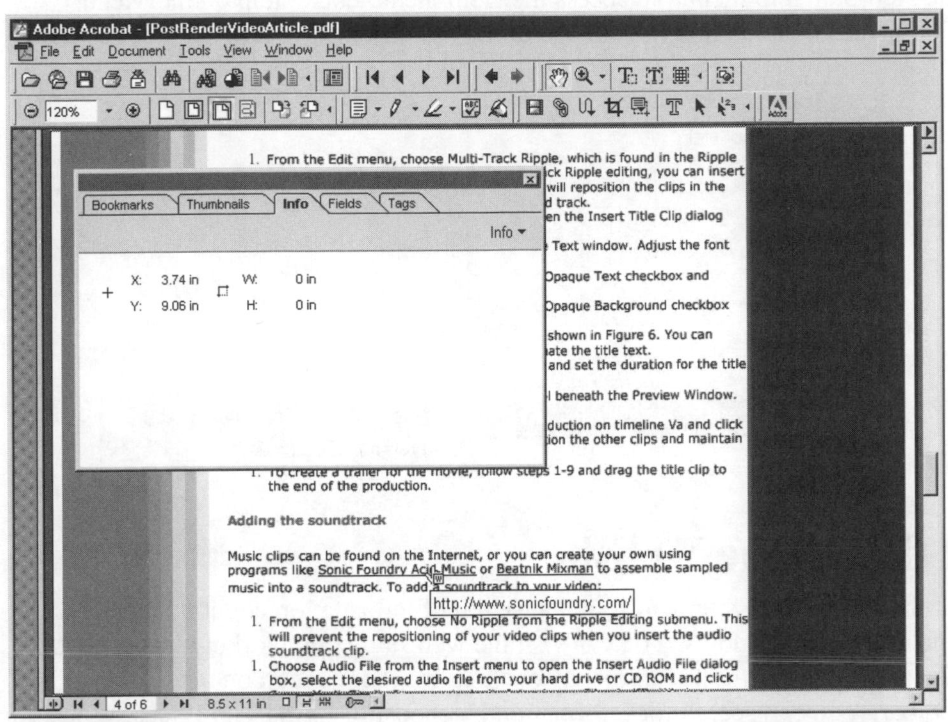

FIGURE 2-11 You can create a palette group by dragging-and-dropping one palette onto another.

TIP *If you frequently use palettes (like the Info and Articles palettes), you can dock them within the Navigation pane or leave them floating in the Document pane. To dock a palette to the Navigation pane, choose the desired palette from the Window menu. After the palette appears in the Document pane, click the palette name and drag it into the Navigation pane. The next time you launch Acrobat, the palette will be in its new home.*

Get Online Help

This book covers every major aspect of Acrobat. However, if you need more information about a specific topic, you can search the Acrobat Online Help document (which, of course, is a PDF document), or choose another topic from the Acrobat Help menu. To access the Help menu, click Help on the Menu Command bar and choose from one of the options shown here.

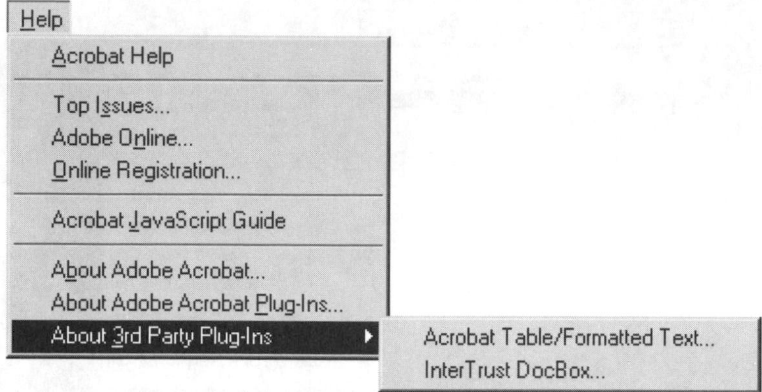

Visit the Adobe Website

At the Adobe web site, you'll find a wealth of information about Acrobat and related Adobe products. You can visit the web site while working in Acrobat if you are logged onto the Internet by clicking the Adobe icon on the Command toolbar. You can search for information by choosing Help | Top Issues. When you select this option, your default Web browser opens, and, if you are connected to the Internet, it opens the support section of the Adobe site in your browser. You can even configure Acrobat to search for updates to your software by doing the following:

1. Choose Help | Adobe Online to open the Adobe Online dialog box shown here.

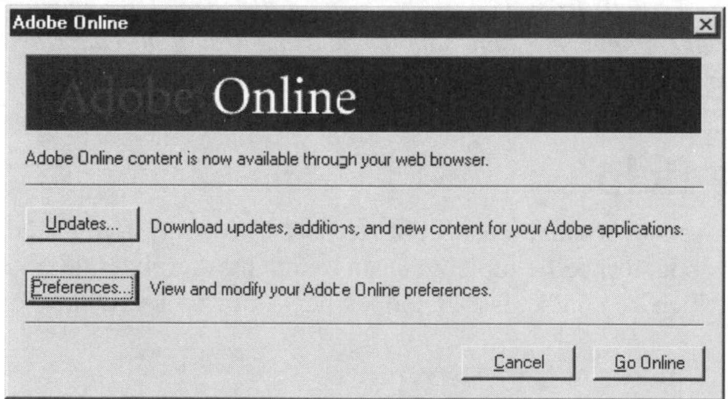

2. Click the Preferences button to open the Adobe Online Preferences dialog box shown here.

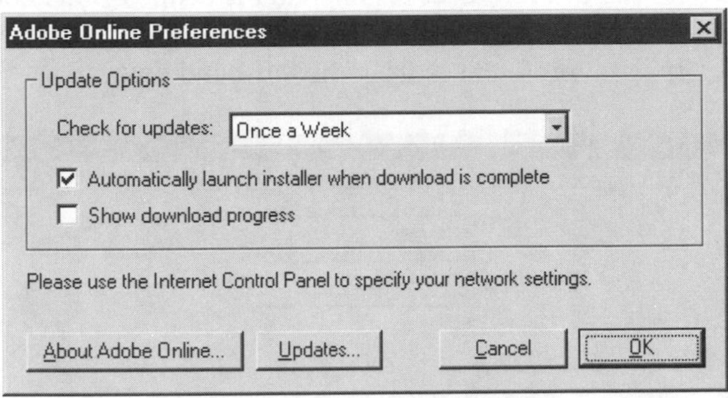

3. Specify how often Acrobat searches for updates.
4. Click OK to apply the changes and close the dialog box.

NOTE *In the Adobe Online dialog box, click the Updates button to download updates for your application, or click the Go Online button and Acrobat will launch your default Web browser and open the Adobe home page.*

Set Preferences

Many people find Acrobat easy to work as it is configured upon installation. However, you can change many Acrobat defaults by selecting the appropriate title in the General preferences dialog box. There is a preference setting for virtually every Acrobat task you perform. Unfortunately, the sheer volume of parameters you can change is beyond the scope of this book. When a preference setting is important to an individual task, it will be covered in that section of the book. Many of the preference settings are easily understood by even casual computer users. However, if you need more information on an individual setting, choose Help | Acrobat Help. After the Acrobat Help file opens, choose Edit | Find and enter the key word or phrase for the specific information you need.

Set General Preferences

As you use different features of Acrobat, you may find that the default settings do not suit your working preference. You can change many of these settings using the General Preferences dialog box. Most of the settings are self-explanatory. When a specific setting in the General Preferences dialog box is relevant to a specific topic, it will be covered in that section of the book. Unfortunately, an in-depth tutorial on setting General Preferences is beyond the scope of this book. To open the General Preferences dialog box shown here, choose Edit | Preferences and then select one of the specific preferences from the left-hand column.

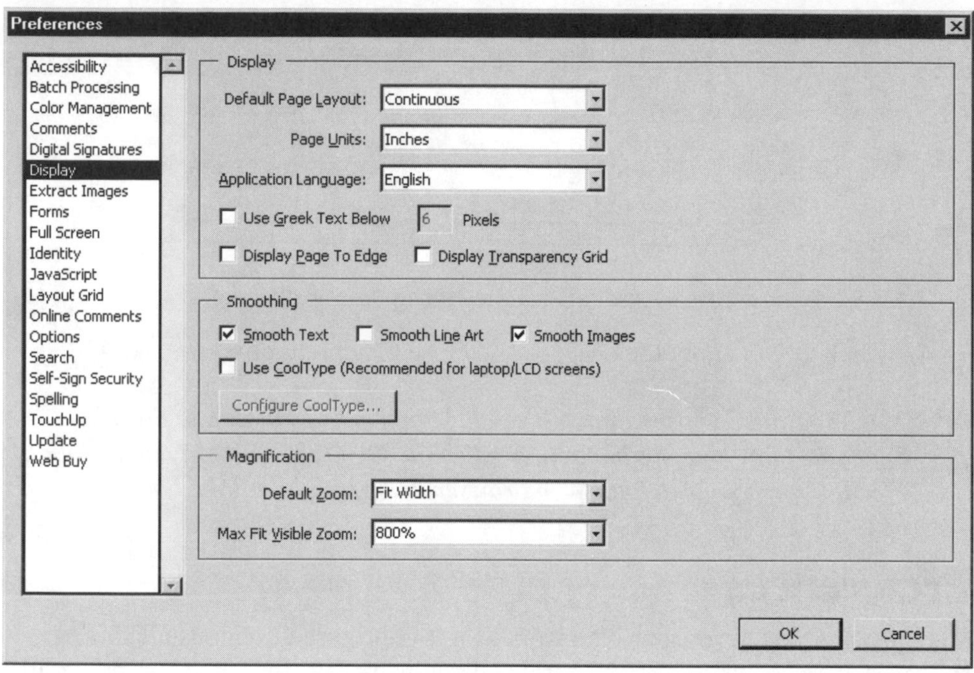

Chapter 3

Read PDF Documents with Adobe Acrobat 5.0

How to…

- Open and navigate documents
- Change Document View
- View multiple documents
- Find keywords and phrases
- Search a PDF Index

You purchased Acrobat—and for that matter, this book—to create and distribute electronic documents. Many people will read your PDF documents in linear fashion from start to finish—which is fine with a one- or two-page document, but cumbersome when reading a large document. When you publish documents with several hundred pages, your readers can choose which parts of the document they view. Acrobat and Acrobat Reader can be used to read PDF files. Both programs have the tools you need to navigate to specific parts of a document, or find and navigate to keywords or phrases. You can also use the Acrobat and Acrobat Reader Search feature to query an index of several PDF documents. In this chapter, you'll learn how to use Acrobat and Acrobat Reader to view a document. In this chapter, Acrobat will be used generically to refer to both Acrobat and Acrobat Reader. When a feature is specific to either program, it will be noted.

Open a PDF Document

Authors of PDF documents can specify what viewers will see when they open a PDF document. A PDF document can be set to open to a certain page, at a certain magnification, or at full-screen view.

NOTE *If the document opens in Full Screen mode, the toolbar, command bar and other navigation aids are not visible. If you prefer, you can exit Full Screen mode by pressing ESC or by pressing CTRL-L (Windows) or COMMAND-L (Macintosh). You can change how you view documents in Full Screen mode by choosing File | Preferences | General | Full Screen and selecting the desired options from the Preferences dialog box.*

To open a PDF file, choose File | Open and use the Open dialog box, shown in Figure 3-1, to navigate to the PDF file you want to view. Select the files you want to view and then click Open.

NOTE *You can quickly open a recently viewed document by choosing File and then clicking the document filename. The last eight documents you viewed appear at the bottom of the menu.*

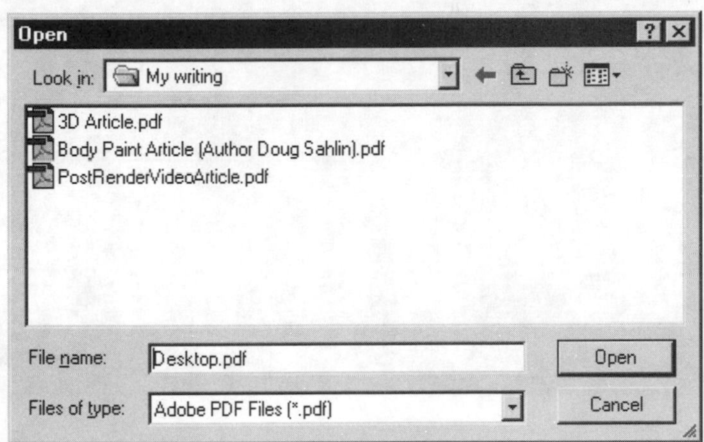

FIGURE 3-1 Use the Open dialog box to open PDF files you want to view or edit.

If you prefer, you can access the Open dialog box by clicking the Open tool, as shown at left.

Alternatively, you can launch Acrobat and open a file by double-clicking a PDF file icon on your desktop, as shown here.

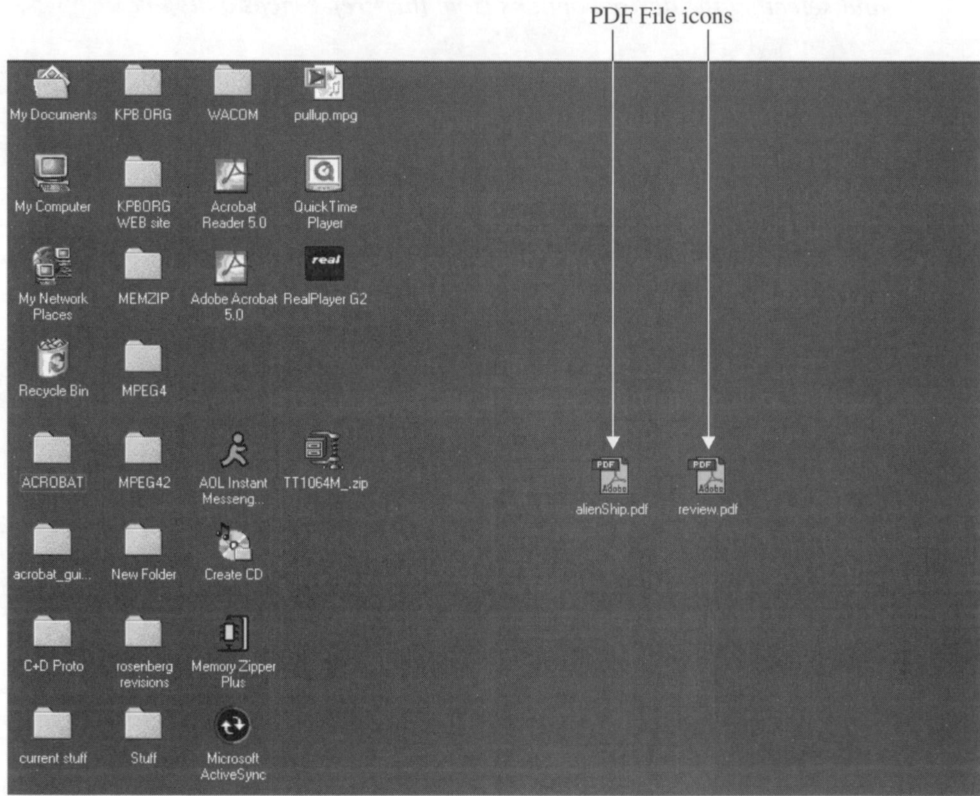

Navigate the Document

After you open a PDF document, you can begin viewing the first page, or you can use the Acrobat viewing tools to navigate to specific parts of a document. If you are viewing an eBook or similar document, you may find a menu or index that you can use to navigate to specific pages. If this is not the case, you can use the Navigation pane palettes for navigation. Acrobat Reader has two palettes named Bookmarks and Thumbnails; Acrobat has two additional palettes named Comments and Signatures. The Comments palettes will be covered in Chapter 12; Signatures palettes in Chapter 13.

Navigate to a Bookmark

You use the Bookmarks palette to navigate to bookmarks within the document. Bookmarks are similar to chapters and section headings in a book. The number of bookmarks is determined by the method used to create the document. When Acrobat Distiller converts a document to PDF format, it uses features from the original document to create bookmarks. For example, if a PDF author uses PDFMaker (the Microsoft plug-in that launches the Acrobat Distiller) to convert a Word document to PDF format, a bookmark is created wherever a Word Heading style is used. If you use the application's Print command to launch the Acrobat Distiller, no bookmarks will be created. When you open a PDF document, the Bookmarks palette usually appears in the Navigation pane. If this is not the case, you can open the Bookmarks palette by choosing Window | Bookmarks. Alternatively, you can press F5. A typical Bookmarks palette is shown in Figure 3-2.

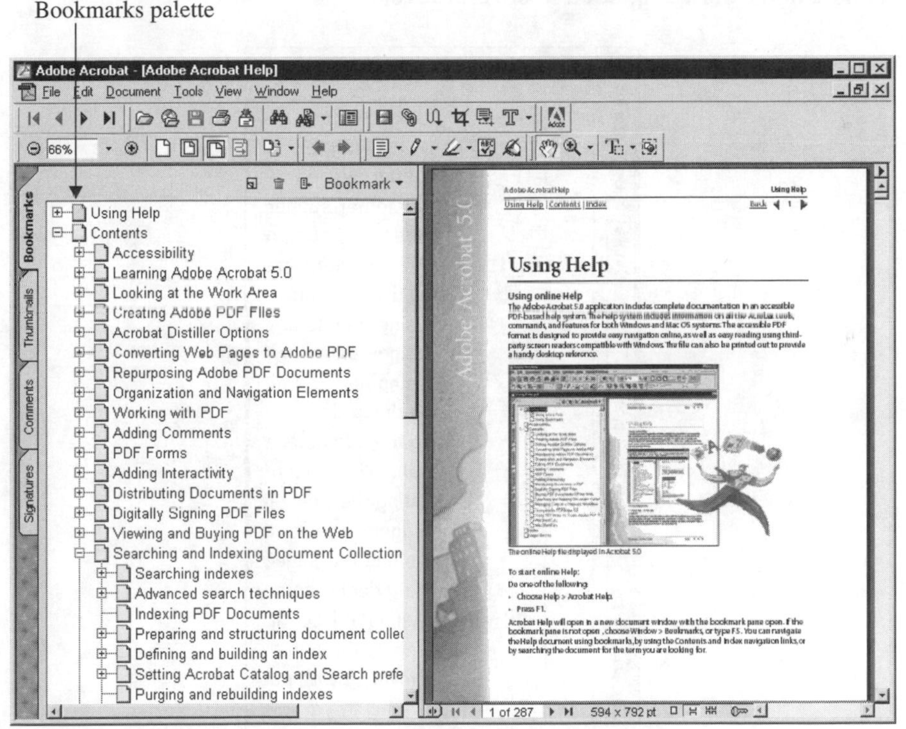

FIGURE 3-2 You use the bookmarks in this palette to navigate to a specific page in a PDF document.

A bookmark is a link to a specific point in a document. To navigate to a bookmark, open the Bookmarks palette and click the desired bookmark icon (it looks like a document with one corner folded), and Acrobat will display the bookmarked page or view.

Expand a Bookmark

Many PDF documents you view have bookmarks with a plus sign (+) beside them. This designates that the bookmark can be expanded to show more bookmarks. Bookmarks give a document structure and make it easier for you to find specific information. To expand a bookmark, click the plus sign (+) and Acrobat will display the bookmarks related to the subject heading. If you are viewing a complex document with several heading levels, the expanded bookmark may include bookmarks with additional subheadings that are also signified with a plus sign (+). To view the additional subheadings, click the section heading plus sign (+). The following image is a bookmark expanded to several levels.

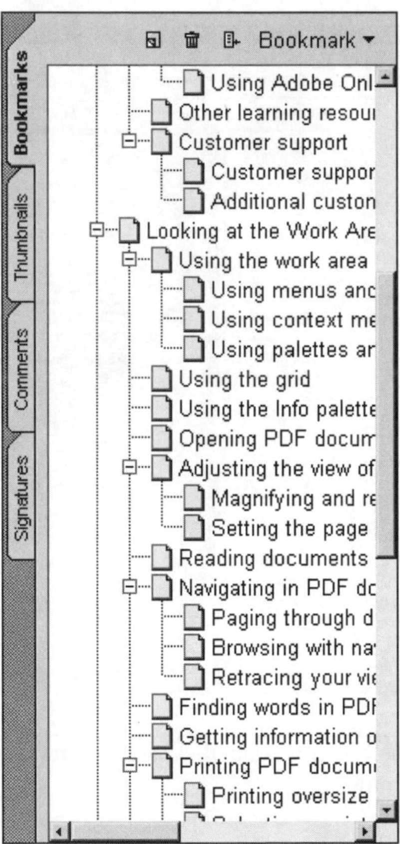

Collapse a Bookmark

When you view a complex document with several heading levels and expand the bookmarks, you end up with an indented treelike structure that displays all of the document bookmarks. You know a bookmark can be collapsed when you see a minus sign (–) to the left of the bookmark. When you expand several bookmarks, the Bookmark palette becomes quite cluttered, making it difficult to find a specific bookmark. You can easily regain control by clicking the minus sign (–) to the left of a bookmark to collapse it.

Use the Bookmarks Palette Menu

You can also navigate to expand and collapse selected bookmarks by choosing commands from the Bookmarks palette menu. To open the Bookmarks palette menu shown here, click the Bookmark icon at the top of the Bookmarks palette.

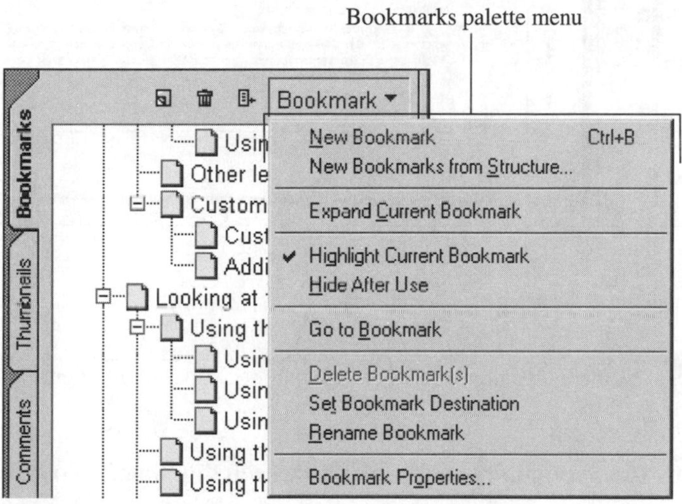

Navigate to a Thumbnail

When Acrobat Distiller or PDFMaker is used to convert a document to PDF format, it creates a thumbnail of each document page. A thumbnail looks like a miniature snapshot of a full-size PDF page. You find document thumbnails in the Thumbnails palette, which is a tab in the Navigation pane. Unless the author of the PDF file specified otherwise, the Navigation pane opens when the document does. To access the Thumbnails palette shown in Figure 3-3, click the Thumbnails tab in the Navigation pane. Alternatively, choose Window | Thumbnails.

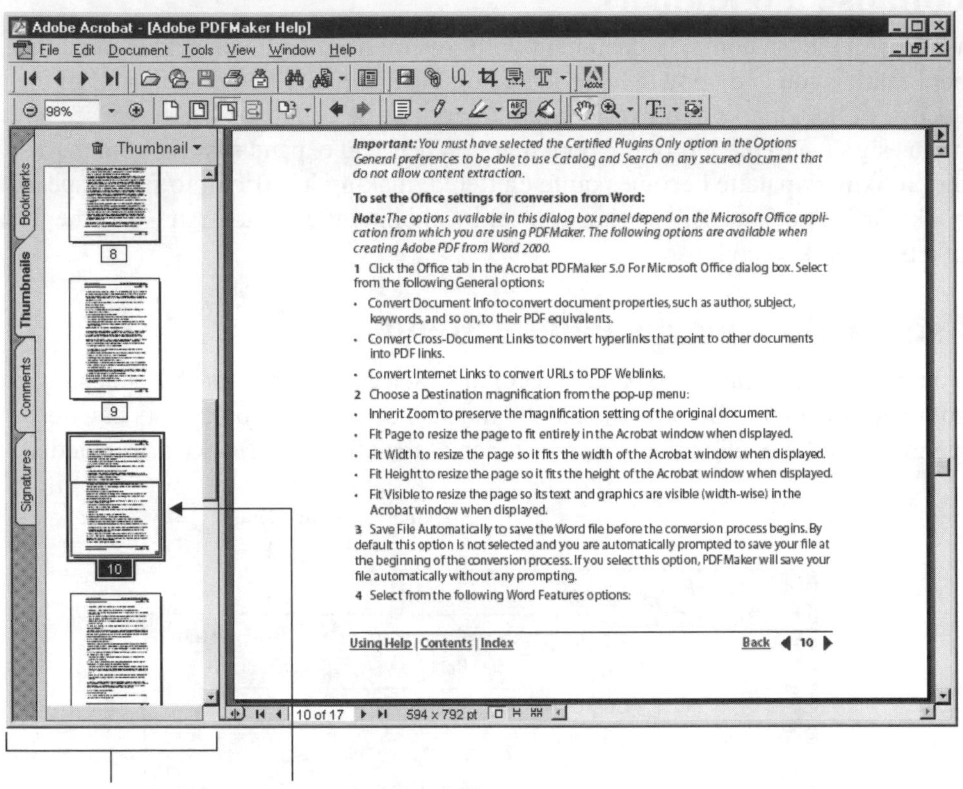

FIGURE 3-3 You can use thumbnails to navigate to a document page.

Notice that the page number is listed below each thumbnail. You can navigate to a specific page by clicking its thumbnail. Acrobat displays a black border around the current page's thumbnail and highlights the page number, as shown next.

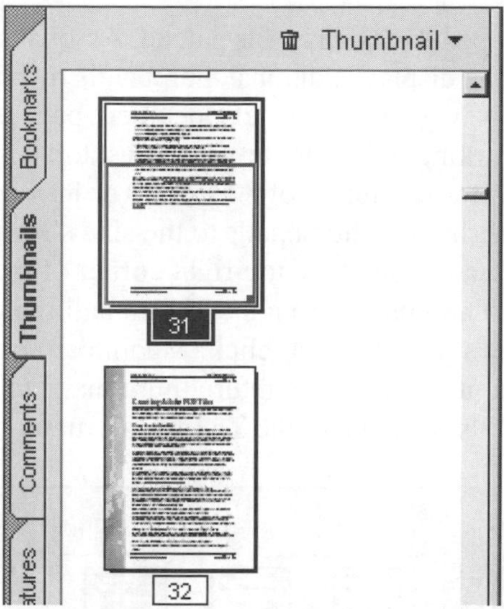

If you are in a magnified view of the page, Acrobat displays a red rectangle within the thumbnail that shows you a miniature representation of the page as displayed in the Document pane. You can use the red rectangle to scroll the page by clicking either the top or the bottom border of the rectangle and dragging, as shown in the following image; or you can resize the view by clicking and dragging the red square at the bottom-right corner of the rectangle.

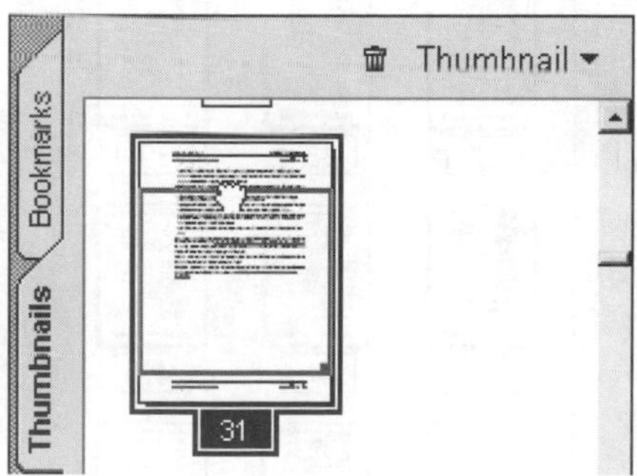

When you initially open the Thumbnails palette, Acrobat displays the thumbnails in a neat column. You can display additional thumbnails by clicking and dragging the border between the Navigation pane and Document pane. However, this may not be feasible if you are working on a monitor with a desktop smaller than 1024 × 768. If you work with a monitor resolution of 800 × 600 or less, you can shrink the size of the thumbnails. To shrink the thumbnails to the size shown in the following image, click the Thumbnail icon at the top-right corner of the Navigation pane, and then choose Small Thumbnails from the Thumbnail menu. Alternatively, you can right-click (Windows) or CONTROL-click (Macintosh), and choose Small Thumbnails from the context menu. To return thumbnails to their original size, choose Large Thumbnails from either the Thumbnail menu or context menu.

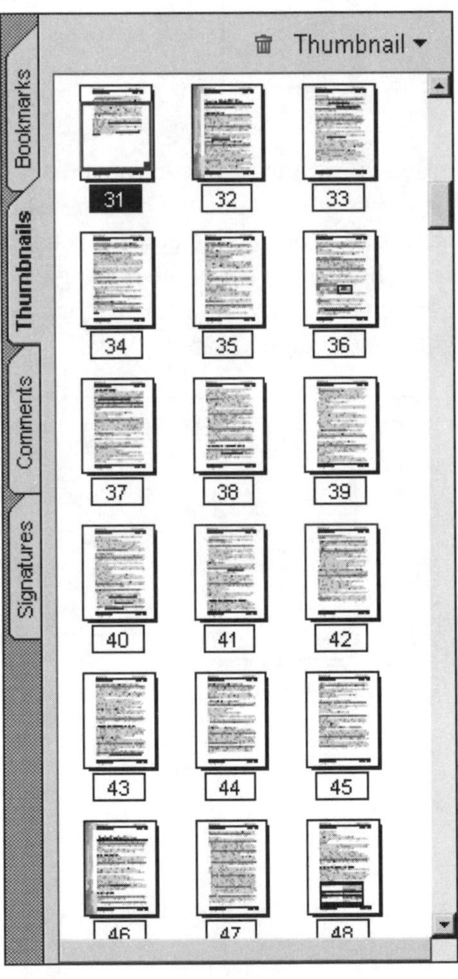

Navigate to a Page

You can use the tools in the Viewing and Viewing History tool groups, previously discussed in Chapter 2, to navigate a PDF file in linear fashion, or jump to and return to previous views you specified. At the lower-left corner of the Document pane, you'll find a group of tools that duplicate the Viewing tools along with other tools that add additional flexibility to your viewing and navigation needs. Use the navigation tools in this group, as shown in the following image, in the same manner as the tools in the Viewing group. In the middle of the navigation tools is a window that displays the current page of the document. Enter a page number in this window, and then press ENTER or RETURN to navigate directly to that page. If you enter a value larger than the last page of the document, Adobe displays a warning message telling you the page is not in the document.

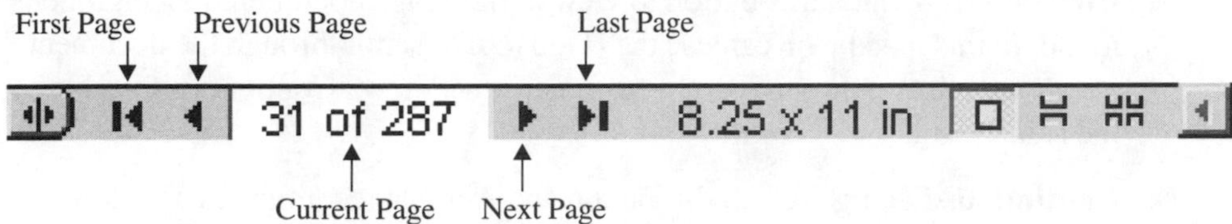

Change Document View

When you view a PDF document, you have a wide variety of viewing options available to you. Unlike a printed document, where you have to contend with the font size and page size chosen by the author, you can modify the magnification of the PDF document, change how much of the document is displayed in the Document pane, change the number of pages displayed in the Document pane, and rotate the document. You can use tools, menu commands, or context menus to change the way Acrobat displays a Document.

Change View Options

As discussed previously, you can use the tools at the lower-left corner of the Document pane to navigate to specific pages of a document. You can also use tools in this group to change your viewing options. You have the following viewing options at your disposal:

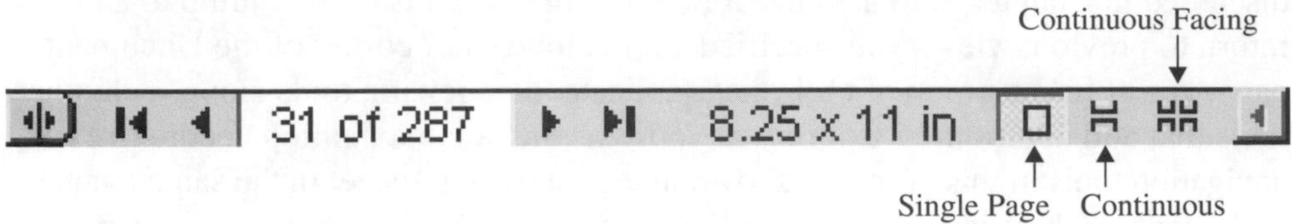

- **Single Page** Click this button to view a single page of the document. You can use the Hand tool to scroll through the page, but not advance to another page. Alternatively, you can choose View | Single Page to enable this mode.
- **Continuous** Click this button to view a multipage document in Continuous mode. In this mode, you can use the Hand tool to scroll through the document a page at a time. Alternatively, you can choose View | Continuous to achieve the same result.
- **Continuous Facing** Click this button and Acrobat reconfigures a multipage document so that the pages are displayed side by side. In Continuous Facing mode, you can use the Hand tool to scroll through the document. Alternatively, you can choose View | Continuous Facing to view a document in this format. Figure 3-4 shows a document displayed in this manner.

Magnify the Document

You can use Acrobat to view a wide variety of documents created by authors on machines with different desktop sizes. Even though Acrobat is cross-platform, and the document you view is identical to what authors create on their computers, you may find it necessary to make modifications to comfortably view the document. When you view a PDF document with small font sizes or tiny graphics, you can magnify the document. You can choose from preset levels of magnification, or choose to zoom in on a specific portion of a document. When you have finished viewing the magnified document, you can zoom out. You can use tools from the

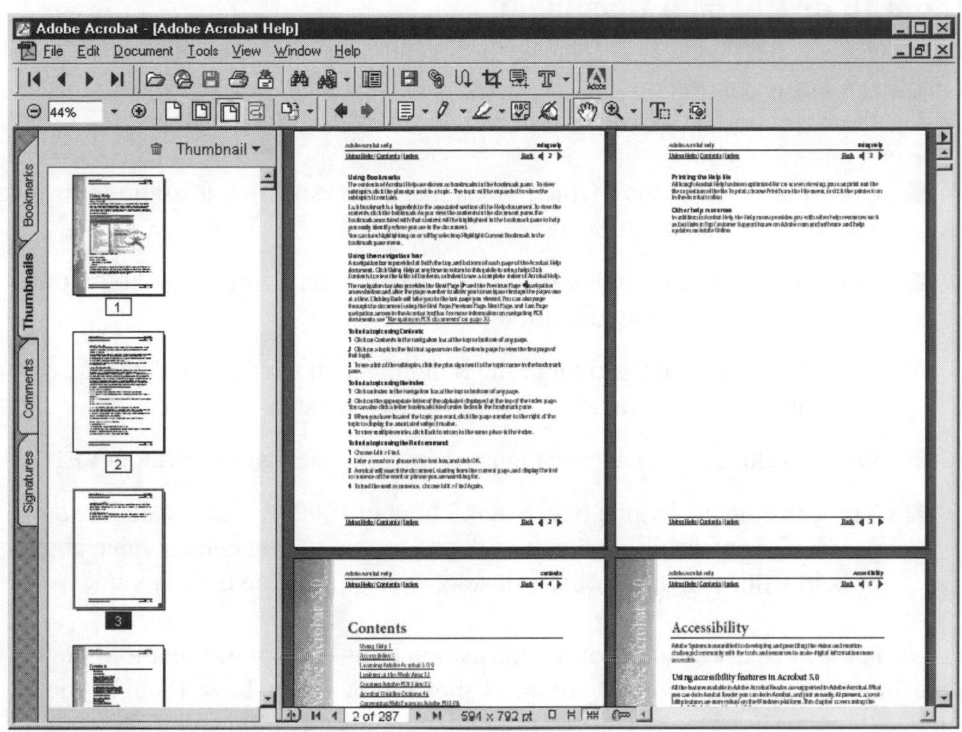

FIGURE 3-4 Display several pages at once by selecting Continuous Facing mode.

Basic and Viewing tool groups, as shown here, or menu commands to change the magnification of a document you are viewing.

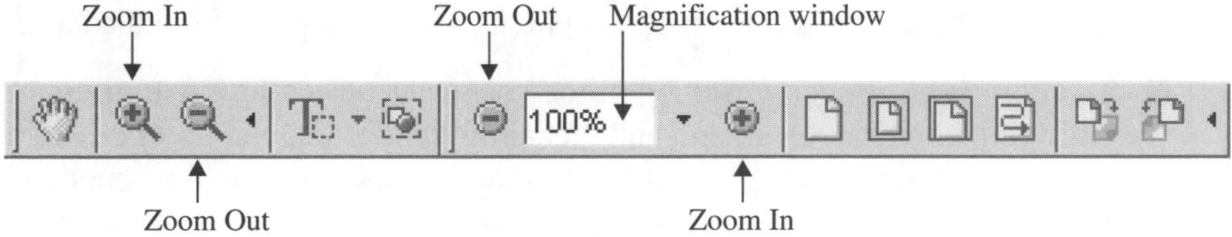

Zoom In or Out on a Document

You have many different ways to change the magnification of a document you view. Your first set of magnification tools are in the Viewing tool group, shown previously. Change the magnification of a document with the following Viewing tools:

- Click the Zoom In tool, which looks like a plus sign (+), to zoom in to a higher level of magnification.
- Click the Zoom Out tool, which looks like a minus sign (–), to zoom out to a lower level of magnification.
- Click the triangle to the right of the Magnification window, and choose a preset magnification value from the drop-down menu.
- Enter a value in the Magnification window, and then press ENTER or RETURN.
- You can enter any value between 8.33% and 1600%. These values are percentages of the original size of the document. If you enter a value above or below this range, Acrobat will select the appropriate default value.

You also have a second set of magnification tools in your Acrobat tool pouch. You find these in the Basic tool group, as shown previously. Even though Adobe refers to these as basic tools, you can use the Zoom In and Zoom Out tools to define the area of the document you want to view. Adobe uses a magnifying glass icon for these tools so you don't confuse them with their identically named counterparts in the Viewing tools group. You change magnification of a document with the following tools:

- To zoom in on a document, select the Zoom In tool and click the document to zoom to a higher level of magnification. When you have zoomed to the maximum level of magnification, the plus sign (+) disappears from the icon.
- To zoom in on a specific portion of the document, select the Zoom In tool, click a point on the document, and then drag right or left and up or down to define the boundaries of the area. As you drag the tool, a rectangular bounding box appears, giving you a preview of the area you are defining. When the bounding box encompasses the area you want to view, release the mouse button and Acrobat zooms to the defined area.

- To zoom out, select the Zoom Out tool and click anywhere inside the Document pane to zoom to the next lowest level of magnification. When you have zoomed out as far as you can go, the minus sign (–) disappears from the icon.
- To zoom out to a specific portion of the document; select the Zoom Out tool and then drag to define the boundary of the area you want to view. As you drag, a rectangular bounding box appears. This bounding box defines an area of the document, however, the tool is zooming out so the bounding box does not designate the area you will actually be viewing when you release the mouse button.

Fit Document in Window

You can change your view of a document so an entire page of the document is sized to the window. You accomplish this by using the Fit In Window tool from the Viewing tool group. To fit a document in the window, click the Fit In Window tool, as shown here, or choose View | Fit In Window.

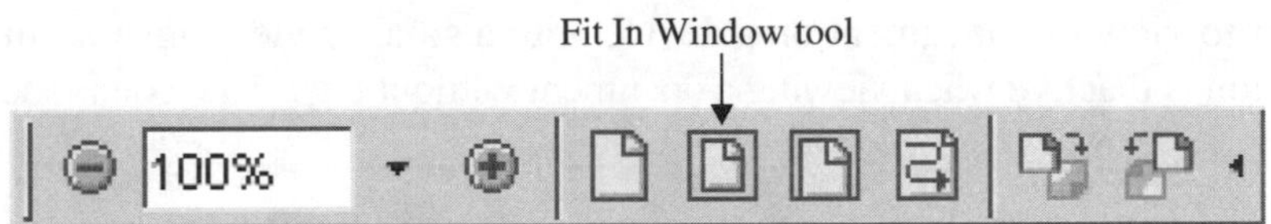

Fit Document to Width

Many of the PDF files you open are narrow, thus formatted for destinations like Internet Web sites. Narrow documents with small fonts present a reading challenge even to people with perfect vision. Fortunately, Adobe has a tool to expand the width of documents and make them easier to read. You can expand the document to fit the current width of the Document Pane by clicking the Fit Width tool, as shown here. Alternatively you can choose View | Fit Width.

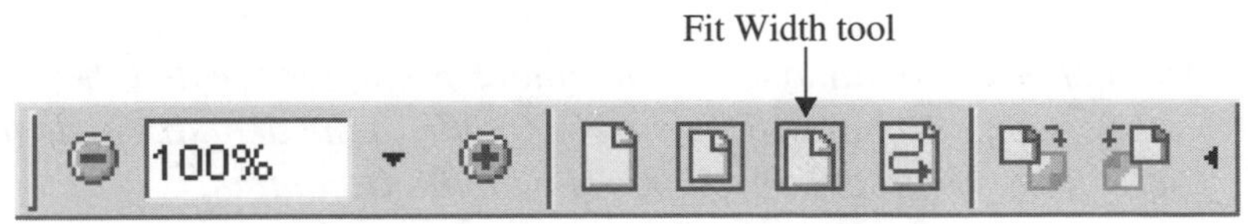

View Document at Actual Size

After viewing a document at a different magnification, you often need to shrink the document back to its original size. You can accomplish this easily by clicking the Actual Size tool, as shown here, or by choosing View | Actual Size.

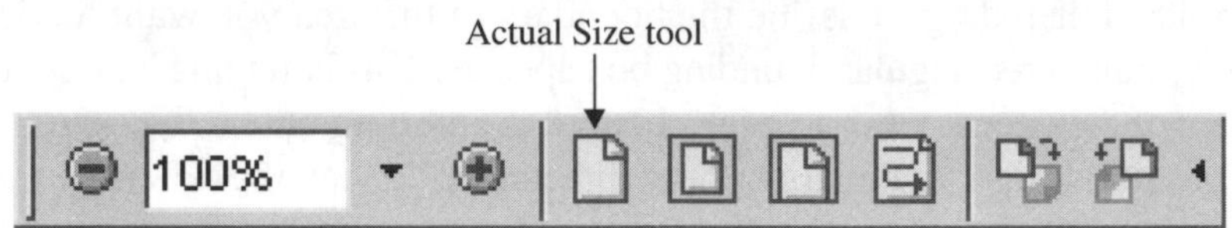

Reflow a Document

In Acrobat and Acrobat Reader, you have a Reflow tool in the Viewing tool groups. The tool icon is identical in both programs; however, it performs different functions. In Acrobat Reader, you use this tool to reflow the width of the document to the current width of the Document pane. In Acrobat, you use this tool to reflow the order of elements in a tagged document (a technique you'll learn in Chapter 12) in order to view the document on a device with a smaller viewing area. In Acrobat, this button is inactive when viewing a document without tags. The icon is shown here.

View Document at Full Screen

If you prefer to read a document without Acrobat toolbars, choose View | Full Screen. When you view a document at Full Screen, it is easier to read. However, it is difficult to navigate if the author has not provided navigation devices such as buttons or text links. To return to normal viewing mode, press ESC.

If you choose Continuous or Continuous Facing mode and then switch to Full Screen, Acrobat will set viewing mode to the default Single mode and you will not be able to scroll pages with the Hand tool.

Rotate a Document

Adobe has also provided you with the necessary tools to rotate a document. You can rotate the view of a document 90° clockwise or 90° counterclockwise by clicking the appropriate tool in the Viewing tool group. To rotate a page an additional 90°, click the button again. The Rotate tools are shown in the following image:

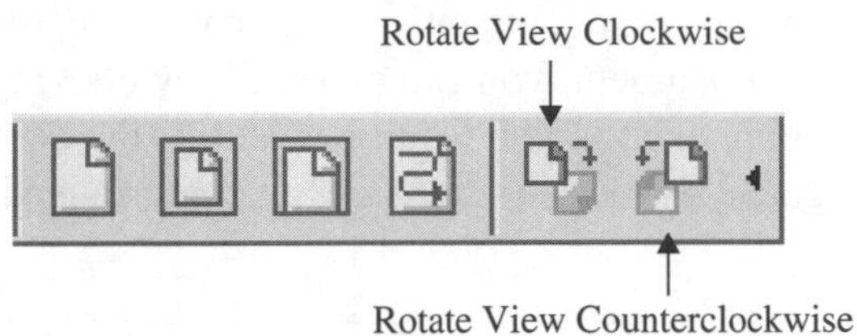

View Multiple Documents

When you do research or create a PDF file that will include several existing PDF documents, it is convenient to work with all of the documents open—or as many as your system resources allow—at the same time. When you have multiple documents open, you can switch from one document to another by clicking Window and then selecting another document from thc list at the bottom of the menu shown here, or you can choose to have Acrobat arrange the documents in a cascading or tiling fashion.

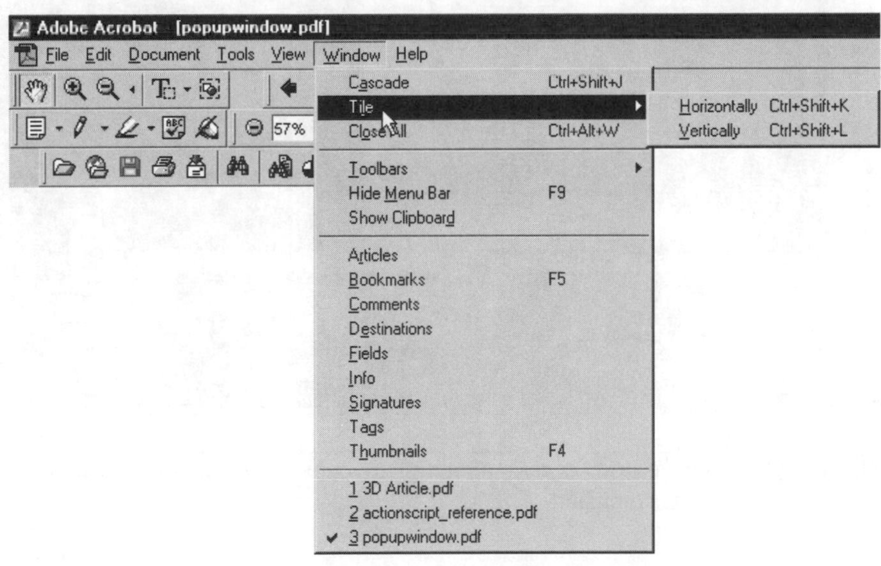

Cascade Documents

When you work with multiple documents, you can speed up your workflow considerably if you have easy access to each document. You can have Acrobat arrange multiple documents in cascading fashion by choosing Window | Cascade. When you choose this viewing option, Acrobat overlaps each PDF file. You can see each document title, as well as its Navigation pane, which is collapsed to conserve working space. To switch to a document while in cascading mode, click its title bar. After you select a document, you can expand it by clicking the Maximize button. Click the Minimize button and Acrobat returns the document to its position in the cascade. In Figure 3-5, you see several documents arranged in cascading format.

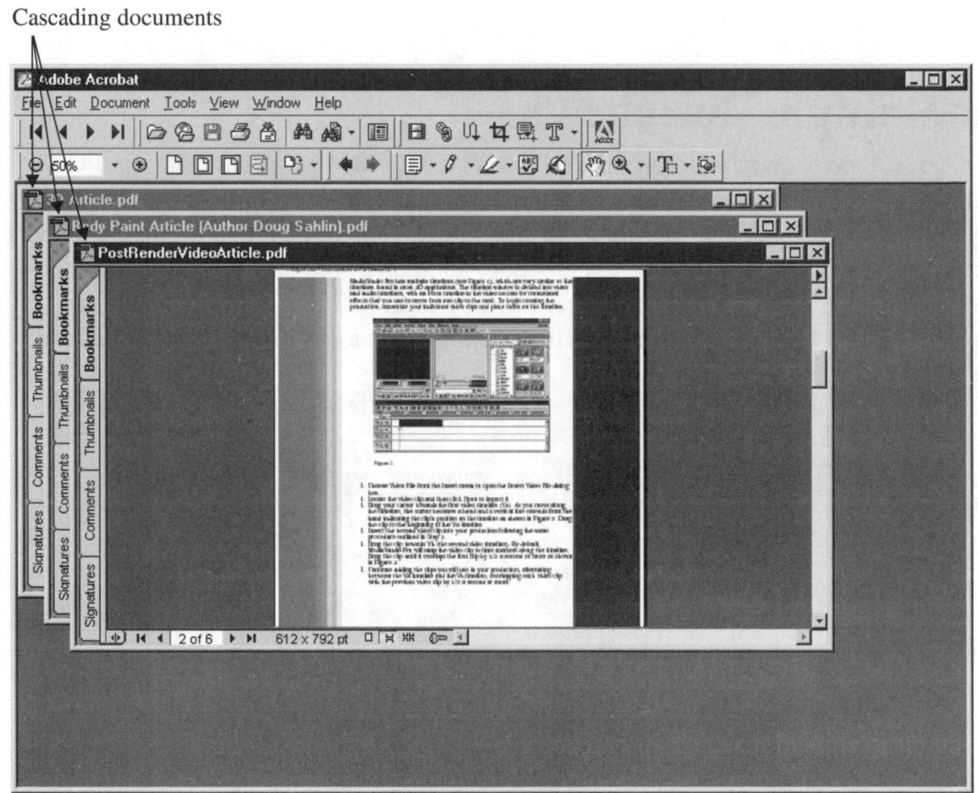

FIGURE 3-5 You have ready access to multiple documents when you choose the Cascade command.

Tile Documents

If you prefer to view multiple documents neatly arranged in checkerboard fashion, choose Window | Tile. Choose this command and you have the following two tiling options available: vertical and horizontal. When you view tiled documents, you can see the document title bar and part of its contents. To select a document, click its title bar. Click the Maximize button to expand the document; click the Minimize button to return it to its tiled position. After you've selected a document from the tile, you can use Acrobat tools to navigate within the document. Figure 3-6 shows several documents tiled vertically; Figure 3-7 shows the same group tiled horizontally.

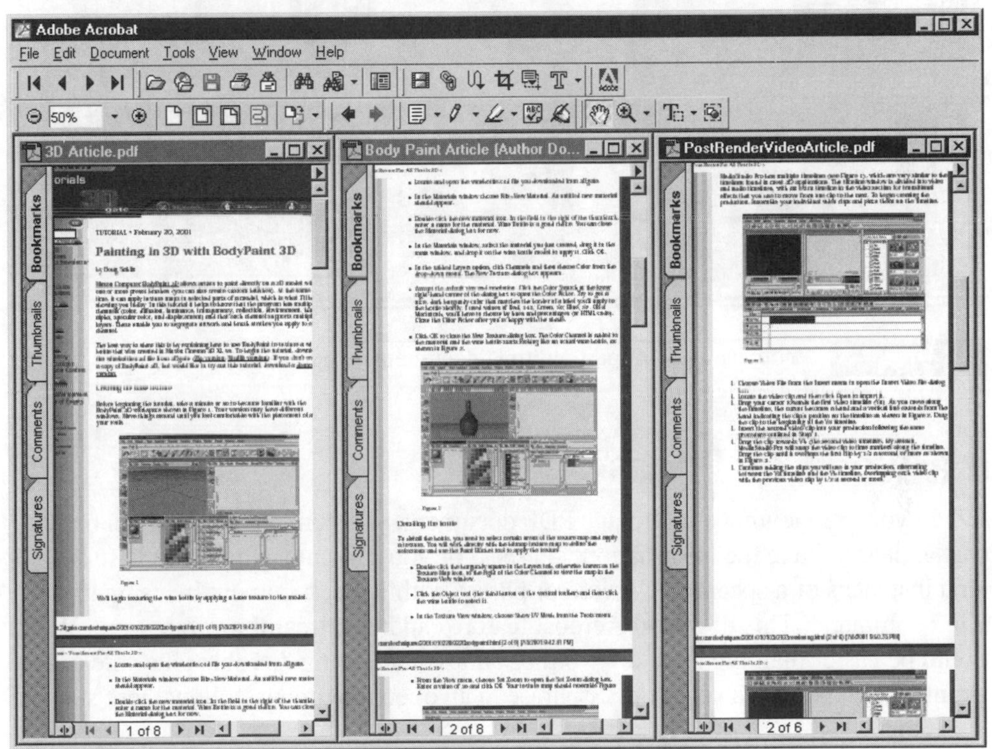

FIGURE 3-6 You can view multiple documents tiled vertically.

FIGURE 3-7 You can view or edit multiple documents tiled horizontally.

Find a Word or Phrase

When you are viewing a multipage PDF document, you can navigate to bookmarks that appear to have the information you seek, or you can cut right to the chase and find instances of a specific key word or phrase within the document by using the *Find* command. This powerful Acrobat feature can help streamline your work. What could be easier than typing a key word or phrase and letting Acrobat take care of the grunt work? To find a key word or phrase in an open document, follow these steps:

1. Click the Find tool that looks like a pair of binoculars. Alternatively, choose Edit | Find to open the dialog box shown next.

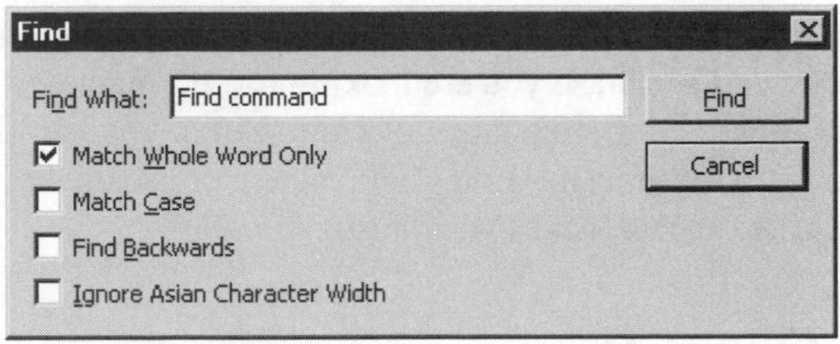

2. Enter the key word or phrase you want to find.
3. Choose from the following options:
   - **Match Whole Word Only** Choose this option and Acrobat only finds matches for the exact word or phrase you enter.
   - **Match Case** Choose this option and Acrobat returns words or phrases that match the case you enter. For example, enter **Query** and Acrobat will only return instances of *Query*, not *query*.
   - **Find Backwards** Choose this option if you want Acrobat to search backward from the page you are currently viewing. With this check box disabled, Acrobat will search forward from the current page.
   - **Ignore Asian Character Width** This option will only apply if you are reading a PDF file in the Japanese version of Acrobat. Use it to distinguish between full- and half-width Kana characters. Choose this option and Acrobat will find an exact match for what you enter in the Find dialog box.
4. Click the Find button to begin the search.

When you use the Find command, Acrobat returns the first instance in the document (or depending on the options you select, the first instance forward or backward from the current page of the document) of the key word or phrase you enter in the Find dialog box. If the key word or phrase does not exist in the document, Acrobat displays that information in a dialog box.

Once Acrobat finds the key word or phrase, it is highlighted on the page. You can then close the Find dialog box to view the results. Alternatively, if you prefer to find another instance of the word, you can use the Acrobat Find Again command. After Acrobat finds the word you are searching for, the Find Again button replaces the Find button in the Find dialog box. Click the Find Again button to find the next instance of the key word or phrase you are looking for. If you closed the Find dialog box after Acrobat found the first instance of your search, you can find the next occurrence of the word by choosing Edit | Find Again, or use the keyboard shortcut CTRL-G (Windows) or COMMAND-G (Macintosh).

Search an Index of Documents

Many authors of PDF documents use Acrobat Catalog to create an index of PDF documents. Acrobat has a sophisticated search function that lets you search for a specific word or phrase in one or more indexed catalogs. To take advantage of this powerful feature, the Search plug-in must be installed on your computer. When you install Acrobat or Acrobat Reader, this is installed by default.

Indexes are created with the *Catalog* command, which is covered in Chapter 15. In order to search an index of documents, you must first specify the list of indexes to search. When you install Acrobat, the Acrobat 5.0 Online Guides index is installed by default.

Add an Index

In order to search other indexes, you add the files to the Available Indexes list. To display the indexes currently available for searching, choose Edit | Search | Select Indexes to open the Index Selection dialog box, as shown in Figure 3-8.

The Index Selection dialog box has a large window that displays the indexes available for search. To add an index, click the Add button. Acrobat opens the Select Index dialog box shown in the following illustration.

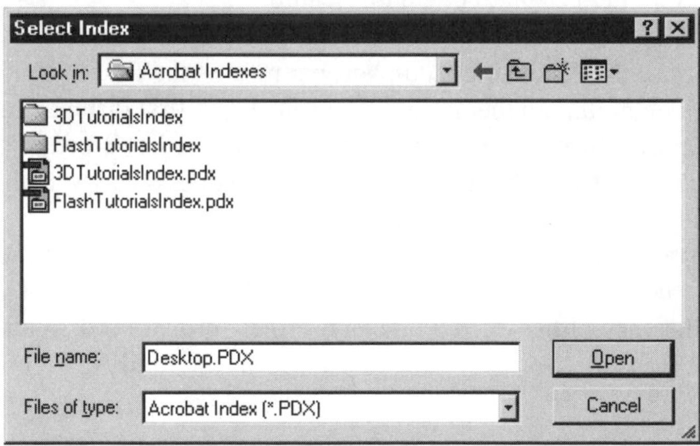

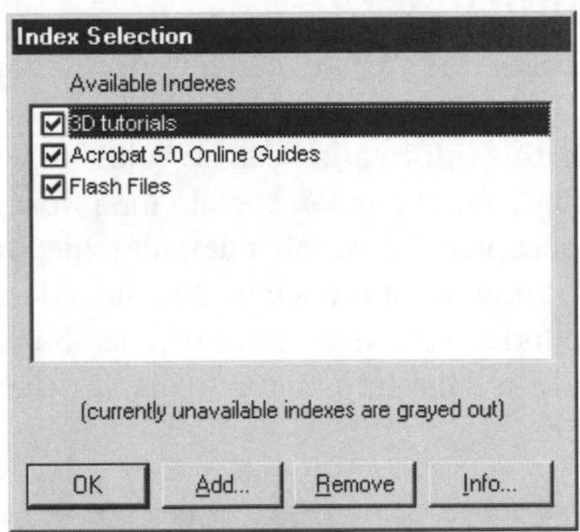

FIGURE 3-8 Use the Index Selection dialog box to add document indexes to the Available Indexes list.

Select the index you want to add and click Open. After you click Open, the Select Index dialog box closes and the newly selected index will appear in the Index Selection dialog box, as shown in Figure 3-8.

Remove an Index

You can enable or disable an index from a search by selecting the check box to the left of the index name. Using the check box is the preferred method of enabling or disabling an index in a search. However, if you are no longer using an index, or have moved it to a different location on your hard drive, you can remove the index. To remove an index from the list, open the Index Selection dialog box shown previously in Figure 3-8, click the index name to select it, and then click the Remove button to delete the index from the list. When you click the Remove button, Acrobat displays no warning and the index is removed from the list. If you inadvertently remove an index, you can use the Add button to restore it to the list.

NOTE *The best way to limit a search is by enabling only the indexes you want Acrobat to use for the search you are performing. For example, if you have ten PDF indexes, but feel only five of them contain information pertinent to your search, disable the ones you don't want Acrobat to search.*

Display Index Information

When an indexed PDF catalog is created, certain information is recorded with the file. If you have several indexes to choose from, or you are sharing indexes with coworkers on a network, this information can be valuable when deciding whether or not the PDF files included in the index contain the information you require. If the author of the index accepted the Acrobat default name of Index, using the Info option is the only way to know what is contained in the index. To access information about an Index, open the Index Selection dialog box, as shown earlier in Figure 3-8; select an index; and then click the Info button to display the Index Information dialog box, as shown here.

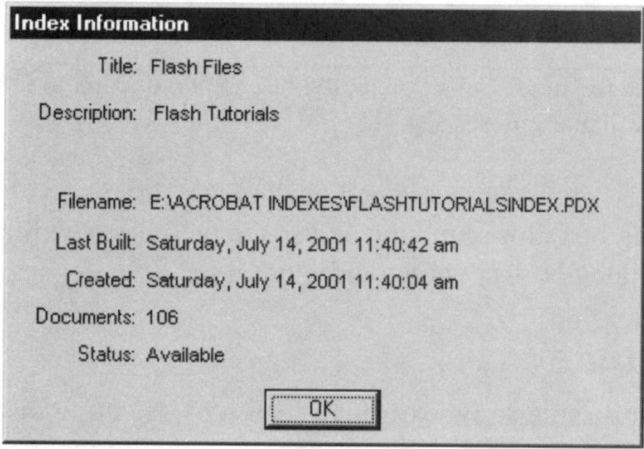

After you open the Index Information dialog box, you have the following information available:

- **Title** This is the title entered by the creator of the index. When you build your own indexes, it is advisable to specify a title that describes the contents of the PDF files being indexed. Refer to Chapter 15 for information on naming an index.
- **Description** This information describes the contents of the PDF index as entered by the author of the index.
- **Filename** This line displays the path to the index and the full filename of the index.
- **Last Built** This information shows you when the index was last updated. If the index has not been updated, the date is the same as when the index was created.

- **Created** This line shows you the time and date the index was originally created.
- **Documents** This line displays the number of PDF files in the index.
- **Status** If Acrobat successfully identified the file when you added it, it is Available. Unavailable indexes are listed as such and are shown dimmed out in the list.

Create a Query

When you search an index of PDF files, you create a query. Your query tells Acrobat exactly what information to retrieve. You can specify which indexes to search and which key word or phrase you want Acrobat to find. You can fine tune the search by specifying whether you want Acrobat to return exact matches or similar matches. To create a query, do the following:

1. Choose Edit | Search | Query to open the Search dialog box shown in the following image. Alternatively, click the toolbar Search tool that looks like a pair of binoculars in front of a document.

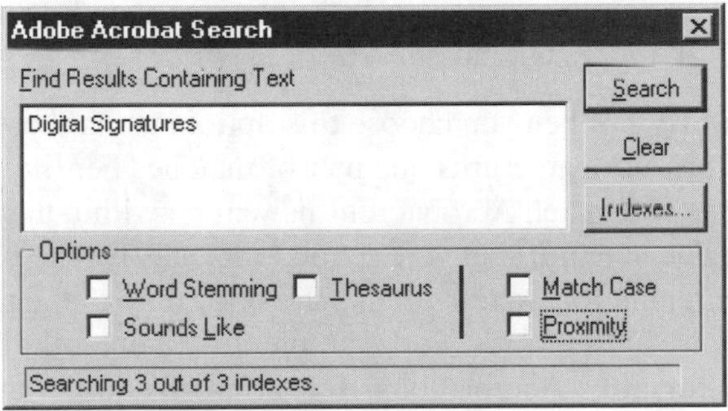

2. If the dialog box contains a key word or phrase from a previous query, click the Clear button to start a new query.
3. Enter the key word or phrase you want Acrobat to search for in the Find Results Containing Text field.
4. Choose from the following options:
   - **Word Stemming** When you select this option, Acrobat will find words that stem from the word you enter. For example, if you enter

the word **index**, Acrobat will return instances of the words *indexed*, *indexes*, *indexing*, *indication*, and *indices* (if these words appear in the indexed files you are searching).

- **Thesaurus** When you select this option, Acrobat will find synonyms of the key words or phrases from the indexes you are searching. For example, if you enter the word **ask**, Acrobat will find the words *call*, *demand*, *interrogate*, *query*, and so on.
- **Sounds Like** When you select this option, Acrobat attempts to find words that sound like the word you entered in the Adobe Acrobat Search dialog box text field. The algorithm used to create this Acrobat option remains a mystery to all except the programmers of the search engine. The Sounds Like option often returns results you do not expect. For example, if you enter the word **look**, you expect Acrobat to find words like *cook*, which rhymes with *look*. Instead, Acrobat returns words that begin with the letter *l* such as the following: *laws*, *looks*, *lock*, *log*, *logo*, and so on.
- **Match Case** When you choose this option, Acrobat matches the case of the word you entered in the Adobe Acrobat Search dialog box text field. For example, if you enter **Adobe**, the search returns instances of the word *Adobe*, but not *adobe*.
- **Proximity** When you choose this option, using the AND Boolean operator, Acrobat returns one pair of matches per file for the words you entered. The match Acrobat returns will be within the first three pages of the document. If there are several matches for the pair of words you are searching for, Acrobat ranks the relevancy of the match on the proximity of the words. For example, if you enter the query **Adobe AND Portable**, Acrobat looks for the words *Adobe* and *Portable* in a document and highlights the first instance of each word, provided they appear within the first three pages of the document. If further instances of either word occur in the document, they are not selected or highlighted, as Acrobat is returning instances of the key words with the closest proximity to each other.

5. Click Search.

Your search results are displayed in the Search Results dialog box that displays a list of documents that contain instances of your query.

You can also add Indexes to the list and choose which indexes to query by clicking the Indexes button. When you click this button, Acrobat opens the Index Selection dialog box previously discussed in this chapter.

About Search Results

After you click the Search button, Acrobat searches for occurrences of your query in the selected indexes. The results Acrobat returns depend on the key word or phrase you entered and the parameters you selected. Results are displayed in the Search Results dialog box shown here.

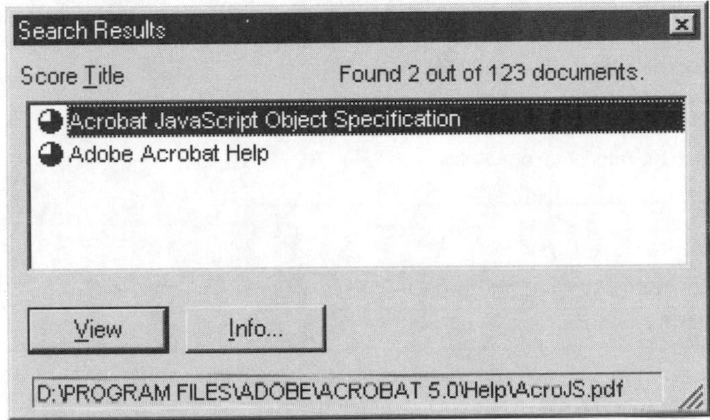

The Search Results dialog box displays the document score in the right column, and its title in the left column. Note that the title is not the document filename, but the title the PDF author specified in the Document Properties dialog box when the document was created or modified.

Your search results are displayed in descending order according to relevancy or score. The documents at the top of the list are more relevant to the parameters of your query; in other words, these documents contain a higher percentage of instances of the key words or phrases in your query. A circular icon appears to the left of a selected document name as shown next. Solid circles indicate the highest score; unfilled circles the lowest score.

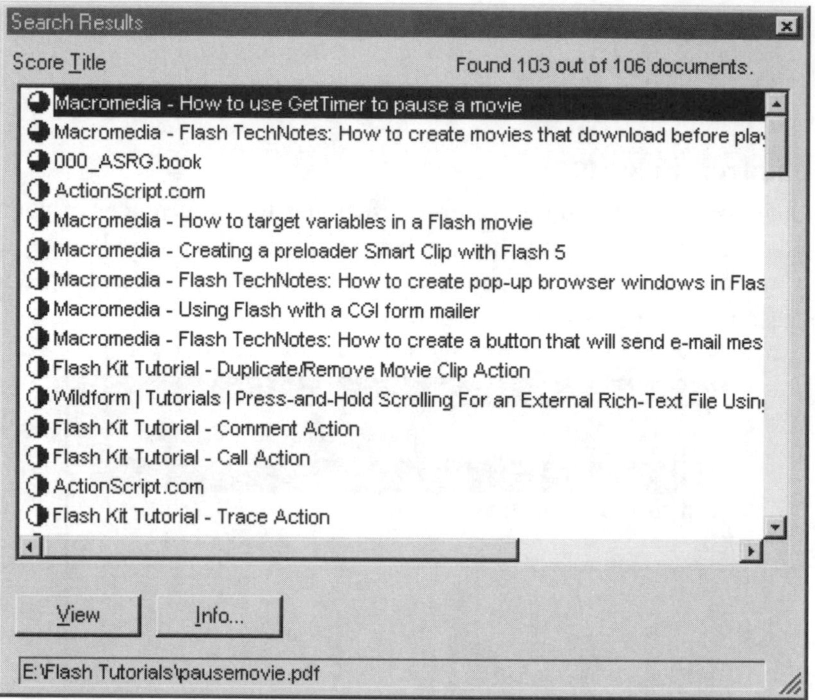

View Query Results

After Acrobat finishes the search, you can select a document from the list by clicking its name. After selecting the document, click the View button and Acrobat loads the file you selected with the first occurrence of your queried text highlighted. At this point, the Search Results dialog box is still visible in the Document pane. If the selected document contains information you want to peruse, you can close the dialog box; if not, click another document to select it and then click the View button to open it.

After you close the Search Results dialog box, you can advance to the next occurrence of your query by clicking the Next Highlight button. After viewing a few highlights, you may want to jump back to a previous highlight, a task you accomplish by clicking the Previous Highlight button. If the Previous Highlight button is dimmed out, you are at the first occurrence of your query in the document. When you reach the last occurrence in a document of the key word or phrase you searched for, clicking the Next Highlight button opens the next document Acrobat returned for your search. The Next Highlight and Previous Highlight tools are shown here.

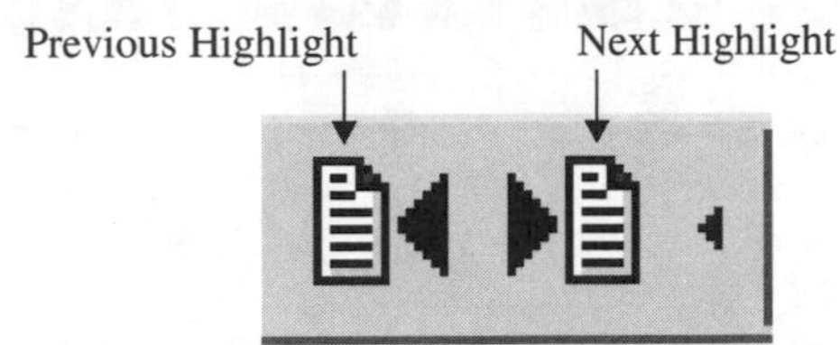

If your search returned several results, and the first few highlights you select do not contain the information you seek, you can reopen the Search Results dialog box and select another document by clicking the Search Results tool, shown on the left, or by choosing Edit | Search | Results. Alternatively, you can open the next document returned in the search by choosing Edit | Search | Next Document. When Acrobat opens the next document, the first occurrence of your query is highlighted.

TIP *If your search yields too many results, you can refine it by choosing Edit | Search | Query. When the Search dialog box opens, press CTRL (Windows) or COMMAND (Macintosh), and the Search button becomes the Refine button. Click the Refine button while still holding down the CTRL (Windows) or COMMAND (Macintosh) key, and Acrobat returns a smaller results list.*

Customize Your Search

The Search dialog box, shown in the previous section "Create a Query," is the Acrobat default. However, you can customize your search by taking advantage of all the available Search command options. You do this by changing your search preferences.

Set Search Preferences

You can harness more of the Search command power by changing your preferences as follows:

1. Choose Edit | Preferences | General, and choose Search, as shown here.

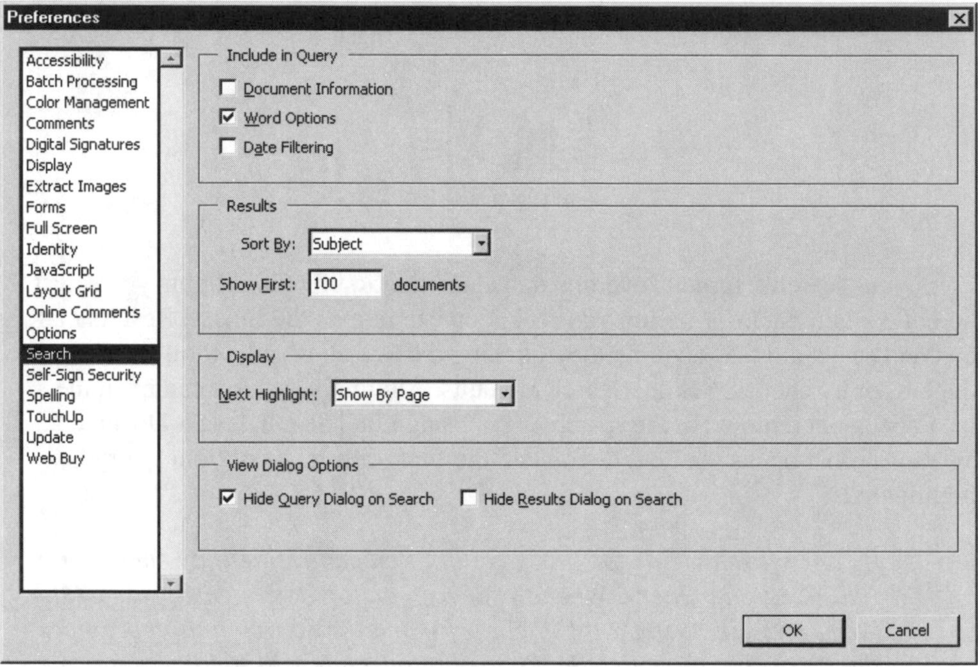

2. From the Include in Query section, choose from the following options:
   - **Document Information** Choose this option to add the Document Information text field to the preset Search dialog box.
   - **Word Options** Choose this option (the Search dialog box default) to enable the Find Results Containing Text field in the Search dialog box.
   - **Date Filtering** Choose this option to add the date filtering fields to the Search dialog box.
3. In the Results section, click the triangle to the right of the Sort By fields and choose one of the following options:

- **Author** Choose this option and Acrobat sorts the results in alphabetical order according to the first word in the Document Summary Author field.
- **Created** Choose this option to have your search results sorted by creation date, starting with the most recent date at the top of the list.
- **Creator** Choose this option to have your results sorted according to the program used to create the PDF file. For example, if the PDF file was created in Microsoft Word, the creator is Acrobat PDFMaker 5.0 for Word.
- **Keywords** Choose this option and have Acrobat display your search results in alphabetical order according to the first word in the Document Summary Keyword field.
- **Modified** Choose this option to display search results sorted in chronological order according to the date the document was last modified, with the most recent date at the top of the list.
- **Producer** Choose this option and your search results are displayed according to the application or driver that produced the file. Producers are programs like Acrobat Distiller or the PDFMaker plug-in for Microsoft Office applications.
- **Score** Choose this option (the Search Command default), and the results of your search are displayed according to relevance; the most relevant documents contain the most matches for the key word or phrase you searched for.
- **Subject** Choose this option and Acrobat displays search results according to the Subject field in the Document Summary dialog box of the file.
- **Title** Choose this option and your results will be displayed in alphabetical order according to the first letter in the Title field of the file's Document Summary dialog box, and score, with the highest scores appearing first.

4. In the *Show First* field, enter the number of PDF documents you want Acrobat to display.

5. In the *Display* section, choose one of the following options:

- **Show By Page** Choose this option if you prefer to have search results displayed with all occurrences of your searched word(s) highlighted on the first page. When you choose this option, all subsequent pages are displayed with searched word(s) similarly highlighted.
- **Show By Word** Choose this option, and Acrobat will highlight only the first occurrence of the searched word(s) when you view the file. Additional instances of the word are not highlighted, but can be selected by using the Next Highlight tool.
- **No Highlighting** Choose this option, and searched words are not highlighted when you view the file; however, you can advance to matches of your search using the Next Highlight and Previous Highlight tools.

6. In the *View Dialog Options* section, choose one of the following options:

- **Hide Query Dialog On Search** Choose this option (the default), and the Search dialog box will close after you click the Search button. Disable this option, and the dialog box will remain open, permitting you to quickly enter new parameters for additional searches.
- **Hide Results Dialog On Search** Choose this option, and the Search Results dialog box will close when you view the first document. Disable this option (the default), and the dialog box will remain open, allowing you to quickly select another document to view.

Conduct an Expanded Search

If you modify the default Search dialog box by changing Search preferences, you can conduct a more thorough and advanced search of an index. With a modified Search dialog box, in addition to searching for documents by key words or phrases, you can use the additional fields (shown in Figure 3-9) to search for documents by Title, Subject, Author, Keywords, or by Date info.

With a modified Search dialog box, you can enter additional information in the following fields:

- **Title** You can enter text in this field to search for documents by their titles.
- **Subject** You can use this field to search for files by subject matter.

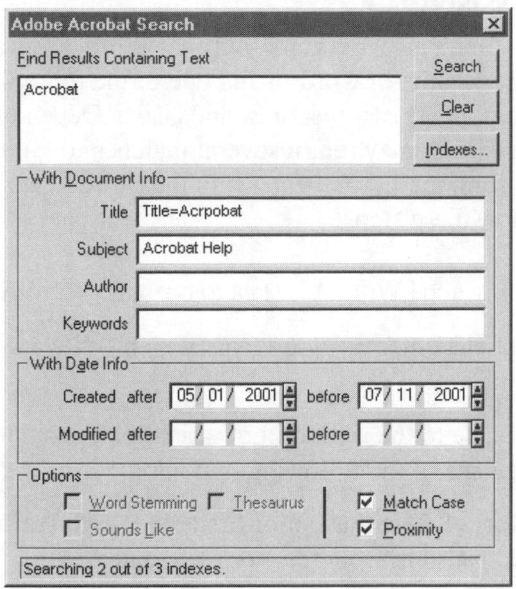

FIGURE 3-9 You can refine a search by using all available fields in the Search dialog box.

- **Author** You can search for PDF documents created by a specific author by entering the name of the author in this field.
- **Keywords** You can use this field to conduct a search based on key words that appear in the file Document Summary dialog box.
- **With Date Info** You can search for documents according to the date they were created or modified. Each option has fields you use to limit your search to documents created *Before* or *After* specific dates. The data in these fields is entered in mm/dd/year format.

Refine Your Search

When you search for information in an index that contains a large number of documents, Acrobat finds every document that matches your query. If the sheer volume of documents is overwhelming, you can fine-tune your search by using the Acrobat Word Assistant or performing a search using Boolean operators. When you use one or both of these tools, Acrobat finds fewer documents; however, the content of the documents provides a better match for the information you seek.

Use the Word Assistant

Your first tool for refining a search is the Acrobat Word Assistant. You use the Word Assistant to build a list of words using one of the following Word Assistant options: Word Stemming, Thesaurus, or Sounds Like. Depending on the word you choose, the Word Assistant may return several matches for your query. You can then choose a word from the list and enter it in the Search dialog box. To use the Word Assistant follow these steps:

1. Choose Edit | Search | Word Assistant to open the Word Assistant dialog box.
2. In the Word field, enter the word from which you want Word Assistant to build a list.
3. Click the triangle to the right of the Assist field. From the drop-down menu, choose one of the following options:
   - **Stemming** Select this option, and the Word Assistant will build a list of words that stem from the word you enter.
   - **Thesaurus** Select this option, and the Word Assistant will build a list based on synonyms of the Word you enter.
   - **Sounds Like** Select this option, and the Word Assistant will attempt to find words that sound like the word you enter. The results returned may not be what you expect, as the Word Assistant builds the list based on the first letter of the word you enter and does not take rhyming into account.
4. Click Lookup and Word assistant builds a list, as shown here.

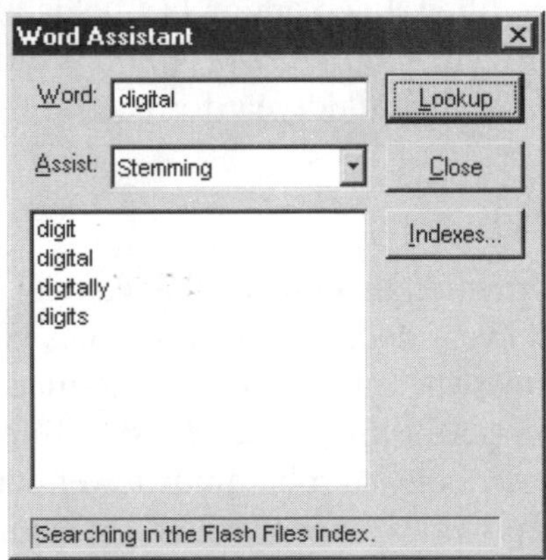

You get the most benefit from the Word Assistant if you use it in conjunction with the Search dialog box as follows:

1. Choose View | Search | Query to open the Search dialog box.
2. Choose View | Search | Word Assistant to open the Word Assistant dialog box.
3. In the Word Assistant dialog box, enter a word, choose an option, and then click Lookup to build a list of words.
4. Double-click a word you want to include in your search. Word Assistant copies the word into the Word text field.
5. Copy the word into the Search dialog box text field, as shown in the next illustration.

NOTE *You cannot use the Acrobat Copy command to copy a selected word from the Word Assistant into the Search dialog box. Instead of manually entering the word, use the keyboard shortcut* CTRL-C *(Windows) or* COMMAND-C *(Macintosh) to copy the word from the Word Assistant to your operating system clipboard. Place your cursor in the Search dialog box text field, and then press* CTRL-V *(Windows) or* COMMAND-C *(Macintosh) to paste the word. Alternatively, you can cut and paste from the context menu.*

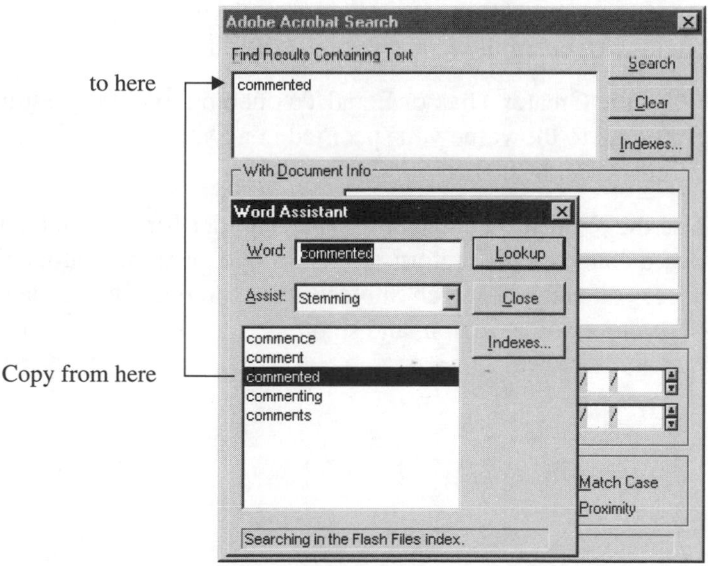

Use Boolean Operators

You can also use Boolean operators to refine a search. When you use Boolean operators, you can reduce the chances of finding irrelevant information, or you can use Boolean operators to expand a search. The Acrobat Search command supports the following Boolean operators:

- **= (equal sign)** Use the Equal To operand to search for words or phrases that are exact matches in a field.
- **~ (tilde)** Use the Contains operand to search for a word or words that are contained within a field, for example, Title~Adobe.
- **!=** Use the Does Not Equal operand to specify a word you do not want included in the results, for instance, Subject!=Adobe Illustrator.
- **!~** Use the Does Not Contain operand to exclude a word from your search results, for example, Title!~Acrobat Reader.
- **<** Use the Less Than operand to modify a search in a date field, for example, Date < 11/25/2001.
- **<=** Use the Less Than or Equal To operand to return a value less than or equal to the contents of a field, for example, Modified<= 12/15/2001.
- **>** Use the Greater Than operand to search for results greater than the value you entered. Use this operand to modify a search in one of the Date info fields, for example: Created>06/01/2001.
- **>=** Use the Greater Than or Equal To operand to obtain results greater than or equal to the value you specified in a Date info field, for example, Modified>=08/15/2001.
- ***** Use the Wildcard character as a placeholder for several characters. The Wildcard character will return results for one or more characters. If, for instance, you create a search Subject=o*n, you receive the matches *on*, *onion*, *opinion*, *observation*, and so on.

- **?** Use this Wildcard character as a placeholder for a single character. If you create a search Title~L?st, your search will return results for documents with titles that contain *Lost*, *List*, *Last*, *Lust*, and so on.

You use Boolean operands in text fields in the Search dialog box. You can apply more than one operand to a field by using them in different text fields, as shown here.

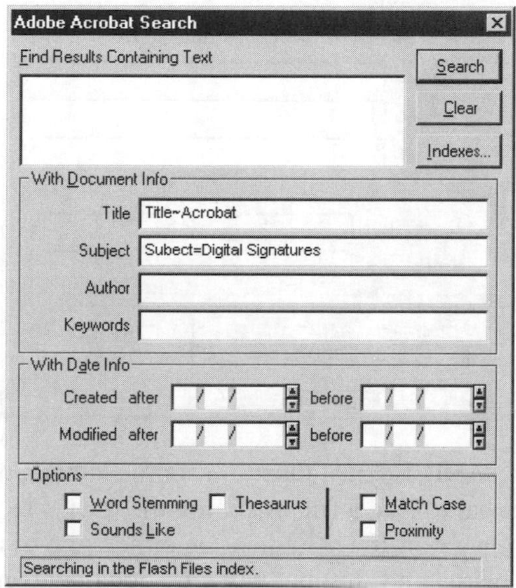

Use Boolean Logical Operators

Another way you can fine-tune a search is to create an expression using *logical operators*. When you use logical operators, you create an expression that must be true for Acrobat to find a particular document in a search. You have three logical operators to work with: AND, OR, and NOT. You can use logical operators to refine or expand a search. For example, if you want to find all documents with titles that contain the word *Acrobat* and that were created after January 1, 2001, you'd create the expression shown here.

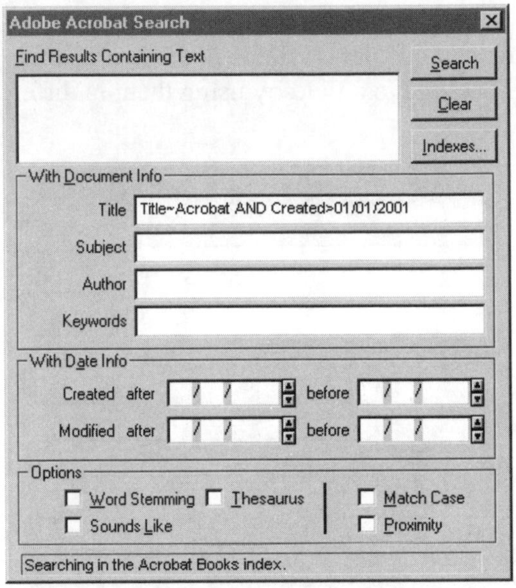

When you use the AND Logical Operator, both statements in an expression must be true for Acrobat to find a file matching the query. However, when you use the OR Logical Operator, if a statement on either side of the operator is true, the expression is true and Acrobat will find documents matching either statement. To find all documents that contain the word *Acrobat*, or were created after January 1, 2001, you create the expression shown in the following image. If you compare this expression with the last expression, you can see that Acrobat can potentially find more documents if the index you search has several documents that match the date parameters but not the title parameters, or match the title parameters but not the date parameters.

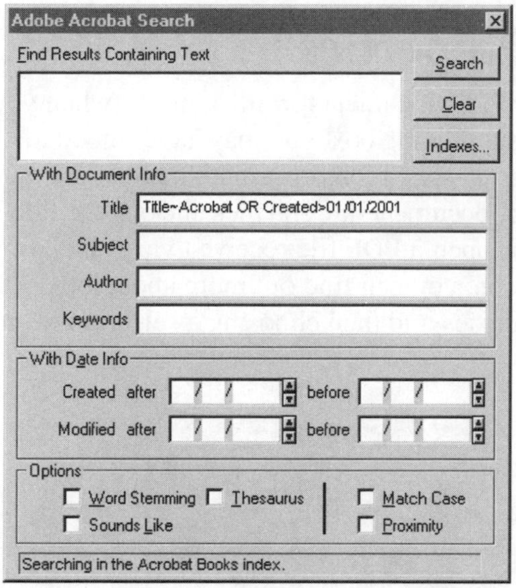

You use the NOT Logical Operator to exclude documents from search results. The statement on the right side of the NOT operator must be false in order for the expression to be true. In the search example directly following, Acrobat will find all documents in the index whose titles contain Acrobat Reader, but that were not created after January 1, 2001. As shown in the following image, the AND logical operator must precede the NOT logical operator.

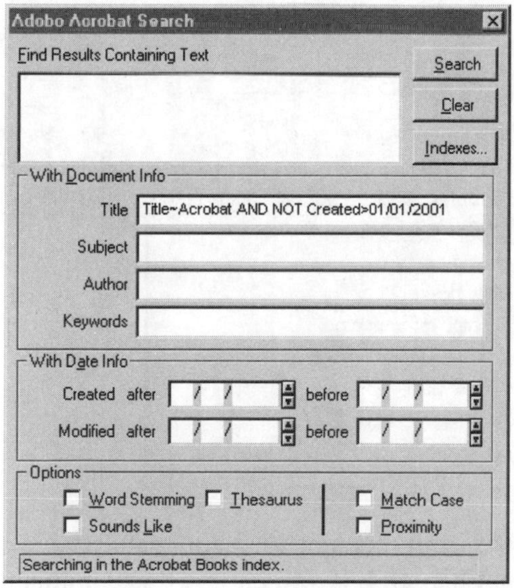

Get Document Properties

When you search for PDF documents from an index, when you see a document's title in the Search Results dialog box, you may have a good idea of what is contained in the document. You can find more information about documents Acrobat finds in a search by clicking the document title and then clicking the Info button, as discussed previously. When you open a PDF file received via e-mail, or one that is part of a multimedia presentation, you can find out more about the document by choosing File | Document Properties and then choosing a selection from the drop-down menu shown here.

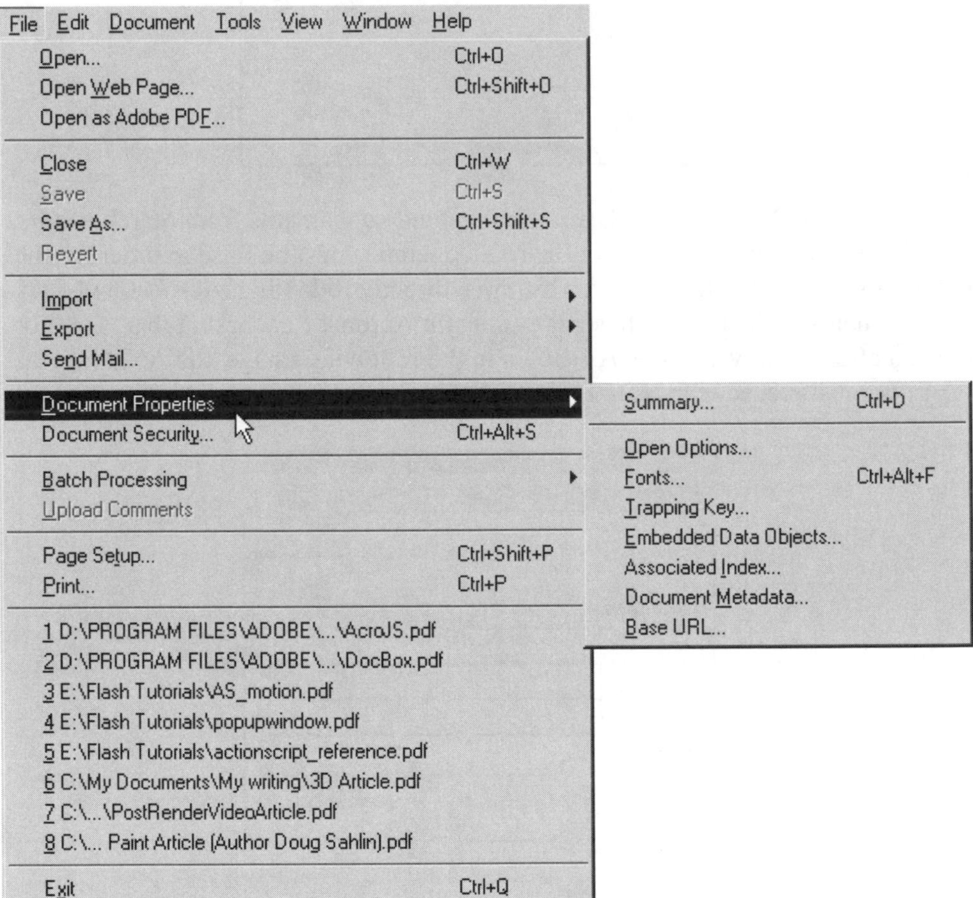

Many of the options from this menu are applicable to creating a PDF document and will be covered in Chapter 4. If you choose this command while using Acrobat

Reader, you only have two options, Summary and Fonts. When you choose one of these options in Acrobat Reader, all of the fields are dimmed out, which means you cannot modify the information. However, in Acrobat, all of the fields are available; you can modify the properties and save them with the document. The next image is a typical Acrobat Document Summary dialog box. Notice that some of the fields are the same ones you specify when conducting a search.

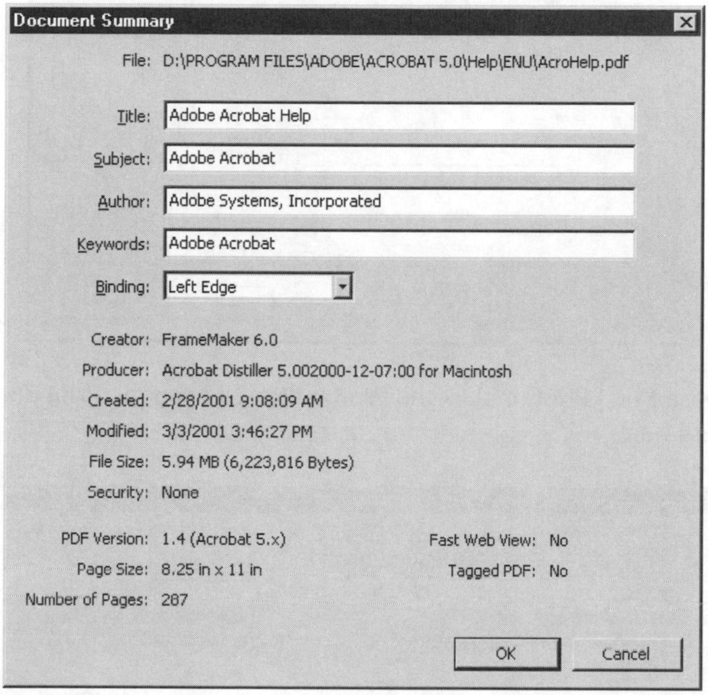

Document Summary

File: D:\PROGRAM FILES\ADOBE\ACROBAT 5.0\Help\ENU\AcroHelp.pdf

Title: Adobe Acrobat Help
Subject: Adobe Acrobat
Author: Adobe Systems, Incorporated
Keywords: Adobe Acrobat
Binding: Left Edge

Creator: FrameMaker 6.0
Producer: Acrobat Distiller 5.002000-12-07:00 for Macintosh
Created: 2/28/2001 9:08:09 AM
Modified: 3/3/2001 3:46:27 PM
File Size: 5.94 MB (6,223,816 Bytes)
Security: None

PDF Version: 1.4 (Acrobat 5.x) Fast Web View: No
Page Size: 8.25 in x 11 in Tagged PDF: No
Number of Pages: 287

OK Cancel

Print PDF documents

After you view a document onscreen, you have the option to print a hard copy of the document. Herein lies another strong suit of Acrobat; the document prints out exactly as it was created on the author's computer. You can set printing options and print a hard copy of a PDF file by following these steps:

1. To open the Print Setup dialog box shown next, choose File | Page Setup. You can use this dialog box to set general parameters for the print job, such as page orientation, size, printer, and so on. After choosing Print Setup parameters,

click OK to close the dialog box. This step is only needed if you want to change the default printer and page size.

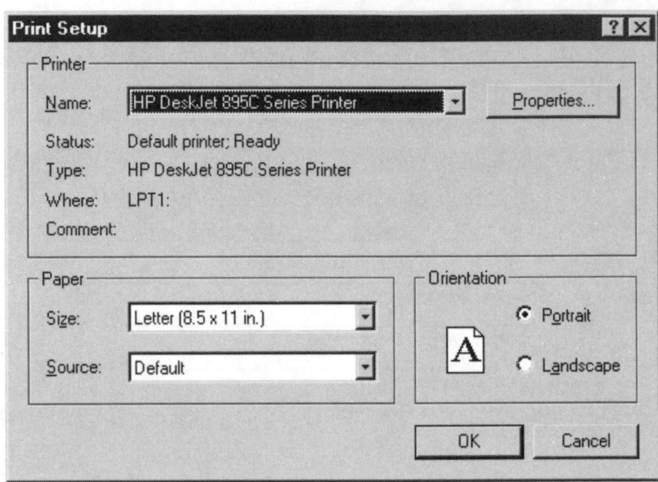

2. Choose File | Print or click the Print button to open the Print dialog box shown here.

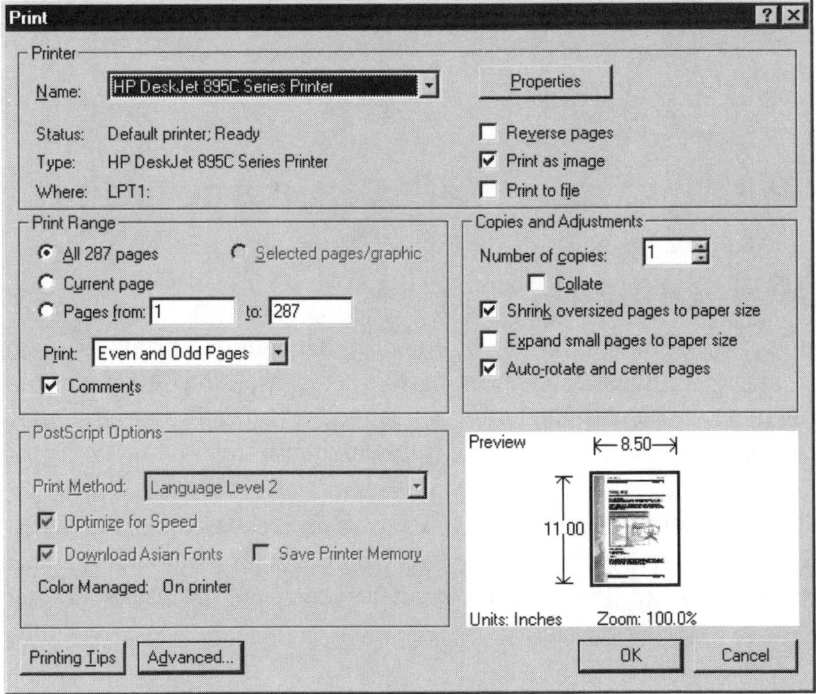

3. In the *Printer* section you can choose from the following options:

   - **Name (Windows) or Printer (Macintosh)** Your system default printer is displayed in this field. To select another printer, click the triangle to the right of the text field and choose a printer from the drop-down menu.
   - **Properties (Windows)** Click this button to set parameters for the currently selected printer. After you click this button, a dialog box will appear that is specific for the selected printer.
   - **Destination (Macintosh)** Your choices are either Printer or File.
   - **Reverse Pages (Windows)** Choose this option, and pages will be printed from last to first.
   - **Print To file (Windows)/ Print Method (Macintosh)** You can use this option to print the document to a file if you experience problems after choosing PostScript options when attempting to print to a device that supports PostScript options.
   - **Print to File** Choose this option to print the document to a file in PRN (Printer Files) format. This is redundant, however, as you already have thc file in PDF format.

4. In the *Print Range* section, you can choose from the following options:

   - **Print Range (Windows)** You can choose to print all pages or current page, or specify a range of pages.
   - **Comments** Choose Comments (the default), and Acrobat will print comment icons as they appear on the PDF document.
   - **Selected Pages Or Selected Graphics (Windows)/ Selected Thumbnails Or Selected Graphics (Macintosh)** If you have selected thumbnails or graphics in the document, this option is available; otherwise, it is dimmed out. Select this option to print selected thumbnails. To select Thumbnails, open the Thumbnails palette in the Navigation pane and click the thumbnails you want to print. Use SHIFT-click to select contiguous thumbnails; use CTRL-click (Windows) or COMMAND-click (Macintosh) to select non-contiguous thumbnails. After selecting thumbnails, you can right-click (Windows) or CONTROL-click (Macintosh), and choose Print Pages from the context menu.

5. In the *Copies And Adjustments* field, choose from the following options:

- **Number Of Copies (Windows)** Enter a value for the number of copies you want to print. If you are working on a Macintosh, you specify this option in the General dialog box.
- **Collate** Choose this option if you are using double-sided printing to properly collate the pages in print order. If you work on a Macintosh, this option appears in the General dialog box.
- **Shrink Oversized Pages To Paper Size** Choose this option, and Acrobat will shrink oversized pages to fit the selected paper size. This option comes in handy if the PDF file you are printing has different page sizes within the document.
- **Expand Small Sizes To Paper Size** Choose this option, and Acrobat will upsize small pages to fit the selected printer paper. Note that if the document you are printing has bitmap images on small pages, choosing this option will cause the images to become pixelated.
- **Auto-Rotate And Center Pages (Windows)** Choose this option if the PDF file you are printing contains pages in both landscape and portrait format. While printing is in progress, Acrobat will change page orientation as needed.

If you are printing to a PostScript device, the PostScript print options become available. You can then choose from available print methods, choose to optimize the operation for speed, choose to download Asian fonts if they are included in the document, and choose to save printer memory.

Part II

Create PDF Documents

Chapter 4

Create a PDF Document

How To...

- Open a file as an Adobe PDF
- Append an existing file
- Use Acrobat Distiller
- Set Job Options
- Set Document properties
- Save PDF files

Acrobat gives you the capability of creating PDF documents from many sources. You can create a PDF file from within many authoring applications (which will be covered in Chapter 5), or you can create documents directly in Acrobat. When you create a document within Acrobat, you have many options available to you. You can save a document using Acrobat defaults, or you can modify the document properties and add security to confidential documents. You can even use Acrobat to save documents in other formats. In this chapter, you'll learn the nuts and bolts of creating a bare-bones PDF file.

Create a PDF File

You can use Acrobat to quickly create PDFs from existing files. Choose between two methods: the Open As Adobe PDF command, or the drag-and-drop method. When you create a PDF file using one of these methods, Acrobat converts the original file into PDF format. After Acrobat converts the file, you can save it in PDF format, or repurpose it to another format. If needed, you can append a document by converting additional files to PDF format. You can also create a PDF document from within an authoring application by exporting the file in PDF format (if supported), or by using the application Print command and choosing Acrobat Distiller as the printing device. Creating a PDF file from within an authoring application will be covered in Chapter 5.

Open a File as Adobe PDF

You use the Open As Adobe PDF command to open files from supported formats. When you choose this command and select a file(s) to open, Acrobat converts the file from its current format into PDF format. You can open the following formats as PDF files:

- **BMP files** You can export BMP files from most popular photo-editing programs, such as Adobe PhotoShop, Corel Photo-Paint, and Macromedia Fireworks. Image files saved in this format can have color depth as high as 24-bit.
- **Compuserve GIF files** GIF (Graphic Interchange Format) files have 8-bit (256-color) color depth. You can open GIF files saved in the GIF 87 format or GIF 89a format as PDF files; however, Interlaced GIFs are not supported. Interlaced GIFs are used primarily for web pages where the image loads into a Web browser in stages. You can also open an animated GIF; however, only the first frame of the animation is converted to PDF format.
- **HTML files** HTML (Hyper Text Markup Language) files are created for use on the Internet. You can open HTML files as PDF documents. When you open an HTML file as a PDF file, Acrobat reads any image tags (<img src= 'yourimage.jpg'>) and converts the associated files to PDF in the exact position they appear when the HTML document is opened in a web browser. If the image is not available, Acrobat creates a bounding box with the dimensions of the image and displays the Alt text. Converting a web page to PDF format is a great way to create a client proof of a website under construction. You can also use the Capture Web Page command to open a web page from your hard drive or download a web page from the Internet. Web capture is discussed in Chapter 6.
- **JPEG files** JPEG (Joint Photographic Expert Group) files are used for web graphics and multimedia presentations. JPEG files are compressed for quick download from the Web or to save file space in a multimedia presentation.
- **PCX files** Image files in the Windows-only PCX (**Pi**Cture E**x**change) format can be exported from most popular image-editing programs. The PCX format is native to the Windows PaintBrush program; however, many applications, such as Corel Photo-Paint, offer full support of the PCX format. Consult your image-editing software user manual to see whether the format is supported. The PCX format supports 24-bit color depth and can be opened directly in Acrobat as PDF files.

- **PICT files** Image files saved in the Macintosh PICT (**pict**ure) format support 32-bit color depth. While PICT files can be created in Windows-based image-editing programs, only the Macintosh version of Acrobat can open PICT images as PDF files.
- **PNG files** PNG (Portable Network Graphics) files are not compressed and support 24-bit color.
- **Text files** You can open text documents saved in .txt format as PDF documents. Text files can be created in programs as sophisticated as Microsoft Word, or as humble as the Notepad utility included with versions of the Microsoft Windows operating system.
- **TIFF files** TIFF (Tagged Image File Format) files are not compressed and support 32-bit color. People who create images in both platforms for print favor this format because of the high image resolution and clarity.

To convert an existing file to a PDF file, do the following:

1. Choose File | Open As Adobe PDF to access the Open dialog box, shown in the following image:

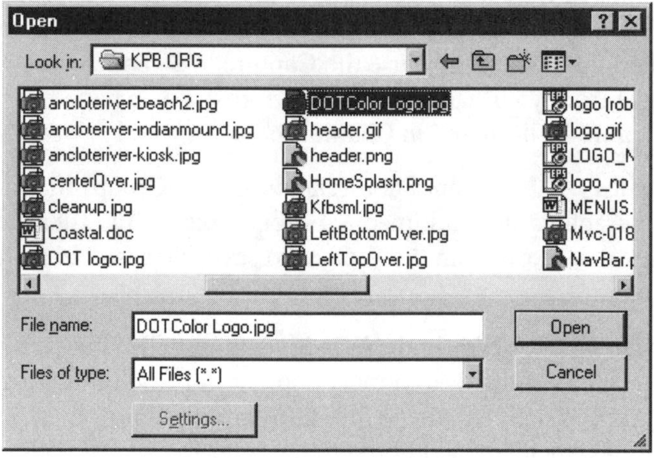

2. Click the triangle to the right of the Files Of Type field and choose an option from the drop-down menu, or accept the default All Files option.
3. Select the file you want to open. To select additional contiguous files, hold down the SHIFT key and click additional files you want to add. To select non-contiguous files, hold down the CTRL key and click additional files you want added to the selection.
4. If you select any image file other than the JPEG format, the Settings button becomes available. When you open an image file as a PDF file, Acrobat uses the JPEG algorithm to compress the image for delivery in PDF format. Click the Settings button to open the Conversion Options dialog box, shown in the following image. Click the triangle to the right of the Grayscale/Color Compression field, and choose either ZIP compression or one of the JPEG compression formats: JPEG (Quality : Minimum), JPEG (Quality : Low), JPEG (Quality : Medium), JPEG (Quality : High), or JPEG (Quality : Maximum). When you choose JPEG (Quality : Minimum), Acrobat applies a high level of compression and image quality is degraded. When you choose one of the higher quality settings, Acrobat applies less compression to the file, and image quality is higher at the expense of a larger file size. Keep this factor in mind if you are opening image files as PDF files that you eventually intend to save in the PDF format and display on the Web.

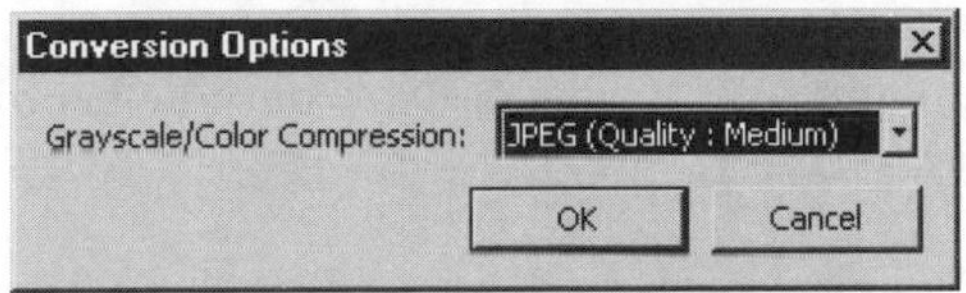

5. Click Open, and Acrobat opens the file in PDF format. Figure 4-1 shows a JPEG image converted to PDF format.

After you open a file in PDF format, you can work with the file directly in Acrobat. You can then save the file in PDF format, or other formats supported by Acrobat. Saving files is covered in future sections of this chapter.

If you already have a PDF file open in Acrobat and then choose another file to open with the Open As Adobe PDF command, Acrobat will display the dialog box

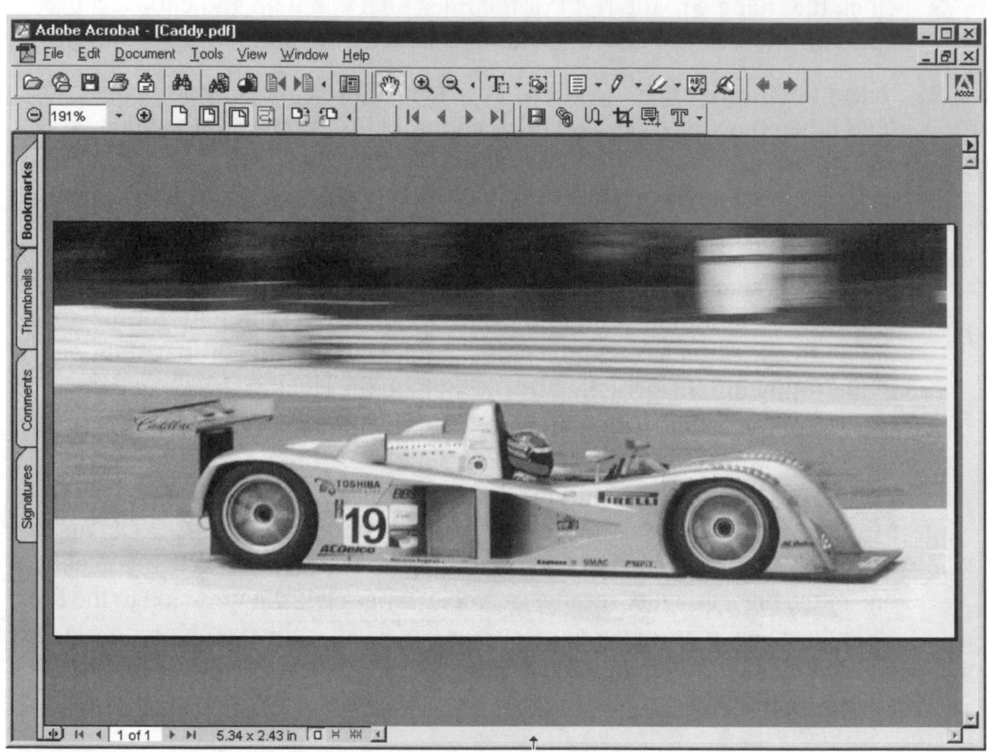

FIGURE 4-1 Use the Open As PDF command to convert other file formats to PDF files.

shown in the following image. Accept the default option (Append To Current Document), and Acrobat will open the file as a PDF and append it to the current document. Choose Create New Document, and Acrobat will convert the file to a PDF and create a new document.

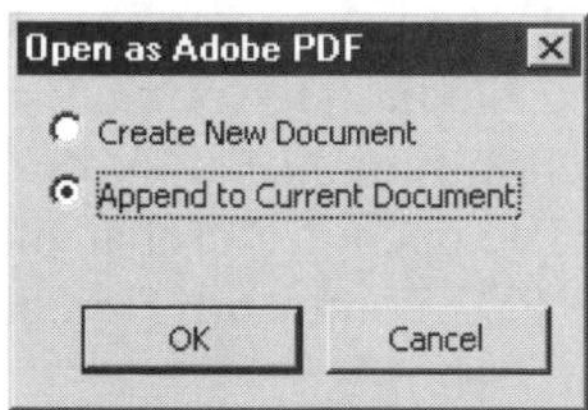

When you invoke the Open As Adobe PDF command with no document open and select several files, Acrobat creates a separate PDF file for each document. However, when you have a document open, and use the Open As Adobe PDF command on several files (with the exception of HTML files, as noted next) and choose the Append Document option, Acrobat creates a new page for each file you convert. If you open files that have the same page size, you can quickly create a multipage PDF document in this manner.

NOTE *If you have a PDF file currently open, and choose the Open As Adobe PDF command and select an HTML file, then you cannot append the current document. If you choose this option, Acrobat displays a warning that says the file is corrupt or not supported. However, you can open the file as a new document by running the command again and choosing the Create New Document option from the Open As Adobe PDF dialog box.*

Create a PDF File by Dragging-and-Dropping

You can quickly open one or several files as PDFs by dragging the file icon from your desktop or an open file folder and dropping it on the Acrobat icon. You can also drag-and-drop a file from a file folder directly into the Acrobat application.

When you create PDF files by dragging-and-dropping, you have the same options and limitations imposed by the Open As Adobe PDF command. If you select several files to open as PDF documents using the drag-and-drop method, Acrobat creates a separate PDF file for each file you select. However, if you open a single document as a PDF file by dragging-and-dropping, and then select additional files to open, you have the option to create separate documents or to append the first document you created. As previously noted, you cannot append an HTML file to a PDF.

Launch Acrobat and Create a PDF File

You can launch Acrobat and create a PDF file on-the-fly by dragging a supported file format onto the Acrobat shortcut on your desktop. This method comes in handy when you work in other applications and decide you need an accompanying PDF file to the one you are currently editing. To open a file in this manner, do the following:

1. Select the file you want to open as a PDF document. You can select one or several files to open.

2. Drag the selected files to the Acrobat desktop shortcut, as shown in the following image, and release the mouse button. After you release the mouse button, Acrobat launches and converts the selected files to PDF format. If you attempt to open a file that is not supported, Acrobat displays a warning dialog box.

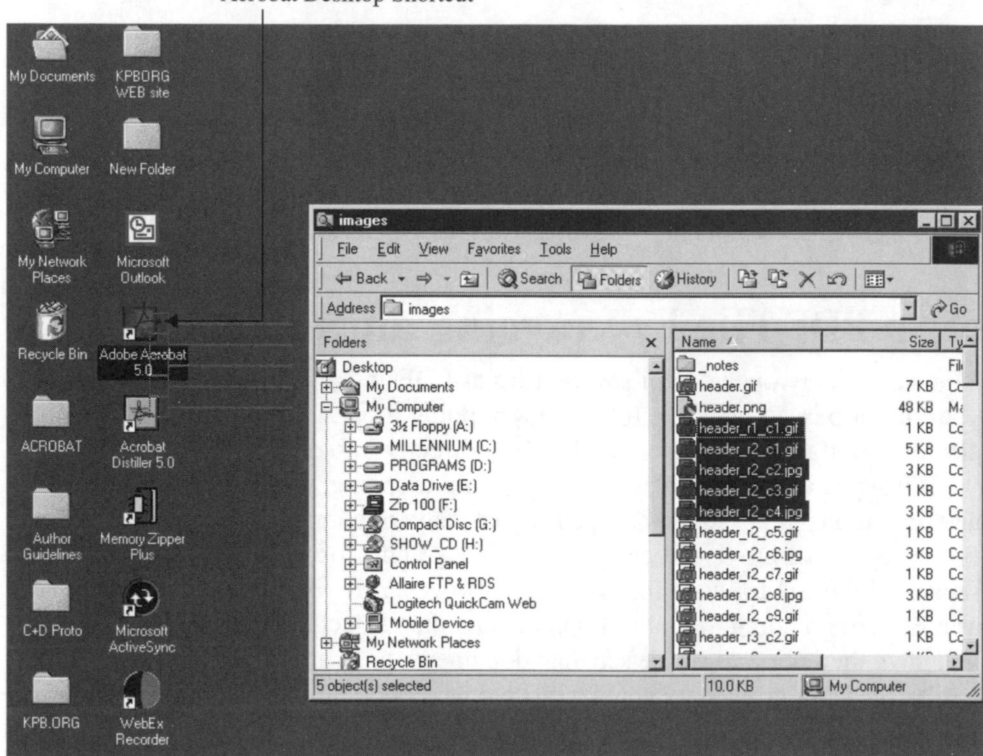

Create PDFs by Dragging-and-Dropping from Folders

When you work on a project and have all of your assets organized in a single folder, you can quickly create PDF files using the drag-and-drop method. This technique works best when the files you convert are stored in a folder on your desktop. Whenever you need to create a PDF document from a file stored in a folder, do the following:

1. Navigate to and open the file folder that contains the files you want to convert to PDF.
2. Resize the folder so that it will fit within the Acrobat workspace.

3. In the file folder, select the files you want to convert to PDF documents and drag-and-drop them into the Acrobat workspace. After you release the mouse button, Acrobat creates a new PDF document for each file you selected.
4. If you have additional files to convert to PDF, you can minimize the file folder to gain maximum workspace in Acrobat. When you need to convert another file to PDF, restore the folder to its previous size within the Acrobat workspace.

If you find that creating PDF documents by dragging-and-dropping them from file folders suits your working preference, consider organizing your work ahead of time. Put all of the project files in a single folder and move them to your desktop. Then resize the Acrobat application and file folder so they are arranged side by side. When you need to create a PDF document from an asset in the project folder, select the file and drag it into the Acrobat workspace. After Acrobat creates the PDF file, you can maximize Acrobat to gain more workspace. Whenever you need to create another PDF file from the folder, click the Restore button, and Acrobat and the project folder will appear side by side as shown in the following image:

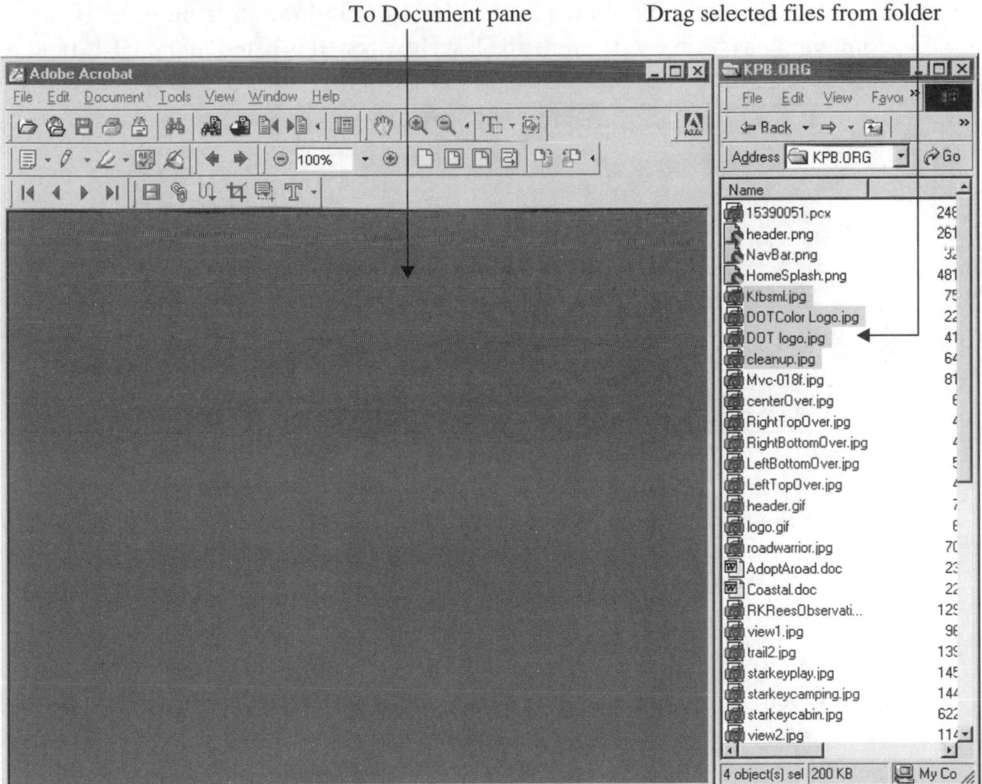

When you work on a PDF file and drag-and-drop files from a folder into the workspace, the Insert Pages dialog box appears instead of the Open As Adobe PDF dialog box. Choose an option to place the converted file in a desired location. The Insert Pages dialog box is associated with the Insert Pages command that is discussed in Chapter 11.

Open Web Pages

If you are a website designer, you can use the Open Web Pages command to create a PDF proof for client approval. This technique shows a customer your design before a web host has been selected. Use this command to convert a single HTML document from your hard drive into a PDF document, or use it to convert the entire site into a PDF document, complete with links. To create a PDF document from HTML files, do the following:

1. Choose File | Open Web Page to access the Open Web Page dialog box, shown in the following image. Alternatively, you can click the Open Web Page button that looks like a file folder with a globe in front of it. If the command has been used before, the last site opened is listed in the URL field.

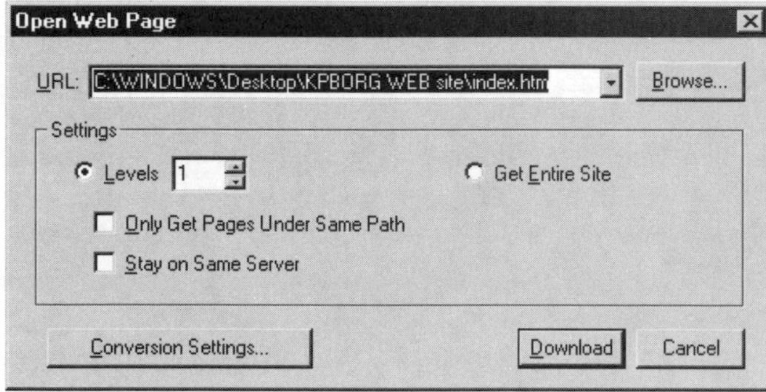

2. If you want to open a single HTML page, accept the default. If you want to open the entire site in PDF format, choose the Get Entire Site option.

3. Click the Browse, button and Acrobat opens the Select File To Open dialog box.

4. Navigate to the HTML file you want to convert to PDF format, and then click Open. If you choose the Get Entire Site option, select the Home page of the site.

5. Click the Download button. If you choose the Get Entire Site option, Acrobat will display a dialog box warning you of a potentially large download. Click Yes to begin the download, click No to abort. When you use this command to convert HTML documents stored in a folder on your hard drive, the download is relatively quick. However, when you download sites from the Internet, the download time depends upon the quality of your connection, your modem speed, your processor, and the size and complexity of the website. Capturing Web pages from the Internet is covered in detail in Chapter 6.

After you click the Download button, Acrobat begins converting the HTML pages into PDF format. Acrobat downloads the entire site, including images and accompanying files. Figure 4-2 shows a website that has been converted to PDF format.

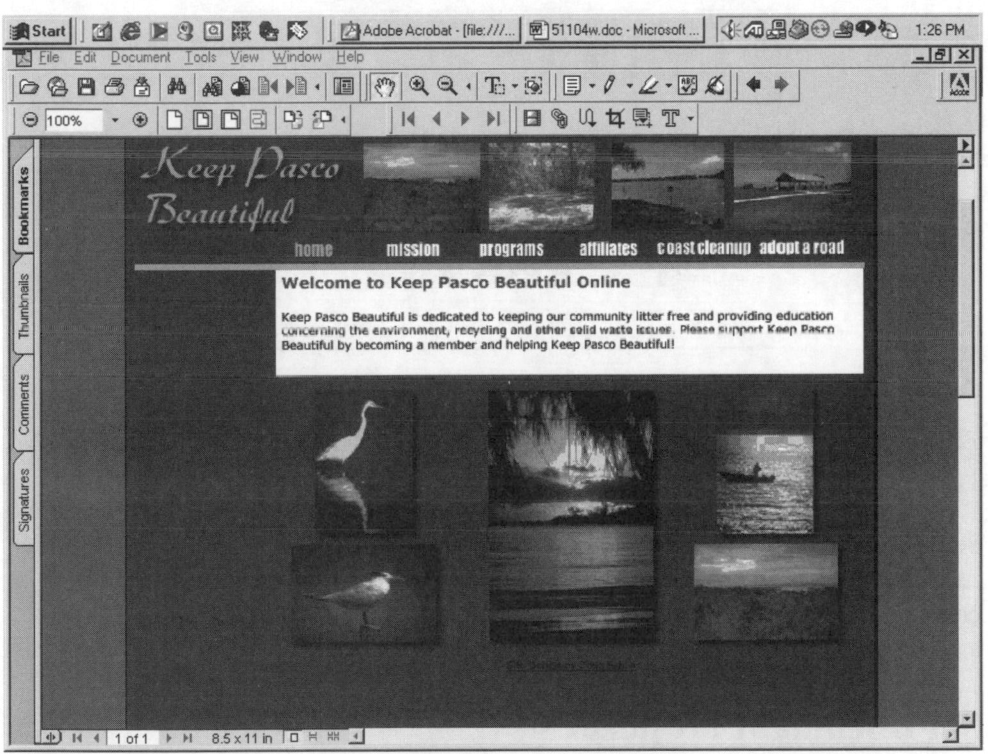

FIGURE 4-2 Use the Open Web Page command to create a customer proof of a Web design.

Save PDF Files

After you convert a file to PDF format, you can save it for future reference. When you save a PDF file, you can either accept the Acrobat defaults, name the file, and save it, or modify the document properties, name the file, and save it. The properties you modify determine how the document appears when opened and what information is available for the Search command (if the document is included as part of a PDF index). To save a PDF file using the Acrobat defaults, do the following:

1. Choose File | Save, and Acrobat opens the Save As dialog box opens, shown in the following image:

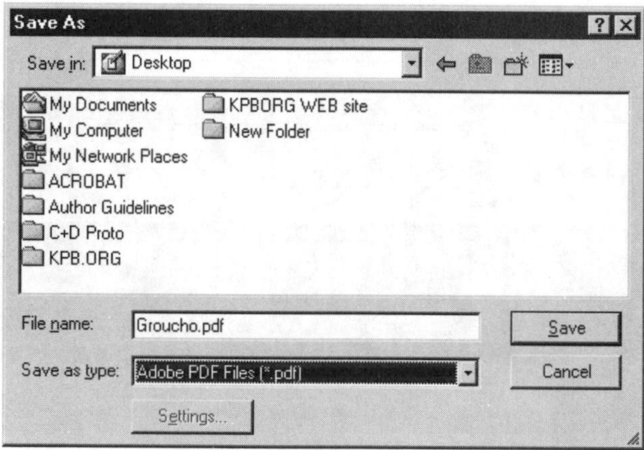

2. Navigate to the folder you want the file saved in, and enter a name for the file. Accept the Save As Type default, Adobe PDF Files (*.pdf), and click Save.

After you click the Save button, Acrobat saves the file in PDF format using the default Document Summary. If you use the document for your own reference, the Acrobat defaults may be acceptable. However, if you distribute the document to colleagues or customers, it is to your advantage to modify the document properties as discussed in the next section.

Set Document Properties

When you convert a file to PDF format, or open a PDF document and modify it, you can change the document properties before saving the document. You can edit the Document Summary to include information you deem pertinent to your viewing audience; you can set the Document Open Options to change or specify what the viewer sees when the document is opened; and you can set Document Security to limit access to the document.

Edit Document Summary

When you convert a file to PDF format, Acrobat creates a Document Summary. The information in the Document Summary is gleaned from the original file. A converted Document Summary tells you when the document was created, the Acrobat method used to create the document, and the document title. If you open a document that has already been saved, the Document Summary may have additional information as entered by the author of the document. You can modify a Document Summary by following these steps:

1. Choose File | Document Properties | Summary to open the Document Summary dialog box shown in the following image:

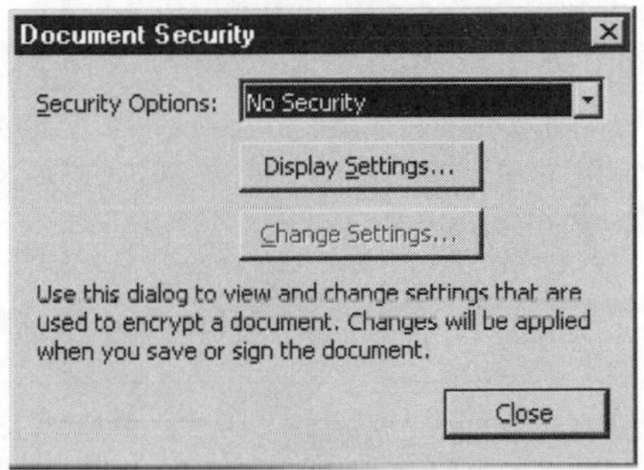

2. Modify the information in any or all of the following text fields: Title, Subject, Author, and Keywords. Remember this information is often the first information your viewers see concerning your document, especially if they use the Search command to locate the information. Keep this information as relevant as possible.
3. Click the triangle to the right of the Binding field and choose Left Side or Right Side from the drop-down menu. Binding is used when thumbnails are displayed, or when a multipage document is displayed using the Continuous Facing mode.
4. Click OK to apply the new information and close the dialog box.
5. Save the document as a PDF file, and Acrobat updates the information you entered along with other Document Summary information, such as the date modified.

When you save a document with pertinent information in the Document Summary, it is easier for other people who view the document to understand the information contained within. Time is valuable. In today's hustle-bustle world, people do not have the time to sift through a document to see whether the information meets their needs. In addition to changing the information in the Document Summary, you can also specify what your viewers see when they open a PDF document. The information you include in the Document Summary can also be used in a search if the document is included in a PDF index. Creating a PDF index is covered in Chapter 15.

Set Document Open Options

If you save a PDF document with Acrobat defaults, when your viewers open the document, then they see the first document page in the Document pane complete with the Navigation pane bookmarks and thumbnails, and all of the Acrobat (or Acrobat Reader) menus and tools. The default open options work fine if you share the document with coworkers or work with a team of authors who will edit the document. However, when you create a document such as an eBook or a multimedia presentation, you can change the default options by doing the following:

1. Choose File | Document Properties | Open Options to open the dialog box shown in the following image:

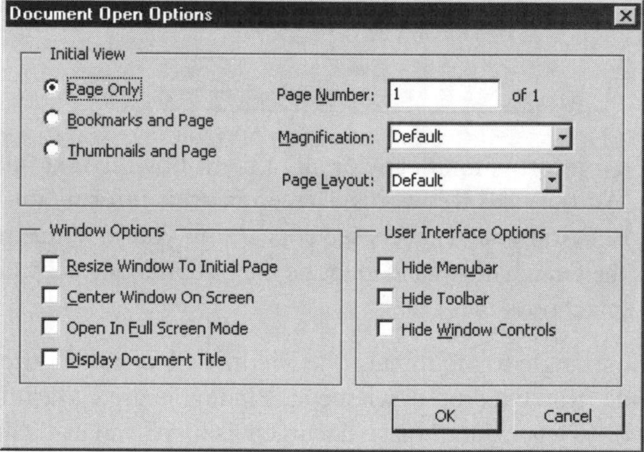

2. In the Initial View section, choose from the following options:

■ **Page Only** Choose this option, and when the document opens, the viewer will see the full page with only the tabs in the Navigation pane visible.

- **Bookmarks And Page** Choose this option, and when the document opens the viewer will see the full page with only the Bookmarks palette of the Navigation pane visible.
- **Thumbnails And Page** Choose this option, and when the document opens the viewer will see the full page with only the Thumbnails palette of the Navigation pane visible.

3. In the Page Number text field, enter the number of the page you want visible when the document opens. If you enter an invalid page number, Acrobat will display a warning to that affect.
4. Click the triangle to the right of the Magnification field and choose one of the following options:
   - **Magnification Levels** Choose one of the preset magnification values, and the document will open at that magnification. These are the numbers followed by the percent symbol. These values represent a percentage of the document size as it was originally published. You can also enter a value between 8.33% and 1600% in the Magnification Levels field to have the document open at a level other than one of the defaults.
   - **Fit In Window** Choose this option, and Acrobat will size the document to fill the entire Document pane when the file opens.
   - **Fit To Width** Choose this option, and Acrobat will fit the document to the current width of the Document pane when the file opens.
   - **Fit Visible** Choose this option, and Acrobat will size the document so that only visible elements fit the width of the Document pane. If you choose this option, no margins will be visible.
   - **Default** Choose this option, and Acrobat will size the document according to the General Preferences of the user.
5. Click the triangle to the right of the Page Layout field and choose a layout option for scrolling. Your choices are
   - **Default** Choose this option, and the page will open to the default layout specified by the General Preferences of the user.
   - **Single Page** Choose this option, and document viewers can use the Hand tool to scroll a single page, but not scroll to the next page.
   - **Continuous Scroll** Choose this option, and document viewers can scroll from one page to the next with the Hand tool.

- **Continuous Facing** Choose this option, and when the document opens, Acrobat will display pages side by side. The viewer uses the Hand tool to scroll to the next set of pages.

6. In the Window Options section, choose from the following options:

   - **Resize Window To Initial Page** Choose this option, and Acrobat will resize the Document pane to fit around the document.
   - **Center Window On Screen** Choose this option, and Acrobat will open the Document pane in the middle of the workspace.
   - **Open In Full Screen Mode** Choose this option, and the viewers will see the initial page in Full Screen mode, without any toolbars, menu bars, or navigation palettes. Unless the viewers have selected Continuous Scrolling from the General Preferences Full Screen section, they will not be able to scroll a multipage document viewed in Full Screen mode. If you choose this option, it is a good idea to create an index or buttons that your viewers can use for navigation.
   - **Display Document Title** Choose this option, and Acrobat will display the document title in the application title bar. If you did not specify a document title in the Document Summary dialog box, the document filename and extension are displayed.

NOTE *You can select every option in the Window Options section. However, when options conflict, Acrobat applies the overriding option. For instance, if you choose both Open In Full Screen Mode and Display Document Title, the document title is not visible because the application title bar is hidden in Full Screen viewing mode.*

7. In the User Interface Options section, choose any or all of the following options:

   - **Hide Menubar** When you choose this option, Acrobat opens the document with the menu bar hidden. Press f9 to unhide the menu bar.
   - **Hide Toolbar** When you choose this option, Acrobat hides the toolbar when the document opens. If you do not choose the Hide Menubar option in conjunction with this option, the user can choose Window | Hide Toolbars to unhide the toolbars or press f8.

- **Hide Window Controls** When you choose this option, Acrobat opens the document with the Navigation pane hidden.

NOTE *Even though it is possible for your viewers to reveal the menu bar and toolbars using keyboard shortcuts, many of your viewers may not know this. Therefore, you may want to consider including some navigation aids for your viewers if you hide either the menu or toolbars.*

8. Click OK to apply the options and close the dialog box.
9. Choose File | Save.

When you save the document, the new Open Options are saved with it and will be applied the next time the document opens. Of course, any of the changes you make to the document can be changed by a viewer with the full version of Acrobat. To prevent viewers from tampering with your handiwork, change the security level of the document.

Set Document Security

You add security to limit access to the document or prevent viewers from editing your document in the full version of Acrobat. You can use Acrobat Standard Security to password-protect confidential documents. When you password-protect a document, you set permissions for document accessibility; for example, you can prevent the document from being printed. Alternatively, you can choose to use Acrobat Self-Sign Security, which requires a user to log in. When you use Acrobat Self-Sign Security, you specify which users can access the document. Both forms of Acrobat Security will be covered in detail in Chapter 13.

Use the Save As Command

You use the Acrobat Save As command to save the same document with different settings under another filename. Use this technique when you need to create different versions of the same document for different destinations, for instance, to save a document optimized for print, or to save a document optimized for a web page. To save the current PDF with a different filename, choose File | Save As to open the Save As dialog box, shown in the following image. Enter the new name for the document and click Save.

You can also use the Save As command to save the document in another format. This is known as *repurposing* content. After you save the file in another format, you can edit the resulting file in a program that supports that format.

Save PDF Files in Other Formats

When you open a document in Acrobat, you can save the file in PDF format, or you can repurpose the document into another format. After you repurpose a document, you can edit the contents in another program. For instance, if you repurpose all of the text in a document by saving in RTF (Rich Text Format), you can edit the text in any word processing program that supports the RTF format. Consult your word processing software documentation to see whether RTF format is supported.

Save Text from a PDF File

Acrobat is a powerful program; but unless you have third-party plug-ins, you will not be able to edit wholesale portions of a document text. However, you can repurpose the document by saving all of the text in RTF format and then edit it in your favorite word processing program. If you use Microsoft Word for your word processing tasks, you can use PDFMaker to export the edited text in PDF format. You can repurpose a PDF document as RTF text as follows:

1. To save the text from a PDF file, choose File | Save As. Acrobat opens the Save As dialog box.
2. Name the document, click the triangle to the right of the Save As Type field, and choose Rich Text Format (*.rtf), as shown in the following image:

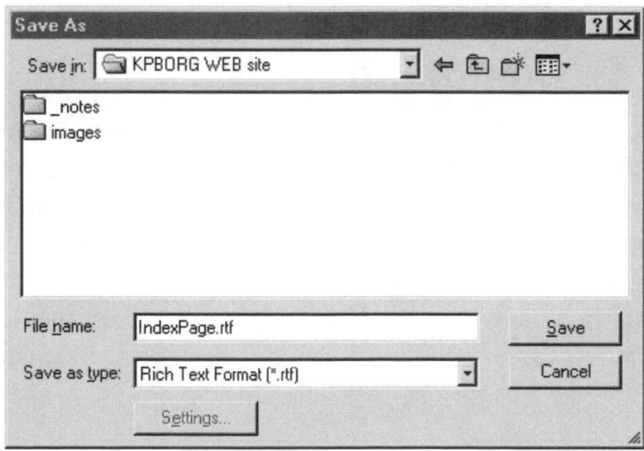

3. Click Save to save the document to file.

Save PDF Files as Images

You can also repurpose PDF documents by saving them in image formats. You can save PDF documents in the following image formats: EPS, JPEG, PNG, PS (PostScript), and TIFF. When you save a document in one of the image formats, you can modify the settings, which differ depending on the image format you use to save the file. The settings you choose determine parameters such as image compression, colorspace, and the resolution of the saved image.

Save as EPS

You can save a PDF file as an EPS for use in an illustration program such as Adobe Illustrator or Macromedia Freehand. When you save a file as EPS, you can modify the output settings to suit your needs. To save a PDF file in EPS format, follow these steps:

1. Choose File | Save As to open the Save As dialog box.
2. Choose Encapsulated PostScript from the Save As Type drop-down menu.
3. Click the Settings button to open the Encapsulated PostScript dialog box, shown in the following image:

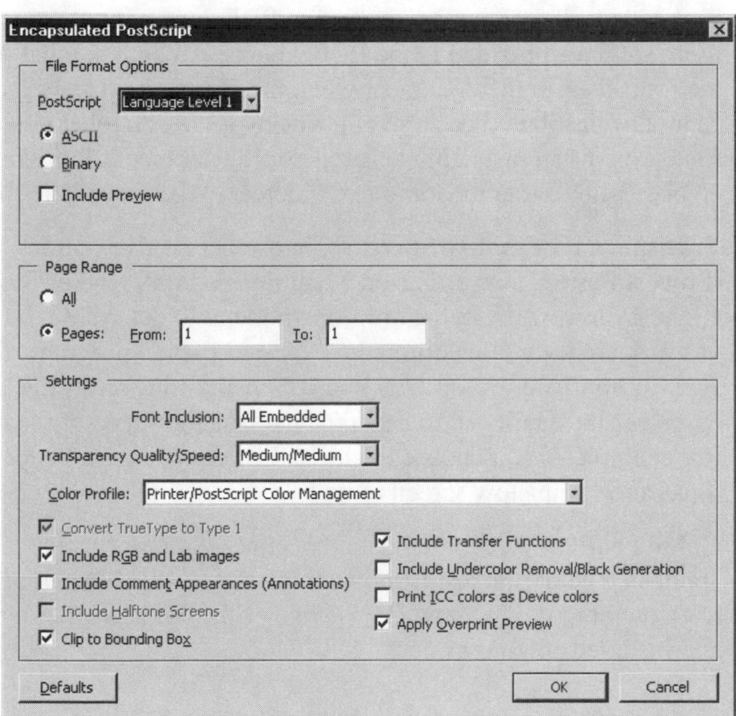

4. In the File Format Options section, choose from the following:
   - **PostScript** Choose one of the following from the drop-down menu: Language Level 1, Language Level 2, or Language Level 3.
   - **ASCII** Choose ASCII if you specified Language Level 1 PostScript.
   - **Binary** Choose this option if you specified Language Level 2 or Language Level 3 PostScript.
   - **Include Preview** Choose this option, and Acrobat will export a screen preview with the EPS file. If you do not choose this option, the preview will be displayed as a gray box when you open the file in another program. If you use Windows Acrobat, you have one choice available: TIFF; with Macintosh, you can choose to generate a PICT or TIFF preview.
5. In the Page Range section, choose All to save all pages in the PDF file, or choose Pages and specify the range by entering values in the From and To fields.
6. In the Settings section, specify the following settings:
   - **Font Inclusion** Choose one of the following options from the drop-down menu: None, All Embedded, or All. If you choose All Embedded, all fonts embedded in the PDF document are preserved. If fonts are not embedded in the PDF, choose All and Acrobat preserves the fonts used in the document when the file is saved as EPS. If a font cannot be distributed because of licensing issues, Acrobat uses a system font to create a reasonable facsimile of the document font you try to embed. Note that embedding fonts increases the size of the file.
   - **Transparency Quality/Speed** Choose one of five options (Lowest/Fastest, Lower/Faster, Medium/Medium, Higher/Slower, or Highest/Slowest) from the drop-down menu to determine the quality of transparency while editing the exported files in programs that support transparency, such as Photoshop and Illustrator. Each option describes the quality of transparency versus the speed of the redraw. For example, if you choose Highest/Slowest, you get a better quality illustration with slow screen redraw as a tradeoff.
   - **Color Profile** Accept the default (Same As Source) and Acrobat applies no color management when the file is saved. Alternatively, from the drop-down menu choose one of the color profiles available and installed on your system.

- **Convert TrueType to Type 1** Choose this option, and Acrobat will convert any TrueType fonts in the document to Type 1 fonts. If there are no TrueType fonts in the PDF document, this option is dimmed out.
- **Include RGB And LAB Images** When you choose this option, Acrobat exports images in these color profiles, as well as images with the CMYK color profile. If you neglect to include this option and there are images with these RGB or LAB color profiles, they are not included when the file is saved. This is especially important if your PDF documents will be printed by a service center. For more information on optimizing PDF documents for print, refer to Chapter 14.
- **Include Comment Appearances (Annotations)** Choose this option, and any comments in the document will be included when the document is saved as an EPS file. To open exported comments, the application you open the EPS file in must be capable of handling comments.
- **Include Halftone Screens** If halftone screens are present in the PDF file, choosing this option keeps them intact when you save the file in EPS format. This option dims out if halftone screens are not present in the PDF file.
- **Clip To Bounding Box** When you choose this option, Acrobat creates an EPS document that is sized to the PDF document bounding box. The bounding box is an imaginary rectangle large enough to surround all of the elements in the PDF document. When you disable this option, the page size of the EPS file is the same size as the PDF document.
- **Include Transfer Functions** Choose this option, and if Transfer Functions are preserved in the PDF document, they will be exported with the EPS file.
- **Include Undercolor Removal/Black Generation** If Undercolor Removal or Black Generation settings are included in the document's images, the settings are preserved when the document is converted to EPS format.
- **Print ICC Colors As Device Colors** Choose this option, and ICC colors embedded in the PDF file will be printed as Device colors. Device colors are derived from the printer's color profiles for grayscale colors, RGB (Red, Green, and Blue) colors, and CMYK (Cyan, Magenta, Yellow, and Black) colors.
- **Apply Overprint Preview** Choose this option, and if Overprint Previews are included in the PDF file, then they will be included with the EPS file.

7. Click OK to close the Encapsulated PostScript dialog box.
8. Navigate to the folder where you want the file saved, name the file, and click OK.

Save as JPEG

When you save a PDF file as a JPEG, you can specify the amount of compression applied to the image. JPEG is a "lossy" format; when the image is compressed, certain information is *lost* to create a smaller file size. Image degradation occurs at high levels of compression. To save a PDF file as a JPEG, follow these steps:

1. Choose File | Save As to open the Save As dialog box.
2. Choose the JPEG Files option from the Save As Type drop-down menu.
3. Click the Settings button to open the JPEG Options dialog box, shown in the following illustration:

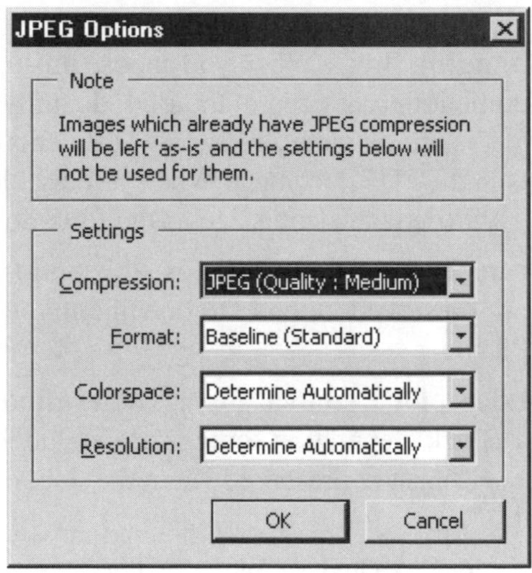

4. In the Settings section, you can either accept the defaults (which work well in most instances), or choose a different setting by clicking the triangle to the right of these fields:

    - **Compression** You can vary the quality of the saved JPEG by changing compression settings. Choose from five settings ranging from JPEG (Quality : Minimum) to JPEG (Quality : Maximum). If you choose JPEG (Quality : Minimum), Acrobat applies high levels of compression and image degradation is likely to occur; if you choose JPEG (Quality : Maximum), Acrobat applies minimal compression to achieve high image quality.
    - **Format** You can specify Standard or Optimized Baseline, or you can choose one of the three Progressive settings {Progressive (3Scans), Progressive (4 Scans), Progressive (5 Scans)}, which are generally used for the Web. When you save an image in the Progressive format, it loads into the viewer's browser in stages.
    - **Colorspace** You can accept the default (Determine Automatically) or choose Color or Grayscale. Unless you want to convert the document from color to grayscale, or vice versa, accept the default setting.
    - **Resolution** When you accept the default setting, the JPEG file is created with the same resolution as the PDF document. If you choose a different resolution than the original from the drop-down menu, Acrobat interpolates the data and redraws pixels as needed.

5. Click OK to close the JPEG Options dialog box.
6. Navigate to the folder where you want the file saved, name the file, and click OK.

Save as PNG

You can save PDF documents in the PNG (pronounced "ping") image format. When you choose this file format, you can interlace the PNG file, and choose the filtering option that supports the device where the PNG file will be viewed. To save a PDF file in PNG format, follow these steps:

1. Choose File | Save As to open the Save As dialog box.
2. Choose the PNG Files option from the Save As Type drop-down menu

3. Click the Settings button to open the PNG Options dialog box, as shown in the following image:

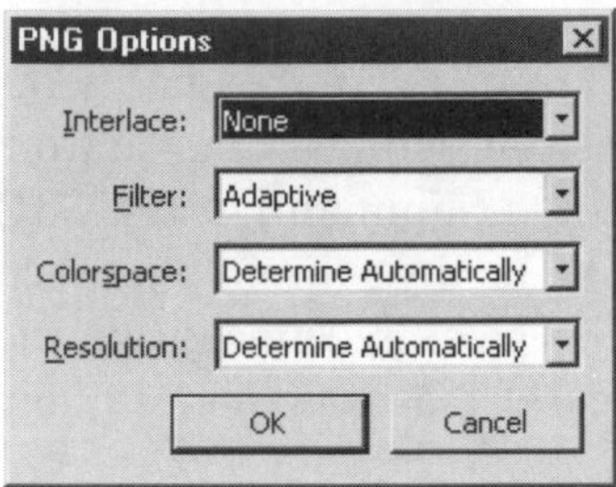

4. Click the triangle to the right of the Interlace field and choose either None (the default) or Adam7. When you choose Adam7 interlacing, the result is similar to an Interlaced GIF image that loads into a viewer's Web browser in stages.
5. Click the triangle to the right of the Filter field and choose a filtering option from the drop-down menu. You generally get good results with Adaptive (the default). However, you may achieve better results with one of the other filtering options. The old trial-and-error method works best here. Save the file using a different filename for each filtering option, and compare the results onscreen to determine which works best for the PDF file you want to save.
6. Click the triangle to the right of the Colorspace field, and choose an option. You have the Colorspace choices as in the JPEG Options previously discussed, with the exception of Monochrome. If you choose this option, the PDF file will be saved as a 1-bit PNG bitmap.
7. Click the triangle to the right of the Resolution field, and choose an option from the drop-down menu. Choose Determine Automatically, and the file will be saved with the same resolution as the PDF document. If you choose another resolution option, Acrobat will interpolate the image data and redraws the pixels to support the different resolution you choose.
8. Click OK to close the PNG Options dialog box and apply the settings.
9. Navigate to the folder where you want the file saved, name the file, and click Save.

Save as PostScript

Converting a PDF file to PostScript (PS) format is like printing a PS file to disk from an illustration program. After you save a file as PS, you can use Acrobat Distiller to save the file with optimized settings for a specific destination, such as a website or multimedia production. To save a PDF file as PS, follow these steps:

1. Choose File | Save As to open the Save As dialog box.
2. Choose PostScript from the Save As Type drop-down menu.
3. Click the Settings button to open the PostScript dialog box, shown in the following image. The file format settings for PS are identical to EPS with the exception of Include Preview, which is not a PS option. Refer to the "Save as EPS section" in the chapter, for detailed information on available options and their settings.

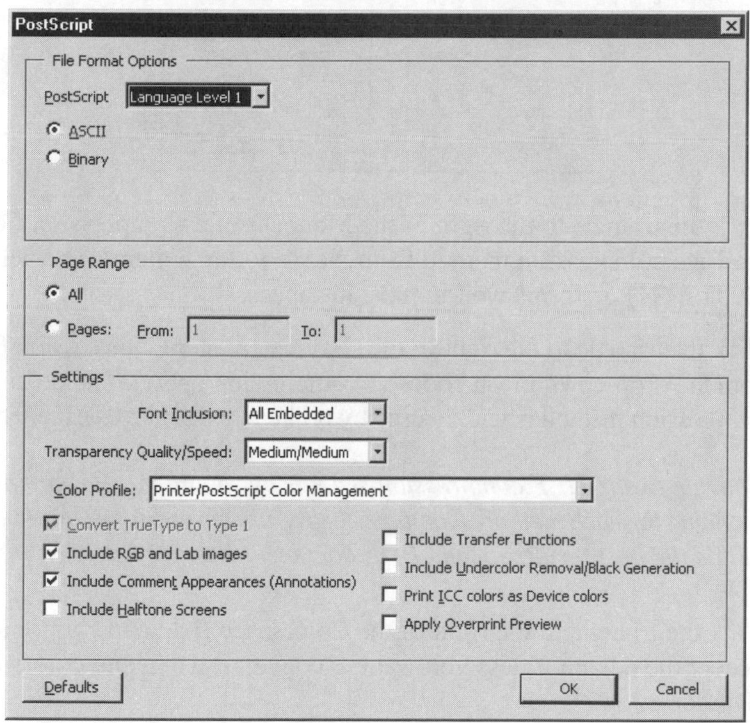

Save as TIFF

When you save a PDF document in TIFF (Tagged Image File Format) format, Acrobat creates a file that is recognized by most image-editing programs. When you save a PDF as a TIFF image, you can specify monochrome and color compression, as well as resolution. To save a PDF document as a TIFF image, follow these steps:

1. Choose File | Save As to open the Save As dialog box.
2. Choose the TIFF Files option from the Save As Type drop-down menu.
3. Click the Settings button to open the TIFF Options dialog box, shown in the following image:

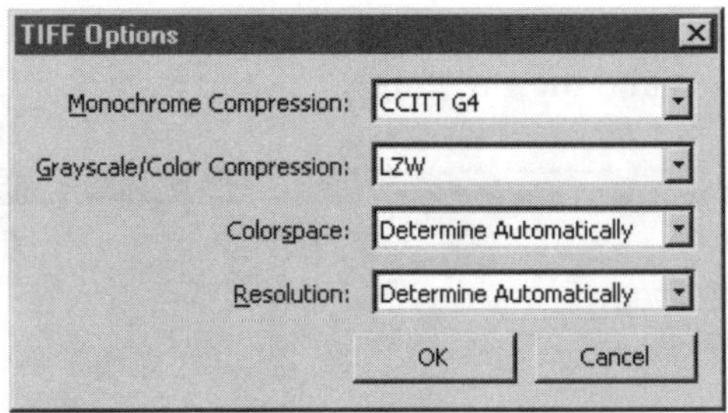

4. Click the triangle to the right of the Monochrome Compression field, and choose a compression method from the drop-down menu. The default (CCITT G4) performs well in most instances.
5. Click the triangle to the right of the Grayscale/Color Compression field, and from the drop-down menu choose a compression option. The default (LZW) compression method is widely used by printers and achieves excellent results.

TIP *You can tweak TIFF compression settings by saving the file with a different filename for each method. Compare the results onscreen to see which method yields the best results for the PDF document you are working with.*

6. Click the triangle to the right of the Colorspace field and choose an option. Accept the default unless you want to convert the existing colors in the PDF document.

7. Click the triangle to the right of the Resolution field and choose an option. Accept the default, and Acrobat will save the file with the same resolution as the PDF document. Choose a different resolution, and Acrobat will interpolate the data in the PDF document and redraw pixels to support the new resolution.

Create PDF Files with Acrobat Distiller

In previous sections of this chapter, you learned to create PDF documents by converting supported file formats into PDF documents and then saving the files from within Acrobat. You can also use Acrobat Distiller to create PDF files. Acrobat Distiller is a separate program; however, you can launch Acrobat Distiller from within Acrobat. When you install Acrobat, Acrobat Distiller is also added as a system printer, which gives you the capability of printing a PDF file directly from within any application that supports printing. Printing from an authoring application will be covered in Chapter 5.

Use Acrobat Distiller

Acrobat Distiller is a separate program that you use to convert EPS and PS files into PDF documents. With Acrobat Distiller, you have preset options available to optimize the file for an intended destination. Optimize a PDF document for a destination by choosing a specific Job Option. The Acrobat Distiller interface is shown in Figure 4-3.

As you can see, there is really not much of an interface at all; just a few menu options, an Info section, and a Progress section. To create a PDF file using Acrobat Distiller, follow these steps:

1. Launch the program by choosing Acrobat Distiller from your operating system program menu. Alternatively, you can launch Acrobat Distiller from within Acrobat by choosing Tools | Distiller.
2. Click the triangle to the right of the Job Options field and, from the drop-down menu, choose the option that best suits the intended destination of the document. Choose from the following:
   - **eBook** Choose this option when creating files for desktop viewing and printing.

- **Press** Choose this option when you need the highest quality images in your files. This option is the way to go if you print your files on a high-end printer with PS capabilities. When you choose this format, minimum compression is applied to images.
- **Print** Choose this option when the file will be viewed on desktops and printed on laser printers without color separation capabilities.
- **Screen** Choose this option when you create a PDF file solely for monitor or web viewing. This option creates a smaller file size by applying higher levels of compression to the graphics of the file.

NOTE *You can modify Job Options to suit the intended destination for the document you distill. Modifying Job Options will be discussed in detail in Chapter 14.*

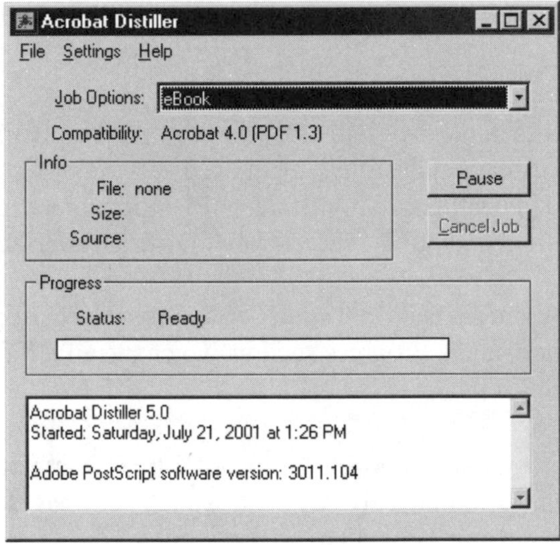

FIGURE 4-3 Create PDF documents from EPS and PS files using Acrobat Distiller.

3. To apply security to the distilled PDF file, choose Settings | Security. For more information about Acrobat Security settings, refer to Chapter 13.
4. Choose File | Open to access the Open PostScript File dialog box, as shown in the following image:

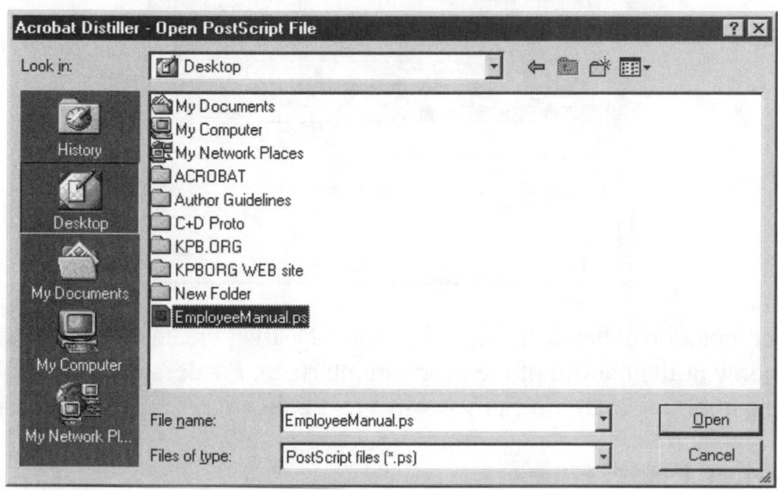

5. Navigate to the PS file you want to convert to PDF format, create a name for the file, and click Open.

After you click the Open button, Acrobat Distiller takes the reins and creates the PDF file. The Acrobat Distiller icon, which looks like a propeller, spins as the file is created. You can view information about the document in the Info section. If you distill a large multipage PS file, the distilling process may take some time. You can monitor the progress by viewing the Status section. In the following image, you see a large distilling job in progress. Acrobat Distiller shows you which page is being printed, the percentage of the job that has been completed, and a visual reference in the form of a blue bar that moves across the window as the file is created.

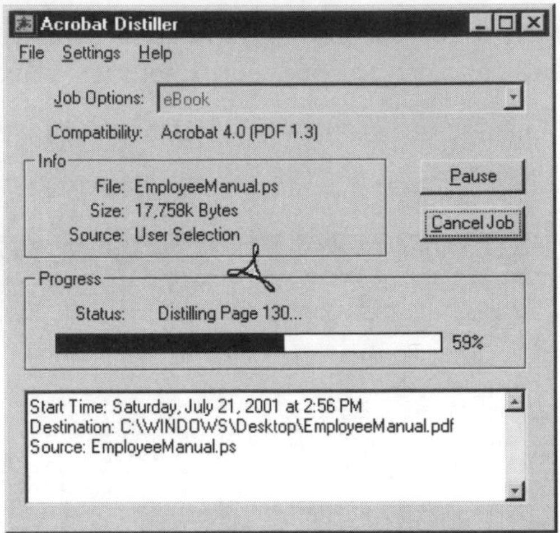

After completion of the distilling job, Acrobat Distiller creates a report that appears in the window at the bottom of the program interface. By default, Acrobat Distiller also creates a job log that you can view in a text editor.

Set Distiller Preferences

When you use Acrobat Distiller, it seems like a straightforward process, and it is—choose a Job Option, load a file, and Acrobat Distiller does the rest for you. The real power of Distiller is in the number of Job Option parameters you can modify, a task you learn to perform in Chapter 14. You can also modify Acrobat Distiller to suit your working preference by doing the following:

1. Launch Acrobat Distiller.
2. Choose File | Preferences to open the Preferences dialog box, shown in the following image.

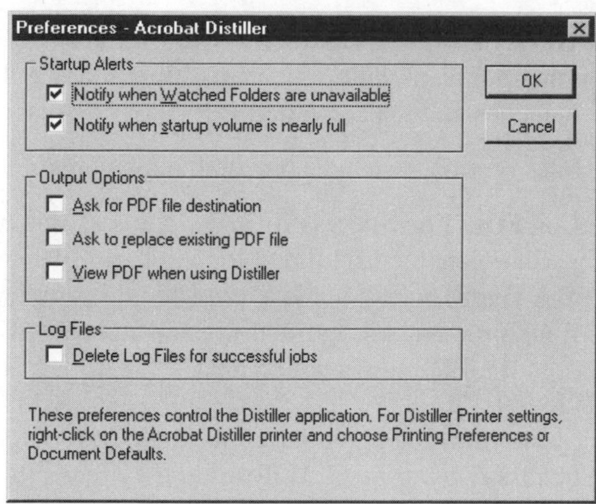

3. In the Startup Alerts section, you can modify the following options:

   - **Notify When Watched Folders Are Unavailable** When you choose this option (the default), Distiller has the capability of monitoring a folder or directory on your computer. Distiller automatically distills PS files placed in Watched Folders. You learn how to create Watched Folders in a future section of this chapter.

   - **Notify When Startup Volume Is Nearly Full** Distiller needs to write temporary files to disk when creating a PDF file. Choose this option, and Distiller will warn you when the startup volume is less than 1MB.

4. In the Output Options section, you can modify the following:

   - **Ask For PDF File Destination (Windows only)** When you enable this option, Distiller will prompt you for a folder to save the converted PDF file in. When this option is disabled (the default), the converted PDF file will be stored in the same location as the PS file.

   - **Ask To Replace Existing PDF File (Windows only)** This option is enabled by default and will prompt you when you try to overwrite an existing file. If you enable Ask For PDF File destination, this option is unavailable.

- **View PDF When Using Distiller (Windows only)** When you enable this option, upon completion of the distilling job, the default Acrobat viewer launches and the converted PDF file is displayed.

5. In the Log Files section, you have one option available:

- **Delete Log Files For Successful Jobs** Choose this option, and Distiller will delete the Log file of the job if the file is successfully distilled. A Distiller Log file is a text file that is created during the distilling process. A Log file is created and records any distilling errors, even if a PDF file is not created.

NOTE *Macintosh Acrobat users do not have the same Preferences options as their Windows counterparts. As noted in the preceding section, several Preferences options are Windows only. The Macintosh menu, however, does have an option not available to Windows users: Restart Distiller After PostScript Fatal Error. When this option is enabled, Distiller will automatically re-launch after encountering a fatal PostScript error.*

Create Watched Folders

If you regularly create PostScript files and save them to certain folders, you can configure Acrobat Distiller to watch these folders and automatically convert PostScript files to PDF files, plus move the original PostScript files to the Out folder or delete them. If you create several Watched Folders, each folder can have unique Distiller settings.

NOTE *If you work in a corporate environment where several authors create PostScript files, you cannot save them to Watched Folders on a network server. Set up a watched folder for converting your own files. Other authors who need to convert PostScript files to PDFs must set up a watched folder at their workstations using a licensed version of Acrobat.*

To create a watched folder, follow these steps:

1. Launch Acrobat Distiller and choose Settings | Watched Folders to open the Watched Folders dialog box, as shown in the following image:
2. Click the Add button to open the Browse For Folder dialog box, shown in the following image.

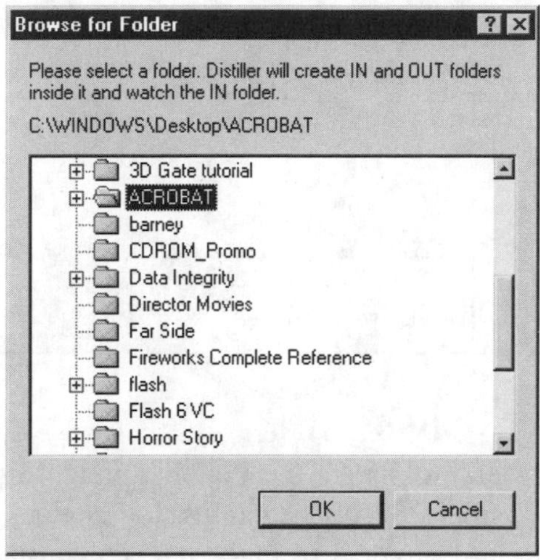

3. Navigate to the folder you want Distiller to watch, select the folder and click OK, and the selected folder is added to the Watched Folders list. After you add the folder, Distiller automatically creates an In and an Out folder within the watched folder.
4. In the Checked Watch Folders Every {___} Seconds: field, enter a value between 1 and 1000 seconds. This value specifies how often Distiller checks a watched folder.
5. Click the triangle to the right of the PostScript File Is Field, and choose an option to determine whether the converted PostScript file is Moved To Out Folder or Deleted.
6. Enter a value between 1 and 999 in the Delete Output Files Older Than {___} Days: field. Distiller uses this value to determine when to delete PostScript files in the Out folder.

7. After you add a folder to the Watched Folders list, you can click OK to close the dialog box, or click the Add button to add additional folders to the list.

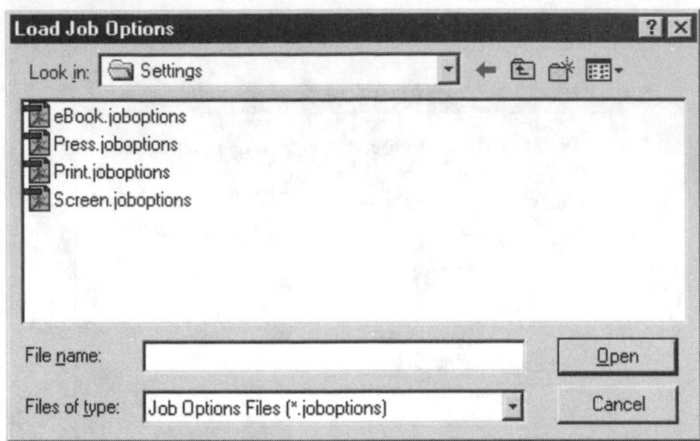

Set Watched Folder Options

After you add one or several folders to the Watched Folder list, you can specify options for each folder, namely, Security Options, Job Options, Load Options, Add additional folders, or Remove folders from the list. To set options for a Watched Folder, do the following:

1. Launch Acrobat Distiller and choose Settings | Watched Folders.
2. Select the Watched Folder whose settings you want to modify. After you select a Watched Folder, additional buttons become available, as shown in the following image, for setting the options that follow.

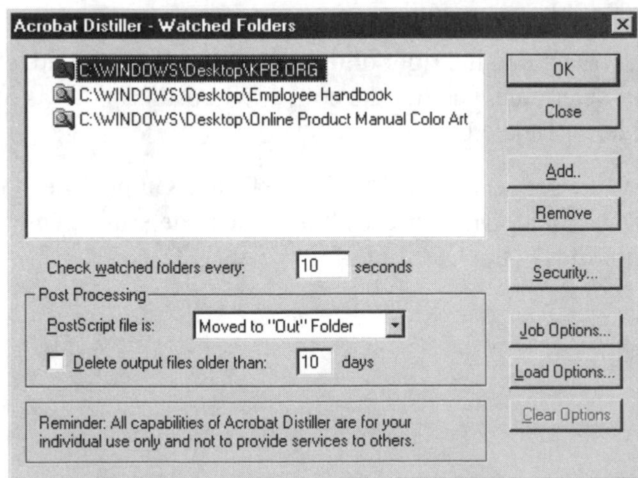

- **Remove** Click this button to remove the selected folder from the Watched Folders list.
- **Security** Click this button to set security for the Watched Folder. After you click this button, the Security dialog box opens. You can apply Acrobat Standard Security to the PDF files that have been distilled. For information on individual security settings, refer to the Use Acrobat Standard Security section earlier in this chapter.
- **Job Options** Click this button to open the Job Options dialog box. Once the dialog box is open, you can specify settings for all files distilled within the selected folder. You can find information for the options in this dialog box in Chapter 14.

TIP *If you create PS files for distillation into PDF files with different destinations, you can copy PS files to different Watched Folders and apply different Job Options to each Watched Folder. For example, you might create one folder for PDF files for the Internet, and another for PDF files that will be printed. Apply the appropriate Job Options to each folder and Distiller takes care of the rest.*

- **Load Options** Click this button, and the Load Job Options dialog box will appear. All of the Acrobat Distiller Job Option presets and any custom Job Options are stored in this folder, as shown in the following image. Click a Job Option to apply its settings to all files distilled in this folder.

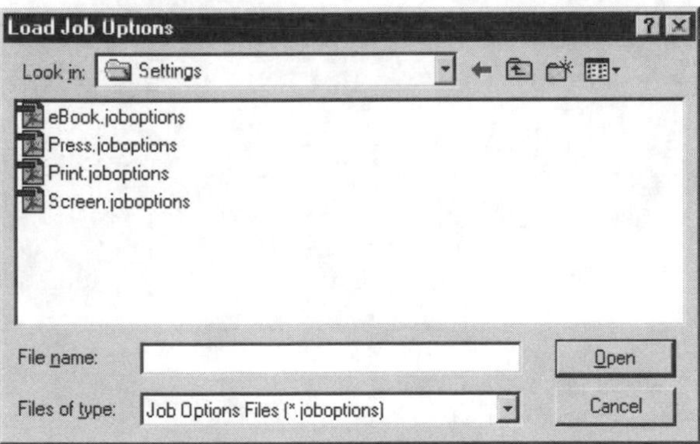

- **Clear Options** This button becomes available after you specify Job Options for files distilled from this folder. Click the button to clear Job Options applied to the PostScript files being distilled from this folder.

3. Click OK to apply the new settings and close the Watched Folders dialog box.

Chapter 5

Create PDF Documents in Authoring Applications

How to...

- Convert Microsoft Office documents to PDFs
- Set Document Conversion Properties
- Convert using the Print command
- Convert a document to PDF and then e-mail

As discussed in Chapter 4, you can use Acrobat to convert supported file types into PDF documents from within Acrobat. You can also create PDF files from within authoring applications. When you create a file in any application that supports printing devices, you can create a PDF file using the application Print command. Other software, such as Freehand and CorelDraw, supports PDF exporting. You can also create PDF files from within Adobe graphics applications. Adobe offers extensive PDF support with many of their image-editing, illustration, and page-layout applications. Adobe has also teamed with Microsoft to create a plug-in that you use to create PDF files from within Microsoft Office applications.

When you create a PDF file from within an authoring application, you gain many benefits. Primarily, you can save the original version of the file in its native format, which makes it available for future editing when needed. Second, you can export the file in PDF format without leaving the host application. If you have several documents to create and convert to PDF format, this is a tremendous time saver. You can also export several PDF files from the original document, each optimized for a different destination.

Create PDF Files from Microsoft Office Software

When you install Acrobat, the install utility searches your machine for Microsoft Office applications. When a supported Microsoft Office application is found, Acrobat installs PDFMaker as a helper utility. With PDFMaker, you can create a PDF file that looks identical to the Microsoft Office file by clicking a Convert To PDF icon that is added to your Microsoft Office program when Acrobat is installed. If you prefer more control of the process, you can also modify the conversion settings to optimize a PDF file for its intended destination.

You can use PDFMaker to create PDF files from within the following Microsoft Office Applications:

- **Word 97 and 2000** Use PDFMaker to convert documents you create with Word to PDF files. The resulting PDF file retains font information, embedded graphics, and Header and Footer attributes.
- **Excel 97 and 2000** Use PDFMaker to convert an Excel spreadsheet to PDF format. The converted PDF file retains column formatting, as well as column and row headers and embedded graphics.
- **PowerPoint 97 and 2000** Convert PowerPoint presentations to PDF files and add additional functionality to the presentation with many features of Acrobat.

The PDFMaker in all supported Microsoft Office applications is identical. The next section will cover all the major features of PDFMaker and show you how to use it to convert documents to PDF format (with examples from Microsoft Word 2000).

Create PDF Files from Microsoft Word Files

When the installer finds a supported application, as previously mentioned, two icons and a menu group are added to the application toolbar. You use the icons shown in Figure 5-1 to convert a document to PDF format, or to convert a document to PDF format and e-mail it. The Acrobat menu group contains commands that duplicate the buttons, allow you to view the converted PDF in Acrobat, and change PDF conversion settings.

Convert Word Files to PDF Files

When you create a document in Word, you can apply styles to the document. When you convert the Word document to PDF format, Acrobat uses these Word

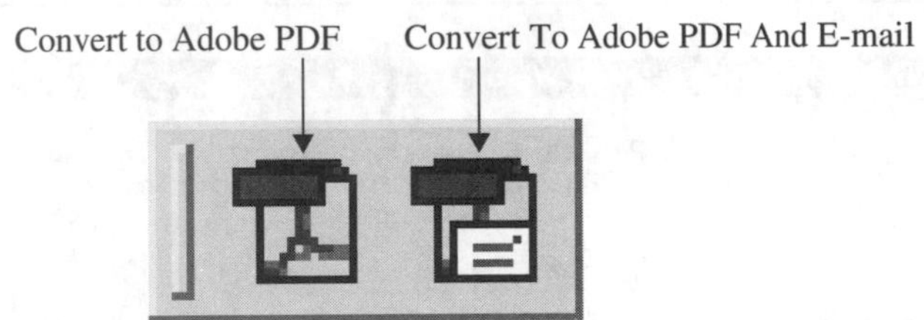

FIGURE 5-1 You can convert a Microsoft Office document to PDF format by clicking one of these icons.

styles to create corresponding bookmarks in the PDF document. The Acrobat default setting uses Heading styles to create bookmarks; however, if desired, you can change the conversion settings to include other styles that exist in the Word document. When you convert the Word file to a PDF file, the resulting file retains the formatting and font information, as well as any graphics you may have embedded in the Word file.

The easiest way to convert a Word file to a PDF file is by using the Convert To Adobe PDF button. You can also use a menu command to achieve the same result. To convert a Word file to a PDF file, do the following:

1. Click the Convert To Adobe PDF button, as shown in Figure 5-1. Alternatively, choose Acrobat | Convert To Adobe PDF.

   If you have not saved the Word document, PDFMaker displays the Acrobat PDFMaker 5.0 For Word dialog box, as shown in Figure 5-2. Click Yes, and the Save PDF File As dialog box opens. Click No, and PDFMaker aborts the conversion process.

2. In the Save PDF File As dialog box, accept the default name (the Word filename) and location (the directory the Word file is saved in), or specify a document name and directory.

3. Click Save to complete the conversion.

After you convert the document to PDF format, you can modify it in Acrobat. You can add interactive elements, such as links to external websites, or add comments, annotations, or multimedia elements to the document. Figure 5-3 shows a PDF file in Acrobat that was converted from a Word document. Notice the bookmarks. PDFMaker created them using Word Heading styles. You learn how to change conversion settings in a future section of this chapter.

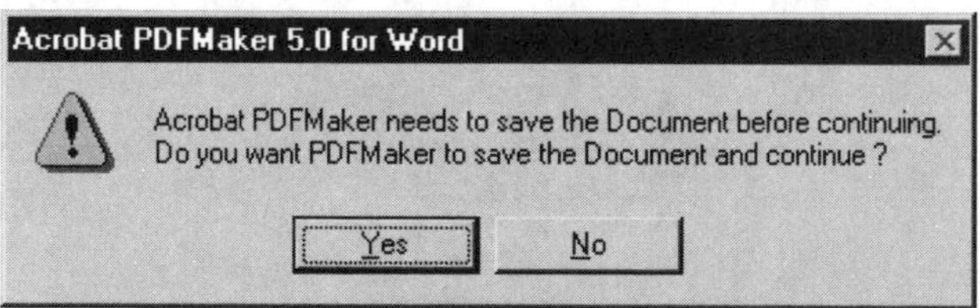

FIGURE 5-2 You must save a document to convert it to a PDF file.

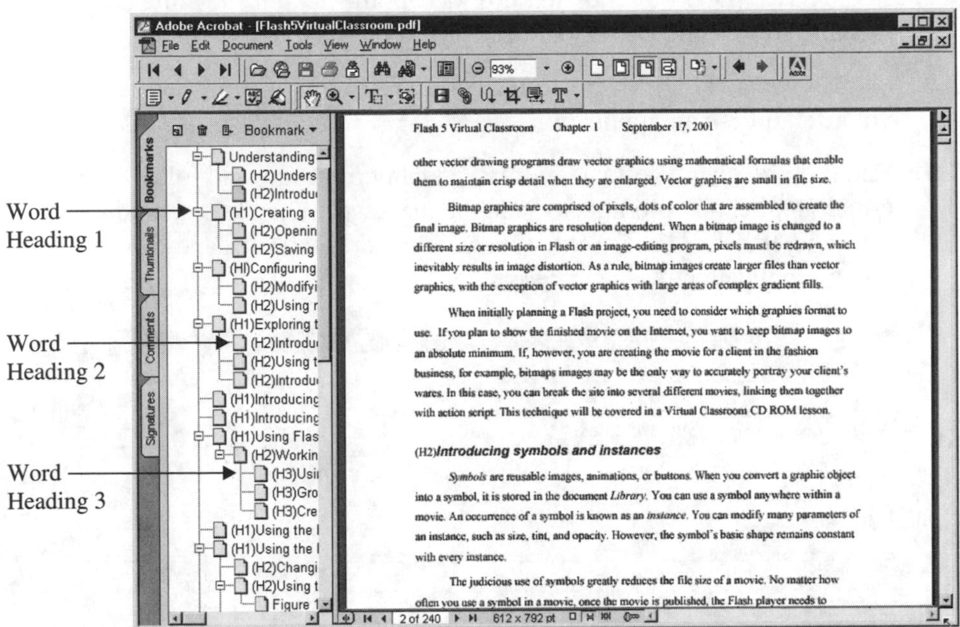

FIGURE 5-3 Use the PDFMaker to convert files from supported Microsoft Office applications to PDFs.

Convert to PDF and Then E-mail

Thanks to the Internet and e-mail, it is now possible to conduct business with faraway clients more efficiently. Whether you are a one-person entrepreneurship, or work in a large organization, you can convert a Word document to a PDF file, and then e-mail it to a client or coworker. To convert a Word document to a PDF file and e-mail it, follow these steps:

1. Click the Convert To Adobe PDF And E-mail button, as shown in Figure 5-1. Alternatively, choose Acrobat | Convert To Adobe PDF And E-mail.
2. If you have not saved the current version of the Word document you are converting, PDFMaker displays the Acrobat PDFMaker 5.0 For Word dialog box shown earlier in Figure 5-2. Click Yes to save the current version of the Word file and open the Save PDF File As dialog box. Click No, and PDFMaker aborts the conversion process.

3. In the Save PDF File As dialog box, accept the default filename and location to save the file in, or specify your own parameters.
4. Click Save, and PDFMaker converts the file to PDF format and launches your default e-mail application.
5. Enter the recipient's e-mail address, add any message, and follow the e-mail application prompts to send the message. When you send the message, the PDF file is sent as an attachment. The Netscape Navigator e-mail application is shown here:

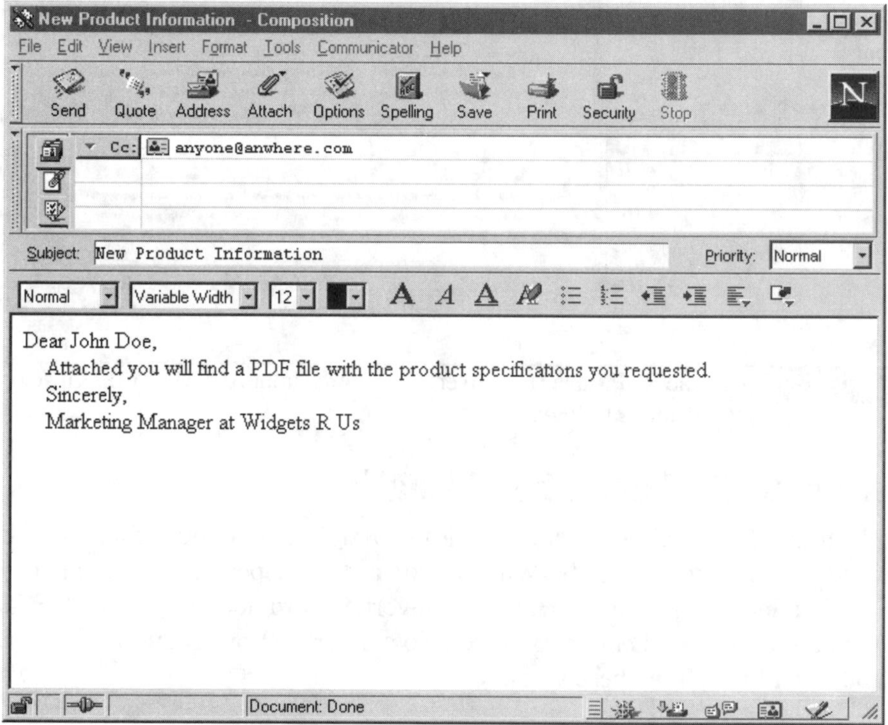

If you are not logged on to the Internet, you can use your e-mail application command to send the message and attached PDF file later.

View Result in Adobe Acrobat

When you convert a Word document to a PDF, you can immediately view the converted file in Acrobat by choosing Acrobat | View Result. When you choose this command, it remains active until you disable it. To see whether the command is active, choose Acrobat. If a check mark appears beside the command, it is active. To disable the command, click it.

When you choose View Result in Acrobat, after PDFMaker completes the conversion process, Acrobat launches and displays the resulting PDF file. After the file opens in Acrobat, you can use Acrobat commands and tools to modify the PDF file.

Set Conversion Settings

When you convert a Word document to a PDF file, PDFMaker uses the currently selected conversion settings. You can modify these settings to change Job Options, to modify document security, to specify how Microsoft Office features are converted to PDF, to specify how PDFMaker creates bookmarks, and to specify display options. You change conversion settings by clicking the appropriate tab in the Conversion Settings dialog box. To open the Conversion Settings dialog box, as shown in the following image, choose Acrobat | Change Conversion Settings.

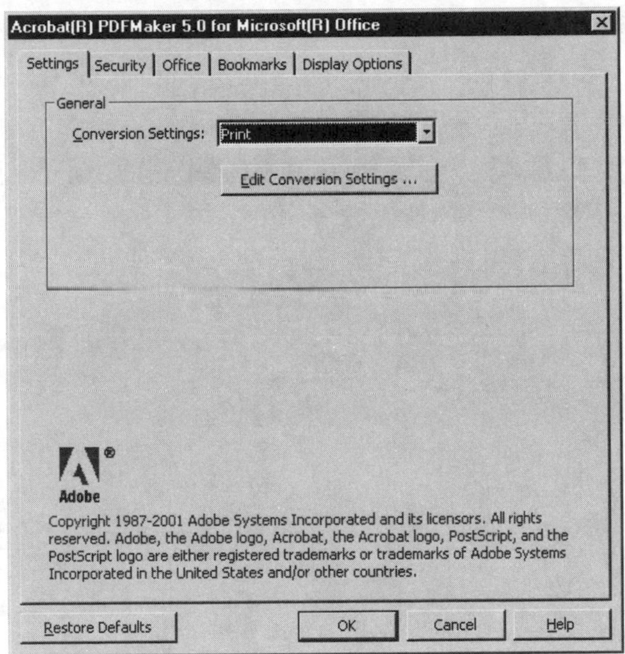

Change Job Option Settings

When you first open the Conversion Settings dialog box, the Settings tab is active. In this section, you'll choose a setting that matches the intended destination of the PDF file. To choose a setting, click the triangle to the right of the Settings field, and choose one of the preset options (eBook, Print, Press, or Screen), or any custom Job Options you created. These options are the same as the Distiller Job Options discussed in Chapter 4. To apply the new settings, click OK. To modify additional conversion settings, click the appropriate tab, and modify the parameters to suit the intended destination of your document.

You can create a custom Job Options file by clicking the Edit Conversion button. After you click this button, PDFMaker opens the Job Options dialog box. For more information on creating a custom Job Options file, refer to Chapter 14.

Change Document Security Settings

When you convert a Word file to PDF format, you can specify document security from within Microsoft Word. You can assign a password to the converted file and limit permissions. Do the following to set document security:

1. Open the Conversion Settings dialog box as outlined previously.
2. Click the Security tab to reveal the security settings, as shown in the following image.

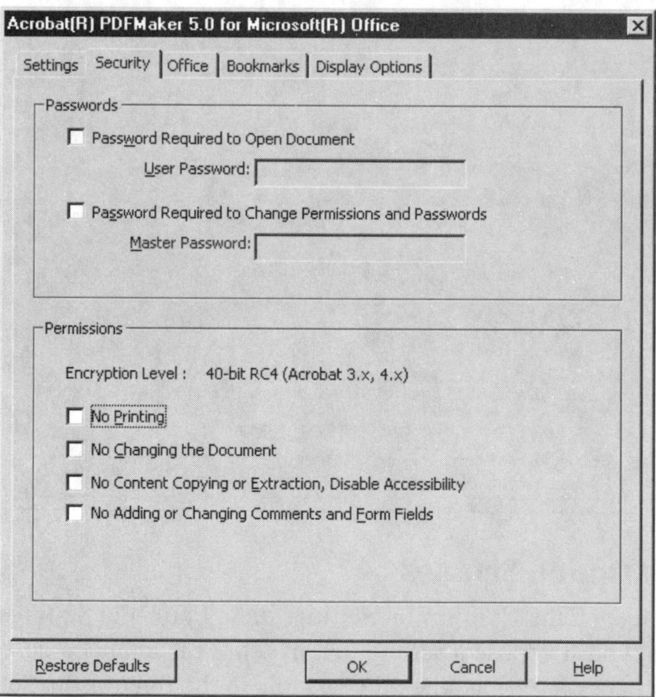

3. To assign a password to the PDF file, choose the Password Required To Open Document option. When you choose this option, the User Password field becomes active.
4. If you choose the Password Required To Open Document option, enter the password in the User Password field.
5. To assign a master password to the PDF file, choose the Password Required To Change Permissions And Passwords option. When you choose this option, the Master Password field becomes available.
6. If you choose a Master Password, enter the password in the Master Password field.
7. In the Permissions section, choose any or all of the following options:
   - **No Printing** Choose this option, and users will not be able to print the document.
   - **No Changing The Document** Choose this option, and users will not be able to edit the document.
   - **No Content Copying Or Extracting, Disable Accessibility** Choose this option to prevent users from extracting graphic or text elements from the document. This option also blocks the user's access to the accessibility interface.
   - **No Adding Or Changing Comments Or Form Fields** Choose this option, and users will not be able to edit document comments or alter form fields; however, a user can still fill in the document form fields.

NOTE *If the settings option you choose uses Acrobat 3.0 or 4.0 compatibility, you can only assign 40-bit encryption to the document. To use 128-bit encryption, you must edit the conversion settings in the Settings section, and choose Acrobat 5.0 compatibility. For more information on modifying document security settings, refer to Chapter 13.*

8. To apply the security settings, click OK. To modify additional settings, click the appropriate tab and modify the parameters as desired.

NOTE *Whether you assign a User Password, a Master Password, or both, you will be prompted to verify the password(s) before the new settings are accepted.*

Change Office Settings

The settings you modify in this section determine how PDFMaker converts Office features and Word features. To change Office settings, do the following:

1. Open the Change Conversion Settings dialog box as outlined previously.
2. Click the Office tab to reveal the settings illustrated in the following image.

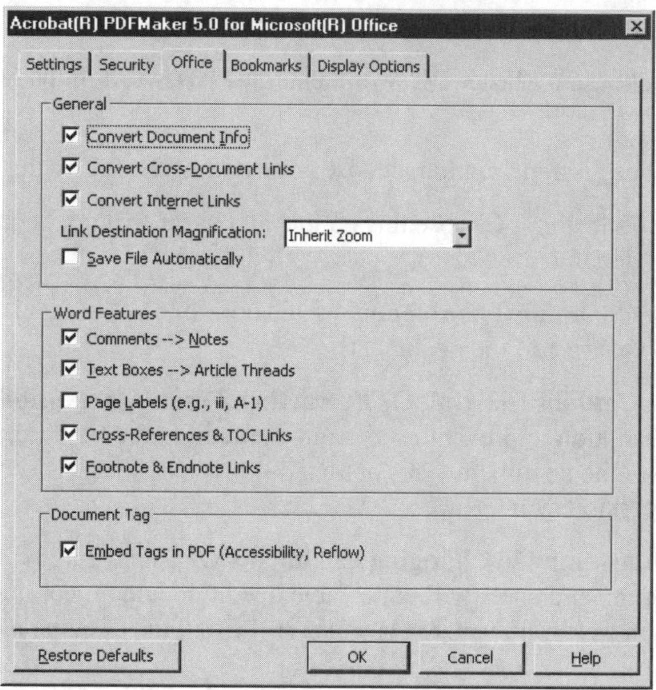

3. In the General section, you can modify the following settings:
   - **Convert Document Info** Choose this option (the default,) and Word document properties will be preserved with the PDF file.
   - **Convert Cross-Document Links** Choose this option (the default), and links to other documents that exist in the Word document will be preserved as links with the converted PDF file.
   - **Convert Internet Links** Choose this option (the default), and Internet links that exist in the original Word document will be preserved as links in the converted PDF file.

- **Link Destination Magnification** Click the triangle to the right of the field and choose one of the five options to determine the magnification of the linked destination.
- **Save File Automatically** The Word document must be saved before PDFMaker can convert it. Choose this option, and Word will automatically save the document when you click the Convert To Adobe PDF button, or choose Acrobat | Convert To Adobe PDF without displaying the warning dialog as outlined previously.

4. In the Word Features section, you can modify the following:
   - **Comments→Notes** Choose this option (the default), and PDFMaker will convert any comments in the Word file to notes in the PDF file. In the PDF file, the comments appear with the default Note icon next to it.
   - **Text Boxes →Article Threads** Choose this option (the default), and PDFMaker will convert text boxes in the Word document to article threads in the PDF file.
   - **Page Labels (e.g., iii, A-1)** Choose this option, and page numbers from the Word document will be preserved in the PDF file.
   - **Cross-References & TOC Links** Choose this option, and any cross-references in the Word document, such as a Table of Contents or Index, will have their links preserved when PDFMaker converts the file.
   - **Footnote & Endnote Links** Choose this option, and any footnote or endnote links will be passed to the PDF document.
   - **Embed Tags in PDF (Accessibility, Reflow)** Choose this option, and any Microsoft accessibility elements in the Word document will be embedded when PDFMaker converts the file to PDF format.
5. To apply the security settings, click OK. To modify additional settings, click the appropriate tab and modify the parameters as desired.

Change Bookmark Settings

The settings you modify in this section determine which Word text styles PDFMaker converts to bookmarks. To change Bookmark settings for the document conversion, do the following:

1. Open the Conversion Settings dialog box as outlined in a previous section.

2. Click the Bookmarks tab, and modify the settings as shown in the following image.

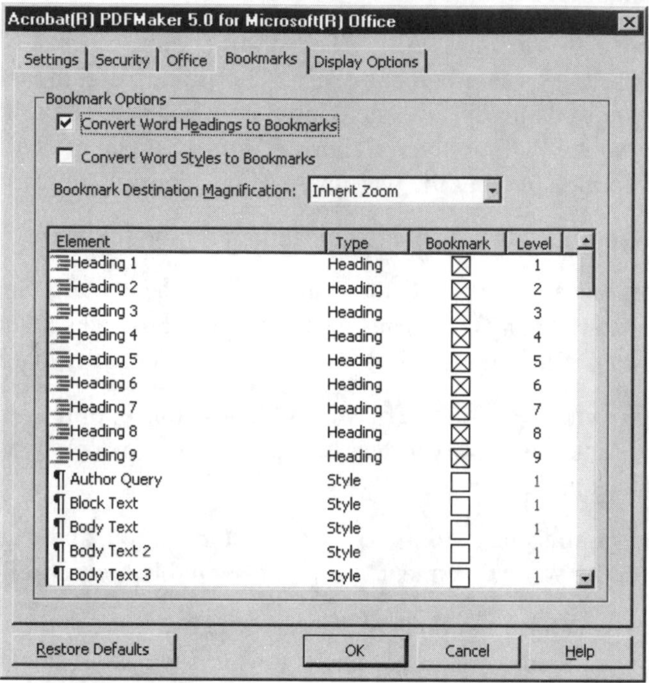

- **Convert Word Headings To Bookmarks** Choose this option (the default), and PDFMaker will convert all Word headings in the document to PDF bookmarks. By default, Heading 1 through Heading 9 styles are converted to bookmarks. To modify which headings are converted to bookmarks, click a heading name in the Bookmark column to select or deselect it.
- **Convert Word Styles To Bookmarks** Choose this option, and all Word styles used in the document will be converted to bookmarks when PDFMaker converts the document. By default, no Word styles are converted to bookmarks. Choose which styles PDFMaker converts to bookmarks by clicking the style name in the Bookmark column to select or deselect it.
- **Bookmark Destination Magnification** Click the triangle to the right of this field, and choose a magnification option for the linked destination. You have five options to choose from (Inherit Zoom is the default).

3. Click OK to apply the new settings, or click another tab to make additional modifications to the document conversion settings.

Change Display Settings

You change the settings in this section to modify the way the converted PDF document opens in Acrobat and how the links are displayed. To change the way the converted PDF document opens and how the links are displayed in Acrobat, do the following:

1. Open the Conversion Settings dialog box as outlined previously.
2. Click the Display Options tab to reveal the settings shown in the following image:

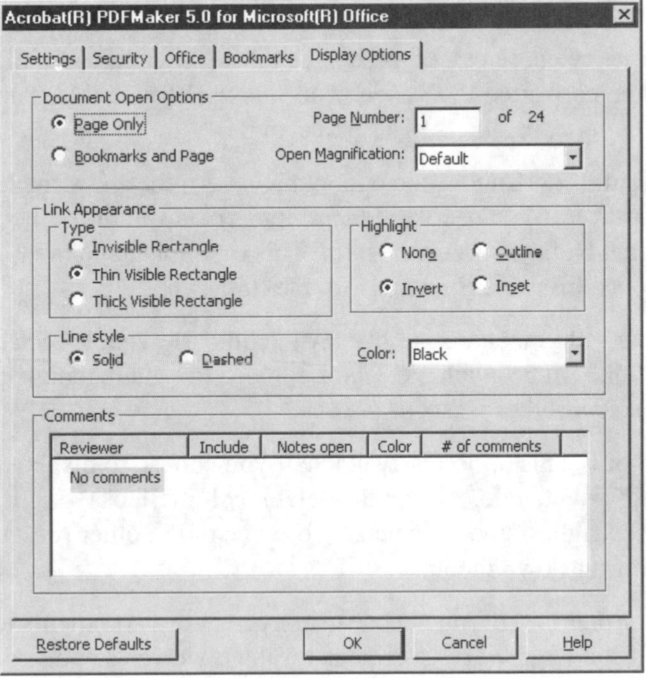

3. In the Document Open Options section, you can modify the following settings:

   - **Page Only** Choose this option (the default), and only the page will be displayed when the converted PDF document is opened in Acrobat.

- **Bookmarks And Page** Choose this option, and the converted document opening page and bookmarks will be displayed when the file is opened in Acrobat.
- **Page Number** If you are converting a multipage document, you can choose which page is displayed when the document opens in Acrobat by entering a valid page number in the text field.
- **Open Magnification** Click the triangle to the right of this field to reveal a drop-down menu. Choose one of the number values to display the document at that percentage of its original size. Choose one of the other options to control how the PDF document is displayed in the Acrobat Document pane. These settings are identical to the Open Options discussed in Chapter 4.

4. In the Link Appearance section, modify the following settings:
   - **Type** Choose one of these three following options for displaying links in the converted PDF document: Invisible Rectangle, Thin Visible Rectangle, or Thick Visible Rectangle.
   - **Highlight** Choose the option that determines how the link is displayed when users roll their mouse over the link. Choose from None, Outline, Invert, or Inset. This option is not available if you choose Invisible Rectangle for the link Type.
   - **Line** If you choose to display the link as a visible rectangle, this option will be available. Choose to display the rectangle border of the link as Solid or Dashed.
   - **Color** This option is available if you choose to display the link as a visible rectangle. Accept the default color (Black), or click the triangle to the right of the field and choose one of the other preset colors from the drop-down menu.
   - **Comments** If you choose to convert Word comments to PDF notes, you can select various options for the reviewer's name, determine whether a particular comment is included in the PDF file, determine whether the note appears as opened or closed in the converted PDF file, and choose a color for the PDF note icon. Also listed is the number of comments for each reviewer.
5. Click OK to apply the new settings, or click another tab to make additional modifications to the document conversion settings.

Restore Default Conversion Settings

After you modify conversion settings, they remain active until you modify them again. To restore the default settings, open the Conversion Settings dialog box, click the Restore Defaults button, and then click OK to complete the restoration. The next document you convert to PDF will be converted with the default PDFMaker conversion settings.

Create PDF Files from Microsoft Excel Files

You can also use PDFMaker from within Excel 97 or Excel 2000 to convert spreadsheets to PDF documents. The only difference you find between PDFMaker in Excel and Word is the available conversion settings. The Excel Acrobat PDFMaker 5.0 For Microsoft Office dialog box has only four tabs: Settings, Security, Office, and Display Options. Within the Office section of the dialog box, there are Excel Features options. Here, you can determine whether to convert the active worksheet to a PDF file, or use the entire workbook to create the PDF file. To convert an Excel spreadsheet to PDF format, follow these steps:

1. Choose Acrobat | Change Conversion Settings to open the Acrobat PDFMaker 5.0 for Microsoft Office dialog box.
2. Modify the conversion settings to suit the intended destination of the file.
3. Click OK to close the dialog box.
4. Click the Convert To Adobe PDF button, or choose Acrobat | Convert To Adobe PDF.

Create PDF Files from Microsoft PowerPoint Files

If you use PowerPoint, you know it is a popular program for creating presentations. It seems that PowerPoint presentations are everywhere these days, even on the Web. You may not think there is any advantage to converting a PowerPoint presentation to PDF format. However, if you want to share a presentation with someone who does not own PowerPoint, or does not have a version of PowerPoint capable of opening your presentation, you can convert it to a PDF. All your recipient needs is Acrobat Reader and they can view your presentation.

You can also convert a PowerPoint presentation to a PDF and enhance it with Acrobat features. For example, you can use the File Attachment tool to open another file during your presentation.

The only difference between the PowerPoint Acrobat PDFMaker 5.0 For Microsoft Office dialog box and the Excel version is the PowerPoint features section behind the Office tab. You have one option, Create Bookmarks.

You can convert a PowerPoint presentation to PDF format by doing the following:

1. Choose Acrobat | Change Conversion Settings to access the Acrobat PDFMaker 5.0 for Microsoft Office dialog box.
2. Modify the conversion settings to suit the intended destination of the converted PDF file.
3. Click OK to close the dialog box.
4. Click the Convert To Adobe PDF button, or choose Acrobat | Convert To Adobe PDF.

Create PDF Files Using an Application Print Command

When you install Acrobat software, Acrobat Distiller is automatically added as a system printer. You can use Distiller to print the authoring application file to disk in PDF format in the same manner as you use a printer to print out a hard copy of a file. You can create a PDF file from any authoring application that supports printing by following these steps:

1. Choose the application Print command.
2. Choose Acrobat Distiller from the application Printer menu. The actual Print dialog box will vary depending upon your operating system and the software from which you are printing the file.
3. Click the Properties button to reveal the Acrobat Distiller Properties dialog box, shown in the following image. As you can see, the dialog box has five sections separated by tabs.

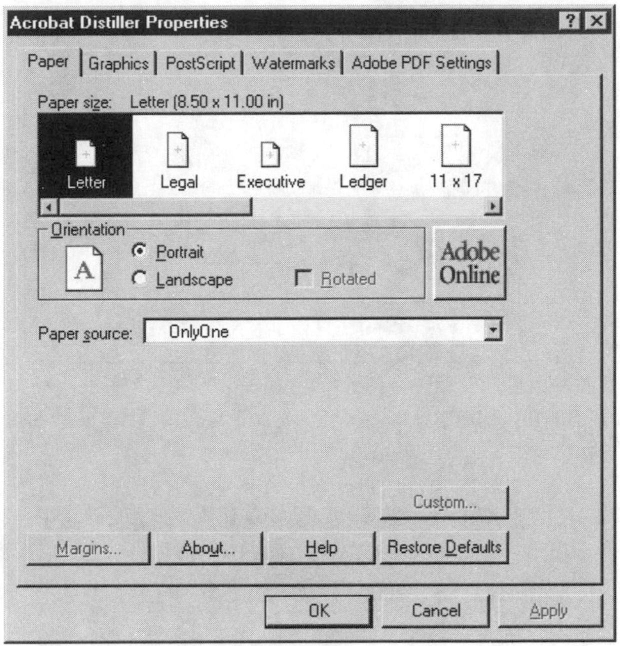

4. In the Paper section, select a paper size and orientation for the PDF document. Match the paper size to the document page size in the authoring application. By default, the Acrobat Distiller will choose Legal Size. If the document you are distilling to PDF is a different size, click the appropriate icon.

TIP

If you are distilling an image from a graphics application, you can create a custom paper size to match the size of the image. In the Paper Size window, scroll to one of the custom p+ icons, click it, and then click the Custom button near the bottom of the Acrobat Distiller Properties dialog box. Enter values in the dialog box, as shown in the following image, to match the size of the image you are distilling to PDF. In this example, the paper size is set at 6 × 9 inches for a custom paper size named Ebook.

5

5. Click the Graphics tab to modify the following graphics settings as in this illustration.

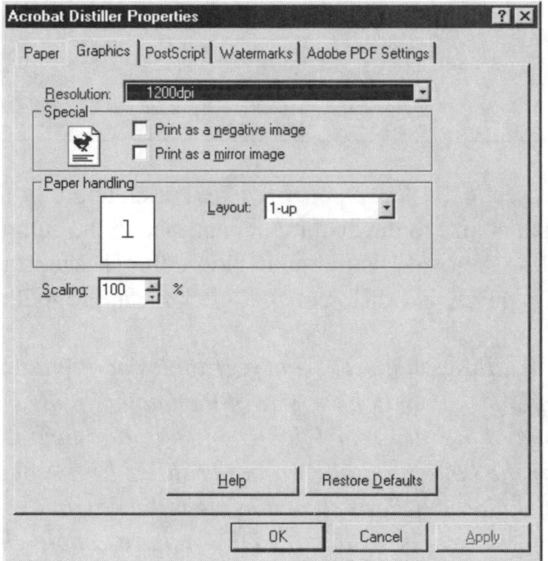

- **Resolution** Click the triangle to the right of this field and choose an option from the drop-down menu. The default resolution, 1,200 dpi (dots per inch), works well in most instances. If the document you are converting to PDF contains vector graphics and you will eventually print the file on a high-end printer, then choose a resolution that closely matches the intended output device.
- **Print As Negative Image** Choose this option, and the PDF file you distill will appear as a negative image. For example, if the page you

are printing contains black text on a white background, choosing this option will result in a PDF file with white text on a black background.

- **Print As Mirror Image** Choose this option, and the distilled file will be the mirror image of the original document.
- **Layout** Click the triangle to the right of this section; and from the drop-down menu, choose to display the document pages as 1-up, 2-up, 4-up, 6-up, 9-up, or 16-up. The default 1-up option will display one document page on one PDF page. If you choose one of the other options, multiple pages of the original document will be displayed on a single PDF page.
- **Scaling** In this field, enter a value between 25 and 400 to magnify or decrease the size of the document when distilled to PDF format. This value is a percentage of the document size as created in the authoring application.

6. Click the PostScript tab; then click the triangle to the right of the PostScript Output Format field and choose an option from the drop-down menu shown in the following image.

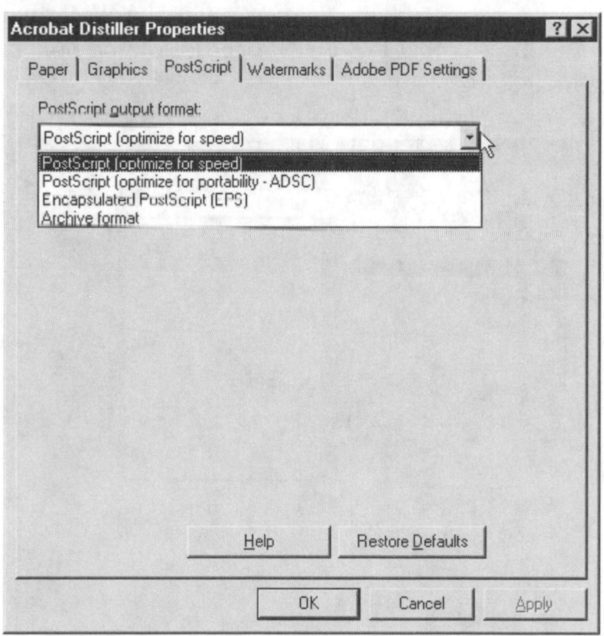

- **PostScript (Optimize For Speed)** Choose this option to speed up the distilling process. However, if you choose this option, you may not be able to take advantage of print spooling if you work on a network.

- **PostScript (Optimize For Portability – ADSC)** Choose this option and the distilled file will conform to ADSC (Adobe Document Structuring Conventions). When you choose this option, each PostScript page is independent of the other pages in the document. Choose this option if you are printing the file on a network spooler. When you use a network spooler, printing happens in the background, which frees up your workstation for other tasks. When you choose this option, the network spools the PDF document one page at a time.
- **Encapsulated PostScript** Choose this option to create EPS files comprised of single pages in the authoring application that you intend to use in documents of other applications. Use this option if you want to create a high-quality image and use it in a document that will be printed from another application.
- **Archive format** Choose this option to improve file portability. When you choose this option, printer settings that may prevent the distilled PDF file from printing on other output devices are suppressed.

7. To apply a Watermark to the document, click the Watermarks tab to open the section of the Acrobat Distiller Properties dialog box shown in the following image:

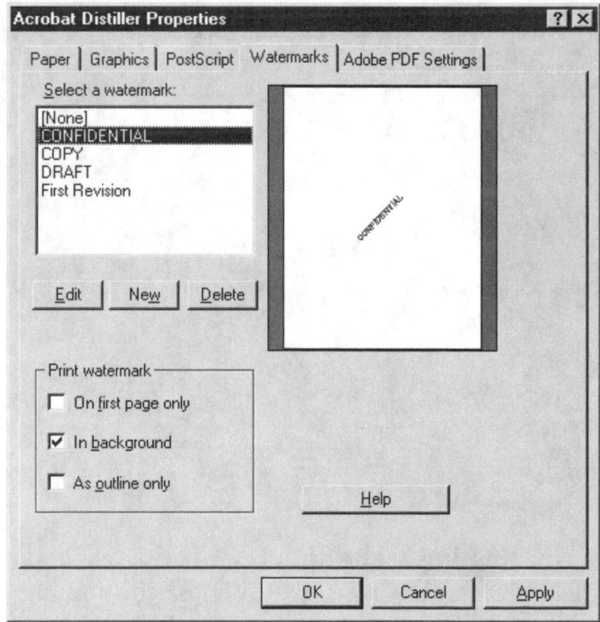

8. Choose one of the Watermark options (the default None prints no watermark on the distilled file). If you choose one of the preset watermarks, the Edit, New, and Delete buttons become active.

- **Edit** Click this button to open the Edit Watermark dialog box. You can modify the settings to change the font style, size, and color used for the watermark, as well as its orientation to the page.
- **New** Click this button to open the New Watermark dialog box, as shown in the following image. In the Watermark Text section, enter the text for the new watermark, and then choose a font type, size, and style. In the Angle section, enter a value for the watermark angle on the page, or drag the slider to set the value. In the Position section, choose to Automatically center the watermark, or choose to Position Relative to Center to enter coordinates in the x and y fields. Enter a value between 0 and 255 in the Red, Green, and Blue fields To determine the color of the watermark. These values are based on the RGB color model. Alternatively, you can click the color button and choose a color from the system color picker. Click OK to add the new Watermark to the list.

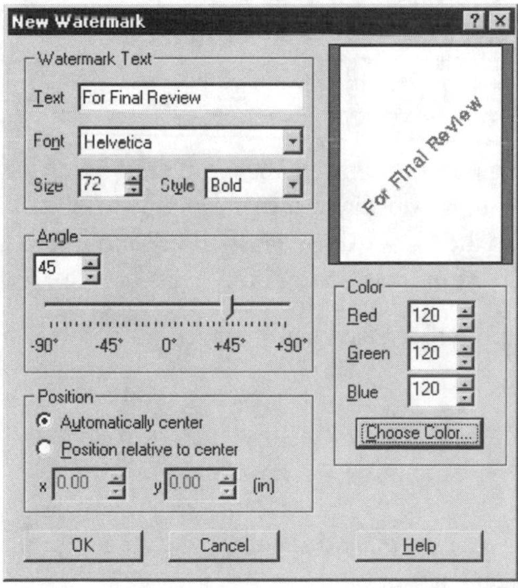

- **Delete** Click this button to delete the selected watermark.

9. In the Print Watermark section, choose one or more of the following three options: On First Page Only, In Background, As Outline Only.
10. Click the Adobe PDF Settings tab to open the section, as shown in the following image:

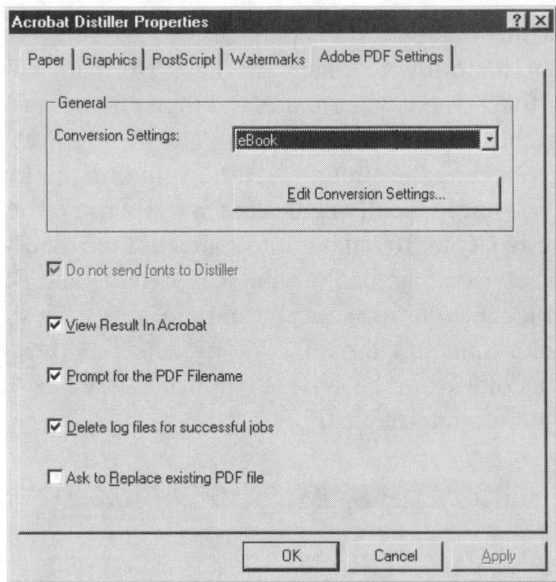

11. Click the triangle to the right of the Conversion Settings field, and choose an option from the drop-down menu. For specific information on each Job Option, refer to the "Use Acrobat Distiller" section in Chapter 4. The remaining options in this section are your Acrobat Distiller preferences.
12. Click OK to apply the settings and close the Acrobat Distiller Properties dialog box.
13. Click OK in the Application Print dialog box to print the document in PDF format.

If you are printing a multi-page document with lots of embedded graphics, the printing process may take a while.

Create PDF Files in Adobe Programs

Adobe has gone to great lengths to enhance interactivity between Acrobat and their graphics software. You can create a PDF file using the following Adobe software:

- **FrameMaker** FrameMaker is a page-layout program suitable for publishing long documents for viewing across multiple media. You can use the program to create content for the Web, CD-ROM and print. FrameMaker offers extensive support for creating PDF documents. To create a PDF file in FrameMaker, you use the application's Print command.
- **Illustrator** Illustrator is a vector-based illustration program. Programs like Illustrator use mathematics to define a shape, which means the shape can be greatly enlarged without loss of fidelity. You can convert Illustrator documents to PDF format using the Save command. Illustrator 9.0 supports transparency, which is preserved when you save a PDF document with Acrobat 5.0 compatibility.
- **InDesign** InDesign is the latest page-layout software from Adobe. InDesign features extensive PDF support. Documents you create in InDesign are converted to PDF format using the Export command.
- **PhotoShop** PhotoShop is award-winning, image-editing software from Adobe. Use the Save As command, and then choose the PDF format to save a PhotoShop file in PDF format. When you use the Save As command to convert a PhotoShop file to PDF, you can specify image compression and the color model. When you save a file from PhotoShop in PDF format, layers are flattened; however, if you open the resulting PDF file in PhotoShop, any layers and objects from the original file are preserved and available for editing.
- **PageMaker** PageMaker is a page-layout program. To create a PDF file from a PageMaker document, use the Export PDF 3.01 plug-in, which can be downloaded from the Adobe Web site http://www.adobe.com.

Although the methods used to create PDF files differ among Adobe programs, many of the options are similar. The following steps illustrate how to export a PDF file from InDesign. To obtain specific information on exporting or saving files in PDF format with other Adobe software you own, refer to the application user guide.

1. Choose File | Export to open the Export dialog box.

2. Enter a name and location for the file, and then choose Adobe PDF from the Save As type menu. Click Save to open the Export PDF dialog box shown in the following image:

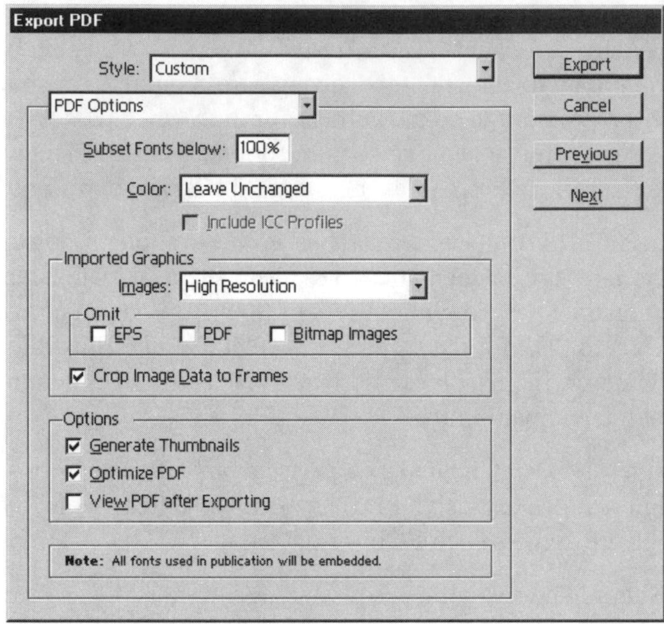

The Export PDF dialog box consists of four sections: PDF Options, Compression, Page And Page Marks, and Security. Unlike the multisection Acrobat dialog boxes, this dialog box has no tabs to navigate from section to section. You use the Next and Previous buttons to navigate to and from the four sections.

1. In PDF Options, enter a percentage in the Subset Fonts field. By default, InDesign embeds all fonts used in the page. However, you can have InDesign subset fonts below the percentage you specify.

2. Click the triangle to the right of the Color field, and choose an option from the drop-down menu. Your choices are Leave Unchanged, RGB, or CMYK. If you have enabled color management, the Include ICC Profiles option becomes available.

3. Click the triangle to the right of the Images field, and choose High Resolution or Low Resolution. If you choose High Resolution, the resolution of imported

bitmaps is unaffected. If you choose Low Resolution, InDesign applies compression to imported bitmaps when the file is converted to PDF.

4. In the Omit section, you can choose to omit EPS, PDF, and Bitmap Images (or any combination thereof) to create a text-only proof in PDF format.
5. In the Options section, you can choose from Generate Thumbnails (the default), Optimize PDF (the default), or View PDF After Exporting. These options are similar to Acrobat Distiller options discussed in Chapter 4.
6. After you finish setting parameters in the PDF Options section, click the Next button; or choose Compression from the drop-down menu, where PDF Options now appears, to reveal the Compression section, as shown in the following image:

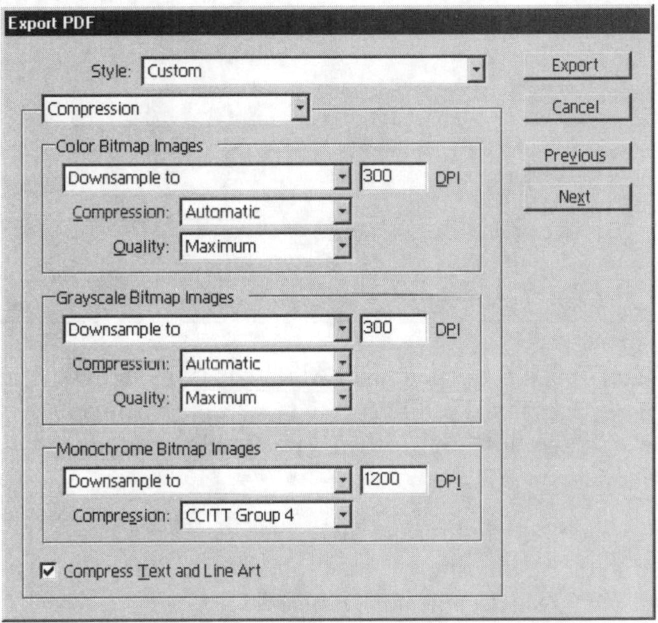

7. Modify the compression settings to suit the intended destination of the PDF document. These settings are similar to the settings in the Compression section of the Distiller Job Options dialog box. For more information on the settings in this dialog box, refer to the Customize Distiller Job Options section in Chapter 14.

8. After you modify the Compression Settings, click the Next button; or choose Pages and Page Marks from the drop-down menu in the second field of this dialog box to reveal the Pages and Page Marks section, as shown in the following image:

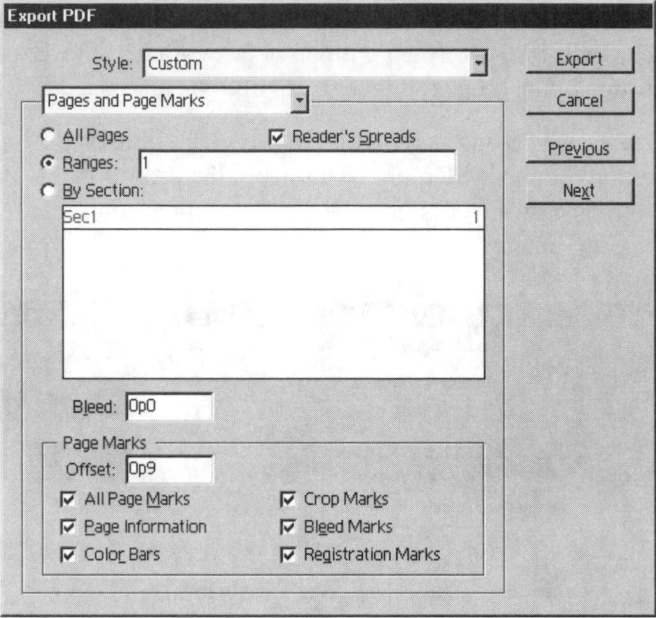

9. Choose an option for page range. All Pages is the default. You can select a range of pages if so specified in the InDesign document. If you choose Reader's Spread, InDesign will create a PDF document in which the pages are printed as spreads.

10. If you included a bleed for the InDesign document, you can specify the bleed amount by entering a value in the Bleed dialog box. The default setting is 0P0, which indicates no bleed.

11. You can specify the distance the document is offset from the edge of the page by entering a value in the Offset field. The default setting of 0P9 is an offset of zero picas and 9 points.

12. In the Page Marks section, choose the printer marks you want to include with the PDF file. Printer marks are useful if you are creating a PDF file for the service center that will print the InDesign document. Printer marks include page dimensions, color model information, and bleed information.

13. After you have finished specifying the Page and Page Marks parameters, click the Next button to open the Security section, as shown in the following image, or choose Security from the drop-down menu in the second field of this dialog box.

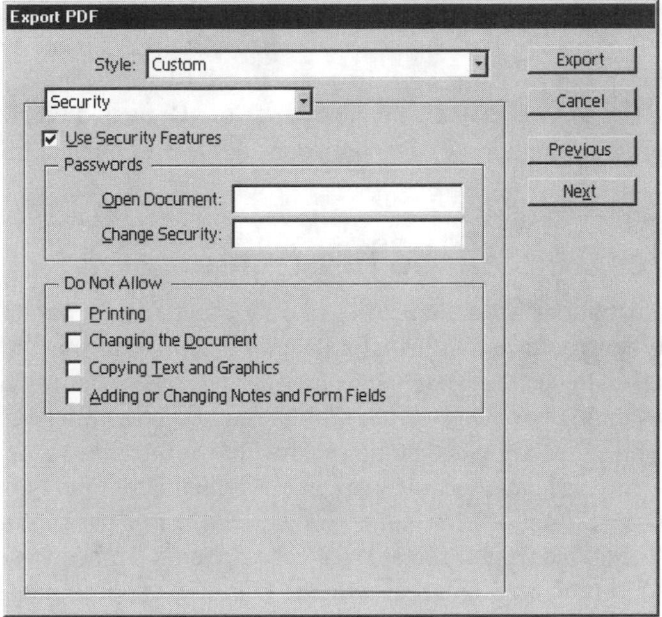

NOTE *The settings in the Security section enable you to apply Standard Security to the PDF document with 40-bit encryption. For specific information on the settings in this dialog box, refer to the Use Set Document Security section in Chapter 13.*

14. Click the Export button, close the dialog box, and export the document in PDF format.

Create PDF Files from Vector Drawing Software

If you create vector-based illustrations, you can convert them to PDF files using one of the following methods:

- Save the file in either EPS or PS format, and then use Acrobat Distiller to print the file.

- Use the vector drawing program Print command, and choose Acrobat Distiller for the printer.
- Export the file in PDF format if supported by the software.

The first two methods of creating PDF files have already been discussed. If you use Illustrator to create illustrations, you can create a PDF document by choosing PDF format from the Save command. Two other vector-based drawing programs offer enhanced support for PDF export. They are CorelDraw and Freehand. If your vector-based program supports PDF export, consult the user manual for specific instructions.

Create Files from Adobe Illustrator

If you create illustrations with Adobe Illustrator, you can save documents in the PDF format. When you save an Illustrator document in PDF format, the Adobe PDF Format Options dialog box appears. There are two sections in the Adobe PDF Format Options dialog box: General and Compression. The settings in the General section allow you to specify whether to save the file with Adobe 4.0 or 5.0 compatibility. You also have the option to preserve Illustrator editing capabilities. When you choose this option, you can open the PDF file in Illustrator and edit layers, objects, text, and so on. You also have the option to embed fonts and subset fonts less than a certain percentage, as with the InDesign export options discussed previously. The Compression section of the Adobe PDF Format Options dialog box is identical to the compression setting of the InDesign Export PDF dialog box, with the exception of an additional option to compress text and line art.

Create PDF Files from CorelDraw Documents

If you use CorelDraw 10 to create illustrations, you may not be aware that the program features extensive support for the PDF format. In fact, PDF documents you create in CorelDraw or Corel Photo-Paint are produced with the Corel PDF Engine. When you want to publish a file from CorelDraw as a PDF document, you do not have to search for a command buried on an obscure menu or choose an option from a Save menu; CorelDraw puts the Publish To PDF file where you can easily find it, on the File menu. To export a CorelDraw file in PDF format, follow these steps:

1. Choose File | Publish To PDF to open the Save As PDF dialog box.

2. To save the file with the current PDF settings, click Save; or to select a preset publishing setting, click the triangle to the right of the PDF Style field and choose one of the options from the drop-down menu shown in the following image:

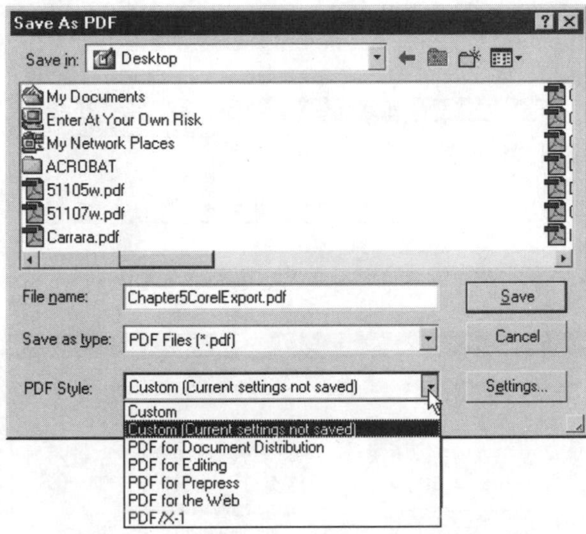

3. To modify a preset PDF style, or create a custom PDF style, click the Settings button to reveal the Publish To PDF dialog box, shown in the following image:

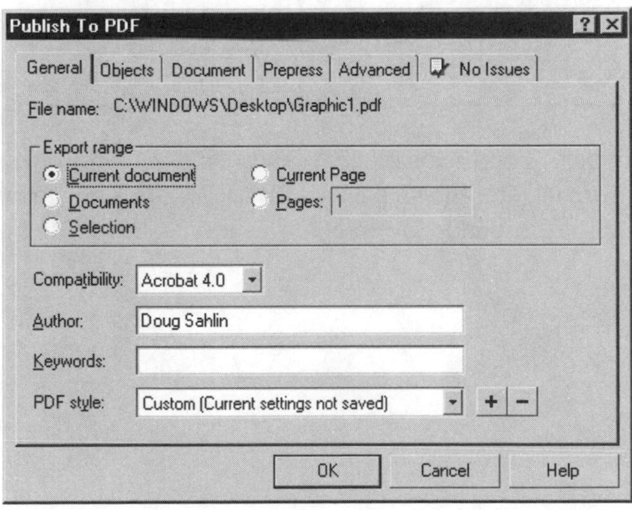

4. In the General section, you can specify the Export range; Compatibility; and other information, such as Author and Keywords, which appear in the PDF Document Summary after the file is converted.
5. If you want to keep the current PDF settings for future use, click the plus sign (+) to reveal the dialog box shown in the following image, enter a name for the new PDF style, and click OK.

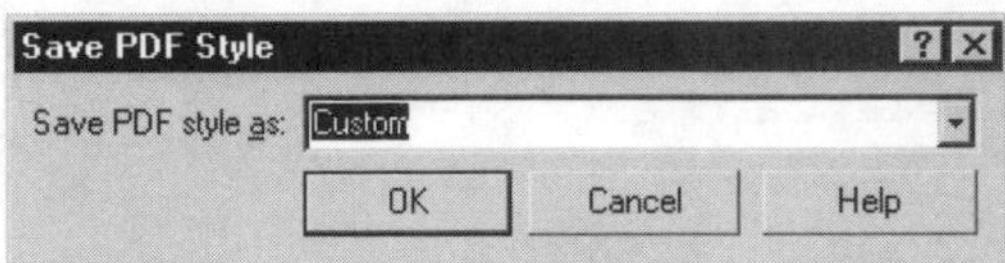

6. Click the Objects tab to reveal the dialog box shown in the following image:

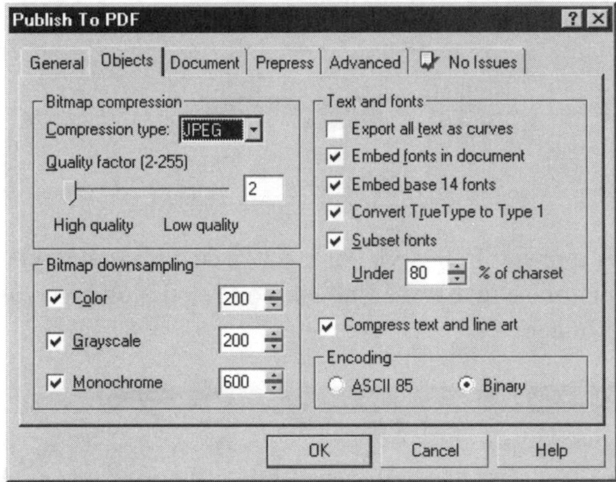

7. In the Bitmap compression section, choose one of the following compression options from the drop-down menu: LZW, JPEG, or ZIP. If you choose JPEG, you can set image quality by dragging a slider. A low setting produces high

image quality with little compression; a high setting with heavy compression degrades image quality, but results in a smaller file size. Specify a higher compression setting if the PDF document will be viewed from a Web site.

8. The remaining settings in the Objects section are similar to the Distiller Job Options discussed in Chapters 4 and 14.

9. After you have completed modifying the options in the Objects section, click the Document tab to reveal the dialog box shown in the following image. In this section, you can choose whether or not to create links, thumbnails, or bookmarks in the published PDF file. You can also specify how the document opens.

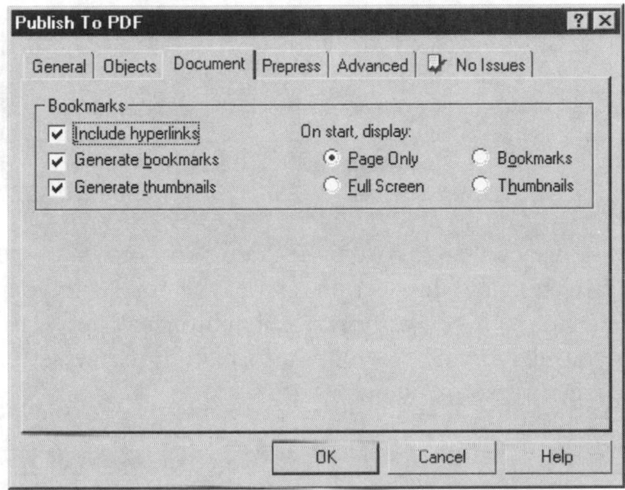

10. Click the Prepress tab to reveal the dialog box shown in the following image. In this section, you can specify which printer marks to include with the document. You can also create a Job Ticket for the file. A Job Ticket is useful when you send a PDF file to a service bureau for conversion to film or plates. You can create a Job Ticket by choosing the Include Job Ticket

option. For more information about the Job Ticket option, refer to the CorelDraw user manual.

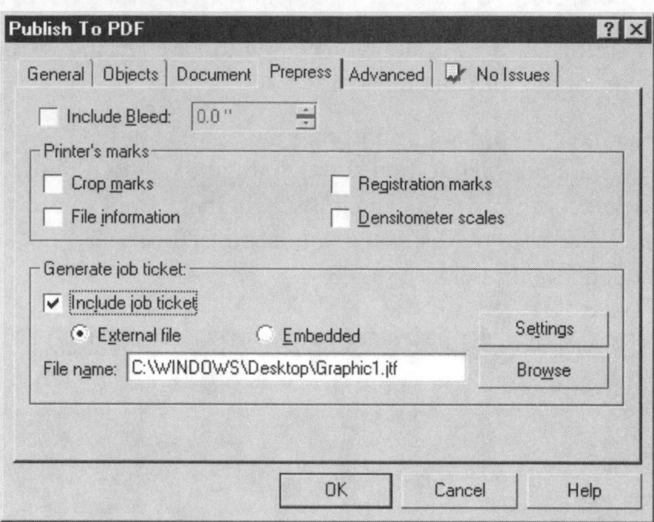

11. Click the Advanced tab to reveal the dialog box shown in the following image. The settings in this section refer to the objects in your CorelDraw document, such as fills, overprints, and halftones. Choose the options that apply to your document. For more information on the settings, refer to your CorelDraw user manual.

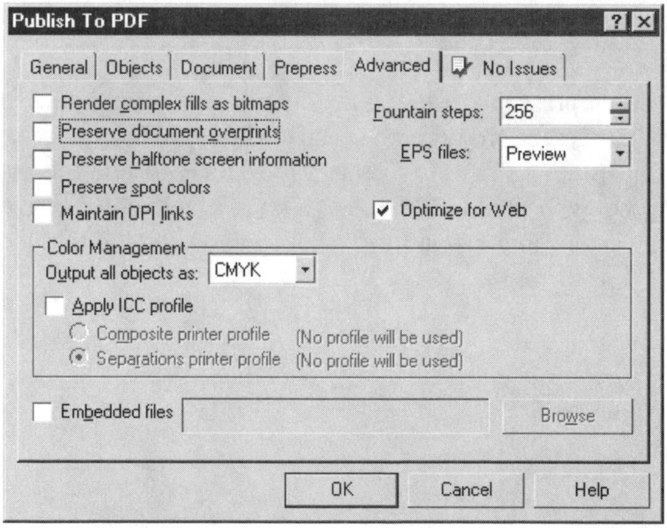

12. The last tab in the dialog box (named No Issues) lists any issues that may cause problems with the file. Click the tab to display the issues pertaining to the document.
13. Click OK to publish the document as a PDF file.

You can also publish a document from Corel Photo-Paint 10 using the Publish To PDF command. The dialog box is almost identical, with the exception of the settings in the Advanced section.

Create PDF Files from Macromedia Freehand Files

If you use Freehand for creating illustrations, you can import PDF documents and edit them within Freehand, and export Freehand documents as PDF files. Freehand supports Acrobat Notes and URLs, and assigns them to separate layers upon import. Note that when you import PDF files into Freehand, if Freehand is unable to determine the path of a note, then it imports them as a rectangular block on the URL layer.

Freehand 10 supports direct export of files as PDF documents. As this is written, Freehand only exports PDF files in Acrobat 4.0 or earlier formats. By the time you read this, there may be a patch available at the Macromedia Web site (http://www.macromedia.com) to support export in Acrobat 5.0 format. Currently, Freehand cannot export the following effects in PDF format:

- Custom fills, PostScript fills, strokes, arrowheads, or textured fills.
- Alpha channel transparency.
- EPS images within the Freehand document. (If the EPS image has a TIFF preview, only the preview image is exported with the file.)
- Text effects, such as drop shadows, highlights and strikethroughs.

To export a PDF file from Freehand, do the following:

1. Choose File | Export to open the Freehand Export Document dialog box.
2. Name the file; select the directory to export to; and, from the Save As Type drop-down menu, choose PDF(*.pdf).

3. Click the Setup (Windows) or Option (Macintosh) button to open the PDF Export dialog box, as shown in the following image:

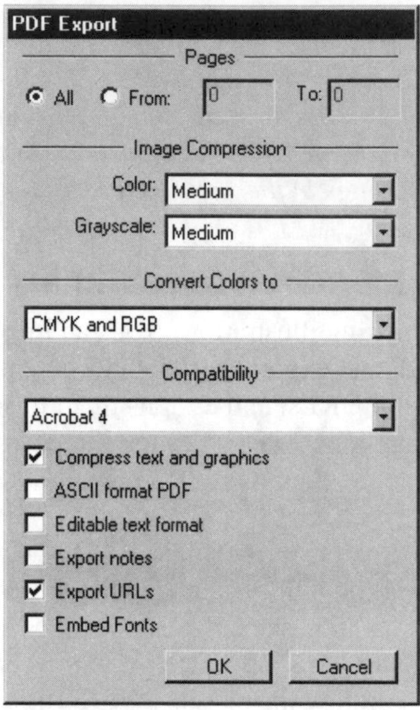

4. In the Pages section, choose to export all pages or select the range of pages you want to export.
5. In the Image Compression section, click the triangle to the right of each color type and choose an option from the drop-down menu. None (no compression) yields the best images at the expense of a larger file size. Maximum (maximum image compression) creates an impressively small PDF file at the expense of image quality.
6. Click the triangle to the right of the Convert Colors To field, and choose an option from the drop-down menu.
7. Click the triangle to the right of the Compatibility field, and choose which version of Acrobat to use for export.
8. Choose Compress Text And Graphics to compress these objects upon export. Freehand uses the PostScript language imaging model for compression. Alternatively, images will be exported with JPEG compression if you selected one of the compression options in step 5.

9. Choose ASCII Format PDF if you anticipate problems sharing the PDF file on an older network or e-mail system.
10. Choose Editable Text Format if you anticipate editing the PDF file in Freehand after export. Note that this option creates a larger file.
11. Choose Export Notes to export Freehand notes as PDF comments.
12. Choose Export URLs, and Freehand will export any URLs in the document as PDF links.
13. Choose Embed Fonts to embed any True Type or Type 1 fonts used in the document with the PDF export.
14. Click OK to apply the settings and close the Export dialog box.
15. Click Save to complete the export operation.

Chapter 6

Capture PDF Documents

How To...

- Capture PDF documents from your scanner
- Capture images from digital cameras
- Use Acrobat Capture
- Use Paper Capture Online
- Capture web pages
- Append web pages

You create most of your PDF documents in authoring applications, and then convert them to PDF files from within the authoring application (if supported) or by using Acrobat Distiller to print the document in PDF format. You can also create PDF files by printing a file to disk in either EPS or PS format, and then using Acrobat Distiller to convert the PostScript file to PDF format. Both of these techniques are covered in Chapters 4 and 5. However, there are other ways to create PDF documents.

You can also create PDF documents with your scanner or by capturing pages from Internet Web sites. Either method is a great way to build an information library. You can scan magazine articles of interest, convert them to PDF format, and discard the original to avoid paper clutter. You can also capture single web pages or an entire website. With the wealth of information available on the Internet, capturing web pages is a wonderful way to build a PDF library on your hard drive. After you capture several web pages, you can use the Adobe Catalog plug-in to create a searchable index of PDF documents captured from the Web. Creating PDF indexes is covered in Chapter 15.

Capture PDF Documents from a Scanner

If you have a scanner attached to your computer, you can capture PDF documents directly from your scanner using the Acrobat Scan plug-in. With the Acrobat Scan plug-in, it is possible to scan a document into Acrobat without leaving the program. After you scan the document, you can use any of the Acrobat tools or menu commands to modify the document before saving it as a PDF file.

Your scanner probably has an interface or other software that makes the scanning process a relatively simple task. Most scanner applications let you crop the image, select a color model, and adjust the image resolution before scanning the document into an application. If your scanner is equipped with similar software, you can adjust the image to suit its intended destination before returning the scanned image to Acrobat.

NOTE

When you scan a document, it is temporarily written to disk before it is converted to PDF format. Make sure you have enough temporary disk space to avoid problems. You can increase disk space by deleting unnecessary temporary files. You can also increase disk space by copying infrequently used documents to a mass storage device, such as a tape backup or zip disk.

Select a TWAIN Device

When you install Acrobat, the install utility detects any TWAIN (Technology Without An Interesting Name) devices you have attached to your computer. As a note of interest, TWAIN originated from Rudyard Kipling's *The Ballad of East and West* ("and never the twain shall meet"), which, when the technology was in its infancy, reflected the difficulties of connecting a scanner to a personal computer. However, many people think TWAIN stands for Technology Without An Interesting Name. A TWAIN device contains the interface and drivers that convert the optical input from a scanner or digital camera into digital format that can be recognized by computer software. The TWAIN devices you have attached to your computer are listed on a drop-down menu in the Acrobat Scan Plug In dialog box.

Capture Images and Text

Once you have a scanner up and running on your system with a TWAIN that Acrobat recognizes, you can scan any document into Acrobat and save it as a PDF file. Unfortunately, if the document you are scanning has text, the text will not be editable and you will not be able to use the Acrobat Find command to search the text for keywords or phrases. To capture a document into Acrobat with your scanner:

1. Insert the document you want to capture in your scanner.

To create a better-looking PDF document, make sure the document is square with the edge of your scanner. If the page is clipped from a magazine, trim and square the edges for better results.

2. Choose File | Import | Scan to reveal the Acrobat Scan Plug-In dialog box, as shown in the following image:

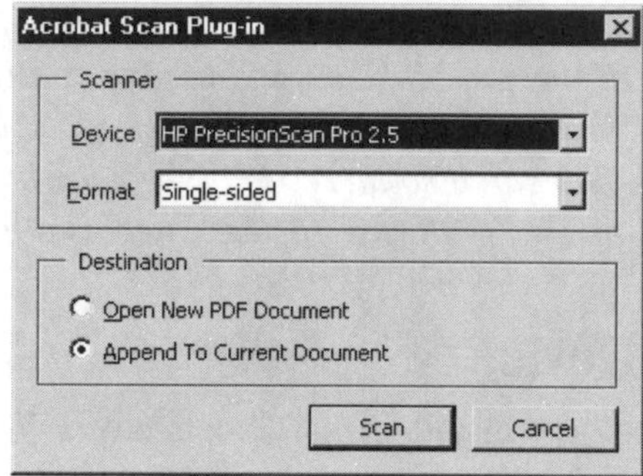

3. Click the triangle to the right of the drop-down menu and choose the appropriate TWAIN device for your scanner.

The menu for TWAIN devices may show two listings for each item. For best results, choose the manufacturer's software for your scanner if it is listed.

4. In the format field, there are two options, Single-Sided (the default) and Double-Sided. If your scanner supports double-sided scanning, choose Double-Sided; otherwise, accept Single-Sided.
5. If no document is currently open in Acrobat, Open New PDF Document is the only option available; otherwise, the Append To Current Document option is available and selected by default. Choose the option that applies, and click Scan.
6. After you click the Scan button, the interface for the TWAIN device you selected opens. Follow the prompts to preview the scan and return it to Acrobat. Refer to your scanner user guide for specific instructions. The following image is the HP Precision Pro 2.5 interface:

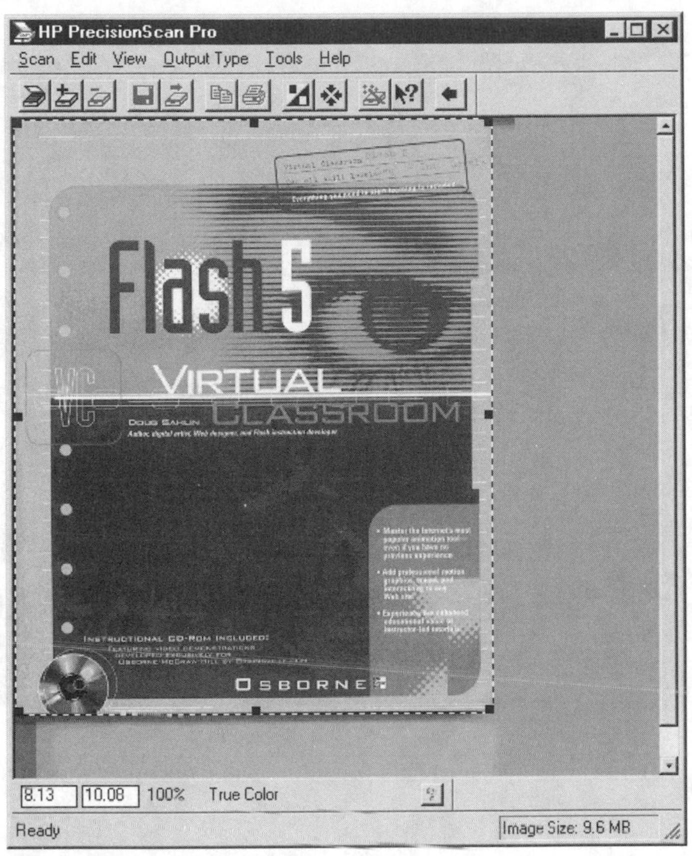

7. After the image is scanned into Acrobat, modify the document as needed and save the image. Figure 6-1 shows a page from a book as captured with the Acrobat Scan plug-in.

Capture Images from Digital Cameras

If you have a digital camera connected to your computer, with a TWAIN driver that is recognized by Acrobat, you can use it to capture images directly into Acrobat. To capture an image from a digital camera, the device must be connected to the computer (the most common hookup being a USB cable), or you must have a device connected to your computer that supports your camera memory cards. To capture an image from your digital camera, choose File | Import | Scan, choose the

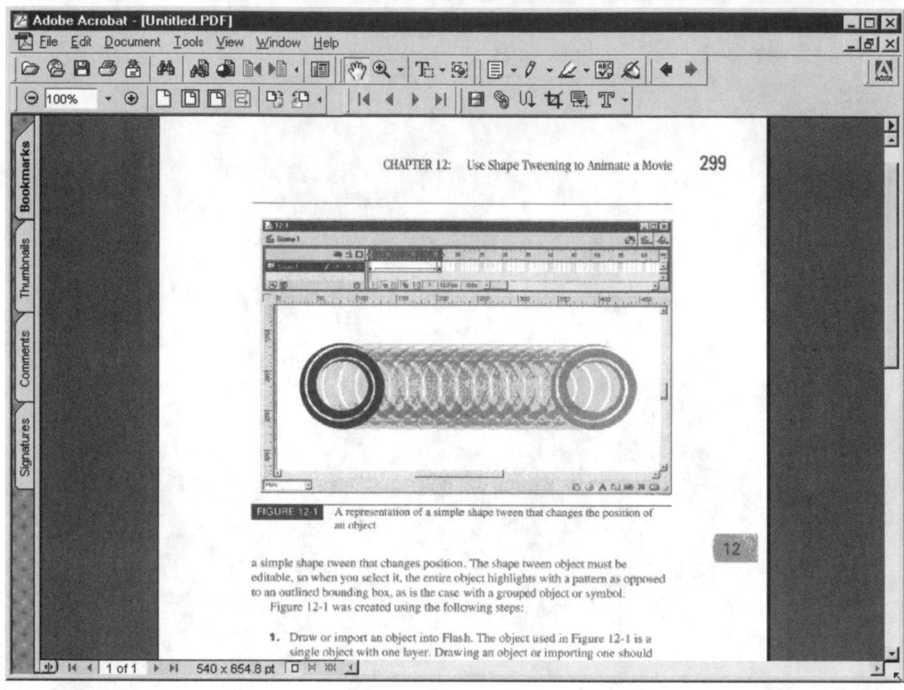

FIGURE 6-1 You can use your scanner to capture paper documents as PDF files.

TWAIN device that supports your camera, and follow the prompts to capture the image. The following is the TWAIN interface for the Logitech QuickCam:

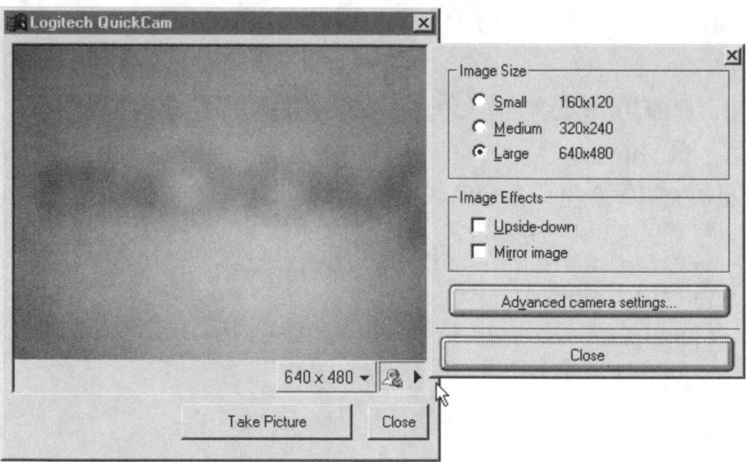

Pictures you take with a digital camera are generally in JPEG format. In the majority of cases, there are better methods for capturing photographs from your digital camera, especially when you have to edit the image after photographing it. However, capturing an image with a digital camera, converting it to PDF, and then attaching it to an e-mail message is any easy way to send images of people or products to friends and coworkers that may not have computer software capable of opening images in their native formats.

Capture Documents as Searchable Text

The Acrobat Scan plug-in does not have OCR (Optical Character Recognition) capabilities, which unfortunately means that documents scanned into Acrobat and saved as PDF files cannot be searched with the Find or Search command. There are three ways you can capture documents and convert them into PDF documents with searchable text. You can use another Adobe program called Acrobat Capture, you can use the Adobe Create PDF Online service, or you can use an OCR program and convert the resulting file to PDF format.

Use Adobe Capture

Adobe Capture is software that converts paper documents into editable PDF documents. Capture was part of Acrobat 4.0; however, this plug-in is not available with Acrobat 5.0. In lieu of the plug-in, Adobe has two versions of Capture available as stand-alone programs: Capture 2.01 and Capture 3.0. Capture 2.01 is available for the following operating systems: Windows 95, Windows 98, Windows NT 3.51, and Windows NT 4.0. Adobe designed Capture 3.0 for users in a network environment. Capture 3.0 is supported by Windows NT 4.0 with Service Pack 3 or later, and by Windows 2000. Capture recognizes most popular scanners with ISIS (Image and Scanner Interface Standard) or TWAIN drivers.

NOTE *Although the Windows 98 and Windows Millennium operating systems are similar, Adobe has not tested Adobe Capture 2.01 with Windows Millennium. The same is true of Windows NT 4.0 and Windows 2000. If you decide to purchase the software and use it with Windows Millennium or Windows 2000 operating system, you do so at your own risk.*

You can use either program to scan a document and convert it to a searchable PDF file. Both programs accurately recognize font styles. Capture automatically creates intradocument links for use as navigation. After you capture a document, you can choose to save the document in one of the following formats:

- **PDF Normal** Choose this option and Capture creates a small, compact, searchable PDF file suitable for viewing on the Web.
- **PDF Image** Choose this option and Capture creates an image of the scanned document suitable for cross-platform viewing.
- **PDF Image + Text** Choose this option and Capture creates a bitmap image of the original document with searchable text in the background and, consequently, also creates the largest file size. Choose this option when you need to preserve the look of the original document.
- You can also choose HTML, ASCII (American Standard Code to Information Interchange), RTF (Rich Text Format), Microsoft Word 6 for Windows, or Corel WordPerfect for Windows.

This technology is not without a price, though. To find out more information about Acrobat Capture and to evaluate whether it's the right solution for your needs, visit the Acrobat Capture Web page at http://www.Adobe.com/products/acrcapture. If your need for creating searchable PDF documents from paper documents is infrequent, consider using the Adobe Create PDF Online service.

NOTE *If you purchased Acrobat 5.0 and still have a licensed version of Acrobat 4.0 installed on your machine, you can use the Acrobat 4.0 Capture plug-in to convert paper documents into searchable PDF documents. Please note that when you upgrade from version 4.0 to version 5.0, you void your license for version 4.0.*

Use the Adobe Create PDF Online Service

You can use the Adobe Create PDF Online service to upload documents or scanned images and have them converted to searchable PDF documents. The Adobe Create PDF Online service supports Microsoft Word documents, graphics formats, and other file types. The fact that you are reading this book means you have the full version of Acrobat; therefore, your only need for the Adobe Create PDF Online service is to convert a scanned document to a searchable PDF file. After the file is converted to PDF, you can choose to download it or have the file e-mailed to you.

As of this writing, you can sign up for a trial membership with the Adobe Create PDF Online service. The trial entitles you to three files converted to PDFs at no charge. With a trial membership, your files cannot exceed 50MB and there is a processing time limit of 15 minutes. Subscriber's files will have priority over trial member's files. If you decide the service is the right solution for your needs, you can subscribe to the service for a monthly fee of $9.95.

You may wonder why you should invest in an online service when you already own the Acrobat software. If you have a full suite of software capable of creating and illustrating, documents and images, you probably do not need the service. If, on the other hand, you occasionally need to convert paper documents into searchable PDF files, the annual cost of the service is considerably less than purchasing either version of Adobe Capture. In fact, at current pricing, you could use Create PDF Online service for over four years and still not equal the investment needed to purchase Adobe Capture 2.01.

Currently, this service is only available in the U.S. and Canada. To find out more about Adobe Create PDF Online or to sign up for a trial membership, go to the Create PDF Online Web page at https://createpdf.adobe.com/index.pl/.

Another way you can create searchable PDF files is to use OCR software.

Use OCR Software

If you use OCR software, you can use it to scan any paper document and preserve editable text. The install utility for many popular OCR programs installs as a helper application for recognized word processing software, such as Microsoft Word or Corel WordPerfect. If your OCR software installs a helper application for Microsoft Word, you probably have an additional menu command named Acquire Text, or something similar. If this is the case, to capture editable text in Word, do the following:

1. Choose the command your OCR software installed to acquire text from the Word menu bar. After you choose this command, your scanner will begin examining the document for recognizable words. The following image is

the OCR Proofreader for ScanSoft's Omni10 Pro software (with a questionable capture highlighted):

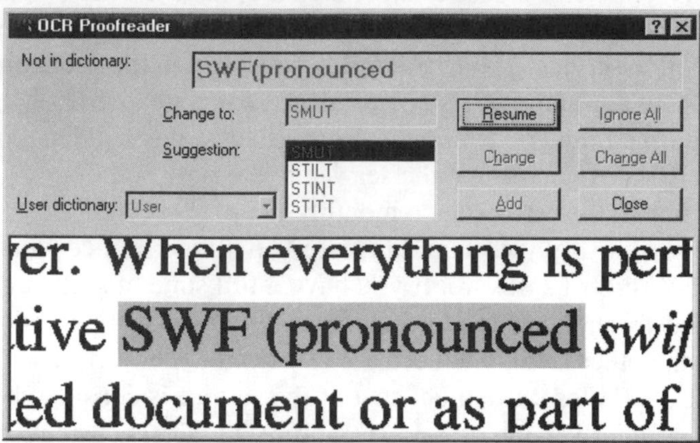

2. Typical OCR software examines the document and automatically recognizes words from the OCR dictionary. If the software doesn't recognize a word or symbol, the unrecognized word or symbol (also known as a *capture suspect*) is displayed and you are prompted to enter a substitute.
3. After the OCR software examines the document, the text is pasted into Word. At this point, it is advisable to proofread the text to make sure it was interpreted correctly by the OCR software. Depending on the OCR software you use, you may also have to clean up some formatting.
4. After proofreading and editing the captured document, click the Convert To Adobe PDF button, or choose Acrobat | Convert To Adobe PDF.

After you save the scanned document to PDF format, it can be searched with the Find command; and, if you add the document to a PDF index, it can be searched with the Search command.

Use OmniPage Pro 11.0 to Convert Paper Documents to Editable PDF (Windows only)

If you have the need to convert paper documents into searchable PDF documents, an alternative to Adobe Capture is OmniPage Pro 11.0 from ScanSoft. You can use this software to scan paper documents into your computer and convert them to editable text, or convert image files with text to editable text. Previous versions of OmniPage Pro have been recognized as the most accurate OCR scanning programs on the market. The engineers at ScanSoft have improved the character recognition engine to such a degree that OmniPage Pro 11.0 boasts a 40 percent increase in accuracy over its predecessors. The software recognizes formatted spreadsheets and documents with formatted tables. You can use the software to convert PDF documents into editable text for use in programs such as Word and Excel. This feature comes in handy when you need to edit someone else's PDF document.

The biggest benefit Acrobat users gain from OmniPage Pro11.0 is the ability to scan a document and convert it to PDF format, or convert an image file with text into an editable PDF. Remember, you can convert an image file into PDF format using the Open As Adobe PDF command, but any text in the file will not be editable. After you launch OmniPage Pro 11.0, converting a paper document or image file into PDF format is a four-step process:

1. Choose the method of transferring the document to OmniPage Pro. You can load a file (OmniPage Pro supports most popular image formats and PDFs), scan a black-and-white document, scan a grayscale document, or scan a color document.
2. Choose one of the OmniPro OCR methods to convert the document into editable text. You can choose from the following: Automatic; Single Column, No Table; Multiple Column, No Table; Single Column With Table; Spreadsheet; or Custom. The Custom option allows you to set up the OCR based on the type of document you want OmniPage Pro to convert to editable text.
3. Choose an export result. You can save the result to disk, e-mail the result, or copy the result to the system clipboard.
4. Click the Start button and the OmniPage Pro OCR engine goes to work. When the software captures text that is suspect (not in its dictionary), you are prompted to change the captured suspect by entering new text, by accepting one of the suggestions, or by ignoring the suspect capture. After OmniPage

Pro finishes recognizing the text, you can save the file in one of the following PDF formats:

- **Adobe PDF** Choose this option and OmniPage Pro 11.0 exports the document in PDF format as it appears in the text editor. You can view the file in Acrobat Reader and edit the file in Acrobat.
- **Adobe PDF With Image Substitutes** Choose this option and OmniPage Pro 11.0 exports the document as an editable Adobe PDF file, but images are substituted for suspect or reject captures.
- **Adobe PDF, Image Only** Choose this option and OmniPage Pro 11.0 exports the document as a non-editable PDF file that can be viewed with Acrobat or Acrobat Reader.
- **Adobe PDF With Image On Text** Choose this option and OmniPage Pro 11.0 exports the document as a PDF file. The exported file retains the look and feel of the original document, but cannot be modified in Acrobat. There is, however, a linked text file with the document, which means the viewer can use the Acrobat or Acrobat Reader Find command to search the document. When Acrobat finds a match for the word or phrase, the found word is highlighted in the image.

As of this writing, OmniPage Pro 11.0 retails for $499.99. If you own an earlier version of OmniPage Pro, the upgrade price is $149.99. For more information, visit the OmniPage Pro page at the ScanSoft website. The URL is http://www.scansoft.com/products/omnipage/pro/.

Capture PDF Documents from Websites

The Internet is a treasure trove of information. You can find out almost anything about any subject by typing relevant keywords into one of the many online search engines. After you submit the search, the search engine usually returns several pages of websites that contain information that pertains to your search. The first three or four pages contain the sites with information that closely matches your query, but searching through 10 or 15 websites can be time consuming. If you have a slow Internet connection, and the returned pages are filled with graphics, this only exacerbates the problem. The solution is to use the Acrobat Web Capture command to download the page into Acrobat. You can download a single page or the entire site. After the download is complete, you can save the page(s) in PDF format for review at your leisure. Figure 6-2 shows a web page that has been downloaded into Acrobat.

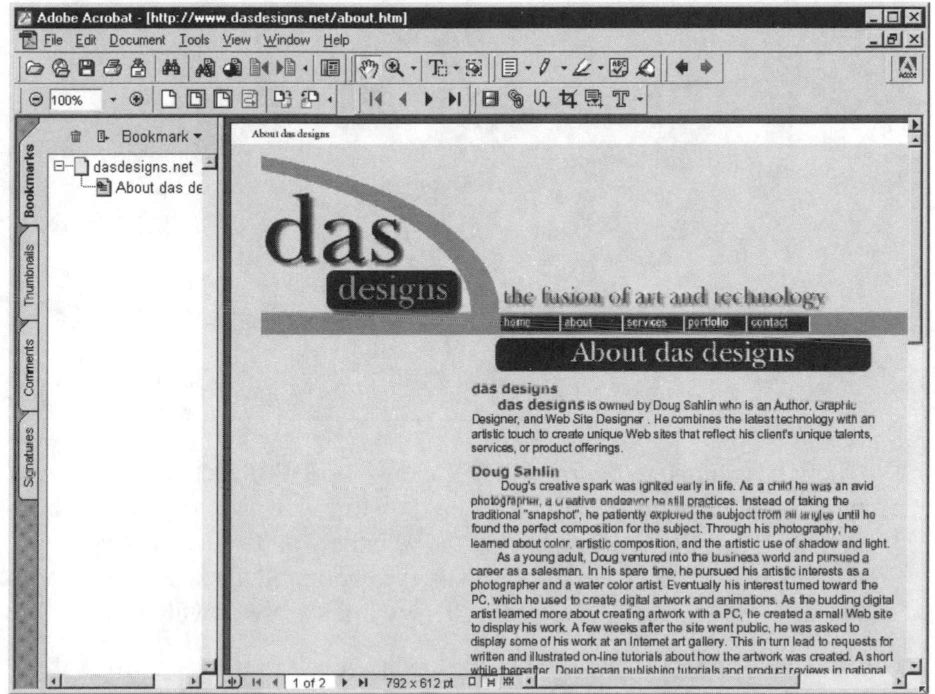

FIGURE 6-2 You can download a web page into Acrobat for future reference.

6

Set Web Capture Preferences

The Acrobat Web Capture is a powerful command that can save you hours of time online. You can configure Web Capture to suit your working style by changing Web Capture Preferences as follows:

1. Choose Edit | Preferences | Web Capture to open the dialog box shown in the following image:

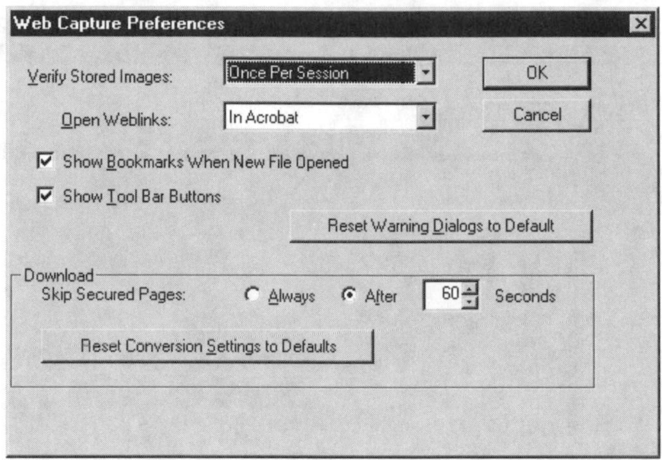

2. Click the triangle to the right of the Verify Stored Images field, and from the dropdown menu choose Once Per Session, Always, or Never. The default, Once Per Session, checks the website you captured pages from to see whether the images stored with the captured pages have changed at the site. If the images have changed, new images are downloaded.
3. Click the triangle to the right of the Open Weblinks field, and from the drop-down menu choose In Acrobat (the default) or In Web Browser. This option determines what device is used to open a page when a captured Web page button or hyperlinked text is clicked.
4. When you enable Show Bookmarks When New File Opened (the default), after the captured web page downloads completely, the Navigation pane opens and the document bookmarks are displayed. Disable this option, and

when the download is complete, the document opens with the Navigation Palette closed; however, bookmarks have been created.

5. If you disable Show Toolbar Buttons, the Open Web Page button—which looks like a file folder with a globe behind—it is not shown on the toolbar. The Open Web Page button is displayed on the toolbar by default.
6. Click the Reset Warning Dialogs To Default button to return all warning dialogs associated with Web Capture to their default settings.
7. Choose a Skip Secured Pages option. Acrobat Web Capture can download secured pages, but you generally need permission to access password protected areas. When you attempt to download a secure page, Acrobat provides a dialog box that you use to enter a Login Name and Password. After you submit this information, Acrobat tries to download the page for the time interval specified in the Seconds field. You can enter a value between 1 and 9999 seconds. If the allotted time has passed and Acrobat has not successfully downloaded the page, a warning message appears and the page is skipped.

NOTE *If the website server is set up to allow only certain web browsers in secure sections of the site, Acrobat may not be able to capture the page, even though the right username and password have been entered.*

8. Click the Reset Conversion Settings To Default, and the settings in the Web Capture Preferences dialog box are restored to the default values when Acrobat is first installed.
9. Click OK to apply the settings and exit the dialog box.

Download Web Pages

Whether you are surfing the Internet for pleasure, or browsing for product information or tutorials, you can quickly download a web page or an entire website using the Acrobat Web Capture commands. When you capture a web page in Acrobat, the entire page is downloaded, complete with images. When Acrobat encounters an unsupported object, such as a Flash movie, a rectangular shape the color of the web page background is displayed in lieu of the unsupported object. If the entire web page is a Flash movie, the captured page shows only the web page background color. If an animated GIF is part of the page being captured, only the first frame of the animated GIF appears after Acrobat downloads the page. When you are on the Internet and find a web page you want to download, do the following:

1. If it is not already open, launch Acrobat.
2. Choose Tools | Web Capture | Open Web Page to access the Open Web Page dialog box, as shown in Figure 6-3. Alternatively, you can choose File | Open Web Page or click the Open Web Page button on the toolbar.
3. In the URL field, enter the URL for the page you want to capture.

Some URLs are very long. Instead of manually entering the entire web address, in your web browser, select the web address and press CTRL-C *to copy the web address to your operating system clipboard. Switch to Acrobat, click in the URL field, and then press* CTRL-V *to paste the URL into the field.*

4. In the Levels field, enter the number of levels to download, or use the Spinner buttons to increase or decrease the value in the Levels field. Alternatively, you can choose Get Entire Site to download every level (and subsequently every page) in the site.

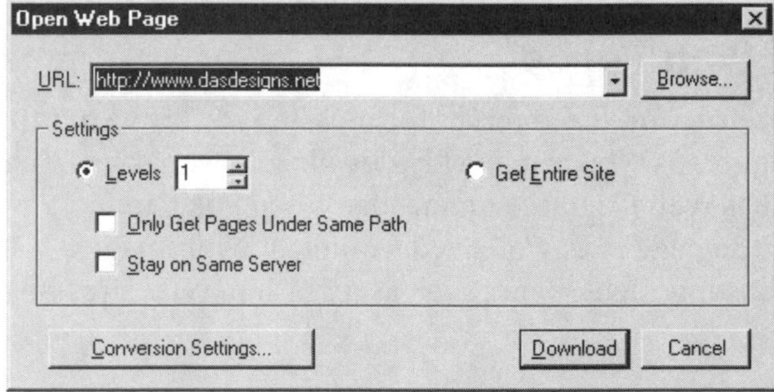

FIGURE 6-3 Enter a URL and specify settings for a web page capture in this dialog box.

CAUTION

Some Web sites are several levels deep; for example, a site home page (Level 1) could branch out to five sections (Level 2). Each section on Level 2 could branch out to other pages (Level 3), and so on. When you download a site that is several layers deep, you use a considerable amount of your system resources, and run the risk of exceeding available system resources and perpetrating a system crash. If you are downloading a site with many levels, you are advised to download the first level, browse through the downloaded page in Acrobat, and then click a link to download an additional page.

5. If you specify the number of levels to download, you can specify the following options:
   - **Only Get Pages Under Same Path** Choose this option, and Acrobat will download all pages along the path of the specified URL.
   - **Stay On Same Server** Choose this option, and Acrobat will only download pages from the server of the specified URL, disregarding links to URLs on another server.
6. Click the Conversion Settings button to modify Acrobat Web Capture conversion settings. This feature is explained fully in an upcoming section of this chapter.
7. Click the Download button to begin capturing the page. As the site is downloading, Acrobat keeps you informed of the download progress by opening the Download Status dialog box, shown in the following image:

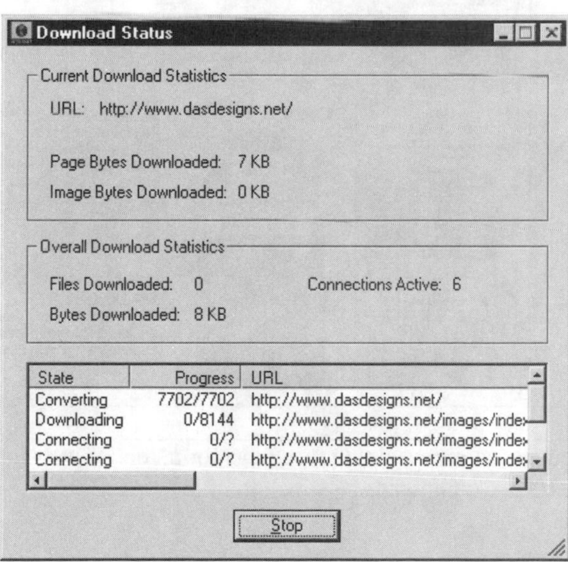

8. To save the captured page in PDF format for future reference, choose File | Save to open the Save As dialog box. Enter a name for the file, specify the folder to save the file in, and then click Save.

After the download is complete, Acrobat displays the captured page in the Document pane according to the specified Web Capture Preferences. Figure 6-4 shows a captured page after download. Note the title above the captured page. This same title is displayed in your web browser when you view the page on the Internet. You can change the document by choosing File | Document Properties | Summary and then entering another name in the Document Summary dialog box Title field; however, this only changes the title as it pertains to an index, to which you may add the PDF file. When you reopen the document after assigning the new title, the title from the web page still appears in the Document pane.

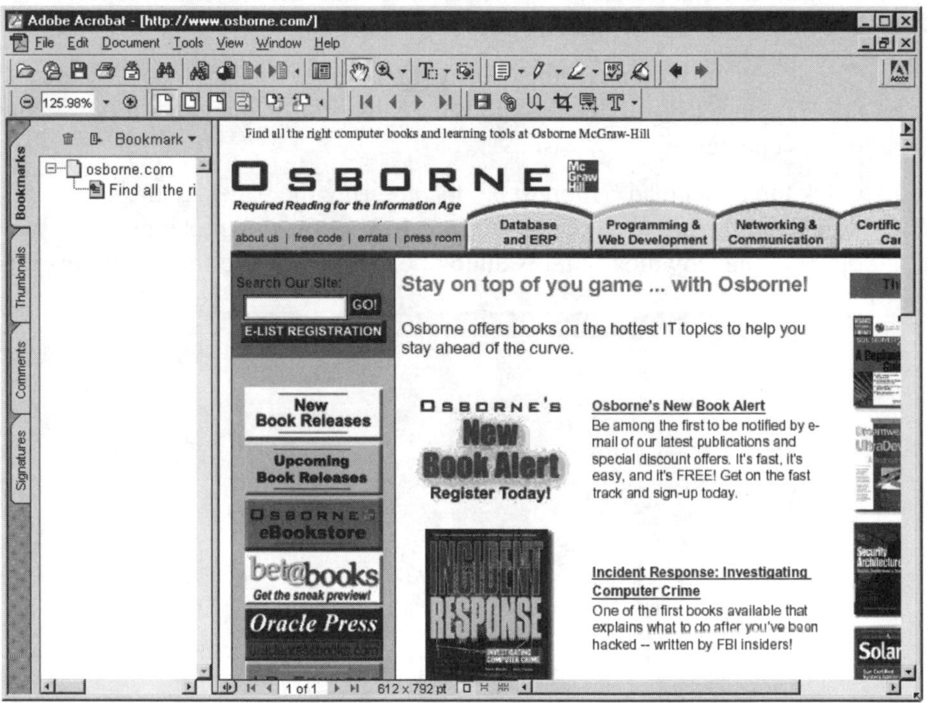

FIGURE 6-4 You can capture a single web page, or an entire website, using the Open Web Page command.

NOTE *Certain web page features will not download, such as pop-up menus. Pop-up menus and similar web page features are created using JavaScript. You should also be aware that Acrobat will not convert Flash SWF files, certain CGI files, Java Applets, or RealMedia to PDF. Although JavaScript is supported in bookmarks, links, and form fields you create in Acrobat, JavaScript features are not downloaded with a web page.*

Append Web Pages

After you successfully capture a web page, you may decide to add additional pages from the same site to the document, download the rest of the site, or append the document with web pages from another site. You can append the current Web page using menu commands, or by clicking links on the captured page.

Append with Web Links

As you view a captured page in Acrobat, you may decide that another page from the same site, or a page from another site that is linked to the captured page, contains information you would like to archive in PDF format. To append a page using a web link, follow these steps:

1. From the captured page, click the link to the page you want to add to the document and Acrobat opens the Specify Weblink Behavior dialog box, as shown in the following image:

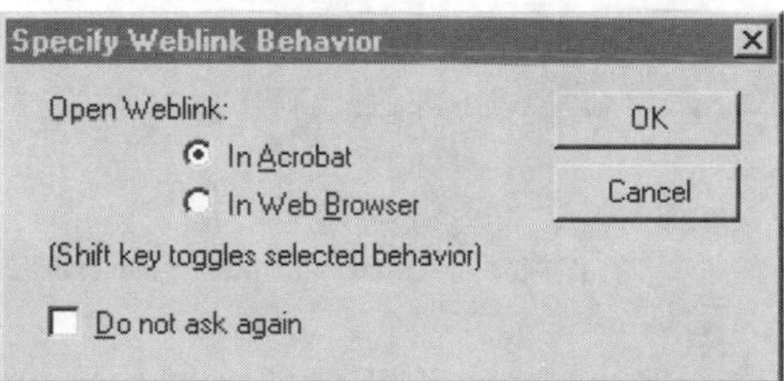

2. To open the link in Acrobat and append the current document, accept the default In Acrobat behavior. If you select the In Web Browser behavior, the linked page opens in your default web browser and is not appended to the current PDF document.

NOTE

The Specify Web Link dialog box appears if you have not modified your Web Capture preferences. After you modify Web Capture preferences, the dialog box no longer appears. If you configure your Web Capture preferences to open links in Acrobat, a plus sign (+) appears when you move your cursor over the link. If you configure your Web Capture preferences to open links in a Web browser, a lowercase w *appears when you move your cursor over a link. To momentarily toggle to the other preference, hold down the* SHIFT *key.*

3. To add another page to the document, click the desired link and accept the default Open In Acrobat behavior, and Acrobat will download the page to the document. Acrobat will create a bookmark and thumbnail for the added page as shown in Figure 6-5.
4. When you have finished adding pages to the document, choose File | Save.

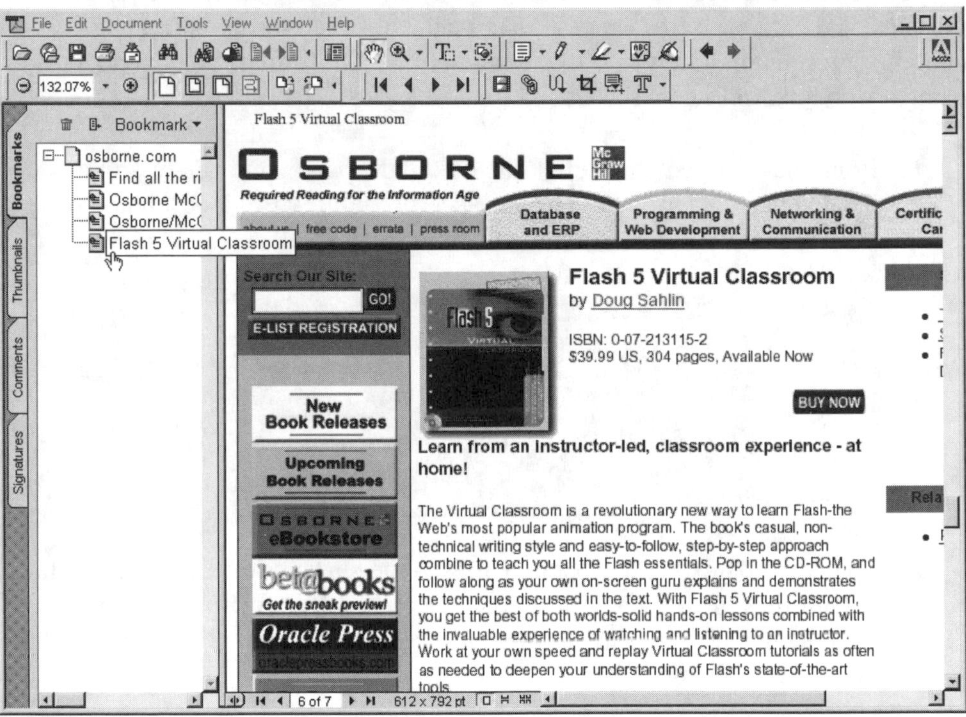

FIGURE 6-5 You can append a captured web page by clicking a link within the document.

Use the View Web Links Command

To view all of the web links within a captured page, you use the View Web Links command. You can use this command to add additional web pages to the document as follows:

1. Choose Tools | Web Capture | View Web Links, and Acrobat opens the Select Page Links to Download dialog box, as shown in the following image:

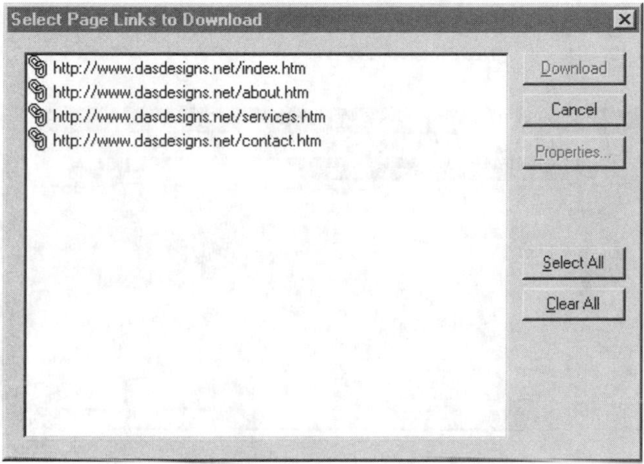

2. To add additional Web pages to the current document, do one of the following:

   - To add contiguous links to the selection, click the link while holding down the SHIFT key. To add noncontiguous links to the selection, click the link while holding down the CTRL key.
   - To select all links, click the Select All button.
   - To clear the selection, click the Clear All button.

3. Click the Download button to begin the download. After you click the Download button, Acrobat opens the Download Status dialog box and displays the progress of the operation. When the download is complete, Acrobat appends the document with the downloaded pages and adds additional bookmarks and thumbnails for the new pages.

Use the Append Web Page Command

You can use the Append Web Page command to add additional pages to the current document. If you are appending the current document with links from within the same site, either click a link within the document, or use the View Web Links command to view the links within the document and then select the links you want to add to the document. However, if the link you want to add to the captured Web page does not appear on the page, then do the following:

1. Choose Tools Web Capture | Append Web Page to open the Append Web Page dialog box, as shown in the following image:

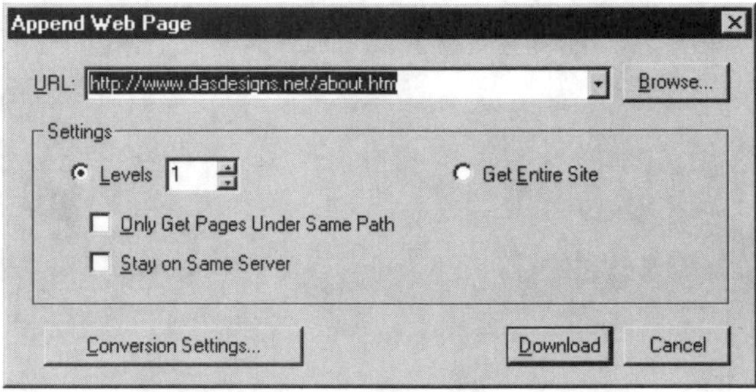

2. In the URL field, enter the address for the web page you want to add to the document.
3. In the Levels field, enter the number of levels to download, or use the Spinner buttons to increase or decrease the value in the Levels field. Alternatively, you can choose Get Entire Site to download every level (and subsequently every page) in the site.
4. Choose Only Get Pages Under Same Path, and Acrobat will download all pages along the path of the specified URL.
5. Choose Stay On Same Server, and Acrobat will only download pages from the server of the specified URL, disregarding links to URLs on another server.
6. Click the Download button to begin capturing the page. Acrobat opens the Download Status dialog box, which you can use to monitor download progress.

7. After the page downloads, you can invoke the command again to add additional pages to the document, or choose File | Save.

NOTE *To enable fast web viewing, use the Save As command to save the captured web pages.*

When you append a captured web page with pages from another website, Acrobat creates a bookmark for the URL of the site. Captured pages from each site are listed under the URL bookmark, as shown in the following illustration:

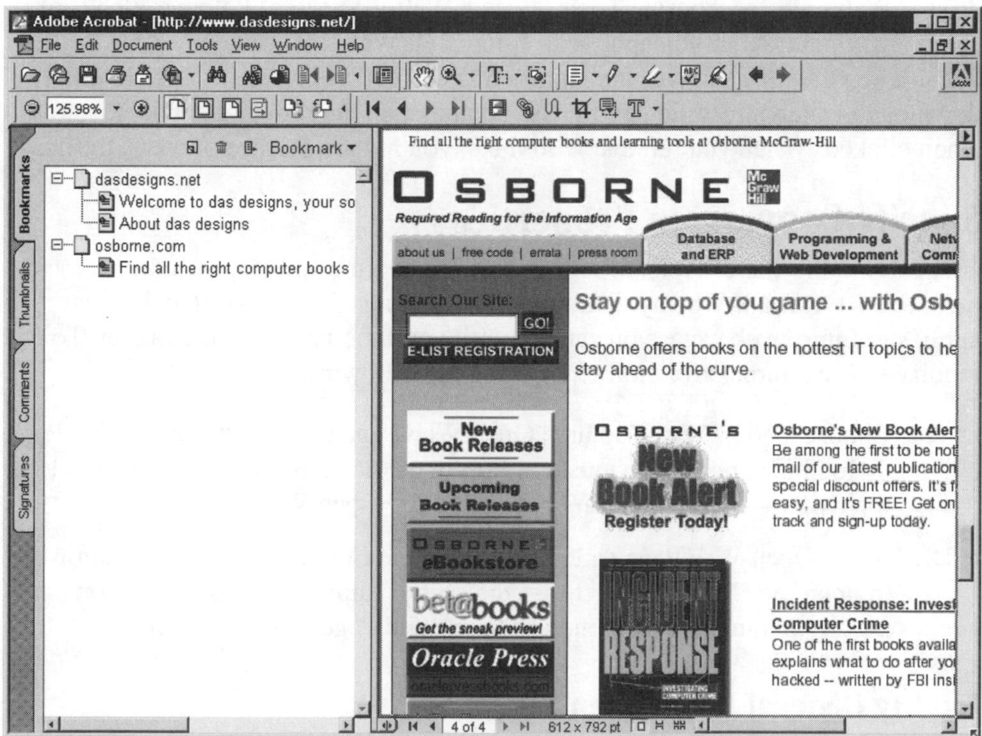

Append All Links on a Page

Once you download a web page, you can use any of the methods previously discussed to append the page, or you can download every page that is linked to the captured page by choosing Tools | Web Capture | Append All Links. After you choose this command, Acrobat downloads the linked pages one at a time and displays the download progress in the Download Status dialog box. This operation may take a considerable amount of time if the page has several links. After the linked pages are downloaded, you can view the downloaded pages by clicking a link in the main page, or by opening the Bookmarks palette or Thumbnails palette and clicking a bookmark or thumbnail. You can apply the Append All Links command on any of the newly downloaded pages to add additional pages to the document.

After you have added all of the desired pages to the document, you can disable Web links by choosing Tools | Locate Web Addresses | Remove Web Links From Document. After you apply this command, Web links will be visible in the document, yet will no longer function as links to URLs. However, links to other downloaded Web pages are still functional and open the proper document page when clicked. When you remove Web links, you reduce the size of the PDF file.

Specify Conversion Properties

You can modify the conversion settings used to capture web pages and convert them to PDF format. When you modify these settings, it is a global action that applies to future web pages you capture until you modify the settings again. To modify web capture conversion settings, do the following:

1. Choose Tools | Web Capture | Open Web Page to open the Open Web Page dialog box, shown previously in Figure 6-3. Alternatively, you can click the Open Web Page button or choose File | Open Web Page.
2. In the Open Web Page dialog box, click the Conversion Settings button to open the Conversion Settings dialog box shown in Figure 6-6. You can modify parameters for General options and Page Layout options.

Modify General Conversion Settings

When you open the Conversion Settings dialog box, the General section is selected by default. As shown in Figure 6-6, the supported file types Acrobat can convert to PDF are listed in the Content-Type Specific Settings window. To modify the General Web Capture conversion settings, follow these steps:

1. Open the Conversion Settings dialog box, as outlined previously. The General tab is selected by default.

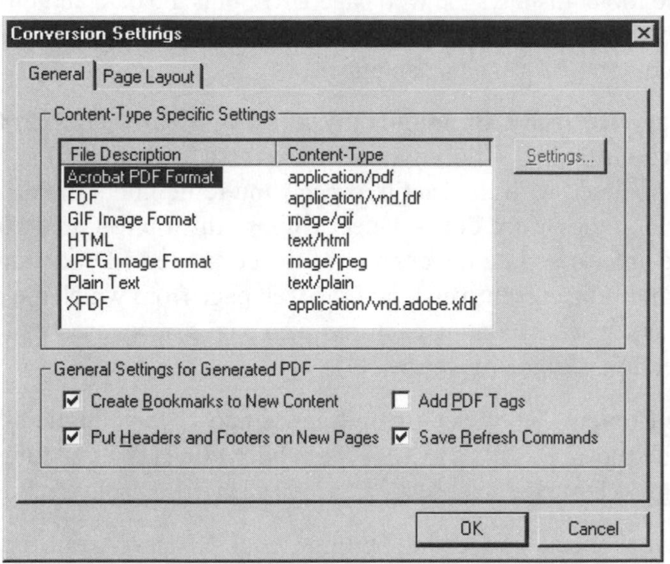

FIGURE 6-6 Use this dialog box to specify how Acrobat converts web pages to PDF format.

2. You can modify the following options in the General Settings for Generated PDF section:

   - **Create Bookmarks For New Content** Choose this option, and Acrobat will generate a new bookmark for each additional page you capture. This option is selected by default.
   - **Add PDF Tags** Choose this option, and Acrobat will create a document structure that conforms to the layout of the HTML document. If you choose this option, Acrobat will add bookmarks for HTML items such as paragraphs, lists, tables, and so on. The tagged document can be reflowed for easier reading on devices with smaller viewing areas. For more information on tagged documents, refer to the "About Tagged Documents" section of Chapter 14.
   - **Put Headers And Footers On New Pages (Windows) or Put Headers And Footers On New Content (Macintosh)** Choose this option, and Acrobat will add a new header and footer to each captured web page. The header shows the web page title as it appears in the browser; and

the footer displays the web page URL, plus the date and time the file was downloaded. If the URL is exceptionally long, it may be truncated to allow room for the page number.

- **Save Refresh Commands (Windows) or Save Update Commands (Macintosh)** Choose this, and Acrobat will save a list of all URLs associated with the captured page and remembers the order in which they were downloaded. Choose this option, and you will be able to update the content of the converted PDF document to match the current version of the web page from which the document was created. Updating captured web pages is covered in a future section of this chapter.

3. In the Content-Type Specific Settings window, you can modify settings for two file types: HTML and Text. To modify the HTML settings and Text settings, refer to the next section "Modify HTML Display Settings."
4. To save General Conversion Settings, click OK and Acrobat closes the Conversion Settings dialog box, returning you to the Capture Web Pages dialog box.

Modify HTML Display Settings

When you capture a web page as a PDF, you can modify the look of the captured page by changing the HTML display settings. You can modify font style; font color; and other parameters of the converted page, such as background color and table cell colors. To modify the display characteristics of captured web pages, do the following:

1. Open the Conversion Settings dialog box as outlined previously.
2. In the Content-Type Specific Settings window, click HTML to activate the Settings button.
3. Click the Settings tab to open the HTML Conversion Settings dialog box, shown in the next illustration.

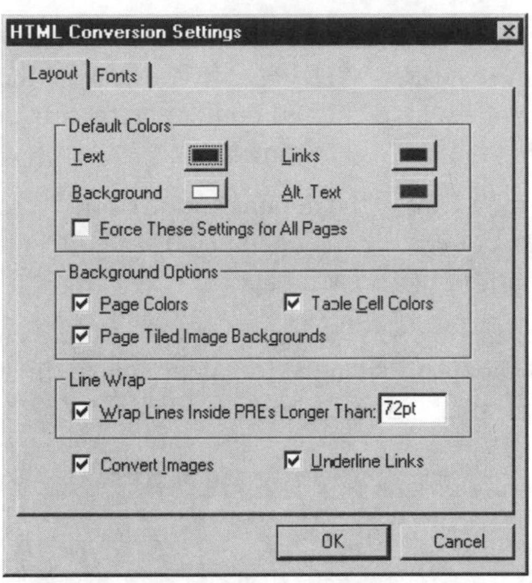

4. In the Default Colors section, you can modify the color of Text, Links, Background, and Alt Text by clicking the color button to the right of an item to open a color palette. Choose a color for the item, and then click OK to close the palette and apply the change. Repeat as needed to change the color of other items.
5. Choose Force Settings For All Pages, and the colors you specified in the previous step will be applied to all pages you capture, regardless of the colors specified in the actual HTML document. If you do not choose this option, Acrobat only applies the colors you specified in the previous step to HTML documents that do not have colors specified in the document HTML code.
6. In the Background Options section, Page Colors, Table Cell Colors, and Page Tiled Background Images are enabled by default. If you disable these options, the captured PDF document may look different from the actual Web Page, but may be more legible when printed.
7. In the Wrapped Lines Inside PREs Longer Than field, enter a value. Acrobat will wrap preformatted lines of HTML longer than the value you specify (10 inches is the default) to fit on the screen.

8. Choose Convert Images (the default option), and Acrobat will include images from the captured Web page. If you disable this option, Acrobat replaces the image with a colored border and the image Alt Text, if specified within the HTML document.
9. Choose Underline Links (the default option), and Acrobat underlines all text links when converting the document to PDF format, whether they are underlined or not in the HTML page.
10. Click the Fonts tab to open the Fonts section of the HTML Conversion Settings dialog box, shown in the following image. In this section, you can modify the font style and size for Body, Heading, or Pre-Formatted Text.

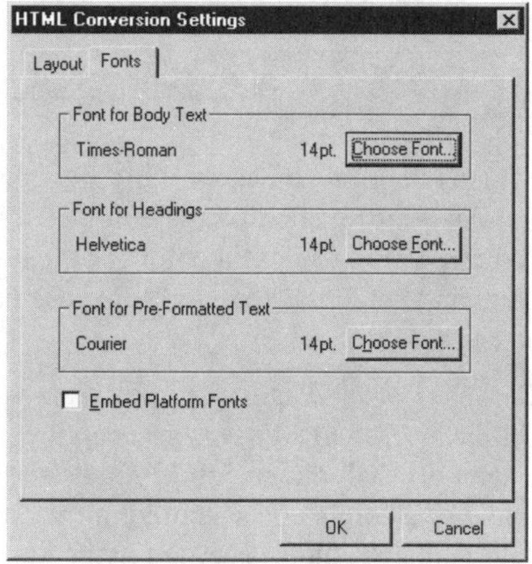

11. If you use Acrobat with the Windows operating system, you can modify a font style by clicking the Choose Font button, and then choosing a font style and size from the Choose Font dialog box. If you use Acrobat on a Macintosh machine, modify the font by selecting from the pop-up menu. Click OK to apply the changes.
12. Choose Embed Platform Fonts if you want the fonts you specify for the captured Web pages to be embedded with the PDF document. Choose this option if the file will be viewed on other machines that may not have the same fonts you have on your machine. Note that embedding fonts will increase the file size of the document. If you embed fonts, make sure you are not violating a font licensing agreement.
13. Click OK to close the HTML Conversion Settings dialog box.

Modify Page Layout Options

In the Page Layout section of the Conversion Setting dialog box, you can modify the size, margins, orientation, and scaling of the converted web pages. These options come in handy if you want to maintain the dimensions of a captured web page. For example, if you know each page in a web site is configured to a certain size, say 760 pixels × 420 pixels (a web browser maximized at an 800 × 600 desktop resolution), you can change the default Acrobat document size (612 pt × 792 pt) to match. To modify the page layout of a captured web page, do the following:

1. Open the Conversion Settings dialog box as outlined previously.
2. Click the Page Layout tab to reveal the Page Layout section of the Conversion Settings dialog box, as shown in the following image:

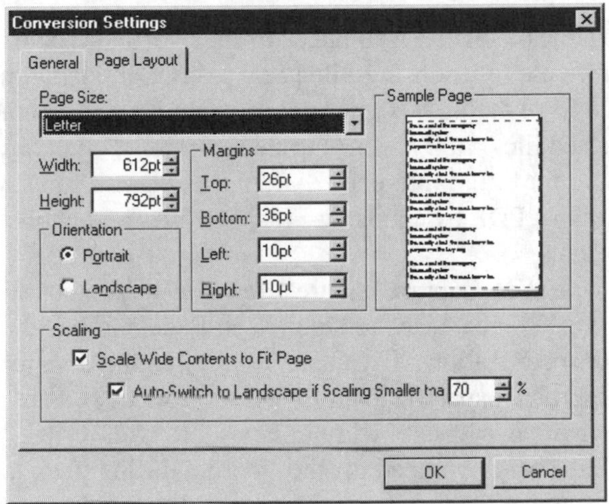

TIP *If the web page you are capturing has no margins, you can duplicate this when you capture the page by entering* ***0pt*** *for each margin setting in the Page Layout section of the HTML conversion settings.*

3. Click the triangle to the right of the Page Size field and choose an option from the drop-down menu. When you select a preset page layout, the values in the Width and Height fields change to reflect your choice.
4. Alternatively, select Custom from the Page Size drop-down menu and specify the page size by entering values in the Width and Height fields.
5. In the Margins section, accept the defaults, or enter your own values in the Top, Bottom, Left, and Right fields.

6. In the Orientation section, choose Portrait (the default) or Landscape.
7. In the Scaling section, you can modify the following options:
   - **Scale Wide Contents To Fit Page** Choose this option, and Acrobat will resize a Web site that exceeds the width of the screen to fit the page.
   - **Auto-Switch To Landscape If Contents Smaller Than** Accept the default value (70%) or enter a value of your own in this field. Acrobat will automatically switch the page layout from Portrait to Landscape if it is necessary to scale the page to a value lower than specified.
8. Click OK to apply the settings and close the Conversion Settings dialog box.

Save Converted Web Pages

After you convert one or several web pages to PDF format, you can save the document for future use by choosing File | Save. After choosing this command, Acrobat opens the Save dialog box and prompts you for a file name and location to save the converted file. After specifying these options, click Save, and Acrobat saves the document for future reference. Alternatively, you can save the document in formats other than a PDF by choosing File | Save As and choosing one of the supported file formats.

After you use the Web Capture feature a few times, you begin to see how useful this feature is. You can use the Open Web Page command to capture a web page with product specifications. If you are contemplating a major purchase, you can download the product specifications of every product you are considering and then compare them at your leisure, without having to wait for the Web pages to download or perhaps being bumped off the Internet during peak traffic.

If you use the Internet for research, capturing web pages is a great way to build a reference library. After you save several (or several hundred) web pages as PDF documents, you can use Acrobat Catalog to build a searchable index. Building a searchable index is covered in Chapter 15.

TIP *If you use Internet Search engines to find web pages that you want to save for reference, after you enter your query, launch Acrobat and choose File | Open Web Page, and then enter the URL for the results page. After Acrobat downloads the page, you can append the document with the results of your search by clicking a link. Download additional web pages by clicking other links. After you have downloaded all the pages you want to save, you can delete the initial search page by clicking its thumbnail and then choosing Document | Delete Pages.*

Update Converted Web Pages

If you surf the Internet frequently, you know it is in a constant state of flux. New Web sites open, old ones disappear, and websites are frequently updated. If you specified Save Refresh Commands (Windows) or Save Update Commands (Macintosh) for your Web Capture conversions settings (see "Modify General Conversion Settings," earlier in this chapter), you can update a captured web page you saved as a PDF document by doing the following:

1. Launch Acrobat and log onto the Internet.
2. Open the PDF file you captured from a web page.
3. Choose Tools | Web Capture | Refresh Pages, and Acrobat will open the Refresh Pages dialog box as shown in the following image:

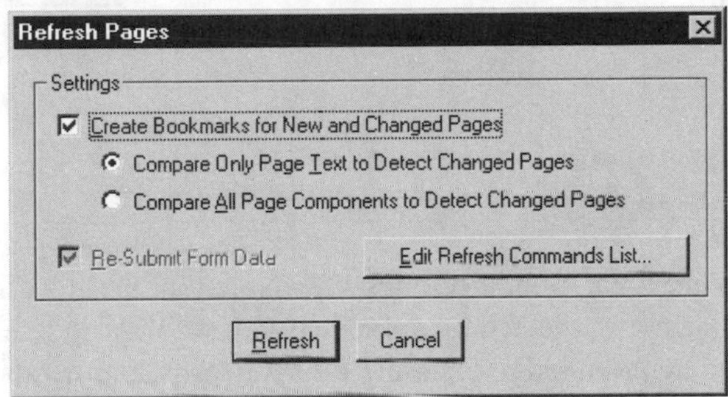

4. Choose Create Bookmarks For New And Changed Pages. When you choose this option, Acrobat creates bookmarks for downloaded pages that have been added to the site or modified since you captured the web page.
5. Choose Compare Only Page Text To Detect Changed Pages, and Acrobat will compare the captured page to the website page and will download the page if the page text has changed.
6. Choose Compare All Page Components To Detect Changed Pages, and Acrobat will compare all elements from the PDF document to the Web site from which the document was captured. The document will be updated if Acrobat senses a change, such as a new image.
7. If the captured web page has a form in it, the Resubmit Form Data option is active. This option is enabled by default.

When this option is selected, any data on the form is resubmitted. If you captured a web page with a form you used to purchase an item, a duplicate purchase may result if you enable this option.

8. Click the Edit Refresh Commands button to reveal the dialog box shown here:

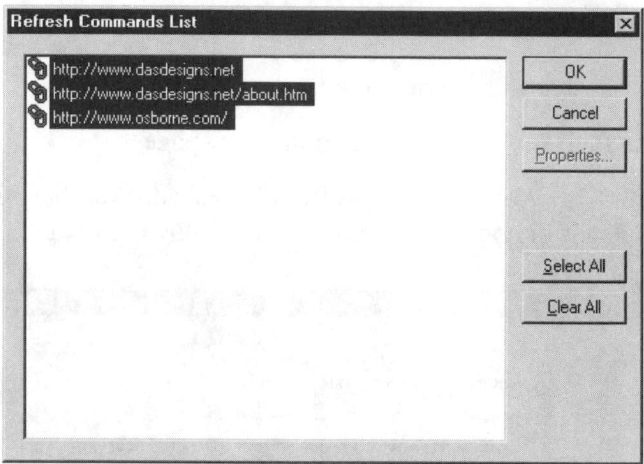

9. To update all links in the list, click OK. Note that all links from the captured page are selected by default. If you want to update all captured pages, you do not need to click the Edit Refresh Commands button. You only need to choose this option to update specific pages from the captured document by selecting the URLs you want to update from the list in this dialog box.

10. Click Refresh, and Acrobat will search for the changes as specified, and will download new or changed pages.

Chapter 7

Create Navigation for PDF Documents

How to...

- Create bookmarks
- Use thumbnails
- Create links
- Create buttons
- Work with Actions
- Work with Page Actions

When you create a PDF document within an authoring application, navigation devices are added to the document. PDF documents have two types of navigation devices that are created automatically: bookmarks and thumbnails. Bookmarks and thumbnails have their own palettes in the Navigation pane.

When you create a multi-page PDF document, one thumbnail is created for each page. Viewers of your PDF documents can navigate to a specific page of the document by clicking its thumbnail. Bookmarks, on the other hand, may or may not be created, depending on how you created the PDF document. If, for example, you use PDFMaker (the Microsoft Office plug-in) with its default settings to create a PDF file from a Microsoft Word document that contains Heading styles, a bookmark appears for each Heading style used in the document. If you use the Word Print command and choose Acrobat Distiller to create the PDF document, no bookmarks are created. Viewers of your documents can navigate to a bookmark by clicking its name in the Navigation pane. For more information on the Navigation pane, refer to Chapter 3.

After you open a PDF file in Acrobat, you can modify bookmarks and thumbnails, as well as create other navigation devices such as text links or buttons. After you create a link (also known as a *hotspot*) or button, you can assign an action to it that determines what occurs when the link or button is activated with a mouse click.

Use the Bookmarks Palette

In Acrobat Reader, you use the Bookmarks palette to navigate to bookmark destinations. In Acrobat, you also use the Bookmarks palette to edit existing bookmarks and to add new ones. The Bookmarks palette is part of the Navigation pane. To open the Bookmarks palette, click the Bookmark tab. Figure 7-1 shows the Bookmarks palette for the Adobe Acrobat JavaScript Guide.

About the Bookmarks Palette Toolbar

Bookmarks are an important part of any multi-page PDF document. Viewers of your PDF files would have a hard time finding what they want without bookmarks. When you create bookmarks, edit bookmarks, or use bookmarks

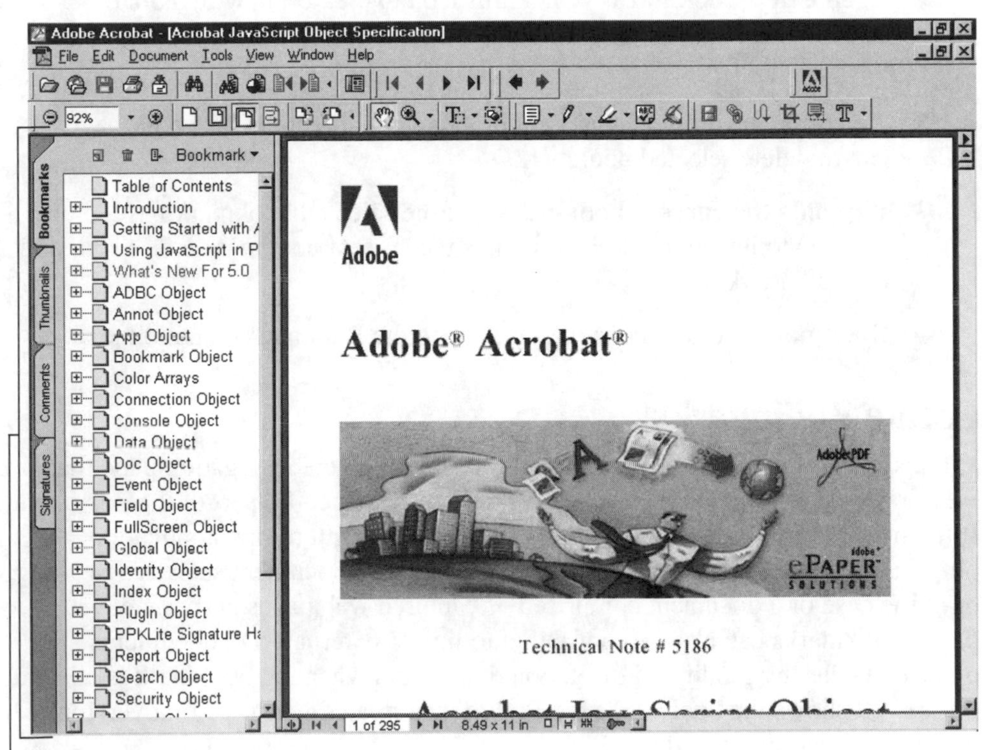

Bookmarks palette

FIGURE 7-1 In Acrobat, use the Bookmarks palette to navigate to, create, and edit bookmarks.

7

to navigate within a document, you can use the Bookmarks palette toolbar to streamline your work. The Bookmarks palette toolbar contains three tool icons and one menu icon, as shown in the following image:

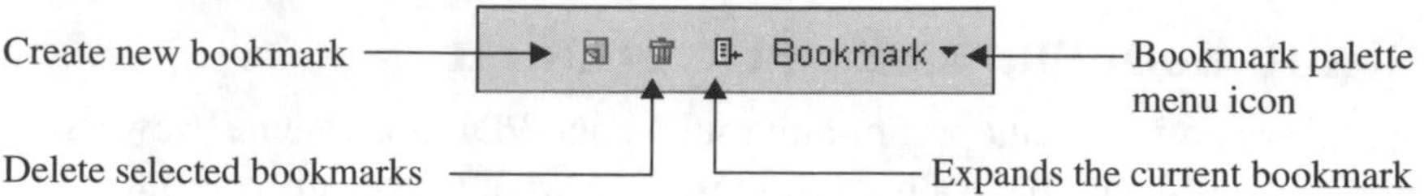

From left to right, you have the following at your disposal:

- **Create new bookmark** Click this icon to create a new bookmark. Specific instructions for creating bookmarks are presented in an upcoming section.
- **Delete selected bookmarks** Click the icon that looks like a garbage can to delete selected bookmarks.
- **Expands the current bookmark** If the selected bookmark has a plus sign (+) to its left, click the Expands the current bookmark icon to expand the bookmark.
- **Bookmark** Click the text icon to open the Bookmarks palette menu.

Create Bookmarks

A bookmark is a text link in the Bookmarks palette of the Navigation pane that viewers of your PDF documents use to navigate to a specific part of the document. If the bookmarks in the document are created from an authoring application plug-in, the bookmark is linked to a specific part of a document such as a heading, or in the case of a document comprised of captured web pages, a specific web page. Bookmarks can also be configured to link to external PDF documents and other PDF files by modifying the action that occurs when the bookmark is clicked. Figure 7-2 shows the bookmarks the PDFMaker created when the first version of this chapter was converted to a PDF file.

You can, however, create your own bookmarks to draw a viewer's attention to a specific view. You can also use bookmarks to open other PDF documents, or open other files. To create a document bookmark, do the following:

1. Open the Navigation pane, and click the Bookmarks tab to open the Bookmarks palette.

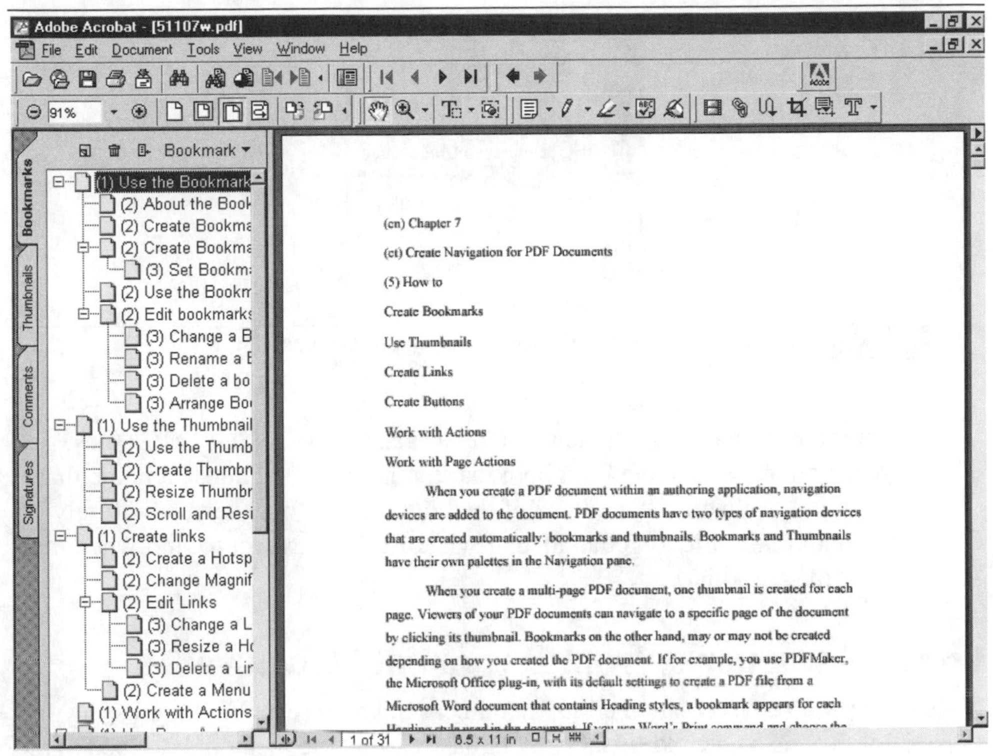

FIGURE 7-2 Use bookmarks to navigate to specific points in a document.

2. Click the bookmark above the place where you want the new bookmark to appear. If you do not specify a place for the new bookmark, it is added at the bottom of the list.

3. Use the Hand tool, Viewing tools, or menu commands to navigate to the part of the document where you want the bookmark to link.

NOTE *Remember, you can also link to a magnified view of a page to direct the reader's attention. You can magnify the page view by using the Zoom tool.*

4. Click the New Bookmark button, as shown in Figure 7-3. Alternatively, click the Bookmark icon and choose New Bookmark from the Bookmarks palette menu. After you click the New Bookmark button, the new bookmark appears below the bookmark you selected when you clicked the button. Acrobat gives the new bookmark the default name of Untitled. The bookmark name is highlighted, as shown in Figure 7-3.

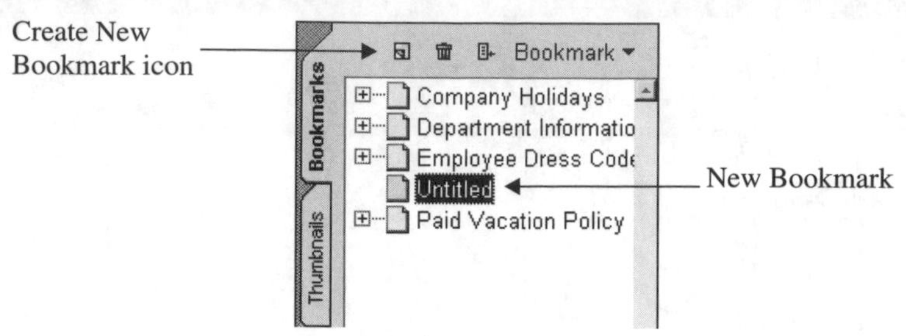

FIGURE 7-3 You can add bookmarks to the document as needed.

5. Enter a new name for the new bookmark, and press ENTER or RETURN. When choosing a name for a bookmark, remember to choose a name that accurately reflects the contents of the bookmark. Your viewers will rely on the bookmark title to get an idea of what they can expect to find when they click the bookmark.

Create Bookmarks from Document Structure

If the program used to create the PDF document did not create bookmarks to your satisfaction, you can add additional bookmarks by using the method described in the preceding section, or you can automate the process by choosing certain elements from the document structure to create bookmarks. To create bookmarks from the document structure, do the following:

1. Open the document for which you want to create bookmarks.
2. In the Navigation pane, click the Bookmarks tab to open the Bookmarks palette.
3. Click the triangle to the right of the word Bookmark; and, from the Bookmarks palette menu, choose New Bookmarks From Structure to open the Structure Elements dialog box, shown in the following image:

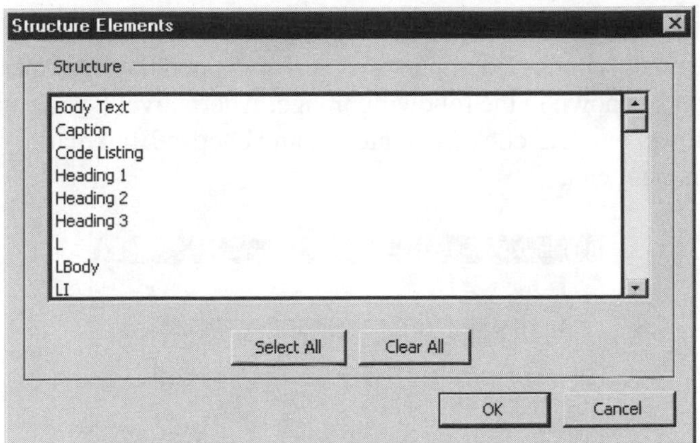

NOTE *The New Bookmarks From Structure command is dimmed if the document does not have elements Acrobat can use to create bookmarks.*

4. Click a structure element name to select it. To add additional structure elements, hold down SHIFT and click to add contiguous elements, or hold down CTRL and then click to add noncontiguous elements. To select all structure elements, click the Select All button.

5. Click OK, and Acrobat scans the document and creates a bookmark for each selected structure element located. The bookmarks are untitled and nested in tree fashion. Click the plus sign (+) to the left of the top element to expand the first bookmark. The bookmarks in the preceding illustration were created from a PDF file of this chapter, as created in Word, using the Caption structure element that notes where the figures and illustrations are inserted.

Modify Bookmark Properties

After you create a bookmark, you can modify the bookmark by changing its properties. You can modify the appearance of the bookmark, modify the view of the link destination, and modify the action that occurs when a user clicks the link. To set bookmark properties, do the following:

1. Click the bookmark whose properties you want to modify.

2. Click the triangle to the right of the word Bookmark; and from the Bookmarks palette menu, choose Bookmark Properties to open the Bookmark Properties dialog box, shown in the following image. Alternatively, you can right-click (Windows) or CTRL-click (Macintosh), and choose Bookmark Properties from the context menu.

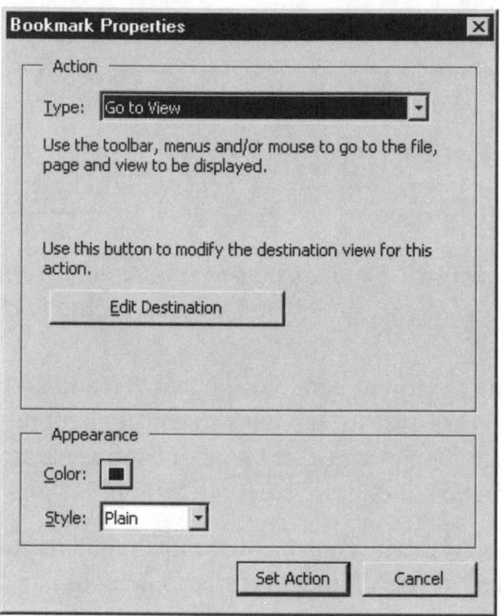

3. When you open the Bookmark Properties dialog box, the currently selected action for the bookmark is displayed. If the bookmark was created in an authoring application, the action is usually Go To View. Click the triangle to the right of the Action field, and choose an option from the drop-down menu. The other available actions are discussed in detail later in this chapter.
4. Click the Edit Destination button to change the link destination.
5. Click the triangle to the right of the Magnification field and choose an option from the drop-down menu. For more information on the magnification options, refer to the "Scroll and Change Page Magnification with Thumbnails" section that appears later in this chapter.

In addition to changing the Magnification of the linked view, you can also change the bookmark's destination page by navigating to a different destination with one of the navigation tools any time before performing step 8.

6. In the Appearance section, click the Color button and choose a color for the bookmark from the pop-up palette. You can choose one of the preset colors, or click Custom to create a custom color from the color picker.
7. In the Appearance section, click the triangle to the right of the Style field; and from the drop-down menu, choose one of the following options: Plain, Bold, Italic, or Bold & Italic. This determines the bookmark text style.

TIP *You can direct a reader's attention to important bookmarks by changing the bookmark text style and color.*

8. Click the Set Action button to apply the changes.

Use the Bookmarks Palette Menu

You use the Bookmarks palette menu to perform functions associated with bookmarks. You can use commands from the Bookmarks palette menu to modify bookmarks, navigate to bookmarks, and maintain the Bookmarks palette. To open the Bookmarks palette menu, follow these steps:

1. In the Navigation pane, click the Bookmarks tab to open the Bookmarks palette.
2. Click the triangle to the right of the word Bookmark to open the Bookmarks palette menu, shown in the following illustration:

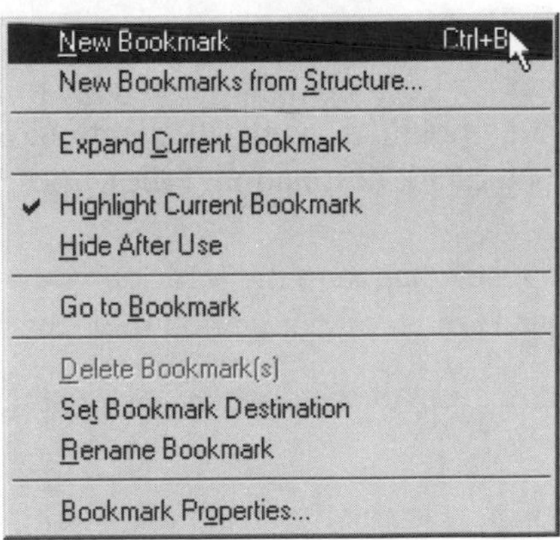

After you open the Bookmarks palette menu, click the menu command you want Acrobat to perform. Some of the commands in this menu have already been presented; others will do the same job as their toolbar counterparts. For example, to expand a bookmark, you can click the Expand Bookmark icon, click the plus sign (+) next to a collapsed bookmark, or choose the Expand Bookmark command from the Bookmarks palette menu. Detailed information about other relevant Bookmarks palette menu commands are discussed in upcoming sections.

Edit Bookmarks

You can edit existing bookmarks by changing the bookmark destination, renaming the bookmarks, deleting selected bookmarks, and rearranging the hierarchy of bookmarks. When you add new bookmarks to a document, you can specify the bookmark destination and view magnification. However, at times it may be preferable to create bookmarks first to lay out the document structure, and then modify the destination and view later. You can use the Bookmarks palette toolbar and menu to edit bookmarks. You can also right-click (Windows) or CTRL-click (Macintosh) to choose a command from the Bookmarks palette context menu, as shown in the following illustration:

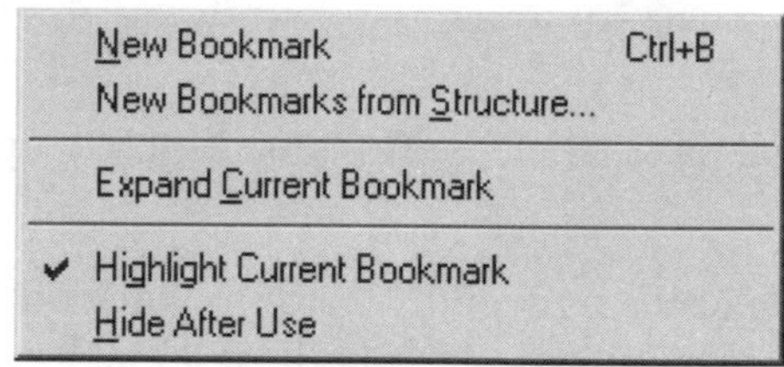

Change a Bookmark Destination

You can change the destination of a bookmark or change its magnification, or both. By modifying the view of a bookmark, you call attention to a specific part of the document. To modify a bookmark destination, follow these steps:

1. In the Document pane, change to the location you want the bookmark to link to by using the Hand tool, navigation tools, or menu commands.
2. Change the magnification of the document by using the viewing tools or menu commands.
3. Choose Set Bookmark Destination from the Bookmarks palette menu, and then click Yes in the Warning dialog box to set the new destination of the link. Alternatively, you can right-click (Windows) or CTRL-click (Macintosh), and choose Set Destination from the context menu.

Rename a Bookmark

Another edit you may need to perform is renaming a bookmark. You have two methods available to change a bookmark name:

1. Select the bookmark, and then click inside the text box.
2. Enter a new name for the bookmark, and then press ENTER or RETURN.

Alternatively, you can

1. Select the bookmark.
2. Choose Rename Bookmark from the Bookmarks palette menu.
3. Enter a new name for the bookmark, and then press ENTER or RETURN.

Delete a Bookmark

You can delete any bookmark. When you delete a bookmark, you do not change the content of a document, you merely remove a link. If you created a PDF document that has several heading levels, you may want to consider deleting a few bookmarks to simplify navigation. To delete a bookmark, follow these steps:

1. Select the bookmark. To add contiguous bookmarks to the selection, press SHIFT and click the bookmark(s) you want to add to the selection. To add noncontiguous bookmarks to the selection, press CTRL and click the bookmark(s) you want to add to the selection.
2. Click the Delete Selected Bookmarks icon, which looks like a garbage can. Alternatively, choose Edit | Delete or choose Delete Selected Bookmarks from the Bookmarks palette menu.
3. Click OK in the Adobe Acrobat Warning dialog box to delete the bookmarks.

Deleting bookmarks cannot be undone.

Arrange Bookmarks

When you create a PDF document, bookmarks are created in descending order from the first page of the document to the last. Acrobat nests bookmarks when you convert a document with multiple heading levels, or if you use the Create Bookmarks From Structure command. You can create your own bookmark nests to organize a cluttered Bookmarks palette. To nest a bookmark or group of bookmarks under another bookmark, follow these steps:

1. Select the bookmark(s) you want to nest. You can select contiguous or noncontiguous bookmarks.
2. Click and drag the bookmarks toward the bookmark under which you want to nest them. As you drag the bookmarks toward another bookmark, a left-pointing arrow appears, as shown in the following image:

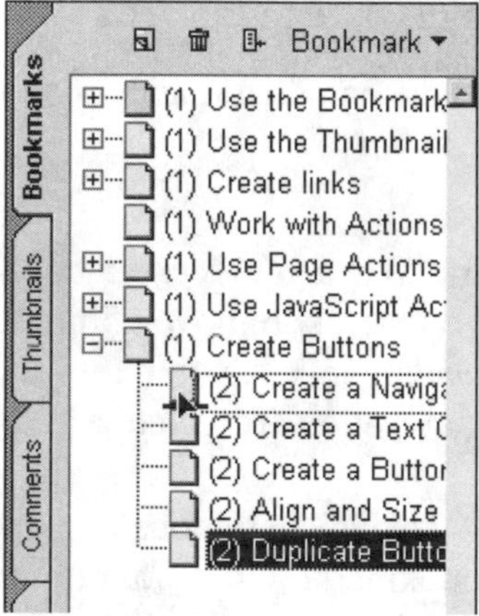

3. Release the mouse button. As soon as you release the mouse button, Acrobat expands the bookmark, as shown in Figure 7-4. You can collapse the bookmark by clicking the minus sign (–).

Remove a bookmark from a nested position by doing the following:

1. Expand the bookmark that contains the bookmark(s) you want to remove from a nested position.
2. Click the bookmark(s) you want to move.
3. Drag the bookmarks to the left and position them under the title of the parent bookmark. You know the bookmarks are positioned properly when you see a black line under the parent bookmark name and a left-pointing arrow, as shown in Figure 7-4.

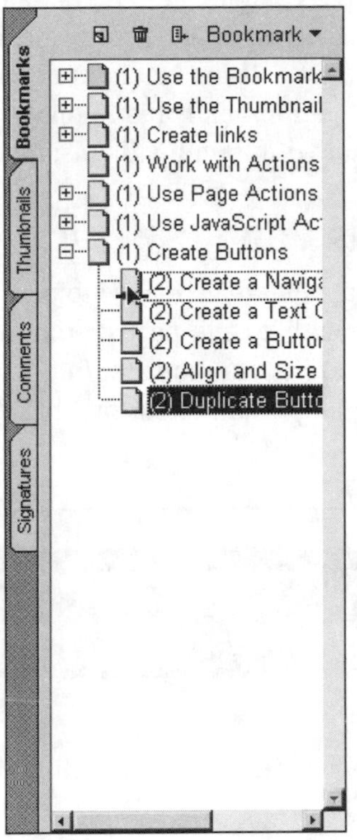

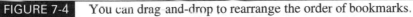

FIGURE 7-4 You can drag and-drop to rearrange the order of bookmarks.

7

NOTE *When you select and drag a branch that has children, the children of the parent are moved as well, maintaining the structure of the branch.*

4. Release the mouse button, and the Adobe Acrobat Warning dialog box appears asking you to confirm that you want to move the bookmarks.
5. Click OK, and Acrobat moves the bookmark(s) out of a nested position.

Use the Thumbnails Palette

When you convert a file to PDF format, Acrobat creates a thumbnail snapshot of each document page. Thumbnails are neatly arranged by page order in the Thumbnails palette, which resides in the Navigation pane. You can use thumbnails as navigation devices when reading a document, as well as to reorder pages, a technique that is discussed in Chapter 11. Thumbnails are also used to print and change the magnification of pages. To access the Thumbnails palette, choose Window | Thumbnails or press F4. If the Navigation pane is open, but another palette is displayed, click the Thumbnails tab to open the palette. Figure 7-5 shows the Thumbnails palette with thumbnails displayed in large format.

Use the Thumbnails Palette Menu

The Thumbnails palette has a menu that you use to perform tasks in the Thumbnails palette. The menu has commands to edit pages, embed or remove embedded thumbnails, and change the size of thumbnails. In upcoming sections, you'll learn to use the commands that pertain to editing thumbnails. In Chapter 11,

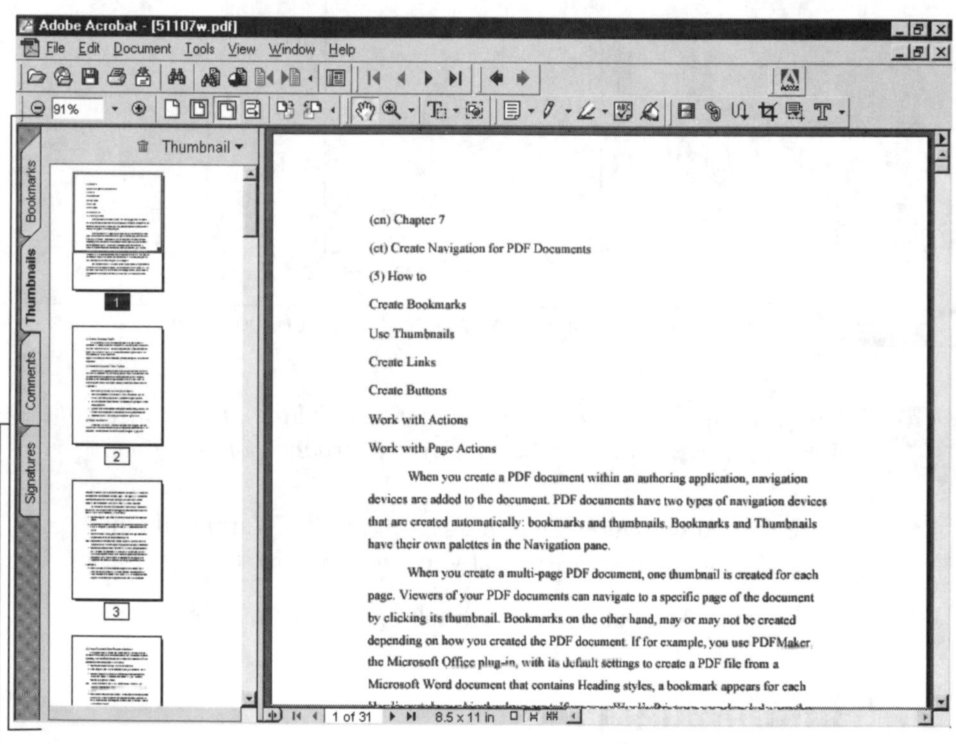

FIGURE 7-5 Use thumbnails to navigate and edit a PDF document.

you'll learn to use thumbnails to edit and reorder document pages. To open the Thumbnails palette menu, do the following:

1. Open the Navigation pane and click the Thumbnails tab.
2. Click the Thumbnail icon to open the Thumbnails palette menu, shown in the following image:

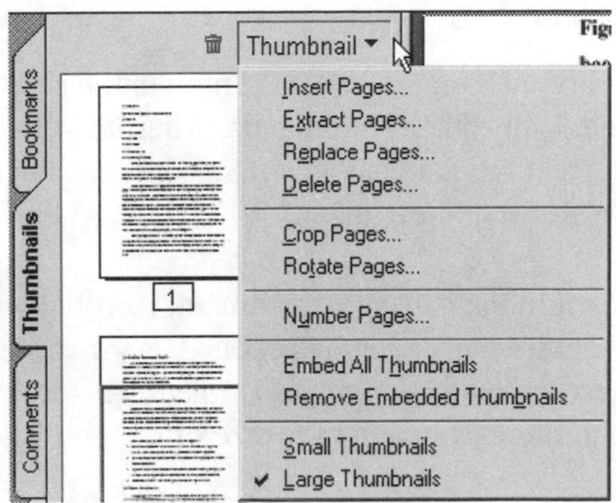

Alternatively, you can right-click (Windows) or CTRL-click (Macintosh) within the Thumbnails palette to open a context menu. The Thumbnails palette context is a watered-down version of the Thumbnails palette menu. However, you may prefer to use the context menu when you need to access its commands quickly.

7

Create Thumbnails

When you create a PDF document in an authoring application or with Acrobat Distiller, you are given the option to create thumbnails or not. Thumbnails increase the file size of the published PDF document by approximately 3K per thumbnail for a page with images; thumbnails for pages with text are only slightly smaller. When you create a document without thumbnails, Acrobat creates them dynamically when you open the Thumbnails palette. This can take several seconds for a large document. You can choose to embed thumbnails to circumvent the redraw every time you open the palette. You can easily remove embedded thumbnails in the future if desired. To embed all thumbnails within a document, follow these steps:

1. Open the Navigation pane and click the Thumbnails tab to open the Thumbnails palette.

2. Open the Thumbnails palette menu and choose Embed Thumbnails. Alternatively, you can choose the Embed Thumbnails command from the Thumbnails palette context menu.

To remove embedded thumbnails from a document, do the following:

1. Open the Navigation pane, and click the Thumbnails tab to access the Thumbnails palette.
2. Click the Thumbnail icon to open the Thumbnails palette menu, and choose Remove Embedded Thumbnails. Alternatively, you can right-click (Windows) or CTRL-click (Macintosh), and choose the Remove Embedded Thumbnails from the context menu.

After you remove thumbnails from a document, Acrobat will create them on-the-fly whenever the Thumbnails palette is opened. As mentioned previously, this may take considerable time with a lengthy document. As a rule, you should only remove embedded thumbnails when the file size of the published PDF document is a factor.

You can also embed or remove embedded thumbnails for multiple PDF files using Acrobat Batch Processing. For more information on Batch Processing, refer to Chapter 11.

Resize Thumbnails

When you open the Thumbnails palette, all thumbnails are displayed at full size. Unless you resize the width of the Navigation pane, large thumbnails are displayed in a single column. If you prefer, you can display more thumbnails in the Navigation pane by choosing Small Thumbnails from the Thumbnails palette menu. After you choose this command, thumbnails are displayed at half their normal size, as shown in the following image. To return thumbnails to their original size, choose Large Thumbnails from the Thumbnails palette menu.

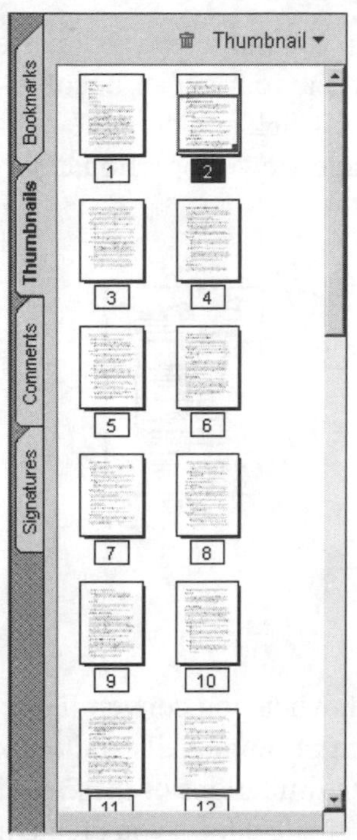

Scroll and Change Page Magnification with Thumbnails

When you view a document page that fits within the confines of the Document pane, a red border surrounds the thumbnail of the page. If you view the page at increased magnification, the red border is cropped and positioned to correspond with the page view in the Document pane. Use this border as a navigation device by selecting the Hand tool, clicking either the top or bottom boundary of the border, and then dragging. Note that if you view the page in Continuous or Continuous Facing mode, you will not be able to advance to the next page by dragging the border boundary.

You can also use the thumbnail border to change magnification of a page. At the lower-right corner of the border is a filled red rectangle. Use this rectangle to resize the red border that surrounds a thumbnail, and consequently change the magnification of the page. As you move your cursor toward the filled rectangle at the lower corner of the border, your cursor becomes a double-headed arrow, as shown in the following image. Click and drag the rectangle to change your view of the page. To change the page view proportionately, click and drag the rectangle while holding down the SHIFT key.

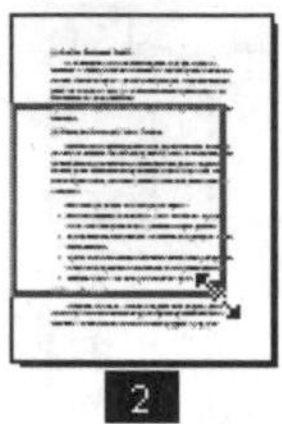

Create Links

As you have already learned, when you convert a document into PDF format, navigation devices in the form of thumbnails and bookmarks are created for you. You can, however, exceed the limitations of these rudimentary navigation devices by creating links. When you create a link, you create a hotspot in the document that changes the user's cursor into a pointing hand when a mouse passes over it; the same thing happens for a link on a Web page. You can create links for text or images in a PDF document, or you can create a link on a blank area of the document. The links you create can be visible or invisible.

Links give you tremendous flexibility. You can create links that change the view of a document, load another document, open a web page, load a multimedia element, and more. You can specify the appearance of a link as a visible or invisible rectangle, as well as specify the type of highlight that appears when a user's mouse passes over the link. The first step in creating a link is to define the active area of the link, also known as a hotspot.

Create a Hotspot

As it relates to PDF documents, a *hotspot* is an active area of the document that, when clicked by a user, links to an action. You create a hotspot with the Link tool, which looks like two interconnecting links of a chain. Use the Link tool to define the boundary of the hotspot as follows:

1. From the Editing toolbar, select the Link tool, as shown in the image on the left. After you select the tool and move your cursor into the Document

pane, it becomes a cross hair. As long as the Link tool is selected, any other links in the document, even invisible ones, are displayed.

2. In the Document pane, click a spot to define one of the hotspot corners, and then drag across and down. As you drag, a dotted bounding box gives you a preview of the area you are selecting, as shown in the following image:

Staff Contact Information

3. When the bounding box surrounds the area you want to define as a hotspot, release the mouse button.

TIP *To create a text link, select the Link tool, hold* CTRL *(Windows) or* OPTION *(Macintosh), and the cursor becomes an I-beam. Click the target text to create a hotspot the exact size of the text.*

After you create the hotspot, the Link Properties dialog box appears, as shown in the following image:

Link Properties

Appearance
Type: Visible Rectangle
Width: Thin
Highlight: Invert
Color:
Style: Solid

Action
Type: Go to View
Use the toolbar, menus and/or mouse to go to the file, page and view to be displayed.

Use the current page's zoom and position in the destination window.
Magnification: Fit View
Page 1

Set Link
Cancel

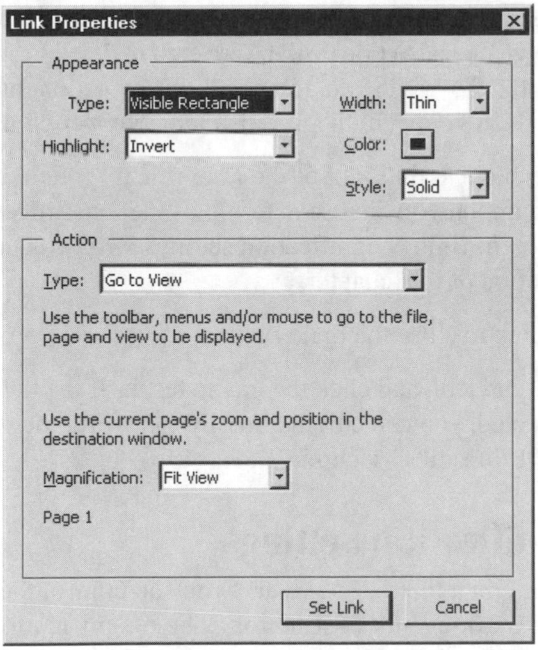

4. Click the triangle to the right of the Type field, and, from the drop-down menu, choose one of the following:
   - **Visible Rectangle** This option creates a hotspot with a visible rectangle at its perimeter.
   - **Invisible Rectangle** This option creates a hotspot that is not visible. If you choose Invisible Rectangle, the Width, Color, and Style options are not valid and are no longer displayed.
5. If you choose Visible Rectangle, click the triangle to the right of the Width field and choose Thin, Medium, or Thick from the drop-down menu. This option defines the thickness of the hotspot border.
6. Click the Color button and choose the rectangle color from the pop-up palette. To choose a color other than the presets, click the Custom button, and choose a color from the system color-picker.
7. Click the triangle to the right of the Style field, and choose Solid or Dashed. This option defines the line style for the hotspot border.
8. The default link action is Go To View. You can choose another action by clicking the triangle to the right of the Type field and selecting an option from the drop-down menu. Actions will be covered in detail in an upcoming section of this chapter. To use the default Go To View action, navigate to the part of the document you want displayed when a viewer clicks the link.
9. Click the triangle to the right of the Magnification field and choose an option. The option you choose determines the magnification of the view connected to the link. Magnification settings will be discussed in detail in the next section of this chapter.
10. Click Set Link to close the dialog box.
11. Select the Hand tool, and click the link to test it. If the link does not perform as you expected, you can edit the link by following the instructions in the upcoming "Edit Links" section.

Change Magnification Settings

When you create or edit a link or bookmark, you can control the magnification setting of the bookmark or link destination. The magnification settings are changed in the Magnification field of the Bookmark Properties dialog box and the Link Properties dialog box. In the Magnification field of either, choose one of the following options:

- **Fixed** Choose this option to display the link or bookmark at the level of magnification and page position that were in effect when you created the bookmark or link. When you choose this option, you can use the zoom tools, view tools, Magnification window in the status bar, or scroll bar to adjust the view before you finish modifying the bookmark or link properties.
- **Fit View** Choose this option, and when selected, the link or bookmark will display the view of the page that was selected when the link or bookmark was created or edited. Note that this view will differ at different monitor resolutions.
- **Fit In Window** Choose this option, and a selected link or bookmark destination will be sized to fit the destination window.
- **Fit Height** Choose this option, and the link or bookmark destination will be displayed at the page height when the bookmark or link was created.
- **Fit Width** Choose this option, and the link or bookmark destination will be displayed at the page width when the bookmark or link was created. If you choose the Fit Width option, images on the page may be pixelated.
- **Fit Visible** Choose this option, and the visible contents of the bookmark or link destination will be sized to fit the Document pane.
- **Inherit Zoom** Choose this option, and the bookmark or link destination will be displayed at the viewer magnification level when the bookmark or link is selected.

NOTE *The Magnification setting you select will stay in effect for future links you create until you change it.*

Edit Links

When the need arises, you can edit any property of a link. You can resize the link, change its destination, change the level of magnification for the link, or change the appearance of the link. When you edit a link, the changes apply only to the selected link.

Change Link Properties

To change link properties, do the following:

1. Select the Link tool.
2. Double-click the link you want to edit and the Link Properties dialog box appears. Alternatively, you can right-click (Windows) or CTRL-click (Macintosh) the link, and then choose Properties from the Context menu.
3. Modify the Link Properties as described in the "Create a Hotspot" section, earlier in the chapter.

Resize a Hotspot

When you use the Link tool to create a hotspot, the resulting hotspot may not be sized properly. When you create a hotspot, it's better to make it a tad larger than needed, unless, of course, you have several hotspots in close proximity. An oversized hotspot gives your viewer a bigger target area. You can change the size of a hotspot at any time by doing the following:

1. Select the Link tool.
2. Click the hotspot that you want to resize. After you click the hotspot, eight handles in the form of solid black rectangles appear on the hotspot perimeter.
3. Click and drag any of the corner handles to create a larger hotspot. If you hold down the SHIFT key while you drag, the hotspot resizes proportionately.
4. Click the handle in the middle of the left or right side of the hotspot, and drag right to make the hotspot wider or left to make it narrower.
5. Click the handle in the middle of the top or bottom of the hotspot, and drag up or down to make the hotspot taller or shorter.

Delete a Link

If you decide a link is no longer needed, you can delete it from the document by doing the following:

1. Select the Link tool.

2. Choose Edit | Delete. Alternatively, select the link, right-click (Windows) or CTRL-click (Macintosh), and choose Delete from the context menu or press DELETE.
3. After you press DELETE, Acrobat displays a warning dialog box, prompting you to verify the deletion. Click OK to delete the link.

Create a Menu Using Links

When you create a PDF document for a specific purpose, such as an employee manual or product presentation, adding a menu is a great way to direct your readers to specific parts of a document. Of course, you can rely on the Acrobat built-in navigation devices, bookmarks and thumbnails. However, if your intended audience is not familiar with Acrobat Reader, your document will be easier to navigate if you create a menu.

If you create a document in a word processing program, you can create a menu page as the first page of the document. On the menu page, list the major parts of the document you want your readers to be able to select by clicking links. Create the rest of the document, and then convert it to PDF using the application's Print command and then choosing Acrobat Distiller; or, if the application supports it, convert the document to PDF using the application's Save As or Export command. Open the document in Acrobat and use the Link tool to create a link for each menu item. After you create the links for the menu page, choose File | Document Summary | Open Options. In the Document Open Options dialog box, choose Page Only. Click OK to close the Document Open Options dialog box, and then save the document. When your viewers open the document, the first thing they will see is your menu page with the Navigation pane closed. Figure 7-6 shows a menu created in Microsoft Word with links added in Acrobat.

Work with Actions

When you create a link or bookmark, the default action is Go To View. However, Acrobat supplies you with a plethora of actions from which to choose. You can also apply actions to form fields and individual pages. When you apply an action to a page, the action determines what the viewer sees or what happens when the page loads.

You set actions for bookmarks and links in the Type field of their respective dialog boxes. You can also add actions to individual pages of the document. For more information on page actions, refer to the upcoming "Set a Page Action"

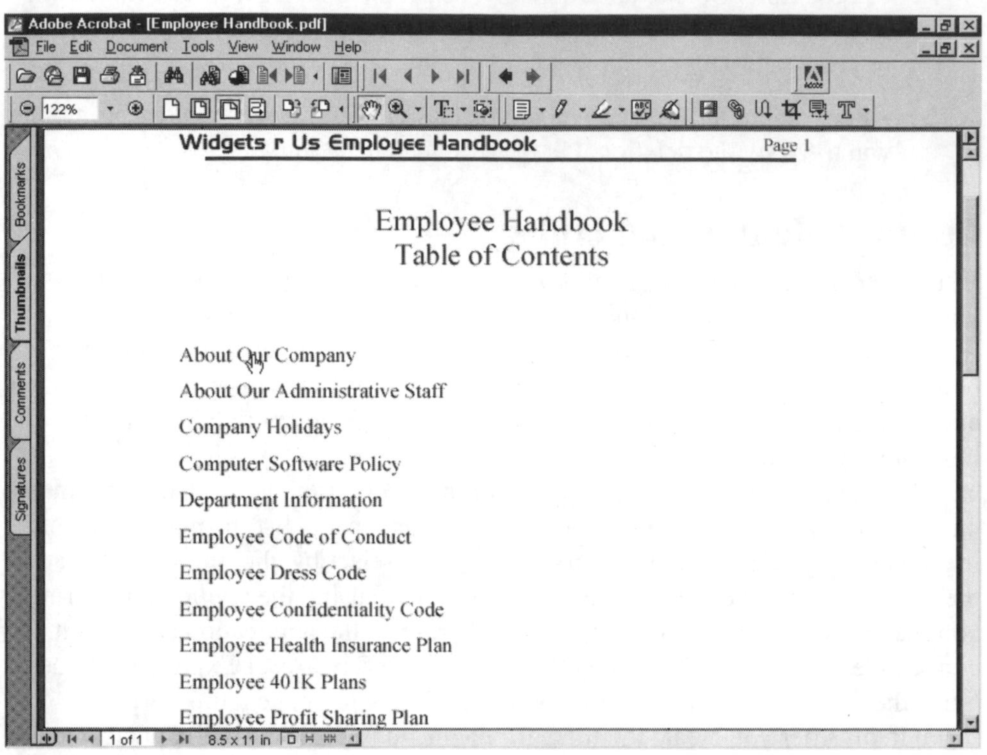

FIGURE 7-6 Create a linked menu to simplify navigation for your readers.

section. To learn more about assigning actions to form fields, refer to Chapter 9. To add interactivity to a link, bookmark, form field, or page, choose from the following actions:

- **Execute Menu Item** Use this action to execute a Menu command. Even though you can choose any Acrobat command to execute as an action, the most logical choices would be to open another file, choose one of the navigation options from the Document menu, or choose one of the magnification options from the View menu.

NOTE *If you distribute your document to users with Acrobat Reader, make sure the Menu command you choose is also an Acrobat Reader Menu command.*

- **Go To View** In most applicable dialog boxes, this is the default action. Use this action to advance to another page or view in the current document or another PDF file.

TIP *To navigate to another PDF file using the Go To View action, select the action and then choose File | Open to open the document you want to open when the action is executed. Navigate to the page of the document you want to appear when the action is executed, and click Set Link.*

- **Import Form Data** Use this action to specify a file from which to import form data. The imported data is inserted in the active form. For more information on working with forms, refer to Chapter 9.
- **JavaScript** Use this action to run a JavaScript. When you choose this option, you can create or edit a JavaScript within a text editor.
- **Movie** Use this action to execute a QuickTime or AVI movie. To use this action, you must have a QuickTime or AVI movie within the document. For more information on adding movies to your PDF documents, refer to Chapter 10.
- **Open File** Use this action to open a non-PDF file. In order for the action to execute, the viewer must have the native application to which the file is associated.
- **Read Article** Use this action to link an article thread within the current document or another PDF document. For more information on creating articles, refer to Chapter 8.
- **Reset Form** Use this action to clear all previously entered data in a form.
- **Show/Hide Field** Use this option to create an action that displays or hides a field in a PDF document.
- **Sound** Use this action to play a sound embedded with the PDF document. For more information on working with sounds in PDF documents, refer to Chapter 10.
- **Submit Form** Use this action with a button to submit data from a form to a URL.
- **World Wide Web Link** Use this action when you need to create a link to a URL on the World Wide Web.

Use Page Actions

You can make your PDF documents more interactive by specifying an action to perform a certain task when a page opens or closes. For example, you can use an action to play a movie when a page opens and play a sound when a page closes.

Set a Page Action

Set a Page Action to execute an action when a page loads or unloads. You can have more than one action occur when a page opens or closes. If you choose multiple actions, you can edit the order in which the actions execute. To set a Page Action, follow these steps:

1. Choose Document | Set Page Action to open the Page Actions dialog box, shown in the following image:

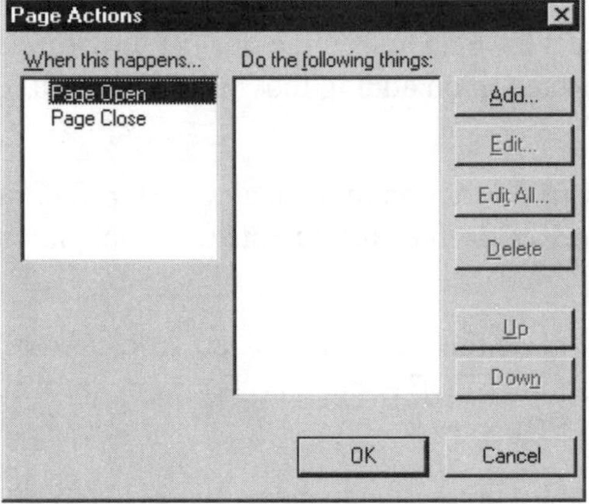

2. Click Page Open to execute an action when a page loads. Click Page Close to execute an action when the page closes.
3. Click Add to open the Add An Action dialog box.
4. Click the triangle to the right of the Type field, and choose an action from the drop-down menu, as shown in the following image:

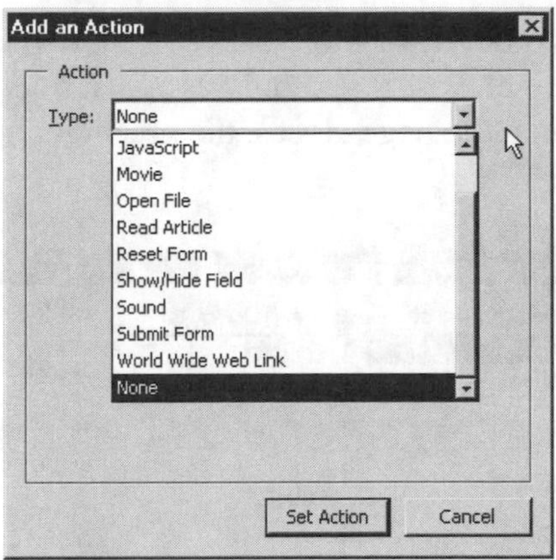

5. Click Set Action to add the action to the events that occur when the page loads.
6. Click the Add button to add additional events to the list.
7. Click OK to close the Page Actions dialog box.
8. Save the document.

The next time you open the document and select the page you applied the actions to, they execute.

Edit Page Actions

The majority of the time, you assign Page Actions and they perform without a hitch. However, sometimes the actions do not execute in proper order, or perhaps you think an action should be deleted or added. When this occurs, you can easily edit Page Actions by doing the following:

1. Navigate to the page whose actions need editing.
2. Choose Document | Set Page Actions to open the Page Actions dialog box. The following image shows the dialog box as it appears when actions are applied to a page. Notice the green dot next to Page Open and Page Close.

The dot signifies that one or more actions occur when the page opens and when the page closes. If you only assign actions to execute when the page opens or when the page closes, the green dot appears next to that particular event.

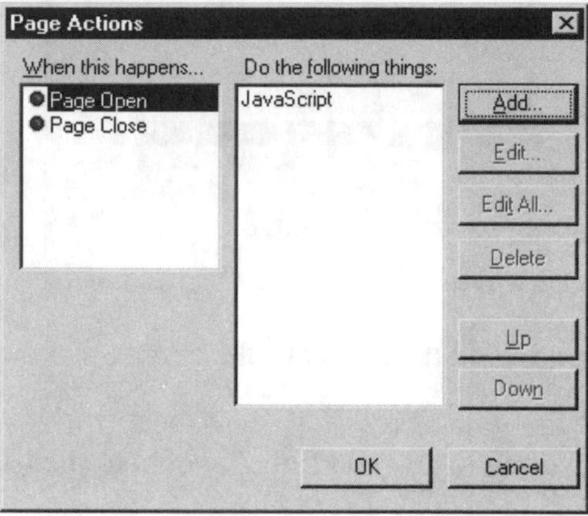

3. In the When This Happens window, select the event you want to modify.
4. To add an action, click the Add button.
5. To delete an action, click the Delete button.
6. To edit an action, click the Edit button.
7. To rearrange the order in which actions execute, select an action, and click the Up or Down button. If the action is at the top of the list, only the Down button will be available, and vice versa if the action is at the bottom of the list. If the action is in the middle of the list, both buttons are available. If only one action is on the list, both buttons are dimmed out, as shown in the previous image.
8. When you have finished editing the page actions, click OK.

Use JavaScript Actions

You can add functionality and interactivity to your PDF document by using JavaScript to access database information, control navigation, access information from the Internet, and more. In Acrobat 5.0, you have more JavaScript actions to work with than ever before.

JavaScript is an object-orientated programming language. If you have designed web pages, you may be familiar with JavaScript. Each JavaScript object has associated methods and properties. Acrobat JavaScript uses standard JavaScript objects and has its own set of unique objects, such as the Bookmark object. Unfortunately, a detailed discussion of using JavaScript with Acrobat is beyond the scope of this book. The definitive resource for using JavaScript with Acrobat is the Acrobat JavaScript guide, a 295-page PDF document. You can access the Acrobat JavaScript guide by choosing Help | Acrobat JavaScript guide.

Create a JavaScript Action

You can use the JavaScript Action with form fields, bookmarks, and links, or create global JavaScript that can be used for an entire document. When you choose the JavaScript action, you create the actual script in a text editor. As previously mentioned, there are myriad uses for JavaScript with PDF documents. The following steps show how to use JavaScript to display the current date when a page loads:

1. Select the Form tool, as shown in the illustration on the left.
2. Navigate to the document page where you want the date to appear.
3. Click inside the document where you want the date to appear, and then drag down and across. Release thc mouse button when the field is appropriately sized and the Field Properties dialog box is displayed, as shown in the following image:

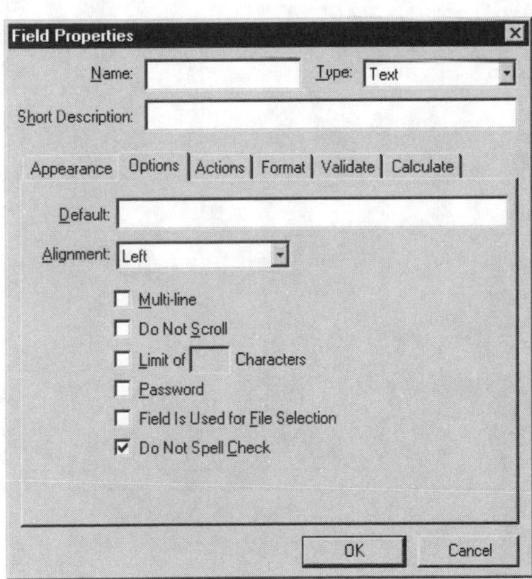

4. In the Name field, enter **'todaysDate'**. This is the name of the form field that will display the current date, which will be retrieved from the host computer using JavaScript you'll create in a future step.
5. Click the Appearance tab, and deselect the Border Color and Background Color.
6. In the Text section, accept the defaults. Alternatively, you can specify Text Color by clicking the button and choosing a color from the pop-up palette. You can also specify the Font Style and Size by clicking the triangle to the right of each field and choosing an option from the drop-down menu.
7. In the Common Properties section, select Read Only. This prevents viewers from entering a value in the field.
8. Click OK to close the Field Properties dialog box.
9. Choose Document | Set Page Action to open the Page Actions dialog box.
10. Click Page Open, and then click the Add button.
11. In the Add An Action dialog box, choose JavaScript from the drop-down menu, and then click Edit to open the JavaScript Edit dialog box, shown in the following image:

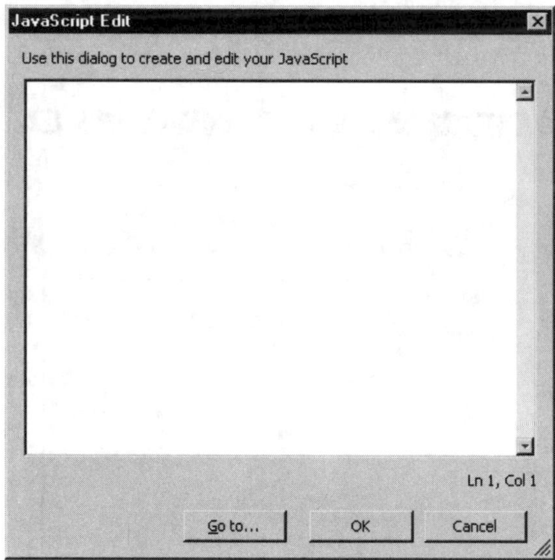

12. In the text edit window, enter the following JavaScript code:

```
var today = util.printd("mmmm d, yyyy", new Date());
this.getField('todaysDate').value = today ;
```

The first line of code creates a variable called *today* and sets its value to the current date (*new Date()*). The first part of the value *printd* method of the *util* object formats the date where *mmmm* is the long form of the month, *d* is the day in numeric form, and *yyyy* is the four-digit representation of the year. The second line of code sets the value of the *todaysDate* field you created in step 4, equal to the variable *today.* To display the day name before the date, modify the code to read as follows:

```
var today = util.printd("dddd, mmmm d, yyyy", new Date());
this.getField('todaysDate').value = today ;
```

NOTE *When you create JavaScript that uses variables, be aware that variables are case sensitive. For example, if you refer to the variable as "today" in one line of code and "Today" in another, the JavaScript will not execute.*

The addition of *dddd* displays adds the name of the day to the value of the variable *today*. The date is returned as text data, or as it is known in the programming world, *string* data. The code between the quotation marks is what returns the current date when the page opens. Notice the addition of commas and spaces. This tidies up the formatting. Without them, everything would run together and the result would be something like, MondayAugust22010 instead of Monday, August 2, 2010.

NOTE *JavaScript programming language has formatting rules, as does the language with which this book was written. In programmer speak, formatting protocol is known as* syntax. *When your JavaScript has a syntax error, it is noted at the bottom of the Edit JavaScript dialog box.*

13. Click OK to close the JavaScript Edit dialog box.

14. Click OK to close the Page Actions dialog box, and then save the document.

The next time you open the document, the date will be displayed where you created the form field. If the date does not appear, or the formatting is incorrect, you will have to edit the JavaScript as described in the next section.

Edit a JavaScript Action

When you create complex multi-line JavaScript code, it's easy to make a mistake. If you mistype a variable name, or choose the wrong method of a JavaScript object, your script will fall flatter than a cake without enough yeast. When this happens, you need to put on your thinking cap, or perhaps deerstalker cap, as you may have to do a bit of Sherlock Holmes–style deducting to figure out where your script went wrong. To edit a JavaScript action, select the link, button, or form field the JavaScript is assigned to; open the Actions section of the dialog box; click the Edit button to reopen the JavaScript Edit dialog box, and then examine the script. Make sure you have chosen the proper object, and the proper method of the object, for the action you want to occur when the script executes. Note that many failed scripts are the result of typographical errors.

TIP *If you prefer working in a text editor when creating JavaScript, choose Edit | Preferences, and then choose JavaScript. In the JavaScript Editor section, choose external editor, and then enter the path of the external editor executable (.exe) file. After changing the preference, whenever you edit JavaScript, Acrobat launches the external editor. After you enter the JavaScript, choose the external editor Save command before setting the JavaScript action in Acrobat.*

How to Master JavaScript

JavaScript is a wonderful tool that you can use to make your PDF documents more interactive. However, JavaScript does have a learning curve. The good news is that you do not have to know all of the JavaScript objects and methods. When you decide to add a JavaScript action to a PDF document, research the Acrobat JavaScript guide to find the proper object and method for the result you want to achieve. Remember, the Acrobat JavaScript guide is a PDF document so you can use the Find command to search for a keyword or phrase. If you want to master JavaScript, take the advice of a major athletic shoe company slogan and Just Do It. You may also want to consider investing in a good JavaScript book to learn the proper syntax of the JavaScript programming language. Ask your local bookseller for a copy of *JavaScript: A Beginner's Guide* by John Pollock (ISBN: 0-07-213140-3) or *JavaScript: The Complete Reference* by Thomas Powell and Fritz Schneider (ISBN: 0-07-219127-9), both published by Osborne McGraw-Hill. You can also order either book online at http://www.osborne.com.

Create Buttons

Buttons are another useful navigation device for your readers. When you create a multi-page document, adding buttons to navigate to the Next and Previous page makes it easier for your viewers to navigate the document, especially if they are not familiar with Acrobat Reader. Buttons are form elements. Buttons, as they relate to forms, will be covered in detail in Chapter 9. The sections that follow show how to create a menu bar for your documents.

Create a Navigation Menu

Experienced Acrobat Reader users are adept at using bookmarks and thumbnails to navigate a document. Bookmarks and thumbnails are even intuitive enough for inexperienced Acrobat Readers to quickly understand how to use the navigation devices. However, if you create a multi-page document for a client, or want to create a professional-looking document, you can create a Navigation menu. A typical Navigation menu functions like a web page navigation bar. The menu has links that connect to specific parts of the document. Most Navigation menus you create for multi-page documents will have a link to the document Table of Contents, a link to the document Index, and links to navigate to the Next page and Previous page.

If you use a Word processing program as the authoring application for your document, you could create a header and footer with the text and graphics needed for the menu. However, this would be tedious work in Acrobat, as you would have to create the navigation bar links for each page of the document. A much simpler solution is to use the Form tool to create the buttons for your Navigation menu.

When you create buttons with the Form tool, you can quickly create a Navigation menu on the first page of the document, and then duplicate it for the remaining pages of the document. To create a Navigation menu, follow these steps:

1. Navigate to the first page of the document.
2. Select the Form tool, shown on the left.

The Navigation menu in this example will have two text buttons, and two buttons with icons. The first step is to create the text buttons.

Create a Text-Only Button

You can use text-only buttons for many purposes. When you create a Navigation menu, you use buttons as navigation devices. You can create a text-only button with either a border or background color, or neither. To create a text-only button, follow the steps:

1. Select the Form tool as outlined previously.
2. Click the spot on the document where you want the button to appear, and then drag down and across to define the button area. You do not have to be precise, as you can resize the button later. After you define the button area, release the mouse button and the Field Properties dialog box opens, as shown in the following image. This image shows the Field Properties dialog box as it appears when creating a button.

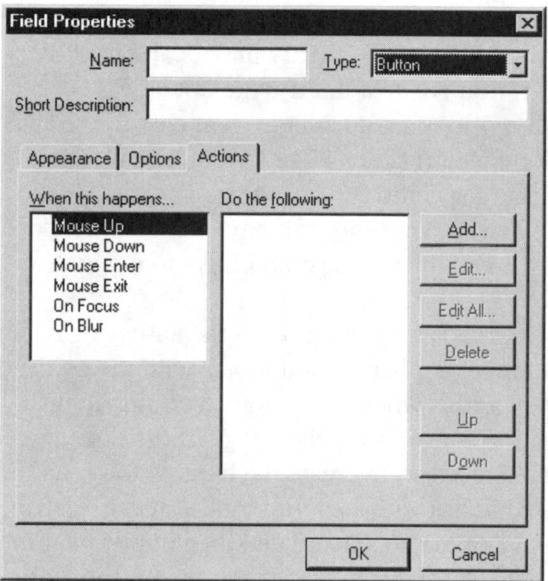

3. In the Name field, enter a name for the button. The name that you choose is only for editing purposes. It is only visible when the Form tool is selected. Choose a name that reflects what the button actually does.
4. In the Type field, choose Button.
5. In the Appearance section, deselect Border Color and Background Color. When you create a Navigation menu, less is more. Adding a border color and background color to the button detracts from the appearance of the menu.

6. Click the Text Color button and choose a color for the button text.
7. Accept the default font style (Helvetica Bold), or click the triangle to the right of the Font field and choose a font style from the drop-down menu.
8. Accept the default font size, or click the triangle to the right of the Size field and choose an option from the drop-down menu. Alternatively, you can enter a value in the field, and press ENTER or RETURN.
9. Click the Options tab to reveal the Options section of the Field Properties dialog box.
10. Click the triangle to the right of the Layout field and choose Text Only from the drop-down menu.
11. In the Text field, enter the text you want to appear on the face of the button. The following image shows the Field Properties dialog box Options section, as it would appear when creating a text-only button that links to a Table of Contents.

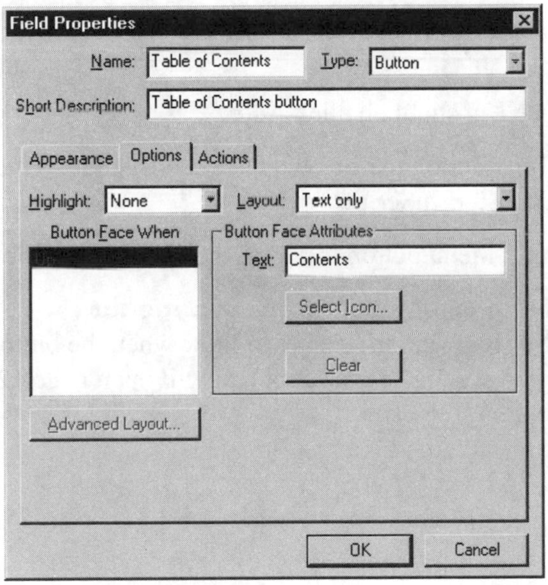

12. Click the Actions tab to reveal the Actions section of the Field Properties dialog box, as shown in the following image:

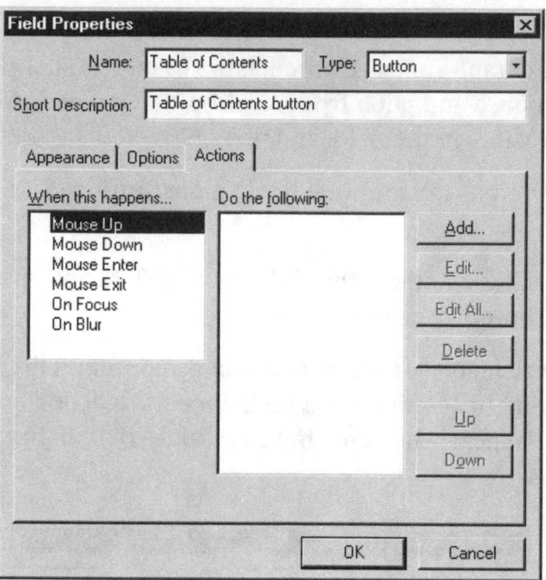

13. Click Mouse Up, and then click Add.

14. In the Add An Action dialog box, click the triangle to the right of the Type field and choose JavaScript.

15. Click the Edit Menu button to reveal the JavaScript Edit dialog box.

16. Enter the following JavaScript: **`this.pageNum = x`**, where x is the page number you want the reader to view when the button is clicked. The following image shows JavaScript that will open page 125 in a document when the button is clicked.

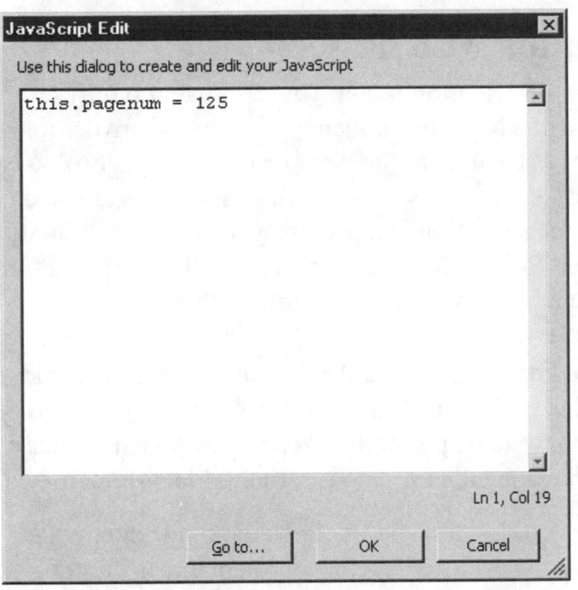

17. Click OK to close the JavaScript Edit dialog box; and, in the Add An Action dialog box, click Set Action.

18. In the Field Properties dialog box, click OK to complete the creation of the button.

To create the next text-only button, which links to the document Index, enter **Index** for the button name in step 3 and step 11. In step 16, modify the JavaScript to reflect the page number of the document Index.

After you create the text-only buttons, you can enhance document navigation further by adding Next Page and Previous Page buttons. You could do this with text or, as shown in the next section, use buttons with icons.

Create a Button with an Icon

When you create a Navigation menu, you can save room by creating buttons with icons. In the case of a Navigation menu, you can use arrows to designate whether the button advances the user to the Next or Previous page. You can get the arrow icons from clipart, or create them in an illustration program such as Illustrator, CorelDraw, or Freehand. You can use images created with the following formats for icons: Acrobat PDFs, BMPs, Compuserve GIFs, JPEGs, PCXs, PNGs, or TIFFs. To create a button with an icon, follow these steps:

1. Select the Form tool, and in the Document pane click and drag a rectangular field at the approximate location you want the button to appear. The field does not have to be perfectly sized or positioned. Release the mouse button to finish creating the field and open the Field Properties dialog box.
2. Click the Actions tab, and in the Name field, enter a name for the button. For the purpose of this demonstration, name the button **Next**.
3. Accept the default Mouse Up option, and click the Add button to open the Add An Action dialog box.
4. Click the triangle to the right of the Type field, and then click the Edit Menu Item button to open the Menu Item Selection dialog box.
5. Choose Document | Next Page, as shown in the following image, and then click OK to close the dialog box.

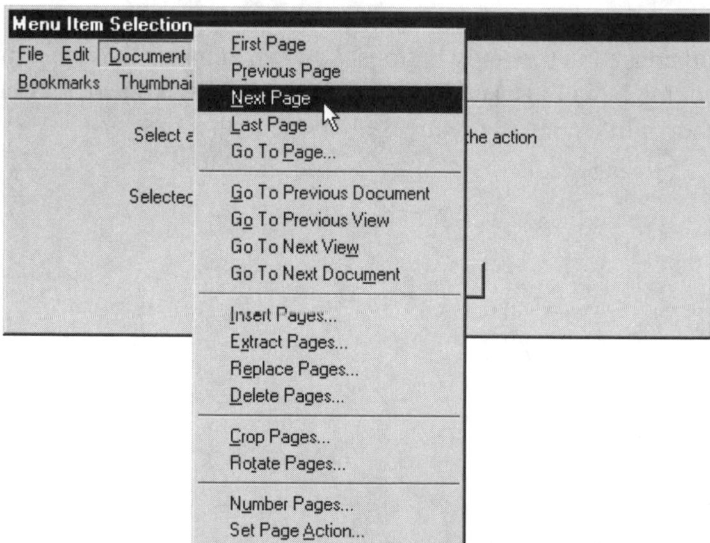

6. In the Add An Action dialog box, click Set Action to apply the action and close the dialog box.
7. Click the Options tab to open the Options section of the Field Properties dialog box.
8. Click the triangle to the right of the Layout field and choose Icon Only from the drop-down menu.
9. Click the Select Icon button to open the Select Appearance dialog box, shown in the following image:

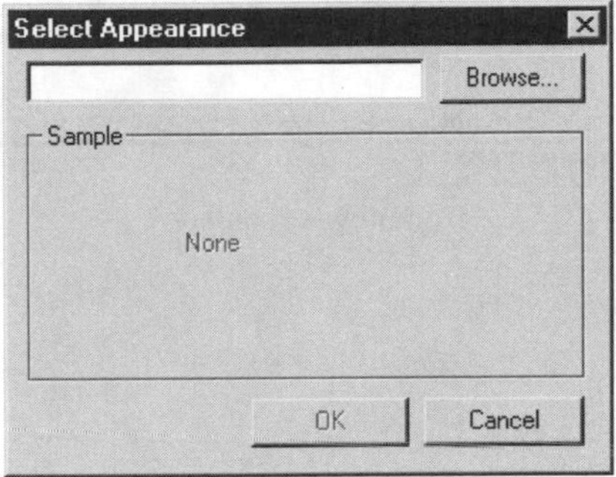

10. Click the Browse button, locate the image file you are using for the button, and then click Select. After you select the button icon, a sample of the icon is displayed in the Select Appearance dialog box, as shown in the following image:

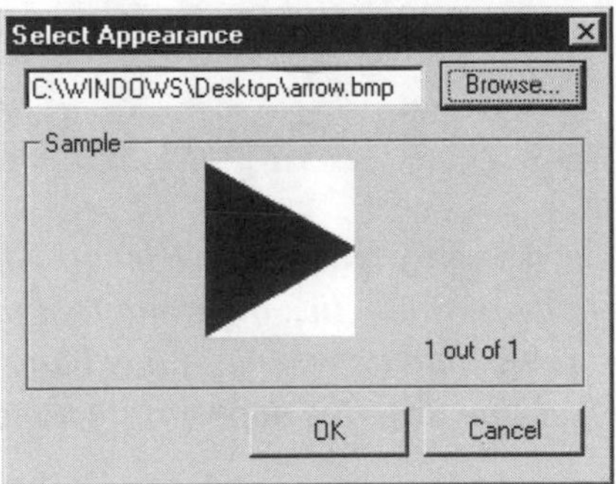

11. Click OK to close the Select Appearance dialog box, and then click OK to close the Field Properties dialog box.

To create the second button, follow the preceding steps, with the exception of giving the button a different name and choosing a different icon for the button. To create a Back button, in step 5, choose Document | Previous Page.

With the Form tool still selected, your Navigation menu should look similar to the following image. All of the buttons are identified by name and are surrounded by the rectangular area you defined with the Form tool. To tidy things up, you need to align and size the buttons.

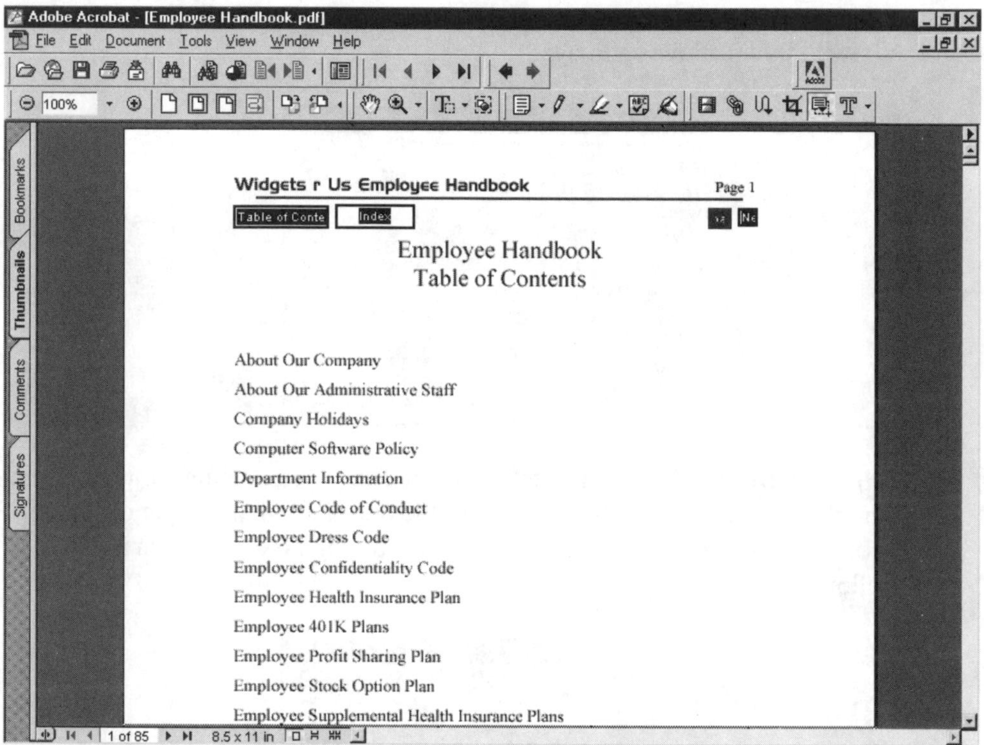

NOTE *If the faces of your text-only buttons have lengthy text, the button may not be wide enough to display it. Click the Hand tool to display the buttons as they will appear in the final document. If any button-face text is truncated, select the Form tool and drag the appropriate handle to resize the form field.*

Align and Size Buttons

You can easily align and size all of your Navigation menu buttons by using menu commands. Before you align and size the buttons, you may need to fine tune the position of one or more buttons. To accomplish this, select the Form tool, click a button, and then drag it to the desired position. After you have positioned your Navigation menu buttons, align and size them as follows:

1. Select the Form tool, and click the first button in your menu.
2. Hold down the SHIFT key, and then click the other Navigation menu buttons. The first button you selected is highlighted in red, with the remaining buttons in blue. When you resize and align the buttons, they will be resized and aligned to the first button selected.
3. Choose Tools | Forms | Fields | Align | Top, and Acrobat aligns the buttons to the top of the first button you selected. Alternatively, right-click (Windows) or CTRL-click (Macintosh), and choose Align | Top from the context menu.
4. Choose Tools | Forms | Fields | Size | Height, and Acrobat sizes all of the buttons to the height of the first button selected. Alternatively, right-click (Windows) or CTRL-click (Macintosh), and choose Size | Height from the context menu.
5. Click the Hand tool to preview the menu. If the Next and Back buttons are not the same size, select the Form tool, select both buttons, and then choose Forms | Fields | Size | Both.

After you position, align, and size the buttons, your only remaining task is to duplicate them for every page of the document.

Duplicate Buttons

After you create a Navigation menu for the first page of your document, you will duplicate your efforts for the remaining pages of the document. You can accomplish this task rather painlessly as follows:

1. Select the Form tool.

2. Click the first button in your menu, and, while holding down the SHIFT key, click the remaining buttons in your menu.
3. Choose Forms | Fields | Duplicate to open the Duplicate Fields dialog box, shown in the following image:

4. Accept All (the default), or select From and specify the range of pages you want the buttons duplicated on.
5. Click OK, and Acrobat duplicates the Navigation menu buttons on the pages specified. Figure 7-7 shows the completed Navigation menu.

TIP *If you want to create an identical Navigation menu at the bottom of the page, navigate to the first page of the document; select all of the menu buttons; and then, while holding down the CTRL key (Windows) or OPTION key (Macintosh), drag the buttons toward the bottom of the page. When you release the mouse button, Acrobat creates a duplicate set of buttons. You can then use the Duplicate command to create copies of these buttons on the remaining pages of the document.*

After you duplicate your Navigation menu on every page of the document, you may want to delete the Back button on the first document page and the Next button on the last document page. To do this, navigate to the first document page, and then select the Form tool. Select the Back button, and then press DELETE. After you press DELETE, Acrobat displays the Warning dialog box, as shown in the following image. Click No to delete only the selected instance of the button. Repeat for the Next button on the last page of the document.

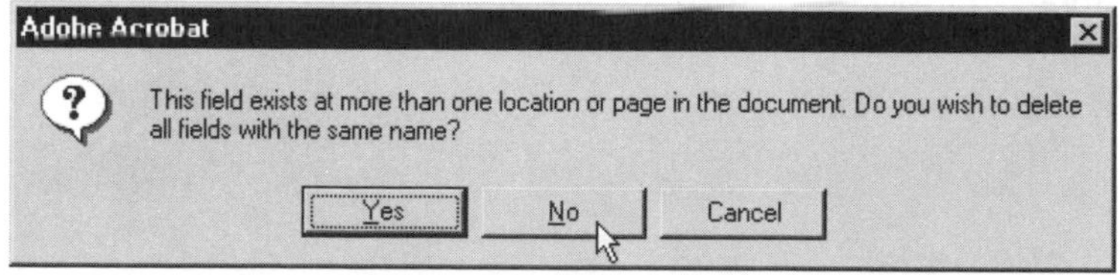

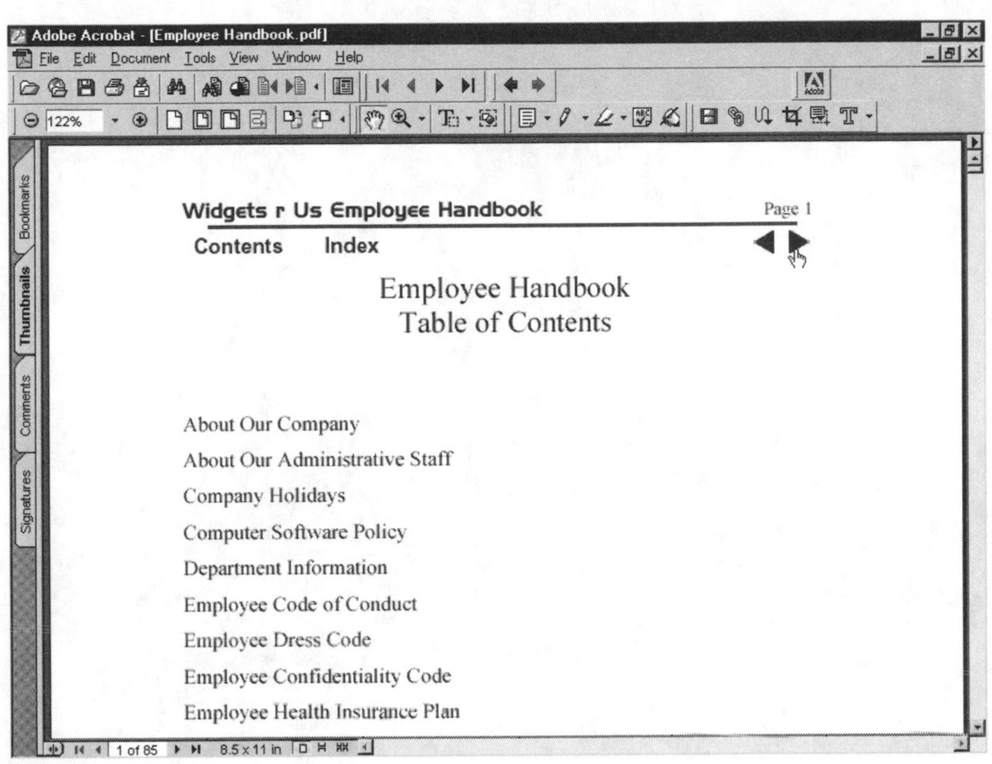

FIGURE 7-7 Create a Navigation menu with buttons to enhance the document usability.

Chapter 8

Create an eBook

How To…

- Create an eBook cover
- Create a thread of linked Articles
- Create a linked Table of Contents
- Create an eBook for Acrobat eBook Reader

When electronic publishing first became available, it was used to publish documents for intradepartmental communication and for publishing computer hardware and software manuals. With the advent of the laptop computer, it became feasible to create electronic books, or eBooks. The original eBooks did not provide a reasonable facsimile of reading a bound book. However, as the technology progressed, eBook publishers made inroads with the general reading public by producing a product that looked similar to a printed book. Users of eBooks could easily create a library of hundreds of books on their computers. A person using eBooks with a laptop can take their virtual library virtually anywhere.

eBook publishers took the medium a step further when they created specialized eBook viewers. An eBook viewer looks similar to a PDA (Personal Data Assistant), a handheld device used to keep track of business contacts, appointments and other items. However, the sole purpose of an eBook viewer is to acquire eBooks (some viewers are equipped with built-in modems), store, and display them. Software manufacturers such as Adobe and Microsoft have created free software to view eBooks with. The increased popularity of the format makes it possible for anyone with a computer to view an eBook.

Many websites distribute public domain fiction in eBook format to increase the popularity of the medium and sell the other eBook titles in their catalog. The greatest potential for eBook publishing is in the technical and educational fields because the content of this material needs frequent updating. eBooks can be quickly updated and redistributed. It is doubtful that the eBook will ever find mass popularity with fiction readers. Avid readers like to spend a cold winter night curled up in an easy chair with a cup of hot chocolate and the latest work of their favorite author. It's hard to imagine someone taking an eBook viewer to bed to read one more chapter before retiring.

In this chapter, you'll learn how to use Acrobat to create an eBook. The material in this chapter will cover creating an eBook for viewing with Acrobat, Acrobat Reader, and Acrobat eBook Reader. Topics covered include creating a cover and navigation devices for the eBook, as well as creating a PDF document that bears some similarity to a conventional book. Distribution and document protection will also be covered.

Create an eBook Cover

There's an old saying that you can't judge a book by its cover, and that still rings true today. Many lavishly illustrated book covers are nothing but window dressing to mask some pretty awful writing. If you have ever picked up a romance or mystery novel with an intriguing cover at an airport bookstore and left it on the airplane after suffering through a chapter or two, you can personally attest to the wisdom of this saying.

It goes without saying that you should publish an eBook with interesting and informative content. However, you still need to do something to attract the reader's attention—especially if you create an eBook with the intent of selling it at an online bookstore. The best way to catch a potential reader's attention is with a well-designed cover.

Design an eBook Cover

Creating a cover for an eBook is similar to designing a Web site. Less is more. If you create a simple design with fewer graphic elements, it has more visual appeal and creates a smaller file size—and file size is a major consideration. You will add the cover to other elements of the eBook: the author's compelling prose, any images or diagrams in the text, and the eBook navigation you create for the document. Remember that your viewers will have to download the document and it will be viewed cross-platform on monitors with different desktop sizes. If you are creating the cover from scratch in an illustration program such as Adobe Illustrator or CorelDraw, use a 256-color palette, or better yet, use the universally accepted 216-color Web safe palette. If you are including images with your cover, begin with the highest resolution images you can get. The images will eventually be viewed at 72 or 96 dpi; however, if you start out with a higher quality image, the cover will look better when compressed into PDF format.

Lay Out an eBook Cover

When you create an eBook cover from scratch, your first consideration is the size of the cover, which will differ depending on whether you create the cover for viewing in Acrobat or create a cover for the Acrobat eBook Reader. Most eBooks created for viewing in Acrobat or Acrobat Reader open in Full Screen viewing mode, which gives the reader the feeling they are actually reading a book and not working with a software program. When you create a cover for viewing in either program, use the following design criteria.

- **Cover dimensions** When you create an eBook specifically for monitor viewing, create a cover with the same proportions as a standard computer monitor. A standard computer monitor is landscape format (as opposed to the portrait format of printed documents). If you create a document 10 inches wide × 7.75 inches high at 72 dpi, or 720 pixels wide × 558 pixels high at 72 dpi, it will be optimized for a monitor with 800 × 600 pixels, and will display well in monitors with smaller or slightly larger desktops. If you use the Fit In Window Open Option, the document will be upsized or downsized to fit the Document pane. As mentioned previously, if you create the image at a higher resolution, such as 300 dpi, the cover will look better when the image is converted to PDF format. The initial file size will be larger; however, when you export the image as a PDF document, you can modify the resolution setting to 72 dpi. When you start out with a higher resolution image, you get a better looking cover when it is converted to PDF format. Consult the user manual of your image editing software for document setup information.
- **Color palette** If the cover for your eBook consists solely of text and vector-based images, use a 256-color palette. If your image-editing software has a 216-color, Web-safe palette available, use it, as these colors will display the same on Windows, Macintosh, and Unix systems.
- **Full-color images** Full-color images look terrific; however, they are not without penalty. Full-color images bloat a file size, even when converted to PDF format. If your client insists on using a full-color image, reduce the size so it doesn't fill the cover. You can always put the cover around the image and center it in a border. After you add text to the cover image, it will fill up nicely. In lieu of a full-color image, consider using vector-based clipart. Most vector based clipart features large areas of solid color that compress well when converted to PDF format. Covers with large areas of solid color will display better when upsized or downsized to fit the window size of the Document pane.

- **Text** If at all possible, stick with standard fonts. Choose a font that will display well onscreen and select a large font size to ensure maximum visibility for visually impaired readers, or readers with small monitors. Highly stylized fonts with long swooping curves should be avoided, as these will not compress well. With highly stylized fonts, you also run the risk of introducing *artifacts*, visual anomalies that distort the text. If you use a standard font such as Times New Roman or Arial, it will display well on most monitors. If you use a nonstandard font, be sure to embed it when you convert the document to PDF format.

You should leave some blank space between the cover objects and the boundary of the document. If you run the text and images right out to the edge of the page, the document becomes hard to read. You also need to leave some blank space at the top and bottom of your document for navigation devices such as menus and buttons. If you are not familiar with graphic design, download a few eBooks to get an idea of how to lay out a cover. Figure 8-1 shows an eBook cover displayed in the Acrobat Full Screen viewing mode.

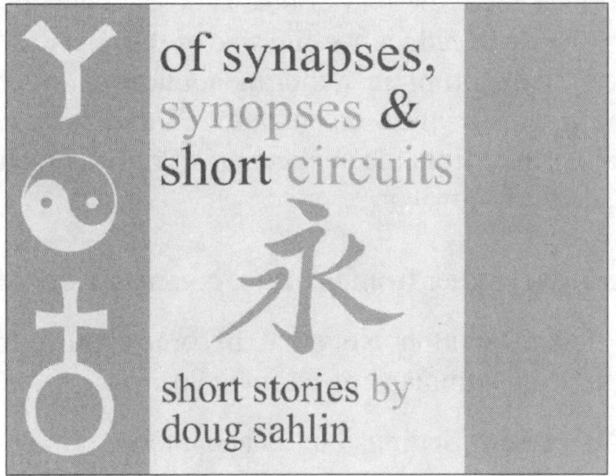

FIGURE 8-1 When you design an eBook cover, create a visually appealing design that downloads quickly.

Export an eBook Cover

After you create the eBook cover, you need to convert it to PDF format. If you use Illustrator, Photoshop, CorelDraw 10, or Corel Photo-Paint 10, you can take advantage of the software PDF export feature. Before converting the file to PDF, it is advisable to save it in the native format of the program. There are two good reasons for doing this. First, if you ever need to modify the cover, you have all of the elements in their native format, which is especially handy if the native software supports layers. Second, image-editing software is notoriously hard on system resources. If your system should happen to lock up while you are converting the cover to PDF format, you can revert to the saved file when you reboot; otherwise, all of your hard work will be lost.

If you create an eBook cover in a program that does not offer PDF support, you can use the application's Print command and choose Acrobat Distiller to convert the file to PDF format. Choose the Acrobat Distiller eBook Job Option.

If you use Acrobat Distiller to create the PDF file, be sure to modify the paper size to conform to the size of your eBook cover. Refer to Chapter 5 for instructions on modifying paper size.

When you export the cover for your eBook, choose 72 dpi, the resolution of most computer monitors. This will reduce the file size of the cover. If you are exporting the image from the PDF export of an authoring application, refer to the program user manual for specific instructions on converting the exported file to 72 dpi. If you choose Acrobat Distiller from the application's Print command to publish the file in PDF format, do the following:

1. Choose Acrobat Distiller from the Print command drop-down menu.
2. Click the Properties button. Note that, in some applications, you have to use the Page Setup command to set up the printer.
3. Click the Adobe PDF Settings button and choose eBook (the default) from the drop-down menu.

4. Click the Edit Conversion Settings button to reveal the eBook Job Options dialog box as shown in the following illustration:

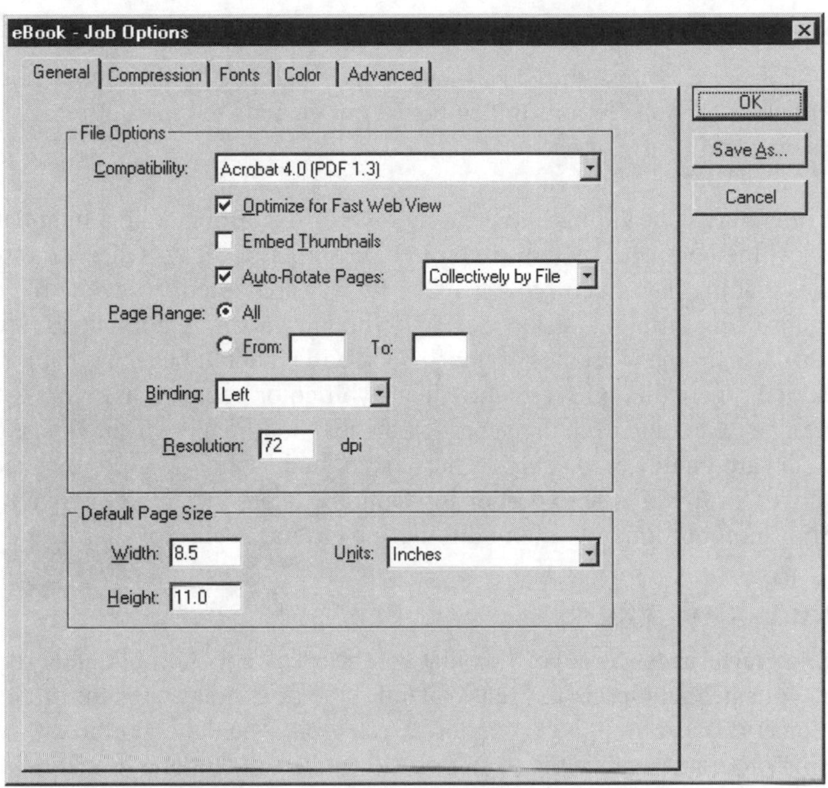

5. If you are converting a document with different page dimensions, enter the appropriate values in the Width and Height fields.
6. Click the Compression tab.
7. In the Color Images section and Grayscale Images section, change the Bicubic Downsampling value from 150 dpi to 72 dpi.

8. Click the Save As button to open the Save Job Options As dialog box.
9. Enter a name for the modified job options; **My eBook.Job Options** is a good choice.
10. Click Save to close the Save Job Options As dialog box, and then click OK to close the Job Options dialog box. Your customized job option file is saved and ready for use.

Before you rush headlong into creating text for the eBook, take a moment or two to view the completed eBook cover in PDF format. This will alert you to any anomalies that my have occurred when the file was converted. View the file on a PC monitor using different desktop sizes. If you have a laptop computer, view the file on that also, as many readers of your eBook will no doubt be using that format. As an added precaution, preview the file at 8-bit color depth (256 colors). In particular, pay attention to the crispness of the text and images. If the image or text borders are muddy, your only recourse is to modify the file used to create the eBook cover, or modify the export or Job Options, to produce a higher quality image. For more information on modifying Job Options, refer to Chapter 14.

Create eBook Pages

When you create pages for an eBook that will be viewed in Acrobat or Acrobat Reader, your best choice is to create a landscape document with the same proportions (4:3) as a computer monitor. If you create the document in a word processing program, modify the page setup to create a document 10 inches wide (25.4 cm) × 7.75 inches high (19.69 cm), or long if you use Microsoft Word.

If the eBook you create has a lot of text, set your page up in landscape format as just described, create the text for the document, insert any images, and then format the document into two columns. If your word processing software has the option, create a line between the columns. This will make the eBook easier to read. The following illustration is an eBook page created in Microsoft Word.

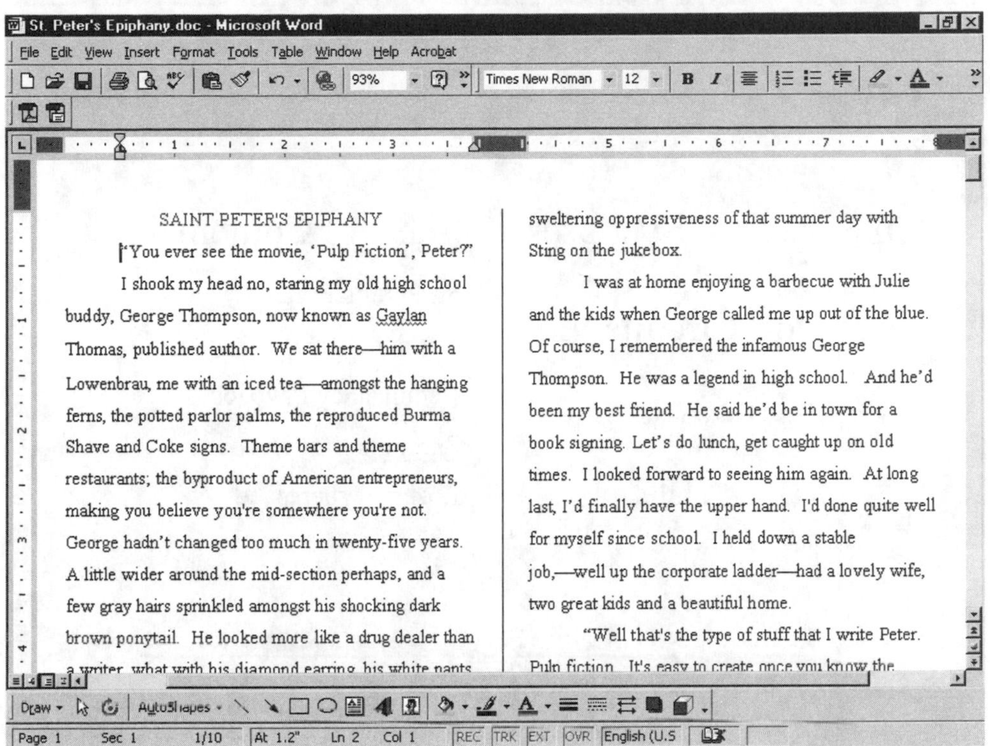

Conventional books generally have a Title Page, Table of Contents, and Preface. You can create these with your word processing software. The Title Page should include the title of the book, the author's name, and any other pertinent information you or the publisher deem necessary. You may want to consider creating a Title Page and a Table of Contents as one page, like the document shown in the following illustration.

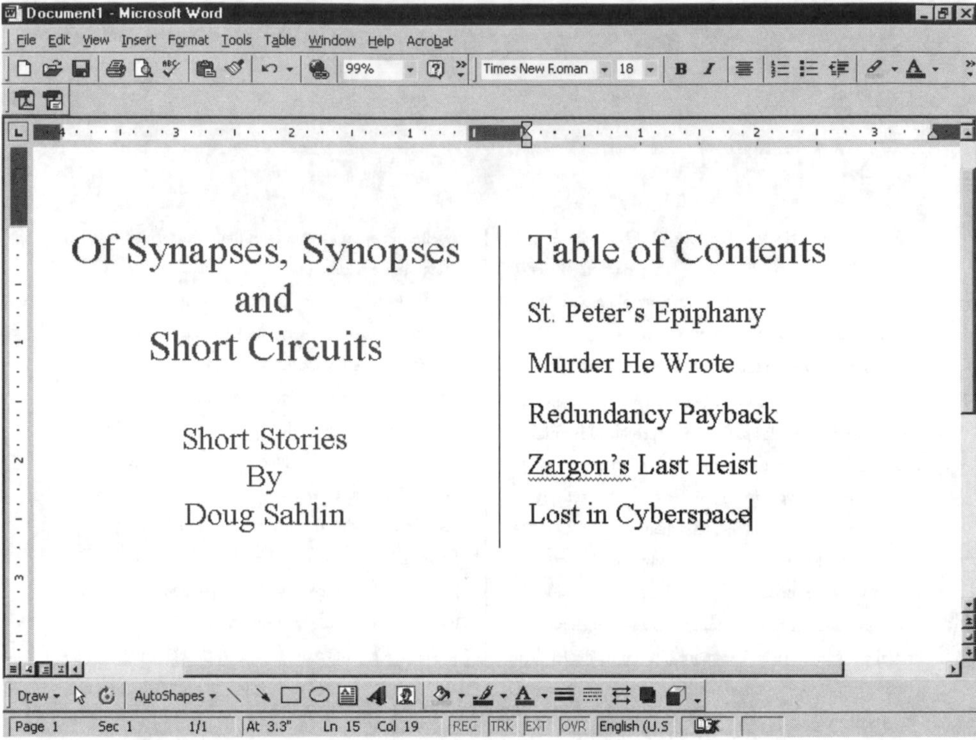

When you create eBook text, here are some criteria to consider:

- **Fonts** If possible, use a serif font if the document will be viewed in printed format, or use a sans serif font for screen viewing if you optimize the document by using the landscape format discussed earlier in this section. Make sure you use a font size no smaller than 12 points, otherwise, the document will be hard to view on smaller monitors.
- **Font Colors** When a conventional book is created, specifying different font colors will run up the printing price tag. However, when you create an eBook, you can change font colors to draw the reader's attention to specific parts of the eBook, such as a chapter title or an image caption, without having to consider the cost of printing those colors.
- **Images** Most word processing software has the capability of including images within the text. If you are creating an eBook for entertainment, images provide visual spice to break up a long chapter. If you are creating

an instructional eBook, images can be used to reinforce the text. It's a well-know fact that we retain more of what we see than what we read. Remember that images will increase the file size, so use them sparingly.

- **Other eBook considerations** When you are creating an eBook as a technical manual or for educational purposes, include sidebars or tips throughout the document. After you convert the document to PDF format, you can use the tips or sidebars to create *article threads*, a topic that will be discussed later in this chapter. Busy readers can often follow an article thread to quickly get the information they need without reading a lengthy document. Also consider the file size of your finished eBook. If at all possible, strive to keep it below 2MB. Remember that most people still download from the Internet using a modem on a dial-up connection. If your finished eBook weighs in at 5MB or more, consider removing some images or modifying compression options. Another alternative is to break a large eBook into two files.

Word processors work well for creating most eBooks. However, if the document you create needs extensive formatting, such as different-sized columns on each page and multiple images of different sizes, you are better off creating the document in a page-layout program such as Adobe Pagemaker or FrameMaker. If you use either Adobe program to create the document, you have the added benefit of being able to export it in PDF format directly from the program.

Converting the Pages to PDF Format

After you create the contents of the eBook, convert it from the authoring application native file format to a PDF document. If you created the document in a program that features PDF export, or has a plug-in like the PDFMaker in certain Microsoft Office applications, create bookmarks for the document. Bookmarks will aid you when you set up the eBook navigation.

If the authoring application you created the text in does not have a method of exporting a file in PDF format, you can use Acrobat Distiller to print the document in PDF format. Use the custom eBook Job Options setting to export the file at 72 dpi, as discussed in "Export an eBook Cover" earlier in this chapter. If you formatted the page to a custom page size, you must change the paper size before printing the document. For detailed information on printing a document using Acrobat Distiller, refer to Chapter 5.

If you create the pages for your eBook in Word, use the Convert To Adobe PDF command to convert the file to PDF format. When you invoke this command, the PDFMaker converts the document and any graphics into PDF format. For detailed information on converting Word documents into PDF format, refer to Chapter 5.

If you use the Acrobat Distiller or Microsoft Office PDFMaker to create the PDF file, choose the eBook Job Option. This Job Option optimizes the file for an eBook.

NOTE *You can modify any Job Option to suit your preference or intended destination. Modifying Job Options will be covered in detail in Chapter 14.*

However, if you changed the document size, you will have to change the document size in both the Job Options settings and the Acrobat Distiller settings as follows:

1. Choose File | Print, and then choose Acrobat Distiller from the printer menu.
2. Click the Properties button to open the Acrobat Distiller Properties dialog box.
3. In the Paper Size section, navigate to the first custom paper icon and click it, as shown in the following image:

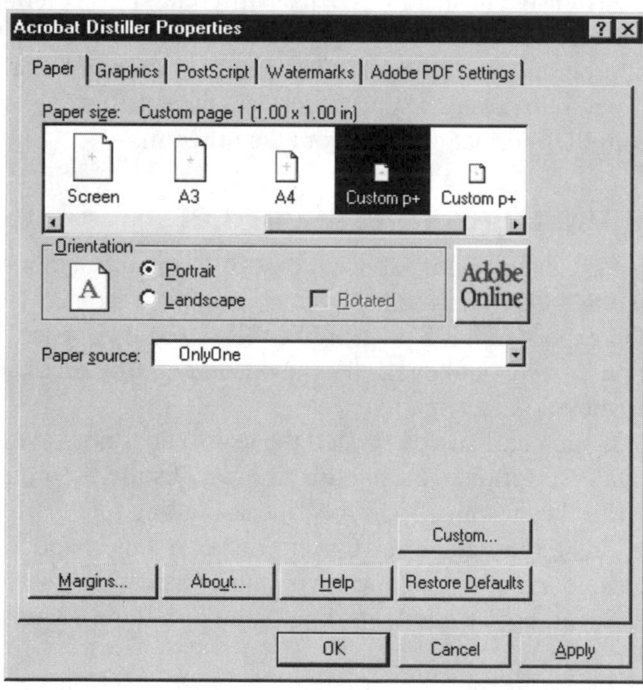

4. Click the Custom button to open the Custom-Defined Size dialog box.

5. In the Width and Height fields, enter the same values you used to set up the page and click OK.
6. Click the Adobe PDF Settings and choose eBook from the drop-down menu.
7. Click the Edit Conversion Settings button to open the eBook Job Options dialog box shown in the following image:

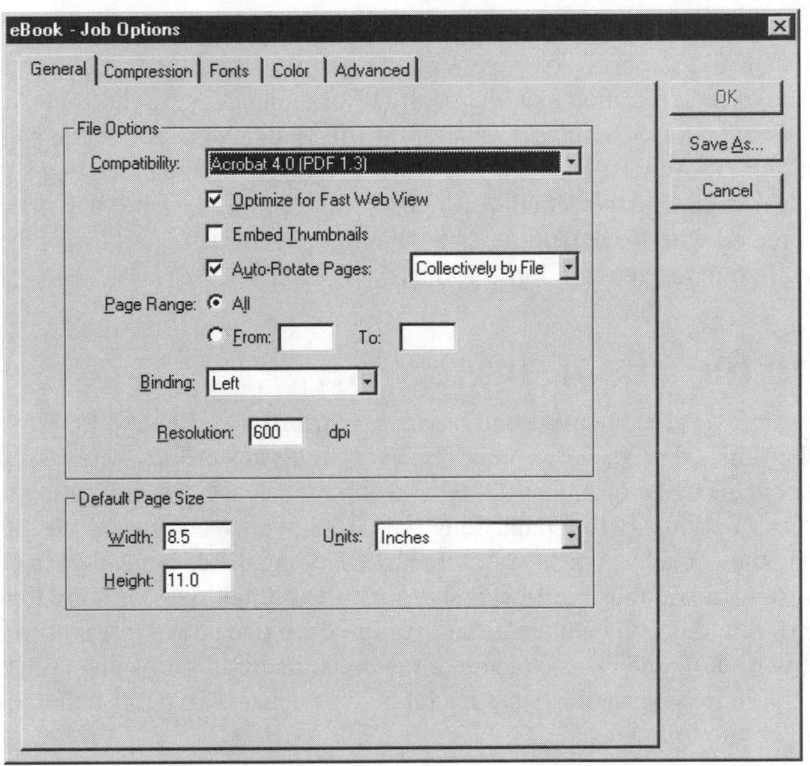

8

NOTE *The dialog box in this image shows a resolution of 600 dpi. This is the resolution for the printing output device. The screen resolution is determined in the Compression section of the Job Options dialog box. The default compression settings for the eBook job option resamples color images to 150 dpi and monochrome images to 300 dpi, higher than 72 dpi monitor resolution. These resolutions make it possible to magnify images in the eBook without distortion. You can, however, change these values to 72 dpi, as outlined in the Customize Distiller Job Options section of Chapter 14.*

8. In the Width and Height fields, enter the values you used to set up the document page.
9. Click Save As to open the Save Job Options As dialog box.
10. Enter a name for the file and click OK. Choose a name that describes the actual page layout, such as eBookLandscape.joboptions.

After you create the new Job Option, you can use it whenever you want to create a PDF file for an eBook page with the custom page layout. You can also choose the same Job Option in a Microsoft Office application by choosing Acrobat | Change Conversion Settings. However, you will first have to define the page size by changing the Acrobat Distiller properties as outlined in the preceding steps. If you neglect to change the default Acrobat Distiller properties, the PDF document will be created with the default Acrobat Distiller page size, regardless of the page size specified in the selected Job Options.

Complete the eBook in Acrobat

After you convert the title page and other elements of the eBook to PDF format, create the finished product by combining everything in Acrobat. After assembling the components in Acrobat, you add other features such as links, navigation buttons, and security options. Before publishing the eBook, you specify what the viewer sees when the document opens in Acrobat by changing the document Open Options. In terms of eBook publishing, this is the equivalent of taking your book to the printer for binding. But with an eBook, you produce one copy, upload it to an eBook distributor, and the customers of the book distributor download the book (hopefully, in mass quantities) and read it at their leisure. To publish the book in Acrobat, do the following:

1. Launch Acrobat and open the document you created for the cover of the eBook.
2. Choose Document | Insert Pages to open the Select a File to Insert dialog box.
3. Navigate to the document that will follow the cover and click Select to open the Insert Pages dialog box, shown in the following image.

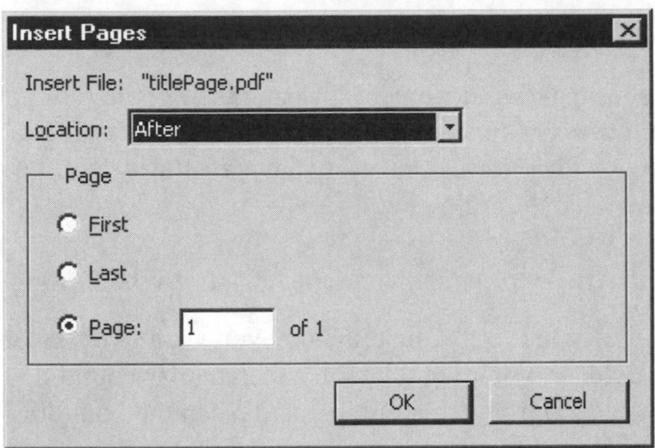

4. Accept the default options, and click OK to insert the page. As you can see, this is only one of many options you can use to insert a page. For more information on inserting and deleting pages, refer to Chapter 11.

5. To insert additional pages in the eBook, navigate to the last page of the document and repeat steps 2 through 4. Your eBook may be comprised of many documents such as cover art, the Table of Contents, the Preface, the Foreword, and individual chapters. Insert the documents in their proper order. If you insert the page in the wrong place, you can always undo the action, or change the order of the pages. You can also delete pages if you insert the wrong document. For more information on editing pages in a PDF document, refer to Chapter 11.

Create a Thread of Linked Articles

You create *articles* to link blocks of text within a PDF file. If you are creating an eBook in magazine format (an *eMagazine,* if you will), an article that begins on page 23 may end on page 54. To make it easy for the reader to navigate from one part of the article to the next, define the block of text that is the start of the article, and then define the additional blocks of text that cover the rest of the article.

If you create an eBook for educational purposes, you can use articles to link chapter summaries together, thus making it easy for the student to skim through the book and locate desired information.

Create an Article

You define articles in a PDF document by using the Article tool to define the boundary of each block of text in the article. The text blocks for each part of the article are linked and the viewer can easily navigate the article. To create an article in a PDF document, do the following:

1. Select the Article tool, (shown to the left), from the Editing tool group.
2. Click and drag the tool around the text you want to define as the first part of the article. As you drag the tool, a rectangular bounding box gives you a preview of the area you are selecting. When the bounding box surrounds the text, release the mouse button and Acrobat defines the first block of the article, as shown in the following image. Notice the article numbering system at the top of the article box. The 1-1 designates the article 1, block 1 has been created.

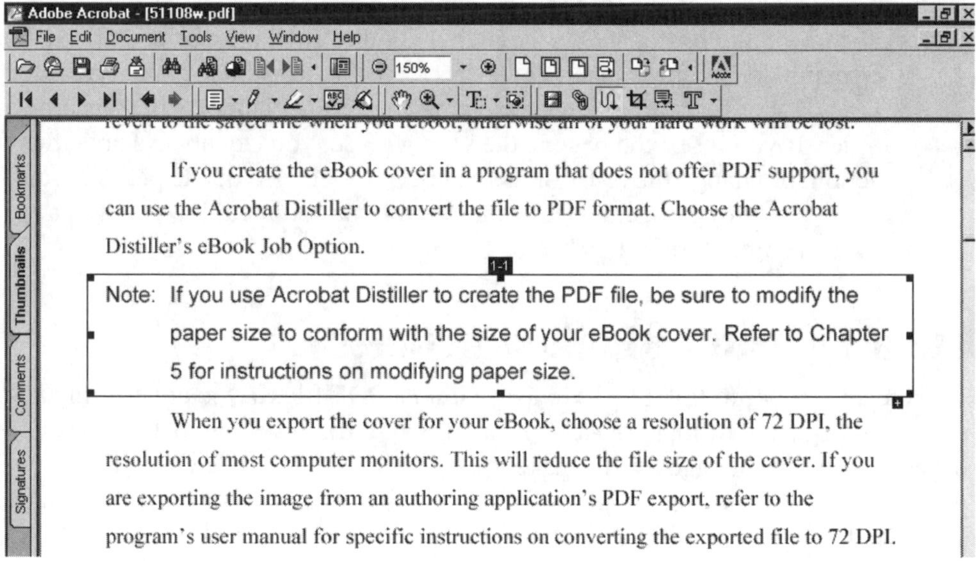

3. After you create the first block of an article, your cursor changes to the icon shown in the image to the left, which means that Acrobat is ready for you to define the next text block in the article. Navigate to the section of the document that contains the next portion of text in the article.
4. Click and drag the Article tool until it encompasses the next text block of the article.
5. Continue in this manner until you have defined all blocks of text in the article, and then press ENTER or RETURN to open the Article Properties dialog box shown here:

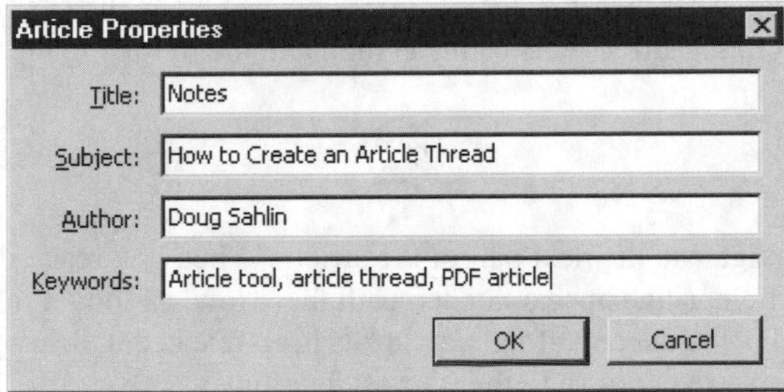

6. Enter the title, subject, and author of the article, plus any other keywords you want associated with the article, and click OK to close the dialog box.

Use the Articles Palette

After you create one or more articles, you can use the Articles palette to test your handiwork. The Articles palette is also used by readers of your document to select an individual article to read. To open the Articles palette, shown in the following image, choose Window | Articles.

8

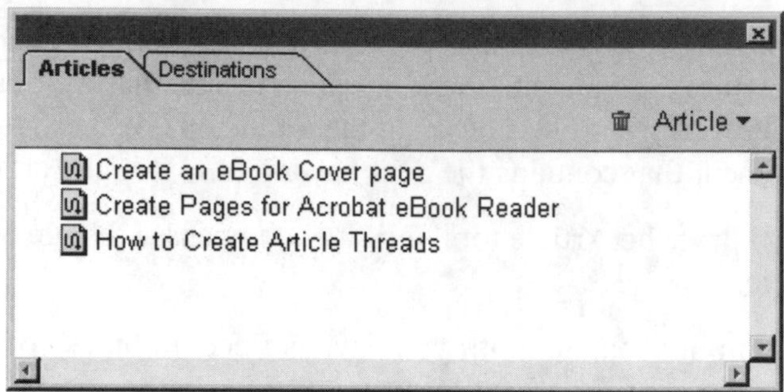

To read an article, double-click its title, and Acrobat displays the first block of text in the article. After the first block of text is opened, your cursor becomes a hand with a down-pointing arrow in its palm, as shown in the following illustration:

Click to navigate to the next part of the article. When you reach the last text block of the article, a line appears underneath the arrow, as shown in the following image. This tells you the end of the article has been reached. Click within the current article thread to return to the start of the article.

Add a Thread to an Article

After you review the article, you may find it necessary to add additional text blocks to the article. You can easily do this by following these steps:

1. Select the Article tool. After you select the Article tool, Acrobat displays the bounding box and number of all articles in the PDF document.
2. Click the text block after which you want the new text block to appear. After you select the text block, a plus sign (+) appears at the lower-right corner of the box, as shown in the following illustration:

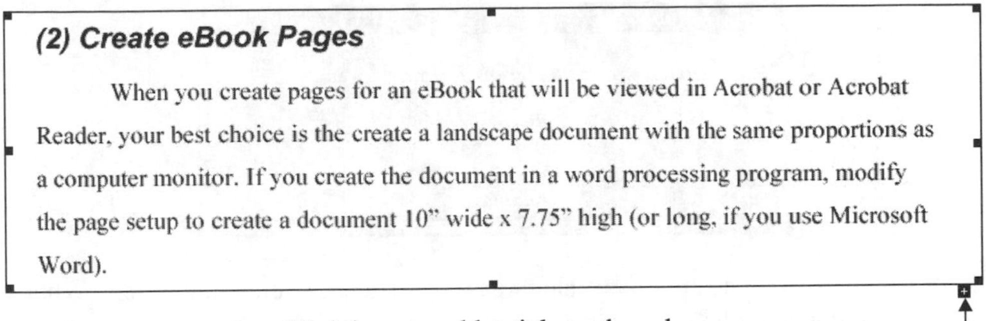

(2) Create eBook Pages

When you create pages for an eBook that will be viewed in Acrobat or Acrobat Reader, your best choice is the create a landscape document with the same proportions as a computer monitor. If you create the document in a word processing program, modify the page setup to create a document 10" wide x 7.75" high (or long, if you use Microsoft Word).

Click icon to add article to thread.

3. Click the plus sign, and then navigate to the text block you want added to the article thread.
4. Click and drag to define the boundary of the box; when the bounding box encompasses the text, release the mouse button.
5. Add additional threads to the article or deselect the Article tool to finish editing the contents of the article. When you add threads to an article, Acrobat automatically renumbers the other threads in the order they appear in the article.

Delete an Article

After previewing the document, you may decide that certain parts of an article thread are not needed. You can easily delete an entire article or article thread by doing the following:

1. Select the Article tool.
2. Click the article thread you want to delete. If you want to delete an entire article, click any thread in the article.
3. Right-click (Windows) or CTRL-click (Macintosh) to open the Article context menu.
4. Choose Delete, and Acrobat displays the dialog box shown in the following image.

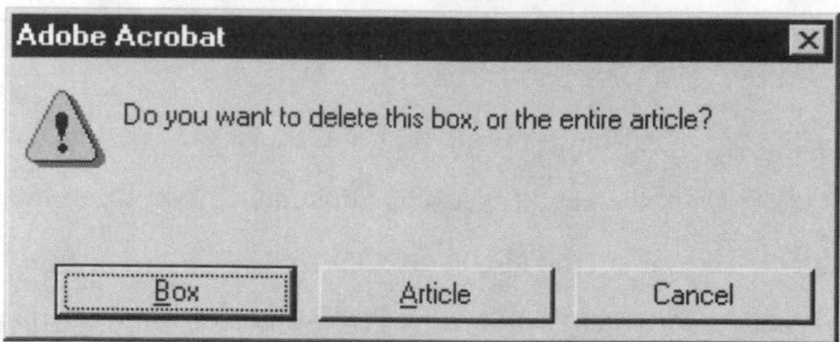

5. Click Box to delete the article thread, or Article to delete the article. When you delete a thread, Acrobat renumbers the remaining threads in the article in their proper order.

Move or Resize an Article Box

When your article thread is viewed, Acrobat magnifies the view to fit the confines of the article box. If, after reviewing the document, you decide the position or size of an article box is off, you can move or resize it. To move the article box, do the following:

1. Select the Article tool.
2. Click the article box you want to move or resize. After you click the box, Acrobat displays eight handles and the plus sign.
3. To move the article box, click inside the bounding box and drag. When you click, your cursor becomes a filled arrowhead. As you drag the article box, a dashed bounding box gives you a preview of the position of the box. When the bounding box is where you want the article box to be, release the mouse button.

To resize the article box, do one of the following:

- Click one of the corner handles and drag to resize the entire article box. Hold down the SHIFT key to resize the box proportionately. Release the mouse button when the box is the desired size.
- Click the handle in the middle on either side of the box and drag right or left to resize the article box width. Release the mouse button when the box is the desired width.
- Click the handle in the middle of either the top or bottom of the article box and drag up or down to change the height of the box.

Edit Article Properties

After you create an article, you can change the title or any other article properties by doing the following:

1. Select the Article tool.
2. Click any thread of the article whose properties you want to modify.
3. Right-click (Windows) or CTRL-click (Macintosh) and choose Properties from the context menu to display the Article Properties dialog box.
4. Modify the article properties as needed, and then click OK.

NOTE *The preceding sections demonstrate how to use the Acrobat Article feature with an eBook. You can, however, use this feature whenever you need to create linked blocks of text. For example, if you are creating a product manual, or online catalog, articles are a great way to link specific information together. Use your imagination to think of new and creative uses for this valuable feature.*

Number the Pages

When you insert pages in a PDF document, Acrobat automatically numbers them in descending order. If you accept this default numbering system, the cover of your eBook becomes page 1, which, of course, is not accurate. The first page of your eBook really begins at the first page of chapter 1. You can, however, easily renumber the pages using thumbnails as follows.

NOTE *The page numbers do not appear on the actual PDF document. When you change page numbers, you change the number in the window at the bottom of the Navigation pane and the page number on each thumbnail.*

1. Open the Navigation pane, and then click the Thumbnails tab. Notice that all of the thumbnails are numbered; the first thumbnail being page 1, and the following thumbnails numbered in descending order.
2. Click the Thumbnail for the cover page of your eBook.
3. Click the Thumbnail icon at the upper-right corner of the Thumbnails palette, and choose Number Pages from the menu to open the Number Pages dialog box shown in the following image. To number more than one

page, select the first thumbnail and then; while holding down the SHIFT key, click additional thumbnails for pages you want to include in the selection. Typically, you number all pages of a section at once, for example, the pages that comprise the Front Matter of the eBook.

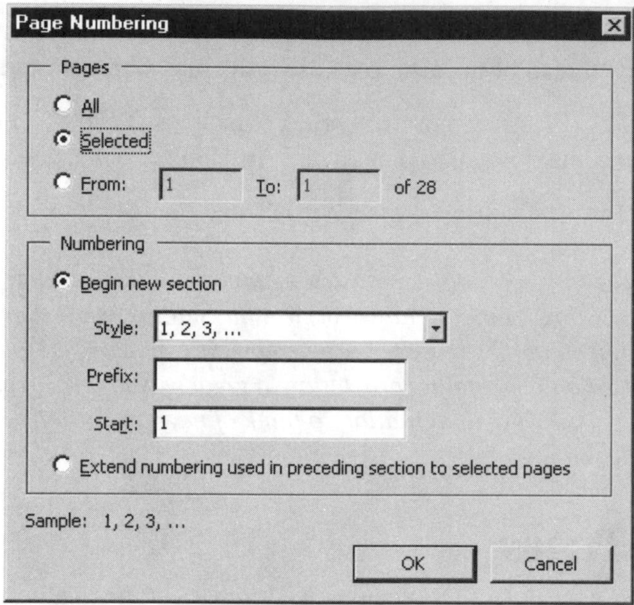

4. In the Pages section, accept the default Selected option. You may notice this dialog box has several options. Numbering pages will be covered in detail in Chapter 11.
5. In the Numbering section, accept the default Begin New Section option.
6. Click the triangle to the right of the Style menu and choose an option from the drop-down menu. You can choose any style you like; however, you may want to consider matching the elements of your eBook to the styles shown here:
   - **A, B, C** Use this style for the cover of the eBook.
   - **a, b, c** Use this style for the inside cover of the eBook.
   - **i, ii, iii** Use this style for Front Matter, such as author information, the Foreword, the Dedication, and so on.
   - **1, 2, 3** Use this style for the pages that comprise the content of the eBook.

7. In the Start field, enter the value that corresponds to the section you are numbering.
   - For the cover and inside cover, enter **3,** and the pages will be numbered with the third letter of the alphabet (*c* for cover).
   - For the Front Matter, enter **1** to begin the numbering with i, or **3** to begin numbering with iii if your document has two cover pages.
   - For the content pages of the book, enter **1**.
8. Click OK and Acrobat renumbers the selected pages to the style selected and renumbers the remaining pages with the default style.

You finish renumbering the pages by selecting the thumbnail that starts each sections and then follow the preceding steps. If you skip a page, Acrobat will not warn you. Make sure you select the beginning page at each section before renumbering a section. Once you have all the pages renumbered, it's time to add some navigation to the document.

Create eBook Navigation

A reader finds a chapter in a book by referring to the Table of Contents to find the beginning page of a chapter. When you create an eBook, you create links in the Table of Contents that open the first page of the chapter when clicked. If you create a product or technical manual in eBook format, you can also create links to article threads.

Create a Linked Table of Contents

The Table of Contents links to individual chapters and sections of the book. If you created the contents for your eBook as a single document and used Acrobat Distiller to convert it to a PDF file, you can create links using the method outlined in Chapter 7. If, however, you created the contents for your eBook in an authoring application that creates bookmarks upon export, or if you created each section of your eBook as an individual document, you can use bookmarks to quickly create menu links for your Table of Contents by following these steps.

1. Navigate to the eBook Table of Contents page.
2. Open the Navigation pane, and click the Bookmarks tab to open the Bookmarks palette.

3. Select the Link tool.
4. Click and drag the tool around an item in the Table of Contents, such as a chapter item. When the linked area has been defined, release the mouse button to open the Link Properties dialog box. Remember, you can press the CTRL key and click the first word in a sentence to create a link the exact size of the text, and then drag the handle at the end of the link box to encompass other words in the sentence.

NOTE *Use the CTRL and drag technique to quickly and accurately highlight text.*

5. Specify the link properties. For complete information on the Link tool and this dialog box, refer to Chapter 7.
6. In the Bookmarks palette, click the bookmark that corresponds to the destination of the link.
7. In the Link Properties dialog box, click Set Link.
8. Continue in this manner to define the rest of the links for your eBook Table of Contents.

As you can see, hop scotching between the Document pane and the Bookmarks palette is a quick-and-easy way to create a linked menu. You can use this method of creating links whenever you work with a document that has bookmarks.

TIP *If your eBook has article threads, instead of creating a link to each article in the document, create a single item on the Table of Contents named **Articles**. When you create the link for the item, instead of choosing Go To View as the Action Type, choose Execute Menu Item. Click the Edit Menu Item button, and then choose Window | Articles. When your readers click this link, the Articles palette opens and they can select an article to read.*

Create Document Navigation

After you create the links for the Table of Contents, you need to create additional navigation items before you publish your eBook. You can use form field buttons to create navigation items for your eBook. After you create the Navigation menu for the first page of the document, you then duplicate it for all the other pages in your eBook. For detailed information on how to create a Navigation menu, refer to Chapter 7.

First and foremost, you need to create Next and Back buttons so the reader has some way to turn the pages of the eBook. Two other necessary navigation items that need to be created are a button that returns the reader to the Table of Contents, and a button to close the book. Use the Go To View Action to create a button that returns the viewer to the Table of Contents, and use the Execute Menu Command Action to create a button that closes the book. To simulate the experience of closing an actual book, you can use two menu commands: Close and Exit. Remember, you will have to add two Execute Menu Command Actions to the button, one for each menu command. For more information on creating buttons and assigning actions to buttons, refer to Chapter 7.

Create Button Tooltips

eBooks are a new experience for many people. Some eBook readers may have a hard time figuring out how to use your navigation devices. You can make the process of using an eBook a simple matter if you create tooltips for the navigation buttons of the eBook. You use form fields to create tooltips. Follow these steps to create a tooltip for a button:

1. Select the Form tool.
2. Click and drag to create a rectangular area near the button for which you are creating the tooltip. After you release the mouse button, Acrobat opens the Field Properties dialog box.
3. Choose Text for the button type and in the Name field, enter a name for the button.
4. Click the Options tab and in the Default field, enter the message you want displayed in the tooltip. Give the user just enough information to know what the button does. Remember the acronym KISS—Keep It Short, Simple.
5. Click the Appearance tab.
6. Enable the Border Color option, click the Border Color button and choose Black.
7. Enable the Background Color option, click the Background Color buttons and choose White.

8. Click the triangle to the right of the Form Field Is field; and from the drop-down menu, choose Hidden, as shown here:

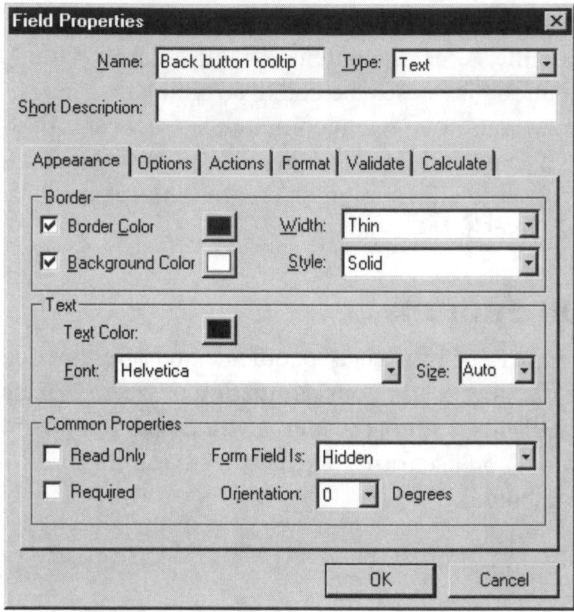

9. Click OK to close the dialog box and apply the properties to the field.

Now that you have created the tooltip, you have to program the button to make the tooltip visible when the user passes the mouse over the button. You do this by adding actions to the button as follows:

1. Select the Form tool.
2. Click the button that will trigger the tooltip you just created.
3. Right-click (Windows) or CTRL-click (Macintosh), and choose Properties from the context menu to open the Field Properties dialog box.
4. Click the Actions tab, and then click Mouse Enter.
5. Click the Add button to open the Add An Action dialog box.
6. Click the triangle to the right of the Type field, and choose Show/Hide Field from the drop-down menu.

7. Click the Edit button to open the Show/Hide Field dialog box, as shown in the following image. Every field you have created in the document is displayed in the large window.

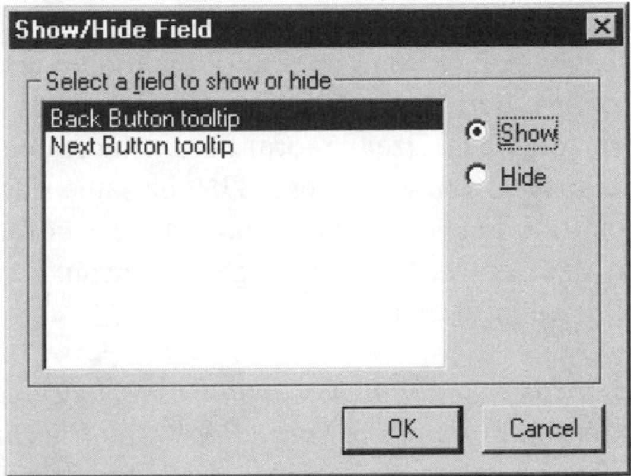

8. Choose the Show option, and then click the name of the field you want displayed when the user's mouse crosses over the field target area.
9. Click OK to close the Show/Hide Field dialog box, and then click Set Action to add the action to the button. The action you just added displays the tooltip; however, you need to add another action to hide the tooltip when the user's mouse exits the field target area.
10. Click Mouse Exit, and then click the Add button to open the Add An Action dialog box.
11. From the Type drop-down menu, choose Show/Hide Field.
12. Click the Edit button to open the Show/Hide Field dialog box.
13. Click Hide, and then select the tooltip's form field name from the window on the left.
14. Click OK to close the Show/Hide Field dialog box, and then click Set Action.
15. Click OK to close the Field Properties dialog box.

After programming the button, you can test your handiwork by selecting the Hand tool. When you move your cursor over the button, the tooltip should display; and when you move your cursor beyond the target area, the tooltip should disappear.

If either action did not execute properly, select the Form tool and then choose Properties from the context menu. Make sure you selected the right action for each event, and then double-check to make sure you selected the right field to be shown or hidden.

Notice that the instructions for creating the tooltip did not specify a font style or color, and accepted the default Auto option for the tooltip text size. When you accept the default options, Acrobat sizes the text to the field. If the text is too small, select the Form tool and resize the form field you created for the tooltip. If you have several tooltips and you want them to be the same size, select the Form tool, select the tooltip form fields, and then choose Tools | Forms | Fields | Size. Alternatively, choose Size from the Form Fields context menu. For more information on creating form fields, refer to Chapter 9.

If the audience for your eBook has limited experience with Acrobat, you can add a Viewing Tips page to your eBook. The Viewing Tips page lets the readers know what shortcuts they can use to advance pages, to zoom in or out on pages, and to fit pages to windows. All of the Acrobat keyboard shortcuts are listed in Appendix A.

Publish Your eBook

After you compile the elements and create navigation for your eBook, you need to apply the finishing touches and publish the document. To properly identify the document, you can change the Document Summary by choosing File | Document Properties | Document Summary. Enter the title for the eBook; the author's name; and any other pertinent information, such as the subject or any applicable keywords. If you have optimized everything using the suggested eBook settings, the document is ready to upload to an online eBook distributor. However, you can have Acrobat perform a final check by using PDF Consultant. Two other items you need to take care of before uploading the document are document security and Open Options.

Optimize Your eBook with PDF Consultant

You use PDF Consultant to audit the document, detect and remove any unnecessary or unwanted elements, and optimize the document. Even though you already optimized the document for online distribution as an eBook, you may have inadvertently created duplicate bookmarks or invalid links when compiling the elements of the eBook.

Audit Space Usage

You can use PDF Consultant to tell you what percentages of the document are devoted to text, images, fonts, and other document elements. PDF Consultant also breaks down each document element into the number of bytes used. To audit document space usage, choose Tools | PDF Consultant | Audit Space Usage. If you have not saved the file before invoking the command, Acrobat displays a warning dialog box. Click OK to perform the audit without resaving the document. Depending on the page size and number of elements in your eBook, the audit may take some time. After Acrobat completes the audit, the results are displayed in the dialog box shown in Figure 8-2.

Detect and Remove Unwanted Elements

You can use PDF Consultant to display a list of elements in your eBook, such as links, image alternatives, JavaScript, and so on. You can then choose which elements, if any, you want to remove from the document. To detect and remove unwanted elements, follow these steps.

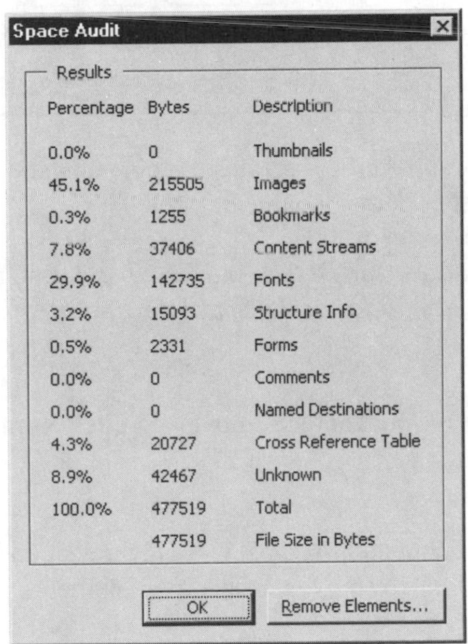

Space Audit
Results
Percentage Bytes Description
0.0% 0 Thumbnails
45.1% 215505 Images
0.3% 1255 Bookmarks
7.8% 37406 Content Streams
29.9% 142735 Fonts
3.2% 15093 Structure Info
0.5% 2331 Forms
0.0% 0 Comments
0.0% 0 Named Destinations
4.3% 20727 Cross Reference Table
8.9% 42467 Unknown
100.0% 477519 Total
477519 File Size in Bytes
OK
Remove Elements...

FIGURE 8-2 Audit space usage to see what percentage of the document is used by images, text, and so on.

1. Choose Tools | PDF Consultant | Detect And Remove to display the dialog box shown in the following image. Notice that all items on the list that appear in your document are selected by default. If you choose to remove all selected elements, you may destroy some of the document functionality. For example, if you have a JavaScript action attached to a button and choose to remove JavaScript Actions, the button will not work properly.

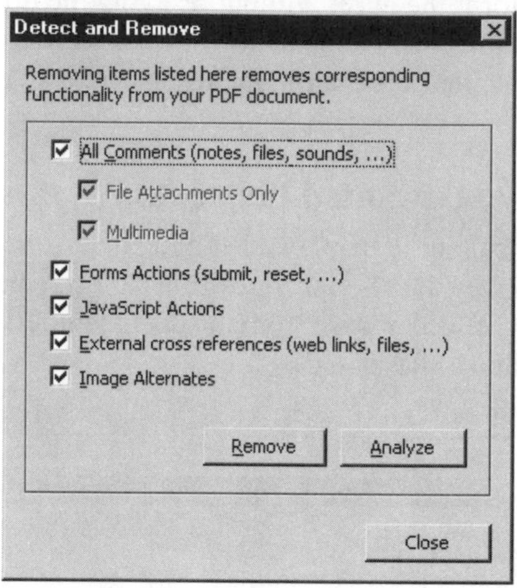

2. Click Analyze, and Acrobat creates a report that shows how many of each element is present in the document.

You can also access the Detect And Remove dialog box by clicking the Remove Elements button in the Space Audit dialog box, shown in Figure 8-2.

3. Choose the items you want to remove and click Remove.

Optimize Space

When you choose this command, Acrobat will only detect and remove the elements you specify, and it will only remove the specified elements if they are extraneous and not needed in the document. This is the safest method of optimizing a document with PDF Consultant. To optimize space in your eBook, do the following:

1. Choose Tools | PDF Consultant | Optimize Space to open the dialog box shown in the following image. If you have not saved the document recently, Acrobat opens a dialog box, prompting you to do so. Click Cancel if you want to save the document before performing the audit; otherwise, click OK to perform the command without saving.

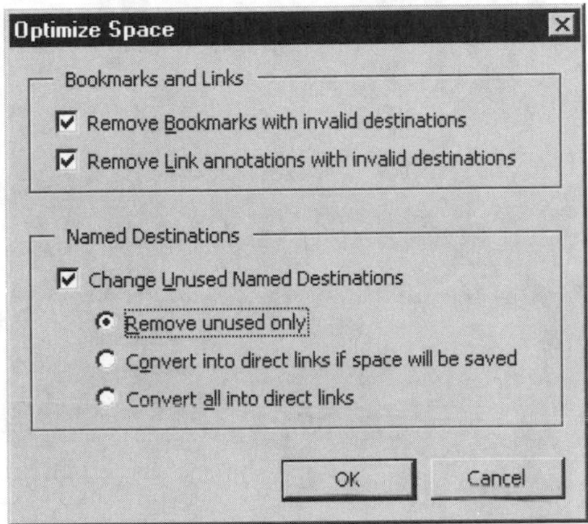

2. In the Bookmarks and Links section, choose which items you want Acrobat to optimize. Bookmarks and Link annotations with invalid destinations are selected by default.
3. In the Named Destinations section, Change Unused Named Destinations is selected by default. Disable this option and Acrobat will not make changes to unused named destinations it encounters.
4. If you choose the Change Unused Named Destinations options, choose one of the following: Remove unused only, Convert into direct links if space will be saved, or Convert all into direct links.

5. Click OK, and Acrobat searches the document for the items you specified. Acrobat displays the dialog box shown in the following image after completing the search:

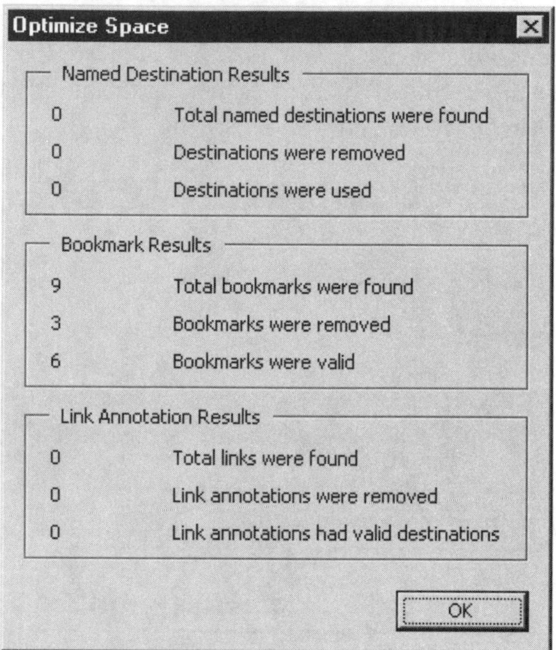

6. Click OK to complete the optimization.

Set Document Security

After you optimize the document, you are on the home stretch. The next task is to set document security. By applying document security, you can limit access to the document, for example, you can disable printing of the document. When you assign security to a document, you can choose either 40-bit or 128-bit security. If you choose 128-bit security, when you save the document, it will be converted to Acrobat 5.0 (PDF 1.4) compatibility.

While Acrobat security limits access to the document, it does not prevent the user from copying the eBook to another machine. If the eBook is being sold for profit, you will lose additional revenue when the eBook is redistributed from one user's machine to another. This loss of revenue can be prevented if the online bookseller who is distributing your book has software that encrypts the eBook to a user's machine. If your distributor has such software, do not apply Acrobat

Security to the document. If you decide to distribute eBooks directly from your Web site, you can subscribe to the Adobe Content Server. Adobe Content Server customers are provided with software that is used to package, distribute, and enable encryption of eBooks to the user's machine. For more information on the Adobe Content Server, you can visit the Adobe Content Server product page at www.adobe.com/products/contentserver.

Set Open Options

Before you save the eBook, you should set the Open Options for the book. When you set Open Options, you control what the viewer sees when the document opens in Acrobat or Acrobat Reader, and how it is displayed in the Document pane. If you created the document to be displayed in Landscape format, you can create an effective eBook using the following Open Options:

- **Page Only** Choose this option and specify the cover page of your eBook, and Acrobat displays the eBook cover while the Navigation pane is closed.
- **Fit To Window** Choose this option, and Acrobat opens the eBook to fit the window. If your eBook is sized proportionately to a computer monitor screen, a single page of the document will fit in the window.
- **Single Page** Choose this option, and Acrobat displays a single page of the document and does not permit scrolling to the next page with the Hand tool. This is the ideal setup if you have added your own navigation devices to the eBook, as outlined earlier in this chapter. Note that if you choose Continuous or Continuous Facing and open the document in Full Screen mode, Acrobat will revert to Single Page mode.
- **Open In Full Screen Mode** Choose this option, and the eBook opens in Full Screen mode with no interface. If you sized the eBook for monitor reading and created navigation devices for the book, this view comes the closest to simulating the experience of reading a bound book.

After you finish this final bit of housekeeping, save the eBook and upload it to the Web site where it will be distributed.

Create an eBook for Acrobat eBook Reader

Adobe created Acrobat eBook Reader as a dedicated software for viewing eBooks. You can find out more about Acrobat eBook Reader and download a free copy of the software at:http://www.adobe.com:80/products/ebookreader/. As of this writing, the latest incarnation of Acrobat eBook Reader, version 2.2, as shown in Figure 8-3, features all of the tools a reader needs to navigate an eBook. For Acrobat eBook Reader users who would rather listen than read, the software comes with a text-to-speech engine. This feature is also handy for the visually impaired. Readers also have the option to zoom in or zoom out on an eBook. The eBook Reader also features a link to the Adobe Web site where additional eBooks may be purchased.

After readers download and install the Acrobat eBook Reader, they can begin collecting a library of eBooks. The cover of every eBook is displayed in the Acrobat eBook Reader Library. To read an eBook, the reader opens the library and double-clicks a cover. As shown in Figure 8-4, the Acrobat eBook Reader menu has options to find out information about an eBook, lend or give an eBook to another reader, and set preferences. After choosing the Info menu option, the readers can click the

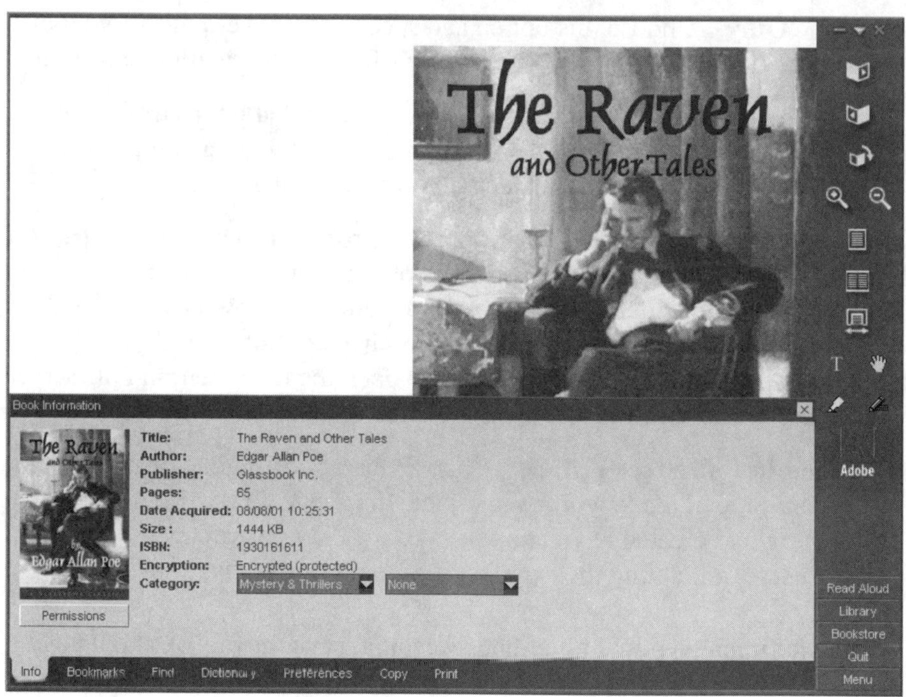

FIGURE 8-3 The Acrobat eBook Reader 2.2 is designed to simulate reading a bound book.

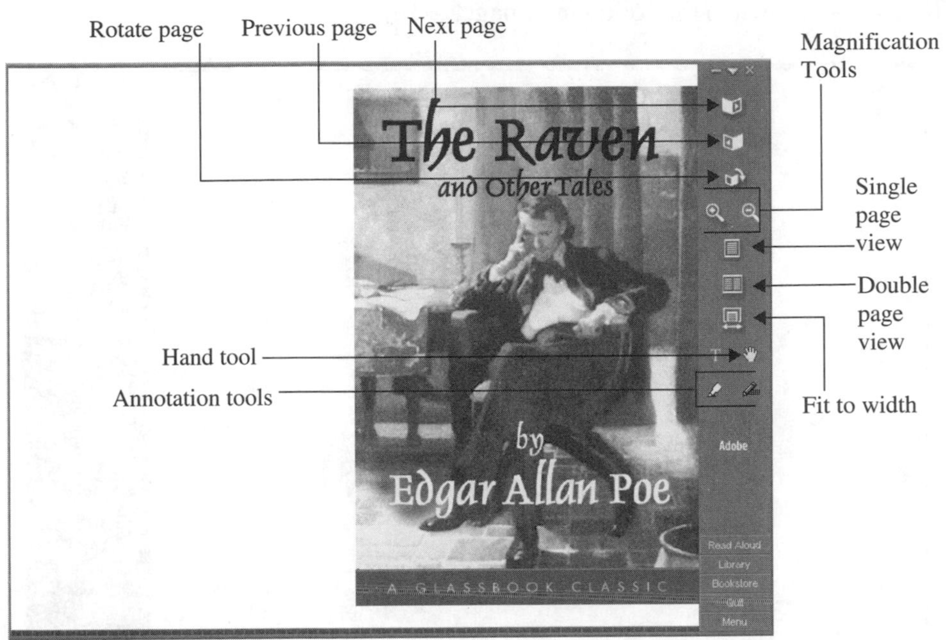

FIGURE 8-4 The Acrobat eBook Reader menu gives the reader access to additional features.

8

Permission button to find out exactly what they can and cannot do with the book. Readers also have access to a dictionary.

Download Books for Acrobat eBook Reader

Readers can download books for Acrobat eBook Reader at the following Web address, which is part of the Adobe Web site:http://bookstore.glassbook.com/store/default.asp. Free titles are available at: http://bookstore.glassbook.com/store/free_title_list.asp. After readers log onto the site and choose a title to purchase, they are prompted for an e-mail address and password if they are returning customers, or for full registration if they are new customers. After choosing one of more eBooks for purchase, readers check out, upon which time an Acrobat Reader

Launcher is downloaded to their computer. This icon is double-clicked while the reader is still online, and the purchase is downloaded directly into Acrobat e-Reader, as shown in the following image.

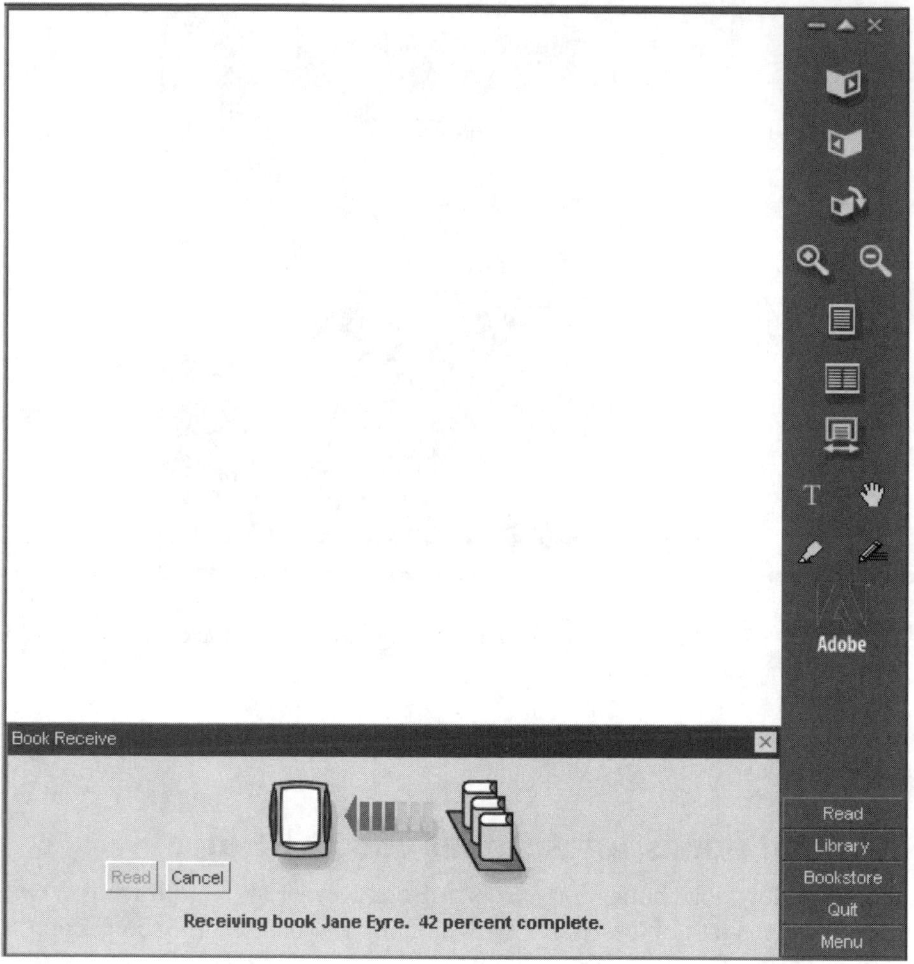

NOTE *eBooks downloaded from the Adobe website are PDF documents; however, if you try to open an Adobe eBook in Acrobat or Acrobat Reader, a warning dialog box appears telling you the document requires the Acrobat eBook Reader.*

Design an eBook for Acrobat eBook Reader

When you design an eBook to be viewed in Acrobat eBook Reader, a few differences apply. First and foremost, you must design the eBook in single-page format. If you design an eBook with two columns facing side by side, the document will not display correctly if the Acrobat eBook Reader user displays the book in side-by-side format. Create a document approximately 6 × 9 inches. The same considerations for fonts and images, as discussed earlier in this chapter, apply to an eBook designed to be viewed with the eBook Reader. You will not need to create navigation devices, as Acrobat eBook Reader has built-in tools to turn pages and magnify the document. Users of eBook Reader can also create their own bookmarks. When you specify Open Options for a document that will be viewed on an eBook Reader, choose Fit To Width. You should also be aware of the fact that Acrobat eBook Reader does not support form field buttons with JavaScript.

When you design the cover for a document optimized for Acrobat eBook Reader, create a thumbnail version of the cover that measures 100 pixels wide. Resize the image so the thumbnail height is proportional to the original image dimensions. After you create the eBook, use the File Attachment tool to attach the thumbnail to the cover page. However, you do not want the File Attachment icon to be visible on the cover so be sure to select an area in the Document pane that is not on the cover when attaching the file. For more information on the File Attachment tool, refer to Chapter 12. The attached JPEG file is what Acrobat eBook Reader sees when the book is added to the user's library.

About Web Buy

Web Buy gives you the ability to purchase and download PDF files that have been encrypted with Adobe Content Server software. Adobe Content Server software has methods for protecting the rights of publishers and authors by locking PDF files to a specific machine. Web Buy makes it possible for you to unlock these files and view them on your computer.

Web Buy Preferences

When you set Web Buy preferences, you specify the information about your machine that sellers automatically have access to when you purchase secure PDF documents over the Internet. If a seller tries to obtain information other than what you specify, a warning dialog box appears in your web browser. To set Web Buy preferences, follow these steps.

1. Choose Edit | Preferences, and then choose Web Buy from the list to open the dialog box shown in the following image.

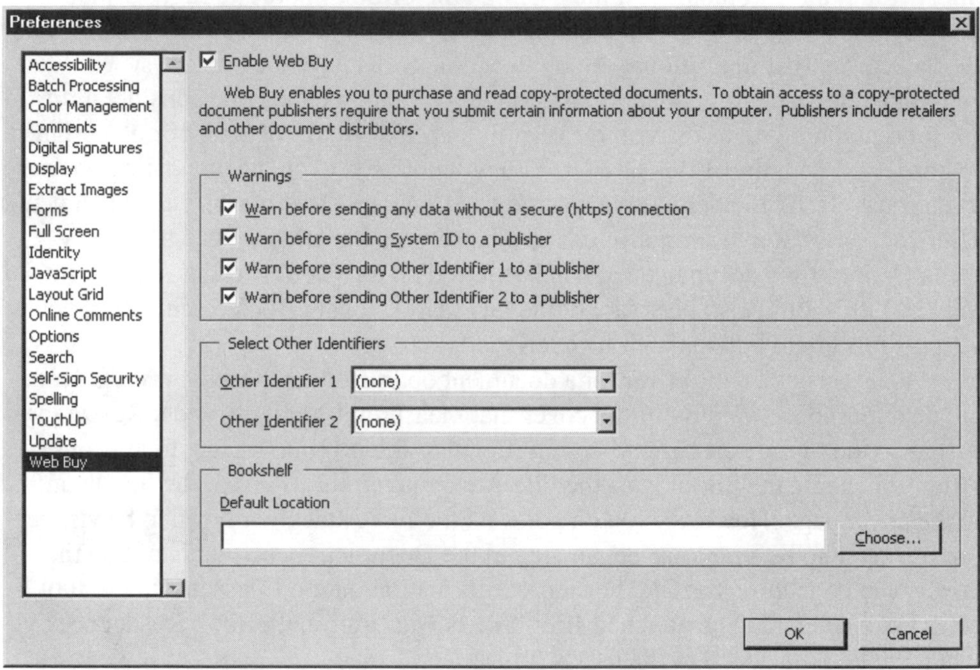

2. Make sure the Enable Web Buy option is selected.
3. Choose the warnings you would like to receive before information from your computer is sent to a seller.
4. In the Other Identifier 1 and Other Identifier 2 fields, choose a preferred storage device. Click the triangle to the right of each field for a drop-down menu that lists storage devices on your computer.
5. In the Default Location field, enter the path to the directory where you would like downloaded PDF documents and their accompanying files stored. Alternatively, click the Choose button, use the Browse For Folder dialog box to navigate to the desired folder, and then click OK.

Chapter 9 Create Forms

How to...

- Add form fields
- Define form properties
- Validate form fields
- Create form buttons
- Submit forms

In previous chapter you learned how to use form elements for navigation. However, this is only part of the functionality form elements lend to your PDF documents. You use form elements to retrieve information from readers of your PDF documents. You can also create forms for orders, questionnaires, and for getting viewer feedback from a website. You can create forms that tally the results of an online purchase and then submit the order to the online seller.

In this chapter, you will learn to use the basic Acrobat form elements to create your own forms. A PDF form is a compilation of data fields that you use to accumulate data from users. The fields can be used to collect text and numeric data. You can specify the field format to control the type and look of the data entered. Your form can be a combination of text boxes, check boxes, combo boxes, list boxes, radio buttons, and signature fields. You can create buttons for the users to submit the data or reset the form. If you create a form for Web use, and the web-host server supports CGI (Common Gateway Interface) scripting, you can have the form results forwarded to a web site or entered into a database.

Create a PDF Form

When you create a PDF form, you can scan an existing paper form into Acrobat and then use the Form tool to create interactive form fields in the same position as the fields in the scanned document. When you create a form in this manner, you have the look and feel of the original form along with the interactivity of the Acrobat form fields. You can also create a form from scratch by creating the textual and graphic elements in an authoring application, converting the document to PDF format, and then using the Form tool to create interactive form fields and elements. Figure 9-1 shows a product registration form that was created by converting a Word document to PDF format and then creating the individual form elements in Acrobat with the Form tool.

Adobe Acrobat - [Product Registration form.pdf]

File Edit Document Tools View Window Help

Widgets r Us Product Registration

Thank you for purchasing a Widgets r Us digitizer. To register your product and receive free 90 day technical support, fill out the following form.

Last Name: First Name: Middle Initial:

Address:

City: State: AZ Zip Code:

Daytime Phone Number: Evening Phone Number:

FAX Number: E-mail:

Product purchased: Serial Number:

Date purchased: Reseller:

What do you use your Widgets r Us digitizer for?

Graphic Arts Architecture

CD ROM presentation Web site design

3D content for multimedia or the Web Other

Would you like to receive our monthly online newsletter? Yes No

Thank you for registering your product. Reset Submit

1 of 1 720 x 558 pt

FIGURE 9-1 You can create PDF forms to collect data.

Fill Out a PDF Form

When users decide to fill out a form, such as the one shown in Figure 9-1, they click inside a field with the Hand tool. When the user clicks inside the form field, the cursor becomes an I-beam. Data is entered from the user's keyboard. To navigate to another field, the user can either click inside another field with the selected Hand tool, or press TAB. When the user presses TAB, the cursor appears in the next field (in the order created within Acrobat). The user can correct an entry error by clicking inside the field with the Hand tool, click and drag to select a word or letter that needs to be changed, and then enter the new data. If the form is equipped with a properly programmed Reset button, the user can start over by clicking the button.

About Acrobat Form Fields

You use the Form tool to create fields in your PDF forms. You specify the type of data the field can accept, or what the form field does. You can assign actions to form fields to create a desired result when a user interacts with the form field. When you create a Form field, it can be in any of the following formats:

- **Button** You can create a text-only button, an icon-only button, or a button with both an icon and text. You can create an invisible button and place it over an existing graphic on a form that you scanned and converted to PDF format. This gives the appearance that the graphic is actually executing the action instead of the form field.
- **Check box** You create a group of check boxes when you want the user to choose from a set of options. For example, if you create a PDF questionnaire, you can create a series of check boxes for the user to select one or more items, such as the publications the user frequently reads.
- **Combo box** When you create a combo box, you give the user a choice of options. A combo box is designated by a downward-pointing triangle. When the triangle is clicked, a menu drops down with a list of available choices.
- **List box** You create a list box to display a list of available choices for the user. You can specify parameters that enable the user to make multiple selections from a list box (something that is not possible with a combo box). If the number of items in the list box exceeds the dimensions of the box, Acrobat provides scroll bars.
- **Radio buttons** You create a group of radio buttons to limit the user's choice to one item per group of radio buttons. For example, if you design an online order form, you can create a group of radio buttons with credit card options. The user chooses the option that applies.
- **Signature** You create digital signature fields for authorized users to digitally sign the form.
- **Text** You create a text field to accept user input, or you can use a text field to display data, such as the current date.

Design a Form

You can create a form from scratch in any existing PDF document. Create the labels for all of your fields by creating read-only text boxes, and then create the fields for user input data. However, the easiest method of creating a form is to lay out the basic design of the form in an authoring application and then to convert the file to PDF format. Then, open the PDF file in Acrobat to add and format the form fields. Another alternative is to scan an existing form into Acrobat and create the necessary form fields.

Use the Layout Grid

Whether you decide to create your form from an existing document or lay out one from scratch, you can use the Layout Grid to provide a visual reference while creating and aligning form fields. To enable the grid shown in Figure 9-2, choose View | Grid.

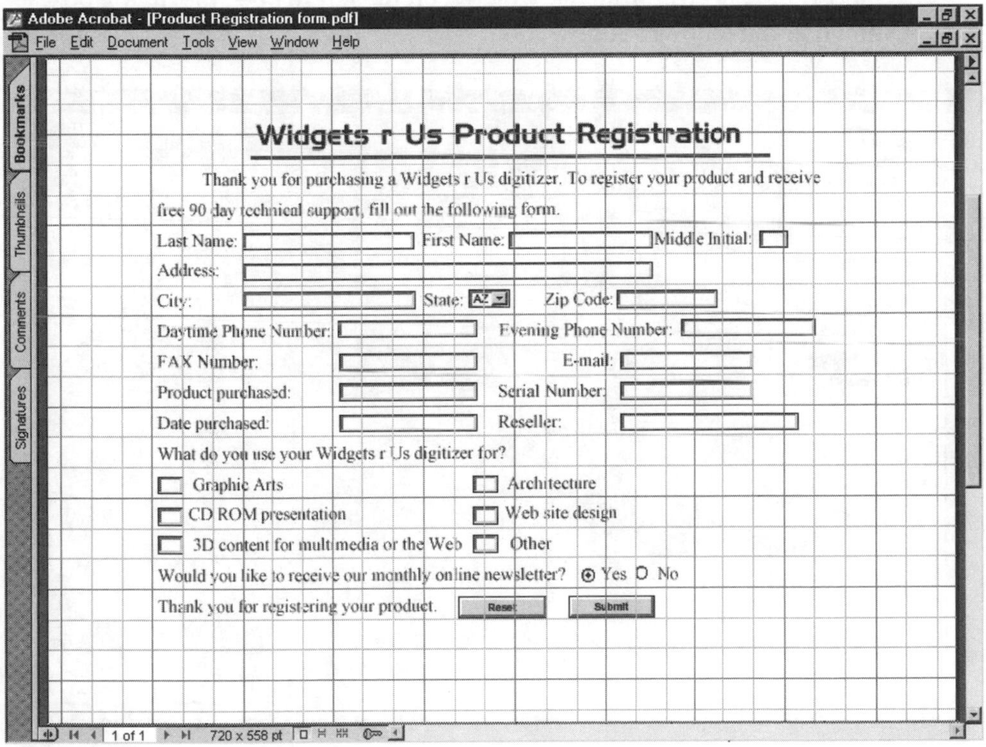

FIGURE 9-2 Use the Layout Grid to precisely place and size form field elements.

Use the Snap to Grid Command

When you enable the Layout Grid, you can visually align and size items to intersecting grid points. Use any of the Viewing tools to zoom in on your work. For exact alignment and sizing, choose View | Snap to Grid. When you use this command, the Layout Grid develops a magnetic personality and any object you create will snap to the grid points.

Set Layout Grid Preferences

The default color and spacing of the Layout Grid works well for most instances. However, if the grid color and spacing are not suited to the document you've work on, you can easily modify the grid by following these steps:

1. Choose Edit | Preferences | General to open the Preferences dialog box.
2. Choose Layout Grid from the window on the left to open the dialog box, as shown in the following illustration:

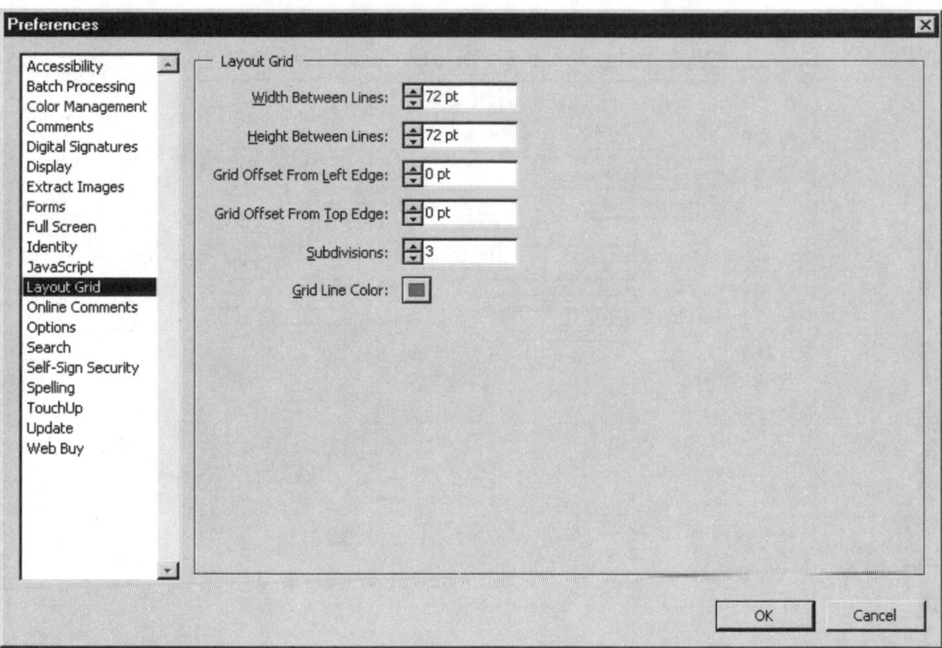

3. To define grid spacing, enter values in the Width Between Lines and Height Between Lines fields. Alternatively, you can use the spinner

buttons to increase or decrease the value. If possible, specify values that will divide evenly into the width and height of the document. You can always change the Layout Grid Preferences when working on a different size document.

4. To change the grid offset from either the top or left side of the document, enter values in the Grid Offset From Left Edge and Grid Offset From Top Edge fields. Alternatively, you can click the spinner buttons to increase or decrease each value. You may be able to compensate for an odd-sized document or line spacing in a scanned document by modifying the grid offset.
5. To subdivide each grid section, enter a value in the Subdivisions field. For example, if you enter a value of 2, the horizontal space between grid lines is divided by 2 and the vertical space between grid lines is divided by 2, effectively breaking each grid space into 4 sections.
6. To modify the grid color, click the Grid Line Color button and choose a color from the pop-up palette, or click the Custom button to choose a color from the system color picker. Choose a grid color that contrasts well with the predominate color in your document.
7. Click OK to complete your modifications to the grid.

Create Form Fields

After you create the PDF document that is the basis for your form, you are ready to start creating interactive form fields. You create form fields by defining the field area with the Form tool. After you define the field area, name the field, and then choose a field type. Each field type has its own parameters that you use to modify the field to suit the needs of the form you create. If the form fields contain text, you can spell check the field as well. To create a form field, follow these steps:

1. Select the Form tool, shown on the left:
2. Click the point where you want the form field to begin, and then drag down and across. When you use the Form tool, your cursor becomes a crosshair. As you drag the tool to define a field, a bounding box gives you a preview of the form field area. When the form field is the desired size, release the

mouse button to open the Field Properties dialog box shown in the following illustration:

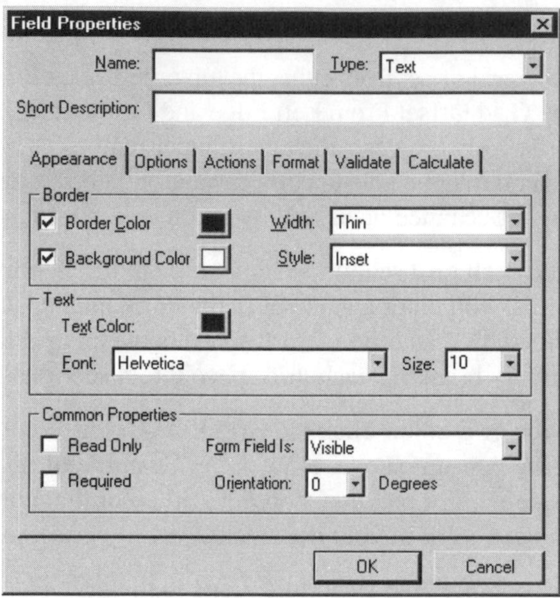

3. In the Name field, enter a name for the field.
4. In the Short Description field, enter any comments or notes that apply to the field (this step is optional). The comments are for reference only, but may come in handy if you need to update the form several months from now, or if you work on a document with other authors. Note that any text you enter in the description field can also be used as a tooltip. If the user holds the mouse over the form field, the description appears in a few short moments.
5. Click the triangle to the right of the Type field, and choose the desired field type from the drop-down menu. Each field type has different parameters that will be discussed in detail in upcoming sections.
6. Click the Options tab and specify the options for the field type. The choices in this tab differ for each field type and will be discussed in detail in upcoming sections.

7. Click the Actions tab, choose an action, and then click the Set Action button. Actions were discussed in detail in Chapter 7 and will be presented as they apply to individual field types.
8. Select the mouse event that will trigger the action. Choose from the following:
   - **Mouse Up** Choose this mouse event, and the action executes when the user releases the mouse button (the upstroke of a mouse click).
   - **Mouse Down** Choose this mouse event, and the action occurs when the user presses the mouse button (the downstroke of a mouse click).
   - **Mouse Enter** Choose this mouse event, and the action occurs when the user passes the mouse over the field boundaries. This mouse event is useful for creating effects like tooltips, which were discussed in Chapter 8.
   - **Mouse Exit** Choose this mouse event, and the action executes when the user moves the mouse beyond the field target area.
   - **On Focus** Choose this mouse event, and the action occurs when the field is selected, either through a mouse action or tabbing.
   - **On Blur** Choose this mouse event, and the action occurs when the field is deselected as a result of a mouse action or tabbing.
9. Click the Appearance tab, and select appearance options for the field. For specific instructions on setting appearance parameters, refer to the next section, "Specify Field Appearance."
10. Click OK to complete the creation of the form field.

Specify Field Appearance

When you create a PDF form, you can change the appearance of a field to suit the document. You can choose to have a border or not and choose to have a background or not and, if applicable, specify border and background colors. You can also control text attributes and determine whether the user is required to fill in the field. To specify the appearance of a form field, do the following:

1. Create a form field, as outlined in the previous section.

2. Click the Appearance tab to reveal the dialog box in the following illustration:

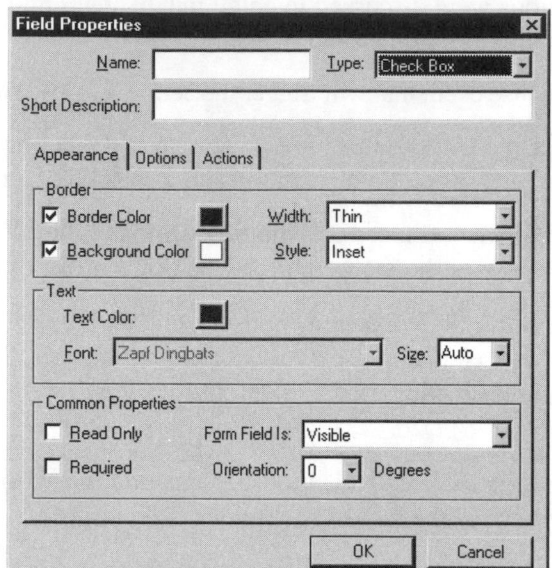

3. In the Border section, choose Border Color to create a rectangular border around the field, choose Background Color to create a field with a color background, or choose neither or both.
4. If you choose to create a field with either a Border Color or a Background Color, click the button to the right of the field and choose a color from the pop-up palette. To create a custom color, click the More Colors button and then choose a color from the system color picker.
5. Click the triangle to the right of the Width field; and, from the drop-down menu, choose Thin, Medium, or Thick. You use this option to specify the width of the border.
6. Click the triangle to the right of the Style field; and, from the drop-down menu, choose Solid, Dashed, Beveled, Inset, or Underlined. The following illustration shows the different styles as applied to a button:

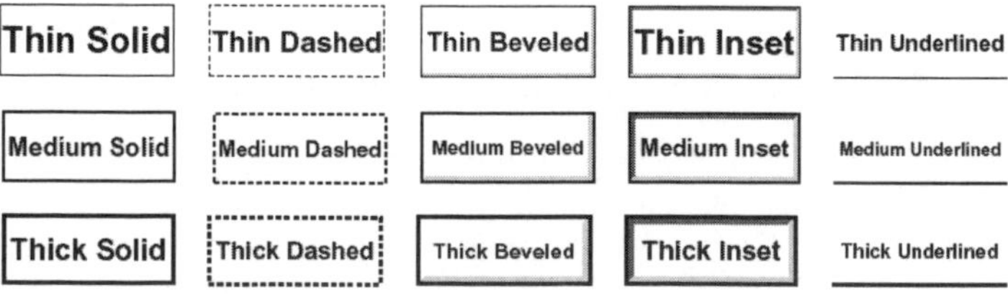

7. If the field type you choose has text, click the Text Color button and choose a color from the pop-up palette. Alternatively, you can click the More Colors button to create a custom color from the system color picker.
8. Click the triangle to the right of the Font field and choose a font from the drop-down menu. Note that if you select a font not available on the user's system, the field font will revert to the user's default system font, or, if able, Acrobat will render a reasonable facsimile of the original font. You can always embed the font, but be aware that font licensing issues may be involved and embedding fonts will bloat the file size.
9. Click the triangle to the right of the Size field, and choose a size from the drop-down menu. Alternatively, you can enter a value no smaller than 2 pts (points) and no larger than 144 pts. If you select Auto, Acrobat will size the text to fit the field with the exception of a text field that is set to display multiple lines. For a text field with multiple lines, the Auto option defaults to a font size of 12 pts.
10. In the Common Properties section, choose Read Only and the user will not be able to alter the contents of the field. Use this option when you create a text field for use as a label, or to display multiple lines of informative text.
11. In the Common Properties section, choose Required if you want the user to fill in the field. When a required field is left unfilled, Acrobat displays a warning dialog box informing the user that the field is empty.
12. Click the triangle to the right of the Form Field Is field, and from the drop-down menu choose one of the following: Visible, Hidden, Visible But Doesn't Print, or Hidden But Printable.
13. Click the triangle to the right of the Orientation field and choose an option from the drop-down menu. Choose any option other than the default to rotate the field 90°, 180°, or 270°.

After you set appearance options for the field, click the other tabs, choose the parameters that apply, and then click OK to complete the field.

TIP *After you create a field, align it, and set up all the parameters, you can prevent accidentally moving or otherwise editing the field. Select the Form tool, click the field, and then choose Lock from the context menu. If you attempt to edit the properties of a locked field, Acrobat displays a warning dialog box telling you the field is locked and edits will not be saved. To unlock a field, select it with the Form tool, and then choose Unlock from the context menu.*

Create a Button Field

You can use buttons for many things in Acrobat. You can use them for navigation devices, as discussed in Chapter 7, and you can use them to submit forms or initiate an action. When you create a button, you can assign different actions to each state of the button. For example, you can have a sound play when the user rolls the mouse over the button. You can even change the appearance of the button based on the interaction of the user's mouse with the button. To create a button field, follow these steps:

1. Select the Form tool and define the boundaries of the field.
2. Click the Appearance tab and specify the applicable appearance options, as outlined previously in the "Specify Field Appearance" section.

If you select the Read Only option, the button will not be interactive and any action you assign to it will not execute.

3. Click the Options tab.
4. Click the triangle to the right of the Highlight tab, and from the drop-down menu, choose one of the following:
   - Choose Invert and the button colors invert when the button is clicked.
   - Choose None and the button appearance does not change when clicked.
   - Choose Outline and the button outline is highlighted when clicked.
   - Choose Push and change the appearance of the button face in the Up, Down, and Rollover states.
5. Click the triangle to the right of the Layout field, and from the drop-down menu, choose one of the following options: Text Only; Icon; Icon Top, Text Bottom; Text Top, Icon Bottom; Icon Left, Text Right; Text Right, Icon Left; or Text Over Icon. Refer to Figure 9-3 for an example of each button layout.
6. In the Button Face Attributes section, if you choose a layout with text, enter the button text in the Text field. If you choose a layout with an icon, click the Icon button and select an image for the button face. For more information on using an image for a button face, refer to the upcoming section, "Create a Custom Multi-state Rollover Button."

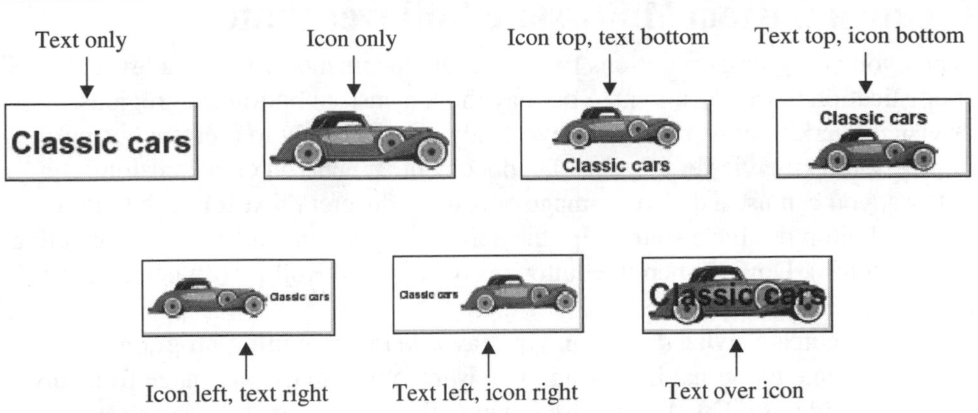

FIGURE 9-3 Customize the appearance of a button by choosing a different layout.

7. If you choose Push for the Highlight option, click one of the three states (Up, Down, or Rollover) and, in the Button Face Attributes section, specify the text and icon decoration for the button when it is in this state. For more information on using the Push Highlight option, refer to the upcoming section, "Create a Custom Multi-state Rollover Button."
8. Click the Actions tab and specify the actions you want to occur when the user interacts with the button. Remember, you can apply multiple actions to the button for each state. For example, on Mouse Enter, you can have a sound play and a tooltip appear; on Mouse Exit, you can hide the tooltip and mute the sound. When you specify different actions and use the Push Highlight option, you create highly interactive buttons that pique user interest. When you add a sound file to a button, use a small file, otherwise the timing may be off as Acrobat has to load the sound and the necessary libraries to play it. For more information on mouse events, refer to "Create Form Fields," earlier in this chapter.
9. Click OK to complete the creation of the button.

After creating the button, you can forge ahead to the next field you need to create for the form. However, it is a good idea to select the Hand tool and test the button to make sure it has the functionality you desire.

Create a Custom Multi-state Rollover Button

When you create custom buttons for your PDF documents, you add a level of sophistication to the document. You may think a custom button is egregious, or visual overkill, however, visual eye candy is more likely to create a lasting impression on the viewer of your PDF document. When you create custom buttons, you can use a different image or display different text for each button state. A button has three states, Up (the default state when a user is not interacting with a button), Down (when the button is clicked), and Rollover (when a user rolls a mouse over a button).

You can create stylized icons in your favorite image-editing program, or use clipart to create the visual impression you want. You can use an image from any file format supported by Acrobat for a button icon. You can also use an image saved in PDF format. Images can be scaled to fit the button area. To create a custom multi-state rollover button, follow these steps:

1. Use the Form tool to define the area for the button.
2. Name the form field, and then choose Button from the Type drop-down menu. If desired, enter a description in the Short Description field. The information you enter in this field makes it easier to identify what a form field does when you create a form with multiple fields.
3. Click the Appearance tab, and specify the Border, Text, and Common Properties attributes.
4. Click the Options tab.
5. Click the triangle to the right of the Highlight field, and choose Push from the drop-down menu. When you choose the Push option, you can display a different image or text for each button state. You have three button states to work with:
   - **Up** The image you choose for the Up state is the default appearance of the button when the user's mouse is not interacting with the button.
   - **Down** The image you choose for the Down state determines what the user sees when the button is clicked.
   - **Rollover** The image you choose for the Rollover state determines what the user sees when mouse is rolled over the button target area.

NOTE *When choosing images for buttons, use your image-editing software to optimize them to the smallest possible file size. If you use a large image file for a button rollover, the action may execute before the image loads.*

6. Click the triangle to the right of the Layout field, and from the drop-down menu choose one of the options that includes an icon. If you choose a layout that involves both text and icon, you can change both attributes in each of the button states.
7. Click the Select Icon button to open the Select Appearance dialog box.
8. Click the Browse button to open the Open dialog box, and then select the image file you want to use for the button face. You can use the following Acrobat-supported image formats for button icons: BMP, GIF, JPEG, PNG, PCX, and TIFF. You can use PDF files for button icons, as well.
9. After you select the image for the button face, it displays in the Sample window. Click OK to apply the image to the icon.
10. In the Button Face When window, select the next button state you want to use.
11. Repeat steps 6 through 9.
12. When you have modified button appearance options for all of the states, click OK.
13. Select the Hand tool and test the button.

When you use an image for a button icon, Acrobat automatically scales it to fit the form field. You can use the Layout Grid to size the form field to the approximate proportions of the icon. To precisely size the form field, refer to "Align, Reposition, and Resize Form Field," later in the chapter.

Rescale a Button Icon

After you test the button, you may find that you need to fine-tune the button face. You can modify the way Acrobat scales the image to the button face by doing the following:

1. With the Form tool, select the button you want to modify.

2. Right-click (Windows) or CTRL-click (Macintosh), and choose Properties from the context menu.
3. Click the Options tab, and then click the Advanced Layout button to open the Icon Placement dialog box shown in the following image:

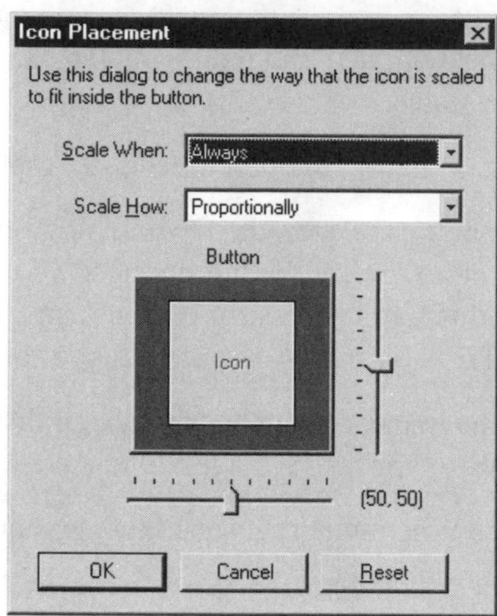

4. Click the triangle to the right of the Scale When field, and choose one of the following options:
   - **Always** Choose this option, and Acrobat always scales the icon to fit, regardless of its size in relation to the form field.
   - **Never** Choose this option, and Acrobat inserts the icon as originally sized. If the icon is too large for the field, it is clipped from top left to bottom right.
   - **Too Big** Choose this option, and Acrobat resizes the icon to the form field if it is larger than the form field dimensions.
   - **Too Small** Choose this option, and Acrobat resizes the icon to the form field if it is smaller than the form field dimensions. Note that if the icon is considerably smaller than the field size, the image will be pixelated.
5. Click the triangle to the right of the Scale How field, and choose one of the following options:

- **Proportionally** Choose this option, and Acrobat preserves the proportion of the original image when resizing it to fit the form field.
- **Non-proportionally** Choose this option, and Acrobat resizes the icon to the proportions of the form field.

6. Drag the sliders in the Button window to determine icon placement in relation to the form field. By default, equal margins are preserved around the button. To modify the margin on sides of the icon, drag the horizontal slider left or right. To modify the margin on the top and bottom of the icon, drag the vertical slider up or down.
7. Click OK to apply the parameters to the button icon.

Create a Check Box

You use check boxes to give the user the opportunity to choose more than one option. For example, if you create a questionnaire, you can use check boxes to collect information about which magazines the user reads. The user selects each applicable magazine, and the results are sent to the location you specify when the form is submitted. To create a check box, follow these steps:

1. Select the Form tool, and define the area and position of the field. Generally, you want to create a square form field for a check box. Remember, you can always enable the Layout Grid and choose the Snap To Grid option for assistance when creating form fields.
2. Enter a name for the form field; and, from the Type drop-down menu , choose Check Box.
3. Click the Appearance tab, and modify the parameters as outlined previously in the section "Specify Field Appearance."
4. Click the Options tab.
5. Click the triangle to the right of the Check Style field, and from the drop-down menu choose Check, Circle, Cross, Diamond, Square, or Star. This option determines what the check box looks like when selected. Note that some of these options may not render properly on different platforms. If possible, test the document on every platform your intended audience may use. When in doubt, Check is usually the best choice.

6. In the Export Value field, enter the value you want exported when the check box is selected. If you create a form where the results will be submitted to a CGI application, check with your web host server to find out the values required and their proper format for the CGI script that you use.
7. Select Default Is Checked and the check style you choose appears in the check box when the document loads; otherwise, the check box is empty.
8. Click OK to complete the check box.

If you create a series of check boxes that are different options for a form element, such as a question, choose the same name for each check box, but specify a different Export Value. For example, if you are creating check boxes to gather a response for a simple question, you create two check boxes for each question and give one a "Yes" export value and the other a "No" export value.

Create a Combo Box

You can use a combo box to display a list of items. Create a combo box when you want the user to select only one item from the list. A combo box functions like a drop-down menu; by clicking a small triangle, the first item on the list displays and you access the menu. To create a combo box, follow these steps:

1. Select the Form tool, and define the area of the field.
2. Enter a name for the field, and choose Combo Box from the Type drop-down menu.
3. Click the Appearance tab and adjust the parameters to suit the style of your form, as previously outlined in the section "Specify Field Appearance."
4. Click the Options tab.
5. In the Item field, enter the first item in your list.
6. In the Export field, enter the export value for the item. If no value is entered, the item is exported with the value listed in the item field.
7. Click Add to add the item to the combo box.
8. Repeat steps 4 through 6 to add additional items to the list.
9. After adding all the items to the list, you can select the following options:

- **Sort Items** Choose this option, and Acrobat sorts the items numerically and then alphabetically.
- **Editable** Choose this option if you want to give users the capability to modify list items or enter their own item.

10. If you did not choose the Sort Items option, you can manually reorder the list. Select a list item and click the Up button to move the item one position higher in the list; click the Down button to move the item one position lower in the list. If the item is at either extremity of the list, the applicable button is dimmed out.
11. Click the Validate tab to restrict the range of data that can be entered in the combo box. For more information on this option, refer to the section, "Validate Form Fields."
12. Click the Calculate tab if you want to use items from the combo box to perform a mathematical calculation. For more information on creating a calculating form field, refer to the section "Calculate Form Fields," in the later in this chapter.
13. Click OK to complete the creation of the combo box. The following image shows a completed combo box:

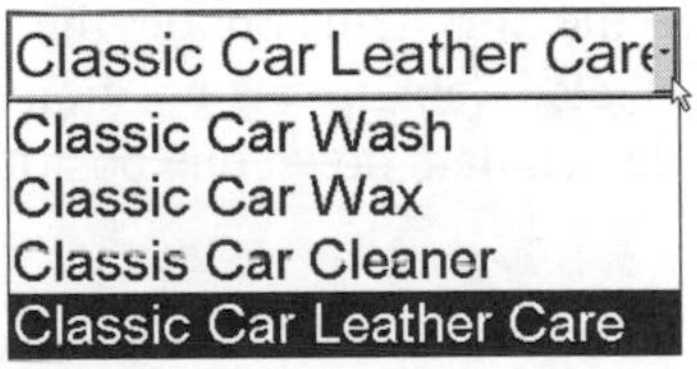

Create a List Box

You create a list box when you want the capability to select multiple items. When you create a list box, you can scroll through the list, as opposed to opening a drop-down menu with the combo box. You cannot edit items in a list box; however, you can select multiple items from the list, whereas only one item can be selected from a combo box. You can use JavaScript to create a custom action when you change the list box selection. To create a list box, follow these steps:

1. Select the Form tool, and define the area and position of the list box.

2. Enter a name for the field, and from the Type drop-down menu choose List Box.
3. Click the Appearance tab, and define the appearance parameters for the list box, as discussed in "Specify Field Appearance."
4. Click the Options tab.
5. In the Item field, enter a name for the first item in the list.
6. In the Export field, enter the export value of the item. If you leave this field blank, the item name becomes the export value.
7. Click the Add button to add the item to the list box.
8. Repeat steps 5 through 7 to add additional items to the list.
9. After you finish adding items to the list, you can choose the following options:
   - **Sort Items** Choose this option, and Acrobat sorts the list items in numerical and alphabetical order.
   - **Multiple Items** Choose this option and you will be able to make multiple selections from the list.
10. If you did not choose the Sort Items option, the Up and Down buttons are active. To move a selected item up one position in the list, click the Up button; to move a selected item down one position in the list, click the Down button.
11. Click the Selection Change tab, and choose one of the following options:
    - **Nothing happens when a list box selection changes** This is the default option, and, true to its word, nothing other than the selection change happens when you change a selection.
    - **This script executes when the list box selection changes** Choose this option, and the Edit button becomes active. Click the Edit button to open the JavaScript Edit dialog box. Create the script that will execute when a list box item changes, and click OK to close the dialog box.
12. Click OK to complete the creation of your list box.

Create a Radio Button

When you create a radio button, you create a form device that enables a user to make a selection. When you create a group of radio buttons for the user to choose an option, only one button can be selected from the group, thus limiting the user to one selection. When you create a group of related radio buttons, each button has the same name but a different *export value*. The export value is used by the CGI application of a Web server to transmit the user's choice as a form result; or, if you are adept at JavaScript, your custom script can use the export value. To create a radio button, follow these steps:

1. Select the Form tool, and define the size and position of the field.
2. Enter a name for the field, and from the Type drop-down menu choose Radio Button.
3. Click the Options tab.
4. Click the triangle to the right of the Radio Style field, and from the drop-down menu choose one of the following: Check, Circle, Cross, Diamond, Square, or Star. This option determines what the radio button looks like when selected.
5. Enter an Export value for the button.
6. Choose Default Is Checked, and, when the document loads, Acrobat will fill the field with the radio style you selected in step 4. If you create a group of radio buttons with the same name, only one button can be set up with the Default Is Checked option.
7. Click OK to complete creation of your radio button.

TIP *To create an exact copy of a field, select the field with the Form tool, and then, while holding down CTRL (Windows) or COMMAND (Macintosh), drag the form field. After you begin dragging the form field, press SHIFT to constrain motion vertically or horizontally. Release the mouse button to complete copying the field. If the copied field is part of a group of radio buttons, choose Properties from the context menu and change the export value of the field but not its name.*

Create a Text Field

You can create text fields to accept user input, or you can use them to display text strings, such as the current date. You can also use text fields to display multiple lines of text. You can limit the number of characters in the field and determine whether the field is visible or not. Invisible fields are useful for creating help options or tooltips. For more information on creating tooltips, refer to Chapter 8. To create a text field, follow these steps:

1. Select the Form tool, and define the area for the field.
2. Enter a name for the field, and from the Type drop-down menu choose Text.
3. Set the Appearance options for the field, as outlined earlier in "Specify Field Appearance."
4. Click the Options tab to modify the following parameters:
   - In the Default field, enter the default value for the field. This value will be submitted unless the user enters different data. Alternatively, you can leave this field blank.
   - Click the triangle to the right of the Alignment field, and choose to align the field contents to the Left, Center, or Right.
   - Enable the Multi-line option to display the contents of the field on multiple lines. If this option is not enabled and the contents of the field exceed the width of the text box, the text will be truncated.
   - Enable the Do Not Scroll option, and users will not be able to scroll through the contents of a multiline text box. This option is deselected by default; users of the form can scroll through the field and edit the contents. Furthermore, if you use the text box to display Read Only text and the Do Not Scroll option is deselected, the user will not be able to scroll the contents of the field, as no scroll bars will be present. If you create a Read Only text box with multiple lines of text, be sure to properly size the box so every line of text is visible.
   - To limit the number of characters a user can enter in the field, enable the Limit of [ ] Characters option and enter a value in the field.
   - Enable the Password option, and each character of text displays as an asterisk. The option is not available until you deselect the Do Not Spell Check option.

- Enable the Field Is Used For File Selection, and a path to a file can be entered as the value of the field. This option is dimmed out until you select the Do Not Spell Check option. It is also unavailable if you have specified a default value for the field or enabled the Multi-line, Limit Of Characters, or Password options. Likewise, it is unavailable if you have defined the field with formatting script.
- Enable the Do Not Spell Check option, and the field will be bypassed when you perform a spell check.

5. Click the Format tab to specify the type of data that will be accepted in the field. For more information on formatting a field, refer to the upcoming section "Format Form Fields."
6. Click the Validate tab if you want to restrict the range of data that can be entered in the field. For more information on this option, refer to the upcoming Validate Form Fields section.
7. Click the Calculate tab if the field will be used to perform a mathematical calculation. For more information on creating a calculating form field, refer to "Calculate Form Fields" later in this chapter.
8. Click OK to create the text box.
9. Select the Hand tool and click the text box to test it.

Create a Digital Signature Field

You can create a digital signature field when you want the user to sign the form. When you create a digital signature field, you can specify what occurs after the field is signed. To create a signature field, follow these steps:

1. Select the Form tool, and define the area for the field.
2. Enter a name for the field, and from the Type drop-down menu choose Signature.
3. Set the Appearance options for the field, as outlined earlier in the section "Specify Field Appearance."
4. Click the Signed tab and choose one of the following options:
    - **Nothing Happens When The Signature Field Is Signed** Choose this default option, and the signature transmits with the submitted form, but nothing else happens.

- **Mark as read only** Choose this option, and you can limit certain fields on the form to read-only status once the document is signed. When you select this option, choose one of the following from the drop-down menu: All Fields, Just These Fields, or All Fields Except These. When you choose either of the latter options, click the Pick button to select the fields to include or exclude.
- **This script executes when the signature is signed** Choose this option to create a JavaScript that executes when the field is signed. After you choose the option, click the Edit button and create the JavaScript in the JavaScript Edit dialog box.

5. Click OK to complete the creation of the Signature field. For more information on digital signatures, refer to Chapter 13.

Spell Check Form Fields

You can spell check form fields and comments you create in a PDF document. You can add words to the Acrobat Spell Check dictionary and edit the dictionary as needed. To spell check form fields and comments in a document, follow these steps:

1. Choose Tools | Spelling | Check Form Fields and Comments to open the Check Spelling dialog box.
2. Click Start to begin the spell check. When Acrobat finds a word that is not in its dictionary, the word is highlighted in the Not In Dictionary field, as shown in the following image. Acrobat supplies a list of suggested replacements in the Suggested Corrections field. You can choose one of the following options:
    - Edit the highlighted word and then click Change.
    - Double-click a word from the Suggested Corrections list to replace the highlighted word.
    - Click Ignore to leave the highlighted word unchanged and continue with the spell check.

- Click Ignore All to leave the highlighted word and all future instances of the highlighted word unchanged.
- Click Add, and Acrobat opens the Edit Dictionary dialog box. Click Add to add the word to your personal dictionary.
- Select one of the words in the Suggested Corrections field, and then click Change to replace the highlighted word.
- Select one of the words in the Suggested Corrections field, and then click Change All to change all occurrences of the highlighted word to the selected correction.

3. Click Done to end the spell check.

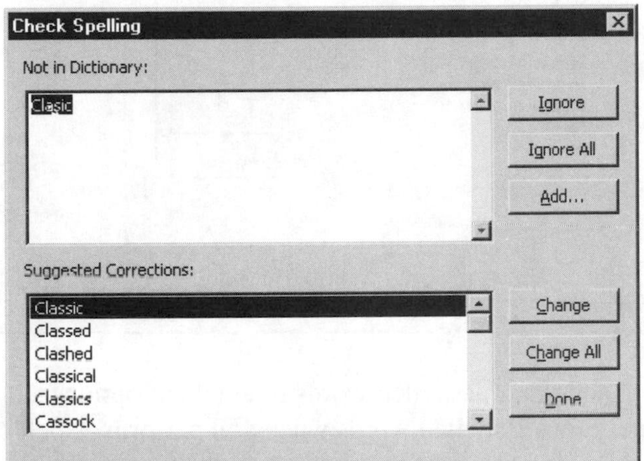

9

Specify Spell Check Preferences

Acrobat Spell Check is a powerful feature that you use to guard against typographical and spelling errors in your form fields and comments. You can configure the Spell Checker to suit your preferences by following these steps:

1. Choose Edit | Preferences | General to open the Preferences dialog box.

2. Choose Spelling from the list in the left-hand window to open the dialog box, shown in the following image:

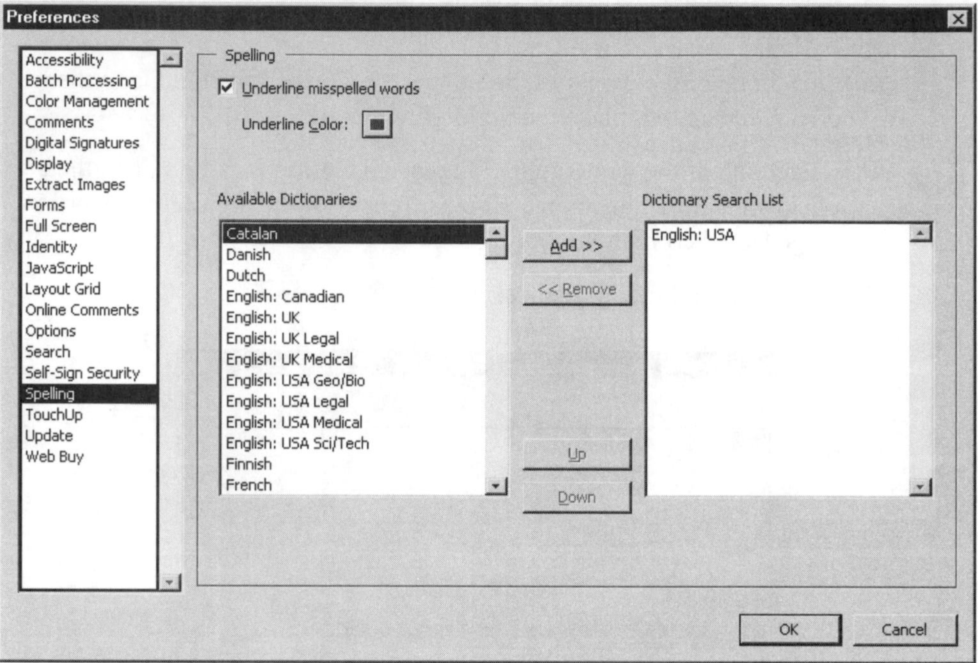

3. Choose Underline misspelled words (the default option) and Acrobat underlines any misspelled words when you perform a spell check.

4. To change the underline color (red is the default), click the Color button and choose a color from the pop-up palette.

5. To add a dictionary to the list, select one from the list on the left and click the Add button. When you have multiple dictionaries, Acrobat searches the dictionary at the top of the list first.

6. To change the order in which Acrobat searches the dictionaries, select a dictionary from the Dictionary Search list; and then click the Up button to move the dictionary toward the top of the list click Down to move the dictionary toward the bottom of the list.

7. To remove a dictionary from the Dictionary Search List, select it and then click Remove.

8. Click OK to apply the changes.

Edit the Dictionary

When you perform a spell check and Acrobat locates a word that is not present in any dictionary in the Dictionary Search List, you have the option to add the word to your personal dictionary. You can add or delete words from this dictionary when they are no longer needed by following these steps:

1. Choose Tools | Spelling | Edit Dictionary to open the dialog box shown in the following illustration:

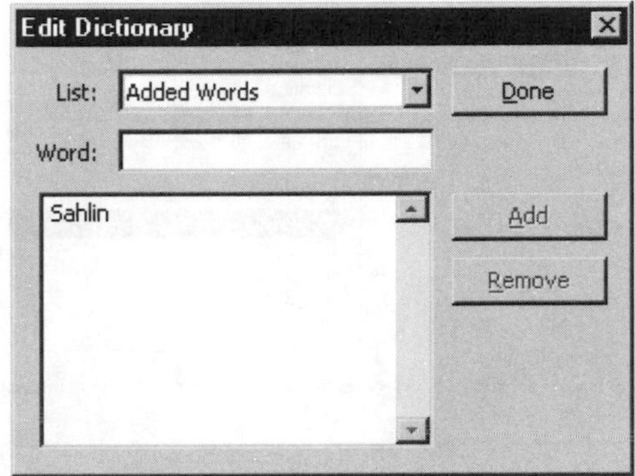

2. To add a word to the dictionary, enter it in the Word field and then click Add.
3. To remove a word from the dictionary, select it from the window on the left and then click Remove.
4. Click Done to finish editing the dictionary.

Format Form Fields

When you create a form field that accepts data input, you can format the field for a specific type of data. For example, if the form field requests the user's fax number, then format the field using the Phone Number option. If the user fills out the form and enters **5555551212**, when the data is submitted, Acrobat reformats the entry to read (555) 555-1212. To format a form field, follow these steps:

1. Create a form field as outlined in the previous sections of this chapter.
2. Click the Format Tab in the Field Properties dialog box.

3. Choose one of the following categories: None, Number, Date, Time, Special, or Custom. Each category has different formatting options. The following image shows the available options for the Number category:

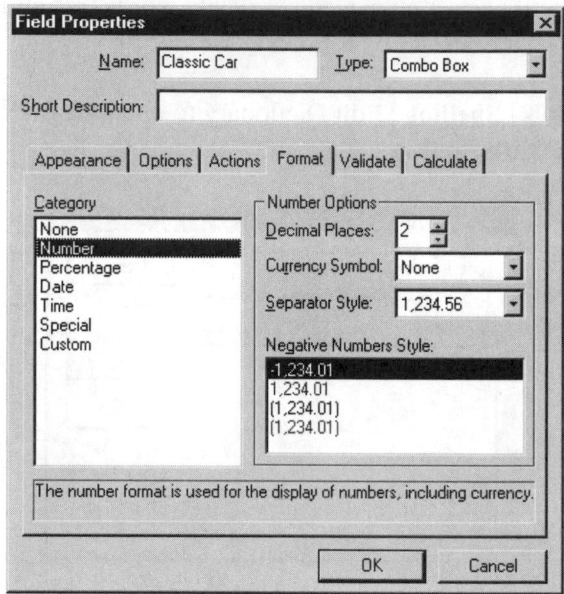

4. Choose the options that best suit the form you are creating.

5. If you choose the Custom category, click the Edit button beside Custom Format Script, or click the Edit button beside Custom Keystroke Script to open the JavaScript Edit dialog box. Enter the script or paste an existing script into the dialog box, and then click OK.

Validate Form Fields

When you create a form field that accepts data, you can limit the amount of data the user enters by validating the form field. Validating a form field is useful when you put a form on the Internet. By limiting the amount of data you let the user enter, you eliminate a potential server bottleneck when a malicious user submits a form with copious amounts of data. You can only validate text and combo box form fields. To validate a form field, follow these steps:

1. Create a form field, as discussed in previous sections of this chapter.

2. Click the Validate tab in the Field Properties dialog box to open the dialog box, shown in the following image. The options you have available will vary depending upon the format you specify. By default, Acrobat does not validate a field.

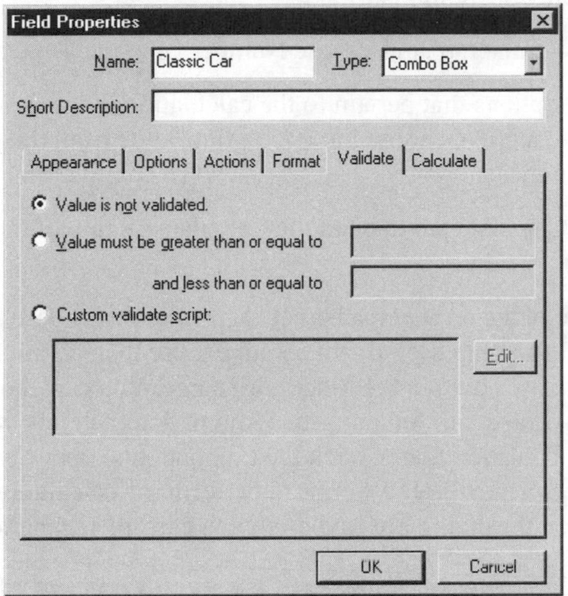

3. If you choose either the number or percentage format (refer to the "Format Form Fields" section earlier in this chapter), you can limit the range of data the user can enter. Enter values in the *Value Must Be Greater Than Or Equal To* field and the *And Less Than Or Equal To* field to define the acceptable range of data.

4. To create a validation script using JavaScript, choose Custom Validate Script and then click the Edit button to open the JavaScript Edit dialog box. Enter the script you want used to validate the form field, and then click OK.

Calculate Form Fields

When you create form fields with numeric data, Acrobat can calculate the value of two or more fields. You can choose from common arithmetic functions, or you can create a complex calculation using JavaScript. To calculate two or more form fields, follow these steps:

1. Create the form field that will display the result of the calculation, as outlined previously in this chapter.
2. Click the Format tab ,and choose Number from the Type drop-down menu.
3. Select the options that pertain to the calculation. For example, if you want to calculate a price, choose the appropriate style from the Currency Format drop-down menu.
4. Click the Calculate tab to open the Calculate section of the Field Properties dialog box.
5. To use one of the present mathematical operations, choose the second option listed; and from the drop-down menu, choose the operation you want performed, as shown in the following image. You can choose from sum, product, average, minimum, or maximum. Alternatively, you can choose Custom Calculation Script, click the Edit button to open the JavaScript Edit dialog box, create the JavaScript to perform the calculation, and then click OK to close the dialog box and apply the custom calculation script.

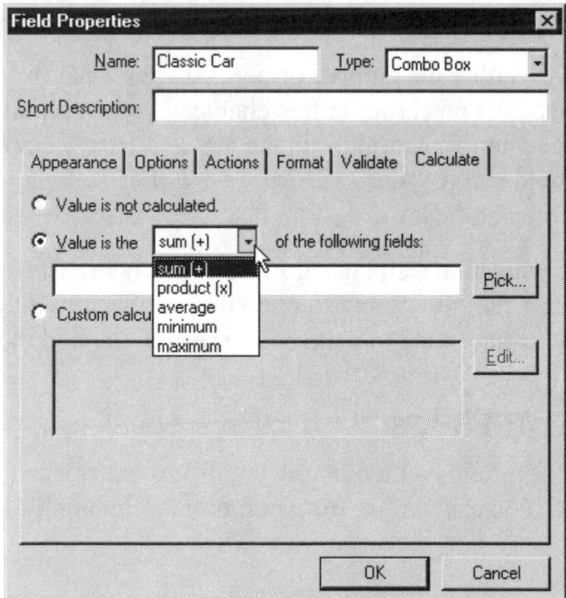

6. Click the Pick button to display the Select A Field dialog box. This dialog box lists all of the fields present in the document.
7. Click a field to select it, and then click Add to use the field in the calculation.
8. Add the other fields necessary to perform the calculation, and then click Close to exit the Select a Field dialog box.

Set Field Calculation Order

When you create a complex form with multiple fields of data that you call upon for calculation, the order in which the calculation performs may differ from the tab order of the fields. To change the order of the calculated fields, follow these steps:

1. Choose Tools | Forms | Set Calculation Order to open the Calculated Fields dialog box. This dialog box shows all of the calculable fields in your form and the order in which the calculations are performed on them.
2. To change a field order in the list, select it, and then click the Up button to move the field one position higher in the list or click the Down button to move it one position lower in the list.
3. Click OK when you finish reordering the fields.

Create a Reset Form Button

If you create a form with multiple fields, you may want to consider creating a reset button. Adding a reset button gives the user the option of starting over again by clicking a button. When you create a reset button, you can specify which form fields are cleared when the button is used. To create a reset button, follow these steps:

1. Select the Form tool, and define the size and position of the field.
2. Name the field (Reset is a good choice), and choose Button from the Type drop-down menu.
3. Modify the button appearance and options to suit your form, as presented in "Create a Button Field" earlier in this chapter.
4. Click the Actions tab, and choose the Mouse Up event.

5. Click the Add button to open the Add An Action dialog box, and from the Type drop-down menu choose Reset Form.
6. Click the Select Fields button to open the Field Selection dialog box and choose one of the following options: All Fields, All Except, or Only These. If you select one of the latter options, click the Select Fields button to open the Field Selection dialog box, as shown in Figure 9-4. Use the Add and Remove buttons to determine which fields clear when the user clicks the reset button, and then click OK to exit the dialog box.
7. Click OK to exit the Field Selection dialog box, and then click Set Action to assign the action to the button.

Create a Submit Form Button

When you create a form for use on the Internet or a local intranet, you can add a Submit Form button to transmit the results to a web server. You can specify the export format and specify which fields are submitted. To create a submit form button, follow these steps:

1. Select the Form tool, and define the size and position of the field.
2. Name the field, and choose Button from the Type drop-down menu.

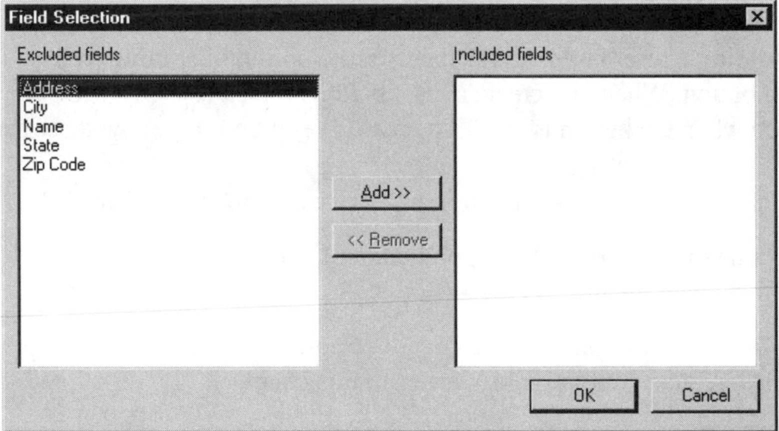

FIGURE 9-4 Specify which fields to include in this dialog box.

3. Modify the button appearance and options to suit your form, as discussed earlier in "Create a Button Field."
4. Click the Actions tab and choose the Mouse Up event.
5. Click the Add button to open the Add An Action dialog box, and from the Type drop-down menu choose Submit Form.
6. Click the Select URL button to display the Submit Form Selections dialog box, as shown in the following image:

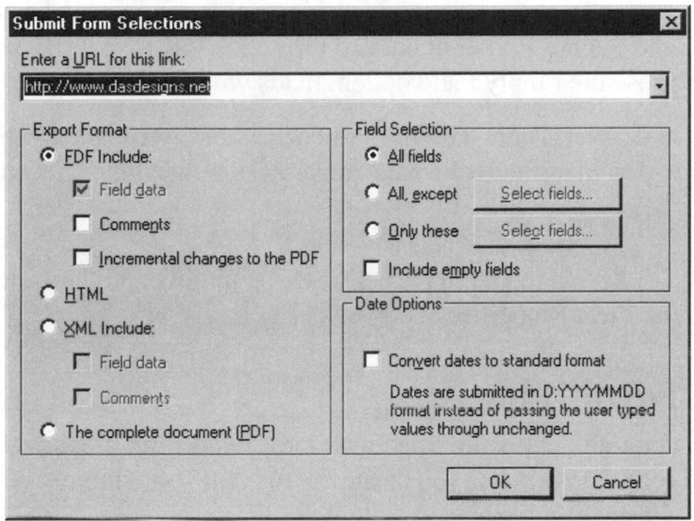

7. In the text field, enter the destination URL for the form results.
8. In the Export Format section, choose one of the following options:
   - **FDF Include** Choose this option, and Acrobat exports the data as an FDF (Forms Data Format) file. With this format, you can choose to export field data, comments, incremental changes to the PDF, or all of the preceding. When you choose the Incremental Changes To The PDF option, data from digital signature fields can be exported in a manner that is recognized by a web server.
   - **HTML** Choose this option, and Acrobat exports the form data in HTML format.

9

- **XML Include** Choose this option, and Acrobat exports the form data as an XML file.
- **The complete document (PDF)** Choose this option, and Acrobat exports the entire PDF file that contains the form data.

9. In the Field Selection section, choose one of the following options: All Fields; All, Except; Only These; or Include Empty Fields. If you select the All Except or Only These option, click the Select Fields button to open the Field Selection dialog box, as previously shown in Figure 9-4. Use the Add and Remove buttons to determine which fields are exported when the user clicks the Submit Form button, and then click OK to exit the dialog box. If you choose the Empty Field option, fields with no data will be exported.
10. Choose Convert Dates To Standard Format and Acrobat exports date information in a standard format, regardless of what the user entered.
11. Click OK to apply the options.
12. Click Set Action to assign the action to the button, and then click OK to close the Field Properties dialog box.

Create a Form Table

You can create a multi-cell table filled with form fields after creating either a row or column of form fields. After you create the first row or column, you use the Form tool to define the table area as follows:

1. Create several form fields next to each other to define the first row of the table, or on top of each other to define the first column of the table. Each cell must have a unique name.
2. With the Form tool selected, press and hold SHIFT, and drag a marquee around the form fields. As you drag, a bounding box designates the area you are defining. When the bounding box surrounds the row or column of form fields, release the mouse button, and Acrobat draws a red rectangle with six handles around the fields.
3. Press and hold CTRL (Windows) or COMMAND (Macintosh), and then click and drag one of the handles to define the borders of the table. Release the mouse button when the table is the size you want.

4. Click inside the red rectangle to finish creating the table of form fields. Acrobat automatically renames the new fields, appending the original field name with a number, as shown in the following image:

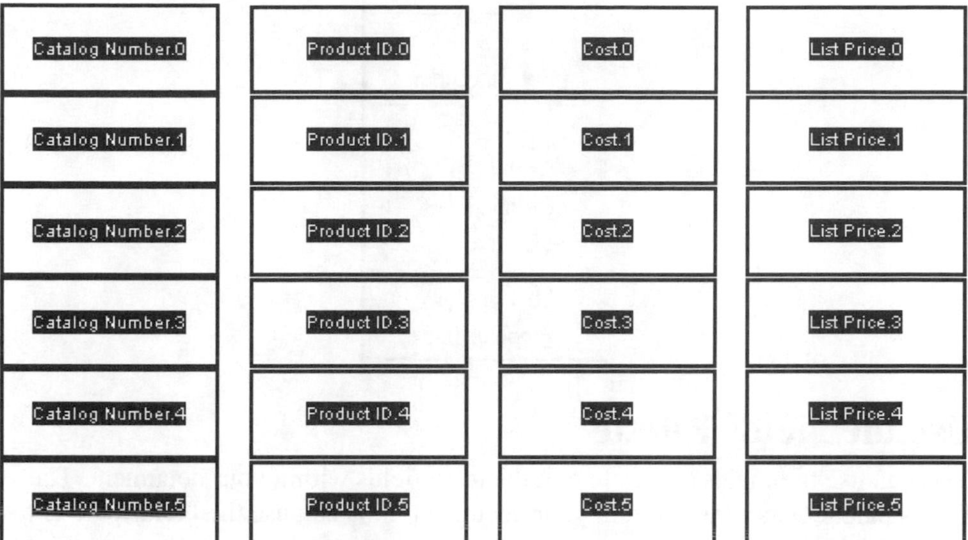

Edit a Form

After you create a form, you may find that you need to edit the form in order to make it more aesthetically pleasing. You can resize, align, reposition, and duplicate form fields to achieve this result. You may also find it necessary to edit the properties of individual fields, if, for example, an action does not execute as planned or a calculation does not give the expected result.

Use the Form Context Menu

You find many of the commands needed to modify forms under Tools | Forms, and then select the desired command from the drop-down menu. You can also quickly access a command from the context menu. To modify a form field with a command from the context menu, select a form field with the Forms tool, and then right-click (Windows) or CTRL-click (Macintosh) and choose a command from the context menu, as shown in the following image. Note that some of these commands are exclusive to the context menu.

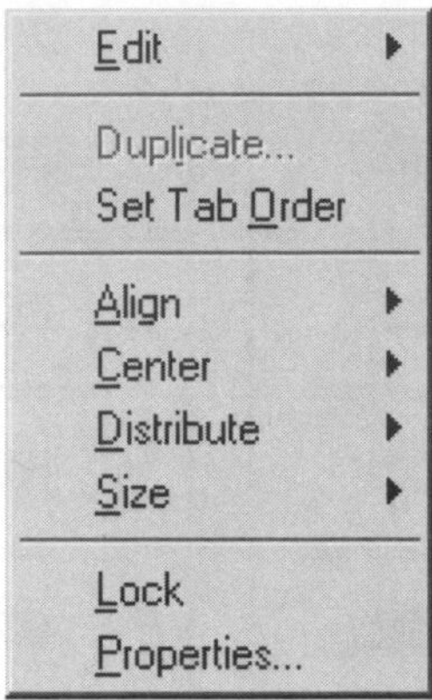

Use the Fields Palette

You can use the Fields palette to edit the form fields within your document. The Fields palette lists every field in your document. You can use the Fields palette to delete fields, navigate to fields, change field properties, and more. Open the Fields palette, shown in the following image, by choosing Window | Fields.

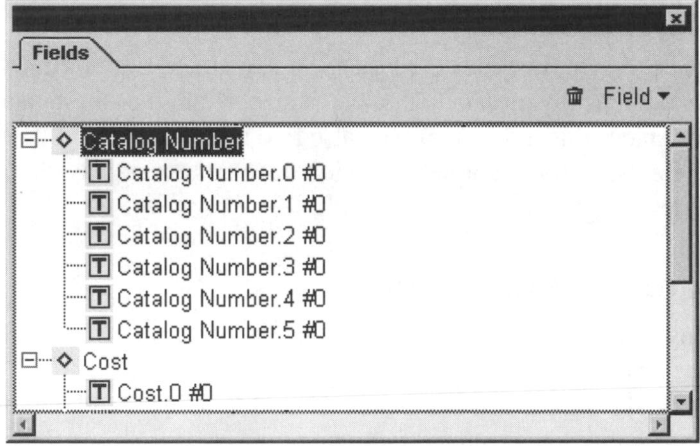

To edit any field from the list in the Fields palette, select the field, click the Field icon in the upper-right corner of the palette, and choose a command from the drop-down menu. Alternatively, you can select a field in the palette, right-click (Windows) or CTRL-click (Macintosh), and then choose a command from the context menu in the following image. The Go To Field command at the top of the menu is unique to the context menu.

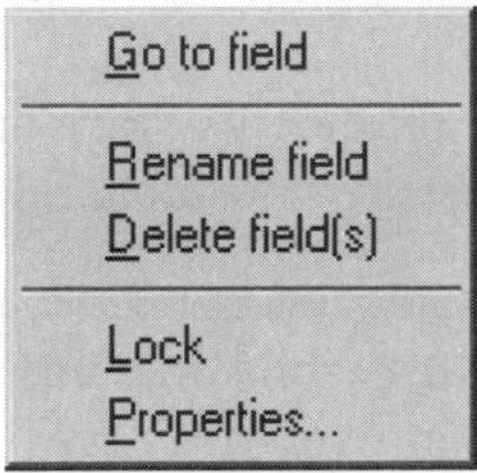

TIP *To delete selected fields, click the icon that looks like a trash can near the top of the Fields palette.*

9

Edit Form Field Properties

When a form works exactly as planned, it's time to move on to the next task, or take a quick break and bask in the glow of accomplishment. However, more often than not, you will need to tweak one or more properties of a form field. To edit form field properties, select the field with the Forms tool, and choose Edit | Properties to open the Field Properties dialog box. Alternatively, you can choose Edit from the context menu.

Delete a Form Field

When you revise a form and no longer need a particular form field, you can easily delete the form field. First, select it with the Form tool, and then choose Edit | Delete. Alternatively, you can choose Delete from the context menu.

Align, Reposition, and Resize Form Fields

If you use the Layout Grid to align and size the fields in your form, you generally end up with a form that is neatly laid out. However, you may still need to make some minor adjustments to the position or size of a field. You can resize individual fields, or select multiple fields and then size and align them to each other.

To resize or reposition an individual form field, select the field with the Forms tool. After you select the field, eight handles appear on the field perimeter. You can then modify the field by doing any of the following:

- To reposition the form field, click the center of the field with the Forms tool and drag the field to the desired location. As you drag the field, a bounding box gives you a preview of the current position of the field. When the field is in the desired position, release the mouse button.
- To resize the field, click any corner handle and drag. To resize the field proportionately, press SHIFT while dragging. As you resize the field, a bounding box appears that gives you a preview of the current size of the field. Release the mouse button when the field is the desired size.
- To modify the field width, click the center handle on either side of the form field, and drag left or right to change the width of the field.
- To modify the field height, click the center handle at the top or bottom of the field, and drag up or down to change the height of the field.

You can also modify the size and alignment of several fields; just select the Forms tool, and then click a form field. The first form field you click is highlighted in red. To add fields to the selection, hold down SHIFT and click the fields you want to add to the selection. All fields will be modified to the applicable parameter of the first field selected. For example, if you choose Forms | Fields | Size | Height, all fields will be resized to the height of the first field selected. After selecting two or more fields, you can do any of the following:

- To change the size of the selected fields, choose Forms | Fields | Size, and then choose Height, Width, or Both.
- To change the alignment of the selected fields, choose Forms | Fields | Align, and then choose Left, Right, Bottom, Top, Vertically, or Horizontally.
- To center the selected fields to the current document, choose Forms | Fields | Center, and then choose Vertically, Horizontally, or Both.
- To equally distribute the selected fields, choose Forms | Fields | Distribute, and then choose Vertically or Horizontally. Note that the fields will be distributed relative to their center points.
- To resize the selected fields, choose Forms | Fields | Size, and then choose Width, Height, or Both.

Set Tab Order

When users fills out your PDF form, they can manually click each field with the Hand tool to select it, or they can advance through the fields by pressing TAB. When a user navigates with TAB, the fields hightlight in the order they were created—in other words, the tab order. If you move a field to a different position, it still retains its previous tab order. If you have repositioned several form fields, you can change the tab order to a more logical progression by following these steps:

1. Select the Forms tool and the boundary of each form field becomes visible.
2. Choose Tools | Forms | Fields | Set Tab Order. After you choose this command, your cursor becomes an angled arrow with the number symbol (#) beside it. Acrobat displays each field tab number in the upper-left corner of the field bounding box, as shown in the following image:

3. To redefine the field tab order, click the field that will be first in the revised tab order, and then click the field that will be second, and so on until you have reset the tab order of the form fields in your document.

9

Duplicate a Form Field

If the information or data entered in a form field needs to be in multiple locations of the document, you can duplicate the form field. You can duplicate a form field on the same page, or across a range of pages. When you duplicate a form field, the field retains all of the attributes you assigned to the original field. When you change a parameter in a field that has been duplicated (in other words, a field with the same name that appears more than once in the document), the parameter changes in the duplicated fields as well. You can duplicate a single form field, or a selection of form fields.

To duplicate form fields on a page, follow these steps:

1. Select the Form tool, and then select the field(s) you want to duplicate.
2. Hold down CTRL (Windows) or OPTION (Macintosh), and drag the selected fields. To constrain the motion of the fields vertically or horizontally, hold down SHIFT, along with CRTL or OPTION, after you begin to drag the fields.

3. Release the mouse button, and Acrobat duplicates the selected fields where you released the mouse button.

To duplicate fields across a range of pages, follow these steps:

1. Select the Form tool, and then select the field(s) you want to duplicate.
2. Choose Tools | Forms | Fields | Duplicate to open the Duplicate Field dialog box, as shown in the following image:

3. Accept the All option (the default) to duplicate the field on all document pages, or choose the From option and enter the range of pages to duplicate the field on.
4. Click OK, and Acrobat creates the duplicates per your specification.

Export Form Data

You can export data from a form for use in other PDF forms that have the same field names. When you export data, you create a smaller file with data only. You can export the data as an FDF file or as an XFDF (an XML representation of the FDF data) file. To export form data, follow these steps:

1. Choose File | Export | Form Data to open the Export Form Data As dialog box.
2. Enter a name for the file and the folder where you want the data file stored. If you do not assign a name for the file, Acrobat uses the current name of the file by default.
3. Click Save.

Import Form Data

You can import FDF files to automatically fill in form fields. When you import an FDF file, Acrobat automatically inserts the data in form fields with the same names. To import data into a PDF document, follow these steps:

1. Choose File | Import | Form Data to open the Select File Containing Form Data dialog box.
2. Navigate to the file containing the data you want to import and select the file.
3. Click Select to open the file.

You can also share form data with other users. For example, if you work in a corporate environment, you can post a form that contains fields pertaining to product information, such as current cost and list price. When the data needs to be updated, you can update the master version of the form and export the data. The version of the form that is posted on the corporate intranet can be programmed to automatically update using the Import Form Data action that you program to execute when the page opens or when the user clicks a button. For more information on Actions, refer to Chapter 7.

Use JavaScript Actions

When you create a form field, you can use the JavaScript action to create a custom script for the field. As you learned in Chapter 7, you can create a JavaScript and assign it to a button for use as navigation. You can also use JavaScript to augment Acrobat mathematical functions. To learn more about JavaScript, choose Help | Acrobat JavaScript Guide. There is additional information on JavaScript in Chapter 7.

Use JavaScript to Subtract and Divide

In the Calculate Form Fields section, you may have noticed, Acrobat does not provide the ability to subtract or divide form fields. In order to perform either operation, you must create a JavaScript. To subtract a text field named *Field B* from a text field named *Field A*, follow these steps:

1. Select the Form tool.
2. Create a form field where you want the results of the calculation to appear.
3. Enter a name for the form field, and choose Text from the Type drop-down menu.
4. Click the Appearance tab, and set the parameters for the field text, background color, and border color.

5. Click the Format tab, and choose a format option for the field. Choose the same format as Field A and Field B. For example, if Fields A and B work with currency value, choose Number, and then choose the currency symbol that applies.

6. Click the Calculate tab, choose Custom Calculation Script, click the Edit button, and enter the following in the JavaScript Edit dialog box:

```
var a = this.getField("Field A");
var b = this.getField("Field B");
event.value = a.value - b.value
```

7. Click OK to exit the JavaScript Edit dialog box.

You can modify the script to perform division by entering the following JavaScript in step 6:

```
var a = this.getField("Field A");
var b = this.getField("Field B");
event.value = a.value / b.value
```

NOTE

Division by a value of zero is not possible. If the user enters a value of zero for the second field, an error message will appear warning that the value does not match the format of the field. To guard against this, click the Validate tab and specify that the number must be greater than or equal to one. Validating the field in this manner will also result in an error message if the user enters a value less than one; this includes dividing by negative numbers.

You can use JavaScript to perform complex calculations involving multiple form fields in a document. Simply create a variable for each form field and use the getField method to get the value of the field. To calculate the result, set the value method of the event object equal to a mathematical calculation using the value of each variable and the applicable operands. For example,

```
var a = this.getField ("Field A");
var b = this.getField ("Field B");
var c = this.getField ("Field C");
event.value = c.value * (a.value + b.value)
```

Chapter 10 Add Multimedia Elements to PDF Documents

How to...

- Work with images
- Extract images from documents
- Add sound to documents
- Add movies to documents

When most people think of creating multimedia presentations, they think of programs such as Macromedia Director. Indeed, Director is one of the most frequently used programs to create full-fledged multimedia presentations. However, with a bit of imagination and a smidgen of JavaScript and Acrobat, you can create impressive multimedia presentations.

When you create a multimedia presentation for CD-ROM, file size is generally not an issue. A CD-ROM can hold 650MB (or 700MB, if you purchase 80-minute CD-ROMs) of data, which means you can fill your PDF documents with stunning full-color images, sound files, and movie files. In this chapte,r you'll learn how to integrate multimedia files into your PDF documents to create full-fledged multimedia presentations.

Work with Images

When you create a multimedia PDF presentation, images are a must. Whether you create a corporate portfolio presentation, educational media, or product catalog, images add visual spice that pique user interest and make the presentation a success. When you prepare images for multimedia PDF presentations, you can crank up the resolution and use file formats that are not compressed; or if you do use an image file that is compressed, you can apply less compression to create a sharper image.

If you create documents with the intention of creating multimedia PDF documents, consider investing in a page-layout program such as Adobe Pagemaker or Microsoft Publisher. When you use a page-layout program, you have better control over image placement, especially when text wraps around the image. In lieu of a page-layout program, many popular word processing applications support embedding images in documents. If the authoring program supports PDF export, export the document with little or no image compression. If you use Acrobat Distiller to convert the document to PDF format, use the eBook Job Option.

Create Images for Documents

When you add images to CD-ROM–based multimedia documents, you can use higher image resolutions when you create images from scratch or when you acquire them with your scanner. Ultimately, you are still dealing with a presentation that will be viewed on a 72-dpi monitor; however, if you start with a high-resolution image and then resample it to 72 dpi, the image will have sharper detail. If your image-editing software supports it, export the file in PDF format. If this option isn't available, use the software Print command, and choose Acrobat Distiller as the printing device to convert the file to a PDF document using the eBook Job Option.

Remember, you can use your image-editing software to create images, save them in an image format, and then choose File | Open as Adobe PDF. You can open the following image formats as PDF documents: BMP (Windows only), GIF, JPEG, PCX, PNG, PICT (Macintosh only), and TIFF files.

If you create an image with image-editing software and intend to use the Open As Adobe PDF command to convert the image file to PDF format, you will get better results if you save the file as a BMP file or an uncompressed TIFF file.

Extract Images from Documents

When you open a PDF document with images, you can extract the images for use in other PDF documents or other applications. You can export extracted document images as JPEG, PNG, or TIFF files. To extract images from a document, do the following:

1. Choose File | Export | Extract Images As, and then choose JPEG files, PNG files, or TIFF files. After you choose an image format, the Extract Images and Save As dialog box appears.
2. Navigate to the folder where you want the extracted images stored.
3. Click the Settings button to apply image compression settings. The dialog boxes for each format option's settings are identical to the dialog boxes previously shown in Chapter 4.

When you extract images as JPEG files and accept the default compression setting, the extracted images may not be acceptable for use in other applications. For the best results, choose the JPEG (Quality : Maximum) compression setting.

4. Click Save, and Acrobat extracts the images to the specified folder.

By default, Acrobat will not extract images smaller than 72 ×72 points, which is equal to one inch at monitor resolution. You can modify this setting by choosing Edit | Preferences. After the Preferences dialog box opens, choose Extract Images, and then choose a different setting from the drop-down menu.

Edit Images Within Documents

After you convert a document to PDF format, you can do minimal editing to images with the TouchUp Object tool. With the TouchUp Object tool, you can select, move, and delete images from a PDF document. You can also use the TouchUp Object tool to edit a selected image in either Adobe Illustrator or Adobe PhotoShop. For more information on the TouchUp Object tool, refer to Chapter 11.

Whenever you convert a document with images to PDF format, it is advisable to keep a copy of the document in its native format, in case you ever have to perform any major image editing or replace an image.

Add Sound to Documents

No multimedia experience is complete without sound. When you add sound to a presentation, you involve another one of the viewer's senses, which, of course, makes the experience more complete. You can use sounds with buttons, when a page opens, or when a page closes. Acrobat only supports sounds in the .wav or .aiff format. When you add a sound to an Acrobat document, it becomes embedded in the document. Adding a sound to a document you plan to display on the Internet would result in an extremely long download, unless the sound file is extremely small. However, when you create a PDF document with sound for a multimedia CD-ROM, Internet bandwidth is no longer a concern.

Add Sound to a PDF Document

You can use the Sound Attachment tool to add sound to a PDF document. However, the Sound Attachment tool (presented in Chapter 12) is better suited for creating audio annotations or adding audio files to a PDF document for internal distribution. When you create a multimedia presentation with sound, you want to control when the sound is played.

There are several ways you can include sound in a multimedia PDF file. One way is to use the Set Page Action command. Add the Sound action, and then choose the sound file you want the user to hear when the page opens. Depending on the type of presentation you create, you can have a short musical piece play when a page opens, or have a vocal introduction. You can also use a sound when the page closes. For more information on Page Action, refer to Chapter 7. A word of caution is in order here. Sound can enhance your presentsentation, but the blatant use of soNote Heading your viewer turning down the speakerPlain Text worse yet, exiting your presentation before it is concluded.

Another method you can use to add sound to your PDF presentation is the button. Create a button and then assign a sound to it. You can assign a sound to the Mouse Enter event to alert viewers that the button warrants their attention, or you can assign the sound to the Mouse Down event, which will alert the viewers that the button has successfully been clicked.

Create Audio Tracks for Your PDF Documents

Acrobat does not have the capability to edit soundtracks. If you intend to use sound extensively when creating multimedia PDF presentations, you may want to consider investing in sound-editing software. You can use sound-editing software to record your own sound clips and then edit them to fit your presentation. Most popular sound-editing software can be used to enhance a recording, remove noise from a recording, add special effects (such as echo or reverb) to a sound recording, and much more. Some sound-editing programs give you the capability of mixing soundtracks with other recordings. There is also software available to create musical soundtracks. Sonic Foundry sells both sound-editing and music-sampling software for Windows-based PCs. For more information, visit their website at http://www.sonicfoundry.com.

If you use sounds for both events, and the sound assigned to the Mouse Enter event is longer than the sound you use for the Mouse Down event, the first sound will play until conclusion. This means that the button action may execute before the second sound ever plays.

If you create a CD-ROM product catalog, or an educational tool, you can have a product description or tutorial play when an image is clicked. To have a sound play when an image is clicked, select the Link tool, and create a hotspot around the image as outlined in Chapter 7. Choose Invisible Rectangle for the Link Appearance type; and from the Action Type drop-down menu, choose Sound, and then select the sound you want to play when the image is clicked.

Add Movies to PDF Presentations

You can also add movies to your PDF documents using the Movie tool. When you add a movie to a PDF document, Acrobat doesn't embed the movie in the document, it adds the relative path of the movie to the document. This is an important factor to keep in mind if the PDF document you create will be displayed on the Internet or from a CD-ROM. The movie will have to be uploaded to the host website with the same relative path, or stored in a folder with the same relative path on the CD-ROM, for the movie to play.

You can also set the path where the files are located by choosing File | Document Properties | Base URL to open the Document Base URL dialog box. Enter the URL where Acrobat can find the external assets linked to the document, and then click OK to close the dialog box and set the base URL for the document.

Add Movies to Documents

You use the Movie tool to add movies to your document. When you add a movie to a document, you specify the appearance of the link that activates the movie. You can also specify the color depth of the movie and whether the movie will display in its native viewer, in the window you create with the Movie tool, or in a floating window. You can add movies to your PDF documents, provided they are in the Windows .avi or QuickTime .mov format.

If you create a movie that will be displayed in the window you create, the window must be sized to fit the movie. You can choose Window | Info to open up the Info palette. The Info palette will display the dimensions of the window you create with the Movie tool. However, the only way to accurately size the window is to use the Layout Grid with the Snap To Grid option enabled. To active the Layout Grid, choose View | Grid and then choose View | Snap To Grid. It will also help if the width and height between grid lines are an even increment of the movie dimensions. Most movies created for computer viewing are sized at 160×120 pixels, 320 × 240 pixels, 400 × 300 pixels, (occasionally) 640 × 480 pixels. If you insert a movie with any of these dimensions, modify the Layout Grid preferences to a width and height of 40 points, and you create a window of the appropriate size. For more information about modifying the Layout Grid, refer to Chapter 9.

When you create a PDF document with a movie, consider your target audience. If the audience of your PDF document does not have the appropriate viewer, they will not be able to view the movie. Another thing you must take into consideration when you add a movie to a PDF document is the codec that was used to compress the movie file. If the movie was compressed with a codec that is not available on the user's computer, the user will not be able to view the document. This is not a problem with QuickTime .mov movies; however, the Windows .avi format has a plethora of compression codecs available.

Once you are sure the movie is viewable by your intended audience, you are ready to add it to a PDF file. Before you actually add the movie to the file, determine how it will be viewed. If the movie will be viewed within a window you create, enable the Layout Grid and the Snap To Grid options, as discussed previously. If necessary, change the grid space width and height dimensions to an even increment of your movie. To add a movie to a PDF file, do the following:

1. Select the Movie tool shown in the illustration on the left.
2. Choose Window | Info to use the Info palette as an aid in sizing the window.
3. Click to define the corner of the movie window, and then drag down and across. As you drag, a bounding box appears giving you a preview of the window size. Release the mouse button when the window is the desired size, and the Movie Properties dialog box shown in Figure 10-1 appears.
4. In the Movie File section, click the Choose button and navigate to a movie. Alternatively, enter the URL where the movie can be found. If you enter the URL, you need to include the exact path, including the movie filename—for example, http://mywebsite.com/movies/intro.avi.
5. In the Title field, enter a name for the movie. By default, Acrobat chooses the movie filename, minus the extension. Do not use spaces in the title, as

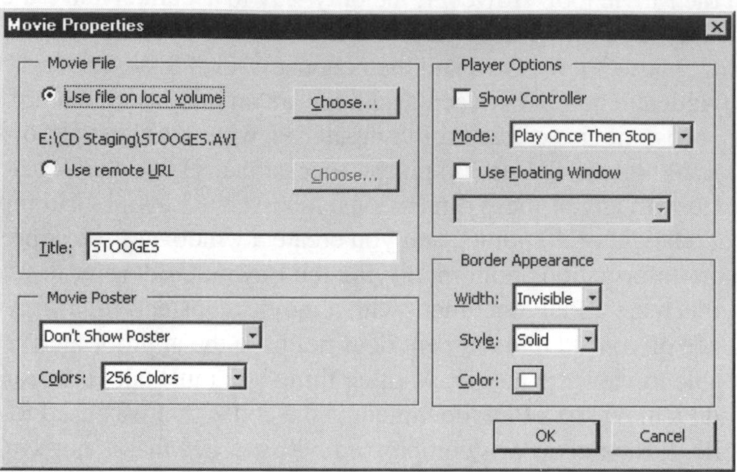

FIGURE 10-1 After you use the Movie tool, the Movie Properties dialog box appears.

certain operating systems add characters where there are spaces that can cause any JavaScript that uses the movie title to be in error.

6. To display the first frame of the movie in the document, choose Put Poster in Document from the drop-down menu in the Movie Poster section, or choose Retrieve Poster from Movie. If you choose to display a movie poster, choose either 256 colors to display the poster as an 8-bit bitmap, or choose Millions of Colors to display the poster at its maximum color depth. Note that if you choose Millions of Colors and the movie is only 8-bit color depth, Acrobat will default to 256 colors.
7. In the Player Options section, choose Show Controller to display a controller at the bottom of the movie window.
8. Click the triangle to the right of the Mode field, and choose one of the following:

   - **Play Once Then Stop** Choose this option, and the movie will play from start to finish and then stop. Unless you include a controller, the user can exit the movie by clicking outside of the movie boundary or by pressing ESC.

- **Play Once Stay Open** Choose this option, and the movie will play in its entirety. If you choose the controller option, the movie remains open at the last frame, giving the viewer the option to play it again by double-clicking inside the movie window, or exit the movie by clicking elsewhere in the document or by pressing ESC.
- **Repeat Play** Choose this option, and the movie will play to the end and then loop back to the beginning. The movie will continue looping until the viewer clicks outside of the movie window or presses ESC.
- **Back and Forth** Choose this option, and the movie will play from start to finish and then plays in reverse. The movie loops back and forth indefinitely or until the user stops the movie by clicking outside of the movie window or by pressing ESC.
- **Floating Window** Choose this option, and Acrobat will play the movie in a separate window. If the movie is in the Windows .avi format, the window is sized to the dimensions of the movie. If the movie is in the QuickTime .mov format, you can choose the size of the floating window from a drop-down menu.

9. In the Border Appearance section, click the triangle to the right of the Width window; and, from the drop-down menu, choose Invisible, Thin, Medium, or Thick.
10. Click the triangle to the right of the Style field, and choose Solid or Dashed.
11. Accept the default border color (White), or click the Color button and choose a color from the pop-up palette. Alternatively, click the Custom button and choose a color from the system color-picker.
12. Click OK.

When you add additional movie clips to a document, you can choose different options; for example, you may decide to show one movie clip in a floating window, and another within a target area you define with the Movie tool.

Play Movie Clips

When a PDF file with a linked movie clip is loaded, Acrobat displays the movie clip by showing the movie poster, or border style, you specify when you add the movie to the document. When the user moves the mouse over the movie target area, the cursor becomes a filmstrip, as shown in the following image:

The user plays the movie by clicking anywhere inside the movie target area. If you choose the Show Controller option, the user will be able to pause and rewind the movie using the native controller for the file format of the file. Figure 10-2 shows a QuickTime movie controller.

Edit Movie Clips

After you add a movie to a document, it's a good idea to test it out to make sure it plays properly. If, after testing the movie, you need to edit any property, do the following:

1. Select the Movie tool.
2. Select the movie in the document, and then choose Edit | Properties to open the Movie Properties dialog box, shown in Figure 10-1. Alternatively, you can double-click the movie clip to open the dialog box.
3. Modify the properties to suit your document, and then click OK to close the Movie Properties dialog box.

To move a movie clip location in the document, select it with the Movie tool and drag it to the desired location. After selecting a movie clip, you can resize it by

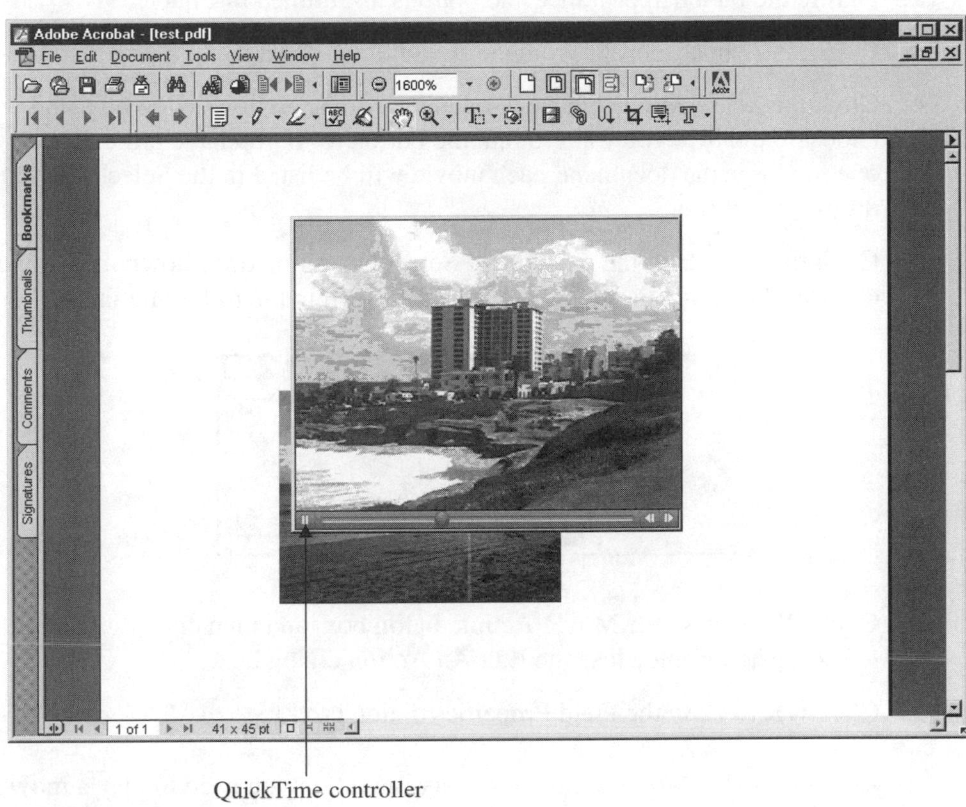

FIGURE 10-2 You can include a movie controller that enables the viewer to pause and replay the movie.

dragging any of the corner handles. However, this is not advised; if you change the proportions of the movie clip boundary, the movie will be distorted.

Control Movie Clips

When you create a true multimedia presentation, you can control the viewer's experience in many ways. For example, you can use a Page Action to play a movie as soon as a page is loaded. You can also create a button that triggers a movie when clicked. When you use a button or Page Action to trigger a movie clip, use the Movie action. To assign the Movie action to a button, do the following:

1. Create a form field, and from the Type drop-down menu choose Button.

2. Define the button appearance and options as outlined in Chapter 9.
3. Click the Actions tab, and from the Action drop-down menu choose Movie.
4. Click the Select Movie button to open the Movie Action dialog box, and choose the movie you want to link the button to. If you have more than one movie in the document, each movie will be listed in the Select Movie drop-down menu.
5. Click the triangle to the right of the Select Operation drop-down menu, and choose Play, Stop, Pause, or Resume, as shown in the following image:

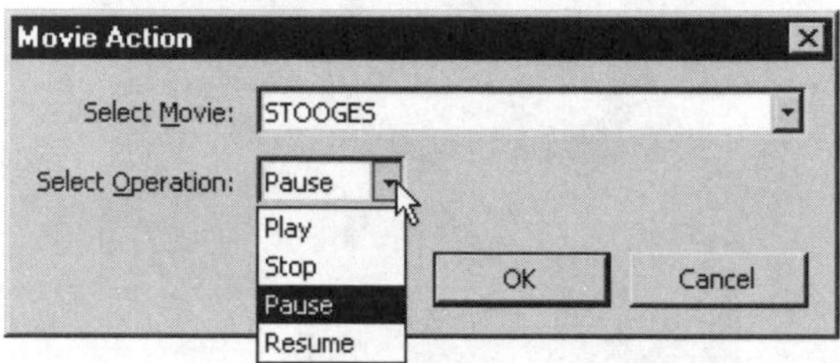

6. Click OK to close the Movie Action dialog box, and then click Set Action to set the action and close the Edit An Action dialog box.
7. Click OK to close the Field Properties dialog box.

As you can see, the Movie action has every operation you need to play a movie except to advance to the end of the movie. By assigning the right action to a button, you can create a Stop, Pause, Resume, or Replay button. You can create a custom controller for your movies by creating four buttons with icon faces and assigning the proper action to each button. Figure 10-3 shows a custom controller created with button text for each button face.

You can use the Movie action to play a movie as soon as a page opens. Use the Movie tool to link the movie to the page. After you have set the movie parameters, do the following:

1. Choose Document | Set Page Action to open the Page Actions dialog box.
2. Select Page Open, and click the Add button.
3. Choose Movie from the drop-down menu, and follow the previous steps to select a movie.

FIGURE 10-3 Create a custom controller to give your PDF presentation panache.

4. From the Select Operation drop-down menu, choose Play.
5. Click OK to close the Page Actions dialog box.
6. Save the document.

When the document is viewed in Acrobat or Acrobat Reader, the movie will play as soon as the page loads. If a large movie file is attached to the page, the movie may take a second or two before it begins playing.

Use the Open File Action

Another action you'll find useful when creating multimedia PDF presentations is the Open File action. You can use the Open File action to open another PDF document or a document not supported by Acrobat, such as a Flash SWF movie or a movie compressed for RealPlayer. When using the Open File action to add content in a different format, make sure your intended audience has the application needed to view the file.

You can use the Open File action as a Page Action or assign it to a button. When the page loads or the button is clicked, the file will open in the application associated with the file type. Note that when you use this action and Acrobat attempts to launch the native player of the application, the Warning dialog box in the following illustration is displayed. Some viewers may find this message disconcerting and not open the file.

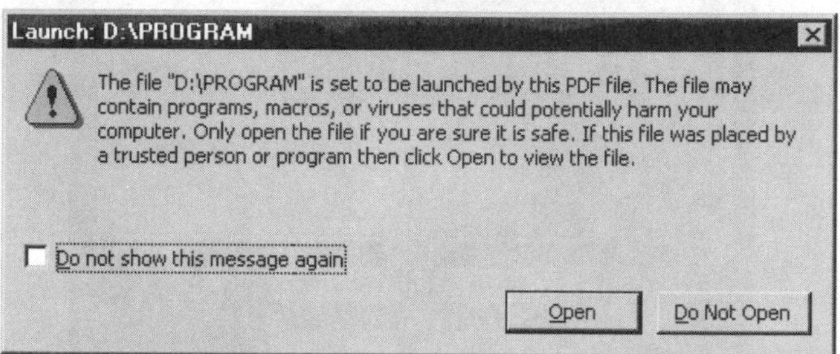

Create a Multimedia PDF Presentation

When you create a multimedia presentation, you may be dealing with hundreds of pages of data. To compile all of the data into a single PDF document would create an unwieldy file that would take a long time to load from CD-ROM. If the file size is too large, it will lock up the user's computer, definitely a result you don't want. To overcome this, break the presentation into a series of linked PDF files. It may help if you think of a large multimedia presentation as you would a large Web site. Each section of the website contains specific information: information about the company, information about company services, information about company products, and so on.

When you need to create a large multimedia presentation, examine the material you need to present and you will have a good idea of how to break the presentation down into sections that will load quickly and not tax the resources of your viewer's computer. After you know how many segments you need for the presentation, you can design a document that contains the navigation elements for the presentation.

Create a Master Document

After you decide how many sections your presentation needs, create a master document with the same dimensions as your presentation. When you create the document, include any necessary items, such as corporate logos or headers. After you create the document in an authoring application, convert it to a PDF file and create a Navigation menu in Acrobat.

Create an Interactive Navigation Menu

In Chapter 8, you learned how to create a basic Navigation menu for an eBook. eBooks are generally downloaded from the Internet, therefore, file size is an important factor. When you create a multimedia presentation for CD-ROM distribution, you have considerable leeway. You can create a menu with multi-state rollover buttons that play sounds, trigger movies, and much more. As long as you can fit the entire production on a 650MB CD-ROM (or 700 if you use 80minute CD-ROMs), you are good to go. Figure 10-4 shows a navigation menu for a corporate CD-ROM presentation. For more information on creating a Navigation menu, refer to Chapter 8.

You can spice up a CD-ROM presentation by adding interactivity to the Navigation menu buttons. When you create a multi-state rollover button for a multimedia presentation, use the Push Highlight option and choose a different image for each button state. For example, you can use an icon for the Up state,

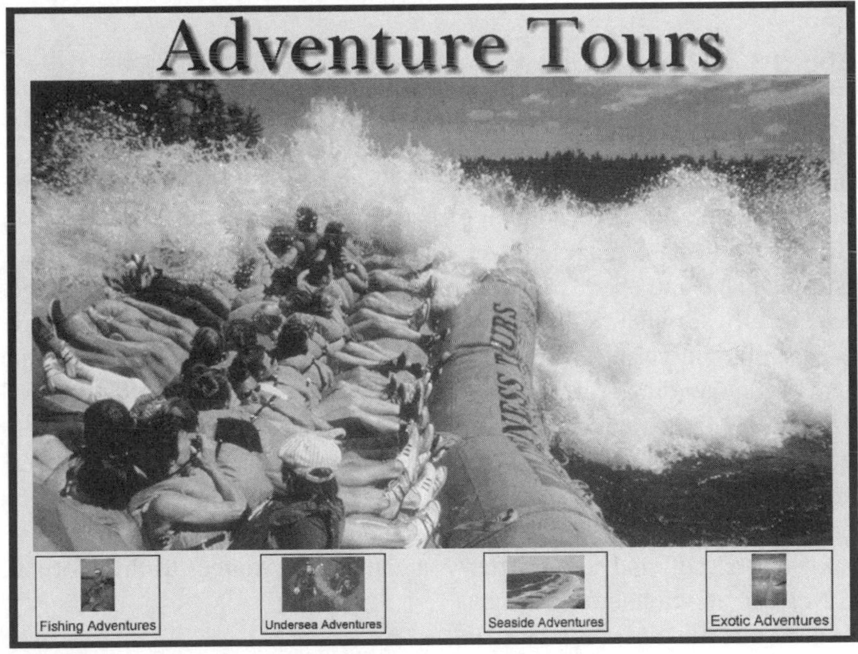

FIGURE 10-4 Create an interactive menu for your CD-ROM presentation.

use an icon with text for the Rollover state, and then use a variation of the icon for the Down state. You can add additional interactivity to the button by assigning multiple actions. For example, you can play a movie file on Mouse Enter, stop the movie file on Mouse Exit, and play sound on Mouse Down. Note that if you use a large movie file with a mouse event, the movie may not load before the user clicks the button. The following image shows a multi-state button that combines an image and text. For more information on creating a multi-state rollover button, refer to Chapter 9.

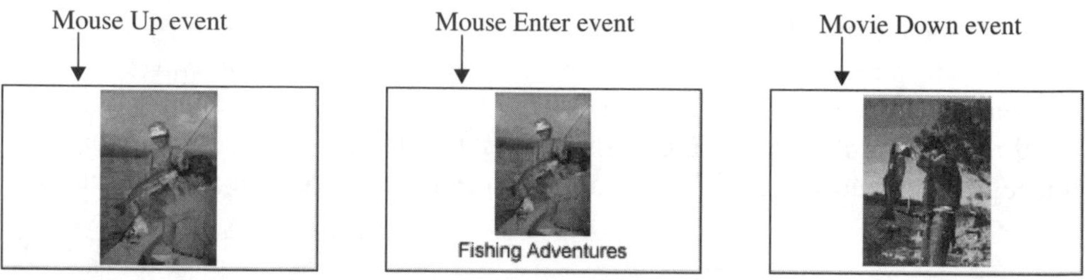

Create an Introduction

You can create an effective introduction to your multimedia presentation by creating a series of pages that will play one after the other, similar to movie credits. After Acrobat displays the last page, you use an action to open the main page of the presentation. The number of introduction pages will vary depending on your presentation. You could create an interesting introduction by gradually increasing the size and opacity of a corporate logo until it fills the entire page. Another visually stimulating introduction for a presentation is to have various images assemble into a splash screen, like the pieces of a jigsaw puzzle coming together. If you have image-editing software such as Adobe PhotoShop, Corel Photo-Paint, or Macromedia Fireworks, you can create the individual images for the introduction. Create the images with the same dimensions as your PDF presentation, and convert each image to PDF format using the eBook Job Option. Name each file in the order it will appear in the introduction, for example, intro1.pdf, intro2.pdf, and so on. After you convert the images to PDF format, launch Acrobat and do the following:

1. Choose File | Open and select the first page of your introduction.
2. Choose Document | Insert Pages and select the remaining pages of the introduction. Accept the default location. Click OK, and Acrobat appends the document with the selected pages.

3. If you are not already there, navigate to the first page of the document and choose Document | Set Page Action. Page Open is selected by default.
4. Click the Add button. From the Type drop-down menu, choose JavaScript, click the Edit button to open the JavaScript Edit dialog box, and then click OK to close the Page Actions dialog box.
5. Enter the following JavaScript code in the text window:

```
var interval = app.setInterval("this.pageNum = this.pageNum + 1;", 3000);
```

6. Click OK to close the JavaScript Edit dialog box, click Set Action, and then click OK to close the Page Actions dialog box and assign the action to the page. Before you go on to the next step, take a look at the preceding JavaScript code. You created a variable named *interval* and set it equal to the *setInterval* method of the *app* object. The *setInterval* method is used to pause the application for a certain amount of time—in this case, 3000 milliseconds, which is equal to 3 seconds. The code in quotation marks executes after the interval has passed. In this case, it increases the value of the *pageNum* property of the document by 1, which advances the document to the next page. The code will continue to execute every three seconds until you stop the code by clearing the interval.
7. Navigate to the last page of the introduction, and choose Document | Set Page Action.
8. Click Add, choose JavaScript from the Type drop-down menu, and then click the Edit button to open the JavaScript Edit dialog box.
9. Enter the following code in the text window:

```
app.clearInterval(interval)
```

10. Click OK to close the JavaScript Edit dialog box. Now that you have created the JavaScript to stop the pages from turning, you need to specify which document will open after the introduction plays.
11. Click Add, and, from the Type drop-down menu, choose Open File.
12. Select the file that you want to open after the introduction plays, click Set Action, and then click OK to close the Page Actions dialog box.

That is all you need to do to create an automated introduction. You could have created each page of the introduction as a separate PDF file and used the Open File action to advance to the next PDF document. However, on all but the slowest computer, the files would open too quickly for the viewer to get a good look at them. When you use JavaScript, you can control the amount of time each page of the introduction is displayed. To increase or decrease the interval time, enter a new value in step 5. Remember that 1 second equals 1,000 milliseconds, and you can precisely control the amount of time each page is displayed.

TIP *You can also use the* setInterval *object to create a slide slow. Assemble the images you want to present, combine them as separate pages of a PDF document, and follow the preceding steps to set the interval between each image. At the end of the document, create two buttons: one to replay the show, and one to exit. For the Replay button, use the Execute Menu Item action and choose Document | Go To First Page; for the Exit button, use the Execute Menu Item action and choose File | Exit.*

Work with Named Destinations

When you create a complex PDF presentation, you may find it helpful to work with named destinations. A named destination links to a specific point in a document. When you work with multiple documents, as is often the case when creating a multimedia presentation, you can simplify cross-document navigation by linking to a named destination. When you link to a named destination, the link remains active even when pages are added or deleted from the target document.

Work with the Destinations Palette

You use the Destinations palette to display and sort named destinations within a document. You also use the palette to rename destinations. To display the named destinations within a document, do the following:

1. Choose Window | Destinations to open the Destinations palette.
2. Click the Scan Document button to display a list of destinations within the document, as shown in Figure 10-5.
3. To sort the destinations alphabetically, click the Name bar near the top of the palette.
4. To sort the destinations by page number, click the Page bar near the top of the palette.

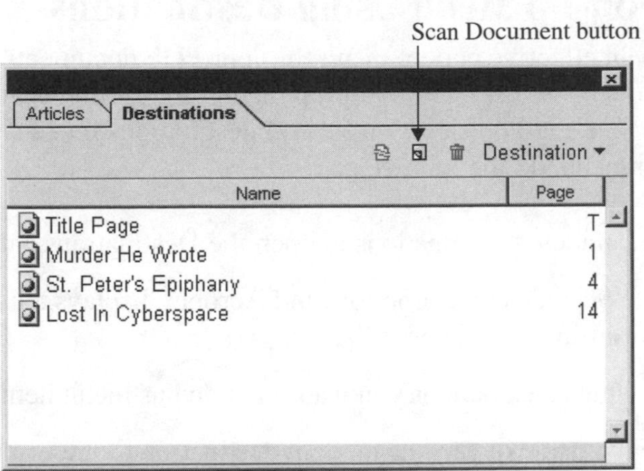

FIGURE 10-5 Scan a document for named destinations with the Desintations palette.

5. To go to a named destination, double-click its name. Alternatively, you can right-click (Windows) or CTRL-click (Macintosh) and choose Go To Destination from the context menu.

6. To delete named destinations, select them and press DELETE. Alternatively, you can click the Delete Selected Destinations button (which looks like a garbage can) or choose Delete from the context menu.

7. To rename a destination, select it, right-click (Windows) or CTRL-click (Macintosh), choose Rename from the context menu, and enter a new name for the destination.

8. To create a named destination, navigate to the document page you want added to the named destination list, set the magnification of the page, click the Create New Destination button, and enter a name for the new destination. Alternatively, you can choose New Destination from the context menu.

NOTE *You must scan the document prior to adding a new destination. If you open the Destinations panel, the Create New Destination button is dimmed out until you scan the document as outlined in step 2.*

Create a Pop-Up Menu Using Destinations

You can create an effective pop-up menu for your PDF documents using named destinations and a bit of JavaScript. Pop-up menus are useful because they do not take up much space and you can cram several destinations into a single menu. To create a pop-up menu, do the following:

1. Choose Window | Destinations to open the Destinations palette.
2. Click the Scan Document button, and Acrobat displays a list of destinations in the document.
3. Decide which destinations you want included as menu items.
4. Change the name of each menu item destination to the name you want to appear on the menu. For example, if the menu item will be called Chapter 1, change the name of the destination to Chapter 1. Note that this technique is intended for desktop viewing. If you create a document for viewing in a Web browser, spaces may cause inconsistent results.
5. Using the Forms tool, create a form field where you want the pop-up menu to appear.
6. In the Field Properties dialog box, enter a name for the field and choose Button from the Type drop-down menu.
7. Define the appearance and options for the button as outlined previously in Chapter 9.
8. Click the Actions tab, select Mouse Up, and then click the Add button.
9. Choose JavaScript from the Type drop-down menu to open the JavaScript Edit dialog box.
10. In the text window, enter the following code replacing the *Dest* designations with the names of your destinations exactly as they appear in the Destinations window. If you have the Destinations palette open when you create the JavaScript, refer to the palette when adding each destination to your code.

```
var c = app.popUpMenu ("Dest1","Dest2","Dest3","Dest4");

this.gotoNamedDest(c);
```

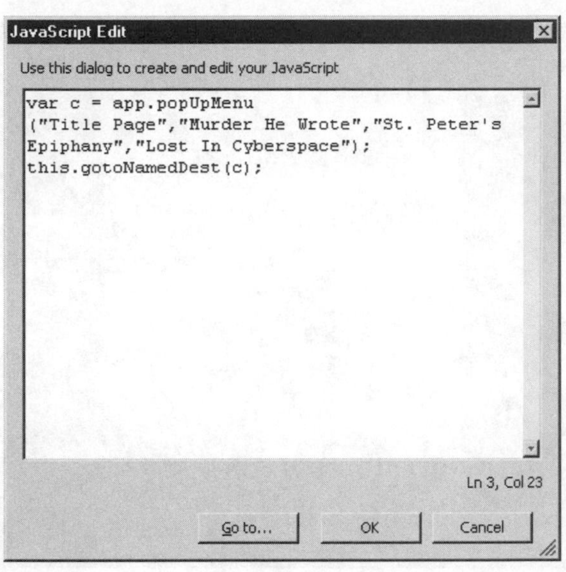
JavaScript Edit
Use this dialog to create and edit your JavaScript
var c = app.popUpMenu
("Title Page","Murder He Wrote","St. Peter's
Epiphany","Lost In Cyberspace");
this.gotoNamedDest(c);
Ln 3, Col 23
Go to...
OK
Cancel

FIGURE 10-6 Create a pop-up menu for your documents using named destinations and JavaScript.

11. Click OK to close the JavaScript Edit dialog box, click Set Action to assign the JavaScript to the button, and then click OK to close the Field Properties dialog box. Figure 10-7 shows the pop-up menu that resulted from the JavaScript shown in Figure 10-6.

NOTE *After you modify document destinations, but before you save the document, choose Tools | PDF Consultant | Optimize Space. In the Named Destinations section, choose Convert All Into Direct Links to prevent inadvertently removing a named destination you plan to use later.*

Create an Auto Run CD-ROM (Windows)

If you create a presentation for CD-ROM, you can create a version of Acrobat Reader to run directly from your CD-ROM. If you own a version of Acrobat 4.0, you may know that there is a folder called CD on the Acrobat 4.0 application CD-ROM. You can copy this folder to your CD-ROM staging area and include it with the other files used to create your multimedia presentation. Users can run

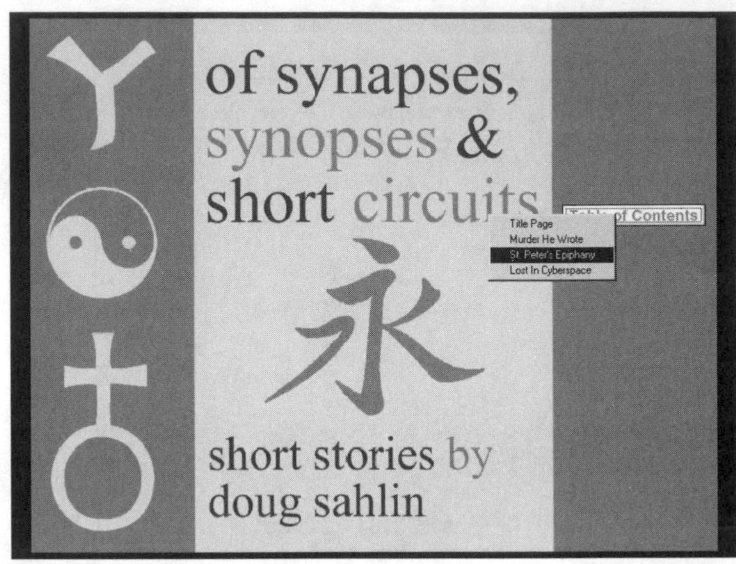

FIGURE 10-7 You can create a pop-up menu using JavaScript and named destinations.

Acrobat Reader directly from the CD-ROM without having the software installed on their computers. You can simplify the process by creating an auto run file that launches Acrobat Reader and opens the first file of your PDF presentation. Unfortunately, the Acrobat 5.0 application disk does not come with a CD folder. The Acrobat 4.0 Reader will work with most of the PDF files you create with Acrobat 5.0. However, if you do not own Acrobat 4.0, you have another option available to you.

Create a Stand-Alone CD-ROM for Acrobat Reader 5.0 (Windows Only)

Although the Acrobat 5.0 Application disk does not come with a stand-alone version of Acrobat Reader 5.0 for CD-ROM, you can create one if you own two computers. On a computer with neither Acrobat nor Acrobat Reader installed, do the following:

1. Insert the Acrobat 5.0 application disk in the computer CD-ROM, and navigate to the Installer directory, which is a subdirectory of the Acroread directory.

2. Click the Setup.exe icon and follow the prompts to install Acrobat Reader.
3. After you install Acrobat Reader, copy the Acrobat 5.0 directory to a mass storage device, such as a zip disk. If you are on a network, you can transfer the folder from one computer to another. If you did a standard installation of Acrobat Reader, the path to the Acrobat 5.0 directory is as follows: C:\Program Files\Adobe\Acrobat 5.0.

On the computer you use to create PDF files and burn presentation CD-ROMs, copy the Acrobat 5.0 folder to the directory where you stage files for the CD-ROMs you create. You will be able to run Acrobat in a directory other than the one it was installed in; however, you will get error messages because Acrobat Reader cannot locate the Fonts folder. In order to rectify this, you need to rearrange the directory structure, as shown in the following steps:

1. Launch Windows Explorer by choosing Start | Programs | Accessories | Windows Explorer.
2. Navigate to the CD Staging directory where you copied the Acrobat 5.0 folder, and expand the directory by clicking the plus sign (+).
3. Expand the Resource directory by clicking the plus sign (+).
4. Click the Reader directory; drag it to the Acrobat 5.0 root and release the mouse button. Your modified directory path will be Acrobat\Reader\Resource, as shown in the following image:

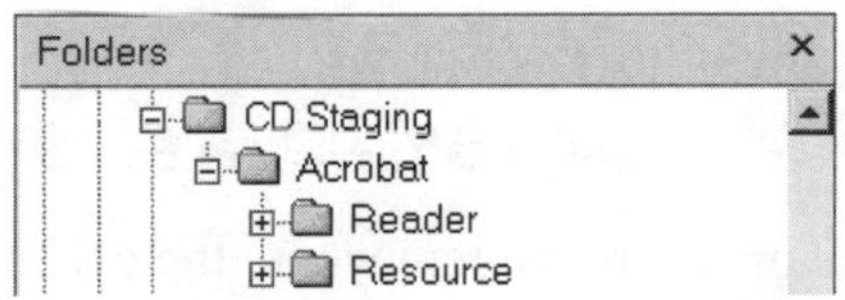

After you modify the directory structure, Acrobat 5.0 Reader will run properly with no error messages. You will not be able to access Adobe Online, but your goal is to create a stand-alone version of Acrobat Reader that will run from a CD-ROM. If your presentation is set up to run in Full Screen mode, the only time your user will be aware that Acrobat is used to view the presentation is when Acrobat launches and the viewer sees the splash screen. After you have a stand-alone version of Acrobat Reader, the only task you have left is to copy the presentation files into the root folder of your CD-ROM staging directory, and create an auto run file as outlined in the next section.

TIP

If you do not have access to two computers or a mass storage device to transport the Acrobat Reader folder from one computer to another, remove Acrobat from your machine using the Windows Add/Remove Programs utility found in the Control Panel. After you delete Acrobat, install Acrobat Reader and copy the folder to your CD Staging folder as outlined previously. Modify the directory structure of the file you copied to the staging folder as outlined previously. Reinstall Acrobat, and you are back in business.

Create an Auto Run File (Windows Only)

Windows 95, 98, Millennium, NT4, and 2000 operating systems have the capability to run a program from CD-ROM as soon as the CD is read. To accomplish this, you need to create an auto run file. The auto run file instructs the operating system which application to launch when the CD-ROM is inserted and which file to open. You can create an auto run file in Microsoft Notepad by doing the following:

1. Launch Notepad.
2. Create one line of text that reads as follows:

   ```
   [autorun]
   ```

   This heading is required and tells the operating system that the lines that follow are instructions on how to launch an executable file on the CD-ROM.

3. Create a second line of text as follows:

   ```
   open=Acrobat\Reader\AcroRd32.exe intro.pdf
   ```

   This line tells the operating system where the executable file is located and which file to open. In this case, a file named *intro.pdf* will open after Acrobat launches. The space between the path of the Acrobat executable file and the file open indicates that the file is in the root directory of the CD-ROM.

4. Create a third line of text as follows:

   ```
   defaulticon=Acrobat\Reader\AcroRd32.exe,1
   ```

   This line indicates the path to the Acrobat Reader icon.

5. Choose File | Save As to open the Save As dialog box.
6. Enter **autorun.inf** in the File Name field, and save the file in the root directory of your CD-ROM staging folder.

After you burn the CD-ROM and a viewer inserts it in a CD-ROM device, Acrobat Reader will launch the PDF file specified in step 3. However, some computer users disable the auto insert function of their CD-ROM player. You can prepare for this possibility by including a Readme file on the CD-ROM telling the viewer how to launch the application.

CAUTION *In order to comply with the Adobe EULA (End User License Agreement) for Acrobat Reader, the EULA must launch the first time the end user plays the CD-ROM. In this regard, do not run the version of Acrobat Reader from your CD staging area; otherwise, you will launch the EULA and it will not be available for the end user to accept.*

Bundle the Acrobat Installer with Your Presentation

If you do not create a CD-ROM with a stand-alone version of Acrobat 5.0 Reader, and you anticipate that members of your viewing audience may not have Acrobat 5.0 Reader installed, copy the Installer folder from the Acrobat 5.0 application disk to your CD-ROM staging area. The path to the Installer folder is as follows: \ Acroread \Installer. When you copy the entire folder, you include the necessary files and documents to comply with the Adobe EULA that allows you to freely distribute Acrobat Reader. If you own software that can create an autorun for your CD-ROM, you can include a link to the Acrobat Setup.exe file as one of the menu choices. It is also a good idea to display a welcome message when the autorun menu launches, telling the viewer they need Acrobat 5.0 installed on their computer to view the presentation.

Part III

Edit PDF Documents

Chapter 11

The Basics of Editing PDF Documents

How To...

- Edit Visually with Thumbnails
- Edit with Menu Commands
- Edit with Batch Processing
- Append PDF Documents
- Touch Up a PDF Document

After you create a PDF document, you can easily edit it. Within Acrobat you can add pages, delete pages, reorder pages, and renumber pages. You can also edit multiple documents by using Acrobat Batch Processing, as well as edit individual objects within the PDF document.

You edit PDF documents by using palettes, tools, and menu commands. Many of the edits you perform with Acrobat tools can also be accomplished by using menu commands or selecting commands from the appropriate palette or context menu. In this chapter you'll learn to edit PDF documents and add pages to PDF documents.

Edit Visually with Thumbnails

Thumbnails are miniature images of each page in a PDF document. Each thumbnail displays with a page number below it. In previous chapters of this book, you have seen thumbnails used as navigation devices. You can also use them to edit your documents. You can use thumbnails to insert pages, delete pages, and change the order of pages. Thumbnails are located in the Thumbnails palette, as shown in Figure 11-1.

The Thumbnails palette is part of the Navigation pane. To open the Thumbnails palette, click its tab. In the Navigation pane, you can open the Thumbnails palette by choosing Window | Thumbnails. The Thumbnails palette has its own menu, a context menu, and one solitary tool.

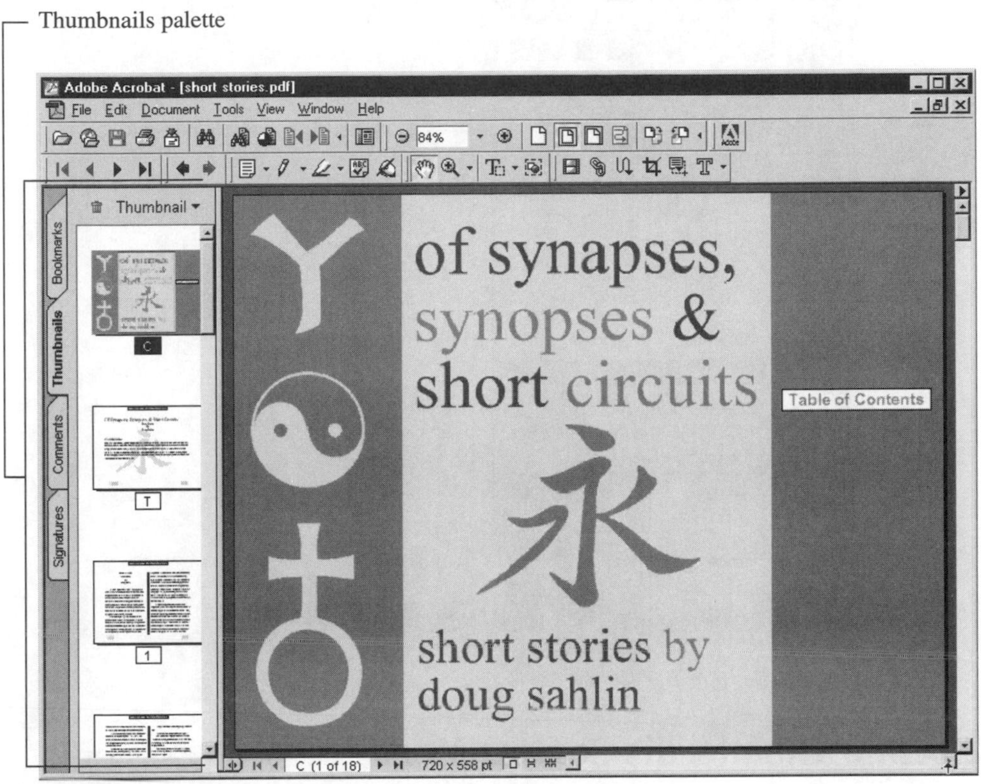

FIGURE 11-1 You can edit pages with the Thumbnails palette.

Use the Thumbnails Palette Menu

You use the Thumbnails palette menu to access certain menu commands that edit a document and work with thumbnails. To open the Thumbnails palette menu, as shown in the following image, click the Thumbnail icon near the upper-right corner of the palette.

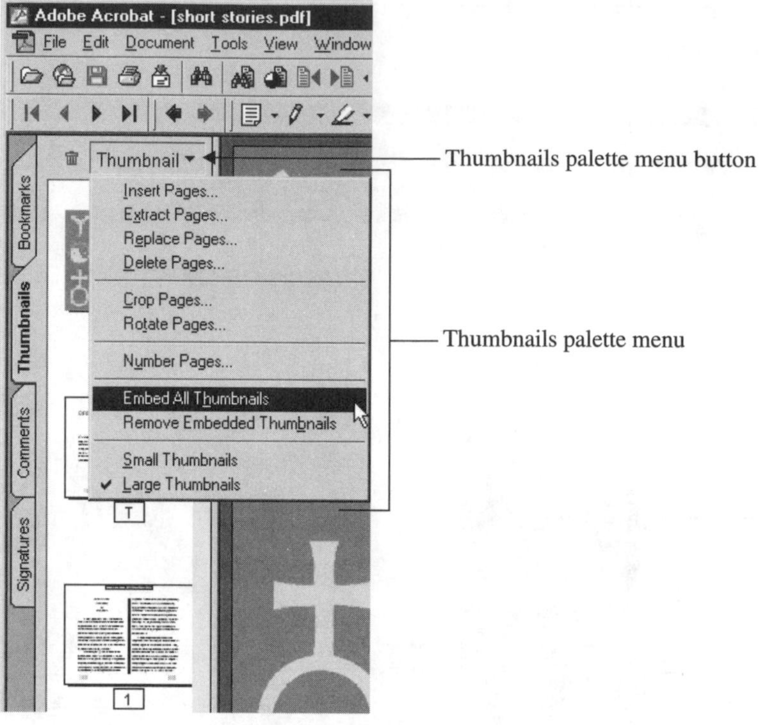

Use the Thumbnails Context Menu

Many of the commands you use to edit PDF documents can be found on the Thumbnails context menu. To access the Thumbnails context menu, as shown in the following image, select a thumbnail and right-click (Windows) or CTRL-click (Macintosh).

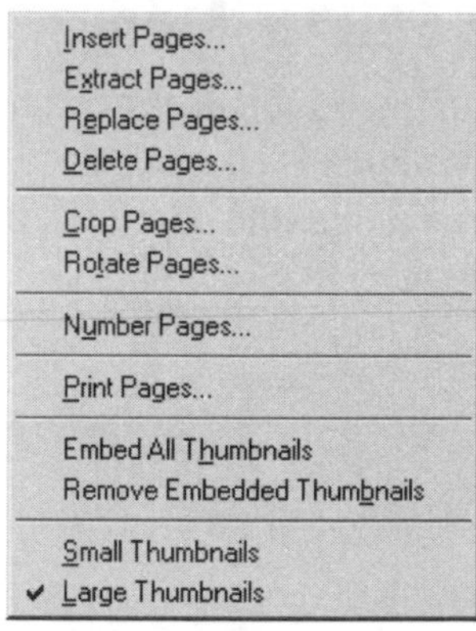

Insert Pages

You can insert pages from within the Thumbnails palette. From within the palette, you click a thumbnail to select a page and then insert pages before or after the selected page. To add one or more pages to your document, follow these steps:

1. Click a thumbnail to select the page before or after the place where the new pages will be inserted.
2. Choose Insert Pages from the Thumbnails palette menu or the context menu to open the Select File to Insert dialog box.
3. Select the PDF(s) file you want to insert and click Select to open the Insert Pages dialog box, as shown in the following image:

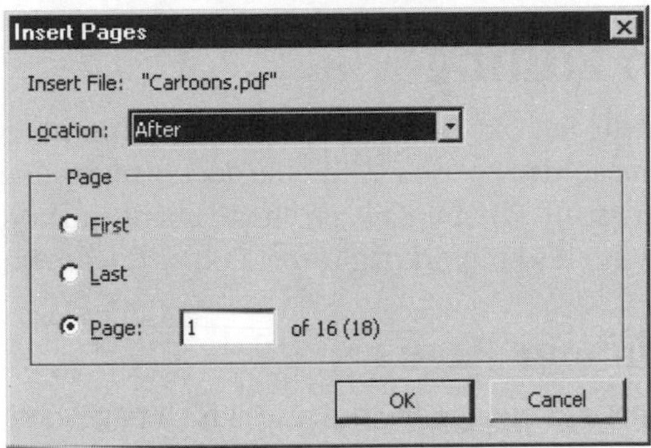

4. From the Location drop-down menu, choose Before or After.
5. Click OK, and Acrobat inserts the selected documents in the location specified and creates a thumbnail for each new page.

Delete Pages

You can also use thumbnails to delete one or more pages. To delete pages from within the Thumbnails palette, do one of the following:

- To delete a single page, click its thumbnail and then click the Delete Selected Pages button, which looks like a trash can, and Acrobat displays a warning dialog box. Click OK to delete the page or Cancel to abort the operation.

- To delete contiguous pages, click a thumbnail that corresponds to a page you want to delete and then, while pressing SHIFT, click contiguous thumbnails to add them to the selection. When you have finished selecting thumbnails, click the Delete Selected Pages button. Click OK to close the warning dialog box and delete the pages.
- To delete noncontiguous pages, click a thumbnail that corresponds to a page you want to delete and then, while pressing CTRL, click additional thumbnails to add them to the selection. Click the Delete Selected Pages button to delete the pages from the document. Click OK to accept the deletion of the pages.
- You can also delete pages by selecting thumbnails and choosing Delete Pages from the Thumbnails palette menu or context menu.

Drag-and-Drop Editing

The Thumbnails palette not only gives you a visual representation of each page in your document, but it can also be used to edit the document by dragging-and-dropping thumbnails. You can use the Thumbnails palette to change the order in which pages display and you can use it to import pages from other documents.

Reorder Document Pages

You can use thumbnails to change the order in which pages appear in a PDF document. To move a single page or a selection of pages to a new position in the document, select them, and then drag-and-drop them to a new location. To change the order of document pages, follow these steps:

1. Open the Thumbnails palette and select the thumbnail that corresponds to the page you want to move. You can move more than one page at a time by selecting contiguous or noncontiguous thumbnails, as discussed previously.

TIP *To view several thumbnails at once, choose Small Thumbnails from the Thumbnails palette menu or the Thumbnails palette context menu.*

2. Click and drag the thumbnails up or down. As you drag the selected thumbnails, your cursor becomes a filled arrow attached to a document,

and a solid blue line appears below each thumbnail to indicate the current position of the thumbnail, as shown in the following image. If the Navigation pane is sized so that more than one column of thumbnails is visible, the blue line appears to the side of each thumbnail.

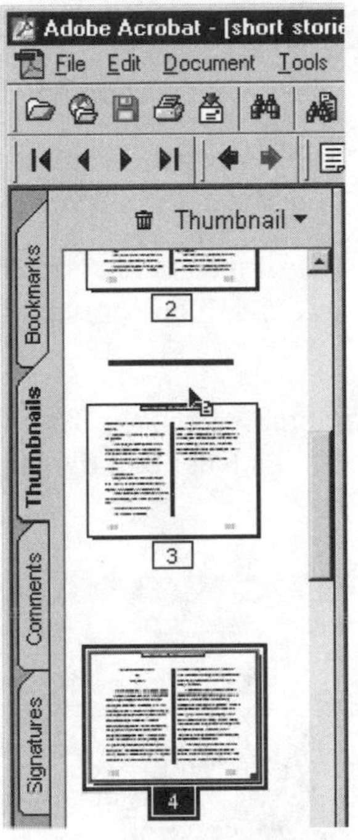

TIP

When you do extensive editing with thumbnails, your work will be easier if you expand the Navigation pane to display more thumbnails. To expand the Navigation pane, click the vertical border between the Navigation pane and the Document pane and drag it to the right.

3. Release the mouse button when the selected thumbnails are where you want them. Acrobat moves the selected pages to their new location and renumbers the thumbnails.

Copy Pages from Other Documents

If you have more than one document open, you can use the Thumbnails palette to copy pages from one document to another. Copying pages is an excellent way to build a document when working with a team of PDF authors. To copy pages from one document to another, follow these steps:

1. Open the source document and target document.
2. Choose Window | Tile and then choose Vertically or Horizontally. Alternatively you can choose Cascading, but you will have to rearrange the documents so each document's Thumbnails palette is visible.
3. If they are not already visible, open the Thumbnails palette of each document by choosing Window | Thumbnails while the respective document is selected.
4. In the Thumbnails palette of the source document, select the thumbnail for the page you want to copy. You can select more than one thumbnail if necessary.
5. Click and drag the thumbnails from the Thumbnails palette of the source document to the Thumbnails palette of the target document, as shown in the following image:

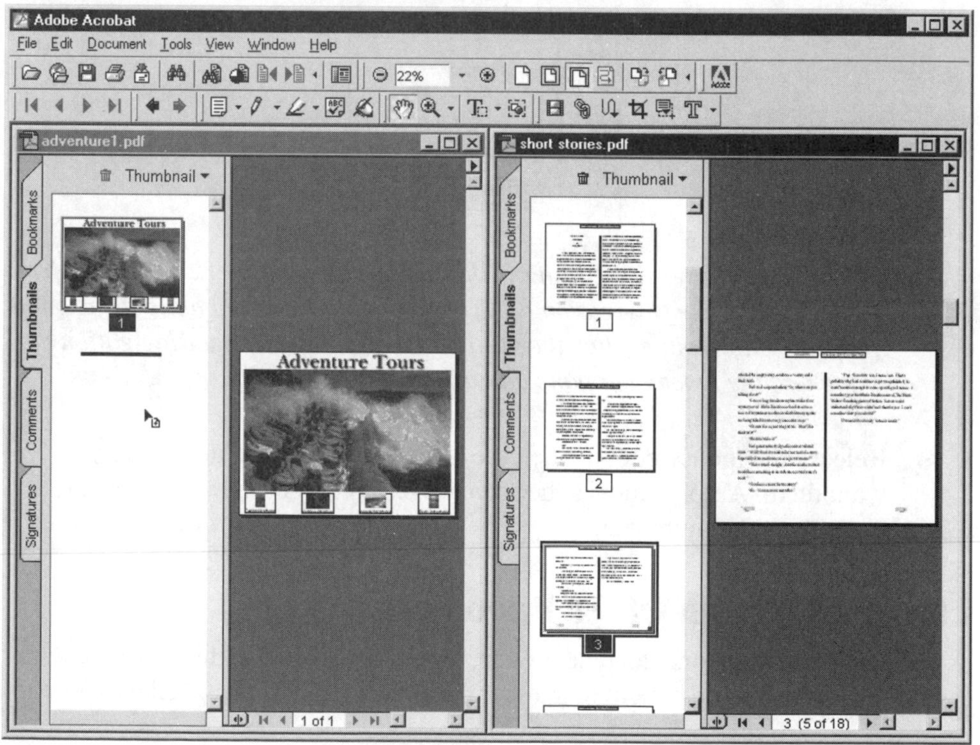

6. As your cursor moves into the Thumbnails palette of the target document, the cursor becomes an angled arrow attached to a document with a plus sign (+) in it.
7. In the palette of the target document, drag the thumbnail to the desired position and release the mouse button. After you release the mouse button, Acrobat copies the selected pages to the target document and then creates numbered thumbnails for the copied pages.

You can move a page from one document to another by clicking its thumbnail, pressing CTRL, *and dragging it to the Thumbnails palette of the target document. An icon that resembles a document page appears under your cursor, signifying that you are moving and not copying a page.*

Edit with Menu Commands

Many of the menu commands that are discussed in the following sections are exact copies of Thumbnails palette menu and Thumbnails context menu commands. When you use these commands in the Thumbnails palette, you work with a single thumbnail or selection of thumbnails. When you use a menu command, you can specify any page in the document. The previous sections dealt with using editing commands in a specific manner within the Thumbnails palette. The following sections show you how to use menu commands to edit selected pages within your documents.

Insert Pages

You can add existing documents to any PDF document using the Insert Pages command. With the Insert Pages command, you specify the exact location within the document where the pages are to be added. To append an existing PDF document using the Insert Pages command, follow these steps:

1. Open the PDF document that you want to add pages to.
2. Choose Document | Insert Pages to open the Select File to Insert dialog box.
3. Navigate to the document page that is before or after the place where you want to insert the pages. This step is optional. You can specify the exact location to add the pages in the Insert Pages dialog box.

4. Choose the file(s) you want to insert and then click Select to open the Insert Pages dialog box.
5. From the Location drop-down menu choose Before or After.
6. In the Page section, choose First, Last, or Page. When you choose the Page option, the pages will be inserted at the current location unless you specify a different location in the Page field.
7. Click OK, and Acrobat inserts the selected pages at the specified location and creates a thumbnail for each added page.

Delete Pages

You can modify a PDF document by deleting unwanted pages. To do this you use the Delete Pages command. This command enables you to delete a single page, a range of pages, or selected pages. To remove pages from a PDF document, follow these steps:

1. Open the document you want to remove pages from.
2. Choose Document | Delete Pages to open the Delete Pages dialog box, as shown in the following image. Alternatively, you can select pages you want to delete by clicking their thumbnails and then choosing Document | Delete Pages.

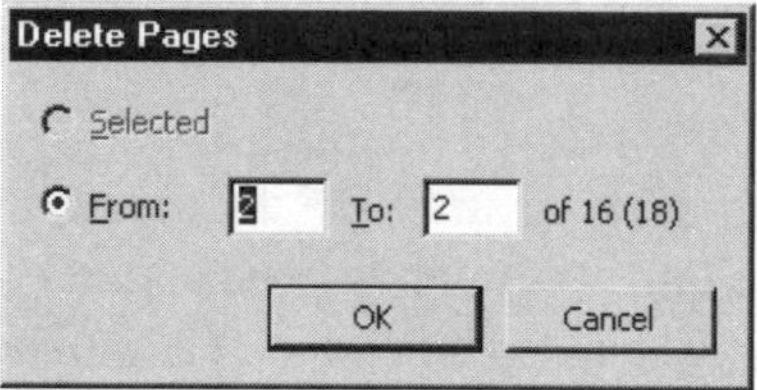

3. If you selected the pages to delete, click OK; otherwise, enter the range of pages to delete and click OK. After you click OK, Acrobat deletes the specified pages and their thumbnails and renumbers the remaining thumbnails.

Replace Pages

You can update a document by replacing a page or a selection of pages. This option is useful when you have a multi page PDF document that needs only minor revisions. Create the pages you need to replace in an authoring application, convert them to PDF format, and then use the Replace Pages command. You can also replace a specific number of pages from one document with a specific number of pages from another document. Acrobat replaces pages on a one-to-one basis. For example, you cannot replace three pages with 50 pages. To replace pages in a PDF document, follow these steps:

1. Open the document that contains the pages you want to replace.
2. Open the Thumbnails palette by clicking its tab in the Navigation pane or choosing Window | Thumbnails.
3. Click the thumbnails that correspond to the pages you want to replace.
4. Choose Document | Replace Pages to open the Select File with New Pages dialog box.
5. Locate the PDF file with the pages that will replace the selected ones and click Select to open the Replace Pages dialog box, as shown in the following illustration:

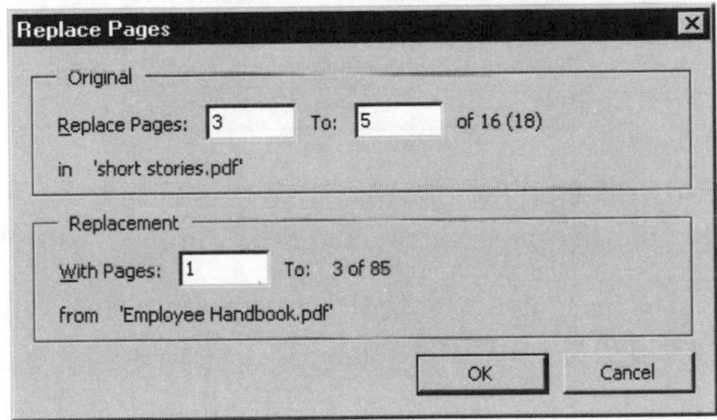

6. If you have already selected the pages you want to replace, go to step 7; otherwise, enter the range of pages you want to replace.
7. In the Replacement section, within the With Pages field, enter the number of the first replacement page of the PDF file you selected. Acrobat automatically calculates the ending page based on the number of pages selected in the original document.
8. Click OK, and Acrobat replaces the pages and generates thumbnails for the replaced pages.

Extract Pages

You can extract pages from an existing PDF document and use them as the basis for a new PDF document. When you extract pages, you can preserve the extracted pages in the original document or delete them. To extract pages from a PDF document, follow these steps:

1. Open the PDF document that contains the pages you want to extract.
2. Open the Thumbnails palette by clicking it tab in the Navigation pane or choosing Window | Thumbnails.
3. Click the thumbnails that correspond to the pages you want to extract. Alternatively, you can enter the range of pages to extract in the Extract Pages dialog box.
4. Choose Document | Extract Pages to open the Extract Pages dialog box, as shown in the following illustration:

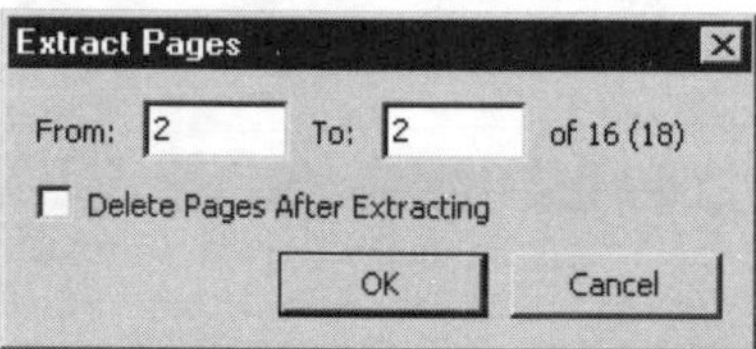

5. If you already selected thumbnails, go to step 6; otherwise, select a range of pages by entering page numbers in the From and To fields.
6. Choose the Delete Pages After Extracting option, and Acrobat will delete the pages when they are extracted.
7. Click OK to extract the pages, and Acrobat opens the extracted pages as a new document.
8. Choose File | Save As and then specify a filename and location where you want the extracted pages saved.

Crop Pages

If you create a PDF document and you find that one or more of the document pages have excessive margins, you can trim (crop) the margins. You crop the margins by using a menu command or a tool. To crop pages, follow these steps:

1. Open the document whose pages you want to crop. Select a range of pages to crop by clicking thumbnails in the Thumbnails palette. Alternatively, you can specify which pages to crop by selecting a range in the Crop Pages dialog box.

2. Choose Document | Crop Pages to open the Crop Pages dialog box, as shown in the following illustrator:

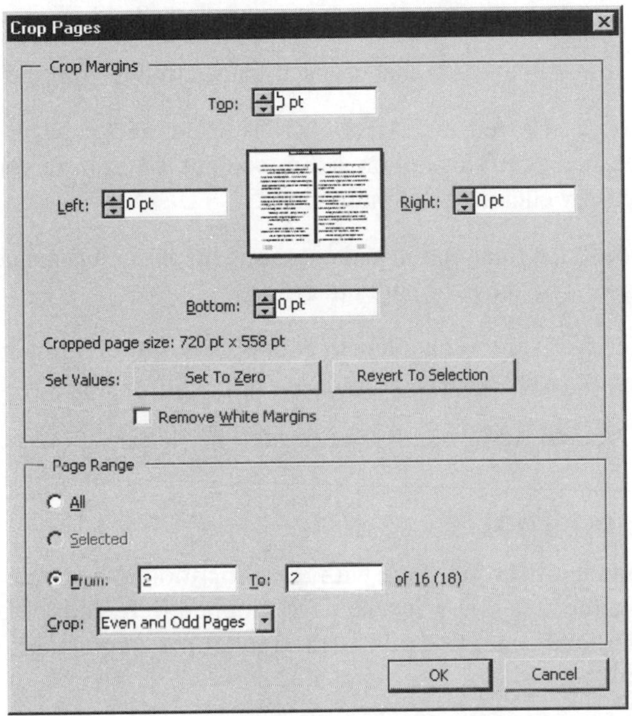

3. In the Crop Margins section, enter a value to crop in any or all of the following fields: Top, Left, Right, Bottom. For example, to crop 6 pts from the top margin enter 6 in the Top field. Alternatively, you can click the spinner buttons to select a value. Press SHIFT while clicking a spinner button, and the values will change in greater increments. As you modify the margin values, a red rectangle appears around the thumbnail in the center of the Crop Margins section changes to reflect the size of the document with the modified margin settings.

   - Click the Set To Zero button to reset the margin values to zero.

- Click the Revert To Selection button to reset the margins to the previous cropping rectangle. This button will reset the margins to zero unless you use the Crop tool to define the cropping rectangle and then modify one of the margins.
- Enable the Remove White Margins option to crop the side margins to the document contents, thus eliminating a white border.

4. In the Page Range section, choose one of the following:
   - Choose All, and Acrobat crops all pages to the specified size.
   - Choose Selected, and Acrobat crops only selected pages to the specified size. This option is dimmed out if you have not selected pages by clicking their thumbnails.
   - Choose the final option and enter a value in the From and To fields to specify a range of pages to crop.
5. From the Crop drop-down menu, choose one of the following: Even And Odd Pages, Odd Pages Only, or Even Pages Only.
6. Click OK, and Acrobat crops the page(s) to the sizes you specified.

Use the Crop Tool

You can also manually crop a page with the Crop tool. When you use the Crop tool, you define the area you want the page cropped to by dragging the tool within the Document pane. Use this method to crop a single page, or multiple pages, as follows:

1. Navigate to the page you want to crop. Alternatively, you can select the page by clicking its thumbnail.

2. Select the Crop tool, as shown at left.
3. Click the point that will define one of the outer boundaries of the cropped page and then drag the tool down and across. As you drag, a bounding box appears, giving you a preview of the area you are defining. When the area is the desired size, release the mouse button, and Acrobat defines the area,

as shown in the following image. Notice the square handles at the corners of the bounding box.

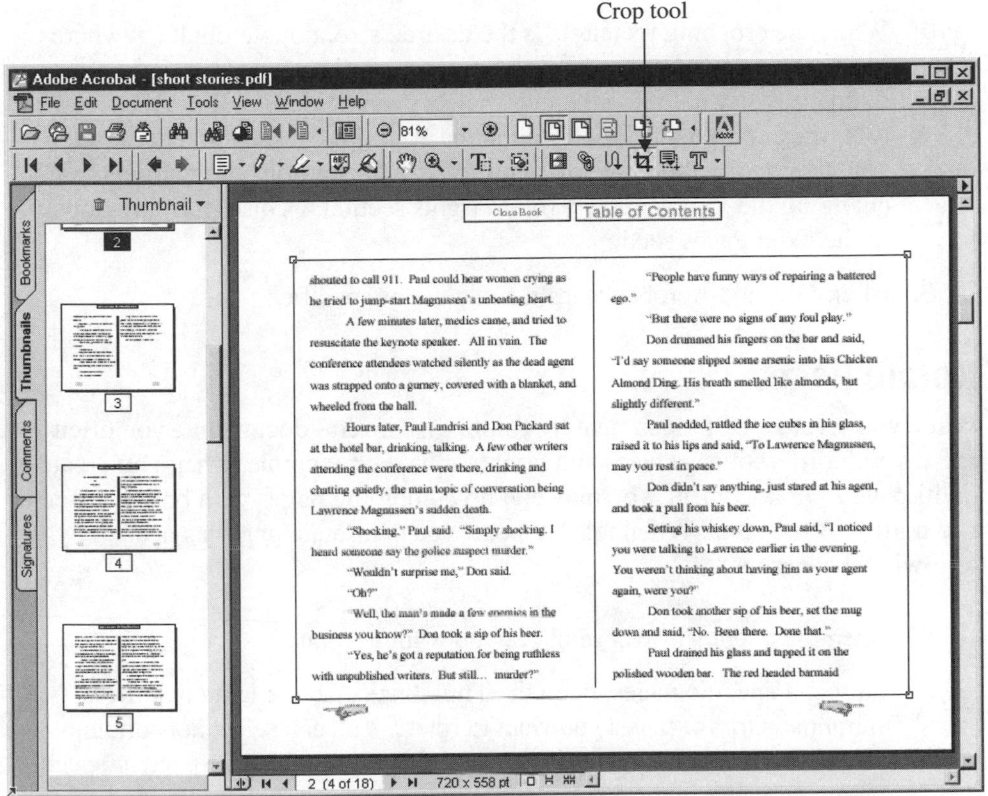

4. With the Crop tool still selected, you can modify the cropping rectangle by doing one of the following:

- To move the cropping rectangle, click inside the rectangle and drag it to a new position. Release the mouse button when the rectangle is in the desired position.
- To change the height of the cropping rectangle, click one of the handles and drag up or down.
- To change the width of the cropping rectangle, click one of the handles and drag left or right.

- To change the size of the cropping rectangle, click one of the handles and drag diagonally. To resize the rectangle proportionately, press SHIFT while dragging.

5. When the cropping rectangle is the desired size, double-click anywhere inside the rectangle, or press ENTER or RETURN to reveal the Crop Pages dialog box. By default, when you select a single page and use the Crop tool, the current page is selected in the Page Range section. If desired, you can modify the range of pages to crop or fine-tune the margins by changing the values in the Crop Margins section, as discussed previously in the Crop Pages section.
6. Click OK, and Acrobat crops the page(s) as specified.

Rotate Pages

When you create a PDF document by combining several documents, you often end up with different page sizes and orientations. For example, when you create a multi-page PDF document, you may end up combining pages with both landscape and portrait orientation. When this happens, you can rotate pages as needed by following these steps:

1. Open the document whose pages you want to rotate.
2. To select specific pages, open the Thumbnails palette and click the thumbnails for the pages you want to rotate. You can select noncontiguous pages to rotate. Alternatively, you can navigate to a specific page or specify a range of pages in the Rotate Pages dialog box.
3. Choose Document | Rotate Pages to open the Rotate Pages dialog box.

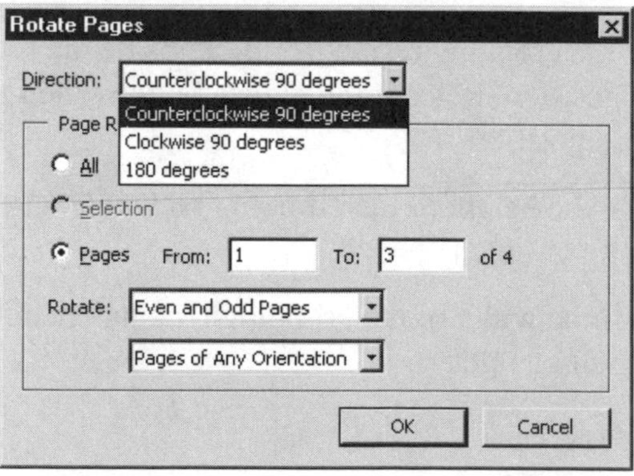

4. Choose one of the following options from the Direction drop-down menu: Counterclockwise 90 Degrees, Clockwise 90 Degrees, or 180 Degrees.
5. In the Page Range section, choose one of the following options:
   - **All** Choose this option, and Acrobat rotates all pages in the direction specified.
   - **Selection** This option is available if you selected pages by clicking their thumbnails; otherwise it is dimmed out.
   - **Pages** This option is selected if you navigate to a specific page before invoking the Rotate Pages command. You can accept the page range (the page you navigated to) or modify the range by entering a page number in the From [ ] and To [ ] fields.
6. In the Rotate section, click the triangle to the right of the first field and from the drop-down menu, choose one of the following: Even And Odd Pages, Even Pages Only, or Odd Pages Only.
7. In the Rotate section, click the triangle to the right of the second field and from the drop-down menu, choose one of the following: Landscape Pages, Portrait Pages, or Pages Of Any Orientation.
8. Click OK, and Acrobat rotates the specified pages to the desired orientation.

Number Pages

When you create a PDF document, Acrobat automatically numbers the pages. When you add pages, move pages, or delete pages, Acrobat updates the page numbers to reflect the order in which the pages appear. Acrobat uses a default integer numbering system, starting with 1 for the first page of the document, and so on. If the document you create has a title page, copyright pages, or similar front matter pages, you can modify the numbering style by following these steps:

1. Select the thumbnails of the pages you want to renumber. Alternatively, you can specify a range of pages to renumber in the Page Numbering dialog box.

2. Choose Document | Number Pages to open the Page Numbering dialog box, as shown in the following image:

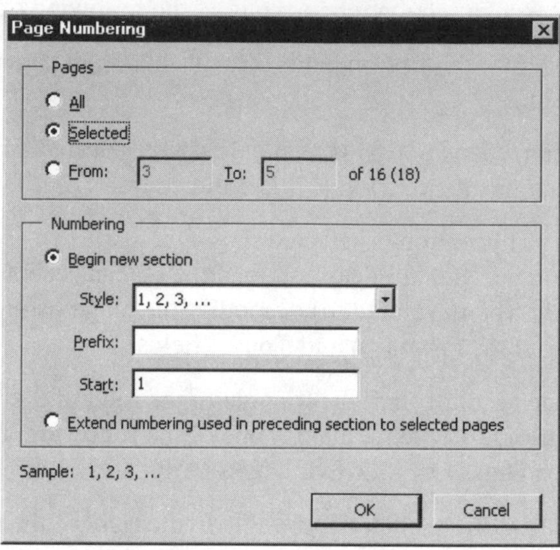

3. In the Pages section, choose one of the following options:

   - **All** Choose this optio,n and all pages will be renumbered.
   - **Selected** This option is available and selected by default when you create a selection of pages by clicking their thumbnails.
   - **From: [ ] To: [ ]** This option is selected by default if you navigate to a page before invoking the Number Pages command. The range of pages will be the page to which you navigated. You can modify the range of pages by entering page numbers in the From and To fields.

4. In the Numbering section, choose one of the following options:

   - **Begin New Selection** Choose this option to begin a new numbering sequence. Click the triangle to the right of the Style field and choose an option from the drop-down menu. To add a prefix to the page numbers, enter the desired prefix in the Prefix field. In the Start field, enter the beginning value for the page sequence.

- **Extend Numbering Used In Preceding Section To Selected Pages** Choose this option, and Acrobat will renumber the selected pages using the same sequence as the preceding pages, numbering the first selected page with the next page number in the sequence.

5. Click OK to renumber the selected pages.

Edit with Batch Processing

When you prepare a large number of PDF documents for a specific audience or destination, you often end up performing the same task on every document, for example, optimizing several documents for Internet viewing. Instead of opening up every document you need to modify and then repeating the same task, you can perform the same command on several documents at once using batch processing. You can choose from preset batch sequences or create your own batch sequence. When you create a custom batch sequence, you can specify the order in which the commands execute. You can also use batch processing to perform a specific sequence of commands on a single document.

Use Preset Batch Sequences

When you choose a preset batch sequence, Acrobat prompts you for the files to process. If a command in the batch sequence requires user input, the applicable dialog box appears. To perform a batch sequence, follow these steps:

1. Choose File | Batch Processing and then choose a preset batch sequence from the menu. If, for example, you want to print the first page of several documents, choose Print First Page Of All. After you select a batch sequence, the Run Sequence Confirmation dialog box appears, as shown in the following image. Note that this image is of the Print First Page Of All batch sequence, which actually uses JavaScript to accomplish the task. The triangle to the left of the actual batch sequence command has been clicked to illustrate the JavaScript used to run the batch sequence.

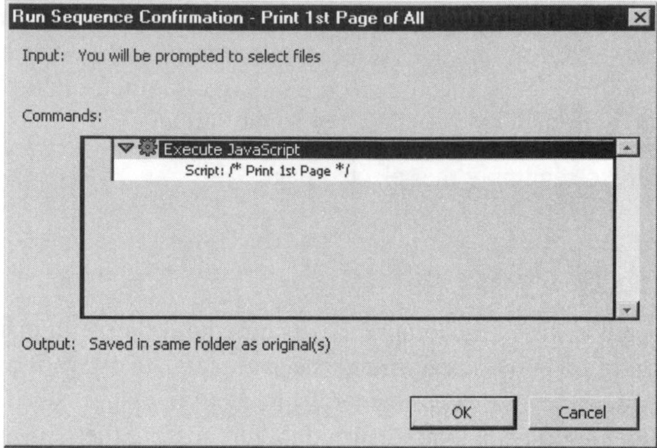

2. Verify that the commands in the Run Sequence Confirmation are the tasks you want to perform. If the batch sequence command has a triangle before it, you can click the triangle to see the exact command Acrobat will perform. If the batch sequence is the one you want, Click OK to open the Select Files to Process dialog box.
3. Select the files you want to process.
4. Click Select, and Acrobat performs the batch sequence commands and saves the modified files in the original folder.

When you choose a preset batch sequence, Acrobat saves the files in the same folder by default. It is advisable to store processed documents in a separate folder. If the batch sequence does not perform as you expected, you can modify the batch sequence and perform it again on the original. You can specify which folder processed files are stored in, as well as other options by editing the batch sequence.

Edit a Batch Sequence

When you edit a batch sequence, you can modify an existing batch sequence, create a new batch sequence, rename a batch sequence, or delete a batch sequence. When you modify an existing batch sequence, you can add or remove commands from the sequence, change the order in which the commands execute, change the files the commands run on, change the folder the files save in, and modify the output options. To edit an existing batch sequence, follow these steps:

1. Choose File | Batch Processing | Edit Sequence to open the Batch Sequences dialog box, as shown in the following image:

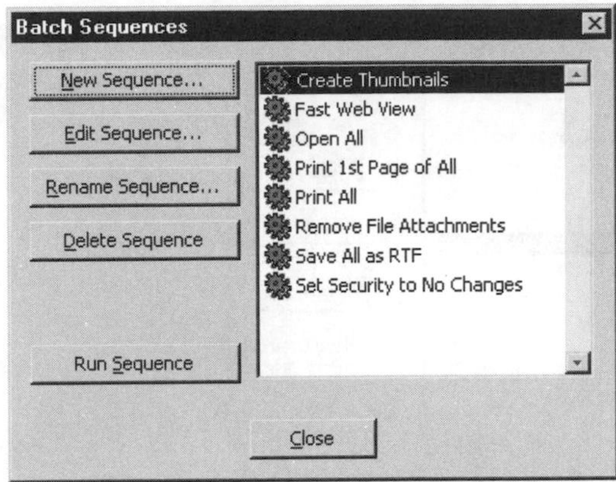

2. Click a sequence to select it, and then click Edit to open the Batch Edit Sequence dialog box, as shown in the following image:

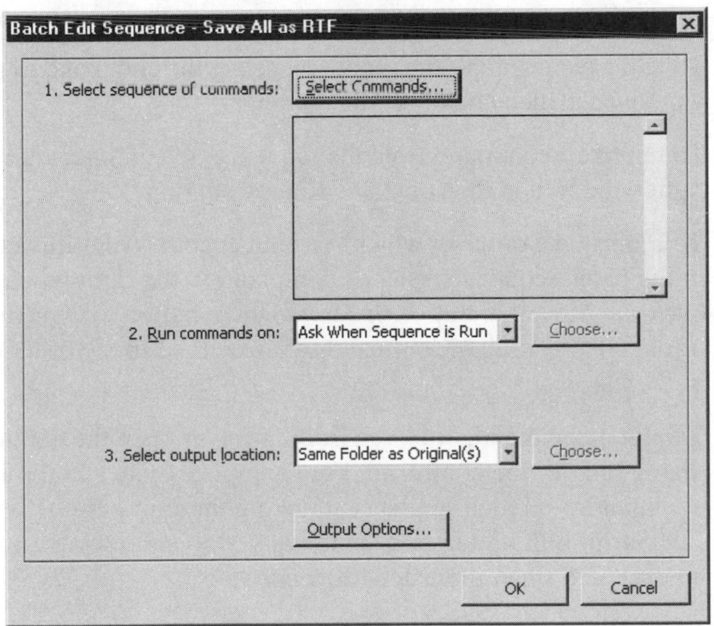

3. To add additional commands to the sequence, click the Select Commands button to open the Edit Sequence dialog box, as shown in the following image:

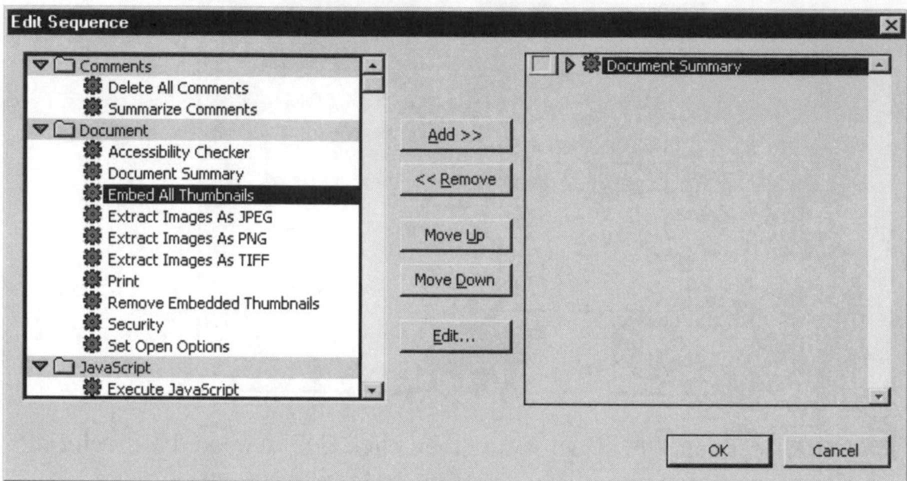

4. In the Edit Sequence dialog box, you can modify the sequence as follows:
   - To add a command to the sequence, select the command in the left window and then click the Add button.
   - To remove a command from the sequence, select the command in the right window and then click the Remove button.
   - To modify the order in which Acrobat executes multiple commands in the batch sequence, select a command in the right window and click the Move Up button or Move Down button to change the order of the command list. Commands are executed in the order they appear in the list.
   - To edit a command, click the Edit button to open the applicable dialog box for the command. For example, if you add the JavaScript command to a batch sequence, clicking the Edit button opens the JavaScript Edit dialog box, enabling you to edit the script that will be executed when the batch sequence runs.
5. Click OK to close the Edit Sequence dialog box.
6. Click the triangle to the right of the Run Commands On field and from the drop-down menu, choose one of the following:

- **Selected Files** Choose this option, and Acrobat runs the sequence on selected files. When you choose this option, the Choose button becomes active. Click the button and choose the files you want the sequence to run on.
- **Selected Folder** Choose this option, and Acrobat executes the batch sequence on all PDF files and other applicable files in the selected folder. After you choose this option, the Choose button and Source Files button become available. Click the Choose button and choose the folder you want the batch sequence commands executed on. Click the Source Files button and choose one or all of the following file formats to run the sequence on in addition to PDF files: BMP files, Compuserve GIF files, JPEG files, PCX files, PNG files, or TIFF files.
- **Ask When Sequence Is Run** Choose this option (the default), and a dialog box appears when the sequence runs, prompting you to select the files to execute the commands on.
- **Files Open In Acrobat** Choose this option and when you choose this batch sequence, it is run on files currently open in Acrobat.

7. Click the triangle to the right of the Select Output Location field and from the drop-down menu, choose one of the following options:
   - **Specific Folder** Choose this option to specify the folder in which the modified documents are stored. After you choose this option the Choose button becomes active. Click it and choose the folder in which to save the output files.
   - **Ask When Sequence Is Run** Choose this option, and Acrobat prompts you for a folder to save the files in when the sequence executes.
   - **Same Folder As Original(s)** Choose this option, (the default) and Acrobat saves the processed files in the same folder as the originals.
8. Click the Output Options button to open the Output Options dialog box. In the Output Options dialog box, you can modify the filename and output options as follows:
   - **Same As Original(s)** Choose this option, and Acrobat saves the processed files with the same name(s) as the original(s). Note that if you choose this option and choose the same output folder as the

originals, Acrobat will prompt you for a new filename as each file is processed, so as not to overwrite the original file(s).

- **Add To Original Base Names** Choose this option, and you can append the original filename by entering a prefix in the Insert Before field or a suffix in the Insert After field. Be aware that depending on your operating system, a long filename may be truncated.
- **Do Not Overwrite Existing Files** Choose this option, and Acrobat will not overwrite existing files with the identical name.

9. In the Output Options dialog box, click the triangle to the right of the Save File(s) As field and from the drop-down menu, choose to save the processed files in one of the following formats: Adobe PDF files, Encapsulated PostScript, JPEG files, PNG files, PostScript file, Rich Text Format, or TIFF files.
10. If you save the files in PDF format, choose Fast Web View (PDF Only) to optimize the files for Internet viewing.
11. Click OK to close the Output Options dialog box, click OK to close the Edit Sequence dialog box, click OK to close the Batch Edit Sequence dialog box, and then click Close to exit the Batch Sequences dialog box and apply the changes.

Note that you can also use the Batch Sequences dialog box to delete a sequence, rename a sequence, run a sequence, or create a new sequence—the topic of discussion in the next section.

Create a New Sequence

You can create a new sequence and tailor it for operations you perform frequently on your PDF documents. When you create a new sequence, you specify the commands that are run when the sequence executes, the order they run in, and how the processed files are saved. To create a new batch sequence, follow these steps:

1. Choose File | Batch Processing | Edit Batch Sequence to open the Batch Sequences dialog box.
2. Click the New Sequence button, and Acrobat opens the Name Sequence dialog box.

3. Enter a name for the sequence and click OK to open the Batch Edit Sequence dialog box.
4. Click the Select Commands button to open the Edit Sequence dialog box.
5. Select the commands you want to execute when the sequence is run. If the command has options, such as the Crop Pages command, you can set the options by clicking the Edit button, or by double-clicking the command name in the right hand window. Remember, when you create a sequence with multiple commands, you can use the Move Up and Move Down buttons to change the order in which the commands are executed.
6. Click OK to close the Edit Sequence dialog box and then follow Steps 6 through 11 in the previous section to specify how and where the files are saved.

After you create a new batch sequence, it is displayed on the Batch Sequence menu list. To run the new batch sequence, choose File | Batch Processing, and then select the name of the custom batch sequence from the list.

Append PDF Documents

You can add pages to a PDF document at any time by using the Insert Pages command, as discussed previously in this chapter. You can append a PDF document by adding existing PDF documents, images, and other supported formats to the document. You append a PDF document by opening it and choosing the proper command.

Combine PDF Documents

You can combine existing PDF documents to create a new file. If you work on a project with several authors, you can combine the files of each author to complete the document. To combine two or more PDF documents, follow these steps:

1. Open the PDF document you want to append.
2. Choose Document | Insert Pages and follow the prompts to add the desired files. For more information on the Insert Pages command, refer to the Insert Pages section previously presented in this chapter.

3. Choose File | Save As and in the Save As dialog box, specify a filename and the location where you want the appended document saved; then click OK.

Add Files to a PDF Document

You can append a PDF document by converting supported file formats to PDF and adding them to the document. To add existing files to a PDF document, follow these steps:

1. Open the PDF document which you want the add the files to.
2. Choose File | Open As Adobe PDF, and Acrobat displays the Open dialog box.
3. Choose the file(s) you want to add to the document and click OK, and Acrobat displays the Open As PDF dialog box.
4. Choose Append and click OK, and Acrobat converts the selected files to PDF format and adds the new pages to the document. For more information on the Open As Adobe PDF command, refer to the Open a File As Adobe PDF in Chapter 4.
5. Choose File | Save As and in the Save As dialog box, specify a filename and the location where you want the appended document saved; then click OK.

When you add files to a PDF document using the Open As Adobe PDF command, the new pages are the same size as the original file. If you want the size of each page in the document to be identical, you will have to use Acrobat Distiller to convert the files to PDF from their native application and specify the page size in the application Print command or Page Setup dialog box.

Touch Up a PDF Document

As you know, PDF documents originate in authoring applications, where they are converted to the PDF format using the authoring application plug-in, an export command, or by using the application Print command and choosing Acrobat Distiller. The converted document retains the look and feel of the original. When you open the document in Acrobat, you can add interactivity to the document, but cannot perform wholesale edits to the document. You can, however, perform minor edits using the TouchUp tools. You can also touch up the order of a tagged PDF document. Tagged PDF documents and the TouchUp Order tool will be discussed in Chapter 14.

Use the TouchUp Text Tool

You use the TouchUp Text tool to perform minor edits to text within a PDF document. You can use the tool to change a word or letter, copy a line of text to the clipboard, fit text within an existing selection, and more. To edit text with the TouchUp Text tool, follow these steps:

1. Select the TouchUp Text tool, as shown at left.
2. Click a line of text to select it. After you select a line of text, your cursor becomes an I-beam, and Acrobat displays a bounding box with two diamond-shaped handles, as shown in the following image:

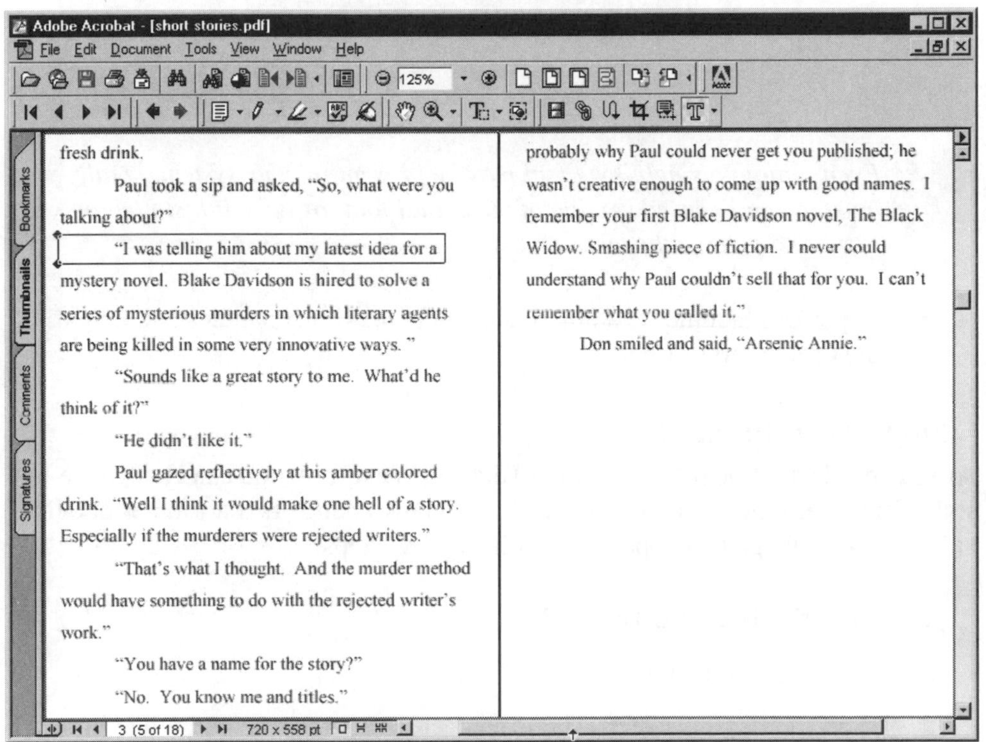

3. To change a letter or word in a text selection, click and drag the tool over the letter or word you want to change. As you drag the tool, your selection

is highlighted. Release the mouse button when you have selected the characters you want to change.

4. Enter new text, and Acrobat applies the edit to the selected text. If the embedded font is not installed on your system, Acrobat displays the warning dialog box, shown in the following image. Click Yes to remove font embedding. If the unembedded single-byte font is not present in your system encoding, you receive an error message saying you cannot edit the font.

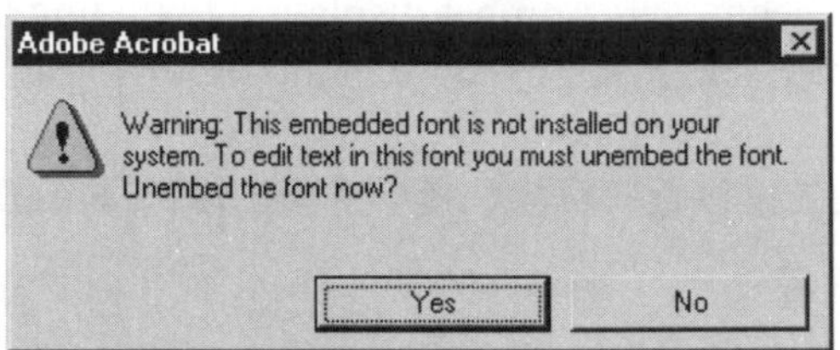

Even though a single-byte font may be present in your system, legally you must own a licensed version of the actual font, or have it installed on your system to change the text.

5. To perform a minor text alignment, click one of the handles and drag the line of text left or right.

Change Text Appearance

After you select a line of text with the TouchUp Text tool, you can change the font style, font size, font color, and more. You can only change text attributes one line at a time. To change text appearance, follow these steps:

1. Select the TouchUp Text tool.
2. Click a line of text to select it.
3. Click and drag to select a single character, word, or the entire line of text. Alternatively, you can place your cursor before a word and double-click to select a single word.
4. Choose Tools | TouchUp Text | Text Attributes to open the Text Attributes dialog box, as shown in the following image. Alternatively, you can

right-click (Windows) or CTRL-click (Macintosh) and choose Attributes from the context menu.

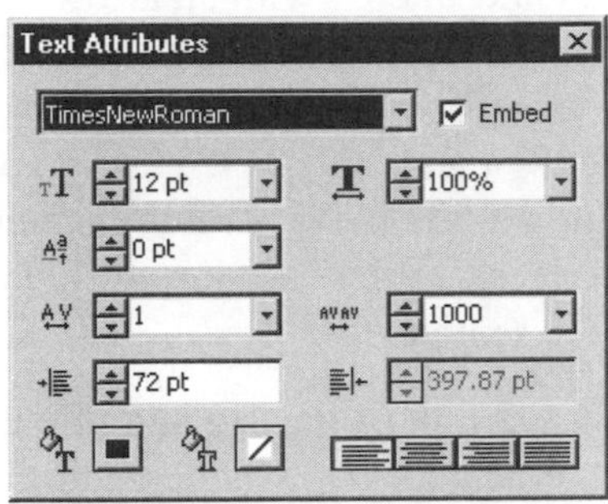

As you change text parameters in the dialog box, the text updates in real time. If the dialog box covers the text, click and drag the dialog box title bar to move the dialog box to a new location.

5. To change the font style, click the triangle to the right of the first field and choose a font style from the drop-down menu.
6. To embed the font, enable the Embed option.
7. To change the font size, click the triangle to the right of the Point Size field, which looks like a small and a large *T*, and choose a size from the drop-down menu. Alternatively, you can click the spinner buttons to increase or decrease the font size or enter a value between 0.01 pt and 1296 pt.

NOTE

If you use Acrobat on a computer with limited processing power, it may take a while for Acrobat to render your font changes, especially when you significantly enlarge the font size.

8. To change the horizontal scale of the selected text, click the triangle to the right of the Horizontal Scale field, which looks like a *T* with a double-headed arrow underneath it, and choose a value from the drop-down menu. Alternatively, you can click the spinner buttons to increase or decrease the scale, or you can enter a value between 0.01% and 32767%. This option changes the proportion between the width and height of the selected text.

9. To change the baseline shift of the selected text, click the triangle to the right of the Baseline Shift field, which looks like an underlined *A* to the right of a lowercase underlined *a* with an arrow beneath it, and choose a value from the drop-down menu. Alternatively, you can increase or decrease the baseline shift by clicking the spinner buttons or by entering a value between –32768 pt and 32767 pt. This option determines where the text appears in relation to the baseline. For example, if you select one word from a sentence and increase the baseline shift, the word appears above the other words in the sentence.
10. Click the triangle to the right of the Tracking field, which looks like an *A* and a *V* with a double-headed arrow underneath them, and choose a value from the drop-down menu. Alternatively, you can click the spinner buttons to increase or decrease the tracking value or enter a value between –1000 and 1000 in the text field. This option determines the spacing between the letters of the selected text.
11. Click the triangle to the right of the Spacing field, which looks like two *AV*s with a double-headed arrow underneath, and choose a value from the drop-down menu. Alternatively, you can click the spinner buttons to increase or decrease spacing or enter a value between –1000 and 1000 in the text field. This option determines the spacing between the words of the selected text.
12. Enter a value in the Indent Left field, which looks like an arrow with a left-indented paragraph next to it, to move the selected line of text. Alternatively, you can click the spinner button to nudge the selected text 1 pt at a time. The Indent Right field, to the right of the Left Indent field, is grayed out unless the text is justified, center justified, or right justified. If the text is right justified, the Indent Left field is dimmed out.
13. To change the font fill color, click the Font Fill Color button, which looks like a bucket pouring color into a solid *T,* and choose a color from the drop-down menu. Alternatively, you can choose a color not listed on the menu by clicking the More Colors icon and choosing a color from the system color picker.
14. To change the font outline color, click the Font Outline Color button, which looks like a bucket pouring color into an outlined *T,* and choose a color from the drop-down menu. Alternatively, you can click the More Colors icon and choose a color from the system color picker.

15. To change the way the selected text is justified, click the appropriate button. There are four to choose from: Left Justified, Center Justified, Right Justified, and Forced Justification.
16. Close the dialog box.

Fit New Text within an Existing Selection

You can fit new text within a selected line by using the Fit to Selection command. This command is useful when you enter new text that has fewer characters than the text you are replacing and you want to maintain the spacing of the rest of the line. To fit new text within an existing selection, follow these steps:

1. Select the TouchUp Text tool.
2. Click the line of text and then select the word(s) you want to change.
3. Choose Tools | TouchUp | Fit Text to Selection.
4. Enter the new text, and Acrobat sizes the text to fit the selection.

Use the TouchUp Object Tool

You use the TouchUp Object tool to perform minor edits to an image or to edit the image in a supported external image editor. As of this writing, you can use only Adobe Illustrator and Adobe PhotoShop as external image editors. The TouchUp Object Context menu has several commands that allow you to perform other tasks with embedded graphics. You can use the TouchUp Object tool to delete or remove an object by performing the following steps:

1. Select the TouchUp Object tool, as shown at left.
2. Click the Object you want to edit. You can select graphic images or entire blocks of text with the TouchUp Object tool. To select more than one object, click and drag the tool around the objects you want to edit. After selecting the object(s), do one of the following:
   - Drag the object to a new location.

- Delete the object by choosing Edit | Delete. You can either press DELETE to remove the selected object from the document or choose Delete from the TouchUp tool context menu.

Use the TouchUp Object Tool Context Menu

When you select the TouchUp Object tool, you have additional options available through the context menu of the tool. Right-click (Windows) or CTRL-click (Macintosh) to open the TouchUp tool context menu, as shown in the following image:

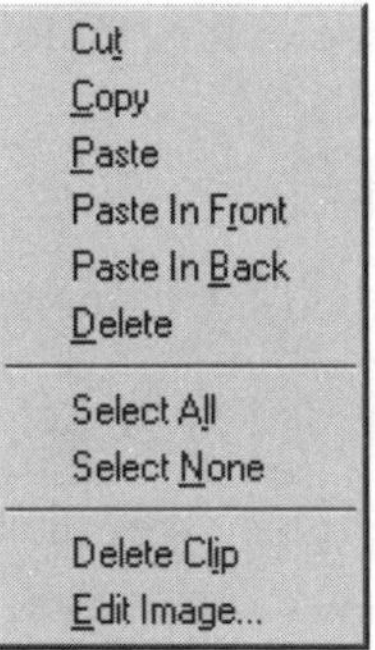

The available Context menu commands will vary, depending on previous actions you have performed with the tool. The following list shows all of the tasks you can perform from the TouchUp Object tool context menu:

- **Cut** Use this command to cut the selected object from the document and place it on the clipboard.
- **Copy** Use this command to copy the selected object to the clipboard while preserving it in the document.
- **Paste** Use this command to paste an object from the clipboard to the document. The command pastes the object in the exact location it was copied from. To move the pasted object, select the object with the TouchUp Object tool and drag it to the desired location.
- **Paste In Front** Use this command to paste a graphic from the clipboard in front of the uppermost object selected on the page. If you paste the object on the same page it was copied from, it is pasted on top of the original object. When you move the pasted object with the TouchUp Object tool, it appears on top of other objects on the page.

- **Paste In Back** Use this command when you want to paste an object from the clipboard and have it appear behind all other objects on the page. When you use this command to paste an object to the page it was copied from, it appears behind the original object. When you move it to a new location with the TouchUp Object tool, it appears behind other objects on the page.
- **Delete** Use this command to remove the selected object from the document. Alternatively, you can press DELETE to remove selected objects from the document.
- **Select All** Use this command to select all graphics objects, including text blocks, from the page.
- **Select None** Use this command to deselect selected graphics.
- **Delete Clip** Use this command to delete any objects that are clipping the selected objects. For example, if modify the size of a text object, and some of the characters are clipped, choosing this command reveals the clipped text.
- **Edit Image** Use this command to launch the supported image or illustration editing application. To specify an external editor choose Edit | Preferences | General and click the TouchUp title. You can then choose PhotoShop for an image editor and Illustrator for a page/object editor. As of this writing, these are the only applications that support this command.

TIP *You can use the TouchUp tool to copy objects from one document to another. Open two documents and then choose Window | Tile (or if you prefer, Window | Cascade). Use the TouchUp tool to select an object and then choose Copy from the Context menu. Click anywhere in the second document and then choose one of the Paste options from the context menu.*

TIP *If you do extensive modifications to a document, and it is not turning out as you planned, you can eliminate all of your modifications by choosing File | Revert. When you choose this command, Acrobat reverts to the* last saved version *of the document.*

Chapter 12

Review PDF Documents

How To...

- Use the Comments palette
- Add Comments
- Use the Note tool
- Add Audio Comments
- Use the File Attachment tool

When you use Acrobat in a corporate environment, you can share information with colleagues in faraway locales. You can send documents via e-mail or a corporate intranet for review and approval. Team members or clients can mark up the PDF document with audio comments, notes, highlighted phrases, ovals or rectangles to highlight items, text boxes, and more. If you ever have sent out an original document for review, and a team member has altered the original by adding comments to the text or modified the formulas of a spreadsheet, you will appreciate how easy it is to create a PDF document from the original and use it to share and receive comments with colleagues using the Acrobat annotation tools.

When you mark up a document, you often need to identify the object you want modified and then create a note or other annotation to reflect the desired change. You can use shapes to identify the object; highlight the object; or point to the object with an arrow, straight line, or squiggly line drawn with the Pencil tool. In this chapter, you'll learn how to use the annotation tools to mark up a document, add comments to a document, and more.

Use the Comments Palette

When you open a document with comments, each comment is noted in the Comments palette. The Comments palette lists the title of each comment and the page number the comment can be found on. You can configure the Comments palette to display comments by Author, Date, Page, or Type. The Comments palette has one tool and a menu that you can use to import comments, export selected comments, find comments, and delete comments. You also use the Comments palette to navigate to comments and change comment properties. To open the Comments palette, as shown in Figure 12-1, open the Navigation pane and click the Comments tab. Alternatively, you can choose Window | Comments.

Comments palette

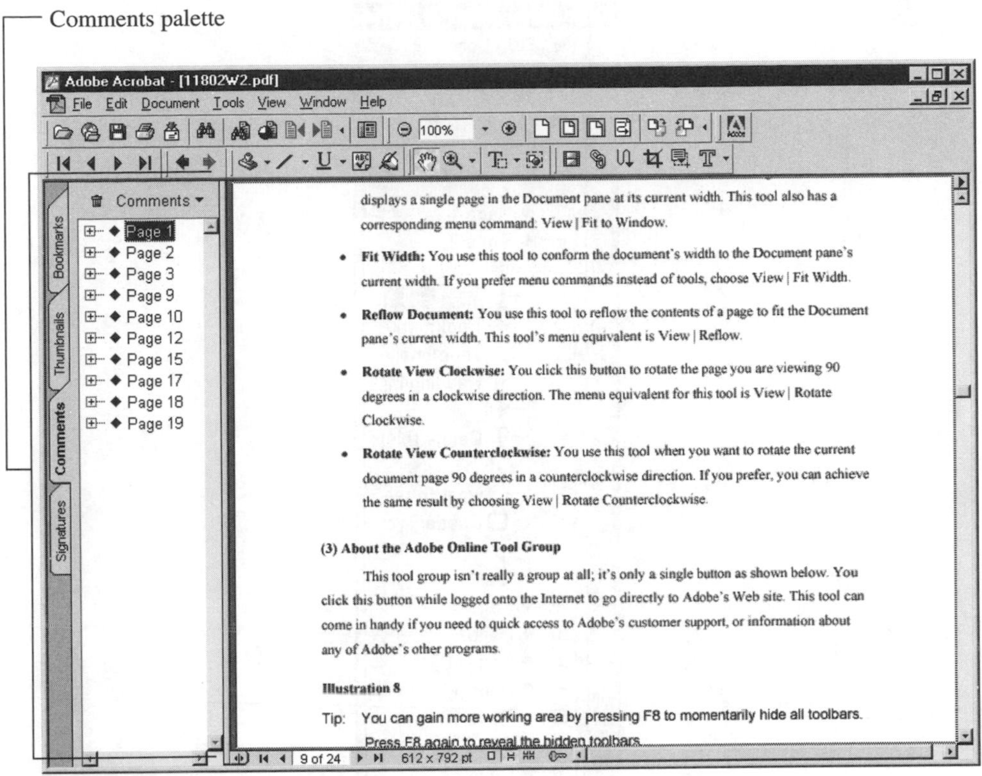

FIGURE 12-1 You use the Comments palette to navigate to document comments.

Navigate to a Comment

When you open the Comments palette for the first time, you get a strong sense of déjà vu. The Comments palette, indeed, bears a striking resemblance to the Bookmarks palette; the differences being the Comments palette displays a different icon for each type of comment and is used to navigate to comments. If there are several comments attached to a page (or author, or type, or date, depending on how you configure the palette to display comments), there is a plus sign (+) next to the heading. Click the plus sign (+) to expand the comment group. After you expand a comment group, a minus sign (–) appears to the left of the comment group heading. Click it to collapse the group to the heading. To navigate to a comment, click the comment icon, or the comment title, as shown Figure 12-2.

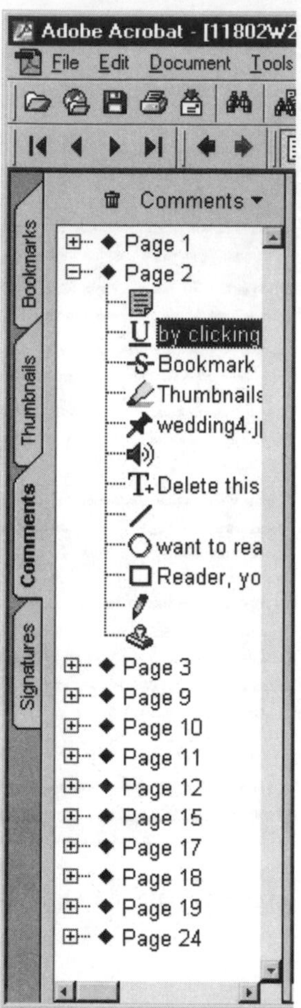

FIGURE 12-2 Use the Comments palette to navigate to comments and edit comment properties.

Notice that the expanded heading in Figure 12-2 has different icons that represent the type of comment in the document. If the Circle tool or Square tool is used to highlight a graphic object, the comment icon type displays in the Comments palette. When you use the Pencil or Line tool to mark up a document, the comment icon type displays in the Comments palette as well. If the document is marked up with the Circle tool, Square tool, Highlight tool, Strikeout tool, or Underline tool, the selected text is displayedin the Comments palette. If you create a comment with the Note tool or the Free Text tool, the comment text is displayed next to the icon. If the text is long, Acrobat truncates the text, displaying only the first several words. When you annotate a document with the Stamp tool or Sound tool, the respective icon is displayed in the Comments palette. If a file is attached to a document, Acrobat displays the filename and extension in the comment palette.

Use the Comments Palette Menu

You use the Comments palette menu to modify the way comments are sorted in the palette, to find comments, to import comments, and to export comments. To open the Comments palette menu, as shown in the following image, click the Comments icon near the upper-right corner of the palette.

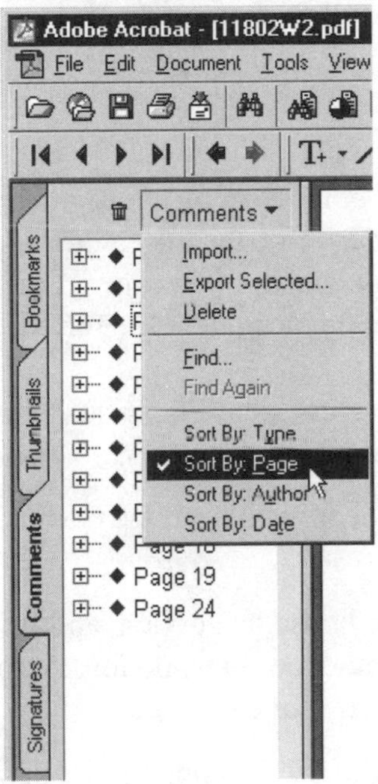

Use the Comments Palette Context Menu

Many Acrobat users prefer the convenience of a context menu to streamline workflow. In the Comments palette, you have two context menus available, one with a full set of commands relating to the Comments palette, and a second with commands used to modify properties of a selected comment or to delete it. To reveal the Comments palette context menu, click inside the Comments palette, and then right-click (Windows) or CTRL-click (Macintosh). To reveal the context menu for editing individual comments, select a comment, and then right-click (Windows) or CTRL-click (Macintosh). The following image shows the Comments palette context menu:

Sort Comments

By default, Acrobat sorts all comments by the page number they appear on. You can, however, change the way Acrobat sorts comments. For example, if you work with a team of authors on a document, you can sort comments by author. To change the way comments in the document are sorted, follow these steps:

1. In the Navigation pane, click the Comments tab. Alternatively, you can choose Window | Comments.
2. Click the Comments icon; and from the Comments palette menu, choose one of the following:
   - **Sort By Type** Choose this option, and Acrobat sorts the comments by type. When you choose this option, Acrobat creates one heading in the Comment palette for each type.
   - **Sort By Page** Choose this option (the default), and Acrobat creates a heading for each page that has comments.
   - **Sort By Author** Choose this option, and Acrobat creates a heading for each author that added comments to the document.

- **Sort By Date** Choose this option, and Acrobat sorts comments by date, creating a heading for each date on which a comment was created. Acrobat displays the earliest date at the top of the palette. Dates are displayed in mm/dd/yyyy format.

NOTE *Alternatively, you can sort comments by clicking inside the Comments palette and choosing one of sort the options from the context menu.*

Delete Comments

When a comment has outlived its usefulness, you can delete it. When you delete comments, you decrease the file size of the document and eliminate having to deal with comments that are no longer pertinent. To delete a comment, follow these steps:

1. In the Navigation pane, click the Comments tab.
2. Select the comment you want to delete and do one of the following:
   - Press DELETE.
   - Choose Edit | Delete.
   - Choose Delete from the Comments palette menu.
   - Choose Delete from the context menu.

Modify Comments

You can modify comment appearance and change the author. You can change the color of any comment, as well as change the default icon used to display a comment created with the Note tool; however, the icons for the other annotation methods are set by default. To modify a comment, follow these steps:

1. In the Navigation pane, click the Comments tab.
2. Select the comment you want to modify.
3. From the Comments palette menu, choose Properties. Alternatively, you can choose Properties from the context menu.

4. After you choose the Properties command, the applicable properties dialog box opens. The following image shows the Note Properties dialog box:

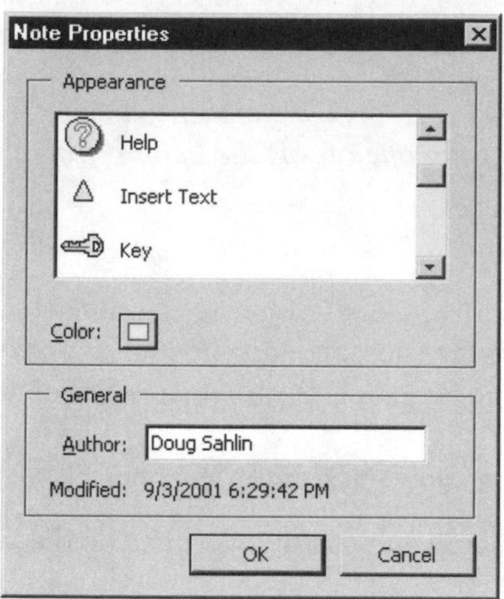

5. Modify the comment as desired, and then click OK to close the dialog box.

NOTE *If Acrobat Standard Security has been applied to the document, and Authoring Comments and Form Fields is not allowed, you will not be able to edit comments unless the settings are changed. If Acrobat Self-Sign Security has been assigned to the document, you will be able to edit comments if the document author grants you permission to edit comments. For more Information on Acrobat security, see Chapter 13.*

Add Comments

When you receive a PDF document, or send a PDF document, you can add comments to the document. Comments are a handy way to communicate between team members or clients. Comments are readily accessible in the Comments palette and can easily be added with the click of a mouse. You can add notes (the PDF equivalent of a yellow sticky note) or audio comments, or create free-standing text.

Use the Note Tool

Use the Note tool when you want to add a quick comment that is specific to a certain part of the document. When you use the Note tool for comments, the reviewer sees an icon that, when clicked, opens a window with the comment. When you create a comment with the Note tool, you can define the size of the window, and the type and color of the note icon, as well as enter your comments. You can also leave a note open, so the comment can be read in full when the user navigates to the note. To add a comment to a PDF document with the Note tool, follow these steps:

1. Navigate to the point in the document where you want to add the note.

2. Select the Note tool, as at the left.
3. Click the point in the document where you want the note to appear. When you create a note in this manner, Acrobat opens a blank note window of the default size. When you use the default window size, scroll bars are provided for use when reading lengthy notes. After you create the window, a blinking cursor appears in the window, signifying that Acrobat is ready for you to enter some text.

TIP *To size the note window while creating it, click a point in the document where you want the note to appear, and then drag down and across. As you drag, a bounding box appears defining the size of the window you are creating. Release the mouse button when the window is the desired size. To constrain the window to a square, press SHIFT while dragging. Acrobat sizes the note window as you specify when the document is next opened.*

12

4. Enter the comments you want to appear in the window.
5. Click the X in the upper-left corner of the note window to close it. Alternatively, you can leave the note open by not clicking the X.

Reviewers of your document read a note by double-clicking it. After you create a note, you can modify the appearance of the note icon and its colors by changing its properties.

Set Note Properties

The default icon for a note looks like a sticky note; and in keeping with that paradigm, the Acrobat designers gave the icon a default color of bright yellow. If you don't like bright yellow or virtual sticky notes, you can change the characteristics of the icon by following these steps:

1. To select the note you want to modify, click its name in the Comments palette, as discussed previously, or click the actual note in the document. You can select the note with either the Hand tool or the Note tool.
2. Choose Edit | Properties to open the Note Properties dialog box, as shown in the following image. Alternatively, you can right-click (Windows) or CTRL-click (Macintosh), and choose Properties from the context menu.

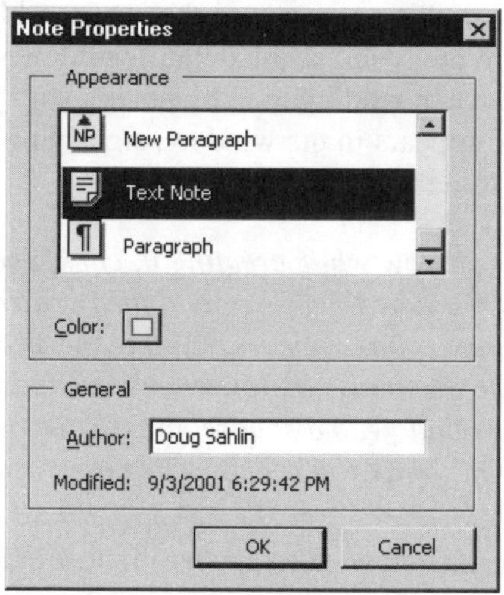

3. In the Appearance section, choose an icon. In addition to the standard note icon, you can select from standard proofreading symbols such as Insert Text, New Paragraph, and Paragraph, as well as a Question Mark icon (?) when you want to ask a question about a certain part of the document.
4. Click the Color button, and choose a color from the pop-up palette. Alternatively, click the More Colors icon, and choose a color from the system color picker.

5. In the General section, you can enter text to change the author name. By default, Acrobat uses the registered owner of the software that created the note as the author name. Notice there is a time stamp at the bottom of this section. After you modify the note properties, the time stamp updates to reflect the time the properties were changed.
6. Click OK to close the Note Properties dialog box, and Acrobat applies the changes to the note. With the exception of a changed author name, the appearance properties of the note are applied to future notes you create until you once again modify note properties.

Edit Notes

In addition to changing the properties of a note, you can change the position of a note, edit its contents, or delete it. In a previous section, you learned to delete a note from within the Comments palette. In this section, you'll learn to delete a note from within the document. To edit a note within the document, select it with either the Hand tool or the Note tool, and perform one of the following tasks:

- To delete a selected note, choose Edit | Delete. Alternatively, press DELETE or choose Delete from the context menu.
- To move a selected note, click the title bar of the note, and then drag it to a new location.
- To change the contents of a selected note, double-click it, edit the contents, and then click the X to close the window.
- To resize the window of a selected note, double-click it, and then click and drag the lower-right handle. To resize the window proportionately, press SHIFT while dragging.

Change Note Window Location

When you open a note, by default, the upper-left corner of the note window appears on top of the note icon. If desired, you can reset the location of the note window by following these steps:

1. Select the Hand or Note tool.
2. Click the Note whose window you want to reposition.

3. Double-click the note; drag the note window to a new location, as shown in the following image; and then release the mouse button.

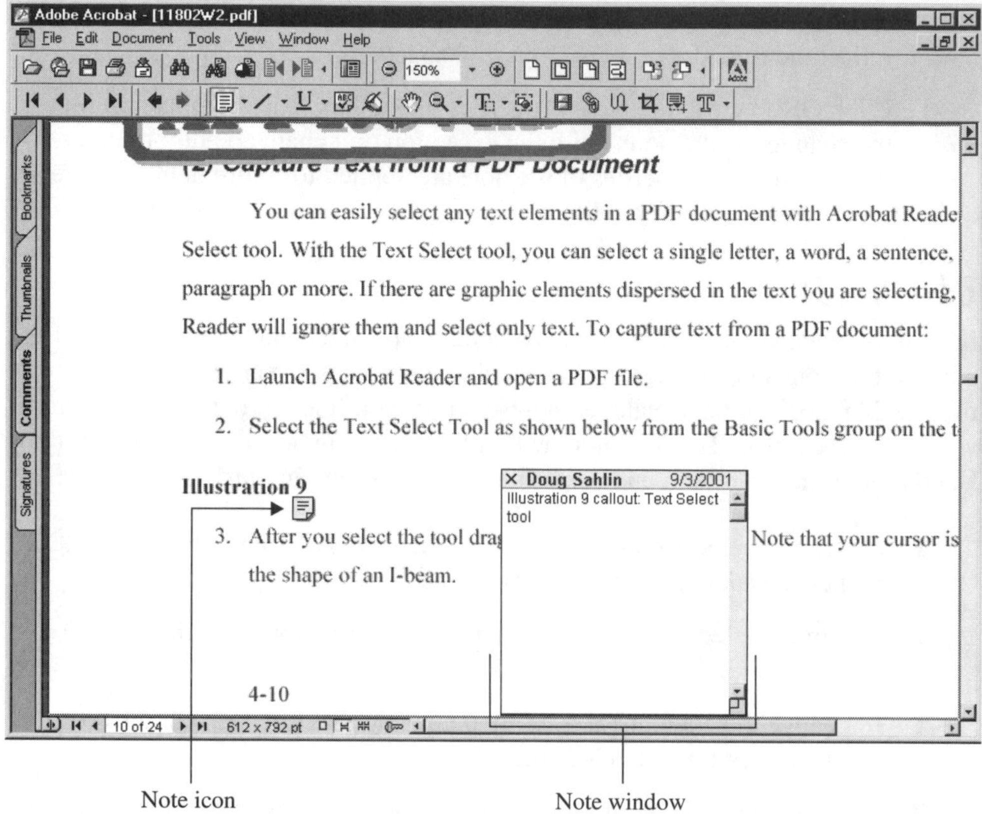

To reset a note window to its default location, select the note with the Hand tool or the Note tool, right-click (Windows) or CTRL-click (Macintosh), and choose Reset Note Window Location from the context menu.

Add Audio Comments

You can also add audio comments to a document. You can record the audio comments through a microphone attached to your computer, or choose an audio

file stored on your system. Whichever method you use, the sound is embedded with the document. You add audio comments to a document using the Sound Attachment tool, as shown at left.

Record a Comment for a PDF Document

If you prefer the spoken word to a written comment, you can record a comment and add it to a document. Audio comments can often be more effective than written comments. You can convey excitement and enthusiasm with a recorded comment. In order to record comments with your PDF documents, your computer must have a sound card and software capable of recording from a microphone. Acrobat relies on your system recording software to create the comment Acrobat embeds with the PDF document. To record an audio comment for a PDF document, follow these steps:

1. Select the Sound Attachment tool.
2. Click the spot in the document where you want to add the audio comment, and the Sound Recorder dialog box appears, as shown in Figure 12-3. This is the Windows version of the recorder. The Macintosh version is slightly different.
3. Click the Record button (the forward-pointing triangle), and speak into the microphone.

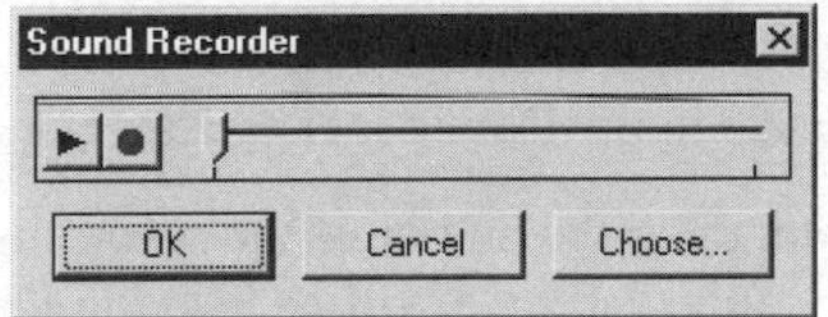

FIGURE 12-3 Add audio comments to your document in this dialog box.

4. Click the Stop button (the filled-in circle) to stop the recording, and Acrobat displays the Sound Properties dialog box, as shown in the following image:

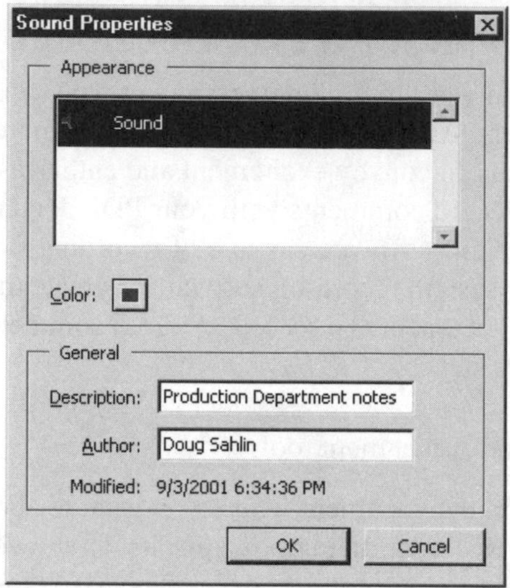

5. Accept the default Sound Attachment icon color (red), or click the Color button to choose a different color from the pop-up palette. Click the More Colors icon to choose a color from the system color picker.
6. In the Description field, enter a description of the recording. The description you enter is displayed in the Comments palette next to the speaker icon, and also functions as a tooltip when a user holds the mouse over the speaker icon in the document. If you do not enter a description, only the speaker icon appears in the Comments palette.
7. In the Author field, enter the author of the recording. By default, the registered owner of the software will be listed in this field.
8. Click OK to embed the sound in the document.

After you finish the recording, Acrobat designates the audio comment with the icon shown at left. To play the recording, double-click the icon. Alternatively, to play the file, click the icon and choose Play File from the context menu.

Add a Prerecorded Audio File to a Document

You can also add prerecorded sound files to a document. In Chapter 10, you learned to use the Sound action to add a sound to a document. You can also add a prerecorded sound as an audio comment using the Sound Attachment tool. To add a prerecorded comment to a PDF document, follow these steps:

1. Select the Sound Attachment tool.
2. Click the spot in the document where you want the audio comment to be available, and the Sound Recorder dialog box in Figure 12-3 is displayed.
3. Click the Choose button to open the Choose A Sound File dialog box.
4. Navigate to the audio comment you want embedded with the document and click Select to close the dialog box; Acrobat opens the Sound Properties dialog box.
5. Modify the sound properties, as outlined in the previous section, and click OK to embed the sound with the document. This may take a few second, depending on the size of the audio file. After the sound is added to the document, the speaker icon designates the audio comment. You double-click it to play the file.

Change Audio Comment Properties

You can perform limited changes to properties of an audio comment. You can change the color of the icon that is displayed in the document and the Comments palette, as well as change the Description and Author information. To change audio comment properties, follow these steps:

1. Select the Hand tool and select the comment in the document. Alternatively, you can select the comment in the Comments palette.

NOTE *You can also use the Commenting tools to select a comment. However, if you click outside of the icon boundary, you end up creating a new comment rather than selecting a comment.*

2. Choose Edit | Properties to open the Sound Properties dialog box. Alternatively, you can right-click (Windows) or CTRL-click (Macintosh), and choose Properties from the context menu.

3. Modify the sound properties as desired, and then click OK to close the Sound Properties dialog box.

You cannot modify the actual audio comment, only its properties. To create a different recording or attach a different prerecorded audio comment to the document, delete the outdated comment and then create a new one.

Create Text Annotations

You have another Acrobat tool at your disposal for adding comments to a document—the Free Text tool. When you use the Free Text tool, it is the equivalent of scribbling in the margins or writing on the document. When you add comments to a document with the Free Text tool, you can specify the style and size of the font. You can create a comment with the Free Text tool that has a border and background, or neither. Figure 12-4 shows the Free Text tool used to point out a change a reviewer wants made.

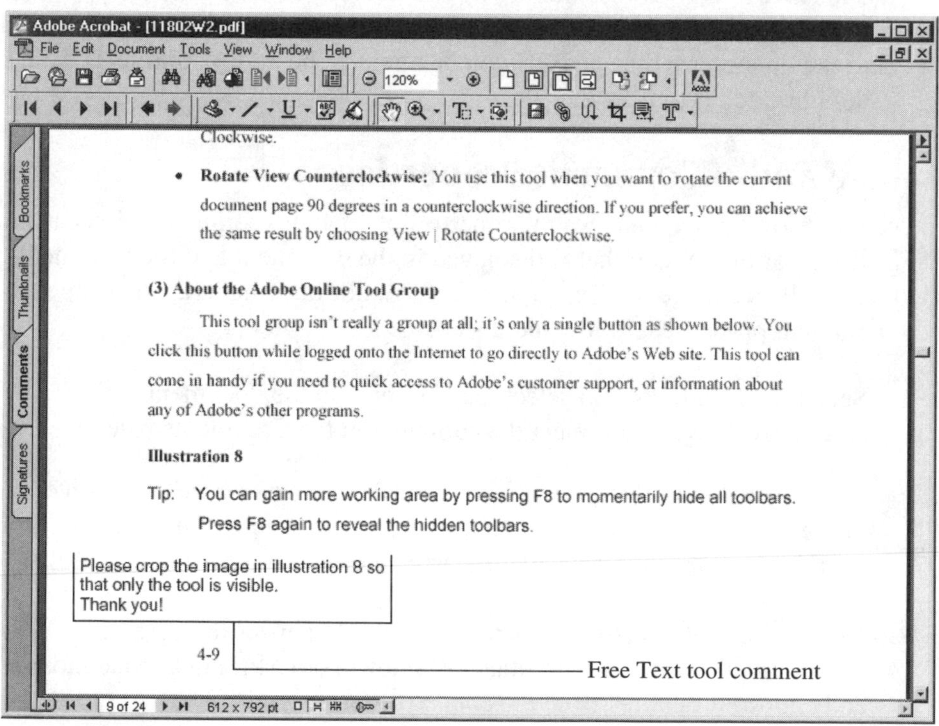

FIGURE 12-4 You can use the Free Text tool to create a comment.

Use the Free Text Tool

You can create a comment using the Free Text tool at any location in the document. When you create a comment with the Free Text tool, the comment appears on top of the actual elements in the PDF document. You can use the Free Text tool to draw attention to a specific graphic that needs to be modified in the original document, or a paragraph you feel needs to be deleted before the publication is finalized.

To add a note with the Free Text tool, follow these steps:

T+

1. Select the Free Text tool, as shown at left.
2. Click the point in the document where you want to add the comment and Acrobat creates a square text box (with default dimensions). A blinking cursor positions in the upper-left corner of the text box, prompting you to enter text.

TIP

If you find the default size of the Free Text tool text box is not to your liking, you can size the box while creating it by clicking in the document and then dragging down and across. As you drag the tool, a rectangular bounding box gives you a preview of the text box size. Release the mouse button when the box is sized to your preference.

3. Enter the text for the comment.
4. After you have written the comment, select the Hand tool to stop entering text.

Modify Free Text Properties

After you create a comment with the Free Text tool, you can modify the properties of the comment. You can change the text attributes and the text box attributes. To modify the properties of a comment created with the Free Text tool, follow these steps:

1. Select the text comment with the Hand tool in either the document or the Comments palette.
2. Choose Edit Properties to open the FreeText Properties dialog box, as shown in the following image. Alternatively, you can choose Properties from the context menu.

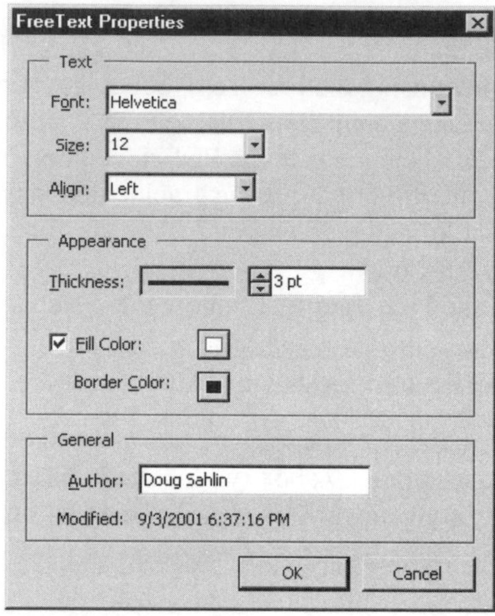

3. To change the font style, click the triangle to the right of the Font field and choose a style from the drop-down menu.
4. To change the font size, click the triangle to the right of the Size field and choose a size from the drop-down menu.
5. To change the alignment of the text, click the triangle to the right of the Align field; and, from the drop-down menu, choose one of the following: Left, Right, or Center.
6. To change the thickness of the border around the free text, click the spinner buttons to the right of the Thickness field. Alternatively, you can enter a value between 0 and 12 pts (points). To create a comment with no border, enter a value of **0**.
7. To change the text box fill color, click the Fill Color button and choose a color from the pop-up palette, or click the More Colors icon to choose a color from the system color picker. Disable the Fill Color option if you want a text box with no background color.
8. To change the border color, click the Border Color button and choose a color from the pop-up palette, or click the More Colors icon to choose

a color from the system color picker. Note that if you create a text box with no fill, it has no border.

9. To change the author of the comment, enter a name in the Author field. By default, the author will be the registered owner of the software.
10. Click OK to close the dialog box and apply the changes.

With the exception of the author's name, the changes you make in the FreeText Properties dialog box will apply to all future comments you create with the Free Text tool until you change the properties again.

Edit Free Text

When you create a comment with the Free Text tool, you can edit the contents of the comment and move the location of the comment; and when the comment has outlived its usefulness, you can delete the comment. To modify text created with the Free Text tool, follow these steps:

1. Select the Free Text tool.
2. Click the comment you want to modify and do one of the following:
   - To select text, click and drag your cursor over the text characters you want to select.
   - To select all text in the box, choose Edit | Select All. Alternatively, you can choose Select All from the context menu.
   - To modify the selected text, enter new text from your keyboard.
   - To delete selected text, press DELETE. Alternatively, choose Edit | Delete or choose Delete from the context menu.
   - To copy selected text to the clipboard, choose Edit | Copy. Alternatively, you can choose Copy from the context menu.
   - To cut selected text to the clipboard, choose Edit | Cut. Alternatively, you can choose Cut from the context menu.
   - To paste text from the clipboard into a selected comment, place your cursor at the point you want to display the text and choose Edit | Paste. Alternatively, you can choose Paste from the context menu. Note that

any formatting applied to the text in another application is lost when it is pasted into a Free Text comment.

You can also change the position and size of a comment created with the Free Text tool. To move a comment, select the comment with the Hand tool, and then drag it to a new location.

To resize the comment box, follow these steps:

1. Select the comment box with the Hand tool, and four rectangular handles appear—one at each corner of the box.
2. Click and drag a handle to resize the box. To resize the box proportionately, press SHIFT while dragging. As you drag, Acrobat draws a rectangular bounding box, which gives you a preview of the current size of the box.
3. Release the mouse button when the box is the desired size.

Spell Check Comments

Before you save a document that you have added comments to, you can spell check the comments. When you spell check comments, Acrobat displays words not found in its dictionary, and prompts you to replace the word with a suggested replacement or ignore the word. You can also enter a word for replacement or add the suspect word to your personal dictionary. To spell check your comments, choose Tools | Spelling | Check Form Fields and Comments or select the Spell Check Form Fields And Comments tool, which looks like the first three letters of the alphabet with a check mark. For detailed information on this command, refer to the "Spell Check Form Fields" and Comments section in Chapter 9.

Attach Files to Document

You can attach any file to a document for use by another reviewer. When you use the File Attachment tool to attach a file to a document, it becomes embedded in the document. Reviewers will need software associated with the file installed on their computer to be able to view the file. To attach a file to a document, follow these steps:

1. Select the File Attachment tool, as shown at left.

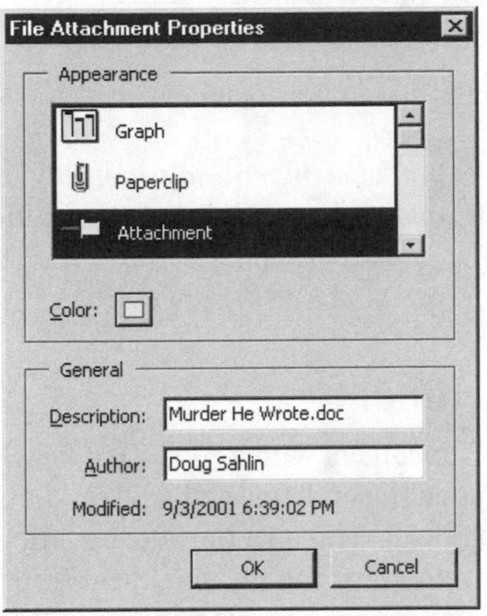

FIGURE 12-5 Choose a file to attach to a PDF document with this dialog box.

2. Click the spot in the document where you want the File Attachment icon to appear, and Acrobat opens the Select File to Attach dialog box.
3. Navigate to the file you want to attach and click Select, and Acrobat opens the File Attachment Properties dialog box, as shown in Figure 12-5.
4. In the Appearance section, select the icon you want to appear in the document. By default, the file attachment icon is a push pin. However, you can choose a different icon if you feel it is a better representation of the type of document you want to attach. For example, you may want to use the graph icon when attaching a spreadsheet.
5. Click the Color button and select a color from the pop-up palette, or click the More Colors icon to choose a color from the system color picker.
6. In the Description field, enter a name. By default, Acrobat uses the filename and extension of the attached document. You can enter any name that you feel describes the document.

7. In the Author field, enter a name. By default, Acrobat fills this field with the name of the registered owner of Acrobat.
8. Click OK to add the file to the document.

NOTE *Attaching a file to a document may considerably increase the document file size. Since Acrobat stores additional information with the embedded (attached) file, the final document file size will be above and beyond the file size of the file you attach to the document.*

Open a File Attachment

When you receive a PDF document with a file attachment, you open the file by double-clicking the file attachment. After you double-click the icon, Acrobat displays a warning dialog box saying that the attached file may contain programs or macros with viruses. If you received the document from a trusted source, click Open to view the file. If you do not know the author of the PDF document, or have reason to believe the attachment may in fact have a virus, click Do Not Open, close the document, exit Acrobat, and then check the PDF document with your virus scanning software. If you decide to open the file, Acrobat launches the application on your computer associated with the file type. When you open an attached file, your operating system creates temporary files, the location of which will vary depending on the operating system you use.

Edit File Attachment Properties

When you use the File Attachment tool to embed a file within a document, you cannot change the embedded file with the File Attachment Properties. Instead, you must make and save changes to the file before attaching it to a document. To delete the previous version of an attached file and embed a different one, select the File Attachment icon with the Hand or File Attachment tool, and delete it by choosing Edit | Delete, pressing DELETE, or by choosing Delete from the context menu. After you delete the incorrect file attachment, attach a different file using the steps outlined in the previous section, "Attach Files to Document."

You can't change the file attached to a document by editing its properties in the File Attachment Properties dialog box. However, you can change the position of the File Attachment icon by clicking it with either the Hand or File Attachment tool, and then dragging it to a different location. You can also edit the properties of the File Attachment icon by clicking the attachment icon and then choosing Edit | Properties to open the File Attachment Properties dialog box, as shown in Figure 12-5. Alternatively, you can access the dialog box by clicking the icon and then choosing Properties from the context menu. Modify the properties, as outlined in the previous section, and then click OK to close the dialog box.

Save a Document to Disk

If you receive a PDF document with a file attachment, you can save the attachment to disk for future use. You can, for example, save a spreadsheet attached to a PDF document to disk for future reference. To save an embedded file to disk, follow these steps:

1. Click the attachment icon that represents the file you want to save.
2. Right-click (Windows) or CTRL-click (Macintosh), and choose Save Embedded File To Disk from the context menu. After you choose the command, Acrobat opens the Extract Attachment To dialog box.
3. Navigate to the folder where you want the file saved, click OK, and Acrobat extracts *a copy* of the file for future use.

NOTE *Even if you know the author of the attachment, it is a good idea to check the file with virus detecting software before opening it in another application.*

Apply a Stamp

When you receive a PDF document for review, you can literally apply a stamp of approval to the document. You apply a stamp to a PDF document using the Stamp tool, the virtual equivalent of a rubber stamp minus the messy ink pad. You can use one of the Acrobat preset stamps on a document, or create your own custom stamp. Figure 12-6 shows a document that has been approved with the Stamp tool.

Use the Stamp Tool

You use the Stamp tool to apply a stamp to a PDF document. You can choose from a large selection of preset stamps. After you stamp a document, you can

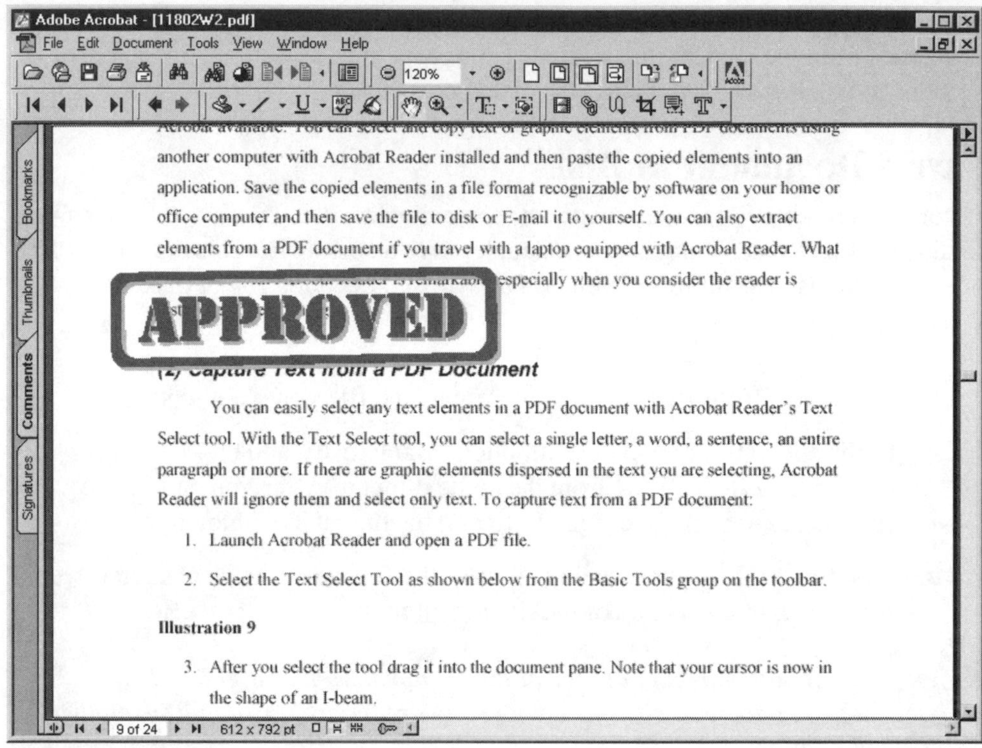

FIGURE 12-6 You can annotate a document with the Stamp tool.

change the color, size, and location of the stamp. You can even attach a note to a stamp. To annotate a document using the Stamp tool, follow these steps:

1. Select the Stamp tool, as shown at left.
2. Click the spot in the document where you want the stamp to appear. By default, Acrobat applies the first stamp named *Approved.*
3. To choose a different stamp, click the stamp and choose Edit | Properties to open the Stamp Properties dialog box, as shown in the following image. Alternatively, you can choose Properties from the context menu.

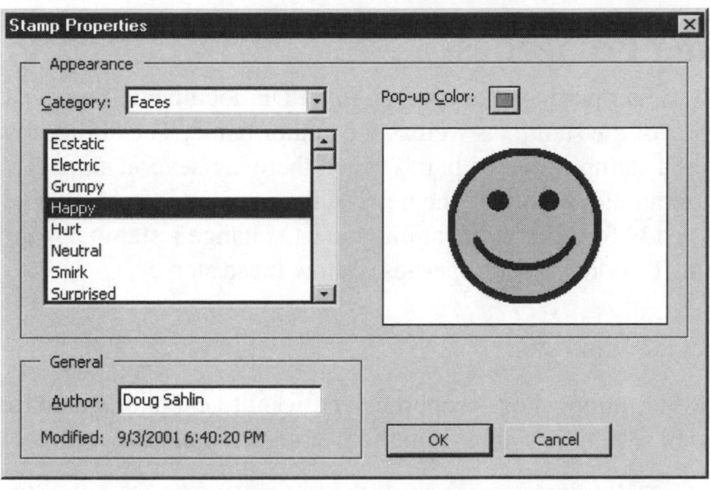

4. Click the triangle to the right of the Category field; and' from the drop-down menu, choose one of the following: Faces, Pointers, Standards, or Words. If you create any custom stamp categories, they also appear in this menu.
5. To change the color of a pop-up note associated with the stamp, click the Pop-Up Color button and choose a color from the pop-up palette, or click the More Colors icon to choose a color from the system color picker.
6. Click a stamp name to select it, and Acrobat generates a preview of the stamp in the dialog box.
7. To change the default author name, enter a name in the Author field.
8. Click OK to apply the stamp to the document.

To move the stamp, select it with the Hand tool and drag it to another location. To resize the stamp, move your cursor toward one of the rectangular handles at each corner of the stamp, click the handle, and drag in or out to resize the stamp. Press SHIFT while dragging to constrain the stamp to its original proportions.

NOTE *You can attach a pop-up note to a stamp. For more information, refer to the section "Attach a Pop-Up Note," later in the chapter.*

Edit Stamp Properties

You can edit the properties of any stamp in a PDF document. You can change the appearance of the stamp, as well as the author name. The ability to change the appearance of a stamp comes in handy when there are several stages in a review process. For example, if you are the head of the review team, and you decide the document is ready for final publication, you can change a stamp appearance from Draft to Final. To edit stamp properties, follow these steps:

1. Select the Hand tool.
2. Click the stamp whose properties you want to change. Alternatively, you can select the stamp from the Comments palette.
3. Choose Edit | Properties to open the Stamp Properties dialog box. Alternatively, choose Properties from the context menu.
4. Modify the properties of the stamp, and then click OK to apply the changes and close the Stamp Properties dialog box.

Delete a Stamp

To delete a stamp, select it with the Hand tool and then choose Edit | Delete. Alternatively, you can press DELETE or choose Delete from the context menu.

Create Custom Stamps

Acrobat provides you with a wide variety of preset stamps. However, if you need stamps for your organization that are not available, you can create custom stamps. For example, you might want every stamp to include your corporate logo. Stamps are PDF documents with one or more pages. When you create custom stamps, you create a new category that appears in the Stamp Properties dialog box. You can create a custom stamp by following these steps:

1. Create the artwork for your custom stamps in an image-editing or illustration program. Create an image approximately 2.00" wide × 1.50" high. Remember that stamps add to the file size of a document. If you create a stamp with complex artwork, it will severely affect the file size of the document—plus, it will take Acrobat a long time to display it.

2. Convert each stamp to a PDF document using the authoring application export function. If the authoring application does not support exporting files in PDF format, print the document using Acrobat Distiller.

3. Launch Acrobat and open one of the documents you want to use as a stamp. Use the Insert Pages command to add the other stamps to the document.

4. Choose File | Document Properties | Summary to open the Document Summary dialog box, as shown in the following image:

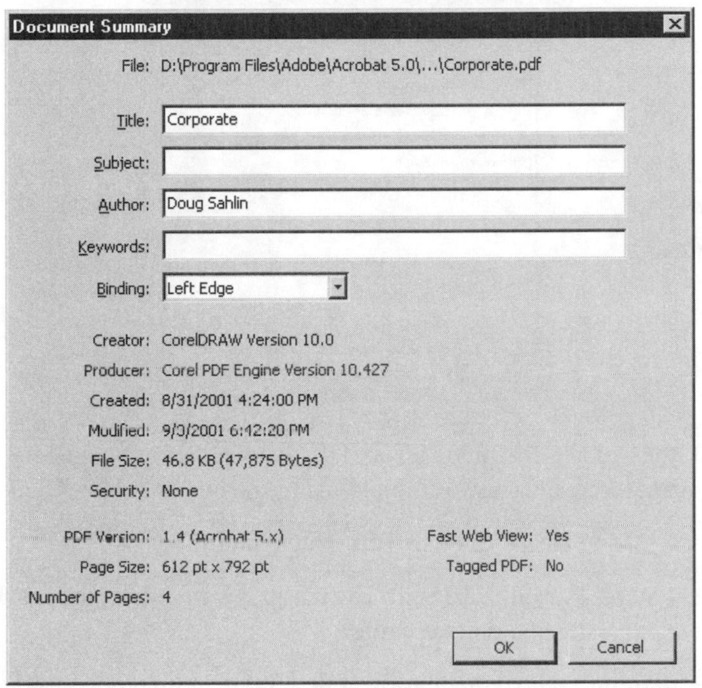

5. In the Title field, enter the category name you want to appear in the Stamp Properties dialog box. Choose a simple name with no spaces, such as *Corporate*. Now that you have named the stamp category, you need to name each stamp. This is the name that appears in the Category section of the Stamp Properties dialog box.

6. Click OK to close the Document Summary dialog box and then navigate to the first page of the document.

7. Choose Tools | Forms | Page Templates to open the Page Templates dialog box.

8. Enter a name for the stamp in the following format: StampName=Stamp Name. For example, if the name you want to appear is *For Review*, you would enter **ForReview=For Review**, as shown in the following image. Notice that both sides of the name tag are the same, except for the lack of spaces to the left of the equal sign (=). The Acrobat programming code uses this nomenclature to display the stamp name in the Stamp Properties dialog box.

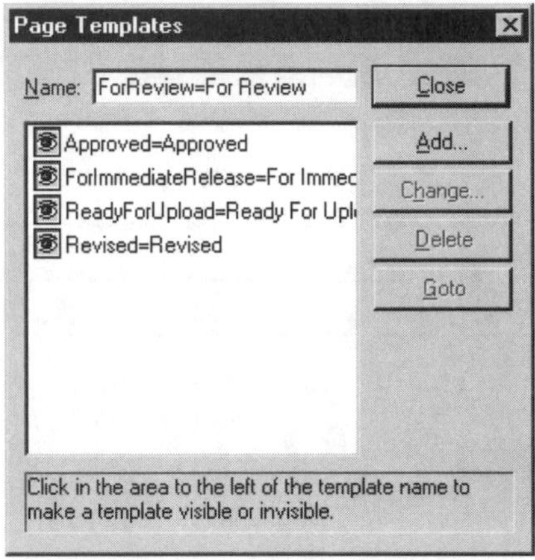

9. Click the Add button, and Acrobat displays a dialog box asking whether you want to create a new template using the current page. Click Yes.
10. Click Close to close the Page Templates dialog box.
11. Repeat steps 7 through 10 for the other pages in the document. Remember to give each stamp a unique name.
12. After naming each stamp, choose File | Save and navigate to the following directory: Acrobat 5.0\Acrobat\Plug-Ins\Annotations\Stamps\ENU.
13. In the File Name field, enter the same name you specified for the Document Title in step 5.
14. Click Save.

After you save the file, your stamps are ready for use. Add a stamp to a document and then follow the instructions in the section "Use the Stamp Tool," earlier in this chapter. Modify the stamp properties, as outlined previously, and choose your custom stamps from the Category drop-down menu. The following image shows a custom stamp applied to a document:

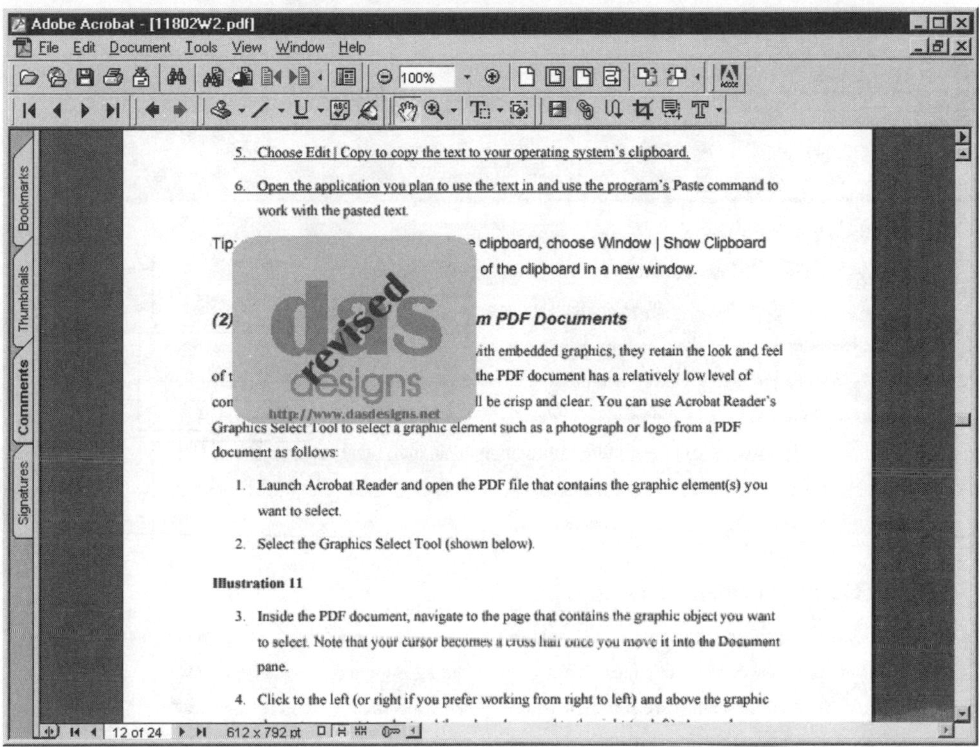

Mark Up a Document

In addition to annotating your documents with notes, stamps, free text, and attached files, you can highlight, strike through, and underline text to create annotations. You can also create graphic elements to mark up a document. You can use a circle, rectangle, line, or a pencil to highlight areas of the document.

Mark Up Text

You can call another reviewer's attention to text that needs to be changed within a document. You can highlight text, strike out text, or underline text. You can create text in a pop-up note that specifies the changes you want made. Figure 12-7 shows the three text annotation methods being used in a single paragraph.

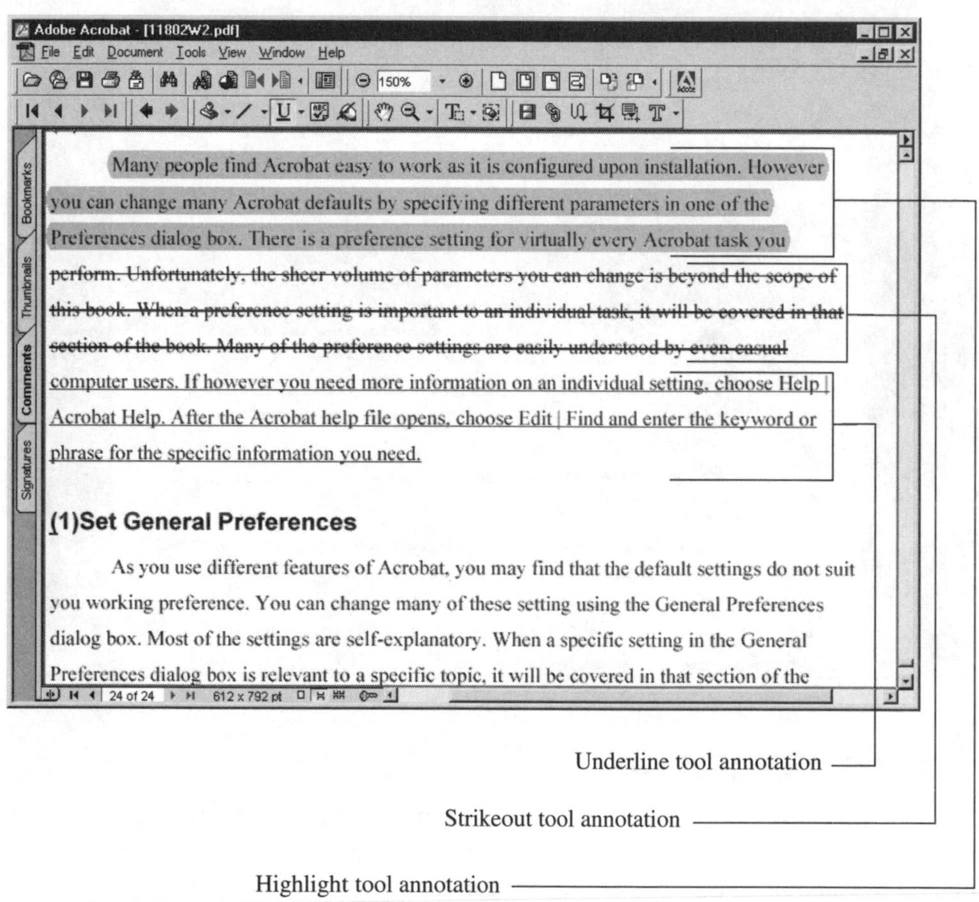

FIGURE 12-7 You can draw a reviewer's attention to text using one of three tools.

Use the Highlight Tool

The Highlight tool is the PDF equivalent of a felt-tipped highlighter. You use it to highlight text within the document. You can highlight a single word, several words, a line of text, or several lines of text. The Highlight tool can only be used to mark up editable text, or text created with the Free Text tool. It will not work on text that is part of an image converted to PDF format. To highlight text, follow these steps:

1. Select the Highlight tool, as shown at left.
2. Move the tool into the Document pane and highlight text by doing one of the following:
   - To highlight a single word, click it.
   - To highlight multiple words or a sentence, click a word and drag. Release the mouse button when the desired words are selected.
   - To highlight multiple lines of text, click a word, drag to the end of the sentence, and then drag down. You can select as many sentences as you want or until a graphic element appears in the document. Release the mouse button when the sentences you want to highlight are selected.

Reviewers of the document can access a pop-up note attached to the highlighted text by double-clicking it. By default, the pop-up note will contain the highlighted text word for word. You can edit the contents of the pop-up note, as described in the section "Attach a Pop-Up Note," later in the chapter.

You can also edit properties of comments created with the Highlight tool by following the steps in the upcoming "Edit Comment Properties section."

Use the Strikeout Tool

Another method you can use to draw a reviewer's attention to text is the Strikeout tool. When you mark up text with the Strikeout tool, a solid line appears through the lower third of the text. A text strikeout is red by default, but you can change that by following the steps in the upcoming section "Edit Comment Properties." To mark up text with the Strikeout tool, follow these steps:

1. Select the Strikeout tool, as shown at left.

2. Move the tool into the Document pane and do one of the following:
   - To strike out a single word, click it.
   - To strike out several words, click a word, and then drag right or left. Release the mouse button when the desired words are selcted.
   - To strike out several sentences, click a word, drag to the end of the sentence, and then drag up or down. You will be able to select sentences until a graphic element appears. Release the mouse button when the desired words are selected.

Notes are attached to text marked up with the Strikeout tool as with highlighted text. By default, the note contains the words marked up with the tool. You can edit the pop-up note by following the instructions in the "Attach a Pop-Up Note," later in the chapter.

You can edit the properties of comments created with the Strikeout tool by following the instructions in the upcoming "Edit Comment Properties" section.

Use the Underline Tool

If you prefer to mark up text so that it is visible to reviewers, use the Underline tool. With the Underline tool, you can underline a single word, several words, or several sentences. By default, the underline is red. To mark up text with the Underline tool, follow these steps:

1. Select the Underline tool, as shown at left.
2. Inside the Document pane, use the tool to do one of the following:
   - Click a single word to underline it.
   - Click a word, and drag left or right to underline several words. Release the mouse button when the desired words are highlighted.
   - Click a word, drag toward the end of a sentence, and then drag up or down to underline several sentences. You will be able to underline consecutive sentences until you encounter a graphic object. Release the mouse button when the desired sentences are highlighted.

By default, a note containing the underlined word(s) attaches to the underlined text. Reviewers can read the note by double-clicking the underlined text. You can change the contents of the pop-up note by following the steps in "Attach a Pop-Up Note," later in the chapter.

You can also edit the properties of comments created with the Underline tool by following the steps in the next section, "Edit Comment Properties."

Edit Comment Properties

Comments created with the Highlight, Strikeout, or Underline tool share the same properties: color and author. To modify comment properties, follow these steps:

1. Select the Hand tool.
2. Select the comment whose properties you want to modify. You can select the actual comment in the document or click its title in the Comments palette.
3. Choose Edit | Properties to open the Comment Properties dialog box, as shown in the following image:

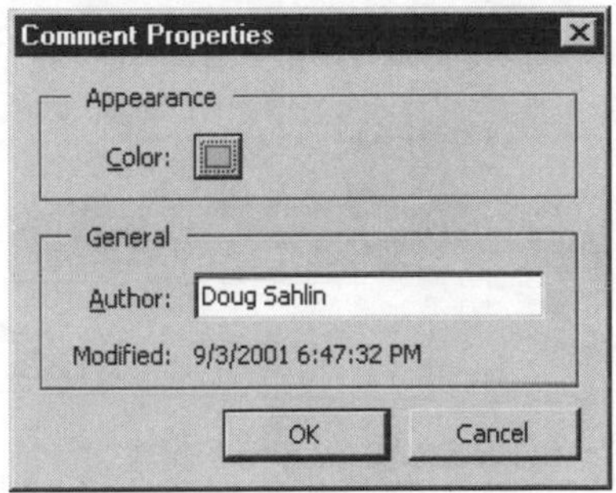

4. To change the color of the comment, click the Color button and choose a color from the pop-up palette, or click the More Colors icon to select a color from the system color picker.
5. To change the author's name of the comment, enter a name in the Author field. By default, the author's name is the registered owner of Acrobat that created the comment.
6. Click OK to apply the changes.

With the exception of the author's name of the comment, the modified properties will be applied to comments created with the applicable tool until you once again select text marked up with the tool and change the comment properties of the marked up text.

Use Graphic Elements

Some reviewers prefer to use graphic elements to mark up a document. You can create graphic elements to mark up a document with one of the following: the Pencil tool, the Square tool, the Circle tool, or the Line tool. When you mark up a document with one of these tools, you can attach a pop-up note, as outlined in the upcoming section "Attach a Pop-Up Note."

Some PDF reviewers prefer to mark up a document with a combination of graphic elements and text created with the Free Text tool. For example, you can use the Circle tool to highlight a graphic element that needs to be modified, and then use the Line tool to point to text created with the Free Text tool, as shown in Figure 12-8.

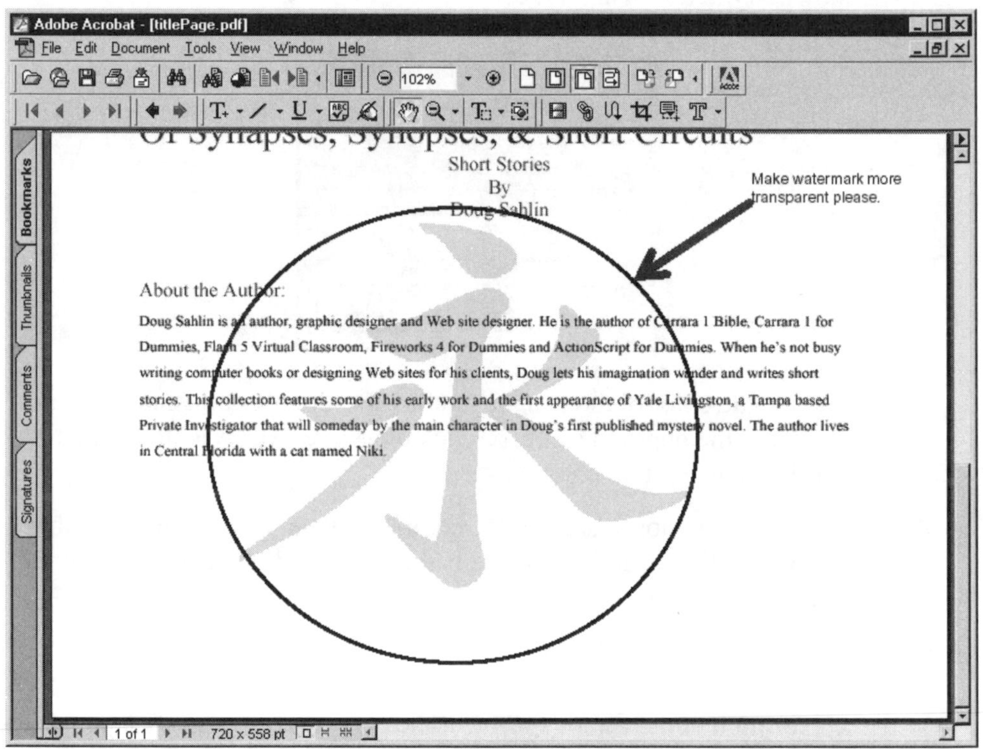

FIGURE 12-8 You can use a combination of comment tools to mark up a document.

Use the Pencil Tool

If you are a card-carrying member of Pocket Pals anonymous, the Pencil tool is right up your alley. You can use it to create expressive squiggles to direct another reviewer's attention to an element you feel needs correcting. When you mark up a document with the Pencil tool, Acrobat smoothes out the rough spots; however, it is not possible to constrain the tool to a perfectly straight line. For that, you use the Line tool. To mark up a document with the Pencil tool, follow these steps:

1. Select the Pencil tool, shown at left.
2. Click anywhere inside the Document pane, and drag to create a line.
3. Release the mouse button to finish drawing with the Pencil tool.

Edit a Pencil Tool Markup

After you create a markup with the Pencil tool, you can move or resize it. You edit a Pencil tool markup with the Hand tool. You could edit it with the Pencil tool, however, if you inadvertently click outside of the markup you want to edit, you create another line. You can edit a Pencil tool markup by doing one of the following:

- To move the markup, select it with the Hand tool, and drag it to another location.
- To resize the markup, click it with the Hand tool, and then click and drag one of the rectangular handles at the corners of the markup bounding box. To resize proportionately, press SHIFT while dragging.

Modify Pencil Properties

You can change the color and thickness of a line created with the Pencil tool, as well as change the name of the author who created the comment. To modify the properties of a line drawn with the Pencil tool, follow these steps:

1. Select the Hand tool.
2. Select the line whose properties you want to change.

3. Choose Edit | Properties to open the Pencil Properties dialog box, as shown in the following image:

4. Click the spinner buttons to the left of the Thickness field to increase or decrease the thickness of the line. Alternatively, you can enter a value between 0 and 12 pts.
5. To change the color of the line, click the Color button and choose a color from the pop-up palette, or click the More Colors icon to choose a color from the system color picker.
6. To change the author of the comment, type a different name in the Author field.
7. Click OK to apply the changes.

The modifications you make to the comment properties (excluding the author's name) will apply to all future lines drawn with the Pencil tool until you select another comment created with the Pencil tool and modify its properties.

Use the Square Tool

Another option you have to mark up a document with a graphic element is the Square tool. You can use the tool to create a filled square with a border, a filled square without a border, or an unfilled square with a border. To mark up a document with the Square tool, follow these steps:

1. Select the Square tool, as shown at left.

2. Click inside the document, and then drag down and across. As you drag, a bounding box appears, giving you a preview of the dimensions of the shape. Press SHIFT while dragging to constrain the shape to a square.
3. Release the mouse button when the square is the desired size.

Edit a Square Tool Markup

You can change the dimensions of a markup created with the Square tool, as well as its location within the document. You can edit a comment created with the Square tool by doing one of the following:

- To move the comment, select it with the Hand tool and drag it to a new location.
- To resize the comment, select it with the Hand tool, and then click and drag one of the rectangular handles at the perimeter of the square. To resize the square proportionately, press SHIFT while dragging.

Modify Square Properties

You can modify the properties of a comment created with the Square tool to change the border thickness of the square, the fill color of the square, and the name of the author who created the square. To modify the properties of a comment created with the Square tool, follow these steps:

1. Select the comment with the Hand tool.
2. Choose Edit | Properties to open the Square Properties dialog box, as shown in the following image:

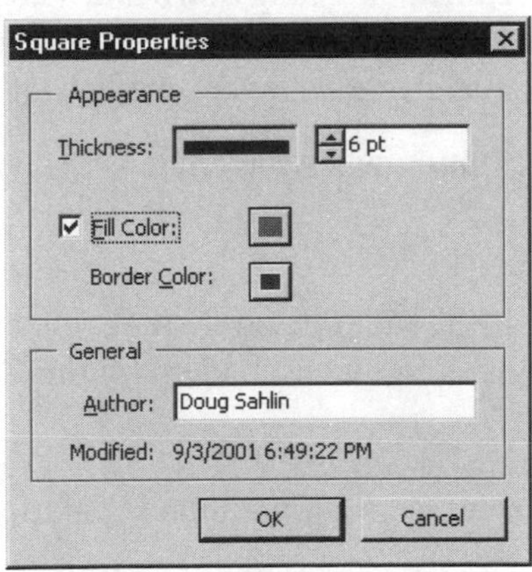

3. Click the spinner buttons to the left of the Thickness field to increase or decrease the border thickness. Alternatively, you can enter a value between 0 and 12 pts.
4. Disable the Fill Color option to remove the fill color from the square. This effectively creates a rectangular border, and the objects below the square are visible.
5. To change the fill color of the square, click the Fill Color button and choose a color from the pop-up palette, or click the More Colors icon and choose a color from the system color picker.
6. To change the author of the comment, enter a different name in the Author field.
7. Click OK to apply the changes and close the dialog box.

With the exception of the author's name, the properties you change will be applied to future squares created with the tool, that is, until you modify the properties of another comment created with the tool.

Use the Circle Tool

If you need to draw a reviewer's attention to a circular element in the document, the Circle tool is the means to your end. With the Circle tool, you can create a filled circle with no border, a filled circle with a border, or an unfilled circle. To mark up a document with the Circle tool, follow these steps:

1. Select the Circle tool, as shown at left.
2. Click inside the document and drag down and across. To constrain the tool to a perfectly round circle, press SHIFT while dragging. As you drag, Acrobat creates a bounding box that gives you a preview of the size of the circle.
3. Release the mouse button when the circle is the desired size.

Edit a Circular Markup

After you mark up a document with the Circle tool, you can change the position or size of the circle. To edit a comment made with the Circle tool, do one of the following.

- To move the comment, select it with the Hand tool and drag it to a new location.

- To resize a circle, select it with the Hand tool, and then click and drag one of the square handles at the corners of the bounding box of the circle. Press SHIFT while dragging to resize the circle proportionately.

Modify Circle Properties

You can change the properties of any comment created with the Circle tool. You can change the thickness of the circle border, the circle fill color, and the name of the author who created the comment. To change the properties of a circle, follow these steps:

1. Select the circle with the Hand tool.
2. Choose Edit | Properties to open the Circle Properties dialog box, as shown in the following image:

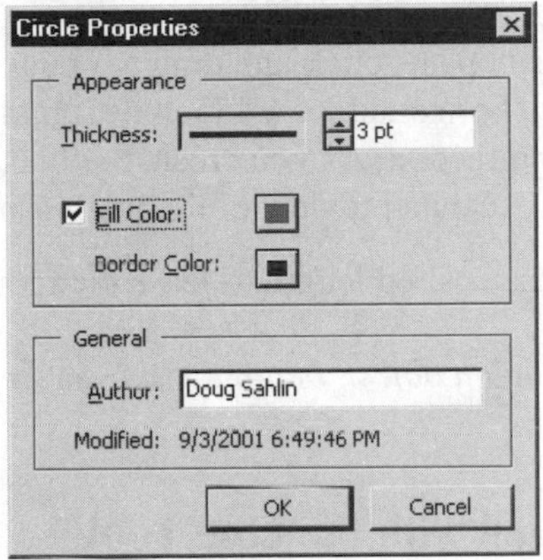

3. Click the spinner buttons to the left of the Thickness field to increase or decrease the thickness of the circle border. Alternatively, you can enter a value between 0 and 12 pts.
4. To change the circle fill color, click the Fill Color button and choose a color from the pop-up palette, or click the More Colors icon to choose a color from the system color picker.
5. To remove the fill from the circle, disable the Fill Color option. This creates a circular border, and the elements under the circle are visible.
6. To change the color of the circle border, click the Border Color button and choose a color from the pop-up palette, or click the More Colors icon and choose a color from the system color picker.

7. To change the name of the comment author, enter a name in the Author field.
8. Click OK to apply the changes and close the dialog box.

With the exception of the comment author's name, the changes are applied to all future comments you create with the Circle tool, that is, until you edit the properties of another comment created with the tool.

Use the Line Tool

When you need to point out an element in a document, the Line tool is an excellent choice. When you mark up a document with the Line tool, you can specify the thickness of the line and the color of the line, and create an arrow on either or both sides of the line. To mark up a document with the Line tool, follow these steps:

1. Select the Line tool, as shown at left.
2. Inside the Document pane, click and drag to create the line. To constrain the line to vertical, horizontal, or a 45° angle, press SHIFT while dragging in the appropriate direction. As you create the line, Acrobat creates a thin black line that gives you a preview of the line position and length.
3. When the line is the desired length, release the mouse button.

To point directly to an object, begin the line at the object perimeter and drag away from it.

Edit a Markup Created with the Line Tool

After you create a comment with the Line tool, you can change the length of the line and the location of the line, as well as the position of the head or tail of the line. To edit a comment created with the Line tool, do one of the following:

- To change the position of the line, select it with the Hand tool, and then click and drag it to a new location.
- To change the position of the head or tail of the line, select it with the Hand tool, click the rectangular handle at end of the line you want to move, and drag it up or down to a new location. As you move one end of the line, the other end stays locked to its original position. When the end of the line is in the desired position, release the mouse button.

- To resize the line, select it with the Hand tool, and then click one of the handles at the end of the line and drag it horizontally. When the line is the desired size, release the mouse button.

Modify Line Properties

When you create a comment with the Line tool, you can modify its properties at any time. You can change the thickness of the line, its color, and whether the line has an arrow on one end, both, or neither. To modify a comment created with the Line tool, follow these steps:

1. Select the comment with the Hand tool.
2. Choose Edit | Properties to open the Line Properties dialog box, as shown in the following image:

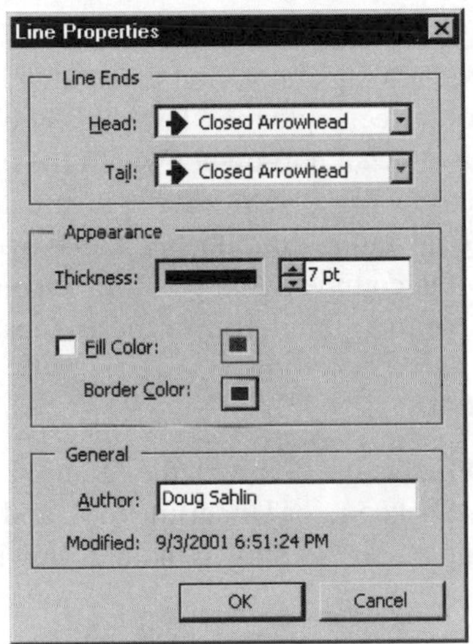

3. Click the triangle to the right of the Head field; and, from the drop-down menu, choose one of the following: None, Open Arrowhead, Closed Arrowhead, Square, Circle, or Diamond.
4. Click the triangle to the right of the Tail field; and, from the drop-down menu, choose one of the same options listed in step 3.

5. Click the spinner buttons to the left of the Thickness field to increase or decrease the thickness of the line. Alternatively, you can enter a value between 0 and 12 pts.
6. Click the Border Color button and choose a color from the pop-up palette, or click the More Colors icon to select a color from the system color picker. There is a fill color option, but it does not function with a line.
7. To change the author of the comment, enter a name in the Author field.
8. Click OK to apply the changes and close the dialog box.

Except for the author name, the modified properties will be applied to all future comments you create with the Line tool, until you select another comment created with the Line tool and modify its properties, as outlined previously.

Attach a Pop-Up Note

You can attach a pop-up note to an annotation created with the Stamp tool, Line tool, Pencil tool, Circle tool, Rectangle tool, Highlight tool, Strikeout tool, or Underline tool. When you attach a pop-up note, with the exception of the default pop-up color, the note window looks identical to one created with the Note tool. When you attach a note to an annotation, it is viewable by double-clicking the comment, or by selecting the comment and choosing Open Note from the context menu. To add a pop-up note to a stamp, follow these steps:

1. Select the Hand tool.
2. Double-click a comment created with the Stamp, Line, Circle, Rectangle, Pencil, Highlight, Strikeout, or Underline tool, and Acrobat opens a pop-up note with a flashing cursor, as shown in the following image:

3. Enter the text for the note, and then click the X in the upper-left corner of the note to close the note.

If you double-click a comment created with the Highlight, Strikeout, or Underline tool, the text selected with the tool appears in the note by default. To enter a new note, drag your cursor over the default text to select it, and enter new text.

Edit a Pop-Up Note

You can edit a pop-up note attached to an annotation by moving it to a new position or changing the text of the pop-up note. You can also reset a pop-up note to its default position. To edit a pop-up note, double-click the comment the note is attached to and do one of the following:

- Click the note title bar, and drag it to a new location.
- Select text to edit, and enter new text.
- Select text to delete, and then press DELETE or choose Edit | Delete.

To reset a pop-up note window to its default position, right-click (Windows) or CTRL-click (Macintosh), and choose Reset Note Window Location from the context menu.

Export Comments

You can export comments from one document and use them in another version of the same document. Exported comments are saved as an FDF (Forms Data Format) file. The comment file contains all of the comments exported from the document in their original positions, but not the actual document elements. You can export all comments from a document, or export selected comments.

To export all comments from a document, follow these steps:

1. Choose File | Export | Comments to open the Export Comments dialog box.
2. Accept the default name for the comments (the document filename) or enter a different name.
3. Navigate to the folder where you want the comment file saved, and click Save.

You can also export selected comments from a document—for example, all comments created by a particular reviewer. To export selected comments, follow these steps:

1. In the Navigation pane, click the Comments tab.
2. Select the comments you want to export.
3. Click the Comments icon and, from the Comments palette menu, choose Export Selected.
4. In the Export Comments dialog box, enter a name for the comment file, navigate to the folder you want to save the file in, and then click Save.

Import Comments

You can import a comment file into a different version of a document. The imported comments appear in their original positions. If you receive several versions of the same document marked up by different reviewers, you can collate each reviewer's comments in a single document. First, export the comments from each document, as outlined in the previous section. Second, open the master copy of the document into which you want to collate the comments. Third, follow these steps:

1. Choose File | Import | Comments to open the Import Comments dialog box. You can now import comments by having Acrobat strip comments from a PDF file or by importing an FDF file.
2. Click the triangle to the right of the Files Of Type field and choose PDF to import comments directly from a PDF file, or choose FDF to import an FDF comment file.
3. Choose the file, and then click Select.

After you invoke the command, Acrobat imports the comments and places them in the exact location they appeared in the document they were extracted from. If you choose to import comments from a PDF file, this may take a while if the document is large and contains many comments.

Compare Documents

When you send a document out for review, and your team has carte blanche access to the document, subtle modifications—such as, touched up text, comments, and modified form fields—may slip past you. If you save a pre-review version of the document with a unique filename, you can employ Acrobat to compare it to the post-review version of the document by invoking the Compare command. You have two methods of comparing documents at your disposal. You can use the Compare Two Documents command to compare two documents with different filenames, or you can use the Compare Two Versions Within A Signed Document to compare a signed document for changes made by other members of the team who digitally signed the document. The latter command will be covered in Chapter 13, along with digital signatures.

When you use one of these commands to compare documents, Acrobat scans each version of the document, comparing the PDF information in each version for any changes. After Acrobat finishes its comparison, it creates a summary page, and then generates a side-by-side comparison of each page in which differences are found. If a reviewer adds a page to the reviewed document, Acrobat generates a blank page in the original document, paired with the added page in the reviewed document. If a page is deleted from the reviewed document, Acrobat generates a blank page in the reviewed document and pairs it with the non-deleted page in the original document. When Acrobat notices a difference, such as a changed word or added comments, the differences on each page are highlighted with bounding boxes, as shown in Figure 12-9.

To compare a pre-review and a post-review version of a document, follow these steps:

1. Choose Tools | Compare | Two Documents to open the Compare Documents dialog box, as shown in the following image:

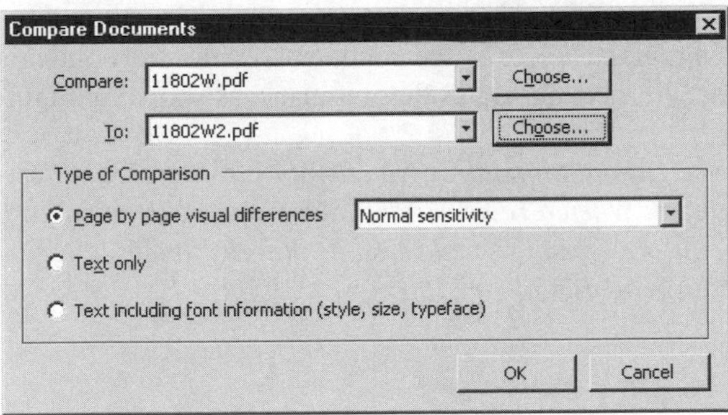

2. Click the Choose button to the right of the Compare field, and open the original version of the document. If you already have a document open in

Acrobat, it is selected by default and displayed in the field. Accept this document, or click the Choose button to open another document.

3. Click the Choose button to the right of the To field, and open the revised version of the document. If you have two documents open in Acrobat, the second document opened is listed in this field. Accept this document, or click the Choose button to open a different document.
4. In the Type Of Comparison section, choose one of the following options:
   - **Page By Page Visual Differences** Choose this option, and Acrobat searches each page for any visual differences, such as a graphic being moved. If you choose this option, click the triangle to the right of the Sensitivity field, and from the drop-down menu choose High Sensitivity (Slow), Normal Sensitivity, or Low Sensitivity (Fast). For the best results, choose High Sensitivity; but as Acrobat warns you, it is slower.

NOTE *To choose the option that is best for you, experiment with each setting while comparing documents you would typically compare. Choose the option that is the right compromise between speed and accuracy.*

   - **Text Only** Choose this option, and Acrobat compares the documents and searches for differences in text content.
   - **Text Including Font Information** Choose this option, and Acrobat scans the documents for differences in text content, as well as differences in font attributes.

5. Click OK and Acrobat begins the comparison. This may take some time depending on the length of the documents. After the comparison is complete, Acrobat generates the summary, as shown in Figure 12-9.

NOTE *If you use Digital Signatures, you do not have to save different versions of a document. When a reviewer digitally signs a document, it is saved. You can recall previously signed versions of a document at any time. For more information on digital signatures, see Chapter 13.*

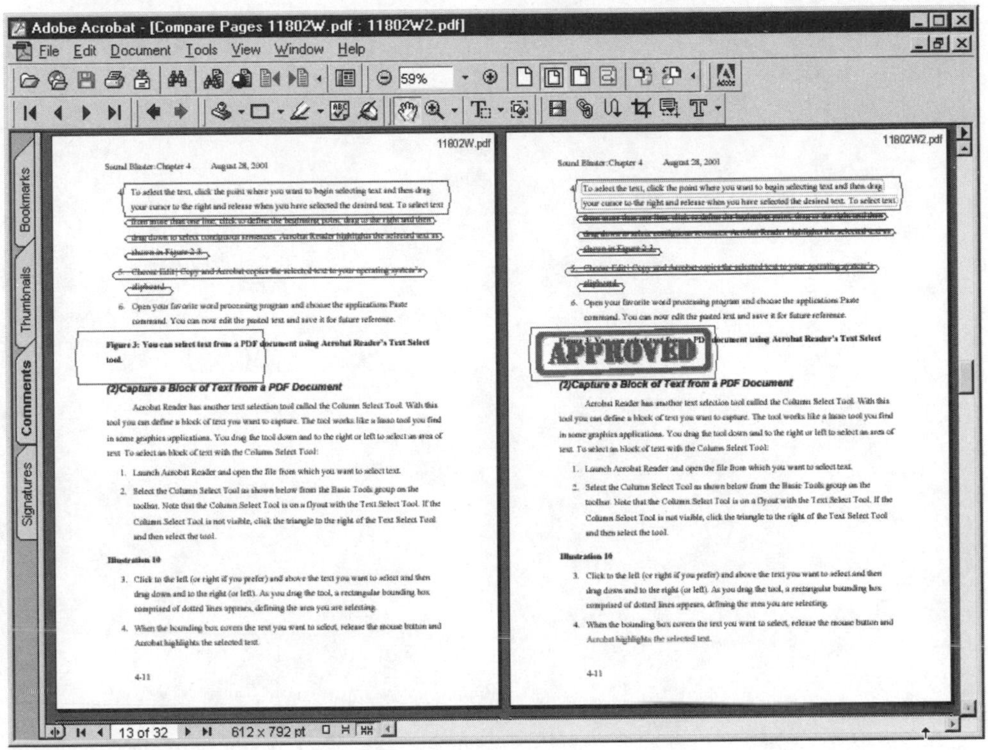

FIGURE 12-9 Compare two versions of a document to highlight changes.

12

Chapter 13

Add Digital Signatures and Document Security

How To…

- Use digital signatures
- Modify signature appearance
- Use the Signatures palette
- Use Acrobat Standard Security
- Use Acrobat Self-Sign Security

When you create a document for use in a corporate environment with several team members, you can keep track of who did what to a document with digital signatures. When a reviewer or team member digitally signs a document, Acrobat acknowledges the reviewer and creates a time stamp. All changes to the document are noted as being performed by the digital signer. When more than one person digitally signs a document, you can compare different versions of the document.

Documents created in a corporate environment are often confidential. When this is the case, you can assign security to a document. When you add security to a document, you limit a viewer's access to the document. When you use Acrobat Standard Security, you can assign a password to the document. Before a document can be viewed, the user must enter the proper password. You can also assign a master password to the document. If a master password is assigned to a document, it must be entered in order for the user to modify any of the security settings. When you use Acrobat Self-Sign Security, you limit access to the document to certain team members. With Acrobat Self-Sign Security, you can create different user permissions for each member of your team. For example, you can disallow editing and printing for certain team members, while giving other team members full access to the document.

About Digital Signatures

In today's economy, corporations often have branches in different counties, states, and countries. Before the advent of e-mail, corporations had to send documents via courier, a very expensive way to communicate. With e-mail, intercompany documents can be sent as e-mail attachments. However, anyone with a bit of computer savvy can access an e-mail message; and if they have the proper software, anyone can view sensitive communications. With Acrobat, documents can be digitally signed. A digital signature is like an electronic thumbprint; it identifies the viewer of the document. It also records any changes made by the signer and stores information about the signer with the document.

When you add Acrobat Self-Sign Security to a document, the only way the document can be viewed is by a team member with an authorized digital signature. Acrobat users with digital signatures can log in before working on documents. Secure documents will open without password verification if an authorized user is logged in.

If you use Acrobat to send contracts to clients, digital signatures can be used to approve contracts. If both parties accept a digital signature as an electronic facsimile of a handwritten signature, a digitally signed contract may be legally binding. Before you accept a digital signature as legally binding authorization to proceed with a contract, it is best to seek the advice of legal counsel. Figure 13-1 shows a document that has been digitally signed.

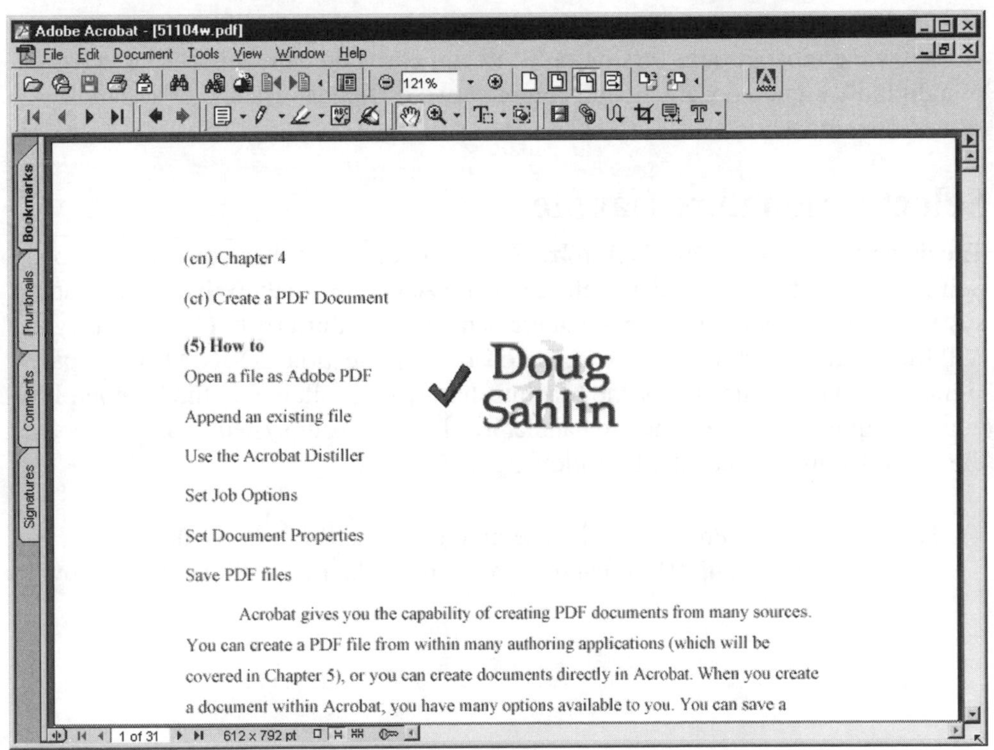

FIGURE 13-1 You can use digital signatures to identify recipients of your documents and limit access to your documents.

Use Digital Signatures

When you decide to use digital signatures to verify the identities of users modifying your documents, you can use the default Acrobat Self-Sign Security or specify a third-party plug-in to handle digital signatures. After you decide on a signature handler, you need to set up your user profile. Your user profile stores information about you. You can use the default Acrobat graphic for a digital signature, or customize the digital signature with a photo or other graphic, such as a logo. When you create a user profile, you can create a list of *trusted certificates*. Trusted certificates are digital signature files in FDF format. Trusted certificates are used to verify digital signatures. You can request digital signatures via e-mail and share your certificate with other users so your digital signature can be verified.

Documents can be signed multiple times by multiple authors. Whenever a document is digitally signed, Acrobat records the changes made since the document was last digitally signed. When you open a document with multiple signatures, you view the most current version of the document. You can view earlier versions of a digitally signed document and compare two different versions of a digitally signed document.

Select a Signature Handler

The default signature handler is Acrobat Self-Sign Security. When you install Acrobat, Self-Sign Security is installed as well. If you use Acrobat with the Windows operating system, you can choose another signature handler from third party plug-ins that you will find in the Security folder of the Acrobat 5.0 application CD-ROM. Third-party signature handler plug-ins for the Macintosh may be available on the Internet. If you have more than one signature handler available on your system, you can choose the default signature handler by following these steps:

1. Choose Edit | Preferences | General to open the Preferences dialog box, and click the Digital Signatures option from the menu in the left window.

2. Click the triangle to the right of the Default Signature Handler field, and choose an option from the drop-down menu. The menu lists all signature handlers installed on your system.
3. Enable the Verify Signatures When Document Is Opened option to have Acrobat automatically verify all digital signatures when you open a document.
4. Click OK to close the Preferences dialog box and set the default signature handler.

Create a User Profile

You create a user profile to create identification and a password that links to your digital signature. You can create more than one user profile if you sign documents in different capacities. To create a user profile, you must be logged in. To create your first user profile, follow these steps:

1. Choose Tools | Self-Sign Security | Log In to open the Self-Sign Security – Log In dialog box, as shown in Figure 13-2. Note that in this illustration, a user profile has already been set up. When this is the case, you can set up an additional user profile by completing the remaining steps.

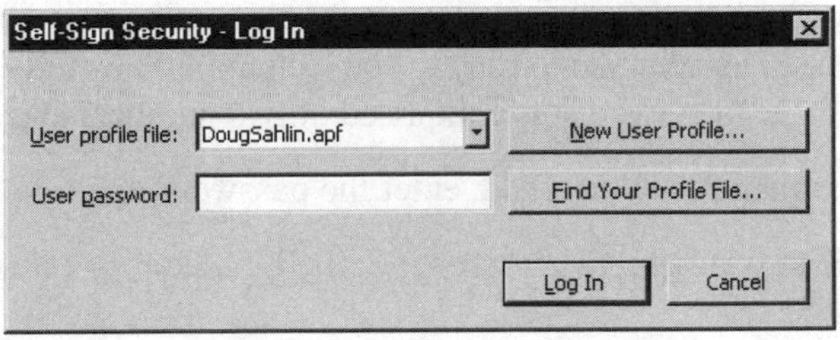

FIGURE 13-2 Use this dialog box to set up a user profile, or log in.

2. Click the New User Profile button to open the Create New User dialog box, as shown in the following image:

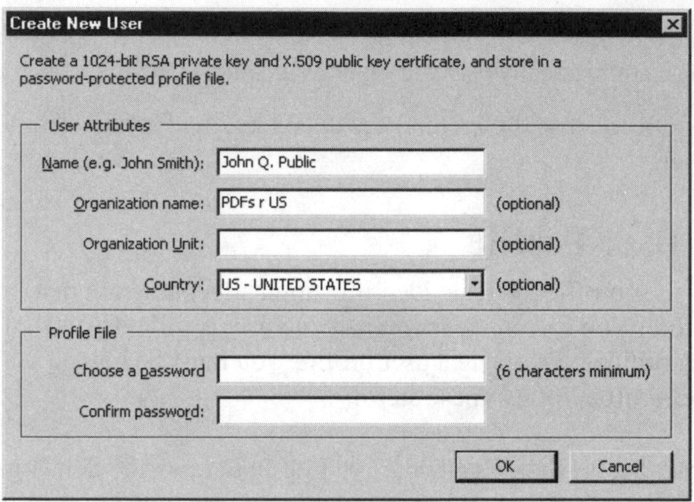

3. In the Name field, enter the name you want associated with the digital signature. If desired, enter attributes for the other fields; however, this is optional.
4. In the Profile section Choose A Password field, enter a password with at least six characters. According to some encryption experts, a password will be harder to crack if it is comprised of two numbers and six letters.
5. In the Confirm Password field, enter the password again.
6. Click OK to open the New Acrobat Self-Sign Security File dialog box, and click Save.
7. After you save the user profile, Acrobat displays an alert telling you, "You are now logged in as 'your profile name.'" Click OK to complete the login process.

Log In

If you work with PDF documents that have been encrypted with Acrobat Self-Sign Security, you can (after modifying the Password Timeout, as discussed in a future section of this chapter) save yourself the hassle of entering a password every time you open a secure document by logging in. After you log in, Acrobat stores your password in memory. When you open a document that you are authorized to access, Acrobat bypasses the Password dialog box and opens the document. To log in, follow these steps:

1. Choose Tools | Self-Sign Security | Log In to open the Self-Sign Security – Log In dialog box, as shown previously in Figure 13-2.
2. Click the triangle to the right of User Profile File field, and choose the user profile under which you want to log in.
3. Enter your User Password and click OK; Acrobat displays an alert dialog box informing you that you are logged in.

Log Out

If you are going to be away from your workstation for a period of time, you can log out to prevent unauthorized users from opening secure documents. You can also log in as a different user if you need to sign documents in another capacity. To log out, do one of the following:

- Choose Tools | Self-Sign Security | Log Out As [your username]. If you log out and there are secure documents open, Acrobat displays a warning to that effect. Click OK to close the document(s) and complete the log out.
- Choose Tools | Self-Sign Security | Log In As Another User to open the Self-Sign Security – Log In dialog box, as shown in Figure 13-2. Choose the user profile you want to log in under, enter the proper password, and click OK to log in with the different user profile.

13

Modify a User Profile

Whatever you create, you can modify; your user profile is no exception. You can change your password, back up your User Profile, change the appearance of the digital signature, and create a list of trusted certificates.

Modify User Information

After you create a user profile, you can back up the file, export your certificate to file, and e-mail your certificate to another user. When you exchange certificates with other team members or clients, you can create a list of trusted certificates to use when encrypting a document with Acrobat Self-Sign Security. To modify user information, follow these steps:

1. If you are not already logged in under the user profile you want to modify, follow the steps in the earlier "Log In" section.
2. Choose Tools | Self-Sign Security | User Settings to open the Self-Sign Security – User Settings dialog box, as shown in the following image:

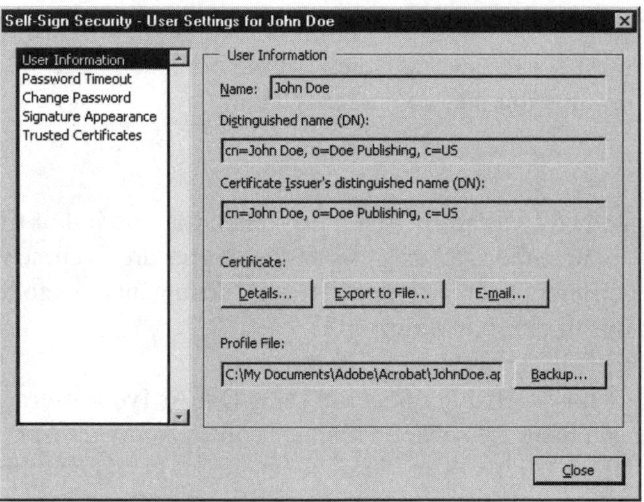

3. Click the Details button to view certificate details.
4. Click the Export to File button to open the Export Certificate As dialog box. Accept the default name and click OK, and Acrobat saves the file as an Acrobat Self-Sign Key (*.fdf) file and displays a dialog box telling you the file has successfully been saved.
5. Click the E-mail button to exchange your certificate with another user. Instructions for exchanging certificates are discussed in detail in the section "Exchange Certificates" later in the chapter.

6. Click the Backup button to create a backup of your user profile and Acrobat opens the Browse for Folder dialog box. Accept the default folder, or choose another folder, and click OK to complete the backup.
7. Click Close to exit the Self-Sign Security – User Settings dialog box, or click one of the other titles to modify a different parameter of your user profile.

Change Password Timeout

By default, Acrobat requires that you enter your password every time you digitally sign a document. You can modify this by having Acrobat prompt you for the password only after a certain period of time has elapsed. To modify the password timeout, follow these steps:

1. Log in under the user profile you want to modify.
2. Choose Tools | Self-Sign Security | User Settings to open the Self-Sign Security – User Settings dialog box, and then click Password Timeout.
3. Click the triangle to the right of Require Password Entry on Signing, and choose one of the options from the drop-down menu. This is the amount of time that must elapse before Acrobat prompts you for a password when digitally signing a document.
4. In the Enter Password field, enter your password.
5. Click Close to close the Self-Sign Security – User Settings dialog box, or click another title to modify another parameter.

Change Your Password

Another user setting you can modify is your password. It is a good idea to change your password periodically to keep security intact. To change your user profile password, follow these steps:

1. Log in under the username you want to modify settings for.
2. Choose Tools | Self-Sign Security | User Settings to open the Self-Sign Security – User Settings dialog box.

3. Choose Change Password to open the dialog box, as shown in the following image:

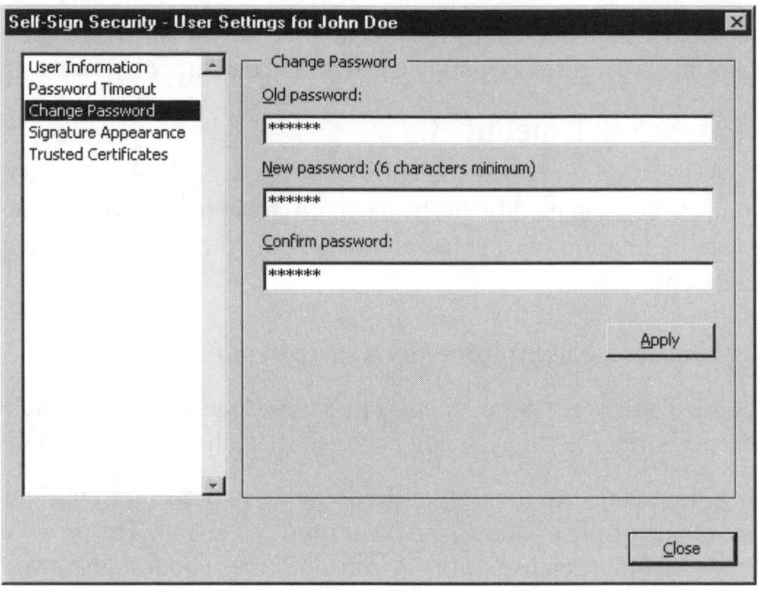

4. In the Old Password field, enter your current password.
5. In the New Password field, enter your new password, and then enter it again in the Confirm Password field.
6. Click Apply to assign the new password to your user profile.
7. Click Close to exit the Self-Sign Security – User Settings dialog box, or choose another option to modify.

Modify Signature Appearance

When you digitally sign a document, Acrobat uses a default text-only signature with the Acrobat logo in the background. You can change the appearance of your digital signature by creating a file in a graphics program and converting it to PDF format. For that matter, you can choose File | Import | Scan, and then scan a copy of your actual signature and save it as a PDF file. After you create a PDF file with the graphic you want to use for your digital signature, follow these steps:

1. Log in and then choose Tools | Self-Sign Security | User Settings to open the Self-Sign Security – User Settings dialog box.
2. Click Signature Appearance, and then click New to open the Configure Signature Appearance dialog box, as shown in the following image. Note that this image shows a custom signature and not the Acrobat default.

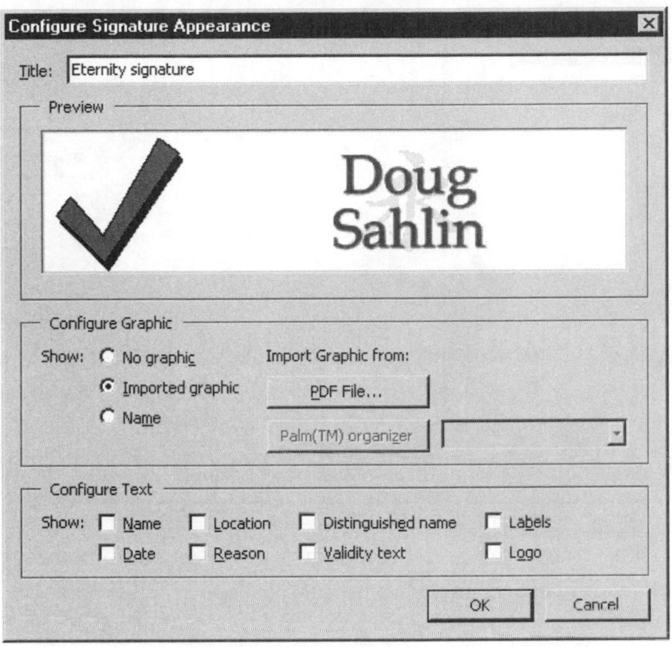

3. In the Title field, enter a name for the signature configuration.
4. In the Configure Graphic section, within the Show options, choose No Graphic, Imported Graphic, or Name. If you choose Imported Graphic, click the PDF File button to open the Select Picture dialog box. Click the Browse button and navigate to the PDF file that contains the image for your digital signature, and then click Select. Acrobat displays a sample of the image in the Preview window. If the image is acceptable, click OK to close the Select Picture dialog box.
5. In the Configure Text section, choose the options you want to appear with your digital signature. Every option is selected by default. As you change the options, Acrobat updates the preview in real time.

6. Click OK to close the dialog box, and Acrobat adds your custom signature to the list, as shown in the following image. Notice that there are options to Edit, Copy, and Delete the custom signature.

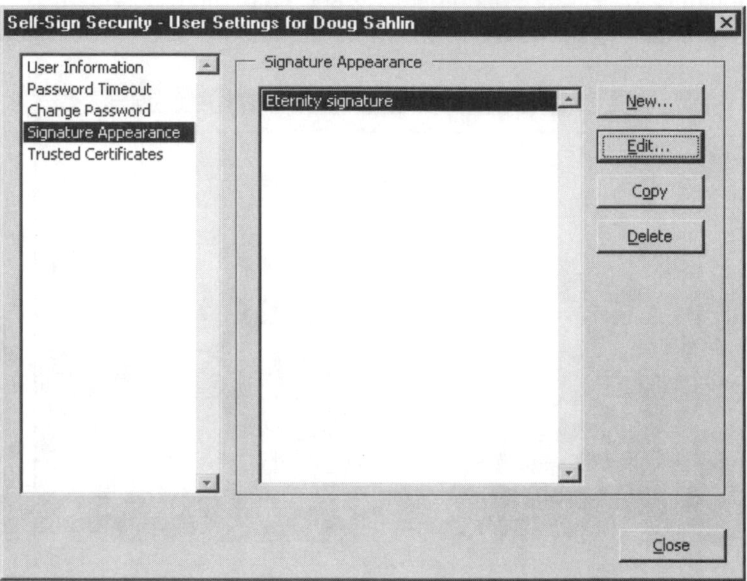

7. Click Close to exit the Self-Sign Security – User Settings dialog box, or choose another parameter to modify.

Sign a Document

After you create a user profile, you can digitally sign documents. When you digitally sign a document, you are required to save it. When you save the document for the first time, Acrobat saves it in an *append only* format. From this point forward, you will not be able to do a full save, as the Save option is not available for a digitally signed document. After you sign a document, your signature appears in the Signature palette, which is discussed in a future section of this chapter. To digitally sign a document, follow these steps:

1. Select the Digital Signature tool, as shown in the following image. Alternatively, choose Tools | Digital Signatures | Sign Document. If you choose the menu command, Acrobat selects the Digital Signature tool for

you and prompts you to drag out the area where you want the signature to appear. When you select the Digital Signature tool, the dialog box does not appear, and you define the area for the signature as outlined in step 2.

2. Click and drag a rectangle inside the document where you want the signature to appear. If you are not already logged in, Acrobat prompts you to log in; otherwise, Acrobat prompts you for a password (unless you have changed user settings for Password Timeout, as discussed earlier in this chapter). Follow the prompts to log in or enter your password to reveal the Self-Sign Security – Sign Document dialog box. When Acrobat opens this dialog box for the first time, you'll see a truncated version that only requires confirming your password. To provide additional information with your digital signature, or to use a custom signature you have created, click the Show Options button to reveal the Self-Sign Security – Sign Document dialog box, as shown in the following image. You can return the dialog box to the abbreviated version by clicking the Hide Options button.

3. In the Confirm Password field, enter your password.
4. Click the triangle to the right of the Reason For Signing Document field, and choose an option from the drop-down menu. Alternatively, you can enter text that describes why you are signing the document.
5. If desired, enter information in the Location field and the Your Contact Information field. These fields are optional.
6. In the Signature Appearance section, accept the default Standard Text signature; or click the triangle to the right of the field, and, from the drop-down menu, choose a signature you have created. If you choose the Standard Text option, you can preview the signature by clicking the Preview button. If you choose a custom signature, you can change the signature by clicking the Edit button. If you do not want to use any of the available signature appearance options, you can create a new signature by clicking the New button and following the steps described previously in the "Modify Signature Appearance" section.
7. Click the Save button to save the document with its current filename. Alternatively, click Save As to save the document with a different filename. If you choose the Save As option, to continue the review process, you will have to save this version of the document, since your digital signature and changes will not appear on the original document. After you save the document, Acrobat displays a dialog box alerting you that the document has been signed successfully.

TIP

To digitally sign a document without adding a signature graphic to the document, choose Tools | Digital Signatures | Invisible Signature and follow the prompts in the Self-Sign Security – Log In dialog box, as discussed previously. Your signature will be invisible; however, all of the information concerning the signing records in the Signatures palette. If you invisibly sign a document, another viewer opening the document may not realize it has been signed. To circumvent this, navigate to the first page of the document and choose Document | Set Page Action, choose the Execute Menu Item page action, choose Window | Signatures, and then save the document. When the document is opened next, the Signatures palette opens and the viewer sees every signature applied to the document.

Use the Signatures Palette

After you, or another author, digitally sign a document, information concerning the signature appears in the Signatures palette. You can select a signature in the palette and find out when the document was signed, who the author was, the validity of the signature, and the reason for signing the document. You use the Signatures palette to manage the signatures in the document, as well as perform other functions. To open the Signatures palette shown in Figure 13-3, open the Navigation pane and click the Signatures tab. Alternatively, you can choose Window | Signatures.

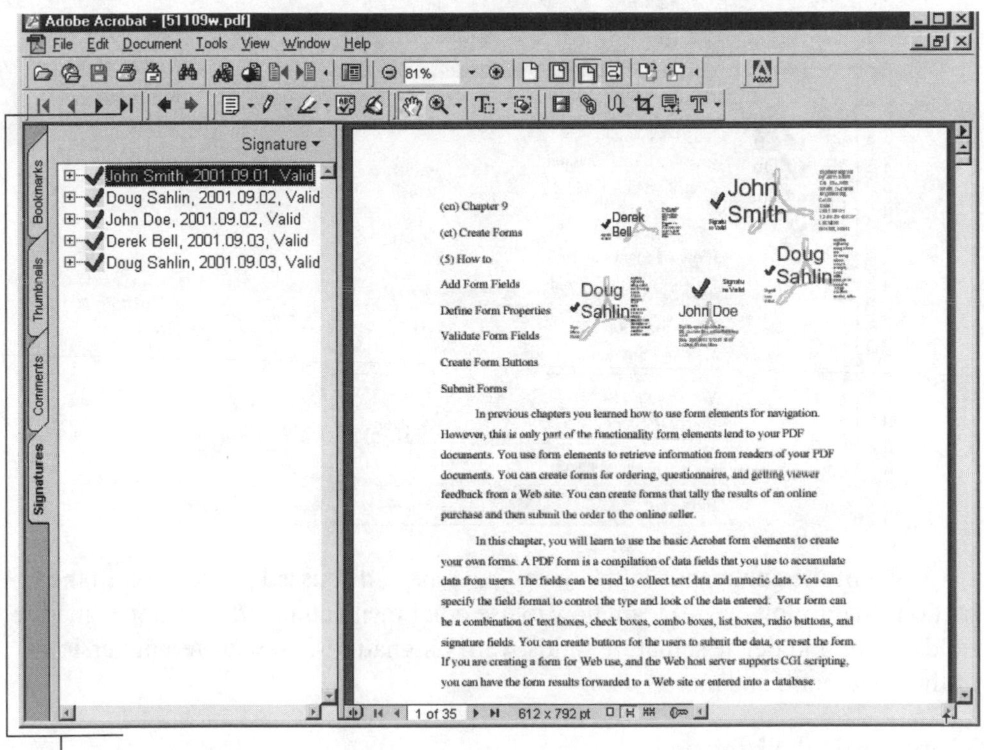

Signatures palette

FIGURE 13-3 You use the Signatures palette to manage digital signatures in your document.

13

You can also open the Signatures palette by clicking the Key icon at the bottom of the Document pane and choosing Show Signatures from the pop-up menu.

The Signatures palette has an extensive menu whose commands duplicate on the Tools menu. To open the Signatures palette menu, as shown in the following image, click the Signature icon in the Signatures palette.

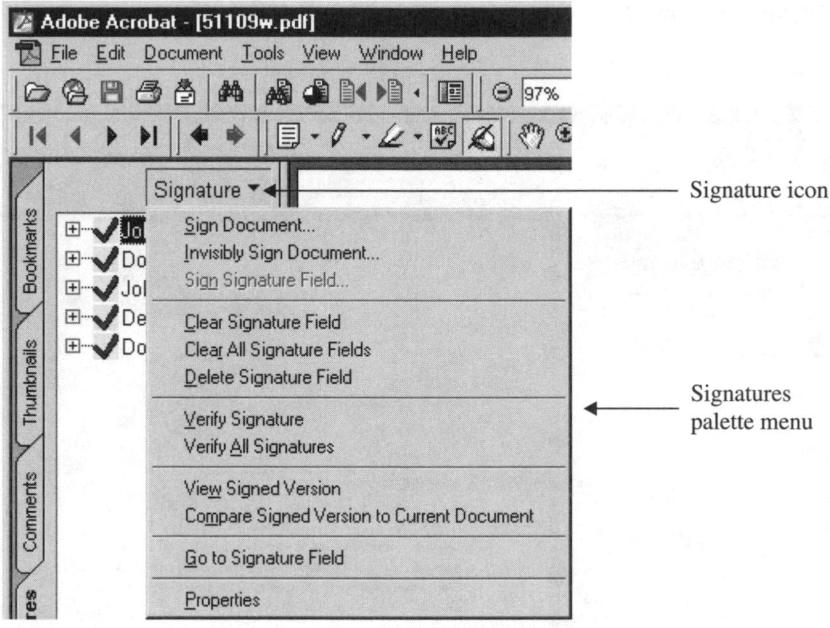

Some of the commands in this menu have been discussed previously. In the sections that follow, you'll learn how to use other menu commands to sign signature fields, clear and delete signature fields, verify signatures, view different versions of the document, and more.

View Digital Signatures

After you open the Signatures palette, you'll see a single listing for each signature in the document. The listing notes the author's name, the verification status of the signature, and the date the signature was added to the document. Verifying signatures is discussed in an upcoming section of this chapter. To the left of the signature is a plus sign (+). Click the plus sign to expand the signature. After you expand a signature, you have access to the information shown in the following image:

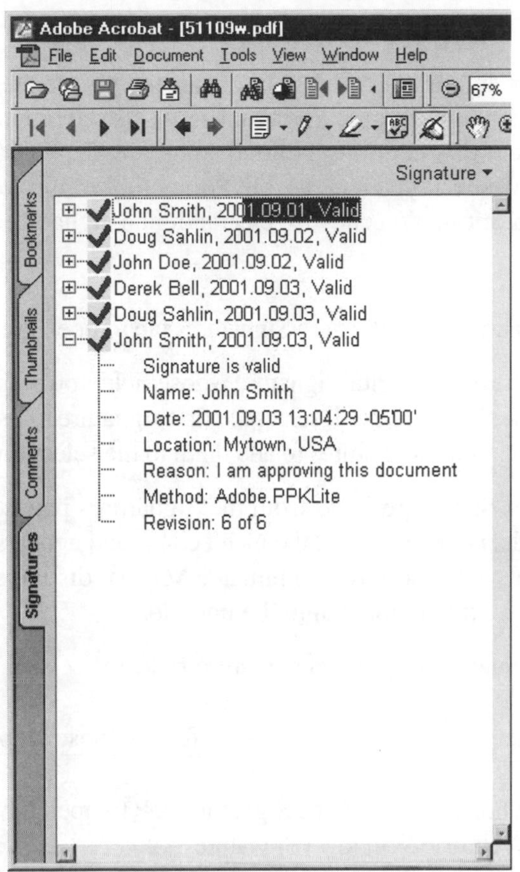

An expanded signature is designated by a minus sign (–). Click the minus sign to collapse the signature.

Sign Signature Fields

When you create a document with a form field requiring a digital signature, you can sign the field in one of two ways: click the field with the Hand tool or choose Sign Signature field from the Signatures palette menu. After you choose to sign the field using one of these methods, Acrobat opens the Self-Sign Security – Sign In dialog box, as discussed previously. Follow the prompts to sign the signature field. For more information on creating signature form fields, refer to Chapter 9.

Clear Signature Fields

When you, or another author, digitally sign a document, you create a field that contains the digital signature. If you select the Form tool, as discussed previously in Chapter 9, you will see each field that contains a digital signature, as well as other form fields in the document. If desired, you can use the Forms tool to move a digital signature field to a different location. You can also clear a digital signature field by following these steps:

1. In the Navigation pane, click the Signatures tab to open the Signatures palette.
2. Click the name of the digital signature whose field you want to clear. To clear more than one signature field, select the first signature, press and hold SHIFT, and click contiguous signatures to add them to the selection.
3. Choose Clear Signature Field from the Signatures palette menu. If you select more than one signature, the menu command appears as Clear Signature Fields. After you choose the command, Acrobat displays a warning dialog box telling you the action cannot be undone.
4. Click OK to clear the selected signature field(s).

To clear all signature fields in a document, follow these steps:

1. In the Navigation pane, click the Signatures tab to open the Signatures palette. Alternatively, choose Window | Signatures.
2. Choose Clear All Signature Fields from the Signatures palette menu, and Acrobat displays a warning dialog box telling you the action cannot be undone.
3. Click OK, and Acrobat clears all signature fields

After you clear a signature field, it is signified in the Signatures palette with a signature icon followed by a title, as shown in the following image. In the document, the cleared signature is a blank signature form field with no border and no fill, hence it is not visible. You can sign a blank signature field by selecting it in the Signatures palette and then choosing Sign Signature field from the Signatures palette drop-down menu.

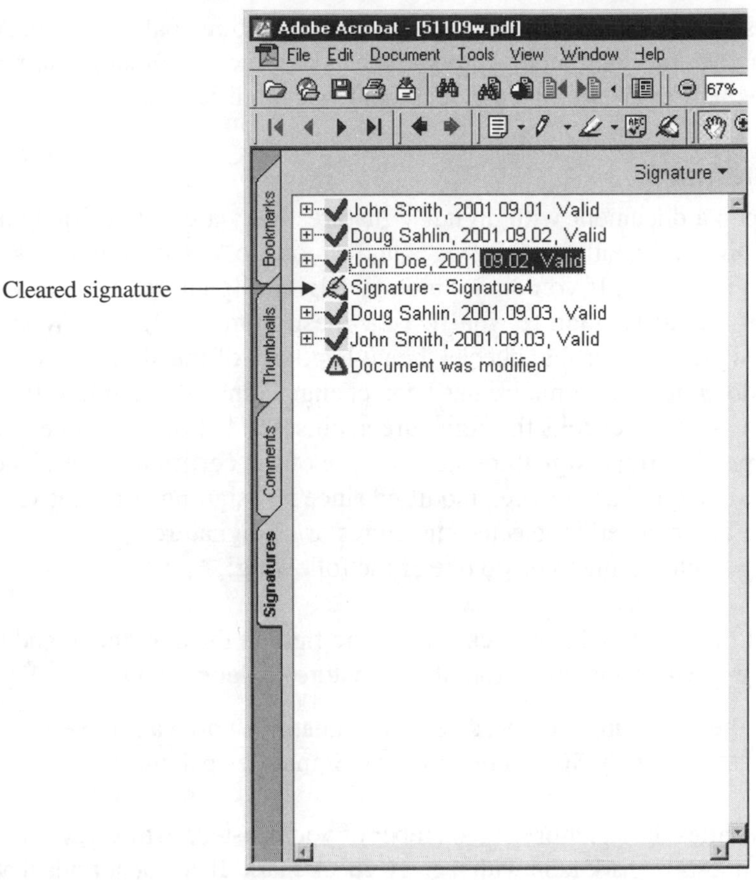

Delete Signature Fields

You can delete one or more signature fields from a document. When you delete a signature field from a document, it is no longer available for future signatures. To delete one or more signature fields from a document, follow these steps:

1. In the Navigation pane, click the Signatures tab.
2. Click the digital signature you want to delete. To add additional signatures to the selection, click them while pressing SHIFT.

3. Choose Delete Signature Field(s) from the Signatures palette menu. After you invoke the command, Acrobat deletes the selected field(s) and notes in the Signatures palette that the document was modified in.

Verify Signatures

When you open a document with digital signatures, they are not verified unless you modify Digital Signature preferences and choose to Verify Signatures when the document is opened. If you do not modify Digital Signature preferences, then to the left of each signature, you'll see a question mark (?) icon. When you verify a signature, Acrobat checks the authenticity of the signature to see whether the document or signature has been changed since the signing. If you are logged on, Acrobat checks the signature against the list of trusted certificates in your user profile. If the signature matches one of the certificates, or if the document or signature has not been modified since last signing, Acrobat verifies the signature. You can verify selected signatures or all signatures.

To verify selected signatures, do one of the following:

- Select the Hand tool and click a signature field in the document, and then choose Verify Signatures from the Signatures palette menu.
- Open the Signatures palette, select the signatures you want to verify, and then choose Verify Signatures from the Signatures palette menu.

Acrobat verifies the signature of a member of your trusted certificates list by replacing the question mark icon with a green check mark. If Acrobat finds that the document has not been modified since the signature, but does not find the signature in your trusted certificates list, Acrobat displays the dialog box as shown in the following image:

To accept the verification and continue working, click the Close button. To verify the identity, click the Verify Identity button and Acrobat opens the dialog box, as shown in the following image. If you can verify the identify of the certificate owner, or if the owner of the certificate is known to you, add the certificate to your list by clicking the Add To List button. For more information on trusted certificates, refer to the section "Exchange Certificates," later in the chapter.

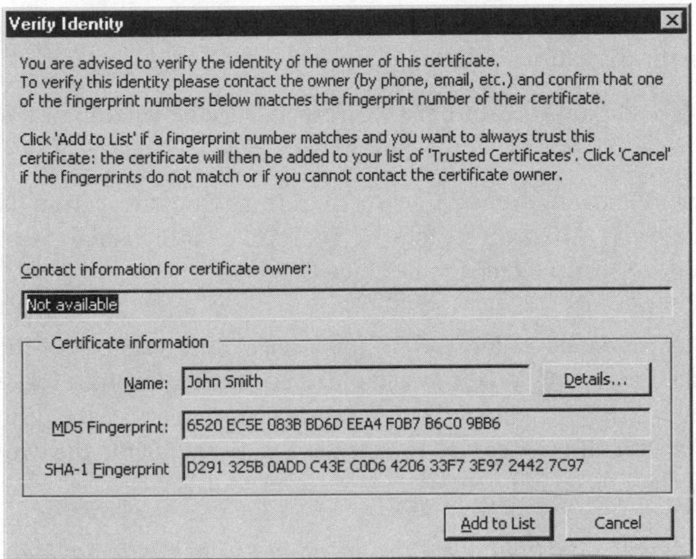

TIP *You can verify any digital signature by clicking it in the document with the Hand tool.*

View Document Version

When a document is digitally signed, Acrobat remembers the exact contents of the document at that stage of the revision process. You can use the Signatures palette or menu commands to view any version of the document, or compare a signed version of the document to the current version of the document. To view a signed version of the document, follow these steps:

1. In the Navigation pane, click the Signatures tab.
2. Click the digital signature that corresponds to the version of the document you want to view.
3. Choose View Signed Version from the Signatures palette menu. Alternatively, you can choose Tools | Digital Signatures | View Signed Version.

After you invoke this command, Acrobat re-creates a version of the document as it appeared at that stage of the revision process, and displays it in another window tiled beside the current version of the document.

You can also compare a signed version of the document to the current version of the document by following these steps:

1. Open the Signatures palette.
2. Click the digital signature that corresponds to the version of the document you want to compare to the current version.
3. Choose Compare Signed Version to Current Document from the Signatures palette menu. Alternatively, choose Tools | Digital Signatures | Compare Signed Version To Current Document.

After you execute the command, Acrobat scans both versions of the document for differences. Depending on the length of the document, this may take some time. After Acrobat finishes the comparison, it displays a summary of the differences, and displays pages with differences side by side in a manner similar to the two Versions Within A Signed Document command, discussed shortly.

TIP

To navigate to a signature field location within the document, open the Signatures palette, select the signature you want to navigate to, and then choose Go To Signature field from the Signatures palette menu. Alternatively, choose Tools | Digital Signatures | Go To Signature Field.

View Digital Signature Properties

You can learn everything you want to know about a digital signature by viewing its properties. When you view a digital signature's properties, you can verify the signature and get information about the author of the digital signature. To view the properties of a digital signature, follow these steps:

1. In the Navigation pane, click the Signatures tab to open the Signatures palette.
2. Click a digital signature to select it.
3. Choose Properties from the Signatures palette menu to open the Self-Sign Security – Signature Properties dialog box, as shown in the following image. Alternatively, you can choose Tools | Digital Signatures | Properties to open the dialog box.

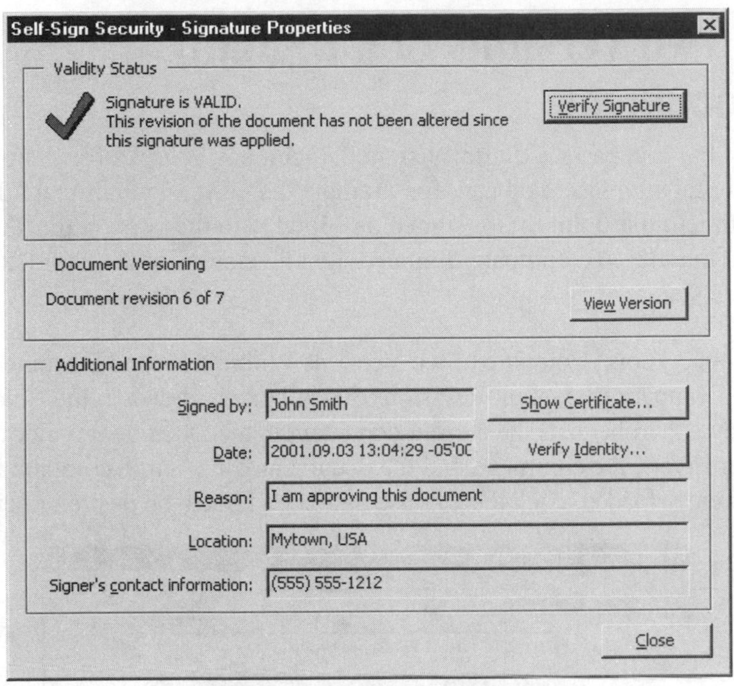

4. Once the dialog box is open, you can perform the following operations:
   - Click the Verify Signature button to verify the digital signature.
   - Click the View Version button to view the document as it appeared when the digital signature was created.
   - Click the Show Certificate button to display the Certificate Attributes dialog box. Click Close to exit the Certificate Attributes dialog box.
   - Click the Verify Identity button to open the Verify Identity dialog box. If the owner of the certificate is not on your trusted certificates list, you have the option to add it in this dialog box. After verifying the identity of the signer, close the dialog box.
5. Click Close to exit the Self-Sign Security – Signature Properties dialog box.

NOTE *To view a digital signature's properties, select the digital signature in the document and then choose Properties from the context menu.*

13

Compare Two Versions of a Digitally Signed Document

When Acrobat compares a digitally signed document, it looks for differences between digital signings. You can, for example, have Acrobat compare the version of the document that John Smith signed on Monday to the version that Jane Doe signed on Thursday. To compare digitally signed versions of the same document, follow these steps:

1. Choose Tools | Compare | Two Versions Within a Signed Document to open the Compare Document Revisions dialog box, as shown in the following image. Acrobat lists the current document in the Document window. If you ever invoke the command and the document you want to compare is not currently loaded, click the Choose button and open the desired document.

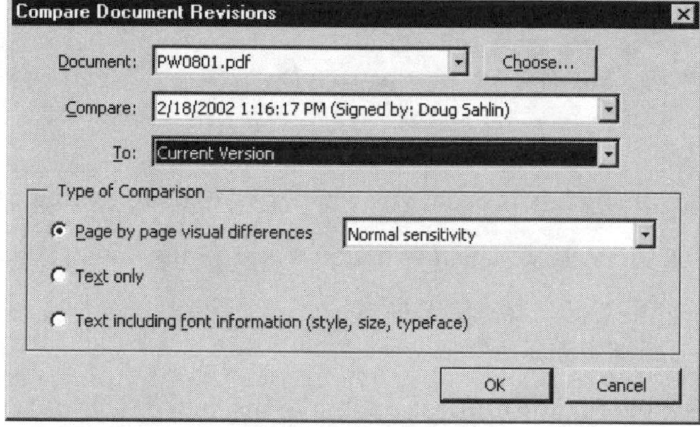

2. Click the triangle to the right of the Compare field; and, from the drop-down menu, choose the version of the document you want as the basis for your comparison. The drop-down menu lists each time the document was digitally signed, as well as the team member who signed it.
3. Click the triangle to the right of the To field, and choose the version of the document you want the other version compared to.
4. Click OK and Acrobat compares the selected version of the document.

About Acrobat Security

When you assign security to a document, you can limit user access to the document. For example, you can prohibit printing of the document and copying elements from the document. You have two versions of Acrobat Security: Acrobat Standard Security and Acrobat Self-Sign Security.

With Acrobat Standard Security, you can password-protect a document, and require a master password in order to change the document password or security settings. When you use Acrobat Standard Security, the same permissions level is granted to all recipients of the document. Acrobat Standard Security is available with 40-bit encryption for Acrobat 3.*x* or Acrobat 4.*x,* and is available with 128-bit encryption for Acrobat 5.0.

If you need to assign different levels of permission for different recipients of your document, use Acrobat Self-Sign Security. When you secure a document with Acrobat Self-Sign Security, the document can only be opened if the user's digital signature appears on your list of trusted certificates. You can assign differing levels of permission for each user on your trusted certificates list, as discussed in the upcoming section "Use Acrobat Self-Sign Security."

Use Acrobat Standard Security

When you use Acrobat Standard Security, you can assign a password to open the document. When a user tries to open a password-protected document, Acrobat prompts the user for a password. When the user enters the correct password, Acrobat opens the document. When you password-protect a document, you can assign permissions, for example, whether a viewer with Acrobat can edit the document or not. To limit access to a document with Acrobat Standard Security, follow these steps:

1. Choose File | Document Security to open the Document Security box dialog box, as shown in the following image:

2. To view current document security settings, click the Display Settings button to open the Document Security dialog box, as shown in the following image.

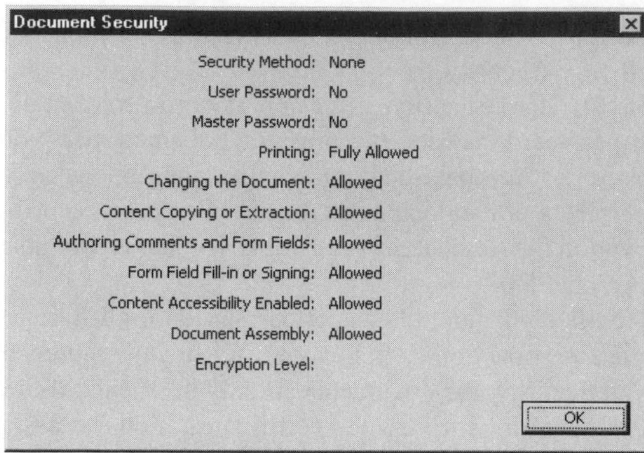

3. Click OK to return to the previous Document Security dialog box.
4. Click the triangle to the right of the Security Options field, and choose Acrobat Standard Security from the drop-down menu. Acrobat opens the Standard Security dialog box, as shown in the following image:

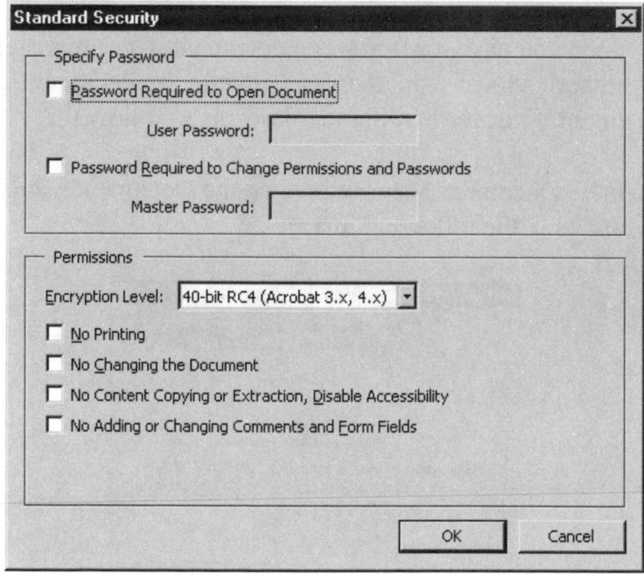

5. To assign a password to the document, choose the Password Required To Open Document option. After choosing this option, the User Password field becomes available.

6. In the User Password field, enter the password that will be required to open the document. As you type each letter of the password, an asterisk appears to prevent prying eyes from seeing the password you enter.

7. To assign a master password to the document, choose the Password Required to Change Permissions and Passwords option and the Master Password field becomes active. When you assign a master password to a document, a user with the regular document password required to open the document cannot change the document password or permissions without entering the master password.

8. In the Master Password field, enter the password that must be entered to change document passwords or permissions. As you enter text in the Master Password field, each letter appears as an asterisk. The document password and master password must be unique. For security reasons, it is a good idea to use dissimilar passwords.

TIP *To protect against being locked out of a document you created, consider copying your document passwords in a safe place, for example, your PDA (Personal Digital Assistant) if you use one.*

9. Click the triangle to the right of the Encryption field, and choose 40-bit or 128-bit encryption. Note that 128-bit encryption is only available to Acrobat 5.0 documents, PDF versions 1.4 and greater.

10. If you choose 40-bit encryption (the default), the following options become available in the Permissions section: 13

    - **No Printing** Choose this option, and users will not be able to print a hard copy of the document. If you do not choose this option, a viewer with the full version of Acrobat is able to print the file using Acrobat Distiller minus any security settings you have assigned to the document, which, in essence, creates an editable version of the original document and disables any other security measures you have assigned to the document.

    - **No Changing The Document** Choose this option, and viewers with the full version of Acrobat will not be able to modify the document.

    - **No Content Copying Or Extraction, Disable Accessibility** Choose this option, and you prevent the user from extracting graphic or text elements from the document. When you choose this option, you also block the user's access to the accessibility interface.

- **No Adding or Changing Comments and Form Fields** Choose this option, and users will not be able to edit comments attached to the document. This option also prevents a user from altering form fields; however, a user can still fill in the document form fields.

11. If you choose 128-bit encryption, the Permissions section of the Standard Security dialog box changes to reflect the following options:

    - **Enable Content Access for the Visually Impaired** This option is selected by default. If you disable this option, the document contents required to support the Accessibility feature are not available.
    - **Allow Content Copying and Extraction** This option is selected by default. When you disable this option, you prevent users from extracting or copying any of the document contents.

12. If you choose 128-bit encryption, click the triangle to the right of the Changes Allowed field, and choose one of the following options:

    - **None** Choose this option to prevent the user from making any changes to the document.
    - **Only Document Accessibility** Choose this option, and users will be permitted to insert, delete, and rotate pages, as well as be create bookmarks and thumbnails.
    - **Only Form Fields and Signing** Choose this option, and viewers of the document will be able to fill in and sign form fields, but will not be allowed to create them.
    - **Comment Authoring, Form Field Fill-in and Signing** Choose this option, and your viewers will be able to add comments to the document, as well as be able to fill in and sign the document, but not create or otherwise alter form fields.
    - **General Editing, Comment and Form Field Authoring** Choose this option, and viewers of the document will have the capability of creating comments and form fields, as well as performing minimal edits. When you enable this option, viewers of the document are not permitted to extract contents or print a hard copy of the document.

13. If you chose 128-bit encryption, click the triangle to the right of the Printing field and choose one of the following options:

    - **None allowed** When you choose this option, you prohibit the viewer from printing a hard copy of the document.

- **Low Resolution** When you choose this option, you permit the viewer to print a low-resolution copy of the document on their system printer. If the document viewer chooses Acrobat Distiller as the printing device, the resulting PDF file is also printed at low resolution, which prevents the user from pirating a high-resolution copy of the document.
- **Fully Allowed** When you choose this option, all printing options are available to the document viewer.

14. Click OK to set document security. If you password-protected the document, the Password dialog box appears, as shown in the following image:

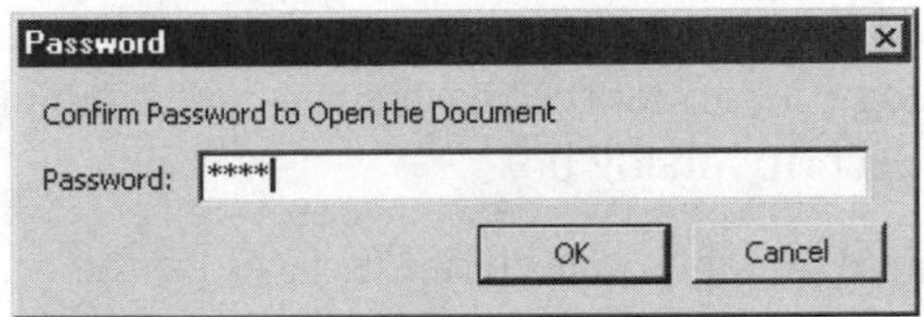

15. Confirm the document Password, and click OK. If you only assigned a user password to the document, the Standard Security dialog box closes. If you assigned a master password to the document, the Password dialog box appears again, prompting you to confirm the master password. Confirm the master password and the Standard Security dialog box closes.
16. Choose File | Save. When the document opens again, the security measures you selected are assigned to the document.

Change Standard Security Settings

When you create PDF files for a corporate environment, things change; employees come and go, people who once had access to certain information are no longer permitted to view it, and so on. When the status of personnel in your corporation changes, it's a good idea to change the security settings of confidential PDF files by following these steps:

1. Open the PDF file whose security settings you want to change.
2. Choose File | Document Security to open the Document Security dialog box. The dialog box lists the currently active Security Option, and the Change Settings button is active, as shown in the following image.

3. Click the Change Settings button.
4. If you assigned a master password to the document, Acrobat opens the Password dialog box. Enter the master password and click OK to open the Standard Security dialog box.
5. Make the desired changes and click OK to close the Standard Security dialog box and then click Close to exit the Document Security dialog box.

Use Acrobat Self-Sign Security

When you use Acrobat Self-Sign Security, you have complete control over who is permitted to open the document and who is permitted to edit the document. You can assign varying degrees of permission as well. This is useful if you create a document that will be distributed in a corporate environment. You can allow complete access to some team members, and varying degrees of access to others. For example, if the document needs to be available to a recent hire, you can disable editing, printing, and extracting elements from the document. When you assign Acrobat Self-Sign Security, you choose the users who have access to the document from your list of *trusted recipients.*

Build a List of Trusted Recipients

Before you can assign Acrobat Self-Sign Security to a document, you need to build a list of trusted recipients. Trusted recipients are Acrobat users who have sent you their *certificate*. When users create a digital signature, they have to option to export the certificate associated with their digital signature to file. You can exchange certificates with other members of your team via e-mail, as discussed in the following section.

Exchange Certificates

The first step in building a list of trusted recipients is to exchange certificates. You can import certificates received from other team members, or you can request a certificate from a recipient via e-mail. To exchange certificates via e-mail, follow these steps:

1. Choose Tools | Self-Sign Security | Log In. If you have more than one user profile, select the one you want to exchange. Follow the prompts to log in, as discussed previously in the "Log In" section of this chapter.
2. After you complete the login process, choose Tools | Self-Sign Security | User Settings to open the User Settings dialog box.
3. Click the E-mail button to e-mail your certificate to another team member. After you choose this option, Acrobat opens the E-Mail Certificate dialog box, as shown in the following image:

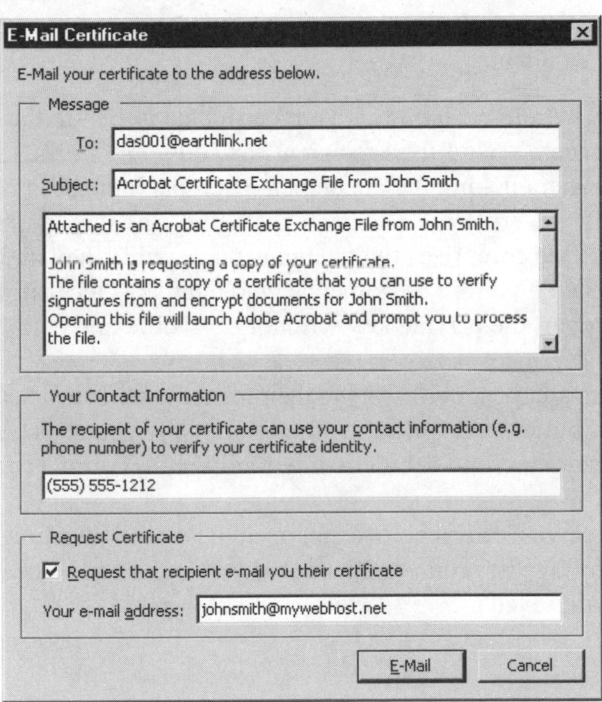

4. After Acrobat opens the E-Mail Certificate dialog box, do the following:
   - Enter the recipients e-mail address in the To field.
   - Accept the default Subject message, or delete the message and enter one of your own.
   - In the Your Contact Information field, enter information that the recipient can verify to ensure the certificate has not been altered.
   - To request a return certificate, choose the Request That Recipient E-Mail You Their Certificate option and enter your e-mail address in the Your E-mail Address field.
   - Log onto the Internet and click the E-mail button, and Acrobat launches your default e-mail application with the recipient's e-mail address filled in along with the subject and message. Use your E-mail application's Send command to send the message and certificate. When the recipient opens your e-mail, the certificate appears as an attachment.

After you click the E-mail button, your certificate is sent to the recipient as an e-mail attachment. Your e-mail recipient can add your certificate by clicking the attachment. After clicking the attachment, Acrobat launches and displays the Self-Sign Security – Certificate Exchange dialog box, as shown in Figure 13-4. Note that a certificate comprises two components, a public key and a private key. The public key can be viewed by someone who intercepts a certificate you send via e-mail. However, the private key will not be visible and cannot be reverse engineered.

Recipients can add your certificate to their trusted certificates list by clicking the Add To List button and following the prompts. If you requested a return certificate, the user can send it by clicking the E-Mail Your Certificate button shown in Figure 13-4.

When you receive a return certificate, open the e-mail attachment, as described previously, and follow the prompts. Make sure you log in under the user profile you want the certificate saved to.

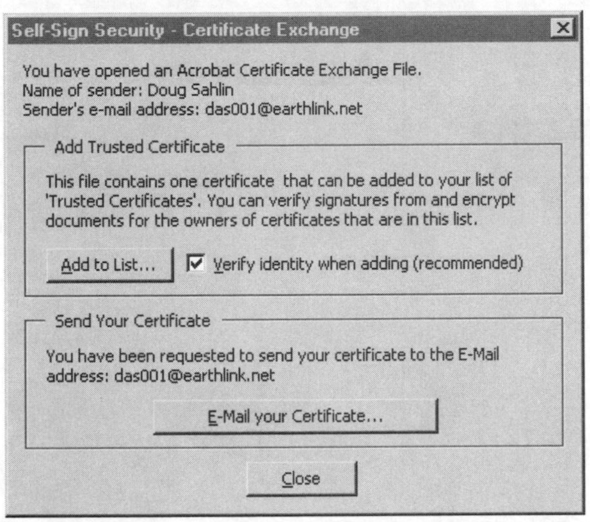

FIGURE 13-4 Use the dialog box to add a certificate to your list or e-mail your certificate to an associate.

Import a Certificate

E-mail is an efficient way to exchange certificates. The files are small and can be sent quickly with even the slowest Internet connection. However, you may receive certificates on floppy disk or other media. When you receive a certificate in this manner, you can import it. To import a certificate, follow these steps:

1. Log in using the user profile that contains the trusted certificate list to which you want to import a certificate.
2. Choose Tools | Self-Sign Security | User Settings to open the Self-Sign Security dialog box.
3. Choose the Trusted Certificates option to open the Trusted Certificates section of the dialog box, as shown in the following image. Note that in this image there is already one trusted certificate in the list.

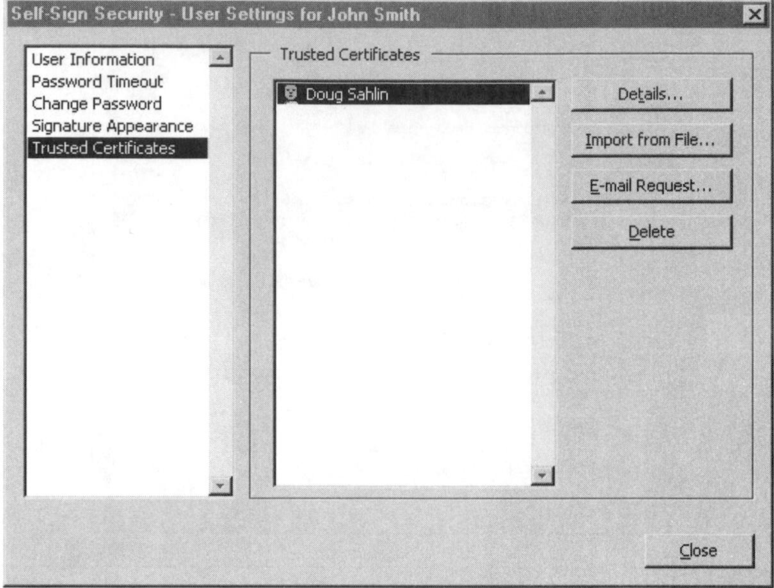

4. Click the Import from File button to open the Import Certificate dialog box. Navigate to the folder where the certificate is located.
5. Click the triangle to the right of the Files of Type field, and choose an option. If the file is an Acrobat Self-Sign Security certificate, choose Acrobat Self-Sign Key (*.fdf). If you use a third-party signature handler, choose Certificate Message Syntax – PKCS#7 (*.p7c) to import files of that type.
6. Choose the certificate file you want to import and click Open, and Acrobat opens the Verify Identity dialog box.
7. If, after viewing the information in the Verify Identity dialog box, you can successfully verify the identity of the certificate author, click Add To List, and Acrobat adds the certificate to your list of trusted certificates.

Add Self-Sign Security to a Document

After the members of your team are added to your list of trusted certificates, you can begin to secure your documents with Acrobat Self-Sign Security. When you set up Self-Sign Security, you do not have to enter passwords. Each team members' password information is stored with their own certificate. All you need to do is determine which members of your list of trusted certificates have access to the document, and the level of permissions each team member will have. To add Acrobat Self-Sign Security to a document, follow these steps:

1. Launch Acrobat.
2. Choose Tools | Self-Sign Security | Log In, and complete the login process, as discussed earlier in the section "Log In." If you have different user profiles, choose the one you want associated with this document.
3. Choose File | Document Security to open the Document Security dialog box.
4. From the Security Options drop-down menu, choose Acrobat Self-Sign Security; Acrobat displays the Self-Sign Security – Encryption Settings dialog box, as shown in the following image:

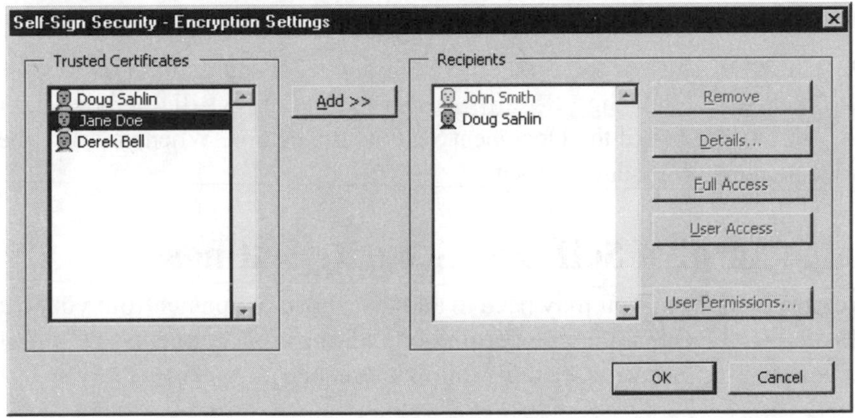

5. In the Trusted Certificates window, select the names of the users that you want to have access to the document and click the Add button; Acrobat add the names to the Recipients list.
6. In the Recipients window, click the name of a recipient. By default, the recipient has full access to the document.
7. To modify the selected recipient's access to the document, click the User Access button; then click the User Permissions button to display the User Permissions dialog box, as shown in the following image.

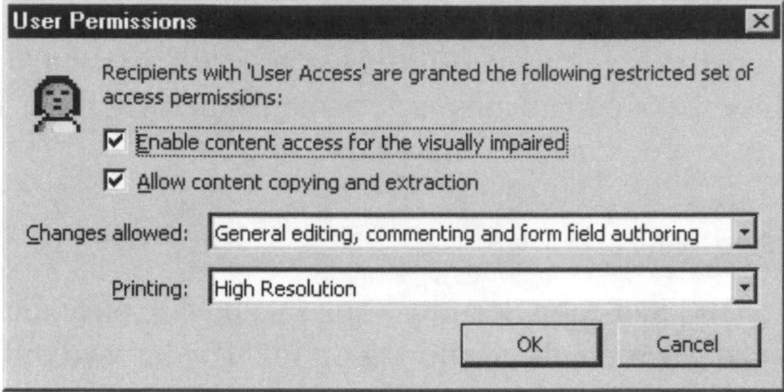

8. In the User Permissions dialog box, modify the parameters for the selected recipients. These options are the same as Acrobat Standard Security, as discussed previously in the section "Use Acrobat Standard Security."
9. Repeat steps 7 and 8 for the other recipients on your list. Remember, you can assign different permissions for each user, which is what makes Acrobat Self-Sign Security such a powerful tool.
10. Click OK to close the the User Permissions Setting dialog box, click OK to close the Self-Sign Security – Encryption Settings dialog box, and then click Close to exit the Document Security dialog box. When you save the document, the security is set.

Change Acrobat Self-Sign Security Settings

As your team changes, you may need to add or remove recipients from your trusted certificate list, as well as change permissions settings for recipients. To modify Acrobat Self-Sign Security settings, follow these steps:

1. If you have not already done so, log in under the user profile that you encrypted the document with.
2. Open the document whose security settings you want to change.
3. Choose File | Document Security to open the Document Security dialog box.
4. Click the Change Settings button to open the Self-Sign Security – Encryption Settings dialog box. Alternatively, you can click the Display Settings button to review the settings currently applied to the document.

5. In the Recipients window, click the name of the recipient whose permissions you want to modify, and do one or more of the following:
   - Click the Remove button to remove the recipient from the list.
   - Click the Details button to review the recipient's certificate.
   - Click the User Access button to modify the recipient's permissions. After you choose this option, you can click the Full Access button to give the user complete access to the document, or you can click the User Permissions button to open the User Permissions dialog box and modify the recipient's level of access.
6. Repeat step 5 for other recipients whose settings you need to modify, or click OK to exit the User Permissions dialog box.
7. Click OK to exit the Self-Sign Security – Encryption Settings dialog box, and then click Close to close the Document Security dialog box. Save the document, and the new security settings are in effect the next time the document opens.

Set Self-Sign Security Preferences

If you use a third-party signature handler, you may have to modify Self-Sign Security preferences in order to create a signature compatible with the signature handler. To modify Self-Sign Security preferences, follow these steps:

1. Choose Edit | Preferences | General to open the General Preferences dialog box.
2. Choose Self-Sign Security from the menu in the left window.
3. Choose one or both of the following options:
   - **Use Certificate Message Syntax (PKCS#7 format) Signature** If you choose this option, Acrobat creates a larger signature file, which may be necessary with certain third-party signature handlers.
   - **Ignore certificate expiration dates when verifying signatures** If you choose this option, Acrobat will verify signatures whose certificates have expired, but may be otherwise valid.

Part IV

Distribute PDF Documents

Chapter 14

Optimize PDF Documents

How To…

- Optimize documents for the visually impaired
- Optimize documents for print
- Optimize documents for CD-ROM applications
- Optimize documents for the Web
- Customize Acrobat Distiller Job Options

When you create a PDF document, you can optimize it for a specific or for several destinations. If you create a document in an authoring application and (if available) use the PDF export feature of the application, or use Acrobat Distiller to print the file, you can modify the output settings for an intended destination. You modify output settings by changing the Job Options. When you change Job Options, you can specify how Acrobat Distiller compresses the images in your document and how it adjusts color settings for the intended destination of the document, and specify whether or not fonts are embedded.

In previous chapters, you learned to use preset Job Options to convert documents into PDF format. In this chapter, you'll learn to fine-tune Job Options to suit the intended destination of the document. Fonts are an important consideration when you create a PDF document. In this chapter, font considerations will be discussed as well as when it is necessary to embed fonts. You'll learn specific strategies for optimizing your documents for an intended destination. You'll also learn how to create a document that can be reflowed for easier reading in devices with different monitor sizes, and how to modify a document for the visually impaired.

About Tagged Documents

When you create a document that will be distributed to users who view the document on devices with a limited viewing area, you can create a tagged document that can be reflowed to any window size. When a user reflows a document, the font size stays unchanged; so it is legible, even on a smaller viewing device. Images, however, reduce in size to accommodate reduced viewing area. If your tagged PDF document will be viewed on devices such as a PalmPilot, or some of the smaller eBook readers,

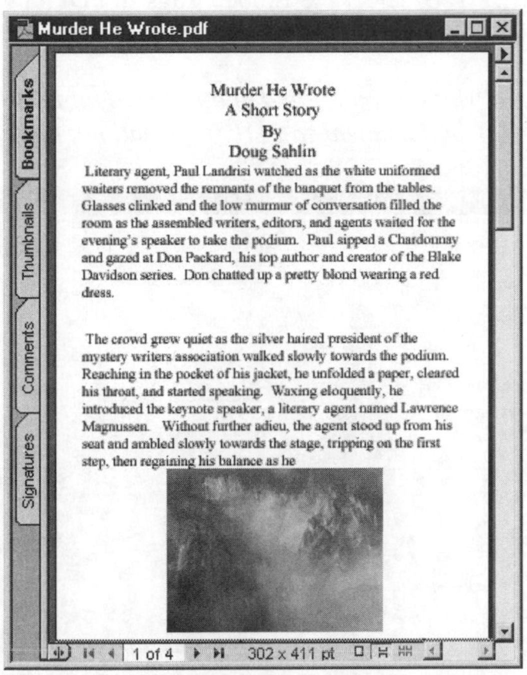

FIGURE 14-1 You can reflow a tagged document to make it easily readable on a device with a smaller viewing area.

viewers can reflow the document to fit the smaller viewing area. Figure 14-1 shows an example of a tagged document that has been reflowed to accommodate a smaller viewing area.

14

Create a Tagged Document

You can create a tagged document by converting web pages to PDF format or by creating a document within a Microsoft Office 2000 application, and then use PDFMaker to convert the document to PDF.

To create a tagged document in a Microsoft Office application, follow these steps:

1. Create a document in a Microsoft 2000 Office application.
2. Within the Office application, Choose Acrobat | Change Conversion Settings.

3. Click the Office Tab, select the Embed Tags In PDF option, and deselect the Page Labels option, as shown in the next illustration:

If you use the Print command and choose Acrobat Distiller to convert a Microsoft Office document to PDF, tags will not be created.

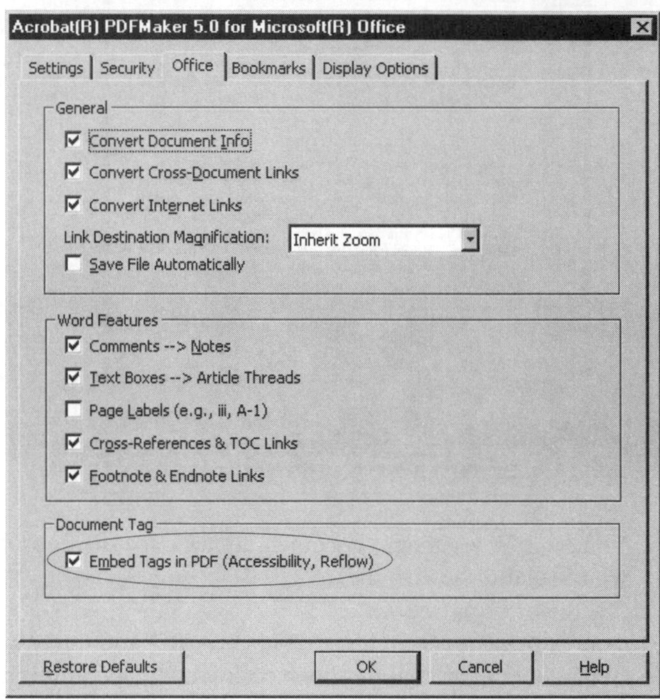

4. Click the Convert to PDF icon and PDFMaker (which is actually Acrobat Distiller working within the auspices of a Microsoft application) embeds the necessary tags to enable reflow of the document. For more information on converting documents to PDF format from within a Microsoft Office application, refer to Chapter 5.

To create a tagged document from HTML pages, follow these steps:

1. Choose File | Open Web Page.
2. In the URL field, enter the URL of the page you want to convert to a tagged document. Remember, you can also capture an HTML document located on your computer by entering the relative path to the file.
3. Click the Conversion Settings button to open the Conversion Settings dialog box.
4. Choose the Add PDF Tags option and then click OK to close the dialog box.
5. Click Download, and Acrobat captures the web page with PDF tags. For more information on converting web pages to PDF documents, refer to Chapter 6.

Reflow a Tagged Document

The recipients of a tagged document can reflow the document to fit the viewing area of the device they use to view the document. Tagged PDF files are optimized for accessibility, making them available to viewers using screen-reader devices. To reflow a document, click the Reflow button, as shown in the following illustration, or choose View | Reflow.

NOTE *If you are distributing a tagged PDF document to users who are not intimately familiar with Acrobat or Acrobat Reader, consider including a readme file or some sort of instruction on how to reflow the tagged document to accommodate a smaller viewing area.*

Use the TouchUp Order Tool

When you create a tagged document, it may not reflow as you expect it to. If this occurs, you can change the order in which elements reflow using the TouchUp Order tool. For example, if an image appears in the center of a paragraph, you can move it below the paragraph for the reflowed version of the document. To change the order in which elements appear in a reflowed document, follow these steps:

1. Navigate to the document page that contains the elements you want to modify the order of.

2. Select the TouchUp Order tool, as shown at left.

   After you select the TouchUp Order tool, Acrobat numbers the tagged elements in their current order, as shown in the following image:

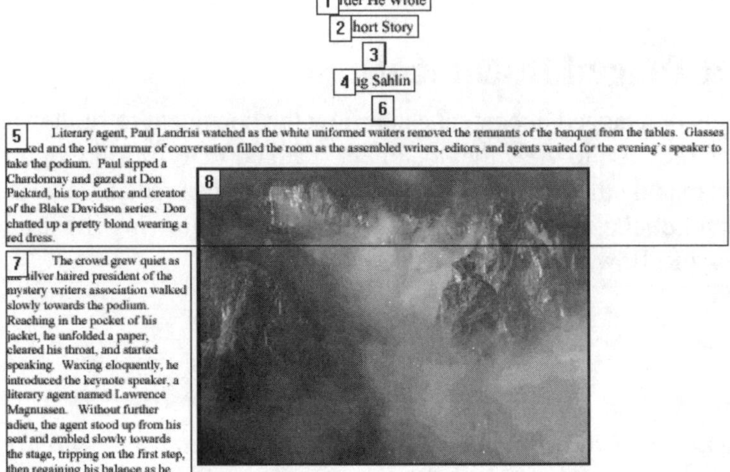

3. Click inside the boxes to change the reflow order. The first item you click becomes the first item in the reflow order, the second item you click becomes the second item in the reflow order, and so on. If you make a mistake, select another tool, and then reselect the TouchUp Order tool and begin anew. Alternatively, you can hold your cursor over the element whose order you

want to change, right-click (Windows) or CTRL-click (Macintosh), and then choose an option from the context menu, as shown in the following image:

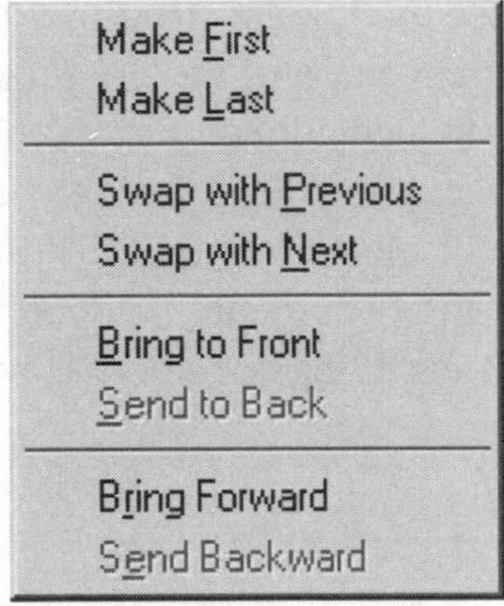

4. Save the document.

The next time you open the document, each element appears as it was created in the authoring application. When you click the Reflow button, the elements display as you reordered them with the TouchUp Order tool.

Optimize Documents for the Visually Impaired

When you create a document that will be used by visually impaired people using onscreen readers, a different challenge presents itself to you—the document will be viewed at varying degrees of magnification. Creating a tagged document will eliminate the problem of reflowing the document, but there is still the issue of images in the document. When a document is greatly magnified, only a portion of the image will be rendered. In order to offset this difficulty, you must provide a way for visually impaired readers to identify what the image is. To accomplish this, provide alternative text for tagged, nontext elements in the document using the Tags palette.

Use the Tags Palette

You use the Tags palette to view the logical order of a tagged document. When you open the Tags palette, you'll see the logical structure of the document, which is a visual representation of the organization of the document elements. You can use the Tags palette to modify tags in a document. For example, many onscreen readers can take advantage of alternate text for a tagged element. The alternate text tells the visually impaired person what the element is about. You can also use tag information to specify the text language of the document. To open the Tags palette shown in Figure 14-2, choose Window | Tags. If the document is not tagged, No Tags Available displays at the top of the palette.

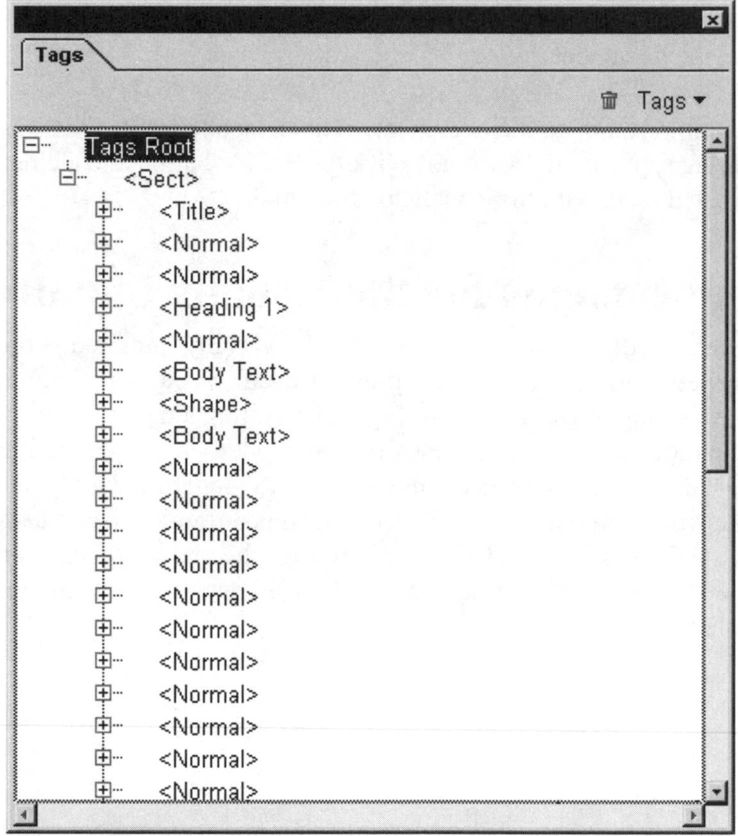

FIGURE 14-2 You use the Tags palette to view the logical structure of a document.

TIP *If you work frequently with tagged documents, you may find it beneficial to add the Tags palette to the Navigation pane. To do so, choose Window | Tags. After the Tags palette opens, drag-and-drop it into the Navigation pane.*

If the document you create will be viewed with onscreen reading devices that have limited graphics capabilities, you can add an alternate tag that describes what the image is about. To add an alternate tag to a nontext element, follow these steps:

1. Open the Tags palette, as previously outlined.
2. Select the tag that denotes the image in the PDF document. If you have a hard time determining which tag is associated with which element in the text, click the Tags icon in the upper-right corner of the palette and choose Turn On Associated Highlighting. When you enable this option, Acrobat highlights the element in the document when you select the corresponding tag.
3. Click the Tags icon and choose Element Properties from the Tags palette menu to open the Element Properties dialog box, as shown in Figure 14-3. Alternatively, you can right-click (Windows) or CTRL-click (Macintosh), and choose Element Properties from the context menu.

NOTE *If you use the Turn On Associated Highlighting command to locate elements in the document, Turn Off Associated Highlighting is the only available menu command. Choose it to turn off highlighting, click the Tags icon again, and all menu commands are available.*

4. In the Alternate Text field, enter a description of the image. For example, if the image depicts the Eiffel Tower you might enter **This image is an illustration of the Eiffel Tower.**
5. Click OK to assign the alternate text to the tag.

14

Current screen readers are designed to read the document in only one language. However, in the future, it is anticipated that screen readers may be able to change languages on-the-fly. In order to benefit from this anticipated technology, you will need to specify the language of the document. To specify the language of the document, follow these steps:

1. Open the Tags palette, as previously outlined.
2. Choose the first tag after the Tags Root listing.

3. Click the Tags icon near the upper-right corner of the palette, and choose Element Properties from the Tags palette menu to open the dialog box shown in Figure 14-3.
4. Click the triangle to the right of the Language field; and from the drop-down menu, choose the language the document is written in.
5. Click OK to apply the change.

Check a Document for Accessibility

After you have modified document tags, you can test the document for accessibility. When you test a document for accessibility, Acrobat informs you of any elements in your document that may deter a visually impaired person's ability to access the

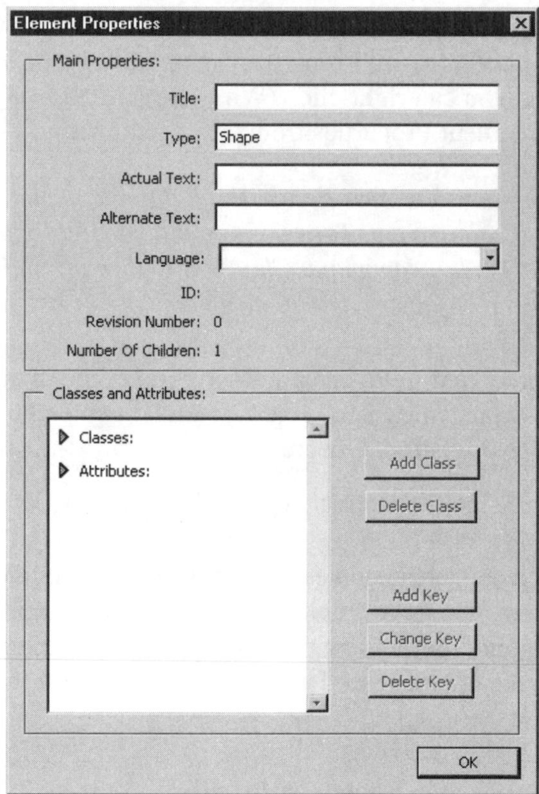

FIGURE 14-3 In a tagged document, you can provide alternate text for a selected image by modifying image Element Properties.

document with an onscreen reader. If Acrobat finds any deterrents to accessibility, you can modify the necessary tags, as discussed previously. To check a document for accessibility, follow these steps:

1. Open the tagged document you want to check.
2. Choose Tools | Accessibility Checker to open the Accessibility Check Options dialog box, as shown in the following image:

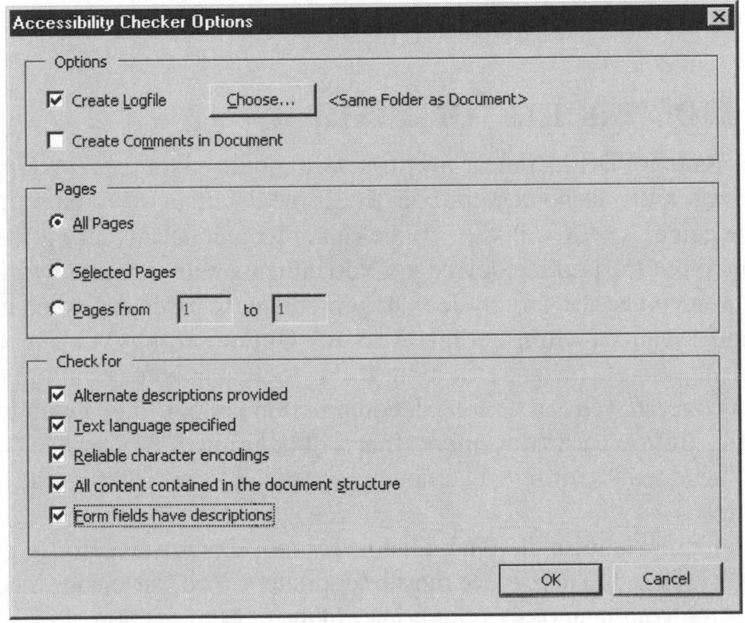

3. In the Options section, choose one or both of the following options:
   - **Create Logfile** When you choose this option, Acrobat creates a text file that lists the problem areas in the document. When you choose this option, you can specify which folder Acrobat saves the file in by clicking the Choose button. By default, Acrobat creates the file in the same folder as the document.
   - **Create Comments In Document** When you choose this option, Acrobat highlights the problem areas in the document and creates a note that describes what will occur if the problem is not rectified.
4. In the Pages section, choose the pages you want Acrobat to check.

5. In the Check For section, choose which accessibility issues you want Acrobat to check for. By default, all options are selected.
6. Click OK and Acrobat checks the document for accessibility issues.

The Accessibility Checker finds any shortcomings that may interfere with a visually impaired person's ability to view the document with an onscreen reader. However, if available, it is highly recommended that you test the document with an onscreen reader. This will give you a visual representation of how your document will appear in an onscreen reader.

Optimize Documents for Print

When you create a PDF document for print, you modify the Press Job Option settings to match the intended output device. If the document is to be printed by a service center, check with the service center technicians to get the necessary information about the printing device your documents will be printed with. This is the information you need to modify Job Option settings, in particular, when modifying the color and advanced settings of the Press Job Option settings. You should also pay careful attention to image resolution. If the document is for print only and file size is not a concern, you can disable all compression options to maintain maximum image quality. If you create documents that will be printed by a service center, or on a printer attached to a different computer, embed all fonts to ensure the document prints properly.

The default resolution of 2,400 dpi is fine for most commercial printing devices; however, it is higher than needed for most laser printers. You can change the resolution setting to match your laser or DeskJet printer in the General section of the Press Job Options dialog box. Modifying Job Options is discussed in detail in the upcoming "Customize Distiller Job Options" section of this chapter. Alternatively you can also choose the Print Job Option as the basis for documents you print in-house on laser or DeskJet-type printers.

Optimize Documents for CD-ROM Applications

When you optimize a document for a CD-ROM application, use the Print job option as a starting point. This option has compression settings with higher resolutions than those generally needed for screen viewing; but when you create a CD-ROM, file size is generally not an issue. If you stick with the higher resolution settings, your viewers will be able to zoom in on document images with little or no loss in quality. In fact, you may want to use the Maximum quality setting and increase the resolution if your CD-ROM presentation has many intricate images, such as maps that beg to be examined at higher magnification settings. You can also disable the Compress Text And Line Art option to produce a document with better detail.

Optimize Documents for the Web

When you optimize documents for viewing over the Internet, begin with the Screen Job Option. The default settings of this Job Option resample document images to 72 dpi. The resulting file is a compromise between file size and image quality. You can decrease the size of the file if you modify the settings in the Compression section of the Screen Job Option dialog box. Experiment with the Low and Minimum settings. If the images in the original document were high quality, you may be able to produce an acceptable document using the Low or Minimum compression settings. You can create a document using the default Screen job option, and then create another document using the Screen job option with modified compression settings. Compare the two documents in Acrobat arranged in tile format and you will be able to see the difference in image quality between the different compression settings.

Enable the Optimize for Fast Web View option and the document will be optimized for *byteserving* (sending a document to a web browser a page at a time) over the Web. A document optimized for fast web viewing downloads a page at a time if the web hosting service supports byteserving. After you convert the document to PDF, open the file in Acrobat, use the PDF Consultant to optimize the file and remove any unused elements, and then save the file. For more information on PDF Consultant, refer to the "Optimize the eBook with the PDF Consultant" section in Chapter 8.

Customize Distiller Job Options

When you create a document for a specific destination using Acrobat Distiller or PDFMaker, you can use one of the preset Job Options in Distiller to convert the file. You can also customize the conversion Job Option by modifying the parameters to suit your needs. When you modify a Job Option, you begin with a preset Job Option, apply the needed changes, and then save the Job Option with a different name. After you save the modified Job Option, it appears on the Job Options menu in Acrobat Distiller, and the Conversion Settings menu in Microsoft Office applications.

Each Job Option is comprised of five tabbed sections. You can modify as many or as few sections as needed to create the optimal conversion for your document(s). To create a custom Job Option in Distiller, follow these steps:

1. Click the triangle to the right of the Job Options field and choose a Job Option from the drop-down menu.
2. Choose Settings | Job Options to open the Job Options dialog box, as shown in Figure 14-4. Note that the dialog box in Figure 14-4 is Print–Job Options. The title of the dialog box changes depending on the Job Option you are modifying; for example if you modify eBook Job Options, the dialog box title reads eBook–Job Options.

When you modify a Job Option from within a Microsoft Office application, you are modifying an Acrobat Distiller Job Option. Job Options created in Acrobat Distiller can be used to convert a document to PDF in a Microsoft Office application and vice versa. To modify a Job Option from within a Microsoft Office application, follow these steps:

1. Choose Acrobat | Change Conversion Settings.
2. Click the triangle to the right of the Conversion Settings field; and from the drop-down menu, choose a Job Option to modify.
3. Click the Conversion Settings button to open the Job Options dialog box, as shown in Figure 14-4.

After you open the Job Options dialog box, modify the Job Options by making changes in each section. To access the settings in each section, click the section tab. In following sections of this chapter, Job Options you can modify will be discussed in detail.

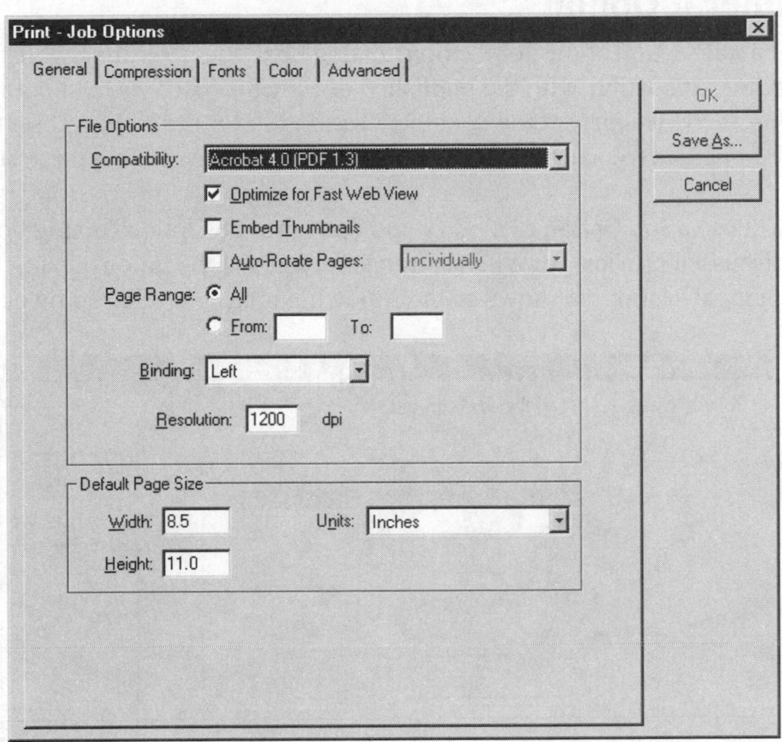

FIGURE 14-4 Modify Job Option conversion settings within this dialog box.

NOTE *Acrobat Distiller defaults to the last Job Option used. Before converting a document to PDF with Acrobat Distiller or using Acrobat Distiller as a printing device, using PDFMaker in a Microsoft Office application, choose the desired Job Option from the Job Options or Conversion Settings menu.*

Set General Options

In the General section of the Job Options dialog box, you determine which version of Acrobat is compatible with the published document. Also, you can optimize the file for fast web viewing, set the document resolution for printing, and set the page size of the published document. To set General job options, follow these steps:

1. Choose a Job Option to modify and open the Job Options dialog box, as discussed previously. When Acrobat opens the Job Options dialog box, the General section, as shown in the following image, is selected by default.

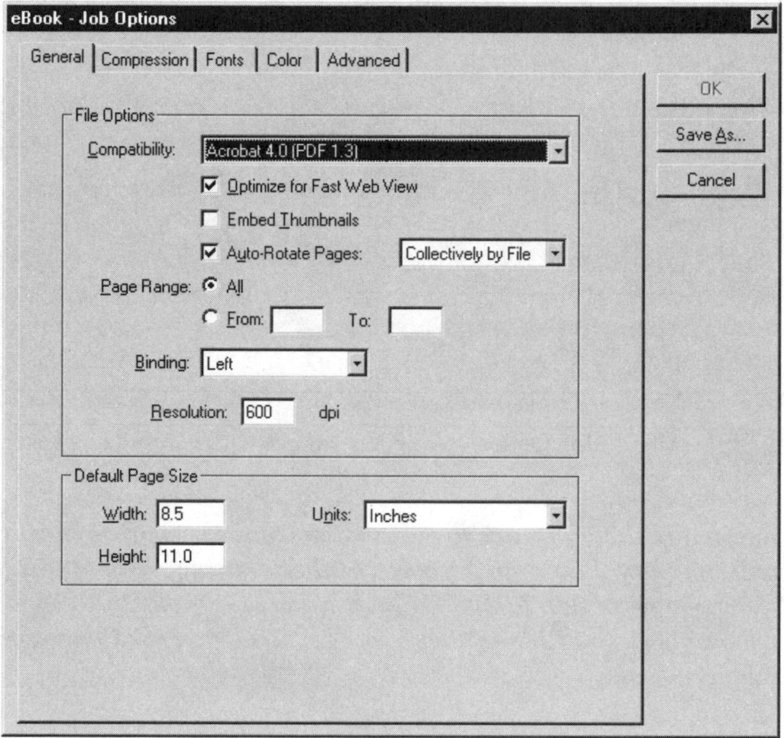

2. In the File Options section, click the triangle to the right of the Compatibility field; and from the drop-down menu, choose the version of Acrobat that you want the published document to be compatible with. You can choose

from Acrobat 3.0, Acrobat 4.0, or Acrobat 5.0. Choose the version of Acrobat that supports the features in the document you have created. Remember to take into account which version of Acrobat the majority of your target audience is likely to have.

3. After you choose the version of Acrobat that documents created with this Job Option will be compatible with, you can modify the following settings:

   - **Optimize for Fast Web View** Choose this option if you create a document to view over the Internet. When you choose this option, Acrobat converts documents created with this job option for page-at-a-time downloading (byteserving) from the host web server. When you choose this option, Acrobat compresses text and line art, regardless of the settings you choose in the Compression section. Choose this option and the document will download quicker from the web server. Note that this option produces a slight degradation of image quality due to the compression used.

   - **Embed Thumbnails** Choose this option, and Acrobat Distiller creates a thumbnail for each page of documents converted to PDF with this Job Option. Remember that this will increase the file size of the published document. If you choose not to select this option, Acrobat automatically generates thumbnails on-the-fly when the document viewer opens the Thumbnails palette.

   - **Auto-Rotate Pages** Choose this option, and Acrobat automatically rotates document pages when the page should be rotated for viewing without scrolling. You can choose Individually to rotate each page based on the page orientation, or Collectively to rotate all pages based on the majority orientation of pages within the document.

   - **Page Range** Choose this option to have Acrobat convert all pages within a document to PDF, or specify a range of pages by entering the first page to convert in the From field and the last page to convert in the To field.

   - **Binding** Choose either Left or Right binding to determine how Acrobat displays the document in Continuous-Facing viewing mode, and how thumbnails are displayed when viewed side by side.

- **Resolution** Enter a value that matches the resolution of the device the document will be printed on. When you create a PDF file with Acrobat Distiller, or Acrobat Distiller in the guise of PDFMaker, the device is actually printing a PostScript file for display in PDF format. The value you enter for resolution emulates the resolution setting of a printing device. If you choose a higher resolution, recipients of your document can print the file on a high resolution device, but the file size will be larger.

4. In the Default Page Size section, enter values in the Width and Height fields, and then choose a unit of measure. The settings you enter here determine the dimensions of the files Acrobat creates with this Job Option. Enter dimensions that match the sizes of documents you create in the authoring application, which you use as the basis for PDF files created with this Job Option. Remember that if you use PDFMaker to convert a Microsoft Office file to PDF format, you must configure Distiller to match the page dimensions specified in the Job Options setting, otherwise, PDFMaker (which is actually using Acrobat Distiller to print the PDF file) reverts to the default dimensions for Acrobat Distiller. For more information on configuring Acrobat Distiller page size, refer to the "Create a PDF File Using an Application's Print Command" in Chapter 5.

After you modify the General settings of the Job Option, you can click a tab to modify other settings, or save the Job Option as described in the section "Save Job Options," later in the chapter.

Job Option Compression Options

When you choose a specific Job Option to create a PDF document, Acrobat compresses the document text, line art, and images using settings deemed optimal for the Job Option. You can, however, modify the compression settings to suit documents you create for specific applications. You can modify the settings to reduce file size or enhance the quality of the published document. With a bit of experimentation, you can modify compression settings for optimal file size while still maintaining a high level of detail in the published document.

Acrobat Distiller Compression Methods

The compression method you choose will greatly affect the overall quality of the images in your published document. When you modify compression settings, you can have Acrobat Distiller automatically choose the compression method deemed right for the images in the document, or you can choose one of following Acrobat Distiller compression methods:

- **ZIP** Use the ZIP (Adobe's variation of the ZIP filter, as derived from the zlib package of Jean-loup Gailly and Mark Adler) method of compression on images with large areas of solid color, such as GIF images. This method of compression works well with simple images created in painting applications such as Windows Paintbrush or Corel Painter. It also works quite well with artwork created in vector-based drawing programs, such as Adobe Illustrator. If the vector images in your document contain complex gradients, choose the JPEG compression method. You can use ZIP compression with 4-bit and 8-bit color depth. If you choose 4-bit color depth on an 8-bit image, you end up with a smaller file size but degrade image quality, as you lose data when the image compresses.
- **JPEG** Use the JPEG (Joint Photographic Experts Group) method of compression on full-color or grayscale images, such as photographs. When you use JPEG compression, you can control the size of the file by telling Acrobat how much compression to apply to the images. You can modify the settings to create a PDF document with high-quality images at the expense of a larger file size, or you can apply a higher level of compression and your published PDF file will be smaller—however, the images will not be as detailed due to the data lost during compression. JPEG compression is also known as *lossy* compression because data is lost when the document images are compressed. Acrobat Distiller has five JPEG compression options. The following graphic shows an image with each compression option applied. The converted PDF documents in the image are magnified to 300% and displayed as tiles in Acrobat. Notice the visible differences in detail around the driver's helmet and the mirrors from Minimum to Maximum. JPEG

compression is best suited for photographs. If you have images with large areas of solid color—such as GIF images—in your document, use ZIP compression.

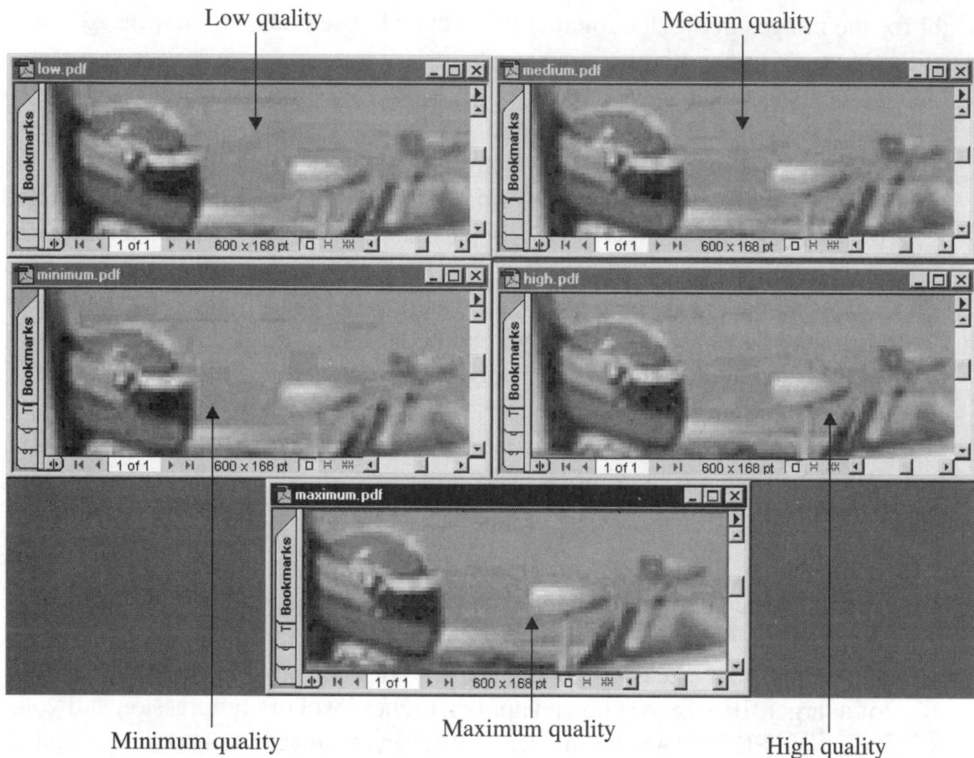

- **CCITT** Use the CCITT (Consultative Committee for International Telephone & Telegraph) method of compression for 1-bit black-and-white images, such as faxes. When you use the CCITT method of compression, no data is lost. Use the CCITT Group 4 method for general-purpose compression of monochrome images; use the CCITT Group 3 method for faxed documents.
- **Run Length** Use this option when your document contains images with large areas of solid black or white. Run Length is a loss-less compression method.

Acrobat Distiller Resampling

When Acrobat Distiller compresses images, it also resamples them. When an image resamples, pixels are either added or removed from the image to change the resolution (pixels per inch, or ppi) the image displays at. When pixels are added to an image to increase resolution, image degradation generally occurs as you ask the software to interpolate between neighboring pixels in order to create new pixels. It is always best to start out with a high-resolution image and then downsample the image when converting it to PDF. You can use specify one of the following interpolation methods to resample images:

- **Average Downsampling** Choose this method and Acrobat Distiller creates new pixels at the specified resolution using the average color of *neighboring* pixels within a given area.
- **Bicubic Downsampling** Use this interpolation method to yield the highest quality images. When you specify bicubic downsampling, Acrobat Distiller creates new pixels at the specified resolution using a weighted average to determine pixel color. In other words, the resultant color is weighted toward the dominant color in each *area* Acrobat Distiller samples. This is the slowest method, yet will give you the best results.
- **Subsampling** Choose this method of interpolation, and Acrobat Distiller creates new pixels at the specified resolution using the color of a pixel in the *center* of the sampled area. Because this method of interpolation uses a single pixel to create new pixels, Subsampling is the quickest interpolation method. Yet, this method of interpolation can lead to images with harsh transitions between adjacent pixels.

Set Compression Settings

Each Job Option has a specific set of compression options that you can modify for documents you create. You modify compression settings to determine the quality of the text, line art, and images in the published PDF document. To modify Job Option Compression settings, follow these steps:

1. Choose a Job Option to modify; and open the Job Options dialog box, as discussed previously.

2. Click the Compression tab to open the Job Options Compression section, as shown in the following image:

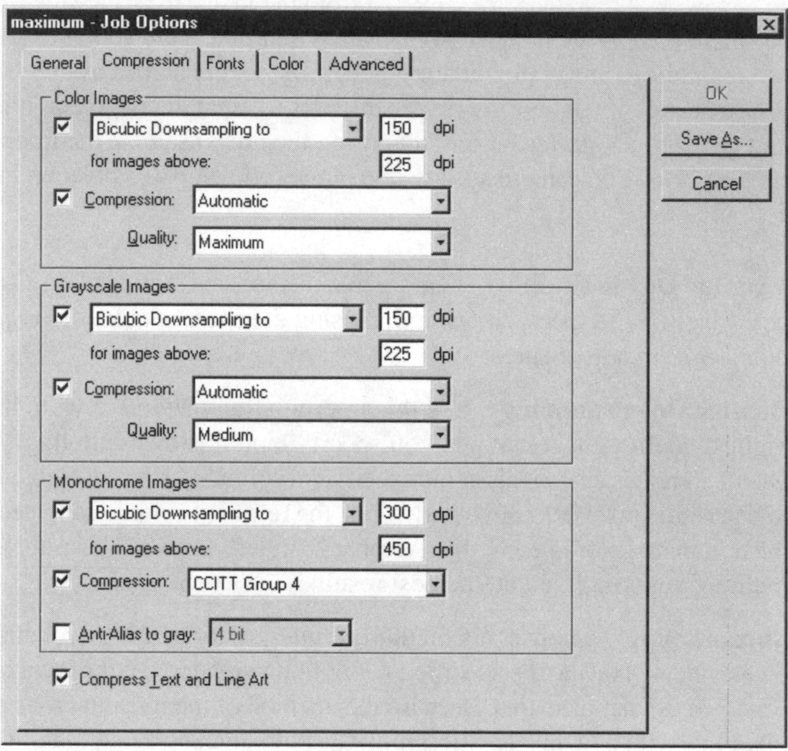

3. In the Color and Grayscale Images sections, choose an interpolation method for downsampling images in the document (the first check box and field in each section). This option is selected by default. Deselect the option and Acrobat Distiller does not downsample images in the document.

4. In the Color and Grayscale Images sections, choose a compression method. By default, Acrobat Distiller compresses and automatically chooses the compression option it deems best for the color and grayscale images in the document. You can deselect the compression option, and Acrobat Distiller converts the file to PDF without compressing it. To choose a compression method other than Automatic, click the triangle to the right of the Compression field and choose the desired method from the drop-down menu.

5. In the Color and Grayscale Images sections, to the right of the interpolation method, enter the dpi value to which you want Acrobat Distiller to downsample color and grayscale images to.

6. In the Color and Grayscale Images sections, enter a value in the For Images Above fields. When you use this job option, Acrobat Distiller downsamples all images above the resolution you enter in this field to the lower output resolution you entered in step 5.

7. In the Color and Grayscale Images sections, click the triangle to the right of the Quality field and choose an option from the drop-down menu. By default, Acrobat Distiller compresses images to Medium quality. Choose High or Maximum to create a better-looking document with a larger file size, or choose Minimum or Low to create a PDF document with a smaller file size and less detailed images.

8. In the Monochrome Images section, choose an interpolation method for downsampling black-and-white images in the document. This option is selected by default. Deselect the option and Acrobat Distiller does not downsample images in the document.

9. In the field to the right of the Interpolation field, enter the dpi value to which you want Acrobat Distiller to downsample monochrome images.

10. In the For Images Above field, enter the value above which you want Acrobat Distiller to downsample images to the value entered in step 9.

NOTE *If a PDF document converted with applied downsampling does not properly display black-and-white images, modify the Job Option and deselect the Monochrome downsampling option.*

11. Click the triangle to the right of the Compression field, and choose an option from the drop-down menu.

12. Choose the Anti-Alias To Gray option, and Acrobat Distiller smoothes the edges of objects in monochrome images. Choosing this option may cause thin lines or small text to blur. If you select this option, click the triangle to the right of the adjacent field and choose 2-bit, 4-bit, or 8-bit. This option determines how many levels of gray are used to smooth the image. Choose 8-bit (256 levels of gray) for the best results.

13. Choose the Compress Text and Line Art option (selected by default), and Acrobat Distiller applies ZIP compression to all text and line art in documents converted to PDF with this Job Option.

Set Fonts Options

When you want to ensure that a document appears exactly as you created it, you embed the font set with the document. When you embed fonts with a document, the document will display and print correctly, even if the user's computer does not have the font installed. Acrobat Distiller can embed Roman Type 1 fonts and True Type fonts. Specify which fonts to embed when you convert documents to PDFs by modifying the Job Option Font settings as follows:

1. Choose a Job Option to modify and open the Job Options dialog box, as discussed previously.
2. Click the Fonts tab to reveal the Fonts section of the Job Options dialog box, as shown in the following image:

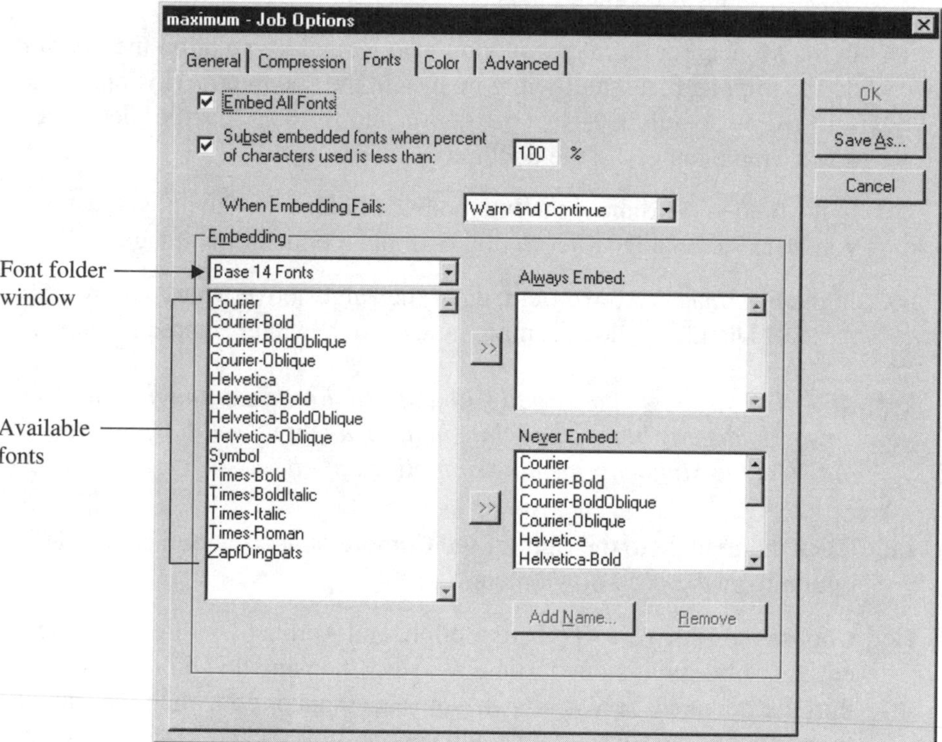

3. Enable the Embed All Fonts option to embed all fonts used to create the document.
4. Enable the Subset Embedded Fonts When Percent Of Characters Used Is Less Than option and enter a percentage value. When you choose this

option, Acrobat Distiller embeds only the characters used to create the document when the percentage of characters used from the font set falls below the value you specify. For example, if you enter a value of 60, Acrobat Distiller embeds only characters used to create the document when less than 60% of the font set is used.

5. Click the triangle to the right of the When Embedding Fails field, and from the drop-down menu; choose one of the following: Ignore, Warn And Continue, or Cancel Job.

6. If you always want to embed a certain font set with documents created using this Job Option, select the font(s) from the left window and click the right-pointing double-arrow to the left of the Always Embed window to add the fonts to the Always Embed list. To remove a font from the Always Embed list, select the font from the Always Embed list and click the Remove button. Licensing issues prohibit you from embedding certain fonts in a document. If a licensing issue exists with a font on your system, Acrobat Distiller displays a lock icon before the font name and a warning dialog box. If you select a font with licensing issues, the button to add fonts is also dimmed out, as shown in the following image:

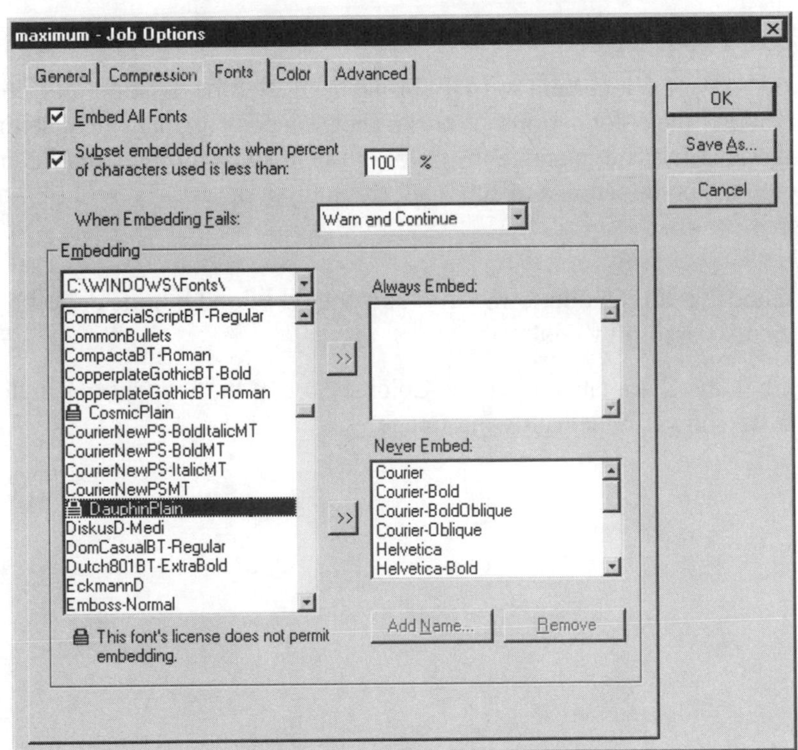

7. To select a different font list, click the triangle to the right of the font folder window; and from the drop-down menu, select a font folder.

8. To add a font to the Never Embed list, select the font from the left window and click the right-pointing double-arrow to the left of the Never Embed window. To remove a font from the Never Embed list, select the font from the Never Embed list and click the Remove button.

After you change the Job Option Font settings, click another tab to modify different settings, or save the Job Option by following the steps in the section "Save Job Options," later in the chapter.

TIP

When you install Acrobat, the install utility locates all of the folders in your system that contain fonts. If you add a new font folder to your system, launch Acrobat Distiller and choose Settings | Font Folders to open the Font Locations dialog box. Click the Add button, navigate to the folder that contains the fonts you want to use with Acrobat Distiller, select the folder, click OK, and then close the Font Locations dialog box. The next time you launch Acrobat Distiller, the font folder will be available.

Set Color Options

When you convert a document to PDF format using Acrobat Distiller or PDFMaker, you can modify the color options. You can choose a color-management settings file and let Acrobat Distiller manage the color of the images during conversion, or you can modify the color settings to suit a specific output device. To set color options, follow these steps:

1. Choose a Job Option to modify; and open the Job Options dialog box, as discussed previously.

2. Click the Color tab to open the Color section of the Job Options dialog box, shown in the following image:

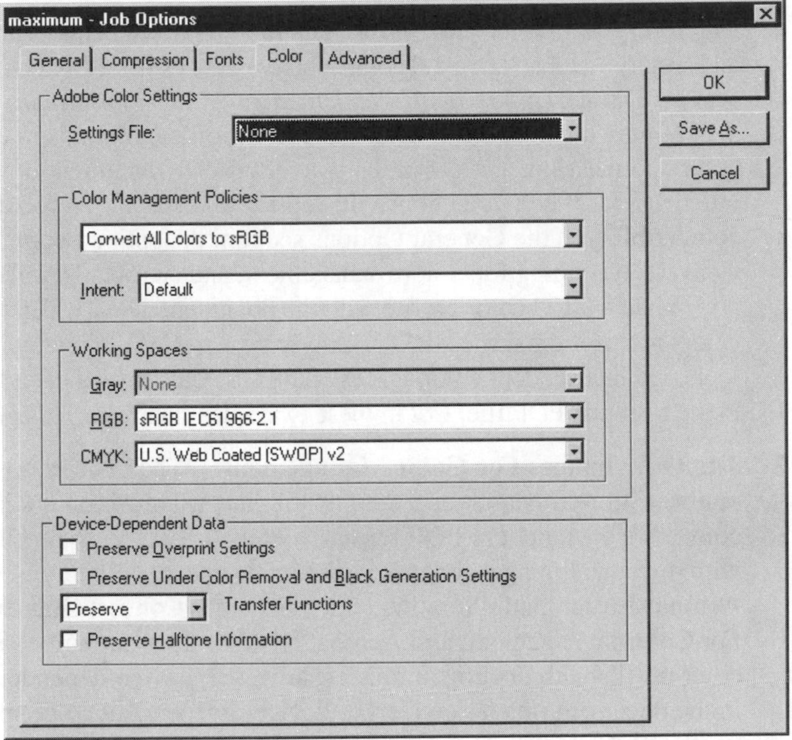

3. To use a preset color settings file, click the triangle to the right of the Settings File field; and from the drop-down menu, choose an option. When you choose one of the color-management setting files, all of the color options are dimmed out. You can choose no color management (None, the default), Prepress defaults, PhotoShop emulation, or web graphic defaults.

4. If you accept the default settings option (None), click the triangle to the right of the Color Management Policies field and choose one of the following:

   - **Leave Colors Unchanged** Choose this option, and Acrobat Distiller does not modify device-dependent colors and processes device-independent colors to the nearest match in the resulting PDF. Use this option if the file will be printed by a color-calibrated device that specifies all color management.

- **Tag Everything for Color Management** When you choose this option and specify Acrobat 4.0 or 5.0 compatibility in the General Options section, Acrobat Distiller embeds an *ICC (International Color Consortium) color profile* with the document. The ICC color profile calibrates image color and makes the colors in the converted PDF document device-independent. When you choose this option and specify Acrobat 3.0 compatibility in the General Options section, the option becomes Convert Everything for Color Management, and Acrobat Distiller does not embed an ICC color profile with the document. Device-dependent colors in the original files (RGB, Grayscale, and CMYK) are converted to device-independent color spaces (CalRGB, CalGrayscale, and LAB) in the resulting PDF file. *Cal* in these examples stands for *calibrated.*
- **Tag Only Images For Color Management** When you choose this option with Acrobat 4.0 or 5.0 compatibility, when Acrobat Distiller converts a document to PDF format, it embeds ICC color profiles with document images, but not with text or line art. When you specify Acrobat 3.0 compatibility, this option becomes Convert Only Images For Color Management, and Acrobat Distiller does not embed an ICC color profile with document images; however, device-dependent colors in the document images convert to device-independent color spaces (CalRGB, CalGrayscale, and LAB) in the resulting PDF file, leaving line art and graphics unchanged.
- **Convert All Colors to sRGB** When you choose this option with Acrobat 4.0 or 5.0 compatibility, when Acrobat Distiller converts the file, all images with RGB and CMYK colors convert to sRGB. If you specify Acrobat 3.0 compatibility, the option becomes Convert All Colors to CalRGB, and Acrobat Distiller converts all RGB and CMYK image colors to CalRGB.

5. Click the triangle to the right of the Intent field to specify how Acrobat Distiller maps color between the color spaces. Choose from the following options:
   - **Default** Choose this option, and the output device specifies the intent, not the PDF file. The majority of output devices use the Relative Colormetric intent.
   - **Perceptual** Choose this option, and the original color values of the document images are mapped to the gamut of the output device. This method preserves the visual relationship between different colors; however, color values may change.

- **Saturation** Choose this option, and the file that Acrobat Distiller produces will maintain the same relative color saturation as the original image pixels. Choose this method when document color saturation is more important than maintaining the visual relationship between colors of the original document.
- **Absolute Colormetric** Choose this option, and Acrobat Distiller disables the white and black point matching when converting colors in the document. This option is not recommended unless your intent is to preserve specific colors used in a trademark or logo.
- **Relative Colormetric** Choose this option, and Acrobat Distiller preserves all colors within the output device gamut range. Colors in the original document that are out of the printing device gamut range convert to brightness values within the printer gamut.

6. If you choose any Color Management Policies option other than Leave Colors Unchanged, then, in the Working Spaces section, you will be able to choose an ICC profile for managing Grayscale, RGB, and CMYK color conversion.
   - **Gray (Grayscale)** Choose None from the drop-down menu, and Acrobat Distiller does not convert grayscale colors. Choose one of the dot gain options to modify the brightness of grayscale images in the distilled PDF document. The default ICC option for grayscale images is Dot Gain 20%. Choose a lower dot gain value to lighten the image, a higher value to darken the image. Choose one of the Gray Gamma options if the document will be viewed on a different platform. Use Gray Gamma 1.8 for Macintosh viewing and Gray Gamma 2.2 for Windows viewing.
   - **RGB** Choose a color management profile from the drop-down menu. The available options are the color profiles installed on your computer. If you are uncertain which profile to choose, the default option (sRGB IEC61966-2.1) will yield good results. Choose None, and Acrobat Distiller does not convert colors in RGB images when distilling them to PDF.
   - **CMYK** Choose one of the options from the drop down-menu to specify how Acrobat Distiller handles colors in CMYK images when converting them to PDF format. If in doubt, choose the default [U.S. Web Coated (SWOP) v2]. Choose None, and Acrobat Distiller does not convert colors in CMYK images when distilling them to PDF.

7. In the Device-Dependent Data section, choose from the following options that pertain to the device that the converted documents will be printed with. These options have no effect on screen viewing.

   - **Preserve Overprint Settings** Choose this option, and Acrobat Distiller will retain any overprint settings from the original file when converting the file to PDF. An overprint is when two or more ink colors print on top of each other to yield another color. If you disable this option and the original document has overprint settings, the underlying colors will not be printed and the converted document colors will not match the original.
   - **Preserve Under Color Removal And Black Generation Settings** Choose this option if the documents you want to convert with this job option are PostScript files that contain Color Removal and Black Generation settings.
   - **Preserve Transfer Functions** Choose this option to preserve transfer functions if they are present in the original file. Transfer functions are traditionally used to compensate for dot gain or dot loss when an image transfers to film. This is the default option. The following two options are alternatives, available from the Transfer Functions drop-down menu:
     - **Apply Transfer Functions** Choose this option, and Acrobat Distiller applies the transfer functions to the file. This option changes the colors in the file.
     - **Remove Transfer Functions** Choose this option, and Acrobat Distiller removes all applied transfer functions when converting the file to PDF. You should choose this option unless the resulting PDF file will be printed on the same device the PostScript file was created for.
   - **Preserve Halftone Information** Choose this option and the resulting file that Acrobat Distiller produces preserves halftone information embedded in the original PostScript document. Halftone screens control the amount of ink deposited in specific locations when the file prints. By varying the dot size, halftone screens simulate the illusion of flowing color and varying shades of gray. CMYK images have four halftone screens, one for each color (Cyan, Magenta, Yellow, and Black).

After you modify the Job Options Color settings, click another tab to modify another setting, or save the Job Option, as outlined in the section "Save Job Options."

Set Advanced Options

The last tab in the Job Options dialog box allows you to modify Document Structuring Convention (DSC) comments that appear in the original PostScript file, as well as other options that affect the conversion from PostScript to PDF. To modify Job Option Advanced Options settings, follow these steps:

1. Choose a Job Option to modify and open the Job Options dialog box, following the steps presented earlier in this chapter.
2. Click the Advanced Options tab to reveal the Advanced Options section of the Job Options dialog box, as shown in the following image:

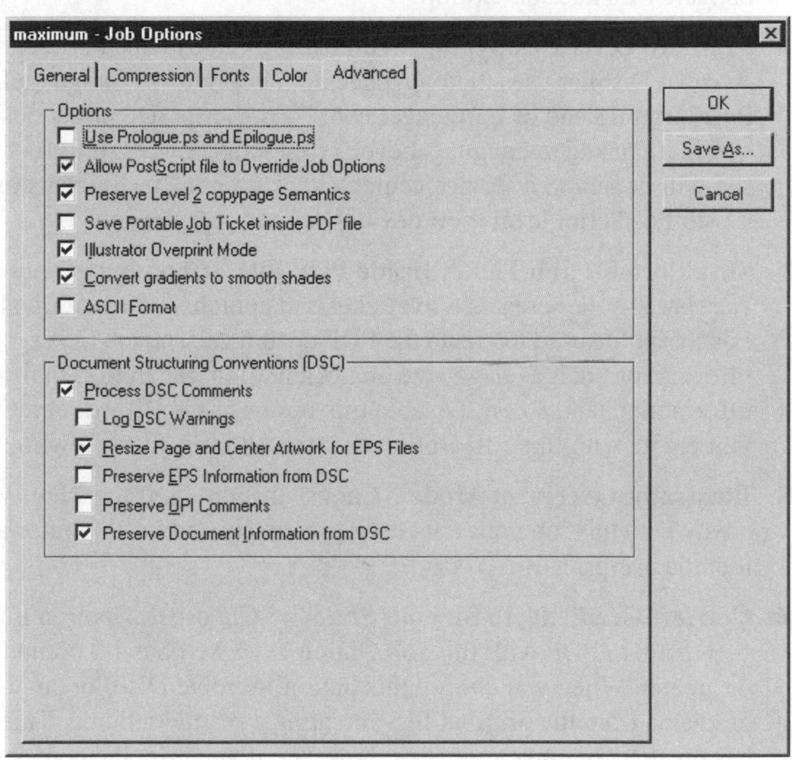

3. In the Options section, choose from the following:

- **Use Prologue.ps and Epilogue.ps** Choose this option to send a prologue and epilogue file with each document Acrobat Distiller converts with this Job Option. Epilogue files can be edited to append information to the PDF file. Prologue files can be edited to resolve procedure problems with PostScript files. Sample Prologue.ps and Epilogue.ps files are located in the Distiller folder. Neither file contains data; however, you can use them as templates. Unless you are familiar with creating PostScript code, it is suggested you disable this option.
- **Allow PostScript File to Overwrite Job Options** Choose this option if you are reasonably certain the PostScript files you convert with this Job Option contain the necessary information for the intended output device. Deselect this option if you want Job Options to take precedence over any settings embedded in the PostScript files that you intend to convert with this Job Option.
- **Preserve Level 2 Copypage Semantics** Choose this option and Acrobat Distiller uses the copypage editor defined in LanguageLevel 2 PostScript instead of LanguageLevel 3 PostScript. Do not choose this option if printing to LanguageLevel 3 PostScript devices. If the converted file will be sent to a service center, check with the technicians to see which PostScript level their devices support.
- **Save Portable Job Ticket Inside PDF File** Choose this option and Acrobat Distiller creates a job ticket that contains information about the PostScript file used to create the PDF document. The job ticket includes information such as page size and orientation, resolution, halftone information, and so on. Disable this option if the PDF documents you create with this Job Option are strictly for screen viewing.
- **Illustrator Overprint Mode** Choose this option if the PDFs you create with this job option were originally created in Illustrator and include overprints.
- **Convert Gradients to Smooth Shades** Choose this option if the files you distill to PDF with this Job Option have Acrobat 4.0 compatibility or greater. When you choose this option, Acrobat Distiller smoothes gradients from the original files, creating a seamless blend. This option has no effect on screen viewing; however, if you print the converted file to a PostScript 3 device, you will notice a marked improvement in quality. Note that if you choose this option, it may take longer for Acrobat to render the gradient onscreen.

- **ASCII Format** Choose this option, and the files Acrobat Distiller converts with this Job Option will be in ASCII text format. Choose this option if the resulting PDF file will be read or edited in a text editor. Be forewarned that this option creates a larger file size.

4. In the Document Structuring Conventions (DSC) section, choose from the following options:

   - **Log DSC Warnings** Choose this option, and Acrobat Distiller displays warning messages about troublesome DSC comments in the original PostScript file and creates a text file log of these errors. Choose this option if the files you process with this Job Option contain DSC comments.
   - **Resize Page and Center Artwork for EPS Files** Choose this option when processing EPS files, and Acrobat Distiller resizes the page to the document artwork and centers the artwork.
   - **Preserve EPS Information from DSC** Choose this option when processing EPS files with DSC comments, and the DSC comments will be preserved when the file converts to PDF.
   - **Preserve OPI Comments** Choose this option, and when Acrobat processes files with FPO (For Placement Only) images or comments, they will be replaced with the high-resolution image located on servers supporting OPI (Open Press Interface) versions 1.3 and 2.0.
   - **Preserve Document Information from DSC** Choose this option and Acrobat Distiller includes the title, creation date, and time information when you use this Job Option to convert files to PDF. When the PDF file opens, this information appears in the Document Summary and can be accessed by choosing File | Document Summary.

5. After setting the Advanced Options, you can click another tab to modify different settings, or save the Job Option file, as illustrated in the next section.

Save Job Options

After you modify a Job Option, you can save it for future use. To save a Job Option and close the Job Options dialog box, follow these steps:

1. Click the Save As button to open the Save Job Options As dialog box. By default, the Job Option you use to create the new Job Option is appended by the next available number, for example, eBook(1).

2. Accept the default Job Option name, or enter a different name. Choose a name that reflects the intended source of documents you create with this job option; for example, if the documents you create with this Job Option will be included on a CD-ROM, choose CD-ROM.
3. Click Save.

After you save the new Job Option, it appears on the Acrobat Distiller Job Options menu. If you use Microsoft Office applications, the Job Option appears on the PDFMaker Conversion Settings menu.

PDF Font Considerations

When you create a document in an authoring application, a little time spent choosing fonts will produce a better-looking document. Try to avoid highly stylized fonts with long swooping curves. They may look great printed, but often they do not display properly on monitors. If you choose a large bold font, when viewed as a PDF file, the center of characters such as *a, o, p,* and so on, fill in and are not legible unless the user greatly magnifies them. When you are in doubt whether a particular font style will display well in Acrobat, create a test document in the authoring application using every character from the font set in both upper- and lowercase. Convert the document to PDF format, and view the document in Acrobat at 100% magnification. One look and you will know whether to use the font or not.

You should also be careful of mixing fonts. If you create a document with multiple fonts, make sure the finished document is aesthetically pleasing. A document with multiple fonts can be hard to read. The actual number of fonts you can safely include in a document is a matter of personal taste and document size. For example, creating a single-page document with more than two fonts would not be a good idea. Also, when you create a document with multiple fonts and embed those fonts, the file size of the document increases dramatically.

When you create a document for print, a service center charges you for every color you use. However, this is not an issue when you create a document for viewing onscreen. You can add a little bit of color to text headings to draw a viewer's attention and spice things up. The tasteful use of color with text can dramatically increase the effectiveness of your document. If you create a document for viewing over the Web, make sure you choose your text colors from the 216-color, web-safe palette.

When you create a PDF document, you view the output on your computer and everything looks as you planned. The images are crystal clear and the text is sharp and stylish. However, if your intended audience does not have the fonts used in the document installed on their computer, the document will look quite different. When you do not embed fonts, and viewers do not have the document fonts installed on their system, Acrobat substitutes either the AdobeSansMM font or the AdobeSerifMM font. MM is an acronym for Multiple Master. Through the use of these fonts, Acrobat tries to create a reasonable facsimile of the original font while maintaining the width of the original font to preserve line breaks from the original document.

Embed Fonts

When you embed fonts, you can rest assured that viewers of your document will see the document as you intended. Embedding several fonts, however, can dramatically increase the file size of the document. You can embed fonts when you set Job Options for Acrobat Distiller. Make sure you do not violate any font licensing agreement when you decide to embed a specific font. For more information on embedding fonts when setting Job Options, refer the earlier section "Set Fonts Options."

You should embed fonts whenever you need the published document to look identical to the original. If, for example, your clients use a font as part of their corporation identity package, embed the font. If you use a stylized font that is difficult for Acrobat to recreate with a MM font, then embed the font.

Subset a Font

When you embed a font, you can reduce the file size by subsetting the font. When you subset a font, you embed only the characters used in the document. You can have Acrobat subset a font when the percentage of characters used drops below a certain value. By default, Acrobat subsets a font when the percentage of characters used drops below 100%. To subset a font, click the Fonts tab in the Job Option you are modifying, choose the option to subset fonts, and then specify the value that Acrobat uses as its signal to embed the entire font set, or subset the font set.

The only disadvantage to subsetting a font is when you edit a document with subset fonts. If you do not have the font set installed on your computer, you have to unembed the font before you can use the text tools to edit the document.

Preview an Unembedded Font in Acrobat

If you have any question as to whether you should embed a font or not, create a test document in an authoring application and view it in Acrobat without using *local fonts*. When you view a PDF document in Acrobat without using local fonts, fonts installed on your system are disregarded and Acrobat goes into font substitution mode. To preview an unembedded font in Acrobat, follow these steps:

1. Create a document in an authoring application using every character of the font set in both upper- and lowercase.

2. Choose Acrobat Distiller from the application Print command; or, if you are in a Microsoft Office application, choose PDFMaker to convert the document to PDF format.
3. Edit the conversion settings; and in the Font section, deselect the Embed All Fonts option, as outlined earlier in the "Set Font sOptions" section of this chapter.
4. Convert the document to PDF format.
5. Launch Acrobat and open the document.
6. Choose View | Use Local Fonts.

When this option is deselected (unchecked), Acrobat substitutes document fonts using MM fonts. You see what the document looks like on a viewer's system without the document fonts installed. When you deselect Use Local Fonts, you can also print a copy of the document using the Adobe substituted fonts. If the test document is not satisfactory, embed the fonts when you create the final document. Figure 14-5 shows two PDFs with several lines of different fonts viewed in the Acrobat tiled format. All fonts in the left window of the document are embedded, the fonts in the right window of the document are not embedded. When this screenshot was created, the Use Local Fonts command was in effect.

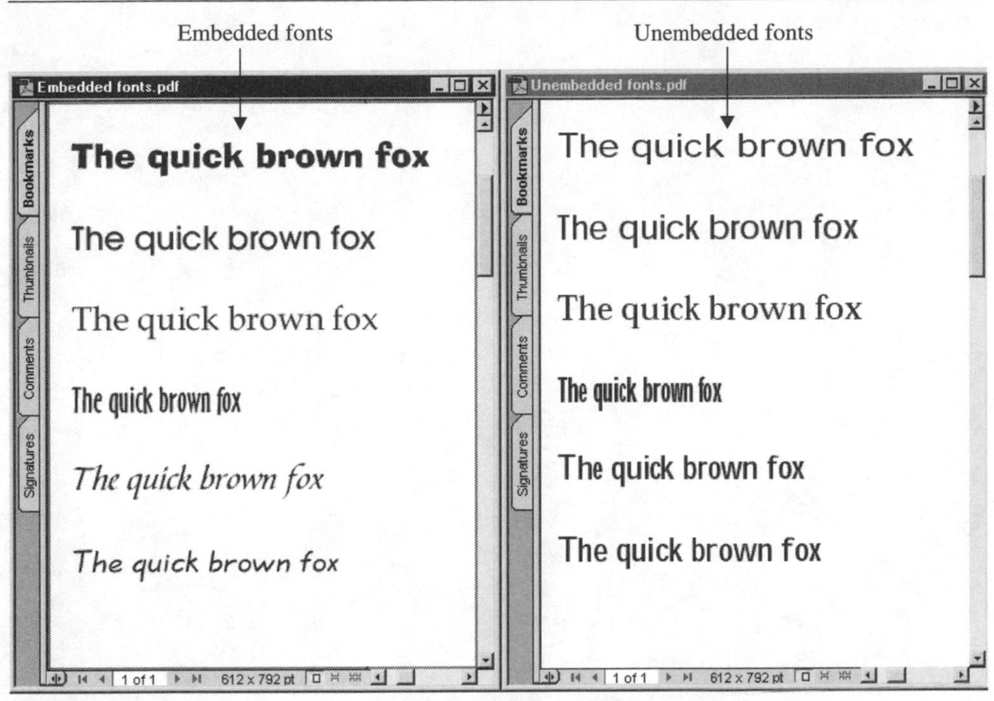

FIGURE 14-5 Decide whether or not to embed a font by deselecting the Use Local Fonts option.

Chapter 15 Create a PDF Index

How To...

- Create an index
- Prepare the documents
- Build an index
- Purge and rebuild an index
- Set catalog preferences

Whether you use Acrobat personally to maintain a collection of information, or you use it to create and maintain documents in a large corporation, you can make the information in your PDF documents more accessible by creating a PDF Index. Whether you use a few, or several hundred PDF documents to create your PDF Index, the result is a searchable database. After you create an index, or several indexes, you can quickly find the information you need using the Search command.

In this chapter, you'll learn how to prepare PDF documents for the creation of a PDF Index. You'll also learn how to use the Catalog command to create a searchable database of PDF documents. In prior versions of Acrobat, Catalog was a separate plug-in that you needed to launch independently of Acrobat. In Acrobat 5.0, Catalog is a Menu command. You'll also learn to use the Catalog command to maintain an index.

Create an Index

To create an index of PDF documents, use the Catalog command. You can create an index of files stored in one folder or several folders. When you create an index from a folder, Acrobat includes all PDF files located in the specified main folder, plus all PDF files located within the main folder subdirectories. You can specify which directories to add or remove from the catalog, as well as specify certain words you want to exclude from the index. Create as many indexes as you want to organize specific documents. For example, you can keep corporate documents in one index, personal documents in another, and research information downloaded from the Internet in yet another index. The long and the short of it is that you can use this powerful tool to create custom PDF indexes to suit your specific needs.

Prepare the Documents

Before you can actually create the PDF index, you need to prepare the documents you want to include in the index. When you create an index, Acrobat creates a PDX (index definition) file and support folders in the same folder as the documents. To prepare your documents for inclusion in a PDF index, follow these steps:

1. Create a folder in which to store the PDF documents you want to index. If you create an index that will be shared cross-platform, choose a folder name with no more than eight characters and no spaces. Also, refrain from including any nonstandard characters, such as $%^&*£$”!.
2. Locate the PDF documents you want to index and move them into the index folder. If desired, break the index folder into subfolders to keep subgenres of the index separated. Be advised, however, that deeply nested folders may adversely affect the performance of the index. If you have deeply nested folders with pathnames longer than 256 characters, you will also get unexpected results. Moving the PDF files to their own index folder is optional, but it is an excellent way to keep track of related PDF files. You can create an index using any folder as the root and Acrobat will index all PDF files in the subfolders you specify.
3. After you add the PDF documents to the index folder, you can begin thc preparation process. Examine the documents in the folder and pay special attention to the following:
   - If you have an exceptionally long document in the index, consider breaking it down into several documents. For example, if you have a manual in the index, break the manual down into individual chapters or sections. This will speed up the search process after you index the documents.
   - Rename any documents that have long filenames. Long filenames may adversely affect the performance of the index when truncated. This is especially true if you share the index cross-platform. Stick with the old tried-and-true DOS naming convention of eight letters followed by the three-letter .pdf extension.

- Rename any documents with spaces using DOS naming conventions. For example, *empbnfts.pdf* would be an acceptable alternative for Employee Benefits.pdf, while *emp bnfts.pdf* would not.
- Rename any documents that use ASCII characters 133 through 159 (as shown in the following table, as Acrobat Catalog does not support these characters.

133	à	134	å	135	ç	136	ê	137	ë
138	è	139	ï	140	î	141	ì	142	Ä
143	Å	144	É	145	æ	146	Æ	147	ô
148	ö	149	ò	150	û	151	ù	152	ÿ
153	Ö	154	Ü	155	¢	156	£	157	¥
158	_	159	*f*						

- If any of the documents need structure editing, perform the edits before renaming and adding the files to the index. If you change the document filename after creating cross-document links and other document structure, the links may not be functional. If a file needs extensive editing and you do not have the time, move the file to another folder. You can always perform the necessary edits, add it to the index folder, and then rebuild the index.

4. After you create the index folder and modify filenames, you can modify the documents for optimal search performance by following the steps in the next section.

Optimize PDFs for the Index

When you create a PDF index, the resulting index will be more efficient if you pay a little attention to detail when preparing the documents that will be included in the index. Acrobat uses the contents of the Document Summary when conducting a user query. For example, a user can search a document by author or keywords—information that can be added to the Document Summary. Recipients of your PDF documents will be able to search more efficiently if you consider the following when preparing your files:

1. Optimize each document for space. This may seem like an arduous task if you have a large document collection to index; however, you can create a batch sequence by choosing File | Batch Processing | Edit Batch Sequences, clicking the New Sequence button, and then choosing the Optimize for Space option

from the PDF Consultant command. When you run this batch sequence on the documents in your index folder, Acrobat removes the following: bookmarks with invalid destinations, link annotations with invalid destinations, and unused named destinations. For more information on creating a batch sequence, refer to the "Create a New Sequence" section in Chapter 11.

2. Optimize each document in the collection for Fast Web View. To accomplish this task quickly, choose File | Batch Processing | Fast Web View and then select the index folder. Optimizing a document in this way decreases the file size, which may be a factor if you create several indexes for CD-ROM distribution. Note that indexes cannot be searched through Acrobat in a web browser. For more information on searching an index, refer to Chapter 3.

3. Audit the Document Summary of each document to be included in the index. This may prove to be a lengthy task with a large document collection. If Acrobat users have their search preferences configured to search by document information, they can search an index by Title, Subject, Author, or Keywords, the same information included in the Document Summary. If you create documents with the intention of including them with an index, you can include the necessary document information when you publish the document. If you index a collection of documents prepared by other authors, or modify your own documents, open each document and then choose File | Document Properties | Summary. Review each Document Summary and pay attention to the following:

   - **Title** Make sure the document title accurately reflects the contents of the document. After a user conducts a search of the index, the document title appears in the Search Results dialog box.
   - **Subject** When you create an index with a variety of documents that contain different subject matter, be consistent with your naming conventions. For example, when indexing documents pertaining to employee benefits, do not use Employee Benefits for the subject of some documents and Benefit Package for others. When users search a document collection, they can click the Info button in the Search Results dialog box to view the subject information.
   - **Author** Include the author's name for each document. Remember that users of the document collection can specify a search by author. If you index a document for a large corporation, remember that personnel frequently change. For this reason, use the department information in this field rather than the author's actual name.

- **Keywords** Acrobat can also use keywords to select documents for a user's search query. Enter the keywords that pertain to the document you include in the collection. Again, be consistent with your naming conventions. If your organization uses a numbering system for memos and correspondence, you can include it in this field.

After you modify a Document Summary for a PDF index, it should contain information similar to what is shown in the following image:

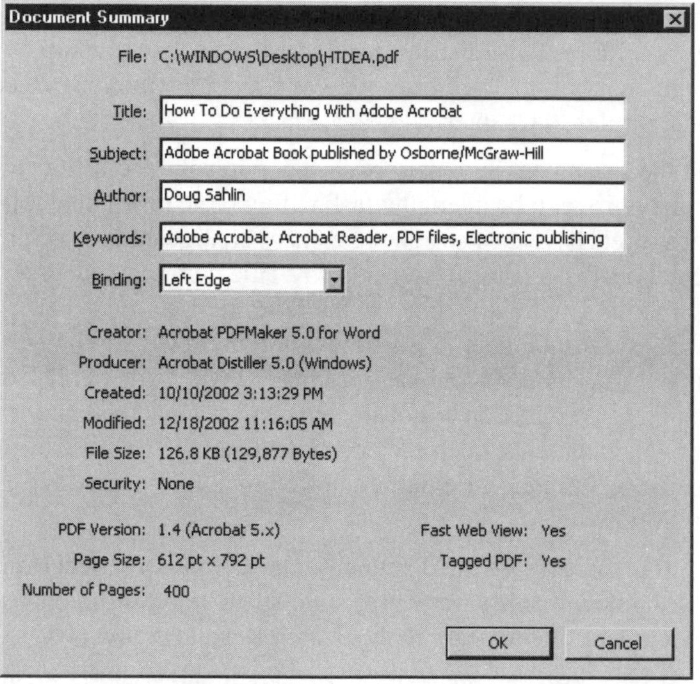

NOTE *You may be tempted to create a batch sequence to modify the Document Summary of several documents at once. If you are intimately familiar with the contents of the documents, this may be feasible; however, the whole point of indexing a document collection is to provide the ability to search the collection for unique information.*

After you audit the documents for the index, consider creating a document that describes the index. The information you include in this document will help users to efficiently search the document index. You can include information about the type of documents in the index, a list of words that have been omitted from the search index, your contact information if a user has questions, and other pertinent information about the document collection. If you index a large document collection, it may be beneficial to include a table listing that includes the following: each document title, each document subject, each document author, and each document keyword. You may also want to include a short tutorial on how to efficiently use the Acrobat Search command, including information about setting Search Preferences, conducting a search using Boolean operators, searching by date, and so on. For more information on the Acrobat Search command, refer to Chapter 3.

Build an Index

After preparing the documents, you are ready to build the document index. Build the document index with the Acrobat Catalog command. When you build the index, you specify a name for the index and the document folders to include in the index. You can also add a description of the index, as well as modify the index options to exclude certain words from a search. To create a PDF index, do the following:

1. Choose Tools | Catalog to open the Acrobat Catalog dialog box, as shown in the following illustration:

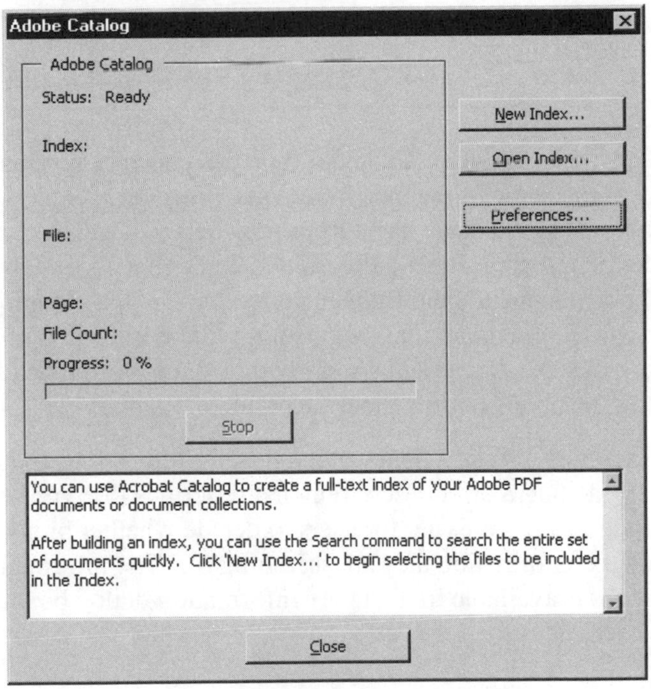

2. Click the New Index button to open the New Index Definition dialog box, as shown in the following illustration:

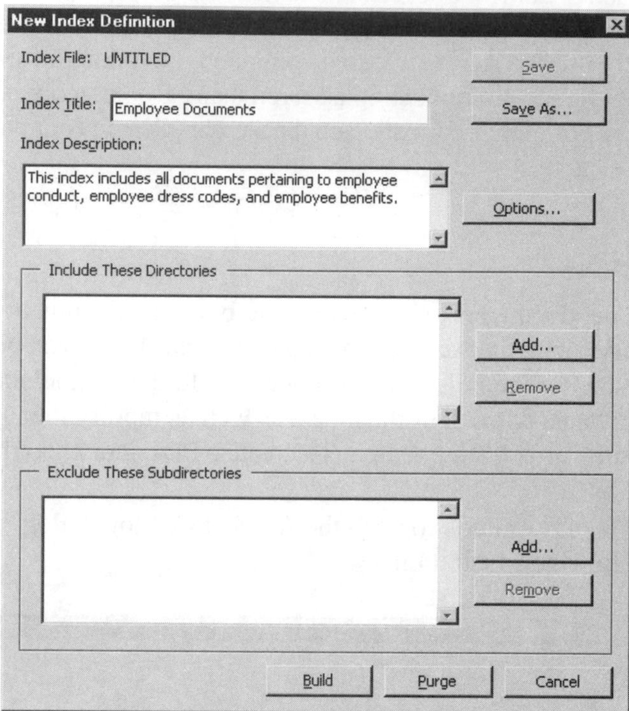

3. Enter a name in the Index Title field. You can choose any name as long as it is not the name of the .pdx index file. However, people within your organization use the index name when they decide whether or not to include the index in a search. Enter a descriptive name that accurately reflects the type of documents in the document collection (such as Employee Benefits Documents). Remember that long names will be truncated on the list of available indexes. Stick with a short two or three word index title that will fit within the bounds of the Index Selection dialog box.

4. In the Index Description field, enter a description. This step is optional. However, adding a brief description that describes the type of documents in the index makes it easier for users to decide whether or not the index contains the information they are searching for. The information you enter in this field is available in the Index Information dialog box that appears after a user clicks the Info button.

5. Click the Options button to open the Options dialog box, shown in the following illustration:

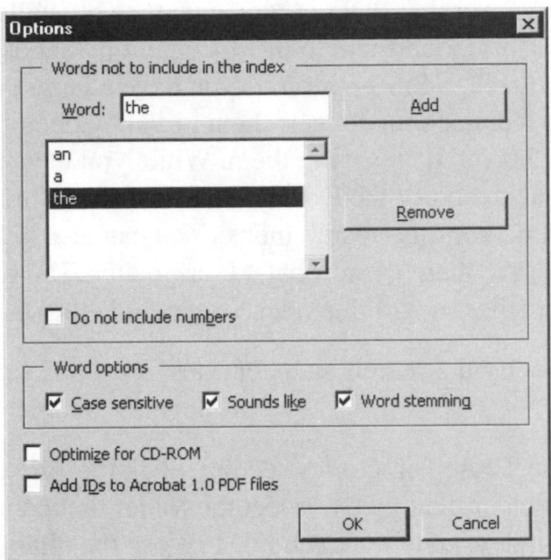

You can fine tune your index by modifying the following parameters:

- To exclude any words from a search, enter them one at a time in the Word field and then click the Add button. To speed up a search, eliminate words such as *a, the, an,* and so on.
- To exclude numbers from the search, enable the Do Not Include Numbers option.
- Change the Word Options parameters to suit the index you build. By default, Case Sensitive, Sounds Like, and Word Stemming are enabled. If you exclude these options, your search index will contain fewer words and users will be able to search the index quicker. For more information on these options, refer to the "Create a Query" section in Chapter 3.
- To optimize the search index for CD-ROM, enable the Optimize for CD-ROM option. This option is disabled by default. When you enable this option, the documents included in the index are arranged for quick retrieval from a CD-ROM. You may want to consider enabling this option if the document is part of an index posted on a network. When a document modified by another team member is searched, Acrobat displays a dialog box to this effect. The dialog box gives the user the choice whether or not to highlight the search results, or whether or not

to cancel, which invariably slows the retrieval of the document. When you enable the Optimize for CD-ROM option, the dialog box is disabled.

- If you have Acrobat PDF 1.0 documents in the collection, you can add cross-platform identifiers to the document by choosing the Add IDs to Acrobat 1.0 PDF Files option. If you have a large quantity of 1.0 files to add to a collection, convert them to 5.0 by opening the documents in Acrobat 5.0 and then saving them. While you have the 1.0 file open, you can also modify the Document Summary information to include pertinent data for the search index. You can also batch process any 1.0 files and save them as Acrobat 4.0 or greater. The resulting PDF file will be smaller as will the index you include the document in.

6. After you modify the search index options, click OK to exit the Options dialog box.

7. In the Include These Directories section, click the Add button to open the Browse for Folder dialog box, select the folder that contains the documents you want to index, and then click OK to close the dialog box. Remember, you can add more than one folder of documents to an index, as long as the additional folders are nested in the main index folder. Acrobat automatically indexes documents in each subfolder of the directory unless you exclude certain subdirectories, as outlined in the step 8.

8. In the Exclude These Subdirectories section, click the Add button to open the Browse for Folder dialog box, select the subdirectory you want to exclude from the index, and click OK to close the dialog box. Repeat as needed to exclude additional subdirectories.

9. Click the Build button, and Acrobat displays the Adobe Catalog dialog box, as shown in Figure 15-1, and begins to build the index. As Acrobat builds the index, the build progress and applicable comments display. You can stop a build by clicking the Stop button. If you stop a build, you can still search the partial index. To rebuild the partial index, choose Tools | Catalog, and then choose Open index. Once the partially built index is open, click the Build button, and Acrobat scans the index to determine how many files were indexed and then completes building the index.

10. Click Close to exit the Adobe Catalog dialog box. Your index is now ready for use.

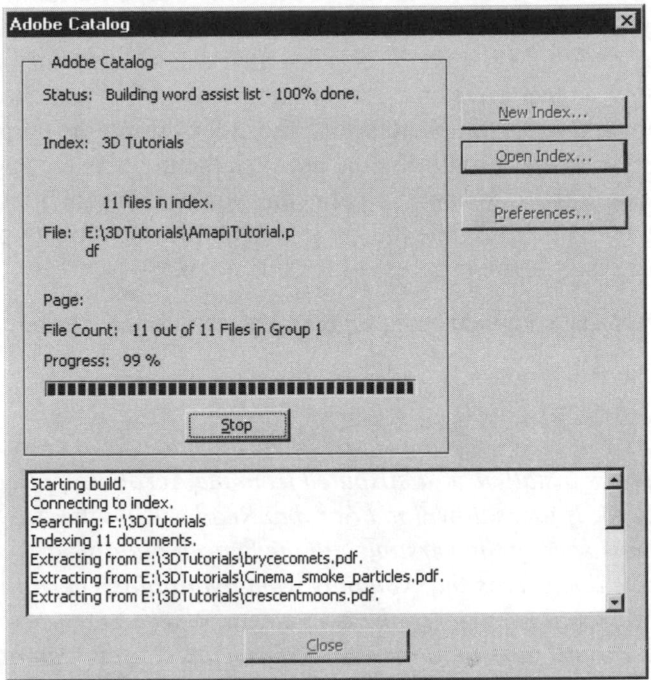

FIGURE 15-1 When you create a PDF index, Acrobat displays the build progress in this dialog box.

Purge and Rebuild an Index

After you create an index, it becomes obsolete as you add and delete documents from the index folder. When you open an index with deleted documents, the original versions of modified documents and deleted documents remain in the index. When you try to select a document whose title still appears in the index, but the document has been moved or deleted, Acrobat displays a warning dialog box to that effect. You should periodically purge an index of obsolete documents and rebuild it to reflect the current content. To purge a PDF index, follow these steps:

1. Choose Tools | Catalog to open the Adobe Catalog dialog box, as shown in Figure 15-1.
2. Click the Open Index button and open the index you want to purge. Remember the index will be in the index root folder with a filename of *index.pdx*.

3. Click the Purge button. After you click the Purge button, Acrobat displays a warning dialog box telling you the build will take 905 seconds (approximately 15 minutes). This is a time delay before the purge starts, which gives other users on a network time to complete searches in progress. If a network user attempts to search the index during the purge, a warning dialog box appears, notifying the user that the index is unavailable. The default time is 905 seconds, a value that you can change by modifying catalog preferences. While the purge is in progress, Acrobat opens a dialog box that displays the progress of the operation.
4. After Acrobat completes the purge, repeat steps 1 and 2 to reload the index.
5. Click the Build button.

TIP *Indexes you create can be searched by anyone with a copy of Acrobat Reader, as installed or distributed from the Acrobat application CD-ROM. If users download Acrobat Reader from the Adobe website, they must specify the version with the Search plug-in. If you have sensitive documents that you only want available to certain parties, then apply Acrobat Security to the documents. When users search an index and Acrobat returns a document with security, users can only view the document if they have the proper password; or in the case of a document with Acrobat Self-Sign Security, users will be prompted to log in. Users not listed on the document author's trusted certificate list will not be able to view the document.*

Set Catalog Preferences

You can modify the default settings Acrobat uses when creating a PDF index. You can modify the size of the index, the default purge time, whether or not to optimize the index for CD-ROM, and more. When you modify catalog preferences, consider the processing power available to users of your document index. If your index will be searched with computers of varying power, always target the lowest common denominator when setting your catalog preferences. To modify catalog preferences, follow these steps:

1. Choose Tools | Catalog to open the Adobe Catalog dialog box, shown in the following illustration:

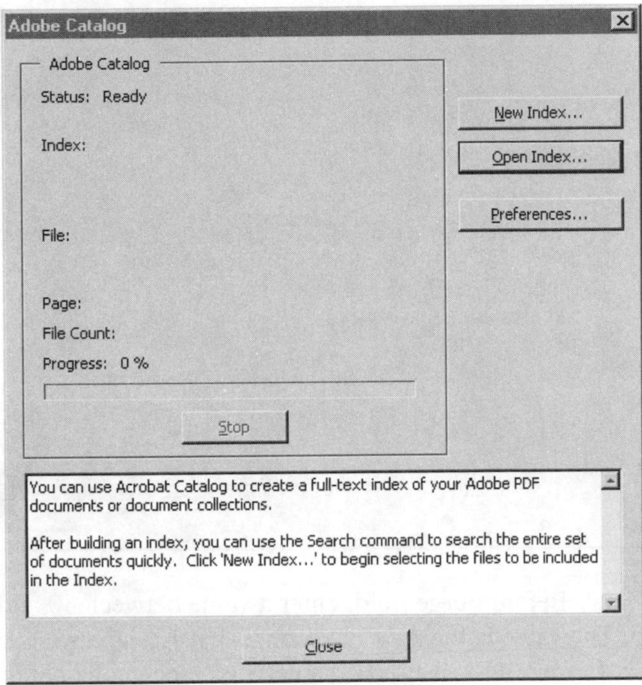

2. Click the Preferences button to reveal the Catalog Preferences dialog box. When you open this dialog box for the first time, it defaults to the General section. You have a total of five sections you can modify. In the five text sections that follow, each of the five General sections will be covered in detail.

Set General Catalog Preferences

15

When you modify General Catalog Preferences, you can fine-tune your index by specifying the delay before purge, the index size, the available memory for building indexes, and more. To modify General Preferences, follow these steps:

1. Open the Catalog Preferences dialog box.

2. If it is not already selected, choose General to open the General Catalog Preferences section, as shown in the following illustration:

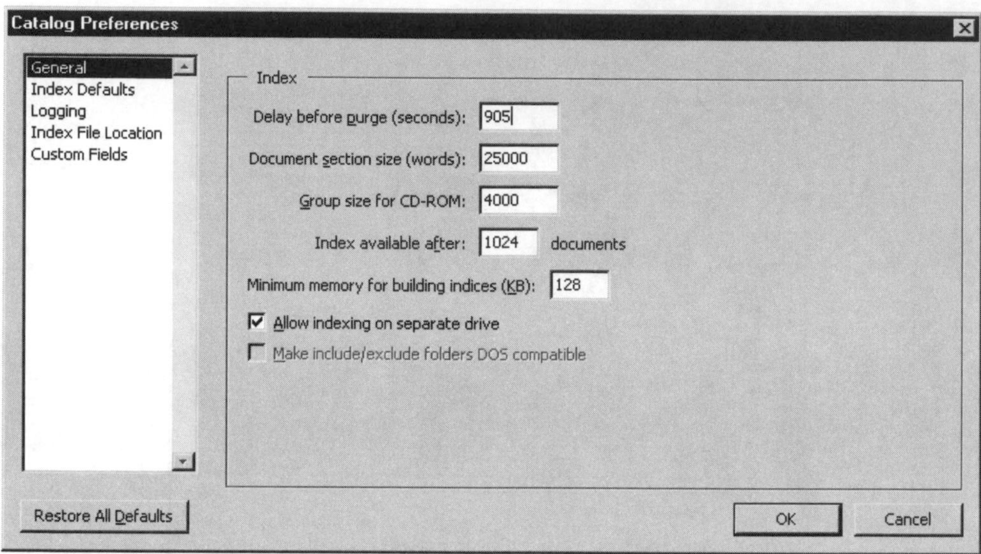

3. In the Delay Before Purge field, enter a value between 30 and 905 (the default). The value is the time in seconds that Acrobat waits before purging an index. If your index is used on a network, accept the default. As mentioned previously, the default value causes Acrobat to pause about 15 minutes before purging, which gives users time to complete searches in progress. If you use the index on a single machine, enter a value of 30.

4. In the Document Section Size field, enter a value between 5000 and 100000. The latter value is the maximum number of words allowed in an index. The default value of 25000 suits most machines. If your network has workstations with older processors and limited memory, enter a smaller value.

5. In the Group Size for CD-ROM field, enter a value between 4000 (the default) and 64000000. This setting determines the maximum number of documents that can be handled reliably on a CD-ROM. It is recommended that you do not exceed the default value of 4000. When creating an index for CD-ROM distribution, it is a good idea to split lengthy documents into

sections. It is also a good idea to split like documents and create several indexes rather than one large index. Splitting the documents into several indexes will speed up an index search from CD-ROMs and similar media.

6. Enter a value between 16 and 4000 in the Index Available After: [ ] Documents field. The value you enter determines how many files the PDF Catalog processes before making a partial index available for search. The default value is 1024. Enter a larger value if you want faster searches. If you have a large index and want users on a network to have quick access to an index during a large rebuild, enter a smaller value. Note that a smaller value will slow the index update and result in longer search times.
7. Enter a value in the Maximum Memory For Building Indices (KB) field. The default value is 128 (kilobytes). If available memory drops below the specified value, the index build stops. Enter a higher value for quicker searches if the workstations in the network, or the machine used to search the index, can support a higher value.
8. Choose the Allow Indexing On Separate Drive option if you work on a Macintosh machine or work with a network server. This option gives you the capability to create indexes on a separate drive and move them to different drives as needed.
9. Choose the Make Include/Exclude Folders DOS Compatible option if you work on a Macintosh machine and you want to build a cross-platform index.
10. Click OK to close the Catalog Preferences dialog box, or choose another catalog preference to modify.

Set Index Defaults Catalog Preferences

You can modify the settings in the Index Defaults section of Catalog Preferences to modify default options and word options. To set Index Defaults Catalog Preferences, follow these steps:

1. Open the Catalog Preferences dialog box.

2. Choose Index Defaults to open the Index Defaults Catalog Preferences section, as shown in the following illustration:

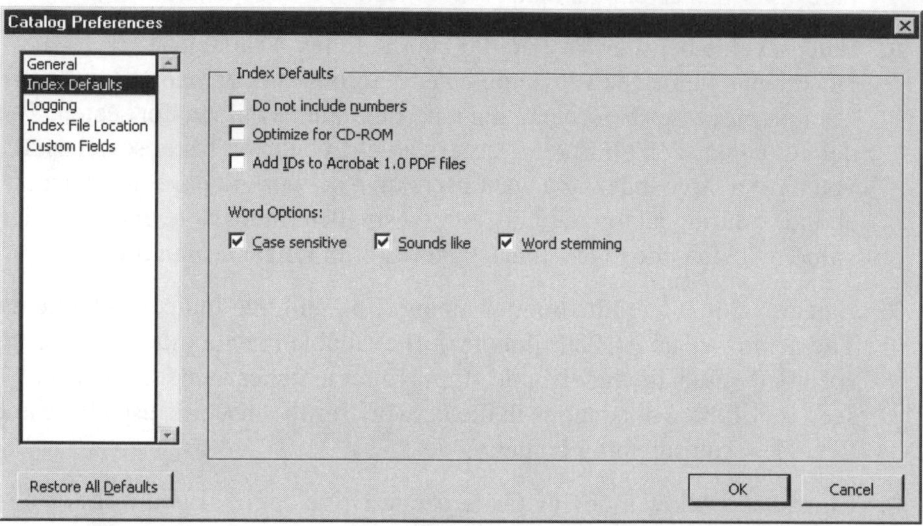

3. Enable the Do Not Include Numbers option, and numbers will be omitted from the indexes you build. Omitting numbers creates a smaller index and speeds up a search. However, you will not be able to perform a search for numbers.
4. Enable the Optimize for CD-ROM option, and the indexes you create will be optimized for CD-ROM distribution. When you choose this option, document files are arranged for quick retrieval and users will be able to search the index quicker.
5. Enable the Add IDs to Acrobat 1.0 PDF Files option if the indexes you build contain Acrobat 1.0 PDFs. When you choose this option, Acrobat adds identification to 1.0 PDFs when included in a document collection.
6. In the Word Options section, choose the options to suit the index you create. All options are enabled by default. Decrease the number of words in an index by disabling any option that does not apply.
7. Click OK to close the Catalog Preferences dialog box, or choose another catalog preference to modify.

Set Logging Catalog Preferences

When you create a PDF index, Acrobat generates a log file. The log file contains information about the index, plus the date it was created. An index log file is a text file that maintains the history of the index. Whenever you purge and rebuild an index, the new information is added to the log file. The following image shows a typical index log file:

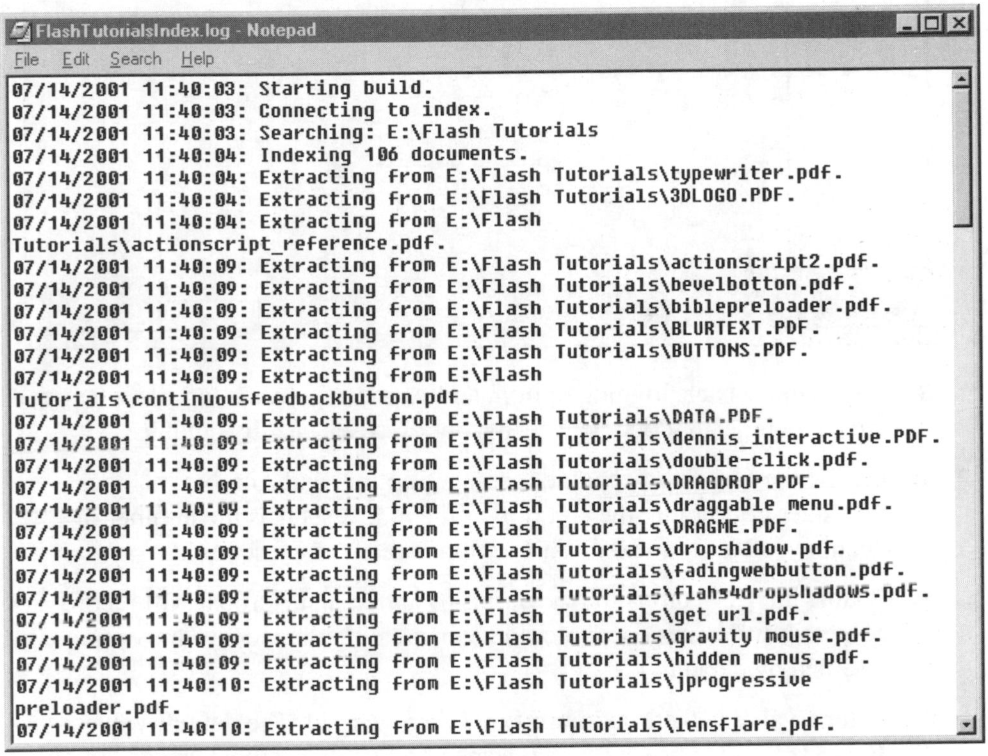

FlashTutorialsIndex.log - Notepad

File Edit Search Help

```
07/14/2001 11:40:03: Starting build.
07/14/2001 11:40:03: Connecting to index.
07/14/2001 11:40:03: Searching: E:\Flash Tutorials
07/14/2001 11:40:04: Indexing 106 documents.
07/14/2001 11:40:04: Extracting from E:\Flash Tutorials\typewriter.pdf.
07/14/2001 11:40:04: Extracting from E:\Flash Tutorials\3DLOGO.PDF.
07/14/2001 11:40:04: Extracting from E:\Flash
Tutorials\actionscript_reference.pdf.
07/14/2001 11:40:09: Extracting from E:\Flash Tutorials\actionscript2.pdf.
07/14/2001 11:40:09: Extracting from E:\Flash Tutorials\bevelbotton.pdf.
07/14/2001 11:40:09: Extracting from E:\Flash Tutorials\biblepreloader.pdf.
07/14/2001 11:40:09: Extracting from E:\Flash Tutorials\BLURTEXT.PDF.
07/14/2001 11:40:09: Extracting from E:\Flash Tutorials\BUTTONS.PDF.
07/14/2001 11:40:09: Extracting from E:\Flash
Tutorials\continuousfeedbackbutton.pdf.
07/14/2001 11:40:09: Extracting from E:\Flash Tutorials\DATA.PDF.
07/14/2001 11:40:09: Extracting from E:\Flash Tutorials\dennis_interactive.PDF.
07/14/2001 11:40:09: Extracting from E:\Flash Tutorials\double-click.pdf.
07/14/2001 11:40:09: Extracting from E:\Flash Tutorials\DRAGDROP.PDF.
07/14/2001 11:40:09: Extracting from E:\Flash Tutorials\draggable menu.pdf.
07/14/2001 11:40:09: Extracting from E:\Flash Tutorials\DRAGME.PDF.
07/14/2001 11:40:09: Extracting from E:\Flash Tutorials\dropshadow.pdf.
07/14/2001 11:40:09: Extracting from E:\Flash Tutorials\fadingwebbutton.pdf.
07/14/2001 11:40:09: Extracting from E:\Flash Tutorials\flahs4dropshadows.pdf.
07/14/2001 11:40:09: Extracting from E:\Flash Tutorials\get url.pdf.
07/14/2001 11:40:09: Extracting from E:\Flash Tutorials\gravity mouse.pdf.
07/14/2001 11:40:09: Extracting from E:\Flash Tutorials\hidden menus.pdf.
07/14/2001 11:40:10: Extracting from E:\Flash Tutorials\jprogressive
preloader.pdf.
07/14/2001 11:40:10: Extracting from E:\Flash Tutorials\lensflare.pdf.
```

When you modify Logging preferences, you can specify which information to include with the log file, as well as the maximum file size of the log file. To modify Logging preferences, follow these steps:

1. Open the Catalog Preferences dialog box.

2. Choose Logging to open the Logging Catalog Preferences section, as shown in the following illustration:

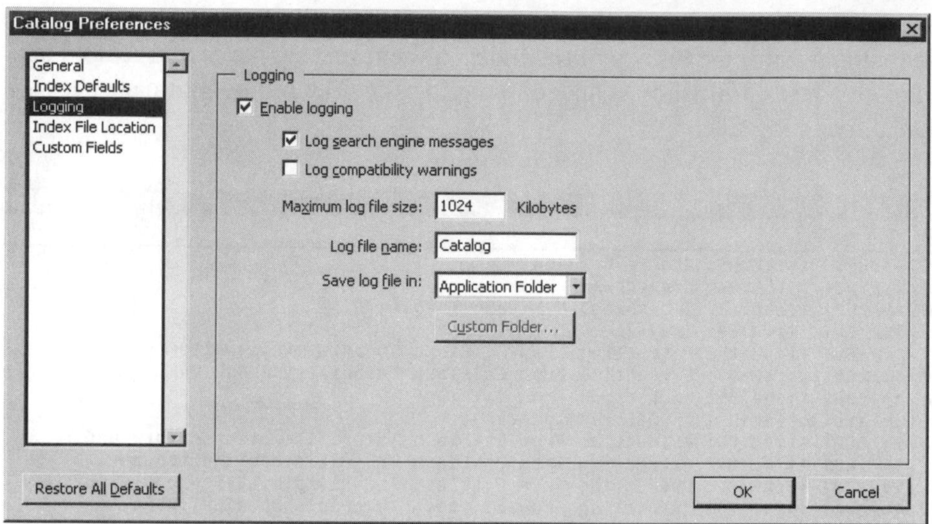

3. Enable the Enable logging option, and Acrobat creates a log file when you create an index of documents. This option is selected by default.
4. Enable the Log search engine messages option, and Acrobat includes messages concerning the creation of the index, such as the number of documents being indexed. This option is selected by default.
5. Enable the Log compatibility warnings option and Acrobat will record any compatibility issues encountered when creating the index. This option is disabled by default.
6. Enter a value in the Maximum Log File Size field. The default value is 1024KB. If a log file exceeds the specified value, Acrobat erases the old log file and creates a new one using the current build information.
7. Enter a name in the Log File name field. The default name is the catalog folder name appended by the index.
8. Click the triangle to the right of the Save Log File In field, and choose one of the following:
   - **Application Folder** Choose this option to save the log file in the Acrobat application folder.

- **Index Folder** Choose this option to save the log file in the same folder as the document collection. This option is the default.
- **Custom Folder** Choose this option, and the Custom Folder button becomes available. Click the button and use the Browse for Folder dialog box to choose the folder you want to save the log file in.

9. Click OK to close the Catalog Preferences dialog box, or choose another preference to modify.

Set Index File Location Catalog Preferences

You can modify the filename of the index and the location it is saved in by modifying options in the Index File Location section. To modify the index file location, do the following:

1. Open the Catalog Preferences dialog box.
2. Choose Index File Location to open the Index File Location Catalog Preferences section, as shown in the following illustration:

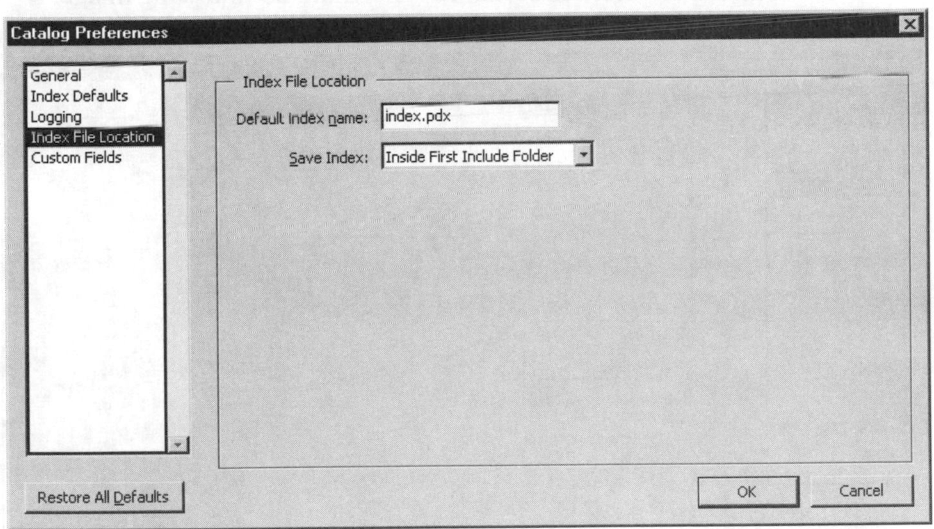

3. Enter a name in the Default Index Name field followed by the .pdx extension to change the default filename of the index file.

4. Click the triangle to the right of the Save Index field, and choose Inside First Include Folder or Outside First Include Folder. The default option, Inside First Include Folder, places the index file with the index document files.
5. Click OK to close the Catalog Preferences dialog box, or choose another catalog preference to modify.

Set Custom Fields Catalog Preferences

You add custom fields after modifying Acrobat with the Acrobat Software Development Kit. To modify the Custom Fields preferences, you need to download the Acrobat SDK (Software Developer Kit). Study the documentation and modify Acrobat before changing the Custom Fields preferences. You should have a good grasp of programming before attempting to create custom fields for Acrobat. To modify Custom Fields preferences, do the following:

1. Open the Catalog Preferences dialog box.
2. If it is not already selected, choose Custom Fields to open the Custom Fields Catalog Preferences section, as shown in the following image:

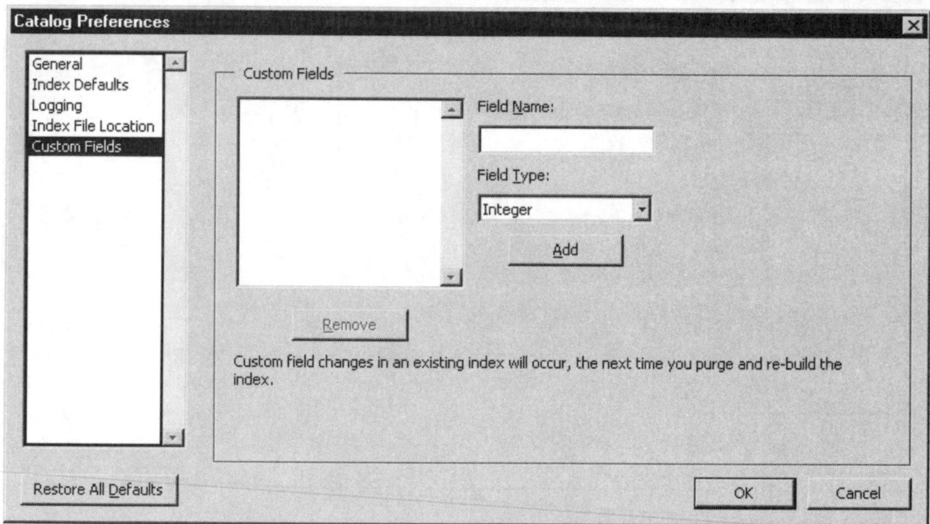

3. In the Field Name field, enter the name of the custom field you want to create.
4. Click the triangle to the right of the Field Type field, and from the drop-down menu, choose one of the following: Integer, Date, or String.
5. Click the Add button to add the custom field. To remove a custom field, select it in the Custom Fields window and click the Remove button.
6. Click OK to close the Catalog Preferences dialog box.

NOTE *If you are adept at programming, you can create plug-ins for Acrobat with the Acrobat SDK. For more information, log onto the Internet and enter the following URL in your web browser: http://partners.adobe.com/asn/developer/. Here, you will find information about the Adobe Developer program, and you can join the Adobe Solutions Network Developer program (ASN). You can either join ASN or download the SDK directly from the following URL: http://partners.adobe.com/asn/developer/acrosdk/acrobat.html.*

Restore Catalog Preference Defaults

You can restore catalog preferences to their default settings. In each section of the Catalog Preferences dialog box, you see a Restore All Defaults button near the lower-left corner of the dialog box. When you click the Restore All Defaults button, Acrobat displays a dialog box asking you to confirm the operation. Click OK to restore the default settings. Note that this action restores the defaults for all five sections of the Catalog Preferences dialog box.

Load a PDF Index

After you create one or more search indexes, you can use them to find information. Conduct a search using one or several search indexes. You can store a PDF index in any location on your hard drive or network server. When you load a PDF index, Acrobat has the necessary path information to access the index.pdx file. To load a PDF index, follow these steps:

1. Choose Edit | Search | Select Indexes to open the Adobe Acrobat Search dialog box, shown in the following image. Alternatively, choose Edit |

Search | Query or click the Search tool. After the dialog box opens, click the Indexes button.

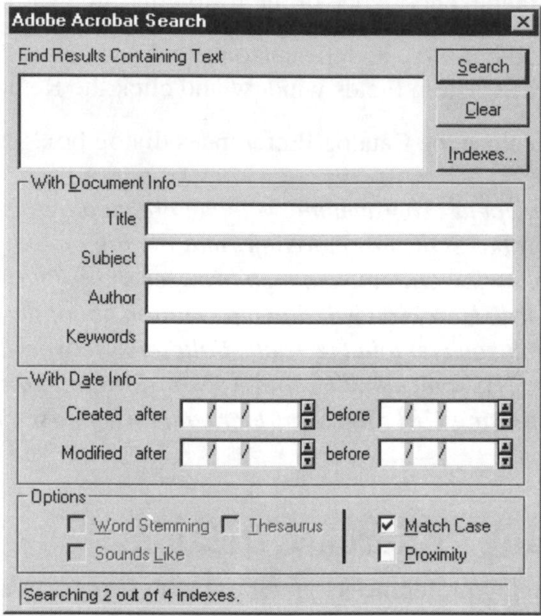

2. Click the Add button to open the Select Index dialog box.
3. Select the index you want to add to the list, and then click Open.
4. To remove an index from the list, select it, and then click the Remove button. When you remove an index from the list, it will not be available for a search until you add it again. Instead of completely removing an index, you can click the check box to the left of the index title to select or deselect the index for a search.
5. To find out information about an index on the list, select it, and then click the Info button to open the Index Information dialog box. The information displayed is a combination of the information entered in the New Index Definition dialog box by the index creator, and the information created by Acrobat when the index was built or last modified.
6. Add additional indexes, or click OK to close the Index Selection dialog box. After selecting indexes, you can use the Search command to create a query. For more information on the Search command, refer to the "Search an Index of Documents" section in Chapter 3.

Move an Index

You can move an index to another folder, another hard drive, or another network server. When you relocate a PDF index, you need to move the index root folder and all associated subfolders. This maintains the necessary links for the index to function properly. The folder structure of a typical index is shown in the following image:

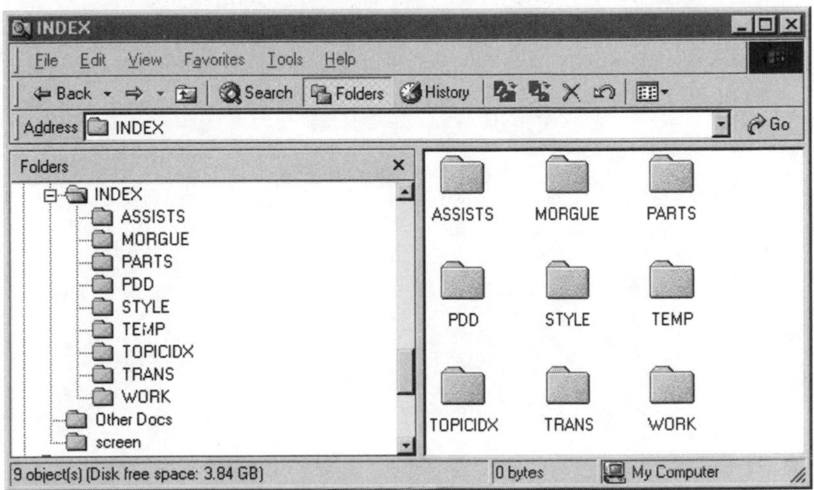

Chapter 16

Create PDF Documents for the Web

How To...

- View PDF documents in a web browser
- Use the Acrobat plug-in
- Prepare PDF documents for the Internet
- Create links to websites
- Work with comments online
- Use PDF forms on the Internet

The power of Adobe Acrobat is not limited to distributing documents within an organization or sharing documents with clients. You can also use Adobe Acrobat to create documents for a website. With Adobe Acrobat, you can create a PDF document from product brochures, product manuals, and other documents. After you optimize it for fast web viewing, post it on your or your client's website, and visitors can view the document in their web browsers. Adobe has an Acrobat plug-in that is compatible with most popular web browsers. In fact, many of the popular web browsers include the Acrobat plug-in as part of the installation package. If a web browser does not have the Acrobat plug-in, it can be downloaded for free from the Adobe website.

In this chapter, you'll learn how to view PDF documents within a web browser, as well as prepare PDF documents for use on the Internet. Also covered are Web browser considerations and information about the Acrobat plug-in. You'll also learn how to work with PDF forms and edit documents in a web browser.

View PDF Documents in a Web Browser

When you view non-HTML documents from a website, your web browser detects the document type and loads the necessary helper application so you can view the document in the web browser. Depending on the type of document you view, the helper application (or plug-in as it's known to web designers) may load within the browser or externally. Some applications give web designers the freedom to embed a document and call up the plug-in interface within the HTML document, or open it in an external window. When you view PDF documents from websites, Acrobat appears in your Web browser. Figure 16-1 shows Acrobat as it appears in the Internet Explorer 5.5 browser. Notice the difference in the available tools and the absence of the Acrobat menu bar.

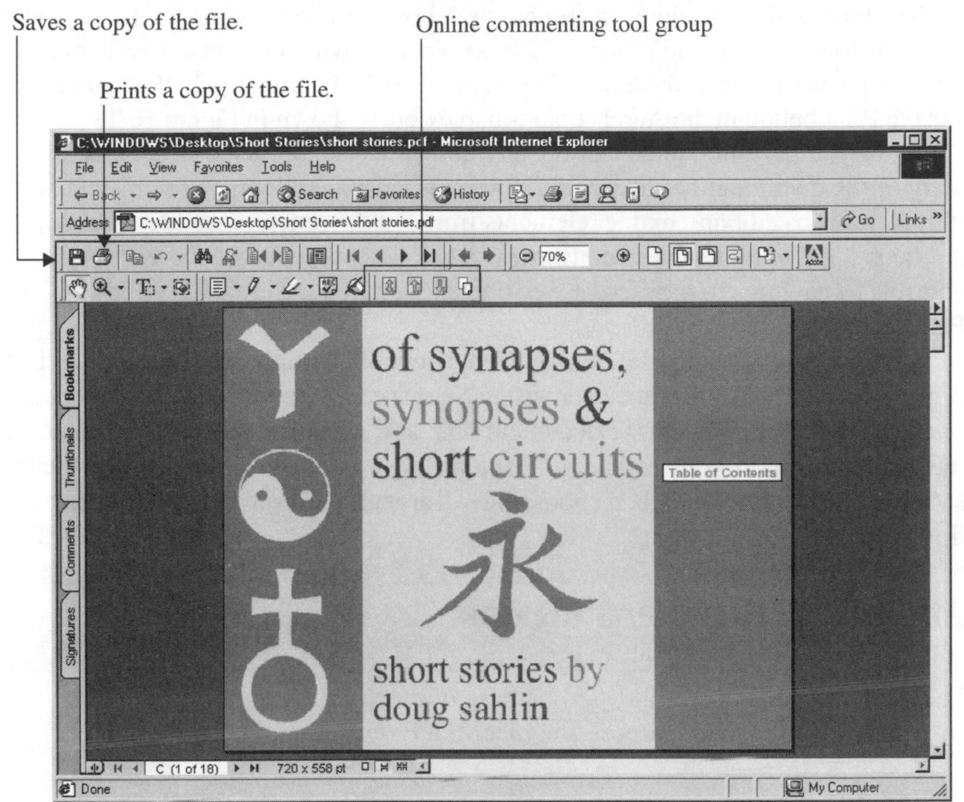

FIGURE 16-1 When you view a PDF document from a website, you can view it within a web browser.

To open a PDF within a web browser, you must specify the path to the document, which consists of the URL and the filename of the document, such as http://www.mysite.net/catalog.pdf. If the file is in the same domain or folder as the HTML document, you can specify a relative URL with just the folder name and the document name. For example, pdfdocs/catalog.pdf, where pdfdocs is the folder name and catalog.pdf is the file that opens when the link is clicked.

When you view documents online, Acrobat provides you with a slightly different set of tools. As shown in Figure 16-1, you still have all of the Acrobat tools, and you also have a set of tools to view and download comments. Also, notice there are no menu commands, only the Acrobat tools and the web browser controls. You only have tools to view the document, save a copy of the document, and annotate the document. There is also the addition of the Online Comments tool group, which is covered in the upcoming section, "Work with Comments Online."

The tools and menus in your web browser, however, do not change. If you use the browser Print command to print the PDF document, it will not print correctly as the browser cannot interpret the binary format of the PDF. To print the PDF document, use the Print button in the Acrobat plug-in, previously shown in Figure 16-1.

After you have the document open within your web browser, you can save a copy of the document for future use. After you save the document, you can open it in Acrobat to edit and extract elements from the document, provided security has not been applied to it. After you finish viewing a document, use the web browser controls to navigate to a different website, or back to the page that called the PDF document.

You can also download PDF documents directly from the Internet to your hard drive. To download a PDF document using Netscape Navigator, right-click (Windows) or CTRL-click (Macintosh) the document link, and then choose Save Link As from the context menu. If you use Internet Explorer, right-click (Windows) or CTRL-click (Macintosh) the link, and then choose Save Target As from the context menu to download a PDF document.

About PDF Browser Plug-Ins

When you install Acrobat, the install utility automatically detects the web browsers installed on your system, and Acrobat is configured as the application for the following MIME (Multipurpose Internet Mail Extension) types:

- **PDF** When you open a PDF file from a website, it is handled by the Acrobat plug-in.
- **FDF** When you receive an FDF file as an e-mail attachment and open it, Acrobat launches. When you send your digital signature certificate via e-mail, it is an FDF attachment.
- **XFDF** When you receive form data via e-mail in XFDF format, the Acrobat program handles the attachment.
- **PDX** When someone sends you an Acrobat index via E-mail, double-clicking the attachment launches the Acrobat program. The Acrobat program also launches if you open a PDX file from within the Web browser. You cannot search a PDX file with the Acrobat plug-in, as there is no Search tool available.
- **RMF** When you purchase locked PDF documents, the seller sends RMF files. This is the licensing information Web Buy uses to unlock the document.

If you install Acrobat on a new system, be sure to install your web browsers first. If you install Acrobat first, in order to view PDF documents in a web browser, you will have to manually configure each web browser on your system.

Download Acrobat Reader

A large majority of Internet users already have a version of Acrobat Reader installed on their systems. If, however, you post a PDF document at your website, or at a client's website whose visitors do not have Acrobat Reader, they will not be able to view your document. In order to accommodate Website visitors that do not have a copy of Acrobat Reader, you can include a link to the Adobe web page where visitors to the website can download a free copy of Acrobat Reader. The following URL takes the viewer to the Acrobat Reader: http://www.adobe.com/products/acrobat/readstep.html

Distribute Acrobat Reader

You can post Acrobat Reader on a company intranet or local network. You can also distribute Acrobat Reader on a CD-ROM, provided you accept the conditions of the Acrobat Electronic End User License Agreement and the Supplement to Permit Distribution.

You cannot distribute Acrobat Reader from a website. Adobe requires that any third-party website must include a link to the Acrobat Reader download page at http://www.adobe.com/products/acrobat/readstep.html. You can include an Adobe Get Reader logo or an Adobe PDF logo, as shown in the following image. Download both logos after you read the information contained in the Get Acrobat Reader and Adobe PDF logos section at http://www.adobe.com/products/acrobat/distribute.html

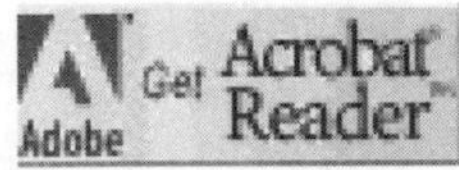

16

Work with Comments Online

When you work within a corporate intranet or on a local network, you can share and edit comments online. To do this you must have a web browser and Acrobat on the same machine. When you share comments within a group, the comment files are FDF (Forms Data Format) files. The basic process involves having PDF documents stored in a folder on the network server. You open a file in the web browser by specifying the path and filename. After you open the file, use the standard Commenting tools to add comments to the document, and then use the Online Comments tools to upload and download comments to the server. Before you can work with comments within a web browser, you need to set your Online Comments preferences to match the server type.

Configure Online Comments Preferences

You configure Online Comments preferences to designate the type of server the PDF documents download from. To configure preferences for sharing comments online, follow these steps:

1. Choose Edit | Preferences | General to open the General Preferences dialog box.
2. Choose Online Comments to open the dialog box, shown in the following illustration:

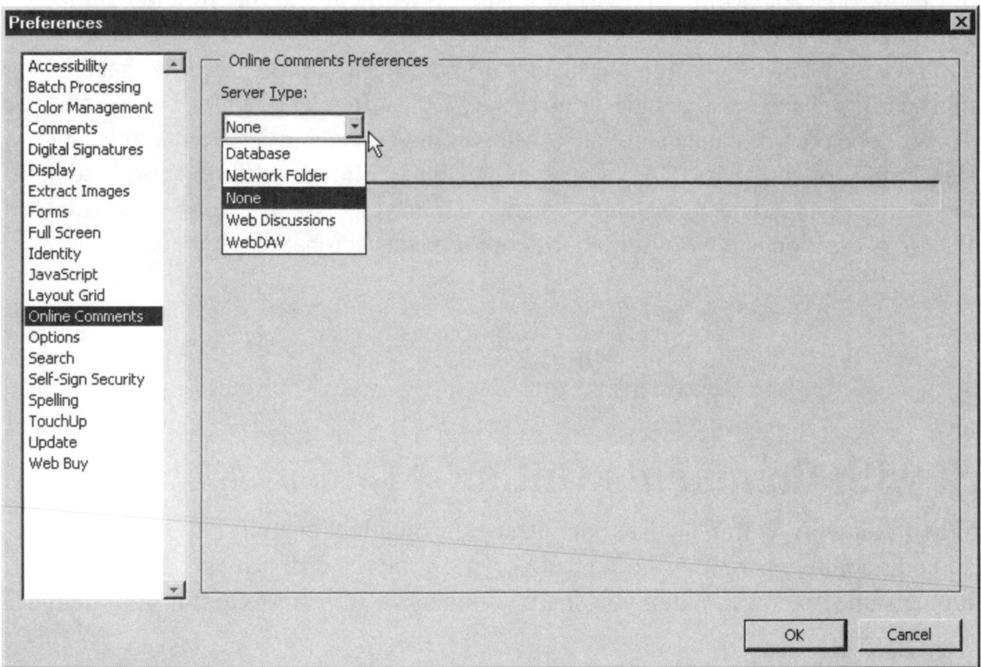

3. Click the triangle to the right of the Server Type field, and choose the option that matches your server type. If you use Acrobat with the Windows platform, you have five choices: Database, Network Folder, None, Web Discussions, and WebDAV (Web-Based Distributed Authority and Versioning). If you use the Macintosh version of Acrobat, you have three choices: Network Folder, None, and WebDAV.
4. Click OK to close the dialog box and apply the changes.
5. If your online collaboration is handled via a web server, contact the administrator to see which server type is used. You will also need the URL if the connection requires a web address. Furthermore, if you use Database, WebDAV, or Web Discussions, these server types have additional parameters that require the assistance of the web server administrator. If you use Web Discussions, you have to configure Internet Explorer as well.

You can find additional information about configuring Acrobat for online comments by reading the Online Comments PDF document located in the Collaboration folder on the Acrobat 5.0 CD-ROM.

Share Comments Online

After you configure Acrobat for the server type, you can begin collaborating with your colleagues online. If you collaborate online with a LAN (Local Area Network), download a PDF file from the network folder. If you collaborate through a network server, log onto the server, launch your web browser, and download a PDF file. Once you have the file open, you can use the tools from the Commenting tool group to create your comments. After you annotate a document, share comments with other team members by using the Online Comments tools, shown in the following image:

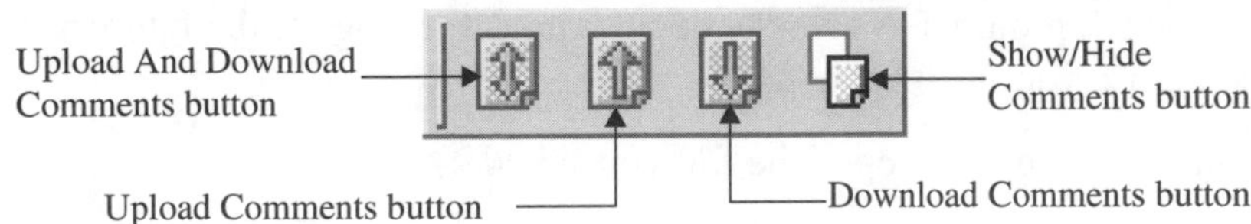

You can use the Online Comments tools to handle the following tasks:

- To upload comments to the server or network, click the Upload Comments button.

- To download comments from the server or network, click the Download Comments button.
- To synchronize comments between the server and the document you work on, click the Upload and Download Comments button.
- To show or hide comments in the document, click the Show/Hide Comments button. This button toggles the visibility of comments in the document.

NOTE

If you close the web browser or navigate to another web page, your annotations automatically upload to the server.

If you keep a working copy of the document in a local folder on your computer, you can delete all comments by choosing Tools | Comments | Delete All. Mark up the document with your own personal comment, and then choose File | Comments | Export to save a copy of your personal comments. If you upload the document to the server, your personal comments are deleted (unless you click the Upload Comments button), but are available in the FDF file Acrobat created when you exported the comments.

Work Offline

You can work on PDF documents when the server is offline. You can create comments offline in Acrobat and then upload them to the web server from your Web browser. To create comments offline and upload them to the server, follow these steps:

1. While working on the Internet, download the document you want to work with offline, and then click the Save button, shown earlier in Figure 16-1.
2. Follow the prompts to save the document to file, log off the Internet, and then close your web browser.
3. Launch Acrobat and open the file you saved.
4. Annotate the document with any tool from the Commenting tool group.
5. After you finish making comments, log onto the server.
6. From within Acrobat, choose File | Upload Comments, and then click Start. After you click Start, Acrobat opens the file in your web browser and closes the file in Acrobat.

7. Click the Upload Comments button to upload the comments to the server.
8. After you upload your comments, they become available for the next reviewer in the cycle. If the review has more than one round, you can download additional comments that have been applied to the document before adding your own. After the document goes through all phases of the review cycle and the comments have been acted upon, they can be deleted before you publish the document. To learn more about comments, refer to Chapter 12.

Prepare PDF Documents for the Internet

When you prepare a document for the Internet, the first step is to optimize the document in the authoring application, as discussed in the "Optimize Documents for the Web" section in Chapter 14. The most important consideration in optimizing a document for the Internet is to get the file size as small as possible. Remember to resample all images to a resolution of 72 dpi and enable Fast Web View when converting the document to PDF format.

You should also consider document security issues, Document Summary information, and how the first page of the document opens when a viewer downloads it. If you include Document Summary information, the website visitor can get an idea of the information included in the document. Add document security if you do not want website visitors to be able to extract content from the document or print the document. If you assign security to the document, be sure to include a master password. For more information about Acrobat security, refer to the "About Acrobat Security" section in Chapter 13. For more information on modifying the Document Summary and document open options, refer to the "Set Document Properties" section in Chapter 4. Note that if you choose the Open In Full Screen Mode Open Option, the document will not be displayed in Full Screen mode when viewed in a web browser.

But that's only the beginning of your task. After you convert the original document to PDF format, you apply the finishing touches in Acrobat.

Create Links to Websites

When you create PDF documents for viewing from a website, you may need to create one or more links to other websites. If you have several interlinked PDF documents, you'll also need to create some sort of link back to the HTML pages of the website. You can ask visitors to rely on the Back button of the web browser. However, if a viewer has navigated through several documents, clicking the Back button several times to exit Acrobat and return to the HTML portion of the website can be annoying. To create a link to a website from within a PDF document, follow these steps:

1. Select the Link tool, and create the rectangular selection that will define your link. Remember, you can create a text link or define the area around an image as the hotspot of the link. For more information on using the Link tool, refer to the "Create Links" section in Chapter 7. After you define the area of the link, the Link Properties dialog box is displayed.
2. In the Action section, click the triangle to the right of the Type field, and choose World Wide Web Link.
3. Click the Edit URL button to open the Edit URL dialog box.
4. In the Enter A URL For This Link field, enter the URL for the link, as shown in the following image:

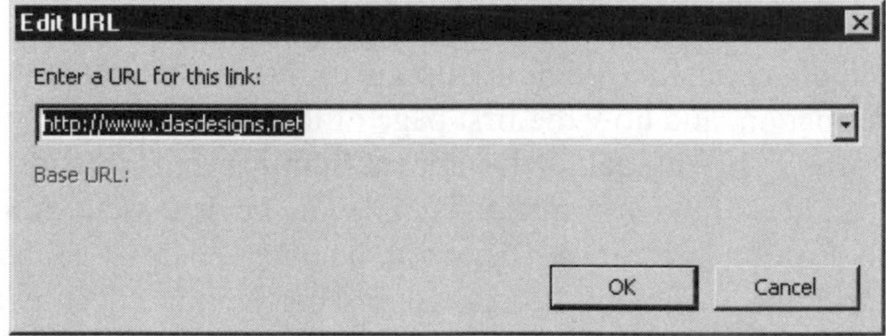

5. Click OK to close the Edit URL dialog box, and then click the Set Link button to close the Link Properties dialog box.
6. After you create the document links, save the document as described in the section "Save the Document for the Internet," later in the chapter.

After you create the link, test it by opening the PDF document in your default Web browser. In Internet Explorer, choose File | Open and navigate to the folder where the document is stored. In Netscape Navigator, choose File | Open Page and navigate to the PDF document. Click OK (Internet Explorer) or Open (Netscape Navigator), and Acrobat will launch in the browser and then open the document. Log onto the Internet and test the link. If you attempt to test the link from within the Acrobat application while logged onto the Internet, Acrobat will download the Web site and append it to the document.

Create an E-mail Link

When you create a PDF document for a website, you can create an e-mail link within a PDF document. When viewers of your PDF document click the e-mail link, their default e-mail application opens with a blank message window addressed to the e-mail address of your choice. To create an e-mail link in a PDF document, follow these steps:

1. Select the Link tool and drag within the document to define the hotspot for the link. After you define the link area, the Link Properties dialog box is displayed.
2. In the Action section, click the triangle to the right of the Type field and choose World Wide Web Link.
3. Click the Edit URL button to open the Edit URL dialog box.
4. In the Enter A URL For This Link field, enter **mailto:** followed by the e-mail address of the intended recipient, as shown in the following image:

5. Click OK to close the Edit URL dialog box, and then click the Set Link button to set the link and close the Link Properties dialog box.
6. Create any additional links and save the document as described in the section "Save the Document for the Internet," later in the chapter. The e-mail link is now ready to use.

In lieu of a link, you can use the Form tool to create a button. After you create the button, add the World Wide Web Link action to the Mouse Up event. Follow steps 3 through 5 from the previous section, and then click the Set Action button. The button you added to the document launches the viewer's default e-mail application when clicked.

Add a Base URL to the Document

If all of the web links in a document are within the same website, you can enter the relative path for the web link. However, if all of your links point to another site, you need to enter the absolute path to the URL. If all of your web links are to the same external site, you can simplify matters by adding a base URL to the document. When you add a base URL, you only need to enter the relative path to the document you want to open; Acrobat automatically links the relative path to the base URL. To specify a base URL for the document, follow these steps:

1. Choose File | Document Properties | Base URL to open the Document Base URL dialog box.
2. Enter the base URL of the document, as shown in the following image:

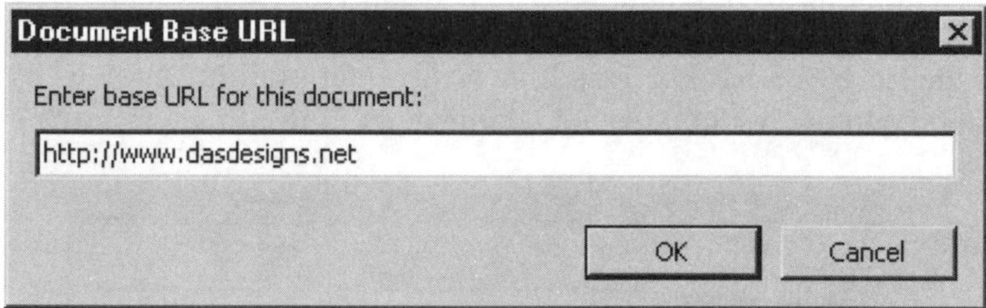

3. Click OK to close the dialog box.

After you set the base URL for the document, whenever you use the World Wide Web Link action to set a URL for a link or button, the base URL appears in the dialog box, as shown in the following illustration, and is added to the web link using the proper HTML nomenclature.

Create Named Destinations and Links

When you create links from an HTML document to a PDF document, the link destination can be the document itself or a named destination within the document. A named destination is a text link to a specific location within a PDF document. When you create a destination, you can change the view to zoom in on a specific image or paragraph within a document.

You can link to a named destination from within an HTML document. Create a named destination for each part of the document that you want to link to from within an HTML document. For example, if you post a PDF product manual on the Web, you can create a named destination for each product. Remember to use proper naming conventions for web browsers as you will be using each destination name as part of a web link. With this in mind, use standard DOS conventions when specifying a name for the destination. In other words, the destination name should be eight characters or less with no spaces. Remember, before you can create a named destination, you must first scan the document for existing destinations, as outlined in the "Work with the Destinations Palette" section in Chapter 10.

You should also create a link within the document that takes viewers back to the HTML page after they have perused the information. You may also need to create links from within the document to other web pages. You can create text links, or use images within the document as links. You can also create a button in the PDF document that acts as a link. However, if you create several buttons within a document, you increase the file size even when you optimize the document for fast web viewing. An increased file size is not a desirable outcome when creating documents for the Web. For more information on creating links, refer to Chapter 7.

Create a Welcome Page

If you have a large PDF document collection at a Web site, you can link the documents together using PDF navigation. When you do this, create a welcome page in PDF format that explains what the document collection is about. On the welcome page, you can create a menu using the Link tool to create links to the other PDF documents. When you create a welcome page in this manner, as long as the other PDF documents are in the same folder, you can use the Open File action to open a specific document when the user clicks the link.

You can also create a welcome page using HTML. Create hyperlinks on the welcome page for each document, as outlined in the upcoming "Create HTML Hyperlinks to PDF Documents" section of this chapter.

NOTE *When you create navigation for a large PDF document collection at a website, after the viewers have followed several links within the document collection, they may have a hard time navigating back to the HTML section of the site. Remember to include a link in each PDF document back to the website home page, or create a PDF navigation menu with links to the major areas of the website.*

Use PDF Forms on the Internet

You can use PDF forms to get feedback from visitors to a website, to conduct an online opinion poll, to build a customer database, and much more. When you create a PDF form for the Internet, create a Submit button to forward the information to the site Webmaster or owner.

When you create a PDF form for the Web, the information the user enters in each field is exported when the form is submitted. Some web hosting services have preformatted CGI scripts that you can modify to forward form results. CGI scripts can be used to password protect websites, create Guestbooks, and much more. In this case you need a CGI script that collects the information from the PDF form and forwards it to a specified person. Create a Submit button that links to the web server script. With most web servers, CGI scripts are stored within a folder named CGIbin. Check with the web hosting service technicians for the relative path to the forwarding CGI script. For more information on creating PDF forms, refer to Chapter 9.

TIP *In lieu of using a CGI script, you can forward the form results to an e-mail address. After you create the Submit button, choose the Submit Form action. Click the Select URL button, and, instead of entering the URL to a Web page, enter* ***mailto:****, followed by the e-mail address of the recipient. When a visitor to the Web site fills in the form and clicks the Submit button, the viewer's default e-mail application opens. The viewer can add a message or send the e-mail as is. When the recipient receives the e-mail, the form results will be attached as an HTML, FDF, or XFDF file, depending on which option you selected with the Submit Form action.*

Digital Signatures on the Web

When you digitally sign a document using Acrobat in a web browser, the Save or Save As buttons are not available. Your only option is to sign the document. After you sign the document, you can save the current version of the document to your hard drive. To digitally sign a document within a web browser, follow these steps:

1. Select the Digital Signature tool, and drag a rectangle on the PDF document where you want the signature to appear.
2. If you are not logged into a profile, Acrobat prompts you to log in. If you have more than one user profile, select the one you want to use when signing the document.
3. After you log in, Acrobat displays the Self-Sign Security – Sign Document dialog box, shown in the following image:

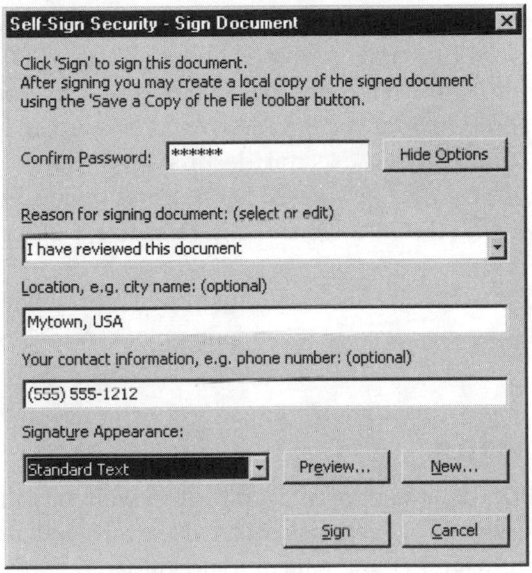

Self-Sign Security - Sign Document
Click 'Sign' to sign this document.
After signing you may create a local copy of the signed document using the 'Save a Copy of the File' toolbar button.
Confirm Password: ******
Hide Options
Reason for signing document: (select or edit)
I have reviewed this document
Location, e.g. city name: (optional)
Mytown, USA
Your contact information, e.g. phone number: (optional)
(555) 555-1212
Signature Appearance:
Standard Text
Preview...
New...
Sign
Cancel

4. Enter a reason for signing the document, and fill in any of the optional fields as desired. If you have a custom signature you want to use on the document, click the triangle to the right of the Signature Appearance field, and choose the desired signature.
5. Click the Sign button, and Acrobat displays a dialog box informing you that you have successfully signed the document.
6. Click OK, and your digital signature appears on the document.
7. To save a copy of the document, click the Save A Copy Of The File button.

Save the Document for the Internet

Before you upload the document to a website, double-check your work. Make sure all links function properly. If any of the document links are to a website, make sure you have the correct URL. There's nothing more frustrating for a web visitor than trying to open a link and getting a Not Found error.

If all of the links are formatted properly, choose Tools | PDF Consultant | Optimize Space. With PDF Consultant, you can remove any bookmarks or links with invalid destinations and reduce the file size. If you created any Named Destinations that you intend to use as link destinations from an HTML or other PDF document, disable the Change Unused Destinations option. For more information on reducing file size with the PDF Consultant, refer to the "Optimize Space" section in Chapter 8.

After you finalize the document in Acrobat, save it optimized for fast web viewing with a web hosting service that supports *byteserving*, as outlined in upcoming sections.

About Byteserving

When you view a PDF document optimized for fast web viewing from a website that supports byteserving, you see a page load almost immediately. If you have ever waited for a 350-page PDF document to download before viewing a single page, you realize the value of fast web viewing. When you optimize a document for fast web viewing, you create a document that can be downloaded a page at a time, provided the hosting service of the website supports byteserving. The website visitor does not have to do anything different to have the pages served-up one at a time. Acrobat or Acrobat Reader communicates directly with the web server. If, for example, a website visitor opens a lengthy PDF document, it opens to the link specified from the HTML document or linking PDF document. If the viewer enters **Page 50** in the Navigation window, then the viewer does not have to wait for the preceding pages to load; Acrobat requests Page 50 from the web server and downloads it.

After the first page of a PDF file optimized for fast web viewing downloads, Acrobat continues downloading the rest of the document by default. To disable this option, choose Edit | Preferences | Options, and deselect Allow Background Downloading.

Create Byteserving PDF Files

Even though you specify Fast Web Viewing when optimizing the conversion of the document to PDF from within an authoring application, after you add navigation links and other interactive features in Acrobat, you must once again save the document in a manner that produces a file optimized for the Web. If you use the Save command to save the document to file, Acrobat does not create a file optimized for fast web viewing. To create a PDF document optimized for fast web viewing, choose File | Save As. By default, the Save As command optimizes a document for fast web viewing unless you disable this option by editing Acrobat General Preferences.

Name the Document

When you name a document for distribution on the Internet, remember that web browsers react differently. Refrain from using spaces within a filename, and always include the .pdf extension. Web browsers are configured to use Acrobat, or Acrobat Reader, as the default application to view PDF files. It is also a good idea to refrain from using long filenames. When in doubt, stick with DOS naming conventions using filenames with eight characters or less and no spaces.

Combine HTML and PDF Files

When you create PDF documents that will be viewed from a website, use HTML pages as the basis for the website and create links within the HTML pages to a PDF document. After you create the HTML pages for your web site, you need to create the links that will open the PDF document in the web site visitor's browser. You can link directly to a PDF document, or you can link to a named destination within a PDF document. You can also create links from within PDF documents to websites.

Create HTML Hyperlinks to PDF Documents

After you create your web pages, you then need to create hyperlinks to open the PDF documents within the web visitor's browser. As long as the PDF documents are stored at the same website as the HTML documents, you only need to enter the relative path to the document when creating the hyperlink. If the PDF documents are in the same folder as the HTML pages, your hyperlink is equal to the filename of the PDF document followed by the .pdf extension. The following example shows a text link to a PDF document. Refer to your HTML editing software documentation for more information on creating hyperlinks.

```
<a href="empman.pdf">Employee Manual </a>
```

Create HTML Hyperlinks to Named Destinations

If the PDF documents you create for web viewing have named destinations, you can create links that open directly to the named destination. When the viewer clicks a link to a named destination, Acrobat launches in the viewer's web browser, and the document opens to the named destination rather than the first page of the document. To create a link to a named destination, follow these steps:

1. Create the HTML page in your HTML editor.
2. Create a hyperlink to the named destination. Format a hyperlink to a named destination the same way as a link to a bookmark within an HTML page. The hyperlink (href) is equal to the filename of the document followed by the extension, which is then followed by the number sign (#) and the name of the destination exactly as it appears in the PDF document. Refer to your HTML editing-software user manual for more information on creating hyperlinks. The following example shows a text hyperlink to a named destination (Cat1) within a PDF document (mydoc.pdf). When you create the hyperlink, make sure you use the proper case for the named destination; otherwise, the document will open at the first page rather than the named destination.

   ```
   <a href="mydoc.pdf#Cat1">Catalog Number 1 </a>
   ```

CAUTION

Linking to a named destination is not supported by some browsers. If your viewing audience is likely to have older web browsers, or web browsers tailored for an Internet Service Provider, add a note telling viewers which web browsers the document is optimized for and provide a link where viewers can download the web browser. Also, tell your viewers they will need Acrobat Reader 4.0 or better to view the document properly, and provide a link to download the proper version.

Create and Distribute PDF Documents via E-mail

As you have learned throughout the course of this book, Acrobat PDF documents can be shared with anyone who has Acrobat or Acrobat Reader installed. PDF documents are often referred to as e-paper, or electronic paper, if you will. What better way to share an electronic document than sending it via electronic mail (e-mail). In Chapter 5, you learned to convert a document from a Microsoft Office application to PDF format and e-mail it to an associate. You can also e-mail any document that you create or append within Acrobat. After you digitally sign a PDF file and add your comments to, or otherwise mark up a PDF document, you can send it via e-mail without leaving Acrobat by following these steps:

1. Log on to your Internet Service Provider.
2. From within Acrobat, choose File | Send Mail. After choosing this menu command, Acrobat launches your system default e-mail application.
3. Within the e-mail composition window, enter any message to accompany the file and then send it. Acrobat automatically sends the PDF document as an e-mail attachment.

NOTE

It is a good idea to save the document before e-mailing it. Acrobat uses a good bit of your system resources. Adding the e-mail application to the tasks the system is already processing may exceed the limits of your processing power and lock up your computer.

Index

A

B

C

D

E

G

H

I

J

L

M

N

O

P

Q

R

S

T

U

V

W

X

Z

INTERNATIONAL CONTACT INFORMATION

AUSTRALIA
McGraw-Hill Book Company Australia Pty. Ltd.
TEL +61-2-9417-9899
FAX +61-2-9417-5687
http://www.mcgraw-hill.com.au
books-it_sydney@mcgraw-hill.com

CANADA
McGraw-Hill Ryerson Ltd.
TEL +905-430-5000
FAX +905-430-5020
http://www.mcgrawhill.ca

GREECE, MIDDLE EAST, NORTHERN AFRICA
McGraw-Hill Hellas
TEL +30-1-656-0990-3-4
FAX +30-1-654-5525

MEXICO (Also serving Latin America)
McGraw-Hill Interamericana Editores S.A. de C.V.
TEL +525-117-1583
FAX +525-117-1589
http://www.mcgraw-hill.com.mx
fernando_castellanos@mcgraw-hill.com

SINGAPORE (Serving Asia)
McGraw-Hill Book Company
TEL +65-863-1580
FAX +65-862-3354
http://www.mcgraw-hill.com.sg
mghasia@mcgraw-hill.com

SOUTH AFRICA
McGraw-Hill South Africa
TEL +27-11-622-7512
FAX +27-11-622-9045
robyn_swanepoel@mcgraw-hill.com

UNITED KINGDOM & EUROPE (Excluding Southern Europe)
McGraw-Hill Education Europe
TEL +44-1-628-502500
FAX +44-1-628-770224
http://www.mcgraw-hill.co.uk
computing_neurope@mcgraw-hill.com

ALL OTHER INQUIRIES Contact:
Osborne/McGraw-Hill
TEL +1-510-549-6600
FAX +1-510-883-7600
http://www.osborne.com
omg_international@mcgraw-hill.com